Internal Principles	Dynamic, structural, sequential systems [pp. 45–59]	Ego, epigenesis, psychosocial conflict [pp. 83–84]	Genetic ultimate (phylogenetic inertia, ecological pressure) [pp. 114–117]	Psychological reality, competence and performance, creativity, synonymy, ambiguity [pp. 141–145]	Activators and terminators, phases of attachment [pp. 170–172]	Differential reinforcement, discriminative stimulus, shaping [pp. 195–200]	Triadic reciprocality [pp. 229–232]	Flow of speech into thought, types of speech, zone of proximal development, genetic law of cultural development [pp. 255–263]	Assimilation, accommodation, and equilibration; organization and adaptation [pp. 285–288]	Cognitive conflict, cognitive development, perspective-taking ability [pp. 328–332]
Bridge Principles	Levels of consciousness, defense mechanisms [pp. 59–62]	Psychosocial stages [pp. 84–92]	Demographic variables, rates of gene flow, coefficients of relationship [pp. 117–118]	Principles and parameters, computational component, logical and phonetic forms [pp. 146–151]	Attachment types [pp. 172–174]	Schedules of reinforcement, generalization, chaining [pp. 200–205]	Differential contributions, temporal dynamics, fortuitous determinants [pp. 232–233]	Phases and stages, functional activities in the ZPD [pp. 264–265]	Schemata, cognitive operations, cognitive structures [pp. 288–306]	Concept of stage, levels and stages, moral types [pp. 332–338]
Change Mechanism	Maturation, psychosexual conflict [p. 62]	Epigenesis, psychosocial conflict [pp. 92–93]	Genetic mutations, sexual recombinations, reproductive success [pp. 118–120]	Innate language faculty, [pp.151–153]	Social instinct [p. 175]	Reinforcement [pp. 205–208]	Acquisition and performance phases [pp. 233–238]	Internalization of language [p. 266]	Maturation, social transmission, physical experience, equilibration [pp. 306–308]	Cognitive conflict [pp. 338–339]

Theories of Human Development

A Comparative Approach

Michael Green
University of North Carolina—Charlotte

John A. Piel
University of North Carolina—Charlotte

Allyn and Bacon

Boston • London • Toronto • Sydney • Tokyo • Singapore

Series Editor: *Tom Pauken*
Senior Marketing Manager: *Caroline Croley*
Production Editor: *Annette Pagliaro*
Editorial Production: *Walsh & Associates, Inc.*
Composition Buyer: *Linda Cox*
Manufacturing Buyer: *JoAnne Sweeney*
Cover Administrator: *Kristina Mose-Libon*
Electronic Composition: *Publishers' Design and Production Services, Inc.*

Library of Congress Cataloging-in-Publication Data

Green, Michael
    Theories of human development : a comparative approach / Michael Green, John A. Piel.
        p. cm.
    Includes bibliographical references and indexes.
    ISBN 0-205-29647-5
    1. Developmental psychology—Philosophy. 2. Child psychology—Philosophy. I. Piel,
John A. II. Title.

BF713.G7 2002
155—dc21

2001041232

Printed in the United States of America
10 9 8 7 6 5 4 3 2 1   06 05 04 03 02 01

CONTENTS

PREFACE

This book is written primarily for psychology and education students whose programs include a course in child psychology, child development, or theories of development. The text may also be used to supplement courses on child development organized thematically or chronologically. Graduate courses in child development may wish to consider this text as a primary synthesis containing more source material and source citations than others of its kind.

The primary aim of the book is to describe what developmental theories are, what they do, where they come from, how they work, and how they are used to explain human nature. To manage the task, we have grouped the theories into three classical "families," which differ in their views about the prime motives underlying human nature. We have tried to consistently show how theories are specific examples of more general points of view called *paradigms*. The theories chosen to represent the three paradigms were selected because they met four criteria: *importance*, as judged by teaching psychologists; *fertility*, as judged by the amount of research the theory has generated; *scope*, as judged by the variety of phenomena the different theories cover; and *family resemblance*, as judged by how well each theory represents its paradigm. Quite aside from these considerations, several of the theories we cover have generated significant controversy in the psychological community. Controversy is often a healthy sign that a theory is taken seriously by psychologists, because it challenges widespread assumptions and commonly held beliefs about human nature. We don't shy away from controversy; we try to explain it in terms of personal assumptions people often make about human nature.

Finally, the lead chapter for each paradigm of theories is presented as the "paradigm case." It is currently accepted as the "best example" for the paradigm. We explain why paradigm cases are important, and we give them more detailed treatment than other theories in the same paradigm. Our treatment of paradigm cases shows students why Freud, Skinner, and Piaget are often considered the "big three" in developmental psychology.

The contents of this text reflect several of our beliefs. For example, we believe it is important for students to understand *why* the study of developmental theory is important, so we take up this question at the outset of Chapter 1.

We believe it is important to understand what the primary purpose of theory is, how theories represent specific examples of larger perspectives, and how theories reflect both philosophical considerations and a theorist's personal life experiences. Consequently, these themes are interwoven throughout the text.

We also believe it is important to understand how developmental theories can be systematically compared both within and across paradigms. For this reason, chapters have been organized in parallel fashion so that each theory can be readily compared with others (inside front and back covers show relevant comparisons).

We believe it is important to be able to evaluate theories independent of one's own personal predispositions and biases. Therefore, we describe and consistently use three different sets of evaluative criteria for the major theories covered. These criteria address issues about *scientific worthiness*, *developmental adequacy*, and *pedagogical usefulness*. It is not our intention to seduce readers into thinking they will become theory experts upon reading the book or to trick them into believing that they can really tell how good a theory is simply by mimicking our ratings. However, it is important for readers to understand that developmental theories differ significantly in how well they incorporate fundamental values of science (scientific worthiness), how well they explain development (developmental adequacy), and how valuable their concepts are in guiding child rearing (pedagogical usefulness).

We believe that developmental theories often reflect issues and concerns that originate in the lives of their authors. For this reason, theory chapters begin with a brief biographical sketch of each author. Theorists' youthful experiences and historical moments are described so that readers can better understand that theories derive from real-life motives rather than from semi-random formulations about "data."

Each of the theory chapters also contains a section that briefly summarizes examples of research that supports the theory. Every theory has generated some supportive research, but the strength of empirical evidence varies from one theory to another. We have chosen to present each theory *in its best light*. Therefore, research findings are presented from the point of view of that theory, and only selected supportive work is described. In addition to supporting research, each theory chapter has a summary section that describes its most enduring contributions and criticisms.

We have given more coverage to the theories of Freud, Skinner, and Piaget because they are the classics. But one reason they are classics is because they represent *paradigm cases*, the best examples, for the major paradigms in developmental psychology. Psychological paradigms and their philosophical antecedents are described early on in order to provide a framework for the theories presented throughout the book.

The book concludes with an examination of two issues not found in any comparable text. The first issue is the perplexing but very important *eclectic versus purist* controversy. We make explicit some of the basic assumptions held by both sides of this debate and describe the best arguments for each point of view. We also describe what we believe are the most compelling arguments in this debate. The second issue is more speculative; it concerns the future of developmental psychology. We describe six emerging trends and attempt to provide some seasoned guesses about their impact on our field of study.

We have improved this text without compromising the most valued qualities of the original, published over a decade ago. We have added chapters on theories by Ainsworth, Chomsky, and Vygotsky. We have also included more real-life examples of theory concepts, many found in the *Sandlot Seminars* adapted from everyday conversations and situations. Updated research references and historical perspectives have been incorporated throughout. And, by incorporating criteria of *pedagogical usefulness*, we have directly addressed the most frequently voiced concern of our own students—how useful is a theory in guiding teaching, parenting, and counseling? Finally, a new closing chapter discusses several important trends and examines their likely influence on the future of developmental psychology.

This book was not a solitary undertaking. We are sincerely grateful to those who reviewed the manuscript with meticulous care and suggested many ways for improving its precision and delivery: Martha Alibali, University of Wisconsin; K. Laurie Dickson, Northern Arizona University; Darryl Dietrich, College of St. Scholastica; Pamela Manners, Troy State University; Gwendolyn T. Sorell, Texas Tech University. Ronald Lunsford (UNC Charlotte), who has published a biography of Noam Chomsky, provided us with significant portions of the chapter on Chomsky's theory. We thank him for his generous and thoughtful help. Finally, we are also indebted to the staff at Allyn and Bacon.

PART ONE

Preliminary Considerations

The study of theories of development requires some familiarity with the general nature of problems, issues, and concerns we encounter in trying to explain human nature. These preliminary considerations are introduced in this section. Many of the major organizing principles used throughout the text are found here.

In Chapter 1 we describe fundamental reasons for studying developmental theories, and provide a working definition of *theory*. In addition, we present structural components common to all developmental theories for later use in describing and comparing individual theories. Finally, we sketch the three major philosophical movements from which modern "families" of developmental theories originated. The organization of this text follows directly from our grouping theories into families according to their predisposing assumptions and claims about human nature.

In Chapter 2 we present a number of important ideas to be used as conceptual tools in determining a theory's value for scientists and for parents and teachers. These ideas are grouped into three discrete sets of evaluative criteria: developmental adequacy, scientific worthiness, and pedagogical usefulness. Throughout the text these criteria are used to evaluate theories systematically. Such evaluations are useful in their own right because they reveal some of a theory's strengths and weaknesses, but they can also be used to make systematic comparisons between different theories.

Developmental psychology today is a fractured mosaic. Sometimes it seems as though there are almost as many theories as there are things to explain. *Function* and *structure* are important, enduring concepts, but today the

> cutting edge of contemporary developmental theory is represented by conceptions of process—how structures function and how functions are structured over time. (Lerner, 1998, p. 1)

The distinction between structure and function is important for developmental psychologists and for their students. But you will not find it in this text. The reason is that developmental psychology, like so many other sciences, has become so spe-cialized that few people have a sense of the geography. What are the landmarks? How is developmental theory organized? What are the recognizable themes that relate one theory to another? Few modern treatments of development theories attempt to answer these questions. We do.

In Chapter 1 we tell you why the study of developmental theories is impor-tant. We understand that the reader may be fulfilling a course requirement or an elective, but either way, readers are entitled to know *why* they should study theo-ries. We answer that question. We also tell you what a theory is and how develop-mental theories are organized into families called *paradigms*. In Chapter 2 we address the question "How good is a theory?" We answer the question in three parts. Is the theory a good scientific theory? Is the theory a good developmental theory? To what extent does the theory have implications for raising or teaching children? These are three important questions many students ask when they study theories of development and learning.

1 Theories as Windows for Looking to See

Preview Questions

Why is it important to understand theories?
What is a theory?
How is a theory different from a model?
What are the structural components of a developmental theory?
Why do theories have jargon?

Why Do We Study Theories?

Charles S. Peirce, one of the architects of American pragmatic philosophy, is credited with the saying that there is nothing more practical than a good theory (Lincourt, 1986). Theories are useful because they attempt to explain things that cannot explain themselves. Many important questions about human nature ultimately require theories rather than facts for answers. For example, why do people remember nothing about their first two years of life? Why do infants form attachment bonds? What is the function of play, for both children and adults? Given such wide variation in childhood experiences, why does language develop so uniformly between the ages of two and five?

Theories attempt to answer these questions. In fact, theories are the hallmark of science. Their importance is so fundamental that they are often a primary focus of the scientific enterprise.

Why do we study theories of human development? Wouldn't our time be better spent learning all we can about the *facts* of development? We can find the answers to these two questions in five basic principles that can help us understand why developmental psychologists spend so much time creating and testing theories. Collectively, these principles imply that any systematic explanation of human development must be preceded by an examination of its theories.

Principle 1—Theories Tell How to Organize Facts and Interpret Their Meaning

Facts cannot explain themselves. They do not organize themselves for our review, and they have no automatic force that indelibly stamps our minds with their meaning. Royce (1975) makes this point directly when he notes that theories are crucial to the conduct of science because facts can mean different things in different theoretical contexts. Theories organize and interpret facts differently, each according to its own principles.

It is a well-known fact, for example, that children around the world acquire the rudimentary grammar of their native tongue between approximately 2 and 5 years of age. While that fact is indisputable, its interpretation is not. Some theorists contend that biological maturation controls language acquisition. Others argue that language acquisition is a product of learning. While the facts of language acquisition are seldom debated, decisions about which body of facts and its theoretical interpretation is most relevant are hotly contested. Facts cannot identify their own causes; that is the role of theory.

Theories shape the collection, interpretation, and meaning of facts, but theories and facts are interdependent. Scientific advancement requires both information and theory. While bad theories are sometimes doomed through a failure to explain data, others are doomed simply because they explain facts later held to be irrelevant for new scientific interests. Moreover, the entire history of scientific ideas marks a trend away from concrete, physical concepts toward more abstract theories in large part because concrete concepts explain only specific phenomena, whereas more abstract theories explain diverse and general phenomena. As researchers collect more and more facts about human development, theories have become increasingly indispensable in organizing and interpreting them. As a general rule, theories make facts important, not the other way around.

Principle 2—Theories Represent Public Knowledge

Virtually everyone attempts to explain human nature by inferring causes and motives for other people's behavior. But when we do that, we invariably rely on either public or private sources of knowledge. Public knowledge is available to everyone and is often found in books and journal articles. This knowledge is easily accessible, readily transferred from one location to another or from one person to another, and openly discussed, examined, researched, criticized, and amended. Theories represent public knowledge and are thus submitted to public scrutiny and debate.

Private knowledge, on the other hand, is only available to individuals. It is inaccessible, difficult to communicate to others, and worst of all, not subjected to public scrutiny. This type of knowledge consists of our personal experiences, ideas, habits, beliefs, and opinions. We often explain others' motivations and actions in terms of our own experiences, attitudes, and memories, and these explanations often have a self-satisfying though unexamined quality about them. While some people still prefer the ease of conjuring up explanations about "Why Johnny can't read," such explanations are generally less reliable and less valid than those that arise through theory testing, careful scrutiny, and informed debate. The absence of reliability can be found in the inconsistency of personal explanations (e.g., "Johnny can't read because his parents don't make him do homework. He doesn't know math because he hasn't applied himself. He doesn't know how to spell because his teachers didn't use phonics."). Personal explanations are often invalid because they are simply untrue.

One of the authors once helped a teacher conduct some simple classroom observations because of her frequent and ardent complaints about how students with disabilities were so disruptive in her classroom. After several weeks of data collection, the embarrassed teacher reported back some insightful news. It turned out that nearly all the class disruptions were produced by her students without disabilities. Her belief that students with disabilities were disruptive was so strong, it had influenced not only what she saw but how she saw it.

The lesson here is that because theories represent public rather than private knowledge, they tend to explain human nature in a less biased, more defensible way. And because they are public, we have the next principle.

Principle 3—Theories Are in Principle Testable

Theories contain various claims about human nature that can, in principle, be tested separately or in combination. Testability provides an element of self-correction for theories not found in private knowledge. A single experiment may at any time disprove one or more claims, but even when a theory is disproved, something about human nature can be learned. Sir Francis Galton put it succinctly: *Truth arises more readily from error than from confusion.* At the same time, however, a theory cannot be proved true; it is virtually impossible to design and carry out all the experiments with all the individuals under all the circumstances needed to exhaustively establish proof. Yet, testability ensures that we can approximate truth by eliminating theoretical claims shown to be false.

What is at issue here is the testability of a theory's claims, the extent to which its claims can be verified objectively. A separate issue concerns the accuracy of those claims. To be sure, the issues are related in that one cannot determine a theory's accuracy unless it is first testable.

Principle 4—Theories Are Less Complex than People

Since the mind cannot produce ideas that are as complex as itself, theories must logically be less complex than the human mind that produced them. Bickard (1978) makes this point directly, noting that any system can itself be known and understood only by a higher-level system. Any level of organization, including the human mind, cannot be perfectly self-reflective: It cannot know its own properties. A higher-level organization is needed to do that. For example, people cognize only the results of their mental processes, not the processes themselves. Accordingly, humans are destined never to realize fully their own true nature. However, because theories of human nature are less complex than actual humans, they can be known and understood. Readers who would skip the study of theories in order to move directly to the "facts" about real people miss this crucial point. Theories are understandable because they are simpler than the phenomena they attempt to explain. Sandlot Seminar 1.1 shows the difficulty of understanding real people.

Sandlot Seminar 1.1

People Are Full of Surprises

Ron (45 years), a successful accountant, and his wife Sara (43 years), a schoolteacher, are having a conversation over dinner at home. Their daughter Fran is a high school junior who plays volleyball on the varsity team. David, their son, is a sophomore at a state university who has recently told his parents about his intention to change his major from engineering to acting. In addition, he visited home this past weekend and caused a major stir when his parents found out he had dyed his hair blue, gotten a tattoo on his ankle, and added a pierced earring.

RON: I can't believe it. I gave him all the advantages money could buy, and this is what he does. I tell you Sara, I won't have it. We raised him to be better than that.

SARA: I understand, dear. But we've always supported his decisions, even if we didn't agree with them at the time.

RON: I know. But this time he's gone too far. We didn't raise him to look like a freak.

SARA: Now, dear, he's not a freak. He's our son. I don't understand it any more than you do, but I figure he's still the same David he's always been, only now he has blue hair and an earring.

RON: It makes me sick. I don't know what possessed him. The blue hair doesn't bother me nearly as much as the earring. It just looks hideous. What was he thinking?

SARA: I really don't understand it myself. But remember, he did call this evening to tell you "happy birthday."

RON: Right. I figure he just called to rub it in my face.

SARA: I don't think so, dear. He knew you were upset when he was home; that's why he wanted you to know that he remembered your birthday. He's still our son, and we'll continue to be supportive even if we don't understand what he's doing.

RON: No son of mine would ever . . .

FRAN (INTERRUPTING): Dad! I don't see why its such a big deal. Lots of kids dye their hair and have body piercing.

RON: Not in this family, they don't.

FRAN: Well, Mom colors her hair, and both of us have pierced ears.

RON: Don't make excuses, Fran. Its not the same thing. He's ruining a perfectly good life. I can't figure out why he wants to throw it all away.

FRAN: He doesn't, Dad. He just wants to live his own life, not the one you've planned for him.

RON: What in the world are you talking about?

SARA: What she's saying, dear, is that engineering was your idea. You told him it was a way to follow his interest in science and make "good money." Making money has always been your bottom line, not his.

RON: He's got to be a able to earn a living when he graduates.

FRAN: Don't you think he knows that?

RON: I don't know what he thinks anymore.

FRAN: Well, I'm not saying that I do either, but I don't see why it's such a big deal.

RON: You wouldn't, Fran. You're still too young to see the big picture. How on earth is he going to be an actor? What I want to know is who put such a silly idea into his head?

SARA: Now, dear, maybe it's been in his head all along, but you just never noticed.

RON: What on earth are you talking about?

SARA: Remember? You're the one who drove all the way to Springfield to see his science project at the regional.

RON: Well, it was a good project. We were all proud of him.

SARA: He was proud too, but even more than the project, he loved being the center of attention. Maybe for him it was his first taste of being on a stage?

RON: Not a chance. He's just throwing away a perfectly good life to do something that he'll never be able to make any money at. I just don't understand why he's done this.

1. Why was Ron surprised by his son?
2. Why do people do unpredictable or unexpected things?
3. Does unpredictability have anything to do with why people are so hard to understand?

Principle 5—Theories Are Generalizable

Theories give us conceptual power because they explain characteristics of human nature that are common to all individuals. Imagine a hypothetical situation in which a well-defined set of theoretical principles perfectly explained the onset, intensity, duration, and objects of attachment among infants whose experiences ranged from highly nurturant at one extreme to abusive and impoverished at the other. If such a theory allowed us to predict and explain each and every infant's attachment formation, no matter what its individual circumstances, then this single theory would be far more powerful than all the circumstantial evidence we might collect about each infant's individual experiences. In short, theoretical power derives from generalization.

Consider another example. Imagine a single theory that explained everything about a particular person with complete accuracy. We could even imagine ten individual theories that explain ten individuals, or a thousand theories that explain everything about a thousand individuals. Eventually, we might imagine a unique theory for each living person. But there is an inherent problem with this approach. When a theory sacrifices generalizability (applicability to large numbers of individuals) for specificity and detail, it soon ceases to be a theory at all. Theories attempt to explain features of human nature that are common to all individuals. They are powerful and efficient, because a small set of principles can explain common characteristics of many individuals, and in doing that, those same characteristics are explained in each individual.

Taken together, these five principles provide strong motivation for studying theories of human development. In fact, some developmentalists devote more time to studying theories than they do to studying the facts of human nature. If psychologists shunned theories altogether and tried to fashion their images of human nature only from the nearly infinite wealth of factual details, their task would rapidly become unmanageable.

Theories as Windows

In many respects, a theory is like looking through a window at human nature to observe, record, and assess human events. Windows and theories are alike in that they both open up certain kinds of events for observation while constraining the view of other kinds of events. They give clear vision to certain phenomena of interest while occluding others that are out of sight (and theoretically irrelevant). Looking through different windows reveals different views of the world outside. What we see and what we cannot see are very much influenced by which window we look through.

A good example of this window metaphor can be found in von Uexkull's (1957) idea of *Umwelt*. Animals possess different receptor systems for perceiving relevant details about their environments. These receptor systems impose on them an *Umwelt*, a world view. Mosquitoes, deer, trout, and earthworms perceive different kinds of worldly events because they are perceptually tuned to obtaining specific types of information about the world, all this in spite of the fact that they may inhabit the same ecological habitat. Like the *Umwelts* of von Uexkull's creatures, theories also function as windows to the world, but these windows do have limitations. Some selectivity always occurs; no theory, receptor system, or window is capable of displaying all the information that is available.

What Is a Theory?

All theories have one overriding purpose—to explain phenomena. The phenomena may be either real, like human nature, or entirely conceptual, like philosophy and mathematics. In order to explain phenomena, three minimal elements are required: phenomena, explanatory concepts, and principles that relate the concepts to their respective phenomena. Hempel's (1966) classic definition recognizes these essential elements, so our definition of theory follows his lead: *a theory is a coherent, integrated set of statements containing internal principles, bridge principles, and an identifiable body of phenomena to be explained*. This rather formidable sounding statement is actually pretty logical.

Internal principles are the primary concepts, the core explanatory principles employed by a theory. They are always abstract ideas, constructs, or processes. These abstract ideas are a theory's "building blocks" in the sense that they cannot be reduced to more fundamental ideas. Internal principles often consist of general laws or functions to which human nature is believed to conform. The reader should not be alarmed by this general definition of internal principles. We will later describe in some detail these concepts for each theory covered in the text.

Phenomena to be explained constitute the essential data a theory attempts to explain and guide theoretically motivated research. Some data may be considered highly relevant by a theory, while other data is deemed irrelevant or peripheral. In addition, some theories may concentrate on explaining phenomena that are highly specific (e.g., infant perceptual acuity), while others address more general phenomena (e.g., personality development).

So far we have outlined two components in our definition of "theory": irreducible basic principles and the human phenomena they attempt to explain. But a theory's abstract ideas and the reality of human nature occupy two sides of a chasm that must somehow be closed. That is the function of a theory's bridge principles.

Bridge principles are secondary or derived concepts used to connect abstract theoretical principles to real-world expressions of human phenomena. Bridge principles often describe how particular internal principles operate in specific situations. Other times they may tell us how internal principles combine in different ways to influence human nature. As with internal principles, we will more completely describe theories' bridge principles in later chapters. For now, it is sufficient to understand that all theories contain bridge principles, and as their name implies, they form connections or "bridges" between a theory's abstract internal principles and the specific phenomena the theory attempts to explain.

Bridge principles are not just excess theoretical baggage; they are absolutely essential to scientific explanation. For example, one of the fascinating events in the modern history of science was the search for an accurate bridge principle to connect the abstract concept of gene with physical manifestations such as hair and eye color. Many researchers had sought this illusive connection until Francis Crick and James Watson discovered the molecular structure of DNA. The double helix strands of coded DNA provided this long-sought bridge and brought Crick and Watson the 1962 Nobel prize in physiology. To take a related example, the Human Genome Project is like a "Lewis and Clark" expedition. Its aim is to identify and "map" the entire set of human genes. When completed, it will have (1) established core, internal principles—all human genes, (2) catalogued the bridge principles— mappings of DNA sequences, and (3) related them to phenotypes—phenomena to be explained. In short, the Human Genome Project is theory building at its finest: establishing what to explain (genotypes) and relating it to regular, lawful patterns.

Any of a theory's essential elements may spawn a unique theoretical terminology called *jargon*. We often think of jargon in rather negative terms, as little more than unnecessary "psychobabble." However, jargon is not just important for a theory; *it is essential*. Specialized vocabularies serve specific purposes. They prevent misconceptions or common biases associated with less-specialized language by providing clear, explicit, unambiguous, and efficient communication. Without theoretical jargon, communication would be needlessly vague, cumbersome, and subject to personal meanings habitually associated with everyday usage. When a theory's concepts are well defined, its specialized vocabulary improves communication efficiency and reduces confusion.

Structural Components of Developmental Theories

In the previous section we saw that three elements were needed to provide a definition of *theory*. This situation is true regardless of the discipline one wants to study. Theories in biology, physics, chemistry, and even art history must contain these three minimum elements. What makes developmental psychology a bit different is its interest in explaining development.

Just as certain components make a car a car (steering wheel, engine, doors, tires) so, too, do developmental theories share certain *structural components*. These components include the three minimal elements needed to define theory. In addition, two other elements, assumptions about the newborn's inherent capabilities and change mechanisms believed to produce development, are needed in developmental psychology. These components may not be clearly identified in a theorist's work; they are often implied and sometimes embedded in a number of different publications. While developmental theories differ from one another in specific content, each theory can be analyzed in terms of these common structural components.

Assumptions.   Theorists seldom make their own assumptions explicit. This situation arises in part because they have grown so accustomed to looking at human development through their own theoretical window that they may be unaware of the implicit beliefs upon which their work is based. Moreover, they may be motivated to place their theory in the best possible light and may not wish to unduly jeopardize its acceptance by dwelling on its assumptions. Nevertheless, all developmental theories are based on unproven beliefs about the nature of the human neonate, the nature of the environment, and the nature of organismic–environmental interactions. One often has to "read between the lines" to identify a theory's assumptions.

Developmental theories typically (but not always) explain human development beginning with birth rather than conception. The assumptions a theory makes about the infant's naturally endowed capacities and characteristics are its starting blocks. They equip a theorist with presumed material from which an explanation of development can be launched. While the exact nature and number of assumptions vary from one theory to another, theorists attempt to make reasonable assumptions given the kind of phenomena they wish to explain. An important goal of this text is to identify the underlying assumptions each theory makes with regard to these infantile capabilities.

Explaining Human Phenomena. Recall that the primary purpose of a theory is to explain phenomena. But in human development as in science, no single theory can explain everything. Consequently, each theory limits itself to identifying a cohesive set of problems that will occupy its attention, although these may be expanded from time to time with new discoveries or theoretical advances. These problems generally entail at least two considerations: a specific body of phenomena that needs explaining and an appropriate methodology for systematically collecting information.

The phenomena to be explained pose problems for the theory because their explanation is not given in the phenomena themselves, nor does information spontaneously organize itself for the theorist's purposes. Theorists identify phenomena based on their own training and interests. Language acquisition, personality development, concept formation, learning, infant attachment, socialization, and moral development have all occupied theorists' attention. Throughout this text we sample from both classical and modern theories that represent the current landscape of important problems of study.

Methodology reflects the tools and strategies used to collect information. Metaphorically, a theory's methods are its "eyes"; they both organize and restrict information to be collected. Consequently, it should come as no surprise that a theory's methodology is matched to the kind of phenomena it attempts to explain. Sometimes different theories will utilize the same methods. Other times, as in the case of Freud's psychoanalysis, highly specialized methods are developed to tap highly specific phenomena that are unique to the theory's purpose. Often the most important information contained in a research article will be the research methodology, which describes how researchers can replicate each other's work. In this text the most typical methods employed within each theory are described. Conscientious readers will take special note of how well a theory's research methods actually match the phenomena it attempts to explain.

Internal Principles. Each developmental theory entails a number of internal principles that comprise the theoretical architecture; these are the *fundamental core concepts* of the theory. Core concepts are usually described in three ways: constitutive definitions (dictionary-like statements of meaning), operational definitions (how a concept is actually measured), and examples or analogies of how the concept works. Because internal principles are conceptual abstractions, they cannot be directly observed or measured. Their action is inferred from measurements that are indirect at best. Internal principles are so important that a theorist cannot afford to have them misunderstood, as often occurs when we encounter concepts already familiar and loaded with prior meanings. Consequently, a theorist tends to give these principles unique names and definitions.

Sandlot Seminar 1.2

Theory Jargon

The power and importance of jargon can be placed in a more personal context. Imagine, for example, that you visit two physicians and report symptoms that include swollen glands, fatigue, and prolonged sleepiness. Each physician orders the same blood tests, for which you are charged $80. The office visit is an additional $50. Each physician asks you to return in three days to learn the results of the lab tests (an additional $40 office visit). On the follow-up visit, the first physician tells you that you are "sick" and that you should go home and rest for six weeks. The second physician reports that you have *infectious mononucleosis* and that six weeks' rest is the only cure. What is your reaction to the two physicians, each of whom charged the same, did the same blood tests, and suggested the same remedy? Which would you be more likely to visit again? Why? The difference between being told that you are "sick" versus telling you the name of your disease is the difference of jargon. As Aristotle noted, *we do not fully understand a thing until we have given it a name.*

To some extent, then, understanding a theory requires a familiarity with the terminology presented in this text. Any reader interested in exploring in detail the terminology used by one or more theorists should examine their original works cited in the references at the end of the text.

Bridge Principles.   The concepts that connect a theory's internal principles to the phenomena it attempts to explain are its bridge principles. Put differently, bridge principles are "show" rules. They show how a theory's most basic principles can be extended, mapped, and projected onto human phenomena. Bridge principles "bridge" the gap between purely abstract concepts and the reality of human conduct. Moreover, because bridge principles play a specialized role within a theory, theorists often invent specialized names for these principles in order to enhance precision and clarity about their theory's meaning. Sandlot Seminars 1.2 and 1.3 illustrate this point.

Change Mechanism.   A unique feature of developmental theories is that, in order to account for development, they must specify some process or mechanism responsible for producing the changes that constitute development. A theory's change mechanism might be thought of as the "motor" that makes development occur. This theoretical component is crucial; how can one explain development without identifying something that brings it about? More often than not, the change mechanism posited by a theory sparks discussion, debate, and criticism, primarily for two reasons. First, it is one of the most critical features of developmental theories, and second, it is often one of the weakest components.

Families of theories can often be identified by their appeal to different mechanisms of change. For example, several theories in one paradigm posit biological maturation as the cause of development, thereby implying that the span of individual growth is relatively fixed and mostly immune to environmental stimuli.

Sandlot Seminar 1.3

Freud's Theoretical Jargon

By the 1920s, Sigmund Freud was well aware that his theory of psychoanalysis extended into uncharted psychological territory. In order to reflect the originality of his thinking, he needed to find theoretical concepts that were both novel and unencumbered with public meanings that might bias or confuse those who read his work.

For example, Freud believed that the human personality was composed of three parts. The part of personality that dealt with motivation and desire he termed the *id*. A more advanced organ that translated desire into action he called the *ego*. Finally, the part of personality that incorporated society's values as a controlling force over our desires was called the *superego*.

In another example, Freud believed consciousness was composed of three layers. The contents of the innermost layer were hidden and inaccessible through normal introspection. The contents of the middle layer consisted of symbols, images, and linguistic terms that could be recalled into memory, although their true meanings could still be hidden from us in the first layer of consciousness. Finally, there was the third layer, the outermost part of consciousness, which contained the ideas and memories of which we are consciously aware. To convey the novelty of these ideas with theoretical precision, Freud used the terms *unconscious, preconscious,* and *conscious.*

The point here is that in the 1920s and 1930s, terms such as *id, ego, superego,* and *unconscious* were all considered by psychologists to be highly technical theoretical jargon knowable only by a handful of specialists in psychiatry, counseling, or developmental psychology. Yet by the latter half of the twentieth century, the fruitfulness of these technical terms proved so useful for public discourse that they are today often used by ordinary citizens to describe elements of human nature. It is true that a degree of theoretical precision and clarity is lost in public use. However, these and other examples illustrate that today's jargon may work itself into the public's everyday vocabulary of the future.

Accordingly, maturational theories hold that the development of such domains as personality, thinking, temperament, language, and morality are the product of an innate plan that governs their timing and form, neither of which can be altered very much by environmental events. In contrast, theories in a competing family may argue that individuals are inherently malleable and flexible. Theories in this family view maturation as setting broad limits on learning, but they contend that it is specific environmental events that govern both the sequence and specifics of development.

Limitations of Developmental Theories

As noted earlier, theories are like windows for looking to see. In certain important ways one theory admits some but not other assumptions, problems, methods, and data. Other theories may admit different assumptions, problems, methods, and data. These limitations *do not invalidate the theory;* they merely require that one understand what theories can and cannot do.

First, a theoretical window precludes certain kinds of information. It defines the kinds of events that are to be recorded and studied. But in any study of human nature, only a fraction of what actually takes place can be recorded. For example, if we are studying how children learn to spell their name, we are likely to ignore a great deal of frequent but irrelevant behavior—yawning, trips to the lavatory, scratching, and fidgeting. At the same time, we are likely to pay attention to such details as pencil holding, writing mechanics, spelling, and eye–hand coordination. Theories make deliberate choices about what data is relevant and what is irrelevant (White, 1976).

Second, human events that become "data" always get distorted to some extent. This distortion is a direct consequence of the methods used by the investigator. Research requires the measurement of bridge principles with certain tools (the researcher's methods) applied under replicable conditions. These methods and conditions act like filters to screen in and screen out certain kinds of information. The information obtained in research studies is always incomplete in terms of the total data available in a given situation. However, incompleteness may be relatively minor, as in the use of a sensitive scale to chart the daily growth of an infant's weight (the distortion occurs in condensing a day's worth of weight gain into a single measure). On the other hand, distortion may be extensive, as occurs when a child's weight is measured annually by a pediatrician; an entire year's growth is condensed into a single moment. Whatever the case, instruments must be used to collect information, but they always provide fractional assessments of the entire event under study. This type of distortion varies from one method to another, but the important point is that it always occurs not as the fault of a particular method but by the very fact of having to use a method at all to collect data.

Third, theories reflect limitations imposed by the assumptions they make. If a theorist assumes that development is driven by internal forces, then external factors will likely be dismissed or discounted. If a theorist assumes that external factors produce development, then internal motives will likely be ignored.

A fourth problem arises when one realizes that *humans* write theories and conduct research. The "facts" collected by researchers are only facts because they reflect a researcher's own interests and attention. After all, researchers could have been interested in and actually have collected different facts. Personal choices like these influence the larger body of theory and information about human nature (Mischel, 1976). Moreover, issues about which facts should be collected ultimately lead to different research programs and to different kinds of theories.

These four limitations mean that theories will probably never provide us with the ultimate truth about human nature (neither can our personal experiences, memories, anecdotes, and the like), though they do provide a systematic means for approaching it. These inherent limitations of theories should not lead to despair of ever fully understanding or appreciating the entirety of human nature. That is because if a theory is genuinely testable, then it provides a way to eliminate the mistaken ideas we hold about human nature. By removing the inaccuracies in our collective knowledge, we can gradually approximate truth. Judicious research gradually chips away at erroneous concepts, thereby leaving a portrait of human nature less tainted with errors than before.

Families and Paradigms of Developmental Theories

Paradigms and Paradigm "Cases" in Developmental Psychology

Using the "window" metaphor developed earlier, we can note that windows in a house sometimes allow similar views of reality, as when, for example, we look out adjacent windows in the living room or kitchen. In this respect, theories of development sometimes share fundamental similarities with other theories; they seem to belong to the same "family." This family resemblance is what scientists call a **paradigm**. *Paradigm* is one of those jargonlike terms that has caught on in recent years. Kuhn (1962) identifies two key features of a paradigm: a collection of beliefs shared by scientists and a set of agreements about how problems are to be investigated. Basically, a paradigm is a body of shared assumptions, beliefs, methods, and interpretations that constitute a particular vision of reality (Royce, 1975). White (1976) provides some insight into how paradigms operate in developmental psychology, noting that different paradigms offer (1) an orientation for viewing the world of human nature, (2) a set of "reals" observable from the orientation, (3) a club of scientists, and (4) mutual agreements among club members about what is and is not considered worthwhile research about the "reals." If one were to walk from one paradigm to another, dramatic changes in methods, jargon, concepts, and theories about the world would be encountered. In this manner, paradigms provide the implicit rules of the game by which scientists tacitly agree to conduct the business of science. A paradigm, then, is a general orientation which may entail several theories, like members of a family.

Philosophical Antecedents of Developmental Theories

Three seminal movements in modern epistemology (a branch of philosophy concerned with explaining knowledge) established the conceptual framework from which psychological paradigms emerged. The following synopsis briefly describes the lines of argument that differentiate these three philosophical approaches and their corresponding paradigms. In developmental psychology, a **paradigm case** is considered the prototype that best exemplifies each paradigm. Table 1.1 summarizes the important elements of this section.

Rationalism and Innate Ideas. Modern philosophy began with the insights of René Descartes, a seventeenth-century thinker whose ideas about the origin of knowledge became known as *rationalism*. In his *Discourse on the Method* (1637),

TABLE 1.1   Overview of Relationships between Epistemologies, Paradigms, and Theorists in Developmental Psychology

Epistemology	Epistemologist	Paradigm	Paradigm Case	Other Theorists
Rationalism	René Descartes	Endogenous	Freud	Ainsworth Chomsky Erikson Wilson
Empiricism	John Locke David Hume	Exogenous	Skinner	Bandura Vygotsky
Constructivism	Immanuel Kant	Constructivist	Piaget	Kohlberg

Descartes set forth his "method of doubt" and the conclusions he drew from its results. Using this method, he simply suspended his belief in anything for which he could imagine the slightest possible doubt. What was left over, beliefs that resisted all doubt, could be considered certain and hence "true" knowledge.

Descartes recalled many occasions when his senses had been fooled into providing false information about the real world. From these lessons he concluded that true knowledge could not derive from sensations, because he couldn't figure out how to tell the difference between accurate and inaccurate sensations. To experience the kind of suspicion Descartes held toward sensations, imagine placing one hand in a pan of cold water and the other in a pan of hot water, each for several minutes. Next place both hands into a single pan of lukewarm water. Each hand will transmit different sensations, yet both hands are subject to the same experience. Which hand is transmitting false impressions? Perhaps both? How, reasoned Descartes, are we to tell when our senses do and do not deceive us if they provide the only information we have for making that judgment? Examining his memories and experiences, Descartes initially concluded that any beliefs about the physical world, God, and even about himself could no longer be justified on the basis of sensation. Since no sensory knowledge was completely trustworthy, he found himself in a position where he could believe in nothing.

Such a preliminary conclusion was short-lived, for Descartes soon noticed that he was at least aware of his ever-present doubting. The brilliance of his discovery lies in the fact that if he was to have any doubt at all, then something must be doing the doubting—*cogito ergo sum* (I think, therefore I exist). Since his own thinking was the only substance that was beyond doubt, Descartes argued that *all external substances must be extensions of one's own reasoning.* Because true knowledge of the world could not be derived from the senses, any knowledge must, like reason itself, have an internal origin. Descartes's *rationalism* is a philosophical position that holds that all knowledge is an extension of internal, *innate reason,* and even knowledge of the physical world is merely an extension of inborn reasoning.

Endogenous Theories.   Rationalism is the philosophical antecedent of the **endogenous** paradigm. The term *endogenous* derives from two roots: *endo*—from within, and

genesis—development. Like rationalism, endogenous theories expla
ment as the result of predominantly internal influences. The family of e
theories places primary emphasis on the organism's internal nature, especially those
inner workings that are believed to produce human development. Moreover, theories in this family employ causal explanations of development and locate the
change mechanism within the internal components of the organism (usually in the
form of a hereditary plan or blueprint for growth). Theories in the endogenous
paradigm typically conceive of development as an unfolding of relatively fixed patterns and being relatively impervious to environmental pressures.

Some endogenous theories, such as those of Sigmund Freud and Erik Erikson,
stress the view that developmental milestones and stages are maturationally predetermined. Endogenous theories that invoke maturation often (but not always)
involve a notion of developmental *critical periods*, biologically timed changes that
result in rapid, specialized learning. The timing of these periods and the objects
of specialized learning are innately determined, as happens, for example, with
imprinting. Sometimes, endogenous theories describe environmental influences
on development, but these influences are invariably subordinated to the natural
plan operating within the organism. The endogenous theories of Freud and Erikson both stress biological maturation as a developmental change mechanism.
Noam Chomsky argues that language is produced by an innate "device" that governs linguistic acquisition and meaning. In contrast to these theorists, Edward
Wilson emphasizes development across the species, *phylogenesis*, rather than development within the individual life span (*ontogenesis*). Wilson emphasizes the roles
of genetic mutation and recombination as change mechanisms from which nature
can do its "natural selection."

Freud's theory of psychoanalysis is the paradigm case (best example) for the
endogenous paradigm. This is because his theory of *infantile sexuality* describes
maturation stages, and maturation is an inborn, biological process.

Empiricism and Learning through Sensory Experience. An important turn in modern philosophy resulted from the efforts of two seventeenth- and eighteenth-century
British writers, John Locke and David Hume, who individually attempted to refute
Descartes's notion of innate reason. Locke's *Essay Concerning Human Understanding*
was a direct effort to demonstrate that knowledge derives from the external world,
not from the mind.

Locke thought of the mind as composed of elements or units called *ideas*. He
wondered how ideas in the mind become connected with each other to form the
meanderings of conscious thought. He began by assuming that things, actions,
events, substances, and processes all have a "real" existence (otherwise one could
not explain how our ideas are so well matched with external reality). His key contribution was the notion of *idea*, which he defined as an object of thought. Ideas constitute the building blocks of knowledge, and they derive from experience, either
directly through sensations or indirectly through reflection, in the following manner. The newborn comes into the world with a *tabula rasa* mind (an empty file cab-
inet or blank slate, available to receive information but possessing none at birth).

Equipped with a *tabula rasa* mind, the infant also possesses a body that, with virtually no effort, comes into contact with a world and thereby senses a great variety of real substances. These contacts constitute experience. The world's substances evoke sensations that are conveyed to the mind, where ideas are formed. An infant first begins to think when the first sensation produces the first idea.

Ideas, however, are of two types: simple and complex. Simple ideas are produced by single, irreducible sensations (a color, a tone, an odor). According to Locke the mind cannot invent new simple ideas; simple ideas can only be produced from sensations. Complex sensations (the smell of breakfast, playing with a parent, listening to a story) are sorted into distinguishable single sensations, each of which gives rise to its arrangement of simple ideas. For simple ideas, the mind acts like a receptacle to be filled. Knowledge of the world is limited by the simple ideas supplied through sensations.

Once a sufficient quantity of simple ideas has been stored, the mind can repeat, compare, and unite the ideas through reflection into virtually limitless combinations, thereby producing complex ideas. By habit, simple ideas gradually become integrated into the unified experience of complex ideas, and through reflection we come to anticipate that things that produce certain sensations will also produce other expected sensations (e.g., the sound of the dentist's drill is accompanied by painful sensations in our teeth).

Locke's *Essay* proposed a radical departure from the path to knowledge forged by Descartes and firmly established the philosophical orientation called *empiricism,* the belief that knowledge derives from experience. Locke failed, however, to explain why ideas occur in an organized rather than random fashion (since simple ideas could be combined with limitless variety). This problem was solved by Hume.

David Hume's *A Treatise of Human Nature* set forth two fundamental principles. First, all ideas derive from sense impressions of the external world or sense impressions of internal states. Consequently, we are incapable of imagining anything (much less understanding it) that we have not experienced. Second, to explain how we get abstract or complex ideas that are organized instead of random, Hume invoked the doctrine of *associationism,* a kind of "mental chemistry" wherein mental elements, in this case ideas, combine with one another into compounds or complex ideas.

The merit of Hume's associationism is that it explained how general ideas could be formulated in an organized manner. Simple ideas get associated with one another through the processes of *resemblance, contiguity,* and *cause–effect* (Lana, 1976). Through resemblance, ideas call up one another when they have derived from similar sense impressions (e.g., girl–woman, car–truck). Contiguity leads to associations between two ideas whose sense impressions occur together in space and time; thus the presence of one conjures up the other (e.g., mother–father, mother–baby, baby–bottle). Cause and effect associations result when the sense impressions underlying one idea compel the sense impressions of a second idea (e.g., needle–pain, hit–hard, drop–fall). Individual associations, through resemblance, contiguity, and cause–effect, gradually interconnect into a network that evokes abstract relationships called concepts. Concepts for Hume were merely the family of associations that existed between individual ideas.

Locke and Hume shaped the modern empiricist movement in philosophy and science. They gave it a forcefulness, an elegant simplicity, and a direction that is clearly evident in the family of **exogenous** developmental theories.

Exogenous Theories.   The term **exogenous** derives from two roots: *exo—*from outside, and *genesis—*development. Theories in the *exogenous paradigm* attempt to explain development as a result of specific environmental factors external to the individual. While these theories recognize that infants are biologically endowed creatures, the biological blueprint is viewed as a malleable plan of possibilities rather than necessities. The newborn is seen as innately flexible and predisposed to conform to pressures exerted by environmental forces. B. F. Skinner's theory of operant conditioning and Albert Bandura's social cognitive theory are good examples of the exogenous perspective, and they propose reinforcement and observational learning, respectively, as mechanisms of development.

Developmental psychology today considers Skinner's operant conditioning as the paradigm case for the exogenous paradigm. No theorist does such an elegantly simple job of showing how the environment controls human nature.

The Nature versus Nurture Controversy.   The **nature-nurture controversy** is a theoretical battle between endogenous and exogenous paradigms over *what facts mean, not what the facts are*. For example, two opposing interpretations have historically been given to account for the fact that high IQ correlations exist between identical twins raised separately. On the one hand, endogenous theorists argue that such a high correlation underscores the importance of a common genetic influence. On the other hand, exogenous theorists point out that identical twins who have been adopted are often raised by families similar in their race and socioeconomic status. These theorists argue that it is the similarity of experiences that accounts for the equally high IQs of such twins. The nature–nurture controversy is a theoretical debate over how best to interpret data. It pivots on what the data mean (theoretical explanations) rather than what the data are (which is commonly agreed upon by different theorists).

Constructivism and the Invention of Knowledge.   The third major influence on modern philosophy was Immanuel Kant, an eighteenth-century philosopher who proposed a critical approach to determining what knowledge the mind could and could not produce. Kant fashioned the most salvageable ideas from rationalism and empiricism into a synthesis that is *not* a simple adding together of the two positions. His *Critique of Pure Reason* provided the foundation for what is known today as *constructivism*.

By the late eighteenth century, sense experience was widely accepted by most thinkers as immutably linked to the origin of knowledge (Lana, 1976). Kant appeared to accept this limited proposition, though he extended it by asking how sense experience itself could lead to genuine knowledge. The challenge he set for himself was to explain how humans could understand such abstract ideas as logic and mathematics, neither of which derive from sense impressions and hence cannot derive from associations of simple ideas.

Kant began his *Critique* by showing that the senses and the intellect are not capable of the same type of knowledge; each produces different qualities and is constrained by different restrictions. Kant believed that in order to know and to act, it is necessary both to sense and to think. This point is crucial. Where Descartes viewed sensation as an extension of the mind, and where Locke and Hume reduced thought to reflections of the senses, Kant maintained that neither sensation nor thought could be derived from each other. Kant reasoned that knowledge derived from the conjoint application of two components—sensibility and understanding. Simply put, *the mind without sensation is empty; sensation without the mind is blind*.

Kant argued that what is innate is not reason or knowledge but rather innate *categories* that act like filters to analyze information from sensory input. The categories are very different from the kinds of ideas described in rationalism and empiricism. They are processors for *constructing* knowledge from sensations. These categories contain rules for putting sensations together in ways that make sense. For example, imagine two objects moving toward you on a racetrack. You may recognize these objects as sprinters. Your innate categories contain spatial and temporal rules that help you make sense of your sensation in the following ways.

The larger object is in front of the smaller object.
The larger sprinter is closer than the smaller sprinter.
The closer sprinter will cross the finish line first.
The closer sprinter is faster than the farther sprinter.

Kant's innate categories are fundamentally different from sensations because they are concepts of a higher order than can come from direct experience. Like intuitions of space and time, the innate categories have to do with the form of experience rather than its material substance. These categories supply no knowledge of particular things (a rejection of rationalism), and empirical sensations provide only the aliment or food for "digestion" and are not themselves knowledge of the external world (a rejection of empiricism). For Kant, knowledge must be a *synthetic construction* deriving from the application of innate categories that confer meaning on the content of particular sensations.

Constructivist Theories. Constructivist theories *describe* the course and constitutive properties of development. Rather than being either innately or environmentally determined, development is viewed as a **synthesis** of progressive organizations and reorganizations that are **constructed** in the process of adapting to and interacting with the external world. The constructivist paradigm is the most complex of the three paradigms in developmental psychology. Here is a simple example of constructivism.

We all know that the elements hydrogen and oxygen are colorless gases without taste or smell. Yet, if these elements are combined under sufficient heat and pressure, they produce a new molecule: H_2O. H_2O is water, which exists in a liquid state. The question here is, does water's liquidity originate in the hydrogen or the oxygen atom? Where does liquidity come from? It can't come from either the hydrogen or the oxygen atoms, since each is a gas. Liquidity must be a synthetic property, reducible to neither atom, but which is created anew in the heat–pressure synthesis of hydrogen and oxygen.

Constructivism is the psychological equivalent of chemical synthesis. As in chemistry, new characteristics are created when individuals act on their environment. People invent knowledge, and their inventions are gradually adjusted to reality.

The theories of Jean Piaget and Lawrence Kohlberg represent relatively pure examples of constructivist theories. Each proposes that development is a natural consequence of solving problems. Piaget is considered the paradigm case for the constructivist paradigm because his theory does the best job of showing how knowledge is constructed through an individual's activities.

While there are many developmental theories one might study, those selected for inclusion in this book meet several conditions that make them important. First, each one attempts to explain universal elements of human nature rather than individual or culture-specific characteristics. Second, each theory is a relatively good example of its paradigm family. This is important because if one can learn about paradigms by studying specific examples, then learning about other theories within the same paradigm is much easier. Third, each theory in this book has easily identifiable structural components, and this is what enables us to compare theories both within and across paradigms. Fourth, each theory has generated a sufficient body of supporting research to give it at least a threshold level of scientific validity. Fifth, each theory has provoked enough interest in the academic community to sustain continued research beyond the work of the original theorist. Sixth, each theory has made enduring and distinctive contributions that have enlarged our understanding of human nature.

Summary Points

1. Five principles tell us why we should study theories of human development. Theories (1) give meaning to facts, not vice versa, (2) represent public rather than private knowledge, (3) are testable, (4) are less complex than people, and (5) are generalizable.
2. Paradigms contain multiple theories, a set of observable "reals," and mutual agreements about reality. Paradigms are the framework within which a theory operates.
3. Theories, such as von Uexkull's *Umwelts,* are windows for looking to see.

4. A theory is a coherent, integrated set of statements containing internal principles, bridge principles, and an identifiable body of phenomena to be explained. This definition implies that developmental theories have common structural components (assumptions, problems of study [phenomena and methods], internal principles, bridge principles, and change mechanisms) although the content of these components differs from theory to theory.

5. Developmental theories have inherent limitations: incompleteness of information, distortion of information, and subjective and personal choices by scientists about what information to collect.

6. Developmental theories reflect three major philosophical considerations about the source and nature of knowledge: rationalism, empiricism, and constructivism.

7. Psychological paradigms are matched to philosophical positions as follows: endogenous—rationalism, exogenous—empiricism, and constructivist—constructivism.

SUGGESTED READINGS

These selections are among the classical readings in developmental psychology.

Hanson, N. R. (1958). *Patterns of discovery*. Cambridge, England: Cambridge University Press.

Kuhn, T. S. (1970). *The structure of scientific revolutions* (2nd ed.). Chicago: University of Chicago Press.

Lana, R. E. (1976). *The foundations of psychological theory*. Hillsdale, NJ: Lawrence Erlbaum.

Looft, W. R. (1972). The evolution of developmental psychology. *Human Development, 15,* 187–201.

Reese, H. W., & Overton, W. F. (1970). Models of development and theories of development. In L. R. Goulet & P. B. Baltes (Eds.), *Life-span developmental psychology*. New York: Academic Press.

Wartofsky, N. W. (1968). *Conceptual foundations of scientific thought*. London: Macmillan.

2 Evaluating Developmental Theories

Preview Questions

What important values of science are embodied in the concept of *scientific worthiness?* How do we assess a theory's scientific worthiness?

What characteristics are implied in the concept of development? How can a theory's developmental adequacy be assessed?

How might we determine a theory's usefulness for parents and teachers?

Values of Scientific Worthiness

Most scientists and philosophers hold certain beliefs about the relationship between theory and data. Collectively, these beliefs help define the enterprise of science and guide expectations about what constitutes an adequate, scientific explanation of reality. According to Hempel (1966), science attempts to explore, describe, explain, and predict worldly events. While science depends on empirical evidence to verify its claims, theories are also necessary because they propose themes for organizing and explaining evidence.

In the following section, several of the most important values of science are described. These values are in one sense arbitrary and in another sense pragmatic. They are arbitrary in the sense that they represent tacit agreements about how to pursue science; in a different time and place these principles could have been (and historically have been) different. However, the same values are also pragmatic, since they define the goals of scientific theorizing and the rationale for its pursuit.

Throughout this book we evaluate each theory's *scientific worthiness* in terms of its adherence to five basic tenets of science. The discussion that follows derives in part from treatments of logic and scientific explanation given by Hempel (1966), Hurley (1982), and Quine and Ullian (1978). This material should be learned because it will be used throughout the book. Table 2.1 on page 24 shows the three sets of evaluative criteria used throughout this text.

TABLE 2.1   Three Sets of Criteria for Evaluating Theories

Scientific Worthiness	Developmental Adequacy	Pedagogical Usefulness
Testability	Temporality	Interpretability
External Validity	Cumulativity	Versatility
Predictive Validity	Directionality	Availability
Internal Consistency	New Mode of Organization	Guidance
Theoretical Economy	Increased Capacity for Self-control	

Testability

A theory should in principle be testable in order to verify the claims it makes about human development. In order to be testable, a theory must provide a degree of clarity for its concepts, because only then can its proposals be checked against the actuality of human nature. Testability is probably the most important measure of a theory's scientific worthiness. A theory that is testable can be objectively verified. We may learn in testing a theory that one or more of its claims are wrong. But if a theory is untestable, we have no way of finding out if it is wrong or right. In this sense, a theory that is testable but false makes a greater scientific contribution than a theory that is untestable (even though it may be right, no one would ever know).

Two requirements must be met for a theory to be testable. First, its constructs and claims must be measurable. The measurement need not be quantitative, but it must derive from observable events. Science relies on measurement for precision and accuracy. Second, a theory's claims must be specific enough to allow us to make predictions: "If I do *A*, then *B* will happen." A theory may be testable but wrong, but its testability must be established before its accuracy can be determined. Testability and accuracy are separate issues. Accuracy is taken up later under the criteria of *external validity* and *predictive validity*.

It is important to recognize that sometimes theoretical claims are not testable simply because they are definitions. Definitions are accepted by any scientist who uses the theory. So long as a theorist is consistent in the employment of a definition, it need not be testable. One may agree or disagree with theorists' definitions, but a theorist is usually granted flexibility in defining concepts in almost any way that is reasonable. Other theoretical claims may not be testable because they are circular. For example, a theory might define an angry person as one who fights rather than talks through conflict. Such a claim cannot be tested because an angry person could not, by definition, choose to talk through a conflict. There would be no way to find angry negotiators, since they have been defined out of existence.

External Validity

External validity refers to a theory's accuracy; it means that a theory provides accurate descriptions of *what we already know* about human nature. Because a theory is limited, it need only account for the phenomena it attempts to explain. Two or more theories may rate high on this criteria because they may explain with equal accuracy different kinds of human phenomena. Most research with human subjects (infants, children, adolescents, or adults) attempts to test the external validity of a theory—does the theory explain the facts of human development?

Predictive Validity

Predictive validity reflects a second kind of accuracy, the accuracy of *foretelling new phenomena* that are not already known. While external validity refers to how well a theory explains what we already know, predictive validity is a measure of a theory's capacity to generate new facts and new knowledge.

Scientific predictions consist of "if . . . then" statements; *if* certain conditions are established, *then* some predicted phenomenon will occur. The more specific the prediction, the greater the predictive validity (all other things being equal) of a theory. Note that it is not the human scientist, but the theory that makes the prediction; any scientist can make an accurate prediction, but if the prediction cannot be clearly derived from the theory in question, its predictive validity has not been strengthened.

Another element of predictive validity is sometimes referred to as *fruitfulness*. Fruitfulness is not explicitly an index of a theory's accuracy; rather, it denotes the amount of research a theory generates. A theory is said to be fruitful if it suggests new ideas for future research and if it leads to the discovery of new facts (Hurley, 1982).

Internal Consistency

Internal consistency refers to the *principle of noncontradiction*. It holds that a theory should not be self-contradictory. In other words, various parts of a theory (assumptions, internal principles, bridge principles, change mechanisms) should be rationally interconnected in such a way that they are logically compatible (Hurley, 1982). The purpose of a theory is to unify and thereby explain a body of data. Consequently, if theoretical concepts are not rationally interconnected, there is no way to explain the data with the theory. This quality of interconnectedness is sometimes called integration (Quine & Ullian, 1978), which implies that each part of a theory should be related to all other parts.

There are at least three general indicators that flag a theory's internal consistency: (1) the number of exceptions acknowledged, (2) relative simplicity (more complex theories increase the probability of inconsistency), and (3) adherence to a central theme or line of reasoning (the more identifiable this central theme, the more likely it is that deviations from it will not tend to contradict one another). In other words, internal consistency requires that the theoretical rules of the game don't change without good reason. Inconsistency would result, for example, if a theory proposed one kind of change mechanism for a certain type of human conduct and an entirely different mechanism for a very similar type of behavior. For example, a hypothetical theory that proposes that all personality traits are formed by the same underlying mechanism, say maturation, would rate high on internal consistency. In contrast, one that proposed that introversion is caused by maturation while claiming extroversion is learned would probably rate low.

Theoretical Economy

Theoretical economy is a measure of efficiency as determined by the relationship between the phenomena explained by a theory and its underlying assumptions. Theoretical economy can be figured in two ways. First, two theories may explain exactly the same phenomena but make different assumptions. In that case, the one with fewer assumptions or with less-complex assumptions would have greater theoretical economy (as an analogy, imagine that two cars travel the same distance, but the one with the better fuel mileage uses less gas). Second, two theories may make exactly the same assumptions, but one may explain more phenomena than the other. In that case, the one that explains more phenomena reflects greater theoretical economy (analogously, of two cars using the same amount of gas, the one with greater fuel economy will travel farther than the other).

Sometimes the term *simplicity* or *parsimony* is used to express the idea of theoretical economy. *Morgan's Canon* expresses this basic idea a little differently: If two explanations of phenomena fit all the facts equally well, then the more economical explanation is to be preferred. In other words, science constitutes the most complete explanation of facts with the least expenditure of effort.

Theoretical economy is relative, not an absolute scientific value. It requires a certain degree of balance between theoretical assumptions and principles and the number, kind, and complexity of phenomena explained. Moreover, assessments of theoretical economy are probably more subjective, reflecting elements of aesthetic and personal impression, than the other criteria of scientific worthiness. Nevertheless, this criterion is widely used under one rubric or another in science.

Developmental Adequacy

The term *development* is used in many different fields, and its usage is accompanied by many different connotations. This state of affairs makes it difficult to derive a formal definition for the concept. In fact, to do so would probably deprive the term of a certain openness and flexibility that has contributed to its appeal. Nevertheless, in a book about theories of development, some attention must be given to defining the concept. We can begin by noting that development is fundamentally a biological concept linked to the idea that certain relatively permanent changes occur over time in the organization of living structures and life processes (Harris, 1957, p. 3).

Not only do developmental theories have to explain something about human nature, as do other psychological theories, but they also have to explain how it gets that way. To accomplish this task, most developmental theories (Wilson's sociobiology, which explains development in a species, is an exception) attempt to explain *ontogenesis,* the relatively permanent changes individuals undergo during their life span. But what do we mean when we claim that a person *develops?* An adequate answer requires that we distinguish between the concept of change and the concept of development. While the concept of development necessarily implies that some kind of change has taken place, the fact that some kind of change has occurred does not necessarily imply that something has developed. For example, filing one's fingernails, brushing one's hair, or waking up in the morning are all manifest changes in the individual's state, but no developmental psychologist would contend that they represent developmental changes.

The concept of development implies the presence of one or more complex changes. The characteristics that follow are usually implicated when the term *development* is used. An advantage of defining development in terms of these characteristics is that they can serve as a set of criteria against which theories can be evaluated for their *developmental adequacy.* That is, theories may represent weak, moderate, or strong developmental explanations, depending on how well they account for these characteristics.

Temporality

All development presumes an element of temporality, which means that changes tend to occur over time (Harris, 1957, p. 3). The duration of time is generally presumed to involve an extended rather than short interval (Harris, p. 10), such as the several years needed to acquire secondary sex characteristics during adolescence. The process of "growing up" and "growing old" is another way of expressing the relationship between time and development, which is not to say that older necessarily means more developed. For example, when we say that interpersonal relationships take time to develop, we don't mean that time alone develops a relationship, only that time provides the opportunity for events, decisions, and experiences that contribute to development.

Cumulativity

Cumulativity means that developmental changes result in the addition of some new feature(s) to the organism: First one thing, then another is acquired. Developmental acquisitions imply a degree of permanence. They in turn modify later acquisitions, thereby altering the shape of the individual's entire being (Anderson, 1957). Cumulative changes may be dramatic (acquiring language) or incremental (extending grasping behavior from a spoon to a fork). Some achievements may ultimately be diminished after having served a transitional function for later achievements, as when, for example, crawling gives way to walking.

An important element of cumulativity is that of causal recession (Anderson, 1957), wherein developing individuals will tend to retain some of the effects of past changes. For example, it may be difficult to explain certain behaviors in a given situation (e.g., bad habits) without appealing to some earlier origins in the individual's life history.

Cumulativity is necessary but not sufficient to claim that a developmental change has occurred. After all, hair growth, piling up hours watching television, and learning who is buried in Grant's tomb are all cumulative processes, but they are not particularly developmental in nature.

Directionality

Russell (1945) has argued that organic development must, on logical grounds, implicate a sense of "directedness." The direction may be from the general to the specific (Hamburger, 1957), from less to greater maturity (Gesell & Ilg, 1949), toward greater differentiation and hierarchic integration (Werner, 1957), toward increased efficiency and specificity (Anderson, 1957), or along some other dimension.

Directionality also implies that developmental changes are progressive, relatively durable, and irreversible. The progressive element means that individuals change in ways that are in some respect better or more advanced than previous states. We do not necessarily have to know what the developmental terminus is, nor do we have to specify the precise point of origin (although theories in developmental psychology use birth as their starting point, there is no necessary reason that requires them to do so). What we do have to account for is the direction of development in terms that imply progressive accumulations between two points in time.

The element of durability implies that development results in improvements that facilitate relatively long-lasting, though not necessarily permanent, change. Most developmentalists would argue, for example, that crawling represents a progressive developmental change for infants (though not for adults), even though it eventually gives way to walking. In cases like this, the durability element is preserved in the sense that crawling facilitates the acquisition of balance and coordination needed to walk.

Directionality also implies that developmental changes are relatively irreversible in that they cannot easily be undone. While individuals change in many ways over their lifetimes, only a portion of these are irreversible and thus constitute developmental changes. Growing bald, learning to read, and forming a personality all reflect directional changes (progress, durability, irreversibility). In contrast, joining a political party (reversible), memorizing the definition of *theory* for an exam (probably nondurable), and acquiring more and more credit cards (nonprogressive) do not.

New Mode of Organization

Strong claims of development describe changes that result in new modes of organization (e.g., Meredith, 1957, p. 115; Nagel, 1957, p. 1). This characteristic is different from cumulativity and directionality; it implies the emergence of new phenomena and new properties not found in previous states.

It takes more than the addition of a new behavior or other element (these are included in the cumulativity characteristic) to comprise a new mode of organization.

This characteristic requires a radical alteration or reorganization in the arrangement, constitution, or structure of the individual. In short, the *rules of the system* change. Caterpillars that change into butterflies, maggots that become flies, and children who learn to walk and talk all represent examples of new modes of organization. Theories that explain the development of new modes of organization are more adequate developmental theories than those that do not because they account for these kinds of developmental changes.

There are several issues that are related to this characteristic. One concerns whether or not development should be conceptualized in terms of stages. Without prejudging material presented later, it must suffice here to note that not all developmentalists see human nature in terms of stages. Even those who do may have in mind quite different kinds of stages. For example, Gesell and Ilg (1949, p. 60) define developmental stages as a "level of maturity," simply a "passing moment" in the life cycle. This notion implies temporality, cumulativity, and directionality, but it does not imply that later stages represent new modes of organizations vis-à-vis earlier stages. Rather, stages of this sort reflect incremental, bit-by-bit improvements continuously linked together along a relatively linear, developmental path. In contrast, other theorists may view development in terms of radical transformations and reorganizations of earlier stages into qualitatively different later stages. This latter conception clearly implies that later stages are new modes of organization. A number of theories described later adhere to some sort of "stage" concept. The astute reader will note that a stage in one theory may not have the same properties as a stage in another theory.

A related issue concerns whether or not development is best construed as a continuous or discontinuous process. This is the *continuity–discontinuity* debate, a controversy that has occupied some attention in developmental psychology. The two poles of the continuity–discontinuity debate can be described as follows. On the continuity side are those theorists such as Noam Chomsky (Chapter 6), B. F. Skinner (Chapter 8), and Albert Bandura (Chapter 9) who maintain that development reflects quantitative rather than qualitative growth. In their view, development is viewed as a relatively uniform, *linear progression* from an initial state to a mature state. At the other extreme are theorists such as Jean Piaget (Chapter 11) and Lawrence Kohlberg (Chapter 12) who cast development primarily in terms of a sequence of qualitatively distinct stages. Others (e.g., Pinard & Laurendeau, 1969; Wohlwill, 1966) believe that the issue is essentially a false dichotomy, a conceptual artifact determined by a theorist's level of analysis. Like the nature–nurture controversy, interpreting development as essentially continuous or discontinuous is a theoretical matter rather than an issue of empirical fact (Werner, 1957).

Increased Capacity for Self-control

As individuals develop, they generally increase the number and types of domains in which they can exert control (Flammer, 1995). Put differently, the concept of development implies that as people develop, they become more proactive and less reactive, thereby increasing their capacity for self-control (Harris, 1957). Self-control entails the use of feedback so that one's activities can be continuously monitored and adjusted. While a person does not have to be completely self-controlling at any time, some aspect or function must display an increase in this property.

Biologists refer to self-control as *autoregulation,* an organism's ability to regulate itself within its ecology. But self-control as autoregulation is more than just conscious control, will power, and deliberate action. It implies some mechanism that anticipates the consequences of a particular activity, adjusts the activity to the expected outcome, initiates the activity, monitors the consequences as they unfold, and continuously readjusts the activity to achieve planned consequences. Moreover, higher forms of self-regulation may also involve an ability to anticipate environmental events before they occur (e.g., weather prediction, flood control). The increased capacity to think out solutions to problems and to experiment mentally with ideas before tackling them on a concrete level are both examples of increased capacity for self-control in comparison to, for example, the directed gropings of an infant.

Along with an increased capacity for self-control comes a simultaneous increase in independence from environmental fluctuations. The two achievements go hand in hand. Increasing independence from environmental changes occurs with the ability to foresee, plan, forecast, and anticipate events in the proximal (nearby) and distal (faraway) ecology, which may have important consequences. Through anticipation, individuals can better adjust themselves to avoid any foreseeable adversities and to take advantage of fortuitous events. For example, as children develop, they gradually acquire the capacity to predict the path of a baseball and to spot and avoid hazardous traffic or other situations.

In this book, the five characteristics just described are used as criteria for judging how "developmental" a developmental theory is. Not every developmental theory accounts for each characteristic. To that extent, how many characteristics a theory does explain is an important measure of its *developmental adequacy.*

The use of these characteristics presumes a certain degree of fairness and neutrality to the theories presented in this book. Consequently, the reader should note that nothing requires a theory to include or ignore one or another of these characteristics in its account of development. A theorist is free, within the bounds of good taste and sound judgment, to assemble virtually any explanation of human development. How good that explanation is, however, depends in large part on how completely it explains the five qualities described. These qualities constitute our measure of developmental adequacy.

Pedagogical Usefulness

Whereas scientific worthiness and developmental adequacy express two different dimensions of a theory's explanatory power, a theory's *usefulness* is quite a separate issue. Usefulness is a measure of a theory's helpful, beneficial implications for parents, teachers, counselors, and others who play a role in fostering children's development. In short, usefulness helps us evaluate the extent to which a theory can be used to direct our efforts at influencing human development. For example, does a theory suggest or imply that parents and teachers should do some things but not others to make development "better" for children? If so, what are its implications for pedagogy?

Note that our concern about usefulness has been expressed in terms of "pedagogy" rather than science. *Scientific usefulness* is quite different. That type of usefulness concerns the extent to which psychologists use a theory to generate testable hypotheses for research. This issue was addressed earlier in terms of a theory's predictive validity: its ability to predict new facts about development. In contrast, our concern here with *pedagogical usefulness* is the extent to which a theory guides us in raising, teaching, or counseling children.

To be sure, our discussion of pedagogical usefulness intertwines issues of simply personal taste with professional judgments about a theory's merits. There are no general accounts in the psychological literature that pertain, in a rigorous way, to evaluating a theory's usefulness. This situation arises, in part, because psychologists understand that the primary purpose of a theory is to *explain* phenomena not to guide child rearing. Moreover, in formulating a theory, individuals are seldom driven to address what uses others might make of their work. Consequently, there is no consensus about what constitutes pedagogical usefulness, nor is there any widespread agreement that theories ought to be useful beyond their primary purpose of explaining human development. Given this state of affairs, readers are cautioned that our formulations about pedagogical usefulness are speculative.

Once introduced to a developmental theory, students, far more often than their professors, ask, "So what?" Underlying their question is a concern for "What can I *do* with this theory?" It is this concern with pragmatic utility that has prompted us to evaluate developmental theories for their usefulness. Our intent is not so much to impose an arbitrary set of values on theories (though we nevertheless will do that to some extent) as it is to provide some sense of the pedagogical merits of the theories we describe. In our view, an assessment of pedagogical usefulness must account for at least four elements: interpretability, versatility, availability, and guidance.

Interpretability

A key element of interpretability is a theory's jargon, which reflects both the number and complexity of new ideas needed to explain human development. A theory that is easily interpreted by parents and teachers is more usable than one that is not. Some theories, more than others, express core concepts in terms of readily accessible ideas that can be easily interpreted by naive adults. Other theories incorporate ideas that are hard to interpret. For example, as we saw in Chapter 1, Freud's concepts of *id, ego, superego,* and *unconscious* are widely used today because they reflect readily interpretable meanings. In contrast, Edward Wilson's sociobiological concepts, such as *genetic fitness*, *phylogenetic inertia*, and *ecological pressure* are used only by experts. Consequently, they reflect meanings that are far less interpretable by teachers, counselors, or parents.

A second element of interpretability concerns the extent to which it provides concrete examples of its explanatory concepts. While theoretical principles are necessarily abstract, concrete examples help us clarify and better understand how they work. Concreteness refers to how well a theory shows (in addition to linguistic descriptions of) what it means. Concrete examples go a long way toward helping us "see" how a theory's explanatory concepts work in real life.

Versatility

A theory's versatility is somewhat like having a sharp knife around the kitchen. The knife is a single implement that can be used to perform many different actions: cutting, scraping, poking, pounding, prying. Versatility in this sense means that a theory and its concepts motivate a variety of pedagogical implications. Does a theory do many different jobs (four tools in my toolbox do 90 percent of my "fixit" jobs)? That is, does it provide instruction for those involved in child rearing, teaching, or counseling? Because some theories provide better or more instruction than others, they have greater versatility.

Availability

A theory cannot be very useful if only a few people have the intelligence to genuinely access its formulations. For example, an old academic anecdote tells of Einstein's publication of his theory of general relativity. At the time, only a handful of physicists and mathematicians understood the complex mathematics underlying the theory. These few individuals were the only ones who had intellectual access to Einstein's work on general relativity. But times change. Today, there is widespread intellectual access to that work. The mathematics is considered routine study for mathematicians and physicists, and the original work has been republished and interpreted in countless forms.

In the same vein, the more widely a theorist's work is circulated, discussed, and interpreted, the greater its availability for use. It was his concern for reaching audiences beyond the realm of purely academic research that prompted B. F. Skinner to present his ideas in *Walden II* and *Beyond Freedom and Dignity*, two works known for their nontechnical presentation.

A theorist's work may be available not only at the university library, but also in various technical or lay journals and magazines. Today, for example, many pamphlets, newspaper columns, or magazine articles provide advice to parents on problems ranging from toilet training to adolescent discipline. Most of these cases have replaced appeals to common sense with veiled references to "research studies," which in turn were almost certainly carried out within one or another theoretical framework.

To some extent, a theory's availability may be limited by the theorist's native language. For example, you will discover in Chapter 11 that four decades of Jean Piaget's work in cognitive development did not become available to American researchers until the late 1960s and 1970s. Prior to that, Americans made little use of Piaget's theory because it was written exclusively in French.

There are other factors that may influence a theory's availability to both scientists and the public. These include the amount and technicality of new jargon it contains, the complexity or even testability of its theoretical concepts, and the type or amount of phenomena it attempts to explain.

Guidance

To be genuinely useful to parents, teachers, and counselors, a developmental theory must provide some degree of guidance in working with children. But in the context of child development, we are not involved here with questions of moral values (i.e., how *should* children be raised). The issue is a bit more subtle. What we are interested in is the extent to which a theory's account of natural development contains implicit advice for adults on how to promote the natural course of child development and reduce the chance of developmental retardation or dysfunction.

Of primary importance in evaluating a theory's guidance is its explanation of how development is produced. Recall from Chapter 1 that this explanation is found in the structural component called *change mechanism*. After all, such mechanisms must ultimately be utilized in order to bring about some change in children's development.

For example, as we will see in Chapter 8, Skinner's theory of operant conditioning implies a systematic program called *behavior modification* for changing children's behavior. It's steps are explicit and direct, and it is an excellent example of theoretical guidance. Note that whether or not we *should* use behavior modification with children is a value question that must ultimately be answered on grounds that transcend Skinner's theory. Our concern here is only with the extent to which a theory actually guides child rearing, not whether its advice is good or bad or popular in one context or another.

Ultimately what we are looking for is a theory that will advise us to do some things and not do other things to promote the natural course of children's development. The extent to which we can garner this type of guidance from a theory's structural components is one important measure of it usefulness.

In the preceding section, we have described four distinct characteristics—interpretability, versatility, availability, and guidance—that comprise our view of pedagogical usefulness. Of course, we have not exhausted all that might be considered relevant here. But these four elements provide us with a common basis for judging a theory's usefulness. Individual readers may wish to add their own criteria to this category and use them throughout this text.

The three *sets* of criteria described—scientific worthiness, developmental adequacy, and pedagogical usefulness—provide independent means for answering the question "How good is this theory?" The reader is encouraged to form an independent opinion about how well each theory meets the criteria proposed. In addition, readers might also identify a set of personally meaningful criteria for evaluating theories. For example, we have found a personal interest in evaluating important theories in terms of their *aesthetic appeal*. We look for qualities of texture (richness, depth), novelty (imagination, creativity), interest (attention holding), and revolutionary impact (breaks new frontiers, shows a new way of viewing something). We don't expect others to judge theories on the basis of their aesthetic appeal, nor do we expect them to understand what we mean when we do it. But our notion of aesthetic appeal has influenced our decision to include some theories but not others in this text.

Professionals who plan to use theories in their work might formulate their own set of criteria. These could include, for example, relevance to one's needs, translatability of theory concepts into personally meaningful situations, ease of using a theory's principles, availability of literature about applications of the theory, and adequacy of practical applications (how well the theory works). However, one should expect that whatever criteria are used to evaluate theories, they will have a common grounding in explicit ideas and will be used consistently.

Important Paradigm Patterns

There are several paradigm-related patterns that emerge in our evaluation of theories in this book. These patterns result not from biases on our part but from the kinds of strengths and weaknesses inherent in different paradigms. For example, as a general class of theories, those in the endogenous paradigm (Part II) are consistently the lowest rated for pedagogical usefulness and testability, the most important element of scientific worthiness. The problem with endogenous theories is that they tend to rely on mentalist constructions, which makes testing them more difficult than theories in other paradigms. In addition, because endogenous change mechanisms tend to be relatively immune to environmental influence, they reduce the impact of change agents such as parents and teachers over the course of human development.

In contrast, exogenous theories (Part III) tend to be consistently among the highest rated for their scientific worthiness. This is due to the fact that these theories tend to use research methods that adhere to the three most fundamental components of science: observation, experimental control, and measurement. Moreover, because these theories tend to concentrate on environmental influences, their "problems of study" concentrate on highly visible aspects of human nature that rely on few inferences about invisible, internal processes and mechanisms. Finally, exogenous theories explain development in terms of environmental influences, and that results in a high degree of pedagogical usefulness.

Theories in the constructivist paradigm (Part Four) tend to score highest for their developmental adequacy. The most compelling reason for this is that they tend to view development in terms of qualitatively different stages. The result of this tendency is that one form of complex development in particular, "new mode of organization," is a centerpiece of their explanatory constructions. Sometimes theories in other paradigms are simply indifferent to this characteristic of development. Other times they view what appear to be qualitative differences as the product of smaller, incremental differences in quantity rather than quality.

Summary Points

1. Development always implies some kind of complex change, whereas change does not necessarily imply development.
2. In developmental psychology, the term *development* connotes five characteristics: temporality, cumulativity, directionality, new mode of organization, and increased capacity for self-control.
3. A theory's scientific worthiness is determined by its testability, external validity, predictive validity, internal consistency, and theoretical economy.
4. A theory's pedagogical usefulness can be measured by its interpretability, versatility, availability, and guidance.
5. As a general rule, certain patterns emerge in evaluating theories in different paradigms. Exogenous theories tend to score higher than others for testability and pedagogical usefulness. Endogenous theories tend to score lower than others on these same evaluative criteria. Constructivist theories tend to rate higher than others on criteria of developmental adequacy.

SUGGESTED READINGS

Harris, D. B. (Ed.). (1957). *The concept of development*. Minneapolis: University of Minnesota Press.

Hultsch, D. F., & Hickey, T. (1978). External validity in the study of human development: theoretical and methodological issues. *Human Development, 21,* 76–91.

Reese, H. W., & Overton, W. F. (1970). Models of development and theories of development. In L. R. Goulet & P. B. Baltes (Eds.), *Life-span developmental psychology*. New York: Academic Press.

PART TWO

The Endogenous Paradigm

The endogenous family of theories views development as the product of innate causes. Often these influences are posited as biological templates that dictate specific changes that occur at predetermined times (e.g., Freud and Erikson). Sometimes endogenous theorists pay less attention to timing than to ultimate biological determination (e.g., Wilson and Chomsky). The variety of theories in this section reflects the richness of possible explanations found in the endogenous paradigm.

In the case of Freud and Erikson, human development is described as the unfolding of an innately determined sequence of stages. Each stage in the sequence is a critical period for later development. The order and timing of the stages are immune to environmental input, although the environment clearly influences the kinds of events that occur and individual adjustments to be made during each stage. These personal adjustments, however, do not themselves influence the orderly progression of the stages.

A third, very different, theory of human development is found in Wilson's sociobiology, which in just over two decades has generated tremendous interest and controversy. Sociobiology is a modern evolutionary theory that claims that important qualities of insect, animal, and human social behavior have common roots in the evolution of the species. This theory provides an interesting contrast to the others contained in this book because it focuses on *phylogenesis* (development of the species across many generations) rather than *ontogenesis* (development within an individual's life span). The theory is included in this book for two reasons. First, evolutionary psychology, based on Wilson's theory, has become a mainstay in psychology course work. Second, Wilson's conception of development as evolutionary changes between generations provides a different point of view and supporting research that challenges conventional notions about development as something that occurs within the life span.

The fourth endogenous theory found in this section is Chomsky's theory of generative grammar. The study of psycholinguistics and children's language development owes much of its current program to Chomsky's revolutionary analysis of linguistic structures. According to Chomsky, the most important parameters of language acquisition and use are innately determined, and the innate mechanisms that govern language are universal across all languages.

Part Two concludes with Ainsworth's theory of infant attachment, which had a tremendous impact on developmental psychology during the 1970s and 1980s. Ainsworth views the infant primarily in terms of its social needs. In her view, an infant's relationship with its primary caretaker creates a prototype on which all later relationships are modeled.

CHAPTER

3

Freud and Psychoanalysis

Preview Questions

In what ways did historical moments influence Freud? What two separate lines of work did he unify?

What assumptions underlie psychoanalytic theory?

What major problems does psychoanalysis study, and how are its methods matched to its problems?

What are the theory's internal and bridge principles?

What change mechanisms account for development?

What makes Freud's theory a member of the endogenous paradigm?

What are the important contributions and criticisms of the theory?

How does psychoanalysis rate for scientific worthiness, developmental adequacy, and pedagogical usefulness?

Historical Sketch

In 1856 Sigismund Schlomo Freud was born to his Jewish father's third wife in Moravia (now part of Czechoslovakia). Young Sigismund had two older half brothers (who had grown and left home), five sisters, and a younger brother. As a child, he moved to Vienna, shortened his name to "Sigmund," and later entered medical school at the University of Vienna where he specialized in neurology. His training there stressed biological *determinism*, a view that attributes all human activity to physiological causes, and inspired him to conduct research on brain neurology. About this time Freud took up cigar smoking because, as Gay (1988) comments, the young man was smitten with an ardent yearning for a young woman, Martha Bernays. Freud needed a constant substitute for her absent kisses, and cigar smoking seemed to fit the bill. Following medical school, Freud learned that his Jewish origins would prevent him from pursuing an academic career, so he gave up his research to enter the private practice of treating mental diseases.

Freud finally married Martha Bernays in 1886, shortly after his return from a "clinical internship" in France. Freud had several children, but his most famous,

Anna, was born nearly a decade after Sigmund and Martha married. Anna would later grow up to study psychoanalysis herself, and after having undergone "analysis sessions" with her famous father, she became a genuine influence in the history of psychoanalytic theory.

Until the turn of the century, Freud complained of widespread anti-Semitism that excluded him from learned societies throughout Europe. In 1909 he visited America and delivered a series of lectures at Clark University that propelled him to international fame and later prompted his appointment by the King of Austria to the rank of full professor at the University of Vienna. At the close of World War I, Freud proposed and helped create free clinics for the treatment of war-related and other psychopathologies. Given today's concern about the cost of medical treatment, Freud's idea was ahead of its time. From 1922 to 1936, the staff of Freud's Vienna Ambulatorium treated patients from all social classes free of charge (Danto, 1998).

In 1930 Freud published *Civilization and Its Discontents,* one of the most widely read of all his books. Part of its popularity was the fact that Freud was by now world renowned. Always the pessimist, Freud included in this joyless book his usual attack on and disdain for social niceties. Following on earlier themes, he argued that we humans would always remain ignorant of our true motives, because they were hidden deep inside our psychological self. The *best* we could hope for would be insights that left us feeling common, ordinary, everyday *unhappiness* (Gay, 1988).

When the Nazis finally invaded Austria in 1936, Freud was defiant as usual and initially refused to flee. But two years later, things had changed for him. His daughter was arrested by the Gestapo and barely escaped with her life (Gay, 1988). This event convinced Freud it was time to leave Vienna. Both American and German ambassadors helped Freud flee to London, where he continued his writing and clinical work. Upon arriving in London, the now famous Freud was asked to sign England's "sacred book of the Royal Society," where his signature now appears alongside those of Charles Darwin and Sir Isaac Newton. Relishing the company of such famous people, Freud continued his cigar smoking and later developed cancer of the jaw, for which he underwent numerous operations. To control the pain, Freud began experimenting with cocaine (in those days, Coca-Cola® meant more than just cola), and some historians believe he became a cocaine addict. Nevertheless, by this time in his life, he had already published his most important theoretical ideas. Freud died in London during the Blitzkrieg of 1939. He never knew the murderous fate awaiting his sisters in Nazi concentration camps.

Psychoanalysis developed out of Freud's unique synthesis of two historically independent lines of work—the search for neurological brain structures and the practice of psychic curing. This synthesis combined Freud's deterministic training in neurology with his clinical treatment of mental disorders. Systematic attempts to isolate discrete brain functions marked the *zeitgeist* (historical spirit of the times) of Freud's medical training. About the same time, humanitarian movements in America, England, and France were underway to reform treatment of the insane by invoking a new concept—*mental disease*—that assumed mental rather than physical causes of insanity. We think Freud's contribution to our understanding of human development cannot be fully appreciated without some attention to how these two historical trends were unified in his work.

The Search for Neurological Structures

In the early 1800s there was tremendous controversy in Europe about the bodily locus of the human mind. Many thought the mind was located in the stomach (the source of appetite); others thought it was located in the heart (the source of compassion). A third group argued that both compassion and appetite were mental functions of the human brain. Freud belonged to this third group, and his work with brain neurology led him naturally to work with brain anatomy.

Franz Joseph Gall, together with his student G. Spurzheim, invented the pseudoscience of *phrenology*. They developed a cranial map that located discrete mental faculties in specific areas of the brain (Boring, 1957). While phrenology had tremendous popular appeal at the time, it also provided scientists with testable hypotheses that were easy to disprove. In its wake came the legitimate, truly scientific study of brain anatomy found in the work of John Hughlings Jackson. Jackson, often called the father of neurology, was best known for his meticulous mapping of the nervous system. In the tradition of Jackson's pioneering work, Brucke and Meynert became two of the leading authorities in the field. Freud studied neurology and neuropathology under them, and they infused in him an unshakable belief that *every behavior was strictly determined by inner forces and mechanisms*. With this strongly deterministic orientation instilled in him, Freud became convinced that all human behavior (even slips of the tongue) was caused by some underlying mental agent. Under Brucke's direction, he attempted to determine how the anatomical structure of the nervous system produced psychological phenomena (Fancher, 1979). Meynert was responsible for perfecting Freud's ability to diagnose symptoms of brain damage. For his labors Freud won a fellowship to study in Paris with the celebrated psychic healer Jean Charcot. While working with Charcot, Freud's neurological training became intertwined with the art of psychic healing.

Psychic Healing

By the mid 1700s gravitational and magnetic forces had been well documented. About that time a Viennese physician, Friedrich Anton Mesmer, posited a force called "animal gravitation," a plausible notion at that time coming in the wake of Newton's discoveries about physical gravitation. Mesmer's importance here lies in his attempts to cure mental illness by harnessing "animal gravitation." He believed that a misalignment of the body's magnetic force resulted in certain "mental" diseases and their accompanying symptoms. At first he tried to realign his patients by exposing them to magnetic ores, but he eventually discarded this therapy when he discovered that many of his patients could be cured without magnetic ores; all he had to do was pass his hands over the afflicted areas. Rather than conclude that magnetism was unrelated to healing, Mesmer decided that his own body possessed unusually large amounts of animal gravitation and that he had personally effected the cures. His personalized healing eventually became associated with his name— *Mesmerism*—though his method fell into disrepute when a scientific committee investigated and found no scientific basis for his psychic cures.

With Mesmerism properly debunked, James Braid, a respected physician and interested witness at many public mesmerizings, produced an unexpected discovery. He showed through carefully planned experiments that the mesmerist's trance could be induced through sensory fixation, a technique he termed *hypnosis*. Because it was based on physiological processes rather than animal gravitation, Braid's hypnotism gained an aura of scientific respectability. Eventually two French physicians, Joseph Breuer and Jean Charcot, attempted to use hypnosis with patients suffering from hysteria. Charcot had tremendous personal influence and attracted several very gifted students: Alfred Binet, William James, Pierre Janet, and Sigmund Freud. But it was Pierre Janet who suggested to Freud that ideas themselves could be determinants of hysterical symptoms (Macmillan, 1991). As they say, the rest is history.

Freud's Clinical Work

Freud's fellowship from the University of Vienna allowed him six months with Charcot to learn hypnosis. When he returned home in 1886, Freud entered private practice with the hypnotist Joseph Breuer. Together they refined Charcot's hypnotic technique and published several papers concerning cures for hysteria before theoretical and clinical differences prompted the two men to sever their professional relationship.

Shortly after the break with Breuer, Freud abandoned hypnosis altogether when he discovered that its cures were only temporary. He developed a new technique he called *free association,* which uncovered his patients' memories of childhood and had prolonged healing effects. Sometimes, these childhood memories revealed sexual intimacies between his clients as children and their adult relatives. These revelations prompted Freud to suggest a theory of *infantile sexuality,* a formulation that met with considerable disdain. The severity of public ridicule itself convinced Freud that the strict sexual attitudes of the day were only a mask for buried, disguised sexual passions. However, he suffered a deep personal crisis when he discovered that his patients' memories—the very ones on which his ideas had been based—were almost always *not true*. It turned out that his patients had been imagining sexual intimacies that had never really occurred.

This discovery marked a turning point in Freud's theorizing, because he concluded that "false memories" must serve some purpose (a reflection of his deterministic training) and that some mental force must be hidden beneath the memories themselves. There is some controversy today about Freud's reasons for abandoning his early views of infantile sexuality (see Gelfand & Kerr [1992] for some fresh insights into his thinking), but his discovery of unconscious motivations is one of his enduring contributions to our understanding of human nature.

Structural Components of Psychoanalysis

The deterministic orientation inspired by his medical training, coupled with his clinical practice, prompted Freud to construct a theory of personality development. Because many of his early ideas were later modified, emphasis in this chapter is given to later formulations of the theory.

Assumptions

Scientific thinking in the late 1800s assumed the correctness of Newton's elegantly simple physical laws of the conservation of mass and energy. This scientific zeitgeist influenced Freud by directing his attention to the dynamic, energetic qualities of human nature, in particular the psychic energy Freud called *libido*. But political, cultural, and social customs of the day greeted his insights with derision and scorn (Pines, 1989). Even today, considerations of Freud are a barometer of the scientific and cultural climate of our times (Forrester, 1997), widely discussed in undergraduate classes but equally renounced or censored in some religious circles.

Freud assumed that infants are born with a fixed pool of instinctual or **psychic energy,** the libido, which energizes all human activity. While individuals may vary from one to another in amount, each person maintains the same amount of libido throughout life; thus, in the spirit of Newton, libido is conserved. Psychic energy may be transformed (changed in form), but its total value remains constant. An analogy can be drawn between libido and a reservoir of water. The water possesses potential energy that may be transformed into thermal, kinetic, mechanical, and electrical energy without altering the amount of total energy. Similarly, the libido can be transformed into behavioral and psychic activities without diminishing its total value.

Instinctual energy is of two types. **Eros** is the positive energy of life, activity, hope, and sexual desire. **Thanatos** is a counterbalancing negative energy of death, destruction, despair, and aggression. Eros initiates motion and goal seeking; Thanatos balances Eros by curtailing, revising, or redirecting activity.

Freud also believed that infants were born with a separate primitive mind, the *id*, whose functions were governed entirely by libido. The infant's id is irrational, because it has yet to be socialized by any experience. Freud believed the libido had evolved in the Darwinian sense in just the same way that other physical traits had evolved.

Finally, Freud recognized that infants display instinctual reflexes inherited from their species. In particular, the infant's sucking reflex occupied Freud's attention. Of course, this reflex provides the only mechanism for acquiring nourishment. But in this reflex Freud saw two important aspects of psychological functioning: (1) a primitive instinctual urge to incorporate worldly objects and (2) an equally primitive tendency to seek pleasure though sucking and incorporation.

In sum, Freud posited three basic assumption about the newborn. First, it possessed a primitive and irrational mind. Second, this mind was possessed of libido or psychic energy. Third, the inborn sucking reflex was driven by powerful urges to seek pleasure.

Problems for Study

Freud's medical training engendered in him a belief in *no causes without effects—no effects without causes*. This determinism guided his analysis of dreams and neurotic symptoms. Most of his clinical work consisted of treating middle-class, Austrian women whose afflictions had been diagnosed as imaginary by local physicians because their own medical training had led them to seek only physical causes. One of the great ironies of developmental psychology is that Freud's treatment of women would end up in a theory of development oriented more toward males than females.

Phenomena to Be Explained.   Given his clinical situation, Freud attempted to diagnose the mental causes of psychic symptoms. As his treatments progressed, he gradually became convinced that the underlying causes could always be found in his patients' early traumatic experiences and parental relationships. More specifically, he believed that unfulfilled wishes, needs, and desires (ungratified libidinal instincts) had been repressed because of the pain caused by their unfulfillment.

Freud's immediate clinical problem was to recover an accurate representation of an individual's childhood in order to identify early events that later acted as triggers for particular kinds of symptoms. Thus, the primary phenomena to be explained is the formation of adult personality traits. Ultimately, Freud envisioned an explanation for all behavior, including many previously inexplicable phenomena—tip-of-the-tongue forgetting, Freudian slips, erotic humor, memory distortion, dreams, and abnormal personalities. He believed that the most atrocious human behaviors—torture, genocide, war—could be explained by the same mental forces that motivated the most artistic or benevolent of human behaviors.

Methods of Investigation.   To gain access to childhood memories, three techniques are used. Freud developed *free association* and *dream interpretation* in his own clinical work; *projective tests* are a more recent addition to psychoanalytic methodology.

Free association is a technique used to obtain verbal memory traces of past experiences. Patients, when placed in a calm, quiet, nondistracting environment, are asked to report any ideas that come to mind. All associations are believed to be important, even though their meaning may not at first be recognized. The therapist records associations without interrupting the spontaneous flow of thoughts. Although patients initially censor their thoughts, they become more trusting and candid over time. The therapist looks for tendencies to dwell on certain associations more than others as well as opposing tendencies to delete normal associations. While unusual associations may represent unfulfilled fantasies, deleted ones may reflect unconsciously "forgotten" material. Either type of pattern signals telltale forces at work in the patient's unconscious mind. In this manner, free associations provide data about childhood events that continue to influence a person's behavior.

Dream interpretation consists of the analysis of dream content in terms of both symbolic and hidden meanings (Freud, 1900). Freud's *Interpretation of Dreams* is considered a classic in psychology because it set forth a framework for analyzing the previously unexplored and overlooked territory of dreams. A dream's symbolic content Freud termed **manifest** meaning; it consists of the meanings associated with events, colors, shapes, sizes, relations, words, and people represented in the dream. For example, if a person dreams of falling off a cliff, the manifest meaning consists of the collective meanings of the separate symbols that denote time, place, activity, agents, actions, and feelings involved in the fall.

The **latent** meaning of a dream is the meaning ascribed to the hidden motivations that prompted the dream. Latent meaning is always uniquely personal, because it originates in conflicts experienced early in one's life. This type of meaning has been distorted to make it palatable to the semiconscious of the dreaming mind. Dreams are often illogical, precisely because their unconscious source—the fantasies, wishes, impulses, and repressed desires that motivate them—is not governed by rational control. Latent meaning is the real meaning of a dream, but it is difficult to interpret since its true meaning has been repressed and disguised. For example, falling off a cliff may unconsciously represent a wish to free oneself from family expectations or a fear of unconstrained freedom. However, in interpreting dream symbols, we must keep in mind Freud's caution that "sometimes a cigar is only a cigar."

Contemporary psychoanalysts also use *projective tests,* which consist of pictures containing ambiguous stimuli—inkblots, random shapes, people engaging in ambiguous behavior. Subjects, in describing these stimuli, must supply their own meanings. Since the stimuli themselves are ambiguous, any description given by an individual is believed to reflect deep-seated libidinal forces. Today, normative data from projective tests is used to diagnose individual responses to these ambiguous stimuli.

Internal Principles

Each of the three internal principles that comprise the core explanatory concepts of psychoanalytic theory is like a "minitheory" in itself. The *dynamic system* reflects Freud's concern with the antagonistic conflict between irrational desire and rational control. The *structural system* includes Freud's concept of our mental architecture: *id, ego,* and *superego.* Finally, the *sequential system* is a series of stages that ultimately determine the basic scope, shape, and content of adult personality. Figure 3.1 on page 46 shows that these three systems reflect distinctive but partially overlapping components of personality development.

The Dynamic System. The *dynamic system* consists of the psychic energy that is deeply hidden from our awareness. Psychic energy has been called various names: nervous energy, instinctual energy, drive energy, mental energy, libido, and tension. Freud thought psychic energy was as much a part of human evolution as the organic energy that powers metabolic, respiratory, and other biological processes.

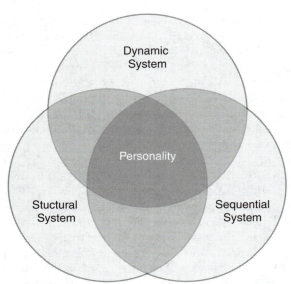

FIGURE 3.1   Three major systems comprising psychoanalytic theory.

The dynamic system is efficient and economical. It directs behavior (both mental and physical) toward objects of desire, whether these objects be imagined or real. Freud believed that this energy motivated the widest variety of phenomena—from acts of war and aggression to acts of benevolent self-sacrifice, from book burnings to creations of artistic masterpieces, from the most intimate expression of love to aggression and torture. Through Freud's eyes the most mundane and the most perverse human activities were viewed as either direct or indirect attempts to satisfy instinctual drives.

The Structural System.   The theory's *structural system* complements the dynamic system. While Freud viewed human nature as driven by powerful forces, he also provided a portrait of mental structures that channel these forces. The *id, ego,* and *superego* comprise the structural system and constitute what Freud envisioned as the architecture of the mind (Freud, 1923).

Id.   Our innate psychic energy empowers the primitive id, which is irrational and unsocialized. Acting in accord with the **pleasure principle,** the id seeks immediate gratification and tension reduction for all its urges (Freud, 1963, p. 311). The primary aim of the pleasure principle is the achievement of tensionlessness (experienced as pleasure) through need gratification (Freud, 1920). Unconstrained by any rules, the id makes no distinction between reality and fantasy. This fusion is the essential quality of **primary process** thought, a primitive form of cognition that directs the id's energy toward pleasure. Id energy is so facile and dynamic that it can be readily channeled from one object to another or from one image to another. Thus an infant beginning to experience hunger may be satisfied momentarily with a pacifier, but as hunger increases, a new object—food itself—must ultimately be forthcoming to satisfy the hunger. In a similar vein, daydreaming is an example of primary process thinking that uses wish fulfillment to partially achieve tension reduction. The id is a seething cauldron of insatiable desires (Freud, 1933a) that continues its unconscious influence throughout our lives.

Because the id's desires are irrational, its needs often do not match what is available in the immediate social and physical environment. For example, a hungry infant, incapable of feeding itself, may not obtain immediate gratification for its hunger. The tension associated with the accompanying hunger pangs unconsciously motivates the infant to discharge energy through crying, sucking, and other activities that may coincidentally signal feeding time to a caregiver. When the infant eats, its hunger decreases, and the unconscious tension subsides. Over time, with repeated episodes like this, the infant gradually comes to associate certain external events (e.g., the mother's appearance) with the repeated discharge of psychic energy. However, the reality of the real world forces the id to adjust itself to external situations, and this is done by harnessing a portion of the id's energy and transforming it into a new personality structure—the ego. This transformation is depicted in Figure 3.2 on page 48.

Ego.   The ego is the organ of reason and sanity (Freud, 1923) which begins developing at around 1 year of age. Its energy derives from libidinal instincts that have been displaced from the id to create a pool of neutralized energy. This displacement turns a portion of the erotic libido into an ego libido, which is accomplished by an abandonment of overtly sexual aims (Freud, 1923, p. 65). The process whereby instinctual energy becomes displaced, neutralized, and transformed into ego functioning is not well understood. In fact, the problem of generating rational thought from irrational desires has led some psychoanalysts to propose alternative hypotheses about the origin of the ego.

In Freud's view, the ego seeks pleasure for the id but in a diminished and delayed capacity in accord with the **reality principle,** that is, within limitations set by surrounding circumstances. The psychic energy of the id gets channeled by the ego and directed at available objects that produce pleasure. Freud uses the analogy of a rider on horseback to characterize this important relationship between the ego and the id. The rider (ego) must control and direct the horse (id), but to avoid being thrown, the rider must sometimes guide the horse where it wants to go; analogously, the ego is obliged to follow the wishes of the id as if they were its own (Freud, 1923). However, circumstances sometimes arise where gratification must be delayed. The result is the arousal of *anxiety,* a psychic tension that acts as the ego's warning that executing certain plans could be either physically or psychologically threatening. Finally, the ego is that personality organ which mediates the conflict between the id's irrational desires and society's restrictive demands.

The ego acts as a remarkably flexible executive decision maker. It operates on the basis of **secondary process** thought, which is more organized, rational, and integrated than the id's primary process (where irrational desires rule). Secondary process thinking is comprised of such intellectual abilities as dreams and dream

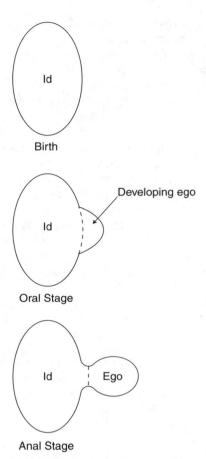

Birth

Developing ego

Id

Oral Stage

Id   Ego

Anal Stage

FIGURE 3.2   Formation of the ego.

censorship, language, sensory perception, problem solving, symbol recognition and use, recognition and recall memory, and reality testing. When the ego is unable to cope with particularly stressful events, it may channel psychic energy to an earlier, regressive developmental mode of coping that is more secure and less threatening. It does not replace the id's primary process thought, but rather adds a new level of organization to it. Consider the examples in Sandlot Seminar 3.1.

In summary, the ego is a constellation of interrelated functions that control mental conflict by mediating the demands of the id and the limitations imposed by external reality. In time, some of the ego's own neutralized energy evolves into a new psychological structure, the *superego*.

Superego.   Whereas the ego evolves from the id by adapting to the situational "here and now," the superego evolves from the ego by adapting to society's "always pre-

Sandlot Seminar 3.1

Stressful Circumstances and Regression

During times of stress individuals often display coping behaviors that would illustrate regression to a more secure and less threatening period of development. Consider the following examples:

1. Just before interviewing for a job an individual finds himself biting his nails.
2. During a final exam, a student finds herself constantly biting and chewing on her lip.
3. When involved in a particularly challenging algebra class, the student cannot keep the pencil out of his mouth, and finds that by the end of the class he has teeth marks all over it.
4. On the way to the doctor for a physical exam and vaccination, the 6-year-old can't keep his fingers out of his mouth, constantly asking, "Mommy, do I have to go to the doctor?"
5. A student, preparing for the defense of her master's thesis, asks a friend for a cigarette, even though she is not a smoker.

In each case the individual, when placed in a particularly stressful situation, regresses to a more secure period of development. How might regressive behavior help an individual feel more comfortable and less stressed?

---

sent" conventions and morals. This evolution begins at around three years of age and is depicted in Figure 3.3 on page 50.

In Freud's view, parents are the primary agents of socialization, and their role in the formation of superego is preeminent. They demand, teach, and encourage certain behaviors in their children while prohibiting and punishing others. In order to conform to parental expectations, a portion of the child's ego gets transformed into what Freud termed superego because it is differentiated from but superior to the ego. The superego contains the *conscience* and the *ego ideal*. The conscience consists of society's moral prohibitions and values incorporated from one's parents, whereas the ego ideal comprises the standards of perfection toward which we strive.

The superego constantly demands that we think and behave in accord with cultural expectations and will punish us with guilt if we give in to the id's irrational, pleasure-driven desires. Moreover, the superego treats thought and behavior in the same way; thinking something is as bad or as good as actually doing it. Freud's recognition of society's role in controlling impulsive, aggressive urges is quite ironic, given the unbridled Nazi terror that surrounded his later years.

The Sequential System.   The third internal principle in psychoanalytic theory is the sequential system of five maturational stages. Before describing each stage, however, it is important to understand what Freud intended by his use of the term *stage*.

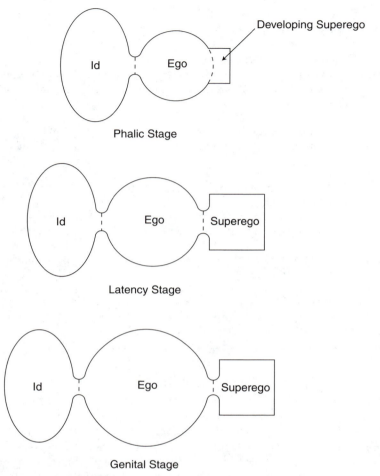

FIGURE 3.3   Formation of superego from ego.

First, the biological determinism ingrained in Freud's thinking is unmistakable in his belief that stages are *critical periods* of development. Critical periods are marked by a biological onset, the rapid learning of some specialized function or ability, and a biologically timed closure. The acquisition of a special function or ability is seen as indispensable to development and often facilitates other changes that occur later. Failure to acquire the critical ability at the proper time also implies both that it cannot be acquired later on and that the individual will be, to some extent, developmentally impaired. For this reason, Freud placed tremendous importance on the early psychosexual stages.

Second, Freud was convinced that sexuality played such a dynamic and vital role in motivating human behavior that he sought to determine the origin of its development in infancy and childhood. While the concept of *infantile sexuality* shocked Freud's Victorian contemporaries, it is understood today not as a literal proposition about adult sexuality present in infants, but as Freud's attempt to emphasize the *nonbiological* sources of pleasure. To make his point, he defined *sexual* to mean a striving for pleasure independent of nourishment (Freud, 1940). When Freud writes about an infant's "erotic" desires, he means precisely that those desires are motivated by the pursuit of pleasure. In short, he believed that infantile sexuality evolves through a series of stages from a state of global, undifferentiated oral pleasure toward the differentiated, mature state of adult sexuality. During each stage along this journey, an individual's sexuality (pursuit of pleasure) is reflected in prototypic patterns of adjustment. "Misunderstanding" seems to be synonymous with Freud. Sandlot Seminar 3.2 illustrates another typical example.

Third, at each stage psychic energy is invested in a particular body region whose increased sensitivity produces an **erotogenic zone** (Freud, 1963, p. 275). This localized energy charges that zone with tension that must be discharged and thereby reduced. Energy discharge and its accompanying tension reduction are experienced as pleasure. The erotic desire associated with a particular erotogenic zone is

---

Sandlot Seminar 3.2

Popular Misconceptions about Freud

Jen Camus and Marta Winegarten get together each morning in Jen's kitchen to share coffee, gossip, and stories about their young children. Jen's 4-month-old Caitlin is asleep upstairs.

MARTA: I think forcing a baby to eat according to a mom's schedule is just crazy in this day and age.

JEN: Speaking of "crazy," I just saw in *TV Guide* that there's a big special coming up on the life and times of Sigmund Freud. Why in the world would anybody want to watch a show about that pervert? He's nothing but sex, sex, sex. Can you imagine anything so absurd as something called infantile sexuality. There is nothing, and I mean *nothing*, he can teach me about my children.

MARTA: You're right about that. I don't know why people keep bringing him up. I thought he died a long time ago. Besides, what in the world could he know about modern children?

JEN: Speaking of . . . guess what? The pharmacy had a special on this new pacifier that guarantees Caitlin will be so relaxed she'll go right to sleep. You know how she is, so fussy all the time. Well, I tried it, and it worked. It's incredible how something so simple could help her go right to sleep. Now if someone would only develop a theory to explain that! Then we'd really be on to something.

1. Why do you think Caitlin went to sleep so quickly with the new pacifier?
2. What might Jen and Marta learn by watching the special on Sigmund Freud?

directly related to the critical period needs of each psychosexual stage. Children's erotic pleasures associated with their erotogenic zones lay the psychological foundation for increasingly adultlike erotic pleasures.

In one of his most quoted statements, Freud offered us *The child is father to the man*. By this he meant that our personality, formed in infancy and childhood, determined what type of personality we would later exhibit as adults. Freud made childhood an object of study, and he helped us appreciate the dynamic and emotional nature of children's feelings. These he attempted to capture with the stages of infantile sexuality.

Oral Stage (birth to approximately 1 year).   The oral stage is a critical period for achieving the ability to "incorporate" external objects as part of oneself. Freud believed that incorporation was prerequisite for later being able to identify with the parents and psychologically incorporate their values as one's own. The infant's erotogenic zone is the mouth, so infantile sexuality is characterized by ingestion-related pleasures.

The infant's mouth, charged with psychic energy, seeks pleasure from stimulation, which may account for why infants suck instinctively even while sleeping. Such stimulation, however, is double edged; it introduces the infant to both pleasure and pain. Pleasure results from eating, biting, gumming, sucking, smiling, and noise making, all of which discharge sexual, pleasure-seeking tensions. While some activities result in satisfaction from hunger reduction, it should be noted that the activities themselves may also be experienced as pleasurable. The infant relates to objects in the world by *cathecting* them, which means that energy is channeled to objects. At the same time, the mouth introduces the infant to pain when teething begins, or when certain objects are ingested (hot formula, medicine). Moreover, anxiety may be aroused when hunger pangs are not immediately satisfied, when weaning occurs, or when regular feeding rituals are interrupted, delayed, or altered.

While the mouth provides both pleasure and pain, the parents also come to represent a similar conflict. They are responsible for meeting the infant's biological needs, and in that capacity, they are seen as pleasure-producing objects. However, with the infant's growing mobility, parents begin to exert increasing control over their child's insatiable desires. Consequently, they become associated with pain when they prevent satisfaction, as occurs when demand feeding is altered to a more regular schedule or when the nighttime bottle is withheld.

The emotion produced by delayed gratification and pain is *anxiety*, which occurs whenever the infant's pleasure is threatened. Throughout infancy, anxiety is experienced when sexual tensions mount and gratification is not forthcoming. Parents too, especially the mother, may provoke feelings of intense anxiety, with her daily comings and goings, a special area of infant psychodynamics extensively investigated by Bowlby (1958, 1969, 1973, 1980).

Important personality characteristics first appear during the oral stage. These may, under certain circumstances, lead to an *oral personality*. For example, the pain associated with teething can be unconsciously transformed into the pleasure–pain of early sadism associated with biting, and the psychodynamic precursors of rejection may be associated with the infant's spitting up of unpleasant foods. Psychoanalytic theory suggests that both passive and active babies may be establishing unconscious patterns of social interaction that will later produce introverted or extraverted personalities. The internal conflicts between satisfaction and anxiety, pain and pleasure, incorporation and rejection all lead to the establishment of patterns for interacting with objects, termed *object relations* (Freud, 1963, p. 288). Too much oral satisfaction results in *fixation*, the cathexis (channeling) of psychic energy to specific objects and a resulting inability to cathect new objects. Fixation may produce neurotic smoking, alcoholism, or obesity in adults. Too little oral satisfaction has its own consequences—a shy, overly dependent, jealous, anxious, or pessimistic personality preoccupied with obtaining oral pleasure. The pedagogical problem here is to ensure an "appropriate" balance between satisfaction and frustration; a mixture of both is needed for healthy mental development. Unfortunately, Freud provided little guidance about how to ensure such a balance.

Anal Stage (approximately 1 to 3 years).   The anal stage is a critical period revolving around acquiring personal power and control. Psychic energy shifts from the mouth to the anus, making it the new center of erotogenic interest and making the bowels highly sensitive to stimulation. Sexual pleasure is associated with elimination of body wastes.

The urge to defecate creates tension. However, this tension produces conflict when parents instigate toilet training because the infant must choose between (1) the pleasure of immediate elimination and pain of parental disappointment or (2) the pain of control and delayed elimination for the pleasure of parental pride and approval. The conflict is resolved by forging a new psychic instrument, the ego, which brings involuntary urges under voluntary control.

In order to control elimination, the ego must channel the id's impulses and direct them toward ends that, on the one hand, are pleasurable, and on the other hand, accord well with the constraints of the external situation. If parents start toilet training in an easygoing, nonthreatening manner, the child should gradually master bowel control and experience the social approval that follows using the "potty." However, if toilet training is premature and demanding, it may create sufficient anxiety to result in later symptoms like fear of authority, paranoia, overdependence, and impulsiveness.

In a larger sense, toilet training's inherent conflict is prototypical of the many conflicts over power and control between parents and their children. These conflicts propel children's growing independence and self-control, which in turn assist them in differentiating between self and external reality (Freud, 1908). Increased mastery over toilet habits, accompanied by enhanced self-control in manipulation, mobility, and delay of gratification, combine to establish a beginning sense of self-identity. By the end of the anal stage, the child knows that pure gratification must be controlled and that negative consequences occur when parental standards are violated. Sandlot Seminar 3.3 on page 54 examines this issue from parents' point of view.

Sandlot Seminar 3.3

Bringing Up Baby

John and Brandon get together every Saturday morning to walk the neighborhood, pushing their strollers in front of them. John's son William is nearly 2 years old. Brandon's daughter Meaghan is 2½.

> JOHN: I've been reading this parenting book, and it says to wait until your kid shows an interest before you start potty training.
>
> BRANDON: Well, that seemed to work with Meaghan. One day she just followed her mom into the bathroom and asked her all kinds of questions. That's when we went and got a training potty and set it up right next to our toilet.
>
> JOHN: Then what?
>
> BRANDON: Then it was almost like she trained herself.
>
> JOHN: How old was she?
>
> BRANDON: Well, she started shortly after her second birthday.
>
> JOHN: How long did it take?
>
> BRANDON: Oh, I don't know. I guess maybe about six weeks before she quit diapers and started wearing panties.
>
> JOHN: Well, I've tried to keep my cool about William and not get too worked up about it. We make suggestions, but he could care less. I sure would like to get done with the diaper scene.
>
> BRANDON: I know. Just give it time.
>
> JOHN: Well, I'm pretty patient, but he hasn't shown any interest at all in the potty chair we bought for him last month. My wife says this stuff is pretty important. We don't want to traumatize him for life.
>
> BRANDON: Well, I wouldn't worry about traumatizing him. I remember this psych course back in college. Seems like all the bigwigs had a theory about something, but believe me, the really useful stuff you could put in a thimble. Anyway, the professor said something about potty training, but I can't recall now what it was. Seems to be the best thing to do is just use common sense.

1. Where does Brandon's "common sense" really come from?
2. Have people always had the same "common sense" ideas about child rearing?
3. Why does "common sense" sometimes change from one generation to the next?

A child may unconsciously adapt to parental authority by becoming irresponsible, sloppy, or narcissistic. Unusually frustrating experiences may result in an anal personality, which tends to be excessively neat, clean, and stubborn and may distort reality by unconsciously making experience conform to neat, unambiguous categories.

Phallic Stage (approximately 3 to 6 years).   The phallic stage is a critical period for the development of sexual identity and socially sanctioned sex roles. Psychic energy is invested in the genitals, making them the dominant erotogenic zone. Genital stimulation produces tension and the accompanying need for tension reduction and pleasure. While unconscious sexual energy is instinctively channeled toward the opposite sexed parent, social taboos prohibit such incestuous relations. According to Freud, the conflict between the unconscious desire to possess and social prohibitions that prevent it brings about permanent and profound changes in the child's personality.

By the beginning of the phallic stage, children generally have a good sense that their identity is different from others. This awareness sharpens and then exaggerates their feelings of love and hate for their parents. For example, a young boy's emotions have differentiated from an initial global state into a complex of interrelated feelings termed the *Oedipus complex,* a name derived from the classic Greek tragedy *Oedipus Rex.*

Oedipus, son of the King of Thebes, spent his life unknowingly fulfilling a fateful prophesy. Upon his birth, an oracle predicted that Oedipus would murder his father and marry his mother. To thwart the oracle, his father abandoned him to die of exposure and starvation. However, Oedipus was found by strangers and raised unaware of his royal heritage. As a young man, he returned unwittingly to Thebes, slayed the King (his father), freed the kingdom from a terrible mythical creature (the Theban Sphinx), and married the Queen (his mother). Only then did Oedipus learn of his fate, and in remorse, he gouged out his eyes to wander blindly through the world. Freud's reference to the Oedipal theme again reflects the determinism of his thinking—males are destined from birth to *unconsciously* want to kill their fathers and possess their mothers.

In seeking the affection and warmth of their mothers, boys become increasingly aware of competition for this love from their fathers. In comparing his own power and size to that of the father, a boy is *unconsciously* compelled by feelings of frustration and inferiority to display aggression toward the father. In spite of cultural taboos, the child pursues his unconscious desires for the mother, thus forcing the Oedipal confrontation between son and father over who will receive the mother's affection.

Throughout this the boy experiences emotional ambivalence, a love–hate relationship with his father, which may be why Freud refers to the Oedipal situation as a *complex*. If the boy is sufficiently fearful of being punished for his erotic (pleasure-driven) desire for the mother, he may experience *castration anxiety,* a special unconscious fear that the father will cut off his penis, the primary zone of erotic pleasure. While the anxiety is unconscious, it is not without some foundation in the real world. Boys are often aware of the fact that they but not females have penises. In a child's mind, it is the absence of a female penis that makes sense as a living example of castration.

Castration anxiety produces an important sequence of events in the child's personality development. Realizing the superior power of the father, the young boy's ego designs a compromise strategy for usurping the power of the father through *identification* with his values, attitudes, behaviors, and habits, and thereby incorporating the father's traits into his own personality. Identification serves both the ego's and the id's purposes. The ego reduces anxiety by repressing desire for the mother, while the id obtains vicarious satisfaction as the child acquires his father's traits.

Identification with the father requires part of the ego to become transformed into a new psychic organ, the superego, capable of representing the cultural values and expectations incorporated from the father. By identifying with the father, the child becomes truly socialized. For the first time he begins to display masculinity, and its accompanying prohibitions and prescriptions, as a part of his own personality.

Freud described a comparable complex in young girls to which the term *Electra* has often been applied. He did not write extensively about it, but what he did say indicates that it is a time of considerable conflict in females. At the beginning of the phallic stage, girls have also begun to realize that there are anatomical differences between males and females. They realize that their clitoris is not as large as the male penis, which they associate with the father's power and strength. The lack of a penis generates unconscious feelings of inferiority, which Freud termed *penis envy*. These feelings intensify desire for the father and rejection of the mother, who is unconsciously held responsible for depriving the young girl of a penis. When the girl realizes she will never have a penis, her erotic desire for the father is channeled into identification with her mother, the primary recipient of the father's attention. By identifying with the mother, the young girl transforms part of her ego into a superego, which in turn brings on genuine socialization and the beginning of femininity.

While the Oedipus and Electra complexes are functionally similar, there is a fundamental difference between boys and girls. In boys, castration anxiety motivates identification with the father, which resolves and thereby *ends* the Oedipus complex. With girls, the unconscious belief that castration has already occurred is an important factor in the *cause* of her conflict.

In recent decades serious objections have been raised about the underlying "sexist" implications of Freud's interpretation of the Oedipus and Electra complexes. Whereas the young male is depicted as fundamentally concerned with erotic pleasure obtained from penile manipulation, the young female is depicted as being preoccupied with the inferiority of her genitalia. Traditional Freudians, for example, believe that girls experience less fear than boys because their lack of a penis precludes castration anxiety and consequently generates less repression. Less repression results in a weaker identification with the mother than the boy experiences with the father. Ultimately this weaker identification in girls is believed to fashion a weaker superego and conscience in them than in boys. Other Freudians argue that the combination of a male-dominant society, nurturant rather than aggressive female sex roles, and the absence of a penis makes the Electra complex much more complicated for girls than the Oedipus complex is for boys.

This brief account of the Oedipus and Electra complexes may lead the reader to the erroneous conclusion that young children have a fairly easy time sorting out the appropriate parent to identify with. Just the opposite is true. Freud believed that young children were to some degree biologically and psychologically bisexual:

> A boy has not merely an ambivalent attitude toward his father and an affection object-relation towards his mother, but at the same time he also behaves like a girl and displays an affectionate feminine attitude to his father and a corresponding hostility and jealousy towards his mother (Freud, 1923, pp. 42–43).

These inherent bisexual urges mean that children always experience some degree of identification with both parents. The two identifications differ depending on such things as the personalities of the parents, the differential strength of masculine and feminine impulses in the child (due to both biological differences and differences in oral and anal experiences), the specific customs of one's culture, and the severity of castration anxiety or penis envy.

The interplay of unconscious desires charged by psychic energy, the exaggerated dynamics of Oedipus and Electra complexes, and the beginning of genuine socialization with the onset of superego make the phallic stage an important critical period with lifelong consequences as the ultimate source of masculine and feminine personalities. Most children experience some degree of emotional difficulty during this stage. At best the resolution of unconscious conflicts represents successful compromises. The interactive patterns that originate in the love–hate relationship with parents influence all later relationships with others, which is why psychoanalysts often attempt to trace adult symptoms back to the conflicts and experiences of the phallic stage.

Latency Stage (approximately 5 or 6 years to puberty). The latency stage is a critical period for expanding relationships beyond the family, developing masculine or feminine personalities, and learning appropriate sex-role habits. Unconscious sexual (pleasure-driven) instincts, strongly repressed by ego from the phallic-stage conflicts, get channeled into learning a variety of social, athletic, and intellectual skills needed for healthy adult functioning. There is no specific erotogenic zone during this stage; hence its name "latency."

Freud identified but gave relatively little attention to this stage of development, largely because he believed this time was marked by sexual quiescence and dormancy (Freud, 1930). There is, however, some controversy over this claim. White (1960, p. 127), for example, believes that Freud (of all people) underestimates the importance of erotic desire during the latency stage. White notes, for example, that anthropological and child development research both show latency-aged children to be intensely interested in sexual matters. While minor disagreements among theorists are common, White's contention poses a major challenge to the Freudian interpretation of latency because it implies that sexual motives are developmentally continuous rather than temporarily interrupted as suggested by Freud.

Parents often have children of different ages who are at various stages of development. Each child faces issues that are influenced by instinctual urges and developing personality organs. Sandlot Seminar 3.4 shows how something as simple as a "boyfriend" reflects these developments.

Genital Stage (onset of puberty to adulthood).   The genital stage is a critical period for establishing patterns of mature heterosexual functioning. This final and most mature form of sexuality is directed toward obtaining sexual pleasure with another person. Psychic energy is again invested in the genitals, making them the erotogenic zone for this stage.

The genital stage is characterized by intense psychic activity, a "lust dynamism" directed toward fulfilling mature sexual desires. The surge of pubertal hormones produces dramatic physical changes in the sex organs and equally dramatic modifications in psychic functioning. For example, the ego attempts to harness and channel these forces into heterosexual love, which Freud believed was the ultimate form of pleasure. At the same time, unconscious libidinal instincts also infuse romantic and sexual meaning into dreams, fantasies, and humor. These meanings are also sought in an attractive partner, someone who unconsciously reminds us of our early parental love objects. Partners may be unconsciously selected because they are dominant or shy, intellectual or weak-minded, liberal or puritan, all depending on the values, attitudes, identifications, and repressed memories acquired during childhood.

Sandlot Seminar 3.4

Psychosexual Stages in a Family's Dinner Conversation

ABBIE (12): Daddy, I've got a boyfriend. His name is Adam, and he's so nice. I'm going to marry him.

CHRIS (8): Yuck, Abbie, you're stupid. Why would you have a boyfriend at your age? I'll never have a girlfriend. I hate girls. They don't even know how to play, and when they do, they're always crying or whining and being yucky. I hate 'em.

AMANDA (4): Daddy, I have a boyfriend too. You're my boyfriend.

DAD: Aren't you a sweetheart, Amanda. That's really nice.

AMANDA: Wait, Daddy. I'm not finished. I want to marry you too.

DAD: What a nice thought, sweetie, but I'm already married. I'm married to Mom.

MOM: Yes, Amanda, Dad's already married to me. What would I do?

AMANDA: Don't worry, Mom. I'm not going to marry Daddy until I grow up. And besides, Mom, by then you'll be dead.

1. How are these children's interests reflective of their psychosexual stages of development?

2. How would you explain Amanda's belief that her mother will be dead?

The five psychosexual stages comprise what Freud termed the *theory of infantile sexuality*. It was, of course, tremendously controversial at the time, and even today it gives rise to uninformed musings and chuckles. But such a view seriously misses the important developmental lesson Freud gave us.

The primary point of the theory of infantile sexuality is to show how mature, heterosexual pleasure evolves gradually, through different forms of pleasure seeking. These forms originate in infancy and represent critical periods of development called psychosexual stages. If one believes that infants and children are naturally motivated to seek pleasure, then there is little controversy to be found in Freud's theory. After all, mature sexuality is clearly a strong human motive. Unless one believes that it appears magically during puberty, without any developmental preparation, then it makes sense to seek its origins in earlier forms of pleasure seeking exhibited in infancy and childhood.

Bridge Principles

Levels of Consciousness. The realm of the id is the psychic **unconscious,** one of Freud's most important discoveries. Unconscious means much more than simple nonawareness. It means that we cannot know about or think about the id's contents or functioning under normal circumstances. Unconscious desires influence psychological and behavioral functioning throughout life. However, as we develop, unconscious motives gain less influence over behavior because they are increasingly controlled by ego and superego. But in spite of these controls, the unconscious continues its influence throughout life as it gains more channels of expression through the ego's coping mechanisms.

The unconscious is *prelinguistic*. It contains no semantic associations, since it existed long before language is learned. But the unconscious storehouses all the "lost" memories repressed by the ego.

The ego resides in the second level of consciousness, the **preconscious,** a region of the mind in direct contact with the immediate "here and now" of one's ongoing experiences. The preconscious stores images, memory traces, words, and symbols that represent both actual experience and unconscious desires. We are not normally aware of the contents of the preconscious, since these have been at least partly repressed, but preconscious content sometimes forces its way into our conscious life in the form of memories of the past, slips of the tongue, and dream symbols. The preconscious also contains the *dream censor*, a specific ego mechanism that channels unconscious sexual energy, originating with the id's erotic desires, into socially acceptable but pleasurable dream processes, images, and symbols. Many people, for example, have experienced dreams in which they act much like a film director in stopping and redirecting certain ongoing or objectionable dream content. When this happens, we are experiencing our ego's dream censor.

The superego resides in the third region of the mind, the **conscious,** which contains only a relatively small and ever-changing portion of an individual's mental life. It holds the immediate, constantly changing sensations, thoughts, and memories that occupy our awareness at any given moment. While id and ego influence the content of our consciousness, neither enters our conscious awareness. "Awareness" is an awareness of the mental conscious.

Freud likened the conscious to an iceberg, with only a tiny portion poking above the water's surface (conscious), with so much more material (preconscious and unconscious content) remaining below the surface of our awareness. Stafford-Clark (1965) suggests the analogy of a performance stage. Mental life is like a vast, dark arena, and consciousness is like the small area lit up by a spotlight. Preconscious material then would consist of the vague, hazy, diffuse images barely discernable at the edges of the spotlight. Portions of the arena, like the psychic unconscious, remain forever out of view beyond the reach of the spotlight.

The three regions of the mind interact with each other in systematic ways. The preconscious contains words and symbols that are socialized representations of unconscious motives, wishes, and desires. In turn, the conscious contains moral imperatives and cultural prescriptions for behavior motivated by unconscious impulses. The unconscious is linked to the preconscious, which in turn is linked to the conscious region of the mind. In contrast, the unconscious and conscious are not directly linked. They interact only through the mediation of the preconscious.

In short, we are always aware of conscious material—it is goal oriented and deliberate. We are seldom aware of preconscious material—it is unconsciously controlled but directed toward realizable goals. We are never aware of unconscious material (although appropriate therapy can gain us insight without direct awareness).

Defense Mechanisms.   As described earlier, insatiable instinctual desires and constant threats from the external world arouse anxiety. The ego attempts to reduce anxiety by employing reality-based problem-solving strategies. However, anxiety is sometimes so overpowering that the ego's strategies prove inadequate. In such cases, energy is channeled into automatic patterns that defend us against the threat of anxiety. These patterns are called *defense mechanisms*. In Freud's view, the presence of defense mechanisms is associated with a weak ego, since a perfectly strong ego is able to adjust to external problems in spite of unconscious memories. Defense mechanisms can function intermittently, or they can become so ingrained in our personality that they operate virtually nonstop. Several of the most notable defense mechanisms include the following.

Repression is probably the most important of all the defense mechanisms. It is the mental inhibition of memories and threatening thoughts that arouse frustration, guilt, or anxiety. By keeping harmful memories buried in the unconscious, the ego protects us from experiencing anxiety. Repression first occurs early in childhood, and it accompanies us throughout our lives. As Sandlot Seminar 3.5 shows, repression is at work when we momentarily forget the name of a close acquaintance, forget an appointment with someone, or fail to remember an event that occurred during childhood. The nature and reality of repressed memories have even been subjects of litigation, particularly in cases in which adults have claimed they repressed for many years memories of childhood sexual abuse by an adult.

Sandlot Seminar 3.5

The Wedding Day

After nearly three years of dating, a young couple decided it was time to get married. A wedding was planned, arrangements were made, invitations were sent, and the ceremony was conducted. In a receiving line, the new bride and groom were greeting their guests when it happened. Spotting Tony, an old "partying" friend from college, the groom felt elated as memories of their exploits together came flooding to mind and prompted this exchange.

GROOM: Tony! It's great to see you. How long has it been?

TONY: Wow, at least six or seven years. Looks like you've put on a little weight there, fella.

GROOM: Oh, yeah. Life has been pretty good.

TONY: I can't believe you are actually married. I didn't think you'd ever settle down. What happened?

GROOM: Well, we did have a great time in those days, didn't we?

TONY: Yup. So, who's the unlucky lady? Aren't you going to introduce me?

GROOM: Of course, I'm sorry. Tony, I'd like you to meet my wife . . .

BRIDE: Hi Tony. I'm happy to meet you. I'm Vicky. I can't believe after all these years, he forgot my name!

GROOM: Oh, Vicky, don't be silly. I'd never forget your name. I just went blank. I was just so surprised to see Tony after all this time.

1. Was it really surprise or something else that prompted the groom to temporarily forget his wife's name? What do you think?

2. Has something like this ever happened to you?

3. Why do you think it happens to most people, usually at an awkward moment?

Regression is the reemergence of early modes of mental functioning and occurs because throughout our lives primitive forms of thinking coexist with more mature forms. If a situation is perceived as threatening and invokes anxiety, the ego may return temporarily to an earlier stage when problems were less complex and fewer controls were placed on problem-solving strategies. For example, some people regress to telling childish nonsense jokes at a party, kicking the family dog for wetting the carpet, or attempting to recreate their own childhood experiences with their children.

Projection is the attribution to others of traits or motives that are unconsciously ingrained in the self. Thoughts and memories that evoke anxiety sometimes get attributed to others, in which case the self may see others as a threat. For example, a married man may unconsciously desire an amorous relationship with an office co-worker, but because his desire provokes anxiety, he may project the desire onto his spouse and suspect her of being unfaithful. In extreme cases, projecting onto others one's own preoccupations may lead to paranoia—the belief that others are preoccupied with oneself.

Reaction formation occurs when the ego disguises an unacceptable impulse in the form of its psychological opposite, often in an exaggerated manner. For example, unconscious jealousy at a mother's attention to a newborn may prompt her husband to become overattentive and overprotective with the infant.

Displacement is the unconscious shifting of psychic energy from one object to another, particularly when it does not belong to the latter. It occurs most frequently in dreams and is the result of the ego's redirecting instinctual energy away from a threatening object toward one that is not threatening. For example, in Ted's dream (which appears as an exercise at the end of this chapter), his ego's dream censor transforms him into a Mafia character in order to achieve revenge by shooting a co-worker who had cut off his fingers. Ted's ego felt too threatened to allow Ted to do the shooting himself, so it displaced Ted's aggression onto the Mafia figure.

Change Mechanisms

Psychoanalysis posits two types of change mechanisms. The most important is biological maturation. It governs the entire scope and sequence of the psychosexual stages, the series of prefabricated critical periods. Because maturation both produces and limits the development of the personality, it is the main developmental mechanism in Freud's theory and is the primary reason the theory is classified as an endogenous theory.

A second mechanism, **psychosexual conflict,** results from the conflicting demands between superego's rigidly conforming mandates and id's irrational impulses and erotic desires. Psychosexual conflict is *intra*psychic, and it results in the formation of defense mechanisms and patterns of adjustment found in one's personality—habits and other symptoms of psychopathology like compulsions, phobias, paranoia, schizophrenia, and Freudian slips.

It is clear that Freud grants a minor role to the environment in how the individual fashions a unique personality. In this vein, environment introduces an element of individual variation in how we develop our personalities. However, the environment is subordinate to the more powerful influence of maturation, which is the unalterable timetable of critical periods that underlie all of human development and create in each of us a common guide path of experiences.

Explaining Human Development: The Research

Psychoanalytic theory has yielded two distinct lines of research. The first consists of extremely rich single subject case studies, some of which are included in Freud's original writings. New insights into psychopathology can be found in reexaminations of Freud's original cases (Gottlieb, 1989; Magid, et al., 1993; Thomas, 1992). Many other case studies can be found in the international journal *The Psychoanalytic Study of the Child,* which contains two recent examples. In one, Kennedy (1986) used psychoanalytic treatment to trace an adolescent's sadomasochistic masturbation fantasies back to a peculiar constellation of early childhood problems: unmet early needs, forced feeding, rigid toilet training, and penile infection followed by circumcision at age two. In another case study, Winestine (1985) found that inappropriate weeping in a preanorexic girl could be traced to a childhood event in which the girl accidentally dropped and broke a glass in a fancy restaurant, an event that prompted the girl's discovery that she would never again be perfect. Since case studies function primarily to exemplify rather than test a theory, they will not be described here.

The second line of research consists of more direct tests of theoretical assertions on groups of individuals. Although psychoanalysis is one of the classical developmental theories, many more systematic studies could be found several decades ago than today, so some of these may appear dated by today's standards. Attention is given here to studies that emphasize recurrent themes in the psychoanalytic literature.

Personality Types

The Oral Personality. The predominant mode of the oral stage is incorporation, a concept whose generality makes it difficult to verify empirically. However, Fisher and Greenberg (1985, p. 84) identify two characteristics of the oral stage that can be scientifically verified: onset (during the first year) and parenting style (resulting in either overgratifying or frustrating the child's oral needs). Additionally, Abraham (1927) extended Freud's analysis of the oral character and identified the following characteristics of the orally fixated individual: (1) one-dimensional traits, such as ambivalence, openness, restlessness, and impatience, and (2) bipolar traits, such as giving–taking, dependence–independence, passivity–activity, optimism–pessimism, and being alone versus belonging to a group. The following clusters of personality traits have been found to exhibit the kinds of intercorrelations expected by psychoanalysis: passivity, dependence, pessimism, egocentricity, and rejection of others (Lazare, Klerman, & Armor, 1966); dependency, pessimism, avoidance of responsibility, demandingness, and envy (Gottheil & Stone, 1968); pessimism, dependency, anxiety, passive hostility, exhibitionism, and impulsive acting out (Finney, 1961a, 1961b); and dependency, need for approval, deference, and conformity (Comrey, 1965, 1966). Because these researchers have employed diverse methodologies in their studies, the relative consistency of these findings indicates some level of support to the typology of an oral personality.

Evidence supporting the early experience determinants of the oral personality comes from studies by Goldman (1950–1951) and Goldman-Eisler (1951), who interviewed mothers to assess the effect of their breast feeding and weaning patterns on 100 adult subjects. Those who had experienced early weaning tended to develop pessimistic traits, whereas those who breast-fed until much later developed optimistic attitudes. In a study of 40 normal preschoolers, increasing levels of dependency were correlated with the severity of weaning (Sears, Whiting, Nowlis, & Sears, 1953). Finally, in a longitudinal study, Heinstein (1963) followed 94 individuals for 18 years and reported correlations between certain oral traits and type of feeding (breast-fed versus bottle-fed), warmth of mothering, and difficulty of weaning.

Other research addresses the question of whether or not oral characters tend to seek excessive oral gratifications. For example, some evidence suggests that obese individuals possess significantly more oral imagery (responses to Rorschach or Thematic Apperception tests) than normal individuals (Masling, Rabie, & Blondheim, 1967; McCully, Glucksman, & Hirsch, 1968; Weiss & Masling, 1970). Similarly, alcoholics possess more oral character traits than do nonalcoholics (Story, 1968), depressed individuals (Weiner, 1956), or psychiatric patients (Bertrand & Masling, 1969). Finally, some studies have identified intense oral motivations among smokers (Jacobs, Knapp, Anderson, Karush, Meissner, & Richman, 1965; Jacobs & Spilken, 1971; Kimeldorf & Geiwitz, 1966; Veldman & Bown, 1969).

In summary, evidence suggests some support for the psychoanalytic construct of an oral personality: its association with early infancy, breast feeding, weaning and mothering styles, and later preoccupation with excessive forms of oral gratification. The diverse methodologies used to explore the oral personality are a source of both strength and weakness for the theory. On the one hand, they provide independent, corroborative external validation for the concept. On the other hand, there is virtually no convincing evidence available about the validity of these measures or the extent to which they are correlated with one another (Fisher & Greenberg, 1985, p. 132).

The Anal Personality.   The evolution of an anal personality is quite similar to that of the oral personality, with two important differences. First, the anal personality is hypothesized to involve a different constellation of traits, and second, its evolution is to be traced to the anal rather than the oral stage. The following cluster of traits are believed to underlie the anal personality: neatness, orderly life-style, excessive control, cleanliness, predictability, precision, trustworthiness, frugality, obstinacy, stubbornness, sadistic and masochistic tendencies, hostile and aggressive fantasies, and obsessive–compulsive habits (Freud, 1908, 1917). Anal character traits should originate in anal stage frustrations or disturbances (Freud, 1909).

Considerable research supports Freud's description of an anal typology. The following examples indicate even more pervasive patterns than those identified with the oral personality: perseverance, orderliness, and cleanliness (Brooks, 1969); neatness, love of routine, meticulousness, and negative impulsivity (Comrey, 1965); orderliness, stinginess, stubbornness, and rigidity (Finney, 1961a); hypocrisy, attention to detail, hoarding, and anal sadism; and orderliness, obstinacy, rigidity, and rejection of others (Lazare et al., 1966).

The early determinants of the anal personality are claimed to lie in particularly frustrating experiences associated with toilet training. Although many studies have attempted to connect toilet training experiences with the later development of anal personality traits (Beloff, 1957; Finney, 1963; Hetherington & Brackbill, 1963; Kline, 1969; Miller & Swanson, 1966; Sears, Rau, & Alpert, 1965), only modest support for a connection has been reported. At the same time, other evidence strongly suggests a connection between individuals' anal personalities and the existence of anal traits in their mothers (Beloff, 1957; Finney, 1963; Hetherington & Brackbill, 1963). While it is reasonable to suppose that anal-oriented mothers would tend to exercise rigid toilet training, it is also likely that these mothers provided a controlling environment throughout their children's youth and not only during the anal stage.

The Oedipus Complex

While Freud made a number of claims about the Oedipus complex, only two have been systematically investigated. First, prior to the Oedipus complex, both male and female children focus their energy primarily on the mother. Second, because girls have no penis to begin with, they should experience relatively greater penis envy and relatively lower castration anxiety than boys.

Focus on Mother.   Studies of pre-Oedipal development suggest that both male and female infants and toddlers prefer their mothers over fathers and others as objects of attachment, especially in situations that provoke anxiety, and this preference appears in American (Ainsworth, Bell, & Stayton, 1972; Bowlby, 1969, 1973), Scottish (Schaffer & Emerson, 1964), and Ugandan cultures (Ainsworth, 1967).

Castration Anxiety and Penis Envy.   One of the striking images in Freud's description of the Oedipus complex is that of the powerful, threatening father, who evokes penis envy in daughters and castration anxiety in sons. Fisher and Greenberg (1985, p. 193) have noted that castration anxiety is often equated with bodily injury and mutilation, and this manifestation has been the object of a number of investigations. For example, boys are more likely than girls to include themes of physical injury in their spontaneous speech (Gottschalk, Gleser, & Springer, 1963) and in stories they are requested to make up (Pitcher & Prelinger, 1963). College males are more likely than females to exhibit castration anxiety responses to projective tests (Blum, 1949; Schwartz, 1956). Finally, men more than women report dream content related to castration anxiety (Hall & Van de Castle, 1965).

Concerning penis envy, Freud theorized that unconscious disappointment accompanies young girls' discovery that they lack a penis. Consequently he claimed that females live out their lives haunted by a negative body image that unconsciously motivates them to seek substitutes for the "loss" of this member. This controversial claim has not been supported by research. In an extensive research review, Fisher (1970, 1973) has concluded that women, if anything, are more comfortable with their own body images and experiences than are men. Moreover, women on the average exceed men in terms of self-awareness, personal security, and flexibility in adjusting to body sensations and appearance (Fisher & Greenberg, 1985).

Dreams

It is important to note that dream research has been handicapped by a particularly vexing problem: determining if the source of dream content is in fact unconscious (another of Freud's important claims). In spite of this problem, dreams are certainly one of the most intriguing of all psychological processes. In Freud's *Interpretation of Dreams*, two major theoretical claims are introduced. First, dream symbols represent both manifest and latent meaning; manifest meaning reflects a disguised "shell" of symbolic content that masks the true latent meaning. Second, dreams serve as a tension vent for the expression of repressed memories and unconscious desires.

Manifest and Latent Meaning.   Because of the difficulty of measuring latent meaning, most investigations of dream content have been correlational. For example, when psychiatric interpretations are used, significant correlations between manifest and latent dream content have been reported for college students (McReynolds, Landes, & Acker, 1966) and psychiatric patients (Sheppard & Karon, 1964). Other correlations have been found between manifest dream content and storytelling themes (Brender & Kramer, 1967; Foulkes, 1969). In a somewhat different vein, a number of research studies have reported correlations between manifest dream content and personality traits such as introversion (Rychlak & Brams, 1963), hostility (Foulkes & Rechtschaffen, 1964), and dominance (Rychlak & Brams, 1963).

Tension Venting.   Freud believed that dreams provide a venting outlet for unconscious impulses. As has been well documented, dreaming takes place at specific times in the sleep cycle and is accompanied by easily detectable Rapid Eye Movements (REM). Psychoanalytic researchers have utilized the REM signal to interrupt sleep and thus deprive subjects of the opportunity to dream (Fisher & Greenberg, 1985), which should preclude the venting of unconscious tensions and result in increased levels of disturbance, irritability, agitation, and anxiety. Not only have such predictions been confirmed (Dement, 1960; Dement & Fisher, 1963; Fisher, 1965a, 1965b), but some instances have been reported of subjects who responded with near psychotic, paranoid suspiciousness (Dement, 1960). Moreover, while sustained dream deprivation does not appear to affect simple cognitive functioning, it greatly increases the degree to which deprived feelings and wishes are produced in response to the Rorschach test (Greenberg, Pearlman, Fingar, Kantrowitz, & Kawliche, 1970). In a typical study of dream deprivation, Fiss, Klein, and Bokert (1966) awakened subjects from both REM and non-REM sleep and asked them to tell stories in response to Thematic Apperception pictures. Story analyses indicated that REM sleep deprivation resulted in more complex, bizarre, and emotionally vivid compositions than did non-REM sleep interruptions. The greater intensity of stories following dream interruption supports Freud's contention that dreams provide a special release function.

Contributions and Criticisms of Psychoanalysis

Contributions

Focus on Infancy and Childhood.   It is difficult to imagine that at the turn of the century, there was virtually no interest in studying the development of infants and children. But it was Freud more than anyone else who focused attention on the importance of development during the early years. He attempted to show how an individual's personality had its roots in the maturation of psychosexual stages. By showing how the infant's primitive instincts gradually unfolded to produce socialization, Freud irreversibly altered the course of developmental psychology. He created widespread public interest in infancy and childhood and made psychology accountable for explaining the influence those years had on adult behavior.

Unconscious.   One of Freud's most enduring contributions is his concept of the *unconscious* mind. Today's widespread acceptance of that idea stands in stark contrast to its original frosty reception. Freud argued that unconscious drives and impulses underlie anthropological phenomena (1913), art (1914), religion (1927), literature (1928), sociology (1930), and both personal aggression and acts of war (1933b). In addition, parents in the last half of the twentieth century became increasingly sensitive to their children's sibling rivalry, sexual curiosity, toilet training, and unrealistic fears in large part due to the powerful impact on child rearing Freud's concept of unconscious has had.

Defense Mechanisms.   Freud's analysis of the ego's defense mechanisms represents another landmark discovery in our understanding of human nature. The role these mechanisms play in the psychopathologies of everyday life (e.g., sexual humor, Freudian slips, tip-of-the-tongue experiences), as well as their role in the more extreme forms of pathology, has gained widespread recognition. The conversational use of such terms as *repression, projection,* and *denial* reflects a recognition of these patterns being displayed in everyday social interactions.

Recovering an Individual's History.   Like Freud, many educated people today believe that children's early experiences are vital in forming lifelong attitudes and patterns of social interaction. Still, psychoanalysis is the only developmental theory whose methodology is specifically designed to recover the individual's memories of childhood experiences. Information garnered through free association and dream analysis is believed to reflect elements of early experiences that have been repressed by the ego. While questions can be raised about the validity of the techniques and the accuracy of our memories, these methods represent original and important contributions for both theoretical and clinical applications.

Pedagogy.   Freud denounced the overly harsh techniques of Victorian child rearing. His work painted a portrait of childhood as teeming with conflicts and frustrations, emotional needs and desires, and wishes and fantasies. His insights fostered a new sensitivity to children's emotional needs. In large part due to Freud, contemporary parents and teachers are generally more sympathetic than critical of the frustrations children experience in such events as the birth of a sibling, toilet training, the Oedipal situation, parental divorce, sexual curiosity, and school learning.

Psychotherapy.   The search for psychic cures to mental illness was one of the early influences on Freud's thinking. His solution to that problem was the development of a therapeutic technique he called psychoanalysis. Psychoanalytic therapy was the forerunner of contemporary psychotherapy, and it is the framework from which many variations have been spawned. In addition, Freud's approach to psychopathology established abnormal psychology as a legitimate subfield within psychology.

Criticisms

Freud (1933a) clearly believed that his theory was not subject to criticism unless the critic had first undergone psychoanalysis. Such a stance notwithstanding, the following problems with the theory have been identified.

Unscientific Concepts.   Many of Freud's most significant theoretical constructs are extremely difficult to measure, and for this reason his work is often dismissed as "unscientific." In fact, the relative absence of empirical science has led some psychoanalysts to question the "place" for Freud's work in psychology (Stone, 1997). For example, it is difficult to imagine how one might directly or even indirectly measure such constructs as unconscious, libido, id, or superego. Most of the evidence described earlier in support of oral and anal personalities and the characteristics of the Oedipal conflict can be challenged on grounds that it is mostly circumstantial. Consider the problem of determining whether and to what extent repressed, unconscious memories motivate dream symbols and content. How does one meaningfully test such a cause–effect relationship? Moreover, how can one establish the prior case that memories have actually been repressed in the first place? The difficulty of establishing reliable and valid measures for psychoanalytic concepts is a major reason many judge Freud's theory to have little scientific merit (Schultz, 1975). In fact, this was also true half a century ago when Freud's ideas, propelled by the power of his writing, were in vogue. When it had become clear that Freud would never win a Nobel prize in medicine, Thomas Mann and other literary greats encouraged his nomination for a Nobel prize in *literature* (Stone, 1997).

Phallocentrism.   *Phallocentrism* refers to Freud's emphasis on the male's penis and his belief in female "inferiority." Some writers have criticized this view of women and derided such ideas as penis envy, castration anxiety, and weak superegos. Such views, argue the critics, reflect unexamined cultural stereotypes, social attitudes, and biases rather than a scientific appraisal of facts. Thompson (1957), for example, argues that while girls may envy boys, their envy reflects jealousy not of the penis, but of the male's privileged social status and relatively greater opportunity for freedom and success. Horney (1967) has further suggested that boys may suffer as much from womb envy as girls do from penis envy.

Massive Errors. In a recent account of Freud's life and work, Webster (1995) takes a unique and extremely pessimistic approach to his "analysis" of psychoanalysis. This analysis traces Freud's religious personality to his childhood and shows how his own dreams influenced the shape psychoanalytic theory was to take. Moreover, Webster argues that Freud was often influenced by purely charismatic theorists and failed to work the very cures he claimed. Although psychoanalytic principles caused Freud (1927) to question the origins and utility of religion, Webster speculates that Freud's sexual theories were actually religious doctrines in disguise. Given the difficulty of reinterpreting history, we may never know if Webster is on to something here or if he is merely "projecting" his own motives onto Freud.

Evaluation of Psychoanalysis

Scientific Worthiness

Testability. Table 3.1 shows that psychoanalysis rates low for its testability, a reflection of Freud's extreme mentalism, the critiques of his theory as "unscientific," and the techniques used to elicit data from an individual's past. To be sure, Freud was aware of such criticisms, but both he and his followers believed that his critics failed to grasp the essential nature of psychoanalytic theory (Gardner, 1995).

Problems encountered in attempting to test some of Freud's most central concepts are pervasive, deep, and essentially unsolvable. In addition, it is sometimes difficult to figure out what Freud means, in part because he often resorted to persuasive analogies (Patterson, 1990) rather than rational analyses to help communicate his ideas.

A second difficulty arises in trying to formulate testable hypotheses; the theory sometimes predicts contradictory but equally likely phenomena. For example, frustration plays an important role in the infant's development. However, frustrating events may lead to habits of conformity and pessimism *or* they may promote the opposite habits of exhibitionism and optimism. Since science presumes

TABLE 3.1   Ratings of Psychoanalysis for Scientific Worthiness

Criteria	High	Medium	Low
Testability			X
External Validity		X	
Predictive Validity		X	
Internal Consistency		X	
Theoretical Economy			X

unique causes for specific effects, there seems to be something logically wrong in attempting to explain opposite effects in terms of the same underlying cause. Consider a second example. Freud explained natural sex play as one manifestation of libidinal energy, but the opposite behavior—puritanical avoidance of sex—is also a manifestation of the same libidinal energy which this time has been channeled through the defense mechanism of reaction formation. The problem is that it is virtually impossible to test a theory that postulates the same underlying cause for diametrically opposed behaviors.

External Validity.   We have judged psychoanalysis to have medium external validity. On the one hand, Freud has captured the infant's oral predispositions (a phenomena other theorists also noticed but explained differently), the child's ambivalent love–hate feelings toward parents, the importance of dreams, the form and function of defense mechanisms, and the role of the unconscious in motivating human activity. On the other hand, it is difficult to believe that latency-aged children suspend all curiosity about sexual matters (see White, 1960), that the complexities of human cognition can be accounted for solely by characteristics of primary process and secondary process thought, and that tensionlessness is an ideal state of pleasure (don't we sometimes deliberately seek certain degrees and forms of tension?). Moreover, by emphasizing exaggerated forms of psychosexual adjustment, Freud may have greatly overestimated their importance during development.

Predictive Validity.   The medium rating for predictive validity derives from a balance of offsetting considerations. On the one hand, many psychologists have worked within the psychoanalytic framework to deduce important hypotheses and to construct new implications. For example, Carl Jung, an eminent student of Freud, derived extensive insight from psychoanalytic theory and extended it through his own analysis of symbolism (Jung, 1953), the psychic unconscious (Jung, 1921), and the psychic complexes (Jung, 1923). Anna Freud (1946) extended her father's work with her detailed analysis of defense mechanisms. René Spitz (1965) made extensive use of the theory in understanding the importance of mothering to infant development. At the same time, many psychoanalists have found it necessary to revise, improve on, or divorce themselves from some of Freud's specific contentions. In some cases, the severity of their differences challenged the predictive validity of Freud's ideas. One prominent example of just such a challenge can be found among the ego psychologists who broke from Freud over disagreements about the properties and development of the ego.

Internal Consistency.   The theory's medium rating for internal consistency derives from concerns described earlier. Recall that Freud sometimes proposes the same cause to explain logically incompatible effects. Such inconsistencies are not unusual in psychoanalytic theory; in fact they occur far too frequently to be occasional exceptions. The theory was not rated at the very bottom of the scale on this criterion because Freud is consistent in other important ways, as when he maintains that the role of the unconscious and the motivating energy of the libido underlie all behaviors.

Theoretical Economy.   We have given the theory a low rating for theoretical economy. The rating reflects the extensive coverage Freud gives to explaining emotions, personality, character disorders, dreams, and the "psychopathology" of everyday life. However, the scope of his theory is tempered by the relatively unwieldy assumptions required to support its internal and bridge principles. Not only does Freud begin with many predisposing assumptions about the nature of the infant, but these assumptions are considerably less orthodox than those made by many other theorists. The ratio of assumptions to explanatory power in the case of psychoanalysis is not impressive; hence the low rating on this criterion.

Developmental Adequacy

The ratings summary for developmental adequacy is shown in Table 3.2. Psychoanalysis actually consists of two types of developmental explanations: the sequential system (maturation) and the structural system (psychosexual conflict). Consequently, separate evaluations are shown.

Temporality.   Psychoanalysis clearly posits a sequence of maturational stages that occur from birth through adolescence. Moreover, the ontogenesis of the personality structures are viewed as time and experience dependent. Thus, each of the two systems posits a temporal component to development.

Cumulativity.   "The child is psychologically the father of the man," wrote Freud in describing how adult personality is determined by maturation and early social encounters. Socialization entails increasingly adaptive habits as children encounter other youngsters, adults, and social expectations outside the family. Simultaneously, the ego evolves from the id and the superego from the ego. Thus, both the

TABLE 3.2   Ratings of Psychoanalysis for Developmental Adequacy

Characteristics	Ratings	
	Sequential System	*Structural System*
Temporality	yes	yes
Cumulativity	yes	yes
Directionality	yes	yes
New Mode of Organization	no	yes
Increased Capacity for Self-control	no	yes

stages and the personality structures do represent new adaptations built on earlier ones.

Directionality.   There is inherent directionality contained in the psychosexual stages—from id-centered autoeroticism toward mature, heterosexual adult functioning. Simultaneously, the evolution of the ego and the superego promote increased socialization. In each case, *progress* is related to increasing psychological maturity and social adjustment.

New Mode of Organization.   Freud's psychosexual stages are organized solely in terms of the predominant erotogenic zone, the libidinal energy that sensitizes it, the objects that provide pleasure, and the instinctual tensions that are the source of psychosexual conflict. While the contents of these organizational properties change from stage to stage, the overall organizational pattern does not. For example, development from the anal to the phallic stage is accompanied by the following changes in organizational content: the erogenous zone shifts from the anus to the penis; the libido energizes a new erotogenic zone; the object of desire shifts from one's feces to one's opposite-sexed parent; and the instinctual tensions shift from conflict over expulsion–retention to the love–hate conflict over one's parents. While these content changes have occurred, the triune organizational *pattern* of instinctual desire, pursuit of pleasure and avoidance of pain, and psychosexual conflict *remain the same throughout each stage*. Because the stages are associated with changes in psychic content without corresponding changes in psychic organization, the theory fails this criterion.

At the same time, the development of the ego and the superego each represents the addition of a fundamentally different type of personality organ that functions according to different organizing principles. The id is guided by the pleasure principle, the ego by the reality principle, and the superego by a conscience principle. These different "rule systems" reflect the type of characteristic addressed by this criterion, so the structural system passes this criterion.

Increased Capacity for Self-control.   The sequential system reflects a biological/maturational blueprint of stages over which the individual has no control. Furthermore, the instinctual desires of each successive stage exert powerful, hidden pressures that can only be controlled by the ego and superego, each elements of the structural system. For this criterion, the "yes" or "no" marks in the respective columns reflect the discrepancy between the sequential and the structural systems' ability to account for increased capacity for self-control.

Pedagogical Usefulness

Summary ratings for the pedagogical usefulness of Freud's theory are shown in Table 3.3.

TABLE 3.3 Ratings of Psychoanalysis for Pedagogical Usefulness

Criteria	High	Medium	Low
Interpretability		X	
Versatility		X	
Availability	X		
Guidance		X	

Interpretability.   We have rated Freud's theory medium for its interpretability because of competing concerns. First, today much of Freud's original technical jargon has become commonplace in everyday conversations. Second, the theory goes a long way in helping adults understand children's emotions and adjust their expectations accordingly. Moreover, specialized training is available for those wishing to make a profession of psychoanalytic therapy. Third, however, the endogenous nature of the theory's stages means that critical period development is immune to the influence of concerned parents and teachers, although this is less true for the formation of the ego and the superego.

Versatility.   Recall that versatility is a reflection of variety or generality. We believe Freud's theory has medium versatility in its usefulness. For example, it is useful in helping parents deal with a variety of developmental phenomena: infant mouthing and frustration, potty training, the ego's push for independence during the "terrible twos," the emotional ambivalence of the Oedipus and Electra complexes, incorporation of parental values and sex roles, and the "lust dynamism" that accompanies the genital stage in puberty. But even these issues are primarily concerned with emotional and personality development. Freud's theory does little to account for other important areas such as physical, cognitive, linguistic, or perceptual development. Consequently, his theory is rated medium for its versatility.

Availability.   Freud's writings have been around for over a century. As a result, his own work and derivative works by others are widely available in campus and many public libraries. Some professional journals are devoted strictly to testing and interpreting his theory (e.g., *The Psychoanalytic Study of the Child*). In addition, popular magazines publish articles discussing Freud's own life and various topics of psychoanalytic theory. Even newspaper columns offer advice to parents about such things as toilet training and sibling rivalry, often without even recognizing that the ideas they contain originated in Freud's work. There is no question that Freud's theory is widely available and therefore garners a "high" rating.

Guidance.   Recall from Chapter 2 that the primary evidence of a theory's guidance will be found in its *change mechanism*. Our question is, does this part of Freud's theory provide tools for parents, teachers, and counselors to influence children's development? In Freud's case, the answer, is both "no" and "yes." Two competing considerations have led us to rate the theory medium on this criterion.

The primary change mechanism in psychoanalytic theory is biological maturation. Maturation is what determines the timing, the scope, and the sequence of psychosexual stages. There is clearly no guidance to be found in how adults might influence children's development through the stages, because maturation is immune to external forces.

However, a secondary change mechanism for Freud is psychosexual conflict between the id and the superego. This internal conflict is what accounts for individual differences in development and is the product of the child's socializing experiences. It is here that adults can find some guidance in child rearing. Such guidance may be highly specific: Delay potty training until the child exhibits curiosity and developmental readiness. Sometimes it may be more general: Infants should experience neither too little nor too much frustration. But the point is that adults can directly influence the quality and intensity of children's psychosexual conflicts.

Summary Points

1. Psychoanalytic theory represents an integration of two historically separate lines of inquiry: the search for brain structures and the search for psychic cures.
2. Freud defined sexuality as the pursuit of pleasure independent of biological needs. His theory of infantile sexuality proposes that adult heterosexual pleasure has evolved through stages from its primitive origins in the infant's simple pursuit of pleasure. Psychosexual stages are psychological critical periods during which libido energizes erotogenic zones, thereby sensitizing them to stimulation.
3. The theory assumes that psychic energy is a biological instinct consisting of a fixed pool of energy that is irrational in nature; functions as the primary, efficient cause of mental and behavioral activity; and directs these activities in the pursuit of pleasure and tension reduction.
4. The clinical problem of psychoanalytic theory is to recover and understand important childhood experiences. The primary methods of investigation include free association, dream interpretation, and projective tests.
5. Psychoanalysis posits three internal principles: the dynamic system (consisting of nonperishable but transformable psychic energy), the sequential system (psychosexual stages), and the structural system (id, ego, and superego). The theory's bridge principles include levels of consciousness and defense mechanisms.
6. Psychoanalysis posits two mechanisms of change. Maturation is the most important of the two. It determines the scope and sequence of development through the series of psychosexual stages. Psychosexual conflict within an individual's mind brings about changes in personality structures (id, ego, superego).

7. Enduring contributions of the theory include its concept of the psychic unconscious, delineation of the defense mechanisms, development of methods
uniquely suited to recovering childhood memories, and pedagogical implications. Recurrent criticisms of psychoanalysis include the difficulty of measuring crucial variables and cultural biases reflected in Freud's "phallocentrism."

8. Overall, psychoanalysis was rated medium to low for its scientific worthiness. Freud's structural system does a more adequate job accounting for development adequacy than does his sequential system. The theory rates medium
for its pedagogical usefulness.

PROBLEMS AND EXERCISES

Class Exercises

1. Ted is 22 years old, the product of a large family (three brothers and two sisters).
He describes his childhood as peaceful, fun, and very normal. His father "brought
home the bacon," and his mother raised the kids. She also "wore the pants in the
family" and was the major disciplinarian. Ted is living with Sue, a woman he
describes as "warm, loving, giving, alive, and the *finest* woman I've ever known,
and I've known quite a few." (Ted implies that Sue is especially good in bed.) One
day Sue goes grocery shopping, leaving Ted only the chore of changing a faulty
light switch. She returns nearly two hours later and discovers him just beginning
to change the switch. In anger, she grabs the screwdriver from his hand, changes
the light switch in a matter of moments, then hands the screwdriver back to Ted
saying sarcastically, "There, now at least that's finished!" That evening when
Ted attempts to engage in sex, he is unable to achieve an erection. He's never
experienced anything like that before and finally falls asleep a little concerned
about his performance. For ten days in a row, Ted is impotent, in spite of a great
deal of help from Sue. On the tenth night, Ted has the following dream, which
exerts therapeutic effects on his love life. The next morning, he is able to perform
sexually as if his impotence had never occurred. Here is Ted's description of his
dream.

> At the end of work one day, this old woman and I started just talking. It was the
> first time we ever talked to each other. Anyway, it was time to go, and we walked
> out together and went over to her car. We were just talking, nothing serious. Well,
> she went and opened her car door, got in, and rolled down the window, so we
> could continue talking to each other. Anyway, I put my hands on the top of the car
> door to lean against it sort of. Next thing I knew, and it all happened in slow
> motion, she reached out and slammed the door shut. It was like I was watching the
> whole thing and not really a part of it. Somehow, I changed from my normal self
> into a classical Mafia type—the hat, the gun, the suit, the sneer, the whole bit. Well,
> I looked down and all my fingers had been cut off by the car door. They were just
> spurting blood. I've never, ever dreamt about even hurting anyone before, but I
> watched from outside myself as I reached in my vest, pulled out a gun, aimed it
> through the window, and emptied it into her shot after shot after shot. I don't
> remember her moving or anything. Then I woke up pretty scared about the dream;
> it was a real shocker.

Given Ted's dream, his upbringing, and the precipitating event, analyze his dream for its manifest content and latent meaning.

2. Alan is a 29-year-old whose background is about as normal and all-American as one could find. He was very proud of his father, who was a decorated hero in World War II. Alan viewed his father as an extremely moral man, one who would stand up for his beliefs. He remembers always wanting his father to be proud of him. When the Vietnam War came along, Alan applied for and was granted Conscientious Objector status, thus exempting him from military service. His father was devastated, disowned Alan, and refused to see, write, or talk to him for nearly six years.

Alan and his best friend Wesley have over the past few years become very good friends (nothing homosexual here, each is going steady with a longstanding girlfriend). Lately, however, both men seem to be becoming increasingly macho in their friendly competitions with each other. Each is engaged in trying to "one-up" or "outdo" the other, and these antics are becoming increasingly antagonistic. Alan and Wesley recognize that their friendship is reaching a crisis and discuss their motives. That night, following this discussion, Alan has the following dream.

A powerful group of whites were coming to take over the island. They knew they'd have to deal with Wesley; he was chief of the native black tribe. That's really weird, why I'd make him black in my dream; he's really white. Well, anyway, Wesley made a bargain with them that he'd lead the tribe in putting all the tourist whites on the island to a test of personal goodness. As part of the bargain, any white who passed the test was to be released and allowed to stay on the island. The powerful whites agreed because they didn't think anyone would pass the test. Well, I remember all the tourist whites had been rounded up and thrown, one by one, into a pit of poisonous snakes. If the person were really a good, moral person, the snakes weren't supposed to bite. Well, Wesley knew I was the only remaining white on the island, but he had made a bargain, so he continued to hunt me anyway. The tribe finally caught me and took me to the pit. I remember Wesley telling me to just project my personal goodness and nothing would happen. I was really scared and let out a huge scream when they threw me into the pit. When I landed, I looked up and was surrounded by snakes. But they didn't seem to mind me; they weren't biting. After a while, I got to my feet and looked up at Wesley, who was standing on the edge of the pit smiling down at me. Anyway, then it was over, and Wesley reached down to pull me out of the pit. Just as our hands met, all the snakes leaped out at him, biting his arm and pulling him down into the pit to kill him.

Considering Alan's background and the precipitating events, analyze his dream for its manifest and latent meaning.

Individual Exercises

1. Most people (both children and adults) are unable to remember any events that occurred before their second or third birthday. This widely recognized phenomenon is called *infantile amnesia*. How would Freud explain this phenomenon?

(Hint: Reexamine the defense mechanisms or review the ego's functions, which begin to develop at around 2 years of age.)

2. *Separation anxiety* is a universal experience that occurs during the second half of the first year of life. During the first six months, infants are not particularly bothered when their primary caretaker leaves them alone in a strange situation. However, between 6 and 12 months, infants become distressed and anxious when temporarily abandoned by a caretaker who leaves the room. Describe how Freud might explain the onset of separation anxiety.

3. Language is a highly efficient social symbol system that children begin to acquire at about 2 years of age. According to Freud's theory, why would we expect language to be acquired at this time rather than earlier or later?

4. Keep a note pad and pencil next to your bed. Each night for two weeks, keep a record of your dreams, and the following morning record any important events that happened the previous day that could have precipitated the dream. Write as much detail as you can. If pencil and paper is too slow for you, talk into a tape recorder. Analyze several of your own dreams for manifest and latent meaning. Several weeks later return and reanalyze the same dreams.

5. For two weeks keep notes of the occasions when you experience a Freudian slip or "tip-of-the-tongue" forgetting. Try to analyze each of these in terms of unconscious motivations.

6. Use the Internet to search for sites related to Sigmund Freud and his theory. You can use Freud's name as well as internal and bridge principles. How do the Internet sites differ in terms of completeness and accuracy of information? What were the best sites you found? What problems did you encounter? What were some of the worst sites (and why)?

SUGGESTED READINGS

More about the Theory

Freud, S. (1962). *The ego and the id*. New York: Norton.
Freud, S. (1935). *A general introduction to psychoanalysis*. New York: Simon & Schuster.
Gay, P. (1988). *Freud: A life for our time*. New York: Doubleday.
Jacobs, M. (1992). *Sigmund Freud*. London, England UK: Sage Publications.

Research Reviews

Fisher, S., & Greenberg, R. P. (1985). *The scientific credibility of Freud's theories and therapy*. New York: Columbia University Press.

Critical Reviews

Eysenck, H. J. (1952). The effects of psychotherapy: An evaluation. *Journal of Consulting Psychiatry, 16*, 319–324.
Hook, S. (Ed.). (1959). *Psychoanalysis, scientific method, and philosophy*. New York: New York University.

CHAPTER

4 Erikson and Psychosocial Theory

Preview Questions

In what ways was Erikson's work influenced by historical and personal factors?

What is Erikson's most basic disagreement with Freud? What implications arise from this disagreement for Erikson's analysis of ego development?

What assumptions underlie Erikson's theory of psychosocial development?

What major problem(s) does the theory address?

What primary method of study does Erikson use?

What are the internal and bridge principles of psychosocial theory?

How does Erikson's view of the social environment differ from Freud's?

What change mechanism accounts for development?

Why is Erikson's theory a member of the endogenous paradigm?

What are the important contributions and criticism of Erikson's theory?

How does psychosocial theory rate on criteria of scientific worthiness, developmental adequacy, and pedagogical usefulness?

Historical Sketch

Erik Homburger Erikson was born in Frankfurt, Germany, in 1902. Following Erikson's birth, his mother married Dr. Homburger, a Frankfurt physician, and together they kept from young Erik the secret that his real father had abandoned him (Erikson, 1972, p. 15). Ironically Erikson, like Freud before him, also suffered from his Jewish ancestry. While his mother and stepfather were both Jewish, young Erik was more Danish in appearance (tall, blond, and blue-eyed), which led to his being called "the goy" (non-Jew) by his Jewish classmates and "the Jew" by his gentile classmates (Erikson, 1972, p. 16).

After high school Erikson skipped college and instead began to wander about Europe in search of purpose and meaning for his artistic talents. Dissatisfied with vagabonding, but possessing a wealth of travel experience, Erikson found a job teaching children in an American school in Vienna. While there, he met Anna Freud, and under her influence, he began to study psychoanalytic theory and even underwent psychoanalysis by her. That experience provided some insight into his childhood experiences and adolescent wanderlust. Subsequently, Erikson enrolled in the Vienna Psychoanalytic Institute where he was taught firsthand by Sigmund Freud. He graduated in 1933, the year Hitler rose to power in Germany.

Erikson makes a particular point about this time in his life. He was profoundly struck by the fact that psychoanalytic theory turns *inward* in order to open up the unconscious world to systematic study, it searches *backward* to find the origin of mental disease, and it pushes *downward* into the instinctual energies humans thought they had overcome. However, he believed that what was needed was a vision of humanity that lead *outward* from the self to mutuality, love, and communality; that moved *forward* from the enslaving elements of the past toward the liberating anticipation of new potentialities; and that looked *upward* from the unconscious impulses to contemplation of one's consciousness (Erikson, 1972, p. 13). This uplifting thread of reasoning later became a guiding principle undergirding Erikson's work.

Fearing the Nazi invasion of Austria, Erikson moved to Boston in 1933 and became that city's first child analyst. Later he enrolled in a graduate psychology program at Harvard but failed to complete it (Brenman-Gibson, 1984). In 1939, the year Hitler invaded Poland, Erikson became a U.S. citizen.

After three years in Boston, Erikson took up a lecturer position at Yale. Two years later he moved to a South Dakota Indian reservation, where he began to experience the Sioux culture firsthand. After later joining the faculty at the University of California–Berkeley, he resumed his psychoanalytic practice and participated in a longitudinal study of normal children in the San Francisco Bay area. In his work, he also collaborated with such distinguished anthropologists as Gregory Bateson, Alfred Kroeber, and Margaret Mead, who together influenced him to begin viewing children's socialization in the context of their own cultural values and customs.

In the 1950s during the McCarthy era, Erikson's own moral principles brought him into direct conflict with his employer, the University of California, when it suddenly demanded a loyalty oath from each of its faculty members. Erikson refused to sign, was fired before his first year was up, but was eventually reinstated when the university administration deemed him to be politically dependable (given his own history of fleeing the Nazis). However, he resigned his position because other politically suspect faculty who had not signed the loyalty oath were not similarly reinstated (Erikson, 1972, p. 20). Returning to Massachusetts, Erikson set up a clinical practice that afforded him the opportunity to write. His most important works were published in the next two decades. These writings made Erikson increasingly popular among psychologists, and in 1960 he was offered a professorship at Harvard University. In 1984, *Harvard Magazine* published an interview with Erikson in which, at the age of 82, he provided an important retrospective on his life, his work, and the importance of the nonviolent ethics of survival preached by Gandhi (Brenman-Gibson, 1984). He died in 1994.

Throughout his professional career, Erikson never attempted to separate himself or his work from Freud. While some of Freud's students later split over profound theoretical disagreements, Erikson located his work in the mainstream of Freudian psychology. His theory was born, like Freud's, in clinical practice. Like Freud, he posits a series of maturational stages. However, where Freud's stages emphasized a sequence of erotogenic zones, Erikson's capture development as a series of crises that occur between the individual and society.

Erikson's psychosocial theory is an example of an attempt to extend psychoanalytic theory rather than modify it, but it does differ from Freud's in several important respects. First, the ego's struggle for identity is emphasized over the id's influence on personality. Second, the healthy, adaptive mechanisms of ego functioning are given priority over the formation of psychopathological symptoms. Third, Erikson casts development across the entire life span rather than concentrating on childhood and adolescence. In the United States, Erikson's theory has gained considerable attention in recent years, in part due to the aging of the American population and an accompanying interest in life-span psychology.

Structural Components of Psychosocial Theory

Erikson embraces important Freudian concepts: the structural and sequential systems, maturational stages, and unconscious motivation. Still, there are important differences between the two which we highlight in the following sections.

Assumptions

Erikson's most important assumption concerns the *autonomous source of the ego*. Where Freud posited only the id's existence at birth, with the ego deriving from id's structure and energy, Erikson assumes that the ego already exists as a functioning organ at birth. This assumption has several important implications. First, since the ego exists independently, there is no need to assume it derives its energy from the id. Second, since the ego does not depend on the id's energy, there is no need to posit intrapsychic conflict. Third, and most important, because there is no antagonism between id and ego, Erikson describes an ego that is *conflict-free*. This is not to say that individuals experience no conflict. Rather, conflict arises between the individual and society, not, as Freud had maintained, between the antagonistic internal forces of id and superego. In this respect, Erikson's theory postulates an ego free of internal conflict, but susceptible in its development to psychosocial rather than psychosexual conflict.

As mentioned earlier, Freud viewed the ego as the personality organ that becomes differentiated through experience from the original id. In contrast, Erikson believes that the ego is the primary organizer of personality and that it functions independently and autonomously from birth. For this reason, Erikson views infancy as far more complex than Freud had. Where Freud's infant is unconsciously driven toward pleasure, Erikson's is driven to establish interpersonal, and therefore adaptive, relationships. An emphasis on social relationships means an ego that is more sensitive to the cultural context of development than the one posited by Freud.

Problems for Study

Phenomena to Be Explained.   Erikson (1980) argues that psychoanalysis has not provided a sufficiently specific theory about the ego's development. In addition, he believes that Freud underestimated the influence of one's cultural environment. To correct these faults, Erikson offers a far more extensive version of ego development within the context of culture and history. In short, the focus of psychosocial theory is to understand the relationship between ego and society (Erikson, 1963).

Both the ego and the culture are in constant flux. Erikson views the dynamic nature of this flux as a series of crises that individuals must resolve and reresolve as they enter new social roles throughout their lives. Psychosocial theory attempts to explain how individuals resolve this sequence of tensions between themselves and society. Implied here is the need to understand (1) the relationship between psychosocial crises and the formation of personal identity, (2) how resolution of earlier psychosocial crises prepares individuals for later crises, and (3) how a sense of personal identity maintains an enduring stability while constantly changing throughout the life span.

Methods of Study.   In the study of identity formation, it is difficult to separate personal growth from social change (a point Erikson tried to make in *Young Man Luther*). It is equally difficult to separate an individual's personal crises from social crises that occur in a historical moment (Erkison, 1968). To overcome these theoretical difficulties, Erikson needed a method for collecting data that would be sensitive to such distinctions.

Calling on his experience with anthropology, Erikson decided that naturalistic observations within different cultures would provide important information about what people say and do in their own cultural context. Naturalistic observations are a particularly good way to gather data about child rearing practices in different cultures.

A second method, called **psychohistory,** was developed by Erikson as a novel analytical technique designed to preserve elements of history, culture, and individuality. Psychohistory is a way of analyzing people's psychological development in terms of their writings, public statements, and activities. It is an alternative to other more personal and subjective methods utilized by psychoanalysis for uncovering a person's history.

Through the psychohistory method, Erikson discovered the ego's resilience to hardship and crisis. To demonstrate this point, Erikson wrote several psychohistories of important figures who experienced and overcame great adversity. Among his published works are psychohistories of Martin Luther, Maxim Gorky, George Bernard Shaw, and William James. His most famous psychohistory, which received a Pulitzer prize and a National Book Award, was about Mohatma Gandhi (Erikson, 1969).

Internal Principles

The Ego.   Erikson's concept of ego derives from Freud with some important differences. One difference is that Erikson posits a conflict-free ego that functions autonomously from the id at birth. A second difference is that he sees ego as more differentiated and more influential in its intrapsychic functions than Freud had. Third, Erikson believes ego evolves continuously throughout the life cycle.

For Erikson, ego is the capacity to unify one's experience in an adaptive manner (1963), and like Freud, he positions ego between the id and superego (1963). He agrees with Freud that ego's function is to balance the extreme demands of id and superego and thereby direct the individual's action by constantly testing reality, selecting memories, and orienting attention to the historical moment. To achieve its purposes, ego may employ defense mechanisms. At this point however, Erikson extends the ego's function beyond the intrapsychic self to include the self in both cultural context and historical moment. The ego's encounters with reality are extremely complex. First, everything is new; the same situation is never encountered a second time. Second, the individual is never the same individual, since earlier encounters bring about ego adaptations to circumstances that can never be undone. Third, different capacities are sensitive to different opportunities (Erikson, 1980).

The Epigenetic Principle. Erikson explains ego development in terms of the **epigenetic principle.** According to this principle, development is the unfolding of a genetically timed plan of development that exposes the individual to environment pressures and influences. For Erikson, the preprogrammed series of crises is innately determined. However, social and historical influences help determine how each stage, once initiated, gets played out in the individual's development. Accordingly, the ego's developmental course is predetermined in the individual's programmed readiness "to be driven toward, to be aware of, and to interact with a widening radius of significant individuals and institutions" (Erikson, 1968). Erikson's epigenetic principle implies that the *scope and sequence* of development is the product of innate laws that determine a fixed sequence of psychosocial stages. These stages are comprised of predictable crises between the individual and significant social figures.

Like Freud's stages, Erikson's crises represent critical periods in the ego's development. However, in contrast to Freud, Erikson recognizes the importance of individual interactions with other people and social institutions, and these interactions produce superficial differences in patterns of adjustment from one culture to another. Nevertheless, Erikson contends that superficial cultural differences do not mask far more important biological laws that fix a sequence of crises between the individual and significant others within the culture to which the ego must adapt.

Psychosocial Conflict.   Erikson (1980) places far more emphasis on the role of society and cultural organization than Freud. He also believes that Freud tended to define the ego too much in terms of its "better-known opposites," the biological id and the societal superego, whose opposition produced the *intra*personal conflict Freud termed psychosexual. While Freud understood the role of parental and societal contacts as immediate sources of superego, Erikson believes he failed to understand the pervasive role culture plays in the larger sense of personality development.

Psychosocial conflict is the mitigating but not the originating factor in each of Erikson's developmental stages. This kind of conflict occurs when the individual's ego interests and society's interests oppose each other. Table 4.1 illustrates the types of social interactions that can produce psychosocial conflict between the self and others. The two essential ingredients in psychosocial conflict are always an individual and some external source of opposition.

TABLE 4.1   Examples of Psychosocial Conflict

- A young girl helping set the dinner table accidentally drops a glass of milk.
- A father does the family laundry but is scolded for folding instead of hanging up his wife's blouse.
- Grandparents take their grandchildren on an outing but bring them home to parents who are upset because they are late for dinner.
- A kindergartner offers a stick of gum to a classmate, who replies, "Yuck! I hate that kind of gum."
- A college student attempts to respond to a professor's question in class. The professor responds, "Does anyone else have a suggestion?"
- A high schooler asks a girl out on a date. She replies, "I'd love to very much, but I have to go with my parents that night to my aunt's. Maybe another time?"
- A newlywed is offered a better job with more money and prestige, but it means moving to a new state.
- A politician considers taking an unpopular stance on an important social issue.

Psychosocial conflict is an inherent part of living and developing. It manifests itself in various ways, including the predominant crises that define Erikson's eight stages. Psychosocial conflict, together with the epigenetic principle and Erikson's concept of the ego, makes up the set of core theoretical concepts used to explain development across the life span.

Bridge Principles

As noted earlier, Erikson accepts many of the tenets of psychoanalysis, including the psychosexual stages, levels of consciousness, and defense mechanisms, all of which comprise the bridge principles of that theory. The bridge principle unique to psychosocial theory is the sequence of eight psychosocial stages.

The Psychosocial Stages.   Erikson's extension of psychoanalytic theory concentrates on the social and historical context of development across the life span. His remodeled developmental stages are cast as a series of psychosocial crises between the individual and society.

Erikson characterizes each crisis in terms of interactions with significant-other persons and the dominant psychosocial activities that occupy the individual's attention. As one matures, later developments are grounded in and dependent on the strengths developed at earlier stages (Erikson, 1984). He often presents a summary of his insights in the form of worksheets. Table 4.2 shows a summary of important elements in psychosocial stages.

Trust versus Mistrust.   The first psychosocial stage parallels Freud's oral stage. But where Freud underscored the need for oral pleasure, Erikson concentrates on the infant's need for continuous care, attention, and protection. Meeting these needs is critical for infants to achieve a sense of peaceful satisfaction and individual security. Herein lies the crisis between a sense of basic trust, being able to predict that one's needs will be satisfied, and basic mistrust, the fear that one cannot count on others for care or affection.

The infant's rudimentary sense of self derives most readily from the mother's consistency in responding predictably to her infant (Erikson, 1963). Consequently, mother is the most important social agent at this time, since she is usually the one to provide comfort, nurturance, and security. The amount of food, attention, or mothering is not crucial; what counts is the quality of the infant–mother relationship. Ideally, this relationship should combine reliability and trustworthiness with

TABLE 4.2   Summary of Erikson's Psychosocial Crises

Age	Psychosocial Crisis	Significant Sources of Psychosocial Conflict
0–1	Trust versus mistrust	Mother
2–3	Autonomy versus shame and doubt	Both parents
3–6	Initiative versus guilt	Family members
7–12	Industry versus inferiority	Neighborhood and school
12–18	Identity versus identity diffusion	Peer groups, out groups, leadership models
20s	Intimacy versus isolation	Cooperation with partner in friendship, recreation, production, sex
20s–50s	Generativity versus stagnation	Sharing child rearing, dividing labor, household responsibilities
50s and beyond	Integrity versus despair	Finding oneself within humanity, civilization, generations

loving attention to the baby's needs within the framework of the culture (Erikson, 1963).

The infant–mother relationship provides the child with its fundamental orientation toward the consistency and dependability of the world. Healthy development comes from a balance between trust and mistrust, from social relationships that are neither too indulgent nor too harsh. The world and its people often act in a predictable fashion, but one may acquire a sense of misgiving if events are not consistently predictable. Some mothers, for example, may unconsciously frustrate their infants' needs (e.g., tardy with feedings, ignoring cries for comfort or emotional longings) and inadvertently produce adults who are largely skeptical about interpersonal relationships and mistrustful of others. Overindulging an infant, however, may produce a gullible individual. Children who are unable to resolve the crisis between trust and mistrust in a positive way may forfeit some progress in later development because the foundation for later resolutions is predicated on successful resolutions of earlier crises. At the same time, even if a child has achieved a good sense of trust, it may be somewhat undermined later by consistent experiences with people who are untrustworthy.

Autonomy versus Shame and Doubt.   Erikson's second stage parallels Freud's anal stage, and both men stress the consequences of the infant's developing digestive system, the growing control over muscles, and in particular the increase of self-awareness over expelling bodily wastes. Children experience a sense of power and pride with growing control over their bodily organs. But Erikson views this experience as a double-edged struggle between achieving a sense of autonomy or ending up feeling shame and doubt about oneself. Children who successfully cope with potty training will experience a sense of power that fuels their maturing autonomy and sense of self-esteem; they learn that they are competent to do certain things for themselves. On the other hand, children who are continually frustrated by their potty training, who are scolded or ridiculed for their failures, may end up feeling shameful and doubting their own abilities. Some balance between cooperation and competition, and between self-expression and self-control, are necessary for a lasting sense of good will and pride (Erikson, 1963).

The child in Erikson's second stage faces the possibility of failure on two fronts if potty training is too rigid or initiated too early. In such a case, the unfortunate child is maturationally unable to control his own bowels and by implication is also unable to control his parents. As shown in Sandlot Seminar 4.1, children require a sensitive balance between parental consistency with limits of acceptable behavior and parental flexibility with freedom commensurate with children's own abilities.

In addition to toilet training, other important forces are at work. Children become aware that they can affect other people in their social world, and they discover how much control they have over their own and others' behavior. They can control their parents' delivery of praise by performing well. They lose approval and risk shame when their performance is not up to parental expectations. Children who are given many opportunities to test the limits of their power and opportunities to succeed as well as fail without retribution will develop a strong sense of

Sandlot Seminar 4.1

"I can do it."
A mother and her toddler enter a grocery store. She places him in the child seat of the cart and begins her shopping. After about five minutes, the child squirms and squeals until she lets him down from the seat with a warning.

MOM: Steven, as long as you hold onto the cart, you can get out of the seat.

STEVEN: Okay.

MOM (a few minutes later, as Steven begins wandering off): Steven, you promised you'd stay next to the cart. Please come closer and hold on.

STEVEN (pointing to the cereal boxes): But I want to go look there.

MOM: Steven, if you don't come hold on, I'll put you back in the cart.

STEVEN: No!

MOM: All right, but don't get lost.

STEVEN: I won't.

Mom continues shopping as Steven "orbits" the cart, each orbit ranging farther away toward new distractions. Finally, Steven stops to watch the lobsters as Mom turns the corner of the frozen food section and disappears from sight. Several moments later, he looks up, but Mom is nowhere to be found.

STEVEN: Mommy! Mommy!

Mom (returning): I told you not to go so far from the cart.

STEVEN (crying and clinging to Mom's slacks): You lost me! I want to ride in the cart.

1. What elements in the supermarket episode might contribute to Steven's sense of *autonomy*?
2. What elements might contribute to *shame and doubt*?

---

personal autonomy. In contrast, overprotection or inadequate opportunities to test one's competence will result in a sense of doubt about personal prowess.

Initiative versus Guilt.   Erikson's third stage depicts the crises that arise as children engage an expanding world of social agents. Children in this stage struggle to achieve independence and attain competence in the commerce of adultlike social transactions. Their social skills take shape as they try to master adult behaviors, and their physical skills mushroom in ways determined appropriate by the culture. These changes are similar to those Freud describes as outcomes of the Oedipal conflict, when superego development prompts children into learning society's sex roles and propels them to internalize a variety of social values and behavioral norms.

Children's guilt arises from the *difference between* the competence needed to perform certain tasks and their self-perceived ability. Preserving children's initiative is important at this time because it motivates them to actively participate in the social world around them. A sense of initiative prompts them to try new things, engage social companions, and master new skills. Given support for such efforts, they will develop a sense of mastery and initiative. At the other end of the continuum, those whose efforts have been frustrated or whose initiative has been punished will experience guilt. While Erikson (1963) believes that the timing of this crisis is maturationally fixed by the epigenetic plan, he also believes that a successful *resolution* is not predetermined. Sandlot Seminar 4.2 illustrates this point.

Industry versus Inferiority.   Erikson's fourth stage parallels Freud's latency period. During this time children learn to pursue social and intellectual activities favored by society: establishing peer groups, attending school, exercising independence in

---

Sandlot Seminar 4.2

Tying Shoelaces

Amanda liked playing with older children except for one thing. They were always telling her she wore "baby" shoes (with Velcro™ fasteners instead of laces). One day, after hearing "Big girls wear shoes that tie," Amanda came home and asked if she could have tie shoes. A trip to the shoe store was planned.

Tying shoelaces proved hard work, but she eventually mastered the task. Although she was very slow, she took great pride in her loose, fall-apart bow-tie knots. Her father even told her that she was the best shoelace tier in the whole family. Swelling with new pride, Amanda tried many new things: setting the table, making her bed, feeding the dog, and emptying the dishwasher. There seemed to be nothing she couldn't do.

This all changed quite suddenly one morning as the family was rushing to catch a Thanksgiving flight to visit Grandma and Grandpa. Amanda sat on the front steps, painstakingly trying to get her shoelaces "just right." Her usually patient father, afraid of missing their plane, just couldn't wait any longer and suggested that she finish tying her shoelaces in the car. Amanda politely refused. Dad couldn't wait any longer. He bent down, tied Amanda's shoes, and carried her kicking to the car for a hurried trip to the airport.

The trip to the airport was full of laughter and conversation from everyone except Amanda. She was mad. Finally, her mom asked, "Amanda, what's the matter?" With tears welling up she exclaimed, "Daddy told me a lie!" "How did I lie to you Amanda?" asked Dad.

"You told me I was the best shoe tier, and I'm not. You tied my shoes for me; so you lied!" Dad thought nothing of it and knew that Amanda would soon forget about the event. He figured that more praise under less harried conditions would lead to new and even better shoe tying behavior. This, however was not the case. In fact, Amanda quit setting the table, making her bed, feeding the dog, and emptying the dishwasher. Whenever she was asked to do a chore, her response was, "I can't. You have to help me."

1. How would Erikson explain Amanda's feelings?

play and learning. Make-believe play is an important milestone of childhood, but excessive use of it may be frustrating for the child who wants to accomplish something worthwhile and thereby gain satisfaction and earn adult recognition.

Because the crisis at this age requires the child to learn cooperation, it is socially the most decisive stage. It marks the origin of the work ethic wherein a sense of what is valued by society is incorporated by children.

Parents, teachers, and other adults who offer worthwhile tasks and meaningful challenges will help foster a sense of industry. However, earlier failures or assignment of tasks that impose greater achievements than the child can accomplish will tend to produce a sense of failure and inferiority. Children's feelings of inferiority due to their social heritage (e.g., racial, class, or sexual differences) may be spawned if consistently linked to lower performance on tasks they think are important.

Identity versus Identity Diffusion. One of Erikson's most important discoveries was the adolescent *identity crisis.* According to Erikson, the onset of puberty brings complex biological/hormonal change. At this time, adolescents also experience a new sense of self-awareness. They gain fresh awareness of themselves as individuals, as potential workers and parents, and as new persons occupying what used to be a child's body. New attractions toward the opposite sex awaken, and more importantly for Erikson, a search for ideas and people who are trustworthy begins. New expectations for the self are adopted, and these ego ideals tend at first to be very flexible, often changing with the time, place, and situation. The cognitive confusion that accompanies these changes Erikson termed the *identity crisis.*

Ego development has up to this point prepared the adolescent for the burden of establishing a genuine self-identity. Earlier resolutions have refined the child's psychological architecture for the intellectual ordeal of establishing a sense of personal identity. These achievements (or nonachievements) of trust, autonomy, initiative, and industry are not left behind. If successful, they promote development *into the future.* If not, they forever limit the possibilities of the future.

The adolescent's identity crisis reflects the opposition between the need to determine a self-identity and the profusion of possible social identities supported by the culture (Erikson, 1963). Youth in industrialized cultures have many role models to choose from; those in more primitive cultures may have far fewer adult roles. Without even knowing it, adolescents may work against identity diffusion by identifying with superheroes, cliques, crowds, and causes, each of which can be a focus of *personal commitment without conviction.* Parents of adolescents know well the sublime irony of that age; teenagers often accuse adults of being intolerant while themselves proclaiming intolerance for those who do not agree with their own stereotyped ideals, fashions, and ideological inclinations.

Adolescents often attempt to resolve their identity crisis by experimenting with different roles, values, and relationships. Those who achieve a sense of personal identity come through the crisis with a sense of self-worth that reflects their self-determined value to society. Those who fail this crisis may continue throughout adulthood to be intolerant and immature in their treatment of and attitudes toward others who are different.

Intimacy and Solidarity versus Isolation.   Unlike Freud, Erikson viewed adulthood as a time of change and transition that gives rise to new opportunities for close interpersonal relationships. However, intimacy can only be established to the extent that self-identity can be shared with the identities of age mates and mentors (Erikson, 1983). The adult with a secure sense of personal identity faces the new task of establishing a close, loving, sexually satisfying, give-and-take relationship with another of the opposite sex. Erikson views the ideal relationship as a satisfying marriage, although he acknowledges that intimacy can also be established outside of marriage. Intimate relationships require one to make a meaningful commitment to another, to invest one's beliefs, feelings, and values in a trustworthy recipient. Such a commitment is possible only for identity achievers, since a secure sense of "self" is prerequisite to being able to commit oneself to another self. Only through commitment is genuine intimacy possible, as is illustrated in Sandlot Seminar 4.3.

Conversely, the lack of a secure, self-determined identity often leads to superficial or selfish relationships with others. The failure to establish intimacy may result in feelings of social isolation, loneliness, or low self-esteem.

Sandlot Seminar 4.3

Do Opposites Really Attract?

Thom, a happy-go-lucky, outgoing computer whiz, and Sheri, an accountant, dated for just over a year before they got married. They were each asked by a friend to describe what it was that attracted them to each other. Thom replied, "I don't know what I want or even what I'm doing half the time. But I know I want Sheri. She is such a good, kind-hearted person. She knows what she wants, and she's happy in her work. She's the 'rudder' in our relationship, the perfect complement to my haphazard life." Sheri's response was quite different: "I'm the serious one. My whole life has been driven by wanting to succeed and get ahead. I'm constantly planning and living for the future. I feel like I'm burdened with responsibilities. Thom is the first person I've ever met who doesn't take himself so seriously. He makes me laugh. We have fun together. I know we'll be happy together."

Several years later Thom and Sheri sought marriage counseling to try and save their marriage. According to Sheri, "Thom has no ambition, can't keep a job, and doesn't know the meaning of the word 'responsibility.' What's worse, he doesn't provide me with any emotional warmth or support. There's no happiness between us any more." Thom agrees with some and disagrees with other elements of Sheri's appraisal, noting: "We don't have any friends, hardly ever go out, and don't have fun together any more. Sheri's right. I do tend to be irresponsible. But I *do* give her emotional support and warmth. After all, we still have a pretty good sex life. It's all the other hassles that are driving us apart."

1. What do you think Erikson would say about Thom and Sheri's relationship?

2. Might either Sheri or Thom (or both) be unable to establish genuine intimacy? What might account for that?

Generativity versus Stagnation.   During the adult years the psychosocial crisis is between the need to be productive both in work and family and a tendency to become self-absorbed with one's personal achievements and life-style. Generative individuals seek productive work, involved child rearing, new adventures and challenges, and important goals. Those who become self-absorbed or fail to incorporate the needs of society into their personal lives tend to become stagnated.

This stage marks the years of primary social production. With confidence in one's ability (favorable outcomes of trust, initiative, industry, identity, and intimacy), individuals can expect success in family and child rearing, work, hobbies and lawn care, and the myriad of adult tasks set by society. Sandlot Seminar 4.4

Sandlot Seminar 4.4

Developmental Interactions

Our colleague Ron Lowery is an elementary schoolteacher in Charlotte, North Carolina. Ron has suggested some interesting ways to think about Erikson's stages, particularly in terms of life-span interactions. For example, consider the implications in each of the following situations.

Situation 1

Two elementary schools are similar in many respects. All the teachers and school administrators are in their forties, have twenty years of teaching experience, and are a dedicated lot. However, imagine that the first school has a staff that successfully resolved the *generativity versus stagnation* crisis in favor of generativity. The second school's staff did not; their egos are in stagnation. Now into these schools walk elementary students who are themselves experiencing a crisis of *industry versus inferiority*. What systematic effects might occur to the students simply because their teachers have different resolutions to their own crises?

Situation 2

Again, imagine two elementary schools that are similar in most respects. This time, however, the first school's staff consists of first-year teachers who have just completed college. These teachers are probably experiencing the *intimacy versus isolation* crisis. In the second school, very experienced middle-aged teachers are experiencing the crisis of *generativity versus stagnation*. All other things being equal, and regardless of how the teachers resolve their respective crises, might we expect systematic differences simply because the teachers are in different stages of their own ego development?

Situation 3

Imagine two high school classes filled with graduating seniors very much in the stage of *identity versus identity diffusion*. Both classes are taught by 25-year-old teachers, each with several years of experience. The only difference is that one teacher has previously resolved the identity crisis in favor of a strong identity, while the second remains in identity diffusion. Even if they're teaching the same subject, how might these two teachers impact their students in different ways?

illustrates the types of developmental interactions that might occur when adults at this stage engage in systematic social exchanges with children at earlier stages of development.

Integrity versus Despair.   Toward the end of the life span, retirement and old age often lead to certain spiritual concerns. Erikson believes that a successful resolution to the crisis of *integrity versus despair* requires an earlier lifetime of successful conflict resolutions as well as a sense of peaceful satisfaction with one's past. The successful aging individual gains a broader vision of life and gains ego strength from this awareness. Lifelong satisfaction can result in ego *integrity,* a sense of personal worth that helps one adjust to the frailties of aging and eventual death. In contrast, despair results when one fears the inevitability of old age and death. Attempts to compensate for lost time at this stage by "trying to catch up" or by "making amends" may prompt feelings of futility, dread, regret, and emptiness—ego despair.

Change Mechanisms

The change mechanisms in psychosocial theory are also among its important internal principles. Erikson describes a primary change mechanism, **epigenesis,** and a secondary change mechanism, **psychosocial conflict**. Each functions differently and results in a different kind or quality of change.

   Epigenesis. As noted earlier, the epigenetic principle is the primary mechanism of development across the life cycle. Epigenesis has its origins in the genetic design containing all the biological information needed to initiate a sequence of critical periods that transcend a lifetime. Biology, not culture, determines when a crisis will occur, what the nature of that crisis will be, and when it will be ended by the onset of a new crisis. Within each crisis, however, social and historical forces influence the individual through a second, subordinate mechanism—psychosocial conflict.

   Psychosocial conflict is a secondary change mechanism in Erikson's theory that always occurs in the context of epigenesis. Psychosocial conflict determines whether a crisis will be favorably or unfavorably resolved. It consists of the day-to-day exchanges between individuals that provide life's interpersonal challenges and frustrations. Social experiences from infancy to old age reflect many cultural events that confront us with higher expectations, that challenge us to do better than our peers, and that motivate us to achieve increasingly complex goals. The ego has a daunting task. On the one hand, it strives for personal identity and self-worth. On the other hand, the same ego battles for conformity in the cultural context of expectations, stereotypes, habits, customs, and skills taught by parents and significant others during one's lifetime. Achieving a balance between self and society is ego's lifelong work.

   It is important to note here exactly what Erikson posits as due to epigenesis and what he posits as due to cultural influence. First, his stages are endogenous in origin; each psychosocial crisis is one manifestation of the fixed, epigenetic plan. Individuals can do nothing to prevent a crisis from occurring or to speed up the sequence of crises. Second, the sequence of crises is universal, not because of necessity or chance, but because of history. Each culture has evolved methods of child rearing that may differ in specifics but that reflect common social spheres in which individuals engage. For example, infants are nursed by mothers, raised by families, work in societies, raise new generations during adulthood, and pass on the cultural traditions. Third, while the sequence and structure of psychosocial crises is universal, specific cultural and individual variations occur within that context. For example, infants in all cultures experience a natural conflict between themselves and their mothers, but how this conflict manifests itself may vary. In some cultures mothers may lavish attention on their infants; in other cultures such attention may be relatively short-lived. Within a culture some infants may experience prolonged nursing, while others may be weaned within months of their birth. In each instance, a crisis of interpersonal trust and dependency is experienced by infants. At the same time, the circumstantial ingredients of this crisis may differ from one infant to another.

An analogy may be helpful in understanding the differential contributions of primary and secondary determinants. Think of your life span as like an extended vacation where your basic plan (the epigenetic blueprint) is the primary determinant of where you go and when. In comparison, psychosocial conflict is analogous to the events that comprise the actual vacation experience. Sometimes events go as planned; often they do not because unforeseen events intervene (e.g., bad weather, missed transportation) to upset and frustrate your plans. The day-to-day experiences and hour-to-hour pressures are like psychosocial conflict in that they influence how well your vacation actually works out. In this way psychosocial conflict is a secondary determinant of development whose effects are subordinated to the primary limitations imposed by epigenesis.

Explaining Human Development: The Research

Aside from some indirect research on infant attachment, there has been very little research that directly tests Erikson's claims about early and middle childhood, adulthood, or old age. In fact, researchers have generally not investigated the predictive validity of the theory in terms of how well it explains successful aging (Ryff, 1982), and while Erikson is often cited in research studies, his theory is seldom studied directly in adults or the aged (Tesch, 1985). However, research on the adolescent identity crisis has occupied a number of researchers. Because of this situation, research that bears on Erikson's claims about adolescent identity formation will be emphasized in this section.

Indirect Research on Infants and Children

According to Erikson, infancy entails a crisis of trust versus mistrust. Given this claim, it is reasonable to expect that infants whose basic physical and emotional needs are met, who are nurtured with tender care, and whose caretakers are consistent in their interactions, would respond by establishing a basic sense of trust in others.

Research on infantile attachments to their mothers has uncovered a number of patterns that bear on the Eriksonian crisis of trust versus mistrust. For example, mothers who are highly affectionate, respond quickly to infant distress, and exhibit emotional and verbal responsiveness to their infants tend to have infants who display more secure attachments than mothers without these qualities (Bates, Maslin, & Frankel, 1985). In fact, the correlation between positive maternal characteristics and quality of infant attachment has proven quite robust. A number of cross-cultural studies have found essentially the same relationship in Germany (Grossmann, Grossmann, Spangler, Suess, & Unzner, 1985) and Japan (Miyake, Chen, & Campos, 1985), and among kibbutz-reared children in Israel (Sagi, Lamb, Lewkowicz, Shoham, Dvir, & Estes, 1985).

Mothering itself should reflect resolutions to earlier trust versus mistrust and autonomy versus shame and doubt crises, at least to some extent. For example, mothers from disrupted families of origin are also less likely than other mothers to talk to, look at, or touch their infants, and they also respond less to their infants' vocalizations, whether fretful or positive (Hall & Pawlby, 1981). There is also evidence that the quality of early attachment experience is correlated with the quality of later marital relations. For example, women who experienced separation or disruption of primary attachments during infancy later tend to experience marital disharmony (Frommer & O'Shea, 1973).

Such research does not directly assess Erikson's contentions about infancy and childhood, but it is suggestive. It indicates that secure attachments are most likely to occur in situations where parents are consistently warm, sensitive, and responsive in meeting their infants' needs, qualities that could reasonably be expected to foster a sense of basic trust.

Ginsburg (1992), in an unusual twist, has shown how Erikson's psychosocial theory could be used to understand and possibly control the frequency and type of childhood injuries typically experienced during the first four psychosocial stages. For example, toddlers in the autonomy versus shame and doubt stage are unconsciously compelled to "let go" of their parents and strike off on their own to establish their independence. Finding themselves in potentially dangerous situations (e.g., walking down a neighborhood street, climbing up a tree, approaching a growling dog) may well be a natural outgrowth of this stage.

Child Rearing

Erikson would predict that children's experiences would impact their later ego development. In this vein, DuCharme, Koverola, and Battle (1997) have found that those who had experienced abuse as children were significantly less likely to establish intimacy as young adults.

Child-care arrangements of infants and young children also have long-term effects on ego development. For example, differences in friendship, identity, and self-confidence among black college students are associated with differences in their child-care arrangements during infancy (Morrison, Ispa, & Thornburg, 1994). Moreover, no day care during infancy followed by part-time day care during the preschool years is a predictor of above-average academic performance in high school (Ispa, Thornburg, & Gray, 1994).

Many researchers have tried to assess the impact parents have on the behavior and personality of their adolescent children. A portion of that work has attempted to examine the relationship between parental characteristics and adolescent identity. La Voie (1976) reports, for example, that male adolescents high in ego identity were less controlled by their parents and received more frequent paternal praise than low ego identity peers. Similarly, high ego identity adolescent females experienced less maternal restrictiveness and closer parental relations than low ego identity females. Other research (Mattheson, 1974; Waterman & Waterman, 1971) supports La Voie's findings and seems to indicate that high ego identity adolescents experience more open parental communication and less restrictive control over their activities than low ego identity adolescents.

As young adolescents change from subordinate to more peerlike relationships, they typically initiate changes in their relationships with parents (Hill, 1980; Youniss, 1980). One indication of this change is reflected in the increase in assertiveness displayed in family interactions by young adolescents (Jacob, 1974; Steinberg, 1981). This growth of autonomy reflects a transformation in the emotional bond with parents rather than a desire for detachment or total freedom from parental influence. Psychosocial theory suggests that parents who are able to adapt to their children's challenge for autonomy create a different family context for development than those parents who are unable to change. Adams and Fitch's (1982) longitudinal study of university students found that parents who tried to inhibit adolescent role exploration had children who experienced early identity foreclosures. Other evidence suggests that identity formation is positively related to supportive, cohesive, and accepting family contexts and to adolescent autonomy (Grotevant, 1983).

Adolescent Identity

An important element of adolescent identity formation is what Erikson (1968) calls a *psychosocial moratorium*. All societies provide a scheduled time for the completion of a personal identity. While considerable cultural variation exists in the timing, duration, intensity, and rituals of adolescence, many societies afford their youth a "time out" during which the adolescent is expected to make certain lifelong commitments and to establish a fixed self-definition (Adams & Montemayor, 1983). This "time out" is the psychosocial moratorium.

The moratorium can be described as commitment without conviction. Adolescents suspend their beliefs in ideas and people in order to search out individuals and points of view that are genuinely trustworthy, that are objectively true rather than subjectively valued. The moratorium may involve a prolonged state of psychological confusion about the many varied roles one might take on in adult society, and it may involve active experimentation with different roles, values, and beliefs in order to "see if the shoe fits."

The psychosocial moratorium is accompanied by a sense of *crisis*, an unavoidable turning point when development has to move in one direction or another (Erikson, 1968). Irreversible adolescent decisions such as moving away from home, relocating for a job or college, getting married, and choosing a career, all pose important dilemmas because once a decision has been made, it is difficult if not impossible to undo it.

Marcia's (1966) research is the most well-known analysis of the identity crisis. He identified four modes of crisis resolution:

Identity diffusion	no crisis and no commitment
Identity foreclosure	commitment without a crisis
Identity moratorium	crisis without a commitment
Identity achievement	both crisis and commitment

Many investigators have chosen to assess Marcia's identity statuses as indirect tests of Erikson's concept of the identity crisis. For example, Archer (1982) examined adolescents in the sixth, eighth, tenth, and twelfth grades in order to determine the age at which identity achievement was reached. Her results indicated that identity achievement was correlated with age; older adolescents were more likely to have attained identity achievement than younger ones. She found similar patterns for boys and girls and noted specifically that identity diffusion and identity foreclosure were more common at each grade level than any other status. In a similar study of 12- to 24-year-old males, Meilman (1979) found that most of his subjects, including young adults, were in either identity diffusion or identity foreclosure. These findings do not, of course, preclude many adolescents from attaining identity achievement later in adolescence or early adulthood. For example, Meilman (1979) also reported that the years between 18 and 21 produced the most significant development in identity formation, with the most prominent shifts being from identity diffusion and foreclosure to identity achievement. Additional support for Marcia's four identity statuses can be found in studies by Toder and Marcia (1973), Adams, Shea, and Fitch (1979), and Waterman and Goldman (1976).

Age alone, however, may not be the only important variable in determining one's identity status. Adams and Fitch (1982) in a two-year study of college students found that approximately half remained stable in their identity status, while the other half either regressed or advanced. Both identity diffused and moratorium students tended to advance. Students who were identity achieved, however, either remained that way or regressed to a moratorium status. An interesting point here has been made by Waterman and Waterman (1971), who have argued that the very nature of college, which stimulates students to reevaluate their beliefs and values, may exert a powerful influence to move toward a moratorium status, whether that status is an advance or a regression. Between the first and last year of college, however, one generally finds an increase in adolescents who have made identity commitments and successfully resolved their identity crisis, and this increase holds up even across three generations of college students (Zuschlag & Whitbourne, 1994). In addition, the quality and intimacy of friendships are positively correlated with the degree to which adolescents have achieved high identity (Moore & Boldero, 1991).

To some extent, the adolescent's achievement of ego identity reflects the developing ability to integrate different social arenas into a coherent whole. In a study of 11,000 high school students, Dukes, Martinez, and Stein (1997) found that gang membership resulted from a lack of social integration. In a very different study, Lightfoot (1997) conducted in-depth interviews about "risk taking" with forty-one 16- to 18-year-olds. Her subjects described various types of "risky" behaviors (drinking, unprotected sex, fighting) as transforming experiences and as a way to establish shared cultural experiences with certain peers. Her results seem to support Erikson's notion that experimenting with different life roles helps adolescents establish a sense of identity.

Cultural Context

The cultural heritage and historical moment during which an adolescent is in the transition from childhood to adulthood has been examined by Paranjpe (1976), who presents several case studies in the form of psychohistories. He shows how several individuals developed a sense of identity achieved in spite of dramatically different personal experiences. Paranjpe's case studies are intriguing because they took place in India, a culture undergoing rapid progress from traditional to contemporary male–female sex roles. Vinu, for example, was a young man who kept diaries between 17 and 27 years of age. During that time, Vinu attended college, attempted to enter a monastery, became celibate, tried a number of religious sects, tried being a teacher, and finally found a sense of occupational achievement as a journalist. It changed Vinu's life. He renounced his celibacy, married a traditional Indian woman his parents had selected for him (according to Indian custom), and finally stopped writing in his diary. In other case studies, two young Indian women, Meera and Sheela, each made personal sacrifices, experienced considerable doubt about their future as women, underwent personal hardship, and ended up choosing diametrically opposing paths to identity resolution. The other psychohistories reported by Paranjpe (1976) also reveal considerable adolescent turmoil, in some cases ending in identity achievement and in others identity confusion. In a different cultural context, Josselson (1973) has reported several case studies of the identity crisis in American female college students, giving careful attention to the ways they examined identity commitments of vocational choice, religion, political ideologies, and sex-role preferences.

Because societies so often differentiate adult roles on the basis of sex, Erikson's theory would suggest that adolescent girls and boys would have different identity experiences. Limited evidence suggests that such a pattern does in fact occur. For example, the identity profiles of late adolescents indicate that males are more focused on career identity issues and that females are more firmly established in their sense of interpersonal competence and identity (Josselson, 1973; Josselson,

Greenberger, & McConochie, 1977). In addition, several researchers have suggested that females resolve relationship and career issues simultaneously while males deal with them sequentially (Hodgson & Fischer, 1979; Thorbecke & Grotevant, 1982).

Adulthood and Aging

The adult stage of generativity versus stagnation involves a conflict between becoming so involved in one's own career and personal preoccupations that normal activities such as fostering, nurturing, and guiding the next generation go unattended. Although child rearing is typical of this stage, generativity can occur in the absence of children (Erikson, 1969) when an adult generates something of lasting significance (e.g., art, literature, ideas, customs). Several studies involving a variety of methodologies have provided various degrees of validation for adult ego development (McAdams, de St. Aubin, & Logan, 1993; McAdams, Hart, & Maruna, 1998; Snarey & Clark, 1998).

In order to assess the relationship between generativity and later ego development, McAdams, Ruetzel, and Foley (1986) examined the identity status of fifty midlife adults and their personal plans for the future. Future plans were assessed in four categories: occupational, interpersonal, recreational, and material. The researchers found that individuals high in ego development also tended to specify a variety of personal goals for the future, whereas those low in ego development described significantly fewer personal goals. Individuals with high ego development also had more complex personalities than did subjects rated low in ego development.

In a different kind of study, Nehrke, Bellucci, and Gabriel (1977–78) found that three independent measures of ego integrity—life satisfaction, locus of control, and the absence of death fear—were positively correlated in a group of forty elderly adults. More recently Walaskay, Whitbourne, and Nehrke (1983–84) examined ego integrity in forty elderly adults who ranged in age from 65 to 90. The researchers reported that integrity-achieving individuals displayed consistently higher late-life adaptation in terms of ego intimacy, ego generativity, emotional balance, and preparation for and acceptance of death than did despairing individuals. These results suggest that elderly people who have achieved ego integrity tend to be better adjusted emotionally than despairing individuals.

Contributions and Criticisms of Psychosocial Theory

Contributions

Healthy Personality.   Where Freud emphasized the ego's function as mediator between the competing demands of id and superego, Erikson concentrates his attention on the ego's role in adaptive personality development. His theory views the ego as healthy and conflict-free. This means that individuals are not doomed to a life of anxiety and impulse-ridden compulsions. People may, depending on their resolutions to the various psychosocial crises, lead lives that are relatively satisfying and happy. Erikson has given the entire field of psychoanalytic theory a choice—a choice that on the one hand leads *inward, backward, and downward* or on the other hand leads *outward, forward, and upward* (Erikson, 1972). Such an optimistic view of human nature is fundamentally different from Freud's.

Stages That Span the Life Cycle. Until the late 1950s and early 1960s, developmental psychologists primarily concerned themselves with infant, childhood, and adolescent development. The explosive surge of interest in life-span human development that has occurred in the past two decades has created an important need. Erikson's psychosocial theory, with its theoretical constructs and unifying lifelong theme (ego identity) allows the developmental psychologist to link elements of adult or old age functioning with earlier patterns of psychosocial adjustment.

Identity Crisis. One cannot outline Erikson's contributions to our understanding of human development without acknowledging the concept of identity crisis. The relevance of his ideas on adolescent identity formation is reflected in the previous section, where it was noted that this concept has occupied more research interest than all other elements of his theory combined. Much of the literature on adolescence acknowledges the importance of Erikson's contribution here. Identity functioning is generally considered to be a vital element of the adolescent experience, and many believe that the ego identity statuses associated with Marcia's work reflect meaningful patterns of identity formation. These in turn have contributed to our understanding of the impact that adolescence has on an individual's functioning later in life.

Psychohistory. It is unfortunate that Erikson's psychohistorical method has been underutilized in developmental psychology, because the method produces extremely rich data. The method provides a way to examine the impact of three separate influences: personal ego identity, one's cultural context, and the historical zeitgeist. In this respect, Erikson overcame two of the criticisms leveled against Freud, namely that the latter relied too heavily on neurotic personalities and failed to adequately account for the role of society in personality development. Erikson not only sampled more widely than Freud, but many of his observations were drawn from different cultures. In that light, the psychohistory method served his purpose well. Reprints of his two of his most famous psychohistories, Martin Luther (Erikson, 1958) and Mahatma Gandhi (Erikson, 1969), can still be obtained in bookstores. No other psychological method produces quite the richness and variety of data for analysis. The method is inappropriate, however, for individuals who have not left written documentation of their thoughts during their psychosocial crises.

Criticisms

Measurability. Erikson's theoretical constructs, like Freud's, have been criticized because they are extremely difficult to measure. Marcia's (1966) analysis of the adolescent identity crisis notwithstanding, only limited empirical studies have been done on infant, childhood, and adulthood psychosocial crises. In large part this shortcoming is due to the difficulty of measuring psychosocial crises. How does one, for example, actually measure whether the infant is experiencing trust, distrust, or a conflict between the two? One can observe an infant's and a child's behavior, note their interests and protests, but aside from direct self-reports, no method has been developed for measuring psychosocial trauma. The problem with being unable to measure theoretical constructs is that researchers cannot establish either the external validity or predictive validity of the theory.

Stage Sequence.   Only limited research supports Erikson's contention that ego identity is prerequisite to being able to form genuinely intimate adult relationships. Moreover, relatively few cross-cultural or longitudinal studies have been conducted to support the claim that psychosocial crises occur in a fixed, universal sequence. Given the importance of this claim for psychosocial theory, the absence of appropriate empirical support cannot easily be overlooked.

Evaluation of Psychosocial Theory

Scientific Worthiness

Testability.   Given the foregoing discussion about the difficulty of measuring Erikson's constructs, it is difficult to imagine how one could test any of the eight psychosocial crises. Various methods have been used to tap ego identity: semistructured interviews, clinical discussions, projective tests, and observations. But these methods simply cannot, for example, test the claim that epigenesis governs the unfolding of psychosocial stages. In addition, attitude and personality measurements are sometimes correlated with age. But such measurements provide only indirect information about an individual's ego status. Even Erikson's belief that ego identity reflects an individual's cultural and historical context is difficult to test, case studies notwithstanding. For these reasons Table 4.3 shows a low rating for the testability of psychosocial theory.

TABLE 4.3   Ratings of Psychosocial Theory for Scientific Worthiness

Criteria	High	Medium	Low
Testability			X
External Validity		X	
Predictive Validity		X	
Internal Consistency		X	
Theoretical Economy			X

External Validity. Erikson's descriptions of psychosocial crises seem intuitively correct: the infant's crisis of trust versus mistrust, the crisis of industry or inferiority of middle and late childhood, the adolescent's identity crisis. Yet, with the exception of the identity crisis, there is relatively little research on childhood and adult psychosocial crises. There are too few cross-cultural studies and virtually no longitudinal studies of psychosocial development in the literature. The identity crisis does, however, appear to be a relatively accurate portrayal of self-searching examination and self-doubt experienced by many adolescents. Given the relative absence of research on the other stages but the relatively good research support for Erikson's portrayal of adolescence, we have judged his theory as medium on this criterion.

Predictive Validity. Because relatively little work has been done to derive empirical predictions of Erikson's concepts, it would rate low on this basis alone. However, Marcia's (1966) derivation of four identity statuses from Erikson's description of the identity crisis is precisely what predictive validity is all about. Given the relatively good empirical support for Marcia's work but the absence of validation in other areas, Erikson's theory is rated as medium on this criterion.

Internal Consistency. Erikson adheres to the majority of psychoanalytic ideas. However, important differences between Freud and him do warrant consideration. Erikson, for example, has consistently posited a conflict-free ego that undergoes a sequence of epigenetically determined crises and whose resolutions to those crises are influenced by the individual's cultural and historical context. The ego is conflict-free in the sense that it is not, like Freud's depiction, constrained to feeding off the id's psychic energy, nor is its primary function to mitigate against the conflicting demands of id and superego. Rather, ego identity uses its own energy to resolve psychosocial crises that occur between the individual and society. Erikson has also been consistent in his description of the kinds of social forces that impact on the various identity crises. On balance, given Erikson's own relative consistency about psychosocial development, we have given the theory a medium rating for its internal consistency.

Theoretical Economy. Erikson's specific assumptions are more restrained than Freud's. His focus on ego development is narrower than Freud's, but his theory covers the entire life span. Psychosocial theory assumes that the ego is both autonomous and conflict-free at birth. These assumptions, together with a general framework inherited from psychoanalytic theory, mean that theoretical economy (a ratio of assumptions to explanatory power) is still comparable to Freud's. Consequently, we have given psychosocial theory a low rating for this criterion.

Developmental Adequacy

Temporality. As shown in Table 4.4 on page 102, Erikson's theory clearly addresses the issue of developmental change over time. Development, in Erikson's view is a lifelong, time-dependent process.

TABLE 4.4   Ratings of Psychosocial Theory for Developmental Adequacy

Criteria	Rating
Temporality	yes
Cumulativity	yes
Directionality	yes
New Mode of Organization	no
Increased Capacity for Self-control	?

Cumulativity.   The theory describes ego development as a sequence of crisis resolutions in which earlier crises have important implications on resolutions of later crises. According to Erikson, successful resolutions at later stages are built upon previous crisis resolutions. Moreover, later crises gradually add to and enlarge one's cultural–historical identity. For example, research indicates some support for the claim that establishment of interpersonal intimacy is predicated on successful identity achievement. Consequently, the theory passes this criterion.

Directionality.   Erikson claims that the development of ego identity occurs through the resolution of crises, which increasingly expands the individual's sense of self in both cultural and historical contexts. Beginning with infancy, the individual is involved in a crisis of trust versus mistrust, a crisis that requires it to form its original interpersonal relationship with its mother. By the time the infant has reached old age, many interpersonal crises have been faced, each expanding its sociocultural sense of self and responsibility to include ever-widening spheres of personal identification. Thus, Erikson's theory does imply a direction to development—a move from self-centered concerns to humanity-centered concerns, and so it passes this criterion.

New Mode of Organization.   Erikson's theory stresses the continuity of ego formation throughout the life span. However, one does not leave behind a well-adapted identity in order to forge a new one; rather the new one is forged within the limits established by previous identity successes. At successive stages the ego undergoes continuous adjustments to new social influences (cumulativity), but new organizational schemes are not imposed on old ones. New elements of identity functioning incorporate rather than replace old ego adaptations. Epigenesis is a continuous unfolding of ego crises that incorporate earlier achievements rather than reorganize previous resolutions. Consequently, Erikson's theory does not explain this characteristic of development.

Increased Capacity for Self-control.   It is helpful to review what is meant by this criterion. Increased capacity for self-control means that as individuals develop, they acquire certain skills or abilities that improve the regulation of person–environment interactions. Because of competing concerns, we cannot decide if Erikson's theory should pass or fail this criterion, so we have left a question mark for future research to decide. The competing concerns are these. Although individuals enlarge their psychosocial spheres, they do not necessarily exert an increased capacity to control their own destinies. For example, individuals whose resolutions to earlier crises were unsuccessful tend toward unsuccessful later resolutions, no matter how much will power they might exert. In a similar manner, later stages do not necessarily imply an increase in self-control, since ego functioning occurs below the level of awareness. Finally, individuals are influenced indirectly by their cultural and historical zeitgeist, each of which is beyond personal control. To the extent that individuals are capable of free choice, their choices are always constrained to a large degree by previous crisis resolutions, culture, and historical context. One cannot, for example, simply decide to choose generativity over self-absorption (stage VII crisis) or integrity over despair (stage VIII crisis) as a way of ego functioning. These arguments notwithstanding, it is also the case that the development of ego identity, especially when crises are resolved favorably, results in adaptive patterns of social adjustment in which people choose the kinds of activities they engage in and the types of people they come into contact with. Because Erikson places more emphasis on the former concerns than the latter, and because it is the latter that are related to increased capacity for self-control, we remain undecided on his rating for this criterion.

Pedagogical Usefulness

Interpretability. One need only read some of Erikson's original works to appreciate his mastery of commonsense language. For all its complexity, ego development is explained with only a minimal influx of technical vocabulary and jargon. *Crises* are conflicts, and *psychosocial* crises are simply conflicts between self and society. Even the names Erikson gives to his stages use descriptive terms from every day language (e.g., industry versus inferiority). The most demanding term employed by the theory is *epigenesis,* which is simply a technical name for a specific type of maturational plan. Occasionally, Erikson surprises us, as when, for example, he uses the term *fidelity* to mean "faithfulness to ideas and ideals" rather than sexual faithfulness to a partner. Still, for a developmental theory, Erikson rates high for theoretical jargon that is easy to understand and interpret (see Table 4.5).

Versatility. Erikson's theory of ego development is far more limited in scope than Freud's. At the same time, it does suggest a variety of different ways adults can interact favorably with infants, children, and adolescents. For these reasons, we have rated psychosocial theory medium for its versatility.

Availability. Unlike Freud's work, Erikson's theory has yet to make its way into the popular culture. The primary places one can find out about psychosocial theory are through Erikson's original writings, professional journal articles, and textbook treatments, such as the one in this chapter. These sources are, of course, primarily available in university libraries. Consequently, the theory is rated low for its availability.

TABLE 4.5   Ratings of Psychosocial Theory for Pedagogical Usefulness

Criteria	High	Medium	Low
Interpretability	X		
Versatility		X	
Availability			X
Guidance		X	

Guidance.   We have rated Erikson's theory medium for its guidance, the implications it has for teachers, parents, and counselors. As some of the Sandlot Seminars have suggested, from infancy until old age, many suggestions are made for self–social interactions that would improve ego functioning and favorable crisis resolution. It is important to point out, however, that there is nothing adults can do to impact the sequence of ego stages or their accompanying crises. These are immune to environmental influence. Overall, Erikson's theory suggests many pedagogical implications for helping youth deal with their various crises.

Summary Points

1. Erikson never rejected Freud as did many other psychoanalysts of the day. Rather, he sought to extend Freud's work by concentrating on the ego's own development. His major differences with Freud include his focus on ego identity, healthy personality functioning, cultural and historical influences, and stages that stretch across the entire life span.

2. The overarching problem of study for Erikson is to understand how the ego adapts itself to a sequence of psychosocial crises. The phenomena to be explained include the status of the ego at any point in the life span, the sequence of crises individuals must resolve, and the historical–cultural context of a person's development. Erikson utilizes naturalistic observations and a method he developed called psychohistory.

3. The internal principles of psychosocial theory include ego identity, the epigenetic principle, and psychosocial conflict. The eight psychosocial stages are the theory's bridge principle.

4. Epigenesis and psychosocial conflict are the change mechanisms that govern the development of ego identity. Epigenesis is the framework of innate stages that determine the scope and sequence of development across the life span. The stages are immune to environmental input. Psychosocial conflict, in turn, influences whether the crises at each stage are successfully resolved.

5. Erikson has made four enduring contributions to our understanding of human nature. He has described how a healthy personality functions and how it

evolves through the entire life span. He has also given psychology the method of psychohistory and an explanation of the adolescent identity crisis.

6. The two primary criticisms of Erikson's theory are its vague, imprecise concepts, which have been difficult to measure, and the universal sequence of his stages, which have not been adequately verified.

7. Overall, the theory rated medium low for its scientific worthiness, medium high for its developmental adequacy, and medium for its pedagogical usefulness.

PROBLEMS AND EXERCISES

1. Many students keep diaries during their adolescent years. If you kept one, reread it now. Evaluate your thoughts and feelings in terms of Erikson's description of the identity crisis. If you didn't keep a diary, try to find several old high school essays you wrote. Evaluate them in terms of Erikson's description of the identity crisis.

2. Spend several hours this week jotting down notes about your parents. Consider the prevailing social climate of their upbringing, the important historical events that accompanied their adolescence (interview them about this), their aspirations about you, and the importance of family or social traditions they wanted you to learn. From your data, see if you can evaluate each of their ego identities in terms of Erikson's last two stages (whichever is appropriate). Be careful not to categorize either one according to any one specific statement or belief; psychosocial identity reflects a complex integration of influences.

3. Compare and contrast Freud's and Erikson's childhood stages. What are their similarities and differences?

4. Analyze the possible consequences on ego development of any of the following pairs of conditions: poverty and wealth, presence and absence of siblings, majority versus minority ethnic group, or urban versus rural environment.

5. Use the Internet to search for sites related to Erikson and his theory. You can use his name as well as key words (internal and bridge principles). How do the Internet sites differ in terms of completeness and accuracy of information? What were the best sites you found? What problems did you encounter? What were some of the worst sites (and why)?

SUGGESTED READINGS

More about the Theory

Erikson, E. (1958). *Young man Luther: A study in psychoanalysis and history.* New York: Norton.

Erikson, E. *Childhood and society* (2nd ed.). New York: Norton.

Gross, F. L., Jr. (1987). *Introducing Erik Erikson: An invitation to his thinking.* Lanham, MD: University Press of America.

Kroger, J. (Ed.). (1993). *Discussions on ego identity.* Hillsdale, NJ: Lawrence Erlbaum.

Research Reviews

McAdams, D. P., & de St. Aubin, E. (Eds.). (1998). *Generativity and adult development: How and why we care for the next generation.* Washington, DC: American Psychological Association.

Waterman, A. S. (1982). Identity development from adolescence to adulthood: An extension of theory and a review of research. *Developmental Psychology, 18,* 341–358.

Critical Reviews

Novak, M. (1985–1986). Biography after the end of metaphysics: A critique of epigenetic evolution. *International Journal of Aging and Human Development, 22,* 189–204.

Roazen, P. (1976). *Erik H. Erikson: The power and limits of a vision.* New York: The Free Press.

5 Wilson and Sociobiology

Preview Questions

What is phylogenesis?

What are the three basic principles of evolution?

How are genotypes and phenotypes related to natural selection?

What assumptions does sociobiology make about human nature?

What problems constitute the purpose of sociobiology, and what types of evidence does the theory consider? What methods does it use?

What are the theory's internal and bridge principles?

What are the theory's change mechanisms?

Why is Wilson's theory a member of the endogenous paradigm?

What are the major contributions and criticisms of sociobiology?

How does the theory rate for its scientific worthiness, developmental adequacy, and pedagogical usefulness?

Historical Sketch

Sociobiology is a theory about the *cultural evolution of social behaviors*. The theory concentrates on *phylogeny* (the development of a species from its origin to its present form) rather than on *ontogeny* (the development of the individual). This is an important point to remember throughout the entire chapter, since the theory views developmental change as something that occurs between generations of individuals instead of something that happens during their lifetime.

The Legacy of Darwin

In 1836 Charles Darwin returned to England from his voyage aboard the *Beagle* convinced that the great variety of plants and animals he had observed did not come into being all in one moment. In his notebook on the "transmutation of species," he recorded his belief that new species were produced from gradual changes in older species, but he had no idea how the changes had been rendered (Gould, 1977). In the following year, Darwin happened upon Malthus's essay on populations and realized that under natural conditions, some individuals in a species tended to survive while others tended to perish in a struggle for scarce resources such as food and water. Darwin concluded that this *natural selection* must be the mechanism of evolution, but for political and religious reasons he delayed publication of his work for over twenty years. *On the Origin of Species by Means of Natural Selection* was published in 1859. It contained his description of evolution and the principle of natural selection. Darwin's theory of evolution is elegantly simple. It embodies three basic ideas: *variation, inheritance of traits,* and *natural selection.*

Darwin knew that individual members of a species varied among themselves in traits such as shape, size, color, strength, and so on. He believed that variation in such traits was passed on from parent to offspring. But he also knew that plants and animals reproduced so rapidly that the whole world could not hold them if all their young survived. This meant that there must be a constant struggle against predators and for resources such as food, water, and shelter. Only the most fit individuals survived this struggle, which Darwin termed *natural selection.*

Modern evolutionary theory, given the post-Darwinian discovery of genes by Mendel, contains the following essential elements. Evolution works on three levels: the genetic level, the individual level, and the species level. Figure 5.1 illustrates how evolution works at each of the three levels.

At the first level, genes are the building blocks of individuals; individuals are the building blocks of species. Evolution requires variations between individuals, because natural selection cannot favorably select some traits over others if every individual is identical. Genes mutate or sexually recombine. They are the original source and basic unit of variation. At the second level, individuals are the units that get naturally selected through predation or the struggle for resources. But individuals grow, reproduce and die; they do not evolve. At the third level, species evolve and are the unit of evolution. It is Wilson's contention that development occurs at the species level, through the mechanisms of evolution.

Mutations are random changes in genetic information that occur in either the ova or the sperm (or both) and are passed along to offspring through sexual reproduction. Most mutations are nonadaptive because they alter a highly complex organization that has already undergone a long period of prior selection for a particular geographical niche. Genetic mutations seldom produce monsters, since they are nearly always small, incremental differences. A second mechanism for introducing variation, *sexual recombination,* occurs when genetic information on the chromosomes is reshuffled through the union of ova and sperm. Natural selection accepts or rejects entire individuals, not specific parts or traits. Only in the very rare case where a cluster of mutations orchestrates an advantageous change in one individual will that person experience more favorable selection than the average individual. To understand how individuals get naturally selected, biologists draw a distinction between *phenotypes* and *genotypes. Phenotypes* are anatomical traits and features. They are physical characteristics that are either directly observable (e.g., body size, hair color, eye color, nose shape) or remain latent and observable only

Level 1: Genes mutate and sexually recombine.

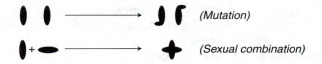

Level 2: Individuals are naturally selected.

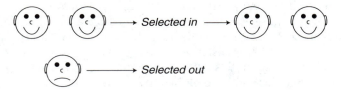

Level 3: Species evolve over many generations.

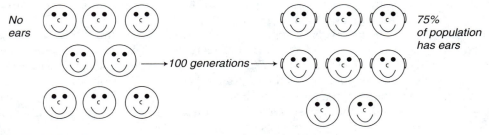

FIGURE 5.1 Evolution exerts influences at three levels.

under special conditions (e.g., maximum power, speed, visual acuity). *Genotypes* consist of the individual's genetic makeup; they comprise the patterns of DNA codes that produce phenotypes. Genotypes are the internal, theoretical causes of phenotypes, a relationship clearly reflective of Descartes's rationalism. No genotype has ever been directly observed nor has its actual connection to a phenotype. It is this link, however, that provides *evolution a means for indirectly selecting genotypes by way of natural selection acting on phenotypes.*

An individual is favorably selected when a new genotype, through mutation or recombination, creates a phenotype that is better adapted to a geographical niche. When a genotype is closely related to a phenotype, the selection is direct. However, since the entire individual is selected, any particular phenotype gets selected only as part of the total arrangement of phenotypes and the entire package of underlying genotypes.

Edward O. Wilson and the Roots of Sociobiology

For over a century after Darwin published *The Origin of Species,* evolutionary theory had remained essentially the same. The publication of Edward O. Wilson's *Sociobiology: The New Synthesis* in 1975, however, is considered a radical departure from traditional evolutionary theory (Caplan, 1978) because it claims that social behaviors, in addition to physical traits, have evolved as phenotypes. In short, sociobiology extends Butler's aphorism—*a chicken is merely the egg's way of making another egg*—all the way to human culture: society is the gene's way of ensuring more genes.

Born in Alabama just before the Great Depression, Edward Osborne Wilson had no siblings. After his family moved to Washington, DC, he frequented the National Zoo and the Smithsonian Institution to satisfy his growing curiosity about plants and animals. The adolescent Wilson spent considerable time collecting and studying insects, eventually deciding to become an entomologist (insect scientist). He attended the University of Alabama and then Harvard University, where he received his doctorate in entomology in 1955 and joined that prestigious faculty in 1958. Fifteen years later he was appointed curator of entomology at the Harvard Museum of Comparative Zoology. Wilson is currently professor emeritus but continues writing for popular audiences about some of the implications of sociobiology (see Wilson, 1998a, 1998b).

One of Wilson's important discoveries back in the 1950s was that ants communicate with one another by means of chemical substances called pheromones. Later, in 1971 he published *The Insect Societies,* a comprehensive treatment endorsed in the *Library Journal* as the finest synthesis of knowledge about the social insects published in the preceding half-century. His analysis of insect societies was extended in the *New Synthesis,* where he catapulted biological evolution all the way from the genes to culture itself.

The central thrust of Wilson's argument is as follows. Over thousands of generations cultures have gradually established certain customs because they express powerful genetic forces. All cultures have, for example, evolved such common practices as personal names, games, superstitions, hospitality rituals, and styles of decorative art. Rituals also exist that represent implicit beliefs—rites of passage, sex-role differentiation, funeral rites, and incest taboos. When customs become so important that we must ensure conformity among individuals, societies erect formal institutions (e.g., government bodies, police) that secure compliance with strong genetic predispositions. *Hypertrophy* is the term Wilson (1975, 1978b) used to describe such extreme phenomena.

Wilson believes that just as the elephant's tusk represents an extreme development of a preexisting tooth, so too do certain institutions reflect extreme, *hypertrophic* social adaptations. For example, schools, law enforcement agencies, judicial hierarchies, religious organizations, and military chains of command all function to ensure conformity in individual behavior. These are hypertrophic adaptations. According to Wilson (1978b), hypertrophy is the key to the emergence of civilization. Relatively simple adaptations of ancient hunter–gatherer tribes have evolved into the complex social institutions of modern societies.

Nowhere is the sweeping stretch of sociobiology more apparent than in Wilson's recent essay on the biological basis of morality. Religious institutions and the moral prescriptions they embody reflect hypertrophic adaptations of dominance hierarchies, with the supreme being at the apex of the dominance ladder. Such phenomena, argues Wilson (1998a), "can all eventually be explained as functions of brain circuitry and deep genetic history" (p. 68). This is the essence of sociobiology, Wilson's theory that social behaviors and rituals, as well as social institutions themselves, are the product of evolutionary forces.

Structural Components of Sociobiology

Assumptions

The assumptions of sociobiology derive from classical evolutionary theory. First, infants are born with a species-specific set of genetic instructions for programming and setting constraints on general modes of behavior. Second, genetic instructions determine the infant's inborn reflexes. This assumption does not require a genetic signal behind every reflex, merely that phenotypes include predispositions to react in certain species-specific ways indicated by the genotype. Third, random mutations of genetic information are assumed to be the source of individual variation. This element must be considered an assumption at this point since it is their *effects* rather than the genes or their mutations that are observable. Fourth, sociobiology assumes that the *potential* for rapid, specialized social learning is programmed by the genotype. Unlike Freud or Erikson, Wilson assumes no stages in development, in part because he directs his attention to change at the species level rather than to individuals.

Problems for Study

Sociobiology's central problem for study is to classify social behaviors into broad, genetic categories and to explain the evolution of behaviors in each category. Identifying genetic categories requires one to isolate qualities of social behavior that have survival value from those that do not. Accordingly, Wilson (1975) posits ten *qualities of sociality*. In addition, however, explaining how these qualities evolved requires further attention to three critical types of evidence to make an argument about evolution: *universality, continuity,* and *adaptation* (Gould, 1977).

Phenomena to Be Explained.   According to Wilson, the ten qualities of sociality, rather than being specific behaviors, are the broad, general conditions that underlie the very idea of what it means to be "social." These qualities are briefly described next.

Group size is a vital quality of a population. A true society requires some minimum number of individuals who interact with one another with sufficient frequency for social behaviors to occur.

Demographic distribution refers to the degree of individual variation according to age, sex, caste, size, marital status, etc. A heterogeneous population can occur only if individuals differ from one another along important, socially relevant dimensions. The larger the group size and the greater its demographic diversity, the more likely it is that adaptive social behaviors will be favorably selected. A very homogeneous group, for example, would exhibit little variation among members, so natural selection of some individuals over others would have little impact on the evolution of the culture in succeeding generations.

Cohesiveness refers to the spatial closeness of group members to one another. It is not the same as psychological closeness or kinship; rather, it is the degree to which individuals occupy the same geographical locale at the same time. A platoon of GIs or sorority sisters exhibit relatively high cohesiveness; farmers and hermits do not. On the whole, human cultures tend to be far less cohesive than a school of fish or an ant colony (Wilson, 1975).

Amount and pattern of connectedness refers to systematic interactions between individuals. Social groups that display hierarchies, chains of command, or castes reflect a high degree of patterned connectedness—the flow of communication is directed primarily toward and from certain individuals more than others. Patterns of connectedness are a reflection of the organization that underlies social behaviors between members (e.g., contrast patterns of connectedness between military ranks versus a frenzied crowd of Saturday bargain hunters at the mall). Wilson believes that advanced societies display a high degree of connected patterning though not necessarily a large amount of it.

Permeability is the degree to which a society is open or closed to communication with and immigration by members of other cultures. A society with high permeability is relatively open to such commerce. Permeability is optimized when the rate of inbreeding within a culture is balanced by the rate of outbreeding between it and other cultures. Even today, wars of genocide between different cultures (often religious) are a reflection of what Wilson calls *low* permeability.

Compartmentalization is the extent to which small groups of individuals operate as discrete, self-contained units within the culture. Families, classrooms, athletic teams, businesses, cities, counties, and states are examples of independently operating but partially overlapping social compartments. Most individuals belong to multiple compartments. This is important, because a culture is maintained through exchanges of members, products, and information between compartments.

Differentiation of roles refers to the kinds of specialized functions individuals perform within a social framework. Societies that are well organized tend to display highly specialized roles. For example, most societies practice some degree of *sex polyethism* (dividing labor according to sex) as well as *age polytheism* (dividing labor by age). But roles may also be differentiated according to other attributes, such as job title, social status, kin relationships, education, or wealth.

Integration of behavior is the tendency of cultures to expect certain roles to fulfill multiple social functions. Parents, for example, may function as caregivers for their children, home managers, employees of some business firm, volunteers in local civic or religious groups, political activists, and innumerable other roles.

Information flow refers to the extent to which members communicate with one another. Wilson views communication flow in terms of the total number of signals, the amount of information per signal, and the rate of signal transmission. Signals can function, for example, to warn of danger, differentiate roles, pass greetings, and increase or decrease permeability. Ants communicate with chemicals called pheromones, but such signals are rigid and convey highly specific information. The information contained in human signals is flexible in both form and content— for example, music, nonverbal gestures, graffiti, and language.

Fraction of time devoted to social behavior is an index of the common elements in cohesiveness, compartmentalization, role specialization, and rate of information flow (Wilson, 1975). Although few members of a culture spend all their time engaging in social behaviors, the more time spent engaging in nonsocial behavior, the less time there is for social interaction. Some cultures are highly socialized because many activities support socializing. In other cultures opportunities for socializing may revolve around a more limited number of activities such as food gathering, cooking, defending, eating, storytelling, and child rearing.

The ten qualities of sociality are not specific behaviors. Rather, they are general attributes that reflect different dimensions of social behaviors. A single behavior typically reflects multiple qualities of sociality. For example, during the course of a high school volleyball game, a high school girl probably engages in most, if not all, of the ten qualities. Fewer qualities would be found when she phones to talk with her best friend after the game.

Kinds of Evidence.   It is one thing to identify qualities of social behavior. It is quite another to claim that they are subject to evolution. Any argument that these qualities have actually evolved over time requires three types of evidence: **universality, continuity,** and **adaptation**.

Universality requires that we identify social behaviors common to all social species. Wilson's *New Synthesis* contains his own classification of social behaviors into the ten qualities of sociality just described. He contends that these qualities, found in both human and primate cultures, are a *necessary but not sufficient condition* for proposing a common genetic evolution for these species.

Continuity requires demonstrating that the factors that influence human social evolution are the same factors that operate on primate social behavior and that influenced early *Homo sapiens'* cultural practices. For example, Hamilton's (1964) notion of *kin selection* holds that by benefiting close relatives, altruistic behaviors in primates actually help preserve the altruist's shared genes with those relatives even if the altruist does not itself produce any offspring. Consequently, an argument for continuity in kin selection can be made by showing that altruistic acts in human societies (as with primates) occur more often between relatives than nonrelatives.

Evidence of *adaptation* requires that we distinguish between adaptive and nonadaptive behaviors in order to show the advantage accorded some individuals through natural selection. Nonadaptive social practices should eventually disappear; adaptive ones should eventually propagate throughout the culture. The sociobiologist's chore is to show how particular qualities provide a more culturally advantageous fit within an environmental niche, thereby affording that individual a greater adaptive advantage in comparison to others.

Methods of Investigation.   Sociobiologists use a variety of research methods. The primary requirement here, due to the theory's phylogenetic approach, is that data collected during one generation be comparable to available data about other generations. Observational methods are often used to gather information about animal, insect, and human social behaviors in different ecological niches. Self-reports and tests may be used to examine how individuals behave in certain situations. Experiments are seldom done with humans because of ethical problems and the inordinately long time spans necessary to examine evolutionary change, so they are carried out most often with social insects and rapidly reproducing animals. In addition, considerable evidence for the theory is borrowed from other disciplines such as biology, economics, psychology, and sociology.

Internal Principles

Sociobiology explains human cultural evolution by introducing two internal principles: **genetic fitness** and **ultimate causes**. Table 5.1 summarizes the important elements of Wilson's theory.

Genetic Fitness.   The most radical part of Wilson's theory is his extension of the traditional definition of phenotype (anatomical traits) to include qualities of social behavior. Wilson believes that individuals initially displaying an adaptive social phenotype tend to produce more offspring than individuals not displaying the phenotype. This reproductive advantage between individuals is called *genetic fitness*. By producing more viable offspring than others, those possessing an adaptive phenotype pass it on to an ever-increasing segment of succeeding generations. In this way, an increase in the adaptive advantage of a phenotype or a combination of phenotypes increases an individual's genetic fitness over others. Finally, individuals need not themselves produce offspring, so long as their close relatives (those sharing common genes) do. This means that an individual can display genetic fitness simply by having siblings who are reproductively successful.

Ultimate Causes.   The *ultimate causes* of social behavior are considered by Wilson to be the "prime movers" of evolution. These causes, **phylogenetic inertia** and **ecological pressure,** operate over very long periods of time on entire cultures, and they ultimately render some phenotypes adaptive and others nonadaptive.

Phylogenetic Inertia.   *Phylogenetic inertia* embodies all the inherited properties of a culture that determine its *resistance to change*. This idea is not the same as popular notions of "genetic endowment" or "genetic heritage," which imply a fixed collection of innate capacities. As Figure 5.2 on page 116 shows, high inertia means that

TABLE 5.1   **Causes and Qualities of Sociality**

Bridge Principles	Internal Principles		Social Quality (to be explained)
Proximate Causes	**Genetic Fitness Ultimate Causes**		
	Phylogenetic Inertia	*Ecological Pressure*	
Demographic variables (reproduction rates, life span, death rates, optimal population size, actual population size)	Genetic variability Antisocial factors Complexity of social behavior	Changing food sources Predation Climatic changes	Group size Demographic distribution Connectedness
		Reinforcing and counteracting selection	Cohesiveness Permeability
Rates of gene flow (degree of inbreeding, outbreeding)		Catastrophes	Compartmentalization
		Intrusions by other populations	Role differentiation
Coefficients of relationship (degree of same genes shared by individuals)		Natural terrain	Integration of behavior Information flow Fraction of time devoted to social behavior

a species is stable and experiences little change over time; low inertia means relatively rapid evolutionary change. There are many sources that contribute to phylogenetic inertia, though three stand out: *genetic variability, antisocial factors,* and *complexity of social behavior.*

Genetic variability reflects the extent to which individuals possess different genes. This variability produces members of a population who display different social behaviors, some of which are more favorably selected through reproductive success than others. Genotypes linked to reproductively successful phenotypes are passed on to increasing numbers of individuals in succeeding generations. Genetic variability directly affects phylogenetic inertia. When evolution works on gene pools with low variability (few differences between individuals), a given number of random mutations affects a larger ratio of genotypes than the same number of

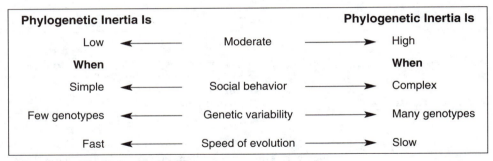

FIGURE 5.2   Phylogenetic inertia.

mutations occurring in a gene pool with high variability. Consequently, low variability is associated with low inertia and rapid evolutionary change.

Antisocial factors, such as disease and geographic isolation, affect the social balance of a population by detracting from the amount of time engaged in social interaction. The result is a decrease in social interaction and in the genetic fitness of the society as a whole. Conversely, prosocial forces move a population toward more social activity, which increases its overall fitness as a society.

Complexity of social behavior refers to the amount of interconnectedness between social behaviors that are suited for different purposes. The more complex a behavior, the more interconnected it is with other behaviors and the higher its resistance to evolutionary change (phylogenetic inertia). In this manner, behaviors that exist in isolation from other behaviors can be easily selected, either favorably or unfavorably. However, behaviors that are highly integrated with others tend to be displayed as an interwoven package, and selection of an integrated behavior is more difficult since it cannot be easily isolated for selection.

Ecological Pressure.   What Darwin called natural selection Wilson more broadly termed *ecological pressure.* It is the set of all environmental forces that enhance or detract from an individual's reproductive success.

Of the main types of ecological pressure discussed by Wilson, three are outlined here. *Changes in food supplies* is an example of an environmental fluctuation that makes previously efficient social behaviors and traits either more or less adaptive in the new context. During times of famine, for example, behaviors that lead some individuals to exploit new food sources will tend to be selected. Moreover, *predation* exerts a very effective selection pressure against some forms of social behavior related to combating predators, signaling their presence, or occupying their hunting territory. Individuals especially adept at utilizing shelter, weapons, or escape strategies would tend to improve their reproductive success in relation to others less well equipped. *Competition* between individual members of a population also acts as a natural selector when it bestows reproductive advantage upon certain members. In polygamous societies, one male weds several females. In that social context, competition for women determines which males will and will not produce offspring. Competition may also occur within cultures for other resources

Sandlot Seminar 5.1

Life and Death in Different Ecological Niches

A well-known example of phenotypic selection through ecological pressure has been described by Barash (1977). Up to 40 percent of some West African populations suffer from a genetic disease called sickle-cell anemia. Because the disease is fatal, one might expect that those who carry its genes would have failed to reproduce, thereby eliminating the disease over time and leaving only healthy individuals to reproduce. Ironically, however, sickle-cell carriers are not susceptible to malaria, another disease that kills many children long before they can reproduce. Instead, sickle-cell children tend to mature and produce offspring who also carry the fatal gene with its malarial immunity. Over many generations the gene for sickle-cell anemia has been retained among West Africans because it has a reproductive advantage for its carriers.

1. Malaria does not exist in the United States. Given this different ecological pressure, is there an adaptive advantage for sickle-cell anemia among U. S. descendants of West Africans?

2. Given your response to the first question, would you expect sickle-cell anemia to exist at the same level among U.S. descendants as it does among West Africans?

such as jobs, money, and status, all of which are essential contributors to genetic fitness.

One example of ecological pressure is illustrated in Sandlot Seminar 5.1. Since malaria is not found in North America, there is no adaptive advantage for sickle-cell anemia. Consequently, ecological pressure selects against carriers of the disease. Among U.S. blacks of West African descent, a much smaller ratio suffer from the disease because, according to sociobiology, the selective advantage of the disease in a malaria-free environment has been eliminated. In addition, the nutritional advantage of North American blacks over West Africans also represents a difference in ecological pressure.

Bridge Principles

Where ultimate causes work their effect over many generations, Wilson uses the term *proximate causes* to refer to the immediate influences on individuals within their own lifetime. Three important proximate causes include: *demographic variables, rates of gene flow,* and *coefficients of relationship.*

Demographic variables directly affect cultures and include such factors as fertility and reproduction rates, individual life spans, death rates, and population size. Cultures also affect individuals by establishing patterns that are more or less beneficial to bearing and raising offspring to reproductive viability. Genotypes underlying adaptive mating rituals and child rearing practices, for example, should be selected for reproductive success, whereas genes of individuals who fail to reproduce or to utilize natural resources efficiently would gradually be selected out of a population.

Rate of gene flow refers to the degree of inbreeding and outbreeding of individuals in a culture. Inbreeding occurs when members of a culture mate with one another; outbreeding occurs when individuals from different cultures mate. The rate of gene flow is a direct reflection of the amount of variation introduced into a population (recall that natural selection operates only when enough variation among individuals exists to produce differential adaptive advantage for some phenotypes but not others). Over many generations, rates of gene flow may either increase or decrease genetic fitness of a culture. Taking a small town as a social unit, if the rate of gene flow is low, the town practices a high degree of inbreeding, which would ultimately reduce the genetic fitness of its successive generations.

Coefficient of relationship is a measure of kinship. The coefficient of relationship can have a profound evolutionary effect on a society. For example, if all members share identical genes, there is no variation, so natural selection cannot work. At the other extreme, if no members share genes, there are no common ancestors, so there would be no altruism or phenotypic continuity. In actuality, social groups invariably exhibit some degree of kinship.

Change Mechanisms

Wilson (1975) uses two change mechanisms to account for evolution: (1) genetic mutations and sexual recombinations and (2) reproductive success through natural selection. Evolution requires that each phenotype display a range of variation within a population so that natural selection has the raw materials upon which it can operate. Genetic mutations and sexual recombinations are the origins of this diversity.

While the creation of genetic variation is highly random, natural selection is not; it results in the very complex, nonrandom systems we call individuals. But there are two kinds of selection. First, *counteracting selection* occurs when ecological pressures on two or more levels of organization (e.g., individual, family, relatives, tribe, population) operate in favor of genes at one level but against genes at another level. For example, children who steal food from the family storehouse during times of famine may enhance their own survival at the expense of other family members. If the tendency to steal is genetically encoded, then stealing may have a later payoff only if it results in greater reproductive success than that experienced by nonstealing family members. Altruism, discussed later, also represents counteracting selection in that no adaptive advantage accrues to the altruist whose actions benefit another.

A second type of selection is called *reinforcing selection*. It occurs when ecological pressures on two or more levels of organization favor genes at all levels, resulting in an acceleration of gene spread throughout the entire population. For example, reinforcing selection might occur when individuals are genetically predisposed to cooperate on a group project. If their cooperation results in greater status for both the individuals and the group as a whole, then all group members would share a reproductive advantage over groups with uncooperative individuals.

Status markers are present in virtually all cultures and subcultures. Sandlot Seminar 5.2 asks you to think about status markers in a typical high school culture.

Sandlot Seminar 5.2

Status Markers

Students in a typical high school are well aware of the various types of status signals that are displayed. For most markers (but not all), a hierarchy of status levels may exist. These displays mark important groups and boundaries. Rarely will a student marked "high" in status enter into any group marked "low" in status, except perhaps to reinforce the difference in their status. Friendships are most often established and maintained among students of similar status. In high school, two general rules seem to apply to status. First, in order to change status groups, a student must earn or display a status signal of another group. Second, almost all students would prefer to move up rather than down the various status hierarchies.

Below are some *types* of status markers students display in high school.

Hair style   Intelligence
Clothing   Athletics
Family income   Cars
Jewelry   Ingroups and outgroups

1. What other types of status markers exist in high school?

2. Can you classify the examples as favoring *reinforcing* or *counteracting selection*?

3. Are tattoos and body piercings status markers? How do they work?

4. Which groups marked for status exhibit high permeability? Low permeability?

5. Why is it that individuals from one status group seldom date individuals from another status group? What happens with friends and family if they do? Why?

6. Do high school teachers exhibit a status hierarchy? How can you tell? What are its signals?

7. Might "friendships" be a status marker? Why or why not?

8. How would you expect status markers to differ between small and large high schools? Why?

The throne of England is subject to a tradition that has kept some royalty from ascending to the rank of king. For example, if a king or prince marries a "commoner," then he forfeits any right to the throne. This is one reason Princess Diana's "royal" ancestry had to be documented and confirmed prior to her engagement and wedding to Prince Charles.

1. How does the English "throne" tradition reflect a status hierarchy?
2. What is the function of such a tradition, according to sociobiology?

In summary, sociobiology posits two basic change mechanisms that oppose each other. First, random mutations and genetic recombinations occur between individuals and their offspring which together produce a never-ending supply of genetic variation. The growth and development of any individual (and hence all individuals) unfolds according to the biological information encoded in their genes. This is an important aspect of sociobiology that marks it as a clear example of endogenous theories. Second, once genetic variation has been supplied, evolution operates on the species through the natural selection of individuals who experience differential reproductive success.

Explaining Human Development: The Research

Five considerations should be kept in mind when examining the research support for sociobiology. First, the theory is directed at explaining phylogenesis rather than ontogenesis. Second, sociobiology attempts to explain general qualities of social behavior rather than any particular behavioral event. A sociobiologist, for example, would be more interested in a general tendency of cultures to establish status hierarchies than with the fact that in some cultures ownership of a Mercedez-Benz accords one more status than does a Ford. Third, Wilson's *New Synthesis* is one of the newest, most comprehensive theories of development of the past quarter-century. Consequently, it has had less time to generate significant research than other theories of development. Fourth, because evidence of universality, continuity, and adaptation are essential to sociobiology, the most relevant research is that which examines social behaviors common to both humans and primates. Fifth, sociobiologists borrow extensively from research in biology, psychology, sociology, and anthropology. While the studies reported here draw from those disciplines, their results are interpreted from the sociobiologist's point of view.

Aggression and Dominance Hierarchies

Sociobiology contends that status signals are highly adaptive for both dominant and subordinate individuals regardless of what forms they take in different cultures (Barash, 1977). Dominants are better off because they gain important resources without having to compete for them each time access is desired, and subordinates, who lose contests most of the time anyway, are better off avoiding the futile costs of unsuccessful challenges to dominant individuals. Accordingly, evolution is assumed to favor societies, both human and animal, that utilize status signals that convey both aggression and dominance.

Lorenz (1963) describes displays of aggression that vary widely in form, from actual fighting at one extreme to strutting or verbal assault at the other as a show of strength. At one extreme of social aggression we have *contest competition* (Barash, 1977), which occurs when individuals compete for freely available resources by displaying status in socially recognized ways (e.g., athletics, wealth, dress style, domicile furnishings, one-upmanship). But even contest competition can have lethal results. Daly and Wilson (1985a) have reported that of 690 nonaccidental homicides in a large urban city, some form of status competition was the underlying motive.

At the other extreme is *scramble competition*. It occurs when individuals compete for vital but limited resources, and it involves attempts to use as much of a critical resource as possible with almost complete disregard for the tacit elements of social gamesmanship. Compared to contest competition, scramble competition occurs relatively infrequently in human cultures. Examples include sibling battles, cheating, gang fights, riots, and wars. But the difference between content and scramble competition may not always be clear-cut, as shown in Sandlot Seminar 5.3.

Kinship Systems and Nomenclature

According to sociobiology, cooperation among individuals should be displayed in direct proportion to their coefficients of relationship. By cooperating with one another, relatives increase the collective fitness of related kin, thereby promoting *kin selection* when any relative behaves so as to enhance the reproductive success of the whole group.

Sandlot Seminar 5.3

Temper Tantrums

Stephanie Hartigen is a stay-at-home mother with two young children, Aimee (age 2½ years) and Tommy (age 4 years). She has become distraught over the past several weeks as Aimee has begun to exhibit some of her older brother's bad habits. This morning she has just returned from the supermarket where both children got into full-blown temper tantrums while waiting at the checkout counter. First, it was Tommy who wanted a brightly packaged lollipop. When Stephanie said "No," he reached out and grabbed one anyway. Of course Stephanie took it away and put it back. But then Tommy flew into a rage, yelling and screaming. When he started kicking the shopping cart, Stephanie gave in and selected a bright yellow lollipop, which she gave to Tommy. Tommy's temper tantrum stopped immediately, but his red eyes still showed a few tears.

Meanwhile, Aimee had been watching the whole episode. From her seat in the shopping cart, she reached and grabbed a huge candy bar. But Stephanie grabbed the candy bar and quickly replaced it with a red lollipop for Aimee. Aimee, of course, didn't want the lollipop and threw it to the floor. Seeing the hopelessness of her position, and enduring the stares of others at the checkout counter, Stephanie caved in and retrieved the candy bar Aimee had wanted.

Back home, with the groceries put away, Stephanie reflected on the rise of temper tantrums whenever she is out in public with her children. See if you can help her understand what is going on by using concepts from sociobiology.

1. Are mothers' and children's self-interests always the same?
2. From the mother's perspective, would a child's tempter tantrum be understood as a form of contest or scramble competition? Why?
3. For a toddler who is not yet fully socialized, do you think a temper tantrum is more like contest or scramble competition? Why?
4. What ecological pressures might select for genotypes that motivate childhood but not adult temper tantrums?

Virtually all cultures recognize kinship relationships by endowing them with special titles—aunt, mother, cousin, brother-in-law. This kinship nomenclature has clear adaptive advantages in bonding together alliances between tribes and provides a means for immigration of tribal members. It also supports the bartering system by which some males achieve dominance and leadership over others. Finally, it helps groups through hard times because it tells individuals who to call on for altruistic assistance (close relatives). In short, kinship customs reflect a genetic pattern of connectedness between families, increase cohesiveness between individuals, frame settings and occasions that promote integration of behavior, and provide opportunities for increasing the amount of time devoted to social behavior.

Youngsters who are adopted or who are raised by unrelated individuals provide an interesting test of sociobiological theory. For example, stepparents in general are far more likely than biological parents to abuse children (Daly & Wilson, 1994; Lenington, 1981; Lightcap, Kurland, & Burgess, 1982), and biological mothers are less likely than stepmothers to abuse children (Lenington, 1981; Lightcap et al., 1982). Preschoolers living with a stepparent are forty times more likely to become child abuse victims than like-aged children living with both natural parents (Daly & Wilson, 1985b). Furthermore, stepfather abuse in Canada and Great Britain is also more likely to be lethal than is genetic father abuse (Daly & Wilson, 1994).

Because natural selection favors those who are socially and physically fit, it should not be surprising that the risk of child abuse is inversely related to family income (Daly & Wilson, 1981; Lenington, 1981), and children with health problems or physical abnormalities are more likely than normal children to experience abuse (Daly & Wilson, 1981; Lenington, 1981; Lightcap et al., 1982). Adoption, an altruistic act, is also more likely among related than unrelated individuals, and biological children tend to be recipients of more frequent and more favorable parental interactions than stepchildren throughout the world (Ainsworth, 1967; Silk, 1980). Interestingly, nonindustrial cultures tend to restrict adoptions to closely related kin (Freedman, 1979). Moreover, adopted children, even when well cared for, often experience a powerful urge to locate their biological parents (Triseliotis, 1973).

Sociobiology also contends that genetically related individuals should exhibit greater degrees of cohesiveness and proximity than unrelated individuals, a pattern that would be expected to increase sociality while decreasing antisocial behavior. A number of direct and indirect tests of such a hypothesis have been undertaken in several diverse cultures. For example, Chagnon (1979, 1981, 1982) studied Yanamamo Indians on the border of Brazil and Venezuela both before and after their villages broke up into smaller villages. He found that villages with higher coefficients of relatedness between individuals tended to grow larger before splitting into smaller villages than those with smaller coefficients. In other words, after splitting of the original village, individuals in each of two smaller villages tended to remain with close relatives of their own and descending generations. Concerning reproductive success, Chagnon also reported that the more resources a male had from kin in his own generation and his ascending generations, the greater his success in finding a mate.

Other studies show that social patterns are different for genetically related and unrelated individuals. For example, Essock-Vitale and McGuire (1980) found that amount and frequency of altruistic acts was higher and that such help was withdrawn more slowly among relatives than nonrelatives. In a similar study, Barkow (1982) reported that among the Migili in Nigeria, resource *donations* were more likely among relatives, whereas resource *exchanges* were more likely among unrelated individuals. Finally, social interactions among Ye'kwana Indians varies in direct proportion to their coefficients of relatedness (Hames, 1979).

Altruism

Sociobiologists define altruism solely in terms of its consequences—being helpful or benevolent toward others; no assumptions are made about the altruist's motives. In more technical terms, altruism is any act that decreases the altruist's genetic fitness while increasing the genetic fitness of the recipient. Sociobiologists are interested in altruism because it is an apparently self-destructive activity, one that presumably cannot be to the reproductive advantage of the altruist. However, if two individuals share the same genes by common descent, and if an altruistic action of one increases their shared genes in succeeding generations, then the tendency toward altruism should gradually be spread through the population due to its adaptive advantage (Wilson, 1975).

Trivers (1971) has explained the evolution of altruism in the following manner. The chances of evolution selecting for altruistic genes would be greatest when (1) there are many potential altruistic situations, (2) altruists interact repeatedly with the same individuals, and (3) pairs of potential altruists can render approximately equal benefits to one another with similar costs. Under these circumstances, reciprocity in altruistic acts would be likely to evolve among intelligent, cohesive species whose members spend a relatively large proportion of time engaging in social activities. Humans have relatively long life spans (much of which is spent in neighborhoods where individuals repeatedly interact with one another) and good, long-term memory capacity. As a result, there is a reasonable expectation that a recipient of an altruistic act will later remember to reciprocate, especially if the two individuals interact on a regular basis. Reciprocal altruism occurs when the recipient later bestows some favor back on the original altruist. The fact that city dwellers are consistently less helpful to strangers in distress than are their rural counterparts (Piliavin, Rodin, & Piliavin, 1969) may be due to the difference in how often the same individuals come into contact with one another as well as the difference in coefficients of relationship normally found in city versus rural residents.

Reciprocal altruism has been empirically studied in the United States and other cultures. For example, in a New York City apartment complex, Thompson (1980) found that reciprocity between individuals mirrored the probability of situation reversal. The more likely it was that others could experience a need for assistance, the more likely they were to help strangers. Moreover, Thompson found, as predicted by Trivers, that reciprocal altruism increased as benefits to the recipient increased, but it declined as cost to the donor increased.

The biological basis of reciprocal altruism has, argues Wilson (1975), led to the evolution of economic mediums of exchange. Exchange mediums make barter and trade possible, and coupled with human memory and written records, allow reciprocal interchanges to be stretched out over time and generations. Currency, for example, represents a culture's hypertrophic adaptation, a simple but effective quantification of reciprocal altruism (Wilson, 1975).

Differential Selection

Males typically suffer a greater mortality rate at an earlier age and for a longer period of time than females. Among humans, 130 males are conceived for every 100 females, but through spontaneous abortions, only 104 males are born for every 100 females. Males experience a higher mortality rate than females, so only by the peak of reproduction is parity reached. Thereafter and with increasing age, females increasingly outnumber males (Freedman, 1979). The point is that males are both born and obliterated at a greater rate than females because selection operates differentially on each sex. Nature treats males as relatively expendable since only a few are biologically necessary for ensuring cultural continuity.

Male and female reproductive success is subject to different ecological pressures. It is an adaptive advantage for males to marry younger females who have more childbearing years left than older females. Similarly, it is advantageous for younger females to marry older males who typically have more resources for child rearing than younger males. This difference in marital ages of spouses is such a strong tendency, it has been given a special name: *hypergamy*.

Although age pairings may vary across individuals, one would expect within a population more younger female–older male marriages than any other age-related pattern. This prediction seems to hold up. Lockard and Adams (1981) sampled 4,048 couples in two Seattle shopping malls. The researchers observed that males were much more likely to be coupled with younger-aged females than with same-aged or older-aged females. Moreover, more children were observed accompanying this selection strategy than with couples exhibiting other age-paired strategies. At the same time, examination of Seattle area divorce records revealed that divorce rates among women tended to rise as they approached menopause. Similar findings have been reported by Paterson and Pettijohn (1982), who found that of the 250 marriage licenses issued in a small Ohio county between 1928 and 1978, most went to males who were marrying younger females.

Considerable evidence suggests that differences in male and female courtship patterns and sexual preferences reflect essential contrasts between their genetically evolved reproductive strategies (Kachigan, 1990). Jewelry, for example, displays important information about status, but the information needs are different for males and females. Along this line, Low (1979) has found that the ornamentation is prevalent in 138 societies, with differences in form associated with sex differences. Specifically, women tend to display jewelry that conveys their marital status, while males tend to exhibit their wealth, power, or sexual potency.

Glenn Wilson's (1997) study of gender differences in sexual fantasies accords well with sociobiology. He found that males are more inclined to fantasize sex with multiple, anonymous partners, which would maximize their reproductive success, since many females could be impregnated in a relatively short period of time. In contrast, females were more likely to fantasize sex with "close-bonded" or famous partners. For females, whose gestation period limits their number of offspring, reproductive success is maximized through the male's resource accumulation and continuing proximity.

As cultures have evolved, different selection advantages are directly related to marriage patterns. For example, polygamy is advantageous for males and older wives, but it disadvantages younger wives. Among the Cameroun (Clignet & Sween, 1974) and the Bedouin (Musham, 1956), monogamous wives tend to average more children than their polygamous counterparts. Just the reverse is true for men in Cameroun (Clignet & Sween, 1974) and Sierra Leone (Dorjahn, 1958), who have greater reproductive success in polygamous than monogamous marriages. Among Sierra Leone polygamous women, senior wives have more children, and junior wives have fewer children than women of the same age in monogamous marriages (Isaac & Feinberg, 1982).

Ecological pressure may also have evolved a number of cultural adaptations found in human infants. For example, newborns react positively to sweet tastes and negatively to salty or bitter tastes (Nowlis & Kessen, 1976); turn away from strong odors (Rieser, Yonas & Wikner, 1976); turn toward loud voices and sounds (Butterworth & Castillo, 1976; Wertheimer, 1961); and even flinch at onrushing objects (Bower, 1972). All these reactions prime newborns for survival and rapid learning about the physical and social qualities of the world that surrounds them. With such reflexes in mind, sociobiologists marshal a *prima facie* case for the genetic control of infant behavior and learning strategies.

Striking differences in newborn capabilities are also believed to be the result of evolution acting on specific cultural phenotypes. Cultural differences found in newborn postures, muscle tone, and emotional temperaments suggest that these phenotypes have undergone cultural evolution (Freedman, 1979). For example, the Navajo and Hopi Indians have historically confined their infants to cradleboards, and unlike other American infants, their babies are capable of holding their heads erect from birth. This specialized infant adaptation serves both mother and infant well (an example of reinforcing selection) since the cradleboard requires erect head posture from the outset. Finally, Freedman (1979) has also reported that aboriginal infants, but not Caucasian or Japanese, display the erect head posture and that temperamental differences exist between Caucasian and Asian infants.

Language

Human speech is believed to represent a dramatic leap in the evolution of communication flow (Wilson, 1975). The human ability to produce differentiated vocal signals accompanies the ability to position signals in relation to one another. This signal pattern is called *grammar;* it is the system of rules that specifies word arrangements that constitute meaningful communication. A number of psycholinguists (e.g., Chomsky, 1957, 1975b; Lenneberg, 1967; McNeill, 1970) have argued that the unfolding of language, particularly elements of grammar and syntax, is innately determined, and although Wilson relies extensively on psycholinguistic evidence to support his theory, psycholinguists do not necessarily endorse sociobiology.

Five types of evidence lend support to Wilson's contention that language is a genetically determined capacity. First, even deaf infants go through the same initial stages of babbling found in normal hearing infants, as if the spontaneous tendency to produce speech was initially dependent on innate instructions rather than imitation of adult speech (Lenneberg, 1967). Second, infants throughout the world develop through the same sequence of stages in sound production, regardless of specific grammatical differences in language content (Lenneberg, 1967). Third, during the first stages, infants from all cultures babble in the same sounds regardless of the unique sounds of their own native tongue (Lenneberg, 1967). Fourth, children acquire the basic grammatical rules of their native language even without specific instruction (Chomsky, 1959). Fifth, children acquire the complete rules of grammar even though, under normal conditions, they have been exposed to only a deficient and limited corpus of linguistic data (Chomsky, 1975b).

It is important to note, however, that while linguists may agree that language acquisition and grammar are under genetic control, they may not explicitly accept sociobiological theory. After all, they are concerned with the ontogenesis of linguistic performance. Wilson is concerned with the phylogenesis of linguistics.

The kinds of social behavior patterns just described represent only a fragment of those actually described by Wilson and other sociobiologists. While a prodigious amount of work on social animals and insects exists in the literature, its relevance is beyond the scope of this text. Because sociobiology is so comprehensive in its explanation of many forms of human, animal, and insect social patterns, new university courses have begun to crop up over the past decade. Psychology courses such as "The Biological Bases of Behavior" and anthropology courses such as "Genes and Culture" are no longer unusual on American campuses.

Contributions and Criticisms of Sociobiology

Seldom has a new scientific field produced such a sharp dichotomy between enthusiasm and dread as that which accompanied sociobiology (Barlow, 1980; Wilson, 1978a). In fact, the initial treatment accorded Wilson is reminiscent of the public ostracism experienced by Darwin and Freud. Still, several contributions will, in our estimation, have an enduring impact on developmental psychology.

Contributions

The Debate.   Two sociobiology debates followed Wilson's *New Synthesis.* The first was sparked by a wave of charges about potential abuse, prejudice, politics, and sex biases perceived to be inherent in the theory (Alper et al., 1978). The essential argument of those attacks maintained that the theory belittled humans by ignoring their free will and that right-wing political and social movements would find ideological support for their positions (Caplan, 1978).

The awarding of the Pulitzer prize in nonfiction to Wilson for *On Human Nature* (1978) may have been something of a vindication for him. The prize underscored the importance of a critical examination of the relation between biology and culture in projecting the future of humanity. In this context, the initial charges against sociobiology seem to have been overblown and exaggerated by many accounts.

The second debate has focused more directly on the theory's claims by challenging its basic principles and evidence. This sociobiology debate (Caplan, 1978) has resulted in (1) improved clarity about what the theory is and is not claiming about human social behavior, (2) increased emphasis on the need for empirically testing the theory's assertions, and (3) better understanding about what does and does not constitute sufficient evidence for a theoretical claim. In recent years, for example, speculative essays seem to have given way to more empirical tests of sociobiology. Thus, the debate itself has been an important contribution to the scientific understanding of connections between culture and evolution.

Unity. A second contribution is the theory's attention to certain principles that tend to unify the continuity between humans and their ancestors. It casts all humans as one basic kind—*Homo sapiens.* Whatever differences may be superficially apparent in cultural, geographical, or ethnic variations, they are insignificant in comparison to the much more important and pervasive ways in which members of the species are alike.

But there is another kind of continuity in sociobiology. It recognizes that modern *Homo sapiens* had ancestors; we are immutably linked with the animal kingdom. In this vein, the theory posits a unifying continuity between humans, primates, and our common ancestors. This phylogenetic continuity helps us understand how the evolution of culture parallels the evolution of the species.

Finally, the theory proposes a unifying theme to the biological and behavioral sciences by synthesizing widely diverse phenomena and their respective disciplines under the single, encompassing umbrella of sociobiology. In spanning the range from ant colonies, at one extreme, to human culture at the other, no other theory rivals sociobiology in explaining such a broad scope of phenomena. This is important. As will be discussed in Chapter 13, psychology is unique in the multiple paradigms that inundate the field. If a truly unifying paradigm is possible, sociobiology is currently the best contender on the horizon.

A New Paradigm Case. Over the past decade, the growth of specialized journals and the increased research attention given sociobiology from different academic disciplines have propelled this theory into the forefront of science. Today, many different lines of study are generating new evidence of connections between genes and human behavior. Those connections can only be enhanced by the work of the Human Genome Project, an exhaustive, federally funded effort to catalog the entire inventory of human genes. As new generations of PhDs enter U.S. universities, we would not be surprised to see Wilson's sociobiology come to replace Freud's psychoanalysis as the preferred paradigm case for the endogenous paradigm.

Criticisms

Two broad categories of criticisms have been mounted against the theory. The first addresses conceptual and philosophical problems; the second concerns the theory's empirical evidence.

Conceptual Problems

Determinism.   Caplan (1978) notes that many scientists have difficulty accepting the endogenous determinism inherent in sociobiology. This extreme form of determinism, while reminiscent of Freud, is perhaps unusual at a time when most scientists tend to think that social behavior is a function of both biology and experience.

Genotype–Phenotype Distinction.   The theoretical link between genes and their phenotypic traits is crucial to the theory. But according to Gould (1980), no matter how adequate a job is done in identifying which behaviors are actually adaptive and which are not, no one can tell if they are genetically programmed. There is nothing given in *behavior* that necessarily ties it in with genetic information in the same way as eye color can be tied to genes; behaviors and physical traits are categorically different. The distinction is vital, since the linkage between social behavior and genes is entirely theoretical rather than empirical. To date the theory has not demonstrated convincingly this invisible linkage when it asserts genetic control over behavior. Perhaps the completion of the Human Genome Project will provide new inroads for testing this important link.

Adaptation.   Sociobiology provides no clear conceptual basis for distinguishing between behaviors that are adaptive and those that are not. The distinction always relies on *post hoc* (after the fact) explanation of the following form: If a behavior leads to reproductive success, it is adaptive; if not, it is nonadaptive. Such an explanation is really no explanation at all, since a behavior that produces differentially more viable offspring is presumed to be adaptive, while any behavior that is adaptive by definition produces more offspring. Such circular reasoning does little to advance our understanding of the concept of adaptation. Since the theory defines adaptation solely in terms of its consequences rather than any constitutive qualities, it is difficult to see how one could establish the predictive validity for the concept of adaptation.

Empirical Problems

Universality. According to Leacock (1980) and Livingstone (1980) sociobiology makes claims about universal sex-role patterns that may not be universal at all. For example, a number of West African societies have dual political systems for men and women, and on the women's side, their interests are represented at all levels (Onkjo, 1976). Women of the Mbuti of Zaire are not housebound; they participate with men in hunting wild animals (Leacock, 1980). In still other cases the biological double standard simply doesn't hold up. For example, in over half of the ninety-three cultures examined by Whyte (1978), no evidence was found for a double standard in sexual restrictions. Moreover, in 54 percent of these cultures, women were allowed to or commonly engaged in extramarital affairs. Such data indicates that the supposed universal practice of male–female stereotyping is not quite so universal after all.

The "universality" of an incest taboo may also be a bit of a myth. Incest occurs more frequently than is generally thought (Sarles, 1975) and is apparently increasing in modern societies (Livingstone, 1980). Some societies include relatively high levels of inbreeding and even prescribe some degree of it. For example, some viable populations in South India have a high frequency of uncle–niece marriage (Sanghvi, 1966) with apparently minimum effects (Rao & Inharaj, 1977).

Continuity. It is unclear how the problem of evolutionary continuity from ancestral origins to current social practices can be adequately addressed. Gould (1980), for example, refers to the practice among sociobiologists of "storytelling," wherein possible events, links, and situations that "might have been" are related to the current status of cultures. Gould's appraisal of the theory in this regard may seem accurate, but it is not clear how any other means of addressing the continuity issue could be more adequate. After all, fossil remains provide physical evidence, but one cannot recover from prerecorded history the bygone behaviors or social practices of human ancestors. While cross-cultural studies provide correlational evidence for many of the theory's claims, there seems to be no means other than reasonable "storytelling" for connecting current data to ancient generations.

Evaluation of Sociobiology

Scientific Worthiness

Testability. The medium rating of the theory for testability (see Table 5.2 on page 130) reflects a trade-off between empirical studies and some of the theoretical criticisms already raised. The tendency of sociobiologists to "tell stories" about hunter–gatherer societies is probably necessary because the fossil record contains no direct evidence of ancient cultural behaviors. Equally important is establishing empirical evidence for the linkage between genotype and social phenotype, yet no

TABLE 5.2 Ratings of Sociobiology for Scientific Worthiness

Criteria	High	Medium	Low
Testability		X	
External Validity		X	
Predictive Validity		X	
Internal Consistency	X		
Theoretical Economy	X		

scientific procedure has been established for testing this theoretical connection. However, sociobiology does make testable predictions about the relationship between adaptation and reproductive success (e.g., reproductive success will occur at different rates for different kinds of phenotypes). And, as shown in the previous section, many other theoretical hypotheses have been empirically tested.

External Validity.   We have rated sociobiology medium for its external validity. As the previous section shows, the comprehensiveness of the theory has been extensively documented by Wilson and other researchers. While some of the claims the theory makes about cultural universals appear to be unfounded, the theory does a remarkable job of accounting for an extremely broad range of social behaviors and qualities.

Predictive Validity.   The theory rates medium for its predictive validity. Concerning anatomical phenotypes, the predictive validity of evolutionary theory has been consistently demonstrated by plant and animal breeders. On the other hand, the difficulty of predicting adaptive social phenotypes cannot easily be overcome because adaptation is a *post hoc* concept. For example, phenotypes that are adaptive in one environment may not be adaptive in another (recall the case of sickle-cell anemia). If a phenotype has evolved, we can look backward and say why it is adaptive, but it is far more difficult to tell if it will be adaptive at some future time. The complexity of interacting ecological pressures contributes to this problem. In terms of potential, sociobiologists are still early in their research agendas, so ratings on this criteria may change in the future.

Internal Consistency.   We have rated the theory high for its internal consistency. Throughout the chapter, a broad array of social behaviors have been explained using the same internal and bridge principles. Few, if any, exceptions need be made by the theory. While sociobiology has been criticized for explaining opposite tendencies of aggression and altruism with the same mechanism of natural selection, there is no necessary contradiction between the two as there was for some of Freud's concepts. It is possible and likely that both aggression and altruism have been selected as complementary (rather than contradictory) behaviors because they have been adaptive in solving different kinds of interpersonal problems in different situations. While Wilson's genetic "determinism" reflects a recurrent criticism of the theory, it also underscores the consistency of his interpretation of social behaviors.

Theoretical Economy. Sociobiology rates high for its theoretical economy. No other theory of human nature approaches it for the breadth of scope in explaining a plethora of human, animal, and insect phenomena. Of course the theory doesn't explain everything. It doesn't tell us why a disproportionate number of college students' grandparents die just before final exams, or why workers call in sick more often on Fridays than any other day of the week, or why adults cannot remember their own infantile experiences. Nevertheless, Wilson's assumptions are minimal in terms of the theory's explanatory power. In addition, relatively few core concepts are needed. The various facets of phylogenetic inertia that determine any individual's fitness in a social–environmental context are clearly important, and the variety of selection pressures set forth by the theory are not burdensome. In short, Wilson's preliminary assumptions deliver superb theoretical mileage; he explains much with relatively few principles and a small list of reasonable assumptions.

Developmental Adequacy

Temporality. The theory passes this criterion (see Table 5.3) because it is an extension of evolutionary biology to human social behavior. It relies on the notion of gradual change over many generations.

Cumulativity. Changes from one generation to the next in human social behavior result from mutations and genetic recombinations. These changes produce small phenotypic modifications that gradually accumulate over time until a new social behavior is formed. For example, the evolution of status hierarchies has taken thousands of generations to change from scramble competition over food, goods, and mates into the contest competition of clothing, etiquette, and cars. In addition, language has gradually evolved from simple signals into what we know as grammar and syntax in modern speech. In these cases and many others, incremental evolutionary changes are added to preceding adaptations, so the theory passes this criterion.

TABLE 5.3   **Ratings of Sociobiology for Developmental Adequacy**

Characteristic	Rating
Temporality	Yes
Cumulativity	Yes
Directionality	Yes
New Mode of Organization	Yes
Increased Capacity for Self-control	Yes

Directionality.   Sociobiology contends that natural selection moves evolution in the direction of increasing adaptation. This is not to say that less-adaptive forms do not occasionally evolve, but as with dinosaurs, when such forms are no longer adaptive within an ecological context, either new adaptations get selected or else extinction occurs. Even a social behavior that is highly adaptive in one context may become nonadaptive if the social context changes dramatically. Consequently, there is no absolute position from which to view the direction adaptation may take. Nevertheless, evolutionary adaptation is one measure of progress, and progress is one of the concepts used to characterize developmental change.

New Mode of Organization.   Wilson believes that evolution has produced forms of social regulation that are more differentiated and more integrated patterns of social interaction than were displayed by cultures even a few thousand years ago. He argues, for example, that new modes of social government mark each of the progressive phases of civilization—from band to tribe, from tribe to chiefdom, from chiefdom to state, and from state to nation. While not every evolutionary change is regarded as a new mode of social behavior, those that do occur are regarded as expressions of the same underlying principles as other adaptations. In our judgment, the theory does an adequate job addressing this characteristic.

Increased Capacity for Self-control.   Humans may well be unique in their capacity to predict and control their environment in many respects. The capacity of humans to erect institutions to control their social interactions (e.g., schools, police departments, courts, social service agencies, churches) means that some environmental pressures can actually be systematically altered to favor rather than oppose human survival. Moreover, the evolution of the human brain has made possible self-reflection, the capacity for rapid specialized learning, and self-control over aggressive emotions. The theory does not hold that every behavior is directly controlled by a gene, only that certain qualities or tendencies in a population have undergone cultural evolution. Human behavior is far less automatic and involves more flexibility and conscious choices than does the behavior of any other animal. These considerations lead us to judge sociobiology as passing this criterion.

Pedagogical Usefulness

It is helpful to recall that pedagogical usefulness is the name we give to a set of criteria employed in judging how helpful a theory is for teachers, parents, and counselors who are interested in influencing children's development. Table 5.4 shows that sociobiology rates low in all but one category. The overarching reason for this is that the theory addresses phylogenetic rather than ontogenetic change. From the theory's point of view, attempts by teachers, parents, and counselors to influence changes within an individual's life span would be considered trivial or misdirected.

Interpretability.   Sociobiological concepts are difficult to interpret. The theory contains a substantial amount of new jargon, and much of it is highly technical.

TABLE 5.4   Ratings of Sociobiology for Pedagogical Usefulness

Criteria	High	Medium	Low
Interpretability			X
Versatility			X
Availability		X	
Guidance			X

Consider the important concept of phylogenetic inertia, one of two ultimate causes. As with physics, the concept of inertia is counterintuitive. High inertia means little evolutionary change over time. Low inertia produces a high degree of evolution. Moreover, the components of phylogenetic inertia are themselves difficult to grasp: genetic variability, antisocial factors, complexity of social behavior. While there is conceptual integrity to these ideas, it is difficult to translate them into the everyday lives of children. For reasons like these, we have rated the theory low for its interpretability.

Versatility.   Sociobiology is perhaps the most comprehensive theory of human development found in the literature today. The variety of phenomena it attempts to explain range from temper tantrums to sibling rivalry to mating rituals to the origins of morality. In terms of sheer scope, no classical or modern developmental theory compares to it. However, recall from Chapter 2 that versatility is an index of how well a theory "instructs" us in a variety of child rearing, teaching, and counseling situations. In this regard, sociobiology is of little value. That is because the theory addresses phylogenetic rather than ontogenetic change. Moreover, because the only sources of change are found in genetic mutations and sexual recombinations, the theory has virtually no value in helping us direct children's development from infancy to maturity. For this reason, the theory is rated low for its versatility.

Availability.   On the one hand, Wilson has made a real attempt to place the case for sociobiology into the public's eye. He has authored a number of nontechnical treatments, including his Pulitzer prize winner *On Human Nature* (1978). A number of articles about the theory have appeared in popular magazines such as *Science, Natural History,* and *Discovery.* On the other hand, these treatments are not so much about the theory of sociobiology as they are about examining one or another of its implications in a nontechnical way. If one really wants to learn about the theory of sociobiology, the primary sources will still be found in monographs and journal articles written for professional audiences. These sources are, of course, located almost exclusively in university libraries. Based on the two types of considerations described here, we have judged the theory medium for its availability.

Guidance.   In accord with our earlier considerations, we have judged sociobiology to have low guidance value for teachers, parents, and counselors. Again, this rating reflects the theory's concentration on phylogenesis rather than individual development.

It is interesting to note that for every criterion, sociobiology was judged to have low medium pedagogical usefulness. But it would be an error to conclude that there must be something "wrong" with the theory. Instead, we should recognize that the theory and our evaluative criteria simply represent different purposes. On the one hand, pedagogical usefulness reflects a concern for influencing people during their life span, while on the other hand, sociobiology is interested in explaining changes that occur over many generations. Should genetic engineering ever progress to the point where social behaviors can be preprogrammed, we might want to reexamine our evaluation.

Summary Points

1. Sociobiology is different from other developmental theories in that it attempts to explain *phylogenesis* (development of the species) rather than *ontogenesis* (development of individuals across their life span). The theory builds on three basic principles of evolution set forth by Darwin: individual variation, inheritance of traits, and natural selection.

2. Wilson advances evolutionary theory by positing social *behavior* as a phenotypic expression of genotypes that have evolved over many generations.

3. Evolution involves three levels of organization: the genetic, the individual, and the species or cultural level. At the genetic level, random mutations and genetic recombinations occur to produce genetic variation between individuals. At the individual level, natural selection operates to accept or reject whole individuals. Favorable selection occurs through comparatively higher reproductive success (genetic fitness). At the species level, evolution operates to produce gradual changes in social behavior over many generations.

4. Sociology attempts to explain ten broad qualities of sociality by demonstrating evidence of universality, continuity, and adaptation. The theory uses data collected from a variety of disciplines such as biology, psychology, sociology, economics, and political science.

5. The theory's internal principles include genetic fitness and two ultimate causes, the "prime movers" of evolution. Ultimate causes, phylogenetic inertia and ecological pressure, exert their influence over long time spans of many generations. The theory's bridge principles include demographic variables, rates of gene flow, and coefficients of relationship, which are seen as the proximate causes of evolution that operate within the lifetime of individuals.

6. The ultimate mechanism of evolutionary change is genetic mutation and recombination, because these are the origins of individual variation. A secondary mechanism, genetic fitness, operates on individuals through their reproductive success.

7. The theory has contributed certain unifying concepts and a clarifying debate about the relationship between evolution and culture. Criticisms of the theory include its biological determinism, its conceptual linkage between genotype and phenotype, the concept of adaptation, and problems with verifying universality and continuity.

8. Overall, we have rated sociobiology medium for its scientific worthiness, high for its developmental adequacy, and low for its pedagogical usefulness.

PROBLEMS AND EXERCISES

Class Exercise

1. Have the class develop a measure of "family tradition" to test the claim that more cohesive families tend to engage in more reciprocal altruism. Also assess the extent to which kin selection leads to reproductive success by comparing the following two groups: (1) average family size of students' uncles' and aunts' families that are highly cohesive versus (2) average family size of students' uncles and aunts that are low in cohesiveness. Do the results support the theory's predictions?

2. Have groups of students go out together and photograph several houses that represent (1) a new neighborhood or housing development, (2) one that is ten to fifteen years old, and (3) an "old" housing development or neighborhood. In class, have them organize their photographs into collections that represent new, middle, and old neighborhoods.

   a. Have students compare collections. Do neighborhoods reflect evidence of social status? If so, how? Does the social status systematically change across the three collections?

   b. Is there systematic change in the presence of fences across the three collections? If so, how would sociobiology explain such differences? What are the adaptive advantages of territory marking? Do humans and other animals have a common "interest" in marking their boundaries? If so, what is it?

Individual Exercises

1. Harry and Beth are killed in a plane crash, leaving behind their three young children. Suppose that a thousand Harry and Beths have the same experience. On the basis of sociobiology, which of the following groups should volunteer most often to raise the three orphans? Justify your answer using internal and bridge principles derived from the theory.

   Harry and Beth's siblings (the children's aunts and uncles)
   Harry and Beth's parents (the children's grandparents)
   Harry and Beth's cousins
   Harry and Beth's best friends
   Harry and Beth's neighbors

2. Many religions rely on some version of the Golden Rule to regulate interpersonal conduct. Outline a sociobiological "story" to describe the evolution of the Golden Rule. (Hint: You'll need to explain why some phenotypes are more adaptive than others and how the Golden Rule is related to phenotypes.)

3. Use the Internet to search for sites related to E. O. Wilson and his theory. You can use his name as well as key words (internal and bridge principles). How do the Internet sites differ in terms of completeness and accuracy of information? What were the best sites you found? What problems did you encounter? What were some of the worst sites (and why)?

SUGGESTED READINGS

More about the Theory

Barkow, J. H. (1989). *Darwin, sex, and status: Biological approaches to mind and culture*. Toronto, ON: University of Toronto Press.

Bell, R. W., & Bell, N. J. (Eds.). (1989). *Sociobiology and the social sciences*. Lubbock, TX: Texas Tech University Press.

Caplan, A. L. (Ed.). (1978). *The sociobiology debate*. New York: Harper & Row.

Kaye, H. L. (1996). *The social meaning of modern biology: From social Darwinism to sociobiology*. New Brunswick, NJ: Transaction Publishers.

Wilson, E. O. (1978). *On human nature*. Cambridge, MA.: Harvard University Press.

Research Reviews

Gray, J. P. (1984). *A guide to primate sociobiological theory and research*. New Haven, CT: HRAF Press.

Kachigan, S. K. (1990). *The sexual matrix: Boy meets girl on the evolutionary scale*. New York: Radius Press.

Wilson, E. O. (1975). *Sociobiology: The new synthesis*. Cambridge, MA: Belknap Press of Harvard University Press. (There is still none more comprehensive than the original.)

Critical Reviews

Gould, S. J. (1978). Biological potential vs. biological determinism. In A. L. Caplan (Ed.), *The sociobiology debate*. New York: Harper and Row.

Ruse, M. (1979). *Sociobiology: Sense or nonsense?* Boston: D. Reidel.

Sahlins, M. (1976). *The use and abuse of biology: An anthropological critique of sociobiology*. Ann Arbor, MI: University of Michigan Press.

Wilson, D. S. (1994). Adaptive genetic variation and human evolutionary psychology. *Ethology and Sociobiology, 15*, 219–235.

6 Chomsky and Generative Grammar

Preview Questions

What influences contributed to Chomsky's interest in language?

What assumptions underlie Chomsky's theory?

What is the problem of study, and how do the research methods match the problem?

What are the theory's internal and bridge principles?

What change mechanism accounts for development?

Why is Chomsky's theory a member of the endogenous paradigm?

What are the important contributions and criticisms of the theory?

How does Chomsky's theory of generative grammar rate for scientific worthiness, developmental adequacy, and pedagogical usefulness?

Historical Sketch

Avram Noam Chomsky was born in Philadelphia on December 7, 1928. His father William published a scholarly edition of medieval Hebrew grammar, an enterprise that afforded young Noam an opportunity to learn some of the historical principles of linguistics. He also helped out with his uncle's newsstand in nearby Manhattan during the depression. As a high school student, Noam later considered emigrating to the new nation of Israel to work for Arab–Jewish cooperation.

Chomsky's early interest in language took hold at the University of Pennsylvania, where he majored in mathematics (Haley & Lunsford, 1994). His mathematics background equipped him with an attitude of mind and formal style of analysis that ultimately led to radically new formulations about the nature of language and new methods of its analysis. However, before all that happened, Chomsky seriously thought about dropping out of college. But in 1947 he made the acquaintance of

Note: This chapter was written with significant help from Ronald Lunsford (English Department, UNC Charlotte), who corrected many of our errors, modernized our understanding of Chomsky's more recent work, and helped clarify much of the material we had originally drafted.

Professor Zellig Harris, a linguist, whose political attitudes meshed with the young Chomsky's, and the 18-year-old began taking graduate linguistic courses with the professor (Haley & Lunsford 1994). This connection started Chomsky on a lifelong career in linguistics, beginning with a 1951 master's thesis on modern spoken Hebrew. Later that same year he became a junior fellow in the Society of Fellows at Harvard, an intellectual society of young scholars usually reserved for bright students with recently completed doctorates.

During the next four years at Harvard, Chomsky capitalized on many new advances that were much in vogue in the early 1950s (Chomsky, 1975a). For example, intellectuals in Cambridge supported interdisciplinary approaches to language, communication, and human behavior at a time when electronic computers were just beginning to have an impact on communication theory, cybernetics, psychophysics, and experimental psychology. In those years, B. F. Skinner's Harvard lectures on science and human behavior were considered the cutting edge of psychological theory.

Chomsky (1975a) recalls that his own reaction to these stimulating ideas was almost wholly negative. He rejected as harmful the agenda of studying problems suggested by available technology, and he believed that a behavioral analysis of language learning was fundamentally incorrect. This belief led him to write a scathing critique of Skinner's *Verbal Behavior* (Chomsky, 1959), a review now considered one of the most influential rejections of behaviorism in academic psychology.

In 1955, Chomsky left Harvard's Society of Fellows to complete his dissertation back at the University of Pennsylvania. Later, he took a position in modern linguistics at the Massachusetts Institute of Technology, where today he holds the endowed Ferrari P. Ward Chair in Modern Language and Linguistics. As a beginning professor, Chomsky delivered a speech about his view of linguistics to his MIT peers. George Miller, the most prominent Harvard language psychologist of the day, was in the audience. Miller later described young Chomsky's speech as the beginning of the "cognitive revolution" in American psychology (Haley & Lunsford, 1994). Revised elements of this speech were later published in *Syntactic Structures* (1957), a work that has spawned nearly five decades of analysis by many linguists. By some accounts Chomsky's analysis of language may have been the single most important force in overturning the then current doctrine of behaviorism. By showing how a behavioral analysis cannot provide an adequate account of language acquisition, he called into question both the behaviorist agenda of research and theory and its explanation of how children acquire new behaviors.

Today Chomsky is unquestionably the world's most renowned linguist. He is credited with turning the study of linguistics away from methods of classification and towards explanatory principles underlying language. His publication of *Syntactic Structures* initiated a new approach to investigating language, one that emphasized a uniquely human mental faculty of biologically determined structures and principles.

Chomsky is also one of America's most outspoken critics of business and government and has been one of this country's prominent intellectual dissidents. For example, he played a leading role in resisting the Vietnam War. His political attitude originated in what he calls "the radical Jewish community in New York." In a documentary film, *Manufacturing Consent: Noam Chomsky and the Media,* Chomsky showed how mainstream news coverage of world events actually works to "manufacture" public support for many special interests that dominate government and business activity in the United States. That film has won fifteen awards, including three Public Choice Prizes and two International Press Prizes.

Chomsky is an intellectual of the highest caliber. He has written more than seven hundred articles and seventy books, an average of approximately twenty articles and two books each year. According to professional citation indexes, he is the most cited living author in the world and ranks among the top ten authors ever cited, just behind Shakespeare, Plato, and Freud. Such a record reflects the fact that his ideas are considered relevant across many different disciplines. As one of the twentieth century's most influential scholars, he has been invited to visit prestigious universities throughout the world. He has delivered the John Locke Lectures at Oxford, been a visiting professor at the University of California for both the Los Angeles and Berkeley campuses, lectured at the University of London, and served as Research Fellow at Princeton's Institute for Advanced Study and Harvard's Center for Cognitive Studies. He is a member of the National Academy of Science, the American Academy of Arts and Sciences, and the British Academy.

Over nearly five decades of productive work, one can find distinct trends in how others write about Noam Chomsky. For example, in the years following *Syntactic Structures* (1957), his ideas were referred to as *transformational* grammar to emphasize the manner in which innate rules governed the meaning of individual sentences. Later, a more general term—*generative* grammar—became the popular phrase for Chomsky's ideas because that term more closely captured the idea that a fixed set of innate rules could generate an infinite number of grammatical utterances. More recently a new term—*universal* grammar—has been used because it reflects the idea that all humans possess a common "system of principles, conditions, and rules that are elements or properties of all human languages" (Chomsky, 1976, p. 29). Today, Chomsky prefers the term *generative* grammar because it captures the most essential task of the theory—to make explicit how a finite set of rules or logical algorithms can generate all possible grammatical sentences of a language and no nonsentences (Haley & Lunsford, 1994).

Structural Components of Generative Grammar

Assumptions

Chomsky (1983) views language as one of many interconnected systems that comprise human cognition. In his view, linguistic knowledge may be seen and studied independently of other cognitive systems such as our knowledge of the number system or visual space.

Chomsky assumes that children possess an *innate language faculty* equipped with at least five procedural rules:

- A technique for representing linguistic sounds
- A way of representing information about these sounds
- A limited set of hypotheses about language structure
- A way to determine implications between hypotheses
- A method of selecting one of the possible hypotheses compatible with linguistic sounds

Taken together, these assumptions paint a picture of a child possessed of a stunning linguistic competence. To account for this level of competence, Chomsky proposes the presence of an innately governed *language faculty*, which functions according to the preceding five procedures (Chomsky, 1965a).

Chomsky's theory reflects his fundamental, two-fold commitment to the value of *economy*. In the first place, science holds the basic position that when faced with two equally tenable explanations, the simpler (more economical) one is always to be preferred. In this vein, it was the principle of economy, not accuracy, that prompted seafarers to reject the charts from Ptolemy's earth-centered universe in favor of equally navigable but far simpler charts derived from a Copernican, helio-centered sky. So, as a basic principle and value, Chomsky wanted to be the architect of a theory with elegant simplicity.

In the second place, the heart of Chomsky's work is the idea of Universal Grammar. This concept entails the belief that every human being is born with a language facility that controls the timing, scope, and sequence of language development. Of course, natural variation exists in the actual languages humans speak, but underlying it is a more general, and therefore more economical rule system—Universal Grammar.

Problems for Study

Explaining Human Phenomena.   From the very beginnings of his work, Chomsky set himself the task of creating a grammar that modeled the cognitive language system in the human brain. This focus led Chomsky to declare very early that his linguistic study was a branch of cognitive psychology, thereby making it what is sometimes referred to as a "hard," or empirical science. As will be shown in the next sections, one of the effects of this declaration was to make his theory vulnerable to empirical research, particularly that being done in the emerging field of psycholinguistics.

Most broadly, the central problem of generative grammar is to explain linguistic knowledge: its nature, origins, and use (Chomsky, 1986). Linguistic knowledge has two major components, syntax and semantics (Chomsky, 1975a). Syntax is the study of language form, and its purpose is to show how the complexity of natural language can be analyzed into simple components. In contrast, semantics is concerned with the meaning and reference of language expressions (sounds, words, phrases). Consequently, an adequate explanation of language would entail formulations about the character of these two components and their lawful relationship to each other.

One of the enduring problems of generative grammar is to explain how it is possible for children to acquire all the capabilities of speaking and understanding a natural language even though they are exposed to a very finite, imperfect set of language constructions during infancy and childhood (Chomsky, 1965a). In this sense, a primary task has been to construct a general grammar of language that characterizes how ideal speakers use rules to relate sound and meaning.

If you think about it, children face a Herculean task in learning their native language. As youngsters, they actually hear only a limited subset of the infinitely possible sentences they could hear. Many times, expressions they hear consist of fragments and deviant wording. Yet, from such deficient linguistic experiences, they develop the linguistic knowledge that allows them to create and interpret meaningful utterances.

Understanding precisely how children come to formulate infinite, grammatically well-formed expressions in the span of only a few short years is the fundamental task of generative grammar (Chomsky, 1972b). In fact, there is a sense in which Chomsky's study of grammar from its beginnings in *The Logical Structure of Human Language* (1975) through *The Minimalist Program* (1995) has been an examination of this question: What does the child really have to learn? That leads to the question of what needs to be specified in the grammar of a given language and what things are governed by the structure of all language—Universal Grammar. As the title of his 1995 book indicates, Chomsky is moving more and more toward a position that brings maximum input for Universal Grammar and minimal input from the particular language of the speaker. Ideally, Universal Grammar would specify all the possible sentences and none of the nonsentences in all language. The elegant precision of such an agenda undoubtedly reflects the impact of Chomsky's background in mathematics.

Methods. Even though language acquisition is at the heart of Chomskyan linguistics, Chomsky does not study children; he studies sentences children (and adults) produce. Why is this? He believes that the native speaker's linguistic competence is an internal system of rules (reminiscent of Freud's mentalism). But since the internal system cannot be directly observed, Chomsky analyzes the sentences it produces instead. Once these sentences are collected, they are examined by native speakers who use their linguistic intuitions to determine whether the sentences are well formed.

Internal Principles

Psychological Reality. Recall from the previous section that Chomsky had set himself the task of devising a grammar that explains the workings of the brain. Toward that end, he invoked powerful and original theoretical concepts such as *deep structure, surface structure,* and *transformations.* A sentence such as "Was the man hit by the ball?" might be said to undergo changes (transformations) that transformed a deep structure version (base meaning) of that sentence into its surface structure (produced) version. Following is a sketch of how such a simple sentence would have been derived in Chomsky's early system.

> *Deep structure—question passive:* the ball past hit the man
> *Passive transformation—question:* the man past be hit by the ball
> *Question transformation:* past be the man hit by the ball
> *Affix hopping:* be past the man hit by the ball
> *Surface structure:* be past the man hit by the ball
>   (was)   (hit)

Soon after Chomsky articulated his theory, psycholinguists began to perform empirical tests involving sentences that were purported to undergo transformations. For example, they recorded how long it took native speakers to understand pairs of sentences with different numbers of transformations. If transformations are psychologically real, if they model what actually takes place in the human brain, then sentences with more transformations should require more processing time than sentences with fewer transformations, all other things being equal. The data did not support this hypothesis.

While no single set of experiments invalidates an entire theory, Chomsky took the results seriously. His goal was to gain insight into what was taking place in the human brain, and such experiments suggested that the early transformational grammar was not modeling the working of the language faculty. The theory had to be modified. In fact, the original grammatical theory outlined in *Aspects* gave way to an entirely different grammar, one that has come to be called *Government and Binding* (Chomksy, 1981). However, the overriding goal of this new grammar is the same as that for transformational generative grammar—to determine how one develops competence in a native language.

While Chomsky's theory has evolved over time, its internal principles have remained intact. For him language is that knowledge that allows humans to create and understand meaningful utterances. Underlying this knowledge is linguistic competence, and its basic characteristics are creativity, ambiguity, and synonymy.

Linguistic Competence and Performance.   Chomsky is careful to distinguish what speakers know about language (their linguistic competence) from what they actually produce (their performance). Even though they may be highly competent speakers of a language, all speakers often deviate from well-formed sentences in various ways. For example, in natural speech we "hem and haw," mismatch subject and verb, and often string together hopelessly long run-on sentences. Chomsky's concepts of competence and performance explain how this can happen.

Competence.   Linguistic competence is a speaker's knowledge of the grammar of a language. How does this knowledge come about? First, individuals are born with innate abilities to learn the grammar of their language. This innate ability takes the form of a linguistic component in the human brain, what Chomsky refers to as the *language faculty*. This faculty, however, must not be confused with a fully developed grammar. It is merely a point of origin. As speakers come into contact with their language—as they hear others speak the language—they gradually develop or "grow" their knowledge of grammar. When that knowledge is fully grown, they possess a grammar of their language. In other words, they are able to create meaningful utterances and to interpret meaningful utterances of other speakers of the language.

Chomsky's concept of linguistic competence has certain properties that may be profitably compared with Freud's concept of the unconscious. For example, both are deeply internal, highly abstract, and very general concepts. Both exert their influence over performance below the level of conscious awareness. Finally, both exert powerful, endogenous motivation to behave in some ways and not others.

There are important differences between Chomsky's and Freud's mentalism, however. Linguistic competence, for example, is far more precise in its operating rules than is the Freudian unconscious. In addition, the unconscious has today attained a degree of unruly familiarity, but the operations of linguistic competence remain the province of Chomskyan linguistics.

Performance.　Linguistic performance is actual speech, the real-life way we talk to and with one another. Performance may not fully reflect our linguistic competence, as would be the case if we were tired, inebriated, or otherwise impaired.

In distinguishing between competence and performance, Chomsky makes clear a critical difference between his study of linguistics and those that preceded him. The linguistic school that preceded Chomsky is often referred to as *descriptive*. The goal of such linguists as Zellig Harris (Chomsky's teacher), Nelson Francis, and Leonard Bloomfield was to describe the linguistic phenomena they observed. These linguists viewed language as the sum total of all behaviors of native users of language.

While Chomsky is also interested in describing language phenomena, he does so as a means to an end. The ultimate goal in a Chomskyan linguistic program is *explanation*. Chomsky wanted to explain how a native speaker is able to do what all native speakers do: create and interpret meaningful utterances in a language. In such a program, language becomes *not* the behavior of individuals who speak a given language, but rather the knowledge possessed in the brains of all speakers of a language—linguistic *competence*.

Creativity.　Chomsky has always been intrigued by the concept that a human grammar has the capacity to "make infinite use of finite means." To put the matter differently, there is a finite number of words in any language and a finite number of rules for putting these words together. However, the native speaker is capable of generating an infinite number of *possible* sentences. In *theory*, the speaker is also capable of generating an infinitely long sentence. We italicize *possible* and *theory* here because what one is capable of in theory is constrained by factors such as time and opportunity. However, our rules of grammar do not preclude us from continuing a sentence indefinitely. For example, we can always add clauses to a sentence with the following structure:

1. The hat that Bill bought Frank, who lives in the house that Betty bought from Tom, who used to live in the house that . . .

Because of his interest in creativity, Chomsky developed what has come to be called a *generative grammar*. It takes this name because its goal is to describe and explain the process by which humans can (in theory) generate an infinite number of sentences and infinitely long sentences.

Ambiguity.   What does the following sentence mean?

2. The six boys and girls left early.

A traditional grammar would assign one structure to this sentence and ignore the fact that it can have two meanings. In one reading of the sentence, there is a total of six boys and girls. In another there are six boys and six girls, twelve people in all.

If a generative grammar is to capture the process by which native speakers assign and interpret meanings for utterances, it has to explain how these two meanings arise. (See Sandlot Seminar 6.1 for an analogy to generative grammar.) In other words, where does the ambiguity come from? Chomsky's original theory posited two different terminal strings (deep structures) for this sentence, as follows:

First meaning   The six (boys and girls) left early.
Second meaning   The six boys and six girls left early.

We do not need to go into the intricacies of the structure that would produce these readings here, though we shall examine phrase structure in some detail. Here we are concerned with the ways in which the principle of ambiguity is central to Chomsky's theory. First, it is central because it explains why one needs an abstract level of grammar to tell us what this surface form of the sentence means. Chomsky used to call this abstract level *deep structure* but now he prefers *logical form*. In either case one surface form (The six boys and girls left early) has two different abstract structures, logical forms, that help account for their two different meanings.

The kind of ambiguity shown is referred to as syntactic because it concerns itself with meanings that come about through changes in the arrangement of words. There is another kind of ambiguity that must be accounted for, as illustrated in such a sentence as:

3. He did not want to go to the bank too early.

In this type of ambiguity, context plays an important role. For example, in one reading we can imagine a store manager waiting to take the day's money to deposit it in a bank. But there is another reading, one in which a fishing enthusiast knows that a prized trout visits the same fishing hole late each afternoon. Ambiguity of this type is called "lexical," because the word "bank" holds open many possibilities.

bank, n   An establishment that handles money
bank, n   The shore of a lake or river
bank, v   To play a pool shot off the side of a table
bank, v   To maneuver an airplane into a sharp turn
bank, v   To count on, or depend on something

The reader can no doubt come up with others. The point here is that lexical ambiguities (sometimes called homonyms) such as these must be accounted for in a generative grammar. This is done at an abstract level where words (technically "lexical items") are placed into the strings.

Synonymy. Just as one surface structure may have more than one meaning, it is possible for two or more surface structures to have the same meaning. Actually, as Chomsky's theory has evolved, he has modified this claim somewhat. In his Standard Theory, Chomsky (1965) posited that such sentences as the following derived from a common deep structure, and that structure accounted for their synonymy:

> 4a. John hit the ball
> 4b. The ball was hit by John

As his theory has evolved, Chomsky has moved further and further away from this premise; two different sentences today would never be considered to be fully synonymous. For example, his grammar is at pains to show that the first two seemingly different sentences that follow differ in meaning (and hence in structure) from the third sentence.

> 5a. John is not easy to please.
> 5b. It is not easy to please John.
> 5c. Not pleasing John is easy.

Sandlot Seminar 6.1

Sandlot Seminar: Linguistics and Chemistry

Chomsky offers an analogy between the job of a linguistic analyst and the job of a chemist who analyzes compounds. Each begins with complex phenomena (speech versus chemical compounds). Each is limited to a finite set of components. The chemist utilizes elements and their laws of interaction, while the linguist uses generative grammar and transformation rules. With her elements, the chemist can generate an infinite set of possible, increasingly complex compounds. The fact that in the real world only a finite set of compounds has actually been generated is a reflection of time and material availability, not theoretical possibility. Similarly, the linguist may use generative grammar, with its components and transformational rules, to analyze all the possible sentences without regard to any special treatment for those that have actually been spoken.

1. Would you consider chemistry to be complex? How about linguistics? What other features of chemistry and linguistics make them complex areas of study?
2. If given sufficient time and materials, could enterprising chemists generate an infinite number of compounds? Why or why not? Would computers help?
3. If given sufficient time, could enterprising linguists generate an infinite number of sentences? Why or why not? Would a computer help?

Bridge Principles

Principles and Parameters.   As one might expect, Chomsky's bridge principles have changed over time as his theory has evolved. Principles that were once integral to Chomsky's transformational generative grammar, such as deep structure/ surface structure and phrase structure rules, have given way to entirely different principles in his minimalist program.

In order to understand the key bridge principles of Chomsky's current theory, one needs to have a basic understanding of his overall program. As we indicated above, Chomsky has continued to be interested in the question of just what needs to be specified in a grammar. Those elements that are a part of universal grammar do not need specification in an individual grammar. This is not to say that the linguist doesn't study these matters. If the structure of language is to be understood, it is crucial that universal grammar be investigated. In doing so, we gain insight into language learning by discovering what the individual does *not* have to learn about language.

But surely there is much to learn about individual languages. From phonetics (e.g., English makes a distinction between the vowel sounds in *beet* and *bit* that Spanish does not), to matters of phrase structure (eg., adjectives come before nouns in English and after nouns in French), to sentence structure (eg., verbs come before objects in English and after objects in Japanese), there is much that does not seem to be specified in universal grammar.

Chomsky divides linguistic study into two parts—the study of *principles,* the basic elements of universal grammar, and *parameters,* the categories within which variation occurs. The concept of parameters presumes that even in those areas in which languages differ, their differences are regular. To return to the preceding example, there is a category of languages in which the verb comes before the object and a category in which the object comes before the verb (similar to active and passive voice in English). When language learners experience their language, they must determine which type of language they are working with and set the parameters in the grammar they are building accordingly.

By way of analogy, imagine workers taking inventory of a huge warehouse. Instead of writing everything down on blank sheet(s) of paper, they are given a large list that includes such items as soaps (liquid, paste, powder), detergents (liquid, powder), bathtub cleansers (liquid, spray, powder), and so forth. Their job is to read the list and make the appropriate tally marks. When they are finished, they will have a complete listing of all the items in this particular warehouse. Likewise, language learners are provided (by universal grammar) with a well-defined inventory that allows them to come up with a complete description of the grammar of their language in an economical fashion.

But what about the principles? What kinds of things do not need to be specified in any grammar because they are principles of human language? Chomsky would be the first to say that any listing of principles at this time must be tentative, but there are certain principles that begin to seem clear. For example, there is a principle that says that language learners can expect linguistic operations to be based on structural descriptions of the items being operated on. While this may seem like so much linguistic "gibberish," the principle involved is actually rather simple. A classic example is the way questions are formed in English. Given such a sentence as

6. John is here.

how do we make it a question? Of course the very easy answer is

7. Is John here?

Suppose a child has seen several very simple declarative/question pairs such as

7a.	John is here.	Is John here?
7b.	The boy is happy.	Is the boy happy?
7c.	The man is my friend.	Is the man my friend?

The child may be well on the way (or so it would seem) to figuring out a principle for forming questions. But then, suppose the child is asked to make a question of such a sentence as

8a. The man who is my friend is here.

The child will not utter such a nonsentence as

8b. Is the man who my friend is here?

But why not? If the child is looking at simple sentences and seeing that in each case the first instance of a *be* (*is*) verb is moved to the front of the sentence, it would seem logical to try this procedure in the complicated sentence. But the child does not? Why not? Because a principle of universal grammar tells us that movements are constrained in certain ways by structure. First, the child intuits that "the man who is my friend" is a constituent (i.e., the words in this grouping go together) in ways that "John is" in "John is my friend" do not. Thus, the child recognizes that in moving the "is" in "John is my friend," we are not pulling an item out of its structure in the same way that we would be doing if we attempted to move the first "is" in "The man who is my friend is here."

We could, of course, write rules that explain how this movement takes place. In earlier versions, Chomsky wrote a rule for creating questions as follows:

SD   NP   *tn*   X

SC   *tn* NP   X

"X" in our example is a variable that stands for any possible sentence completion of a well-formed sentence. The rule then says that to form a question, begin with a sentence that fits the structural description (SD) given—all well-formed declarative sentences will. Then, move the first instance of tense and "be" verb (if there is one) in front of the subject NP. So, if you have

John   is   here

tn be

(*Note:* The be verb "is" contains tense (*tn*), in this case present.)

you get:

Is   John here

tn be

If you have

> 9. The man who is my friend is here.

then, applying the question-forming rule, you get

> 10. Is the man who is my friend here?

Note that we did not move the first verb "is" because it was a component of the entire noun phrase that acts as the subject of the sentence. In this case the second "is" acts as the verb for the sentence, and that is the one that the question-forming rule moves to the front of the sentence.

But what about the 4- or 5-year-old child learning a language? How does this child know what to do (and what not to do) in forming questions? Chomsky would suggest that a basic principle of language is at work here in helping the child know what to do.

Let's look at another basic principle of language. Consider the following sentences.

> 11a.   John likes himself.
> 11b.   John would like Bill to like himself.
> 11c.   John would like Bill to like him.
> 11d.   John thinks that people should like him.

Now, to whom does each of the pronouns in these sentences refer? After careful reflection, we should agree to the following:

> 11a.   "himself" refers to John
> 11b.   "himself "refers to Bill
> 11c.   "him" refers to John (or to someone not mentioned)
> 11d.   "him" refers to John (or to someone not mentioned)

Now, how do we know this? And even more importantly, how does a child of 6 or 7 figure this complicated reference out? When we examine the structures of these sentences, we find that in sentence *11a* both "John" and "himself" are in the same simple clause. In *11b*, "Bill" and "himself" are in the same simple clause. (It should be noted that the concept of clause here differs from a traditional grammar's concept of clause. We understand sentence *11b* to mean Frank wants X, where X stands for a clause: Bill like Bill.) Likewise, in *11c* "Bill" and "him" are in the same simple clause. And in *11d*, "John" and "people" are in different clauses.

If we were to try to state a rule for what is going on here, it would be something like the following:

> When a noun and a pronoun refer to the same person and are in the same simple clause, the pronoun must be reflexive.

If you'll examine the preceding sentences, you will see that this rule holds. But how does our 6-year-old figure this out? No one has taught the child the rule or what clauses are—either in traditional grammar or in transformational theory. So how does the child do it? A principle of universal grammar might be that the young reader understands (intuitively) the concept of clauses. A separate principle might be that the child knows that pronoun reference will be bounded by clauses (e.g., why "himself" refers to John in *11a* but must refer to Bill in *11b*).

The Computational Component. The crucial way in which unique sentences may be formed and assigned meanings requires that there be a system for generating these structures in the grammar of a language. This role is assigned to the *computational component*.

In order to understand just how crucial the computational component is to Chomsky's theory of language, we need to reexamine what it means to call Chomsky's grammar *generative*. In Chomsky's (1957) sense, generative means that one that can abstractly "project" with explicit formal rules. To see what this means, see if you can "project" the next number in the following series:

$$1, 2, 4, 8, 16, 32, \ldots$$

Did you get 64? If so, how did you do it? We projected this number by using a very simple algorithm to solve for any next number in the list:

$$Y = \text{the last number in the list}$$
$$X = 2 \times y$$

This algorithm will project an infinite number of integers that would be members of our series and no numbers that would not be in the series. From early on in his work, Chomsky set himself the task of arriving at an algorithm of sorts that would allow him to generate (or project) every possible sentence in a language and no nonsentences in that language. At the center of that algorithm in his original grammar (Chomsky, 1957) were *phrase structure rewrite rules*. In a very oversimplified form, a sentence such as

12. John likes candy

could be generated with the following phrase structure rewrite rules:

S	$\longrightarrow$	NP AUX VP
NP	$\longrightarrow$	PN
		N
AUX	$\longrightarrow$	Tn
VP	$\longrightarrow$	V (NP)

In regular English, this formula gives us the following information:

(1) A sentence (S) may be composed of a noun phrase (NP), an auxiliary to the verb (AUX), and a verb phrase (VP).

(2) A noun phrase (NP) may be composed of either a proper noun (PN) or a common noun (N). By writing the PN over the N, we symbolize an either/or choice.

(3) An auxiliary may be composed of tense (Tn).

(4) And a verb phrase (VP) may be composed of a verb (V) and a noun phrase (NP). By placing the NP in parentheses, we symbolize that it may be present, but does not have to be.

Clearly, then, this algorithm works to generate (or describe) the preceding sample sentence, "John likes candy."

S

NP   AUX   VP

PN   N   Tn   V   (NP)

John   present   like   candy

(*Note:* When we read a "tree" structure such as this, we should be aware that as we move from one line in a tree down to the next, we are moving from the leftmost term in our algorithm to the terms that tell us what that leftmost term is composed of. The first two lines show us that S may be rewritten ($\longrightarrow$) as NP AUX VP. If you look back at our algorithm, you find that this is the case. The next line shows us that NP may be rewritten ($\longrightarrow$) as PN; that AUX may be rewritten as ($\longrightarrow$) Tn; and that VP may be rewritten ($\longrightarrow$) as V NP.)

We are on our way, then, to coming up with an algorithm that will generate the sentences in English. However, we are far from success. How would the system handle the following sentences:

13a. John is sleeping soundly.

13b. John knows that Bill likes candy.

It would not, and that means that our grammar so far is incomplete. How might we revise it so that it would accommodate these new sentences? The obvious answer is to generate more rewrite rules. Of course, increasingly complex sentences will require even more rewrite rules.

Logical Form and Phonetic Form. As the preceding discussion indicates, Chomsky's early theory of generative transformational grammar embodied two important components: *deep structure* and *surface structure*. These concepts revealed that sentences that look very different from each other may be closely related because they have a common deep structure.

> 14a. John hit the ball.
> 14b. The ball was hit by John.
> 15a. John gave Mary the ball.
> 15b. John gave the ball to Mary.

On the other hand, sentences that look very much alike may be very different structurally. Chomsky's (1957) classic example is the following:

> 16a. John is easy to please.
> 16b. John is eager to please.

A traditional grammar would analyze these two sentences as structurally identical, but a transformational grammar shows that these similar surface forms derive from very different structures. We can illustrate those differences in the following simplified structures:

> For someone or something to please John is easy.
> John is eager for John to please someone.

In his recent work, Chomsky has moved away from the concepts of deep and surface structure. In their place is what he refers to as *logical form* and *phonetic form*. Every sentence must be assigned both a logical form, which assigns meaning to the utterance, and a phonetic form, which assigns sounds to the utterance. By accounting for the interrelations between logical form and phonetic form, the grammar accounts for native speakers' abilities to create and understand meaningful utterances.

Change Mechanisms

Chomsky (1983) views the environment as playing a subordinate, secondary role in language development. He notes that, depending on the region of the country, Americans grow up speaking English with different accents just as East Africans grow up speaking Swahili with different accents. In this he concedes that language specifics may well be a function of one's environment and that different languages may reflect unique, though shallow, differences.

> The child's language "grows in the mind" as the visual system develops the capac-
> ity for binocular vision, or as the child undergoes puberty at a certain stage of mat-
> uration. Language acquisition is something that happens to a child placed in a
> certain environment, not something that the child does. (Chomsky, 1993, p. 29)

This said, Chomsky's primary interest has always been in explaining universal
grammar rather than individual differences. This focus has led him to propose an
innate, biologically based linguistic faculty that determines universal characteristics
of learning and understanding for *any* human language. Experience may "trigger"
and shape this language faculty, but it cannot alter the "intrinsic, genetically determined" structure, function, or content (Chomsky, 1983, p. 49).

This genetically determined capacity for acquiring language is called the *language faculty*. The language faculty provides as "output" a grammar for language, on
the basis of limited language input (from parents, siblings, and others in the infant
and child's experience). Schematically, the language faculty may be represented as
shown in Figure 6.1. In Chomsky's view, the language faculty is directly and
explicitly a reflection of Descartes's rationalist philosophy, which is why the theory
occupies a central position in the endogenous paradigm. Motivated by the language faculty, "learning language is primarily a matter of filling in detail within a
structure that is innate" and biologically determined (Chomsky, 1975b, p. 39).

> Its "initial state" is determined by genetic endowment. Under the triggering and
> (marginally) shaping effect of experience, it passes through a series of states and
> attains a relatively stable "steady state" at about puberty, changing later only in
> peripheral respects. (Chomsky, 1993, p. 47)

While some linguistic data is necessary for language learning, this necessity
may function in one of several ways. It may, for example, simply determine which
of the possible language hypotheses (see Assumptions earlier in chapter) are activated within the developing child. However, it may also be that language experiences are required in order to activate or trigger the language faculty while exerting
no effect at all on the manner of its operation. In short, Chomsky holds open the
possibility that children's linguistic experiences may either initiate the operation
of innate mechanisms or may either influence the direction that innately
programmed learning potential will take.

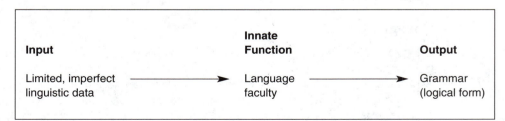

FIGURE 6.1   Schematic of the language faculty in linguistic performance.

The language faculty is characterized by two essential properties. First, it is biologically predisposed to develop a rich, generative grammar (linguistic competence). In Chomsky's view, what differentiates children in Guatemala from those in Lagos from those in the United States is the nuances of their native tongue, not the generative, universal grammar that accounts for that language. Second, the language faculty must be innately programmed to *evaluate* data from a limited and often deficient corpus of linguistic "input." It is this evaluation function that accounts for the language faculty's ability to recognize and produce valid sentences.

As a child matures, the innate language faculty activates (either through linguistic "triggering" or "guiding") linguistic competence. The organizing principles of this competence are not learned; rather, they are what make learning possible (Chomsky, 1986). In short, "We could not have acquired any language unless its fundamental properties were already in place, in advance of experience" (Chomsky, 1993, p. 48). Accordingly, children proceed through a sequence of states, which begins with an initial state S_0 prior to any language learning and terminates at a final, mature state S_f. The final state is attained fairly early in life and does not change significantly from that point on. As Sandlot Seminar 6.2 illustrates, children who suffer severe linguistic deprivation pose an interesting explanatory challenge for Chomsky.

Sandlot Seminar 6.2

Victor and Genie

In 1799, a naked boy was seen running through the woods in France. When captured, this 11-year-old "Wild Boy of Aveyron" (Lane, 1976) seemed to be more animal than human. A young French physician named the boy Victor and tried to socialize him. Over a five-year period, Victor did stop howling like a wolf, and he learned to eat with utensils, wear clothes, and sleep in a bed. But he never learned to communicate effectively.

Nearly two hundred years later, in 1970, a California social worker discovered a 13-year-old girl, Genie, in a back bedroom where she had been kept isolated for over a decade. During the day, Genie was strapped naked to a child's potty, and at night she slept in a crib with wire mesh sides and top. Throughout her childhood, Genie did not speak, nor was she spoken to. Whenever Genie made a noise, her father beat her. At the time of her discovery, Genie could move her hands and feet, but she could not speak or stand erect (Rymer, 1992).

Genie spent years in rehabilitation with Susan Curtiss who attempted to teach her to speak (Curtiss, 1977). Genie eventually learned to walk and use the toilet. She also learned to recognize many words and to speak in rudimentary sentences. First she spoke in one-word utterances and later was able to string together two-word combinations. Then came three-word sentences. But Genie never learned how to ask questions, understand grammar, or distinguish among pronouns or between passive and active verbs. As an adult, Genie still speaks in short, mangled two- or three-word sentences.

1. Consider the likely emotional trauma and absence of "triggering" experiences for Wild Victor and Genie. How might these factors influence language acquisition?
2. In your view, do Victor and Genie's language development support or contradict Chomsky's theory? Explain.

Explaining Human Development: The Research

While Chomsky emphasizes the formal study of *sentences*, rather than studying people or children, some developmental researchers have attempted to test various of his formulations (Crane & Thomton, 1998). Lenneberg (1967), for example, has noted four specific regularities about language that make it unique to humans.

1. The onset of speech is regular.
2. Speech is not, given normal experience, suppressible.
3. Language syntax cannot be taught to other species.
4. Languages everywhere have certain universals.

The first, third, and fourth of Lenneberg's propositions have been subjected to research.

Speech Is Regular

Several classic studies (Clifton & Odum, 1966; Savin & Perchonock, 1965) showed that simple sentences that closely approximate base structures were processed more quickly and were easier to recognize than more complex sentences, suggesting that interpretation relied on base rather than surface structures. In addition, Sachs (1967) found that regardless of the surface structure of a sentence, only its baseline meaning was remembered. Finally, in an ingenious study, if subjects heard a "click" while processing a sentence, they perceived the "click" as having occurred at the nearest constituent boundary (e.g., between clauses or between noun and verb), regardless of when it actually occurred (Garret, Bever, & Fodor, 1966). This last study suggests the brain is innately hardwired to interpret syntactic parsing.

In another series of classic studies, researchers examined children's *overregularization,* the inappropriate application of a grammatical rule. A child might say, for example, "I eated a cookie." Overregularization of inappropriate rules such as this is important because such errors could not derive from adults; rather, they must derive from a premature rule in the latent structure of language. Overregularization has been found in a variety of languages and cultures, including Turkish (Slobin, 1982) and Russian (Slobin, 1966). In a modern recasting of these studies, Morgan, Bonamo, and Travis (1995) investigated the influence of adult corrections on children's language errors. They discovered that parental corrections did not facilitate language learning but actually impeded it.

Nonhumans Cannot Learn Syntax

Chimpanzees have so far shown an ability to learn a limited number of specific signs after prolonged training, but they have not shown any consistent ability to acquire humanlike syntax (Savage-Rumbaugh, 1990; Hulit & Howard, 1997). Finally, studies of language training with chimpanzees show that their semantic acquisitions tend to be stimulus bound rather than generative or creative like human language (Umiker-Sebeok & Sebeok, 1980).

Language Is Universal

Concerning the state of S_0, the initial linguistic state, experimental research has confirmed the infant's early sensitivities to structural aspects of grammar (Mazuka, 1996; Mehler & Dupoux, 1994; Morgan & Demuth, 1996). Such work supports but does not prove Chomsky's claims about the existence of an innate component such as the language faculty. Infants in many cultures perceive relevant acoustic dimensions of language and clearly differentiate between speech sounds and noises made by machines or nature (Molfese, 1989). In addition, infant babbling appears at approximately the same age and in the same form across many languages and cultures (Levitt & Uttman, 1992).

Around the world, across cultures, and in different environments, infants routinely progress through the same sequence of general language stages: crying, babbling, echolalia (imitation), expressive jargon, one-word utterances (Blake & deBoysson-Bardies, 1992; Brown, 1973; D'Odorico, 1984; Stark, Bernstein, & Demorest, 1993). Following infancy, step-by-step language acquisition continues through two-word and three-word utterances until fully grammatical language is acquired (Brown, 1973; deVilliers & deVilliers, 1972). Studies of children immersed in a second language from infancy versus those who attempt to learn a second language later in life show that there appears to be a maturationally determined critical period, after which language acquisition becomes very difficult (Johnson & Newport, 1989). Studies of Genie, who was deprived of almost any linguistic input until age 13, show that even with years of intensive training, she did not acquire control of syntax, even though her semantic and cognitive development advanced normally (Curtiss, 1981).

Contributions and Criticisms of Generative Grammar

Contributions

Historical Impact. Linguistic analysis began as early as 2000 B.C. when Egyptian kings commanded hieroglyphs be encoded onto their monuments. Since that time, many types of systems have been proffered to explain language and its development. Most modern linguists would agree that Chomsky's formulations about generative grammar are the most cogent, most extensive, and most general explanation of language in the history of its study.

Universality. Chomsky's theory is far too expansive to fully understand without a specialized degree in linguistics. Without question he is the most important linguist in modern thought. He turned the study of linguistics away from its historical roots in *semantic* analysis to modern explorations of *grammatical structure*. In doing that he gave modern psycholinguistics an explanatory model of grammar universal to all human language.

Importance.   Virtually all modern linguistics takes place in Chomsky's shadow. Even those who attempt to disprove his theory do so with an eye toward the importance of his work.

Criticisms

The Ideal Speaker.   Agassi (1997) points out that "The most important novelty of Chomsky's work is his idealization of the field by postulating the existence of the ideal speaker–hearer" (p. 136). The fact that real speakers of a language are far less polished in their linguistic output (what they actually say) than Chomsky's ideal speaker is relegated to differences in performance, not competence. But herein lies a problem for developmental psychology, which has an important primary aim in the explanation of real people. It is this abstraction of an ideal speaker that prompts Chomsky to study and analyze *sentences rather than speakers*. As Aggasi (1997) points out, such a theoretical choice leaves serious questions of child development unanswered. For example, how do preverbal infants attend to and select linguistic input from their language environment? How is it that infants acquire "perfect" grammar from impoverished, incomplete, and imperfect language experiences? What important factors "trigger" the language faculty? In this light, the theory of universal, generative grammar tells us relatively little about how children actually acquire language, let alone how real adults actually talk. In fairness to Chomsky, he would probably argue that child development data would be largely irrelevant to the kinds of claims he makes or that whatever data could be discovered would ultimately be no real test of his theory anyway. In our view, a theory of language, including its embedded language faculty to account for language acquisition, is seriously deficient if it does not implicate the serious study of real children. This shortcoming will, of course, impact how we evaluate Chomsky's theory for its external validity in the following section.

Finding Linguistic Competence.   Does linguistic competence reflect mental reality in the same sense that the id and unconscious are psychologically real in Freud's theory? According to Chomsky, no. Generative grammar and linguistic competence do not occupy mental space. Without psychological reality, what good is a theory of generative grammar? According to Chomsky (1983), it is the explanatory power that generative grammar provides in giving an efficient explanation for linguistic evidence that is important. Still, if generative grammar is only a system of explanatory rules, then what gives it any priority in human lives over other systems of rules such as traffic, copyright, or tax laws?

Language Faculty. Some critics of Chomsky doubt that the language faculty can account for cultural differences that convey the same meaning using either grammatical or nongrammatical techniques (Maratsos, 1998; Tomasello, 1995). For example, African languages rely on tone patterns to express articles such as *a* and *the*, while Chinese and Japanese infer them entirely from sentence context.

Others have shown that language acquisition is not completed quite as quickly or as orderly as Chomsky supposed. Complete mastery of some grammatical forms (e.g., *tell* versus *ask, perhaps* versus *will*) is not achieved until well into middle childhood (Green, 1979, 1984; Tager-Flusberg, 1997), suggesting that factors other than biological maturation play important roles in language acquisition. Finally, Givon (1998) argues that the "facts" of natural language grammar cannot support Chomsky's extreme nativist position.

Evaluation of Generative Grammar

Scientific Worthiness

Table 6.1 shows our ratings for the theory's scientific worthiness. It is important to note that the two measures of validity, both of which require research with real people, have received a rating of low. This is due almost exclusively to the fact that the theory eschews children in favor of sentences.

Testability. We have judged Chomsky's theory low for its testability for the following reasons. His extreme mentalism, his reliance on generative grammar and deep structure (later called "initial phrase markers"), makes important elements of his theory difficult to test empirically. In addition, the language faculty, with its genetically determined rules of grammar, is equally immune to empirical study. However, there remain some theoretical issues that are subject to empirical test. For example, what is the extent to which real speakers correspond to ideal speakers in judging sentence syntax? To what extent do real speakers agree with one another on the grammaticality or degree of syntax violation of target sentences? Questions such as these can be answered with empirical evidence.

TABLE 6.1 Ratings of Generative Grammar for Scientific Worthiness

Criteria	High	Medium	Low
Testability			X
External Validity			X
Predictive Validity			X
Internal Consistency		X	
Theoretical Economy		X	

External Validity.   Chomsky makes little attempt to explain the real world of children or to account for their progression from infancy to linguistic competence. His theory emphasizes the role of an "ideal" (e.g., mature) speaker in determining syntactical conformance. Except by way of anecdote, children's speech is not, until it has matured, what Chomsky is interested in explaining. For these reasons, we have judged his theory low for its external validity.

Predictive Validity.   Just as real children are peripheral to Chomsky's current interests, they remain so to his future interests. Virtually no attempts have been made to establish the theory's predictive validity by predicting and discovering new facts about language development. Consequently, we have judged the theory low on this criterion of scientific worthiness.

Internal Consistency.   The theory rates medium for its internal consistency. Language acquisition is governed by the language faculty, an endogenous explanation. Generative grammar reflects linguistic competence, not performance. These are the messages of Chomsky's theory, and he has been pretty consistent about them. With that in mind, his revision of the early concept of deep structure, to dissociate syntactic from semantic aspects of meaning, reflects more of an evolutionary step in the theory's development than it does a conceptual inconsistency in such a complex theory.

Theoretical Economy.   Although Chomsky makes five basic assumptions about the linguistic mind, his theory purports to explain an infinite number of possible sentences. Granted the final details, which would explain as yet undiscovered nuances about natural language, have not yet been written. Still, no other modern theory has for its *current* agenda the task of accounting for all real and all possible phenomena within the problem of study. At the same time, however, language is a limited domain of study. These considerations lead us to rate Chomsky's theory medium for this criterion.

Developmental Adequacy

While Chomsky's theory of generative grammar does an extensive job in describing the various rule systems for formulating and understanding sentences, it is not a very good developmental theory. Except in a formal sense, Chomsky makes few attempts at explaining how children develop from an initial, nonlinguistic state he calls S_o to a mature, final linguistic state called S_f. It is reasonable to expect that this development takes some time, so the theory passes the criterion of temporality. However, the theory offers few insights into the qualities that characterize children's language acquisition. While it can be applied to children, it is not so much about them as it is about the semiautonomous language faculty and the linguistic competence underlying what they say. Based on these theoretical considerations, we have failed generative grammar without further elaboration on the other four criteria of developmental adequacy. Table 6.2 reflects these judgments.

TABLE 6.2   **Ratings of Generative Grammar for Developmental Adequacy**

Characteristic	Rating
Temporality	yes
Cumulativity	no
Directionality	no
New Mode of Organization	no
Increased Capacity for Self-Control	no

Pedagogical Usefulness

Whereas scientific worthiness and developmental adequacy are related to two dimensions of a theory's explanatory power, its usefulness for parents and teachers is not. Rather, this set of criteria evaluates how useful a theory is in directing efforts to influence children's development. In short, does the theory imply that parents and teachers should do some things but not others to make development "better" for our children? Our ratings of the pedagogical usefulness of generative grammar are summarized in Table 6.3.

Interpretability.   Chomsky employs such an extensive taxonomy of theoretical terms that few outside the study of linguistics would be comfortable reading his work. While theoretical jargon serves an important communicative function, too much of it retards a theory's interpretability and makes it less useful for teachers and parents. In this vein, it was little help in 1975 when Chomsky issued his "extended standard edition" of the theory and converted deep structure into "initial phrase markers." Our point here is that generative grammar is not among the more interpretable of developmental theories. Its heavy dosage of technical jargon results in a low rating on this criterion.

Versatility.   It is important to distinguish between (1) a broad theory, such as Freud's or Skinner's, which covers a wide spectrum of phenomena and (2) a narrowly focused theory, such as Ainsworth's or Chomsky's, which covers a restricted

TABLE 6.3   **Ratings of Generative Grammar for Pedagogical Usefulness**

Criteria	High	Medium	Low
Interpretability			X
Versatility			X
Availability			X
Guidance			X

range of phenomena. A broad theory is generally much more versatile, from a pedagogic point of view, than a narrowly focused theory. Chomsky's generative grammar, for example, may well be versatile in dealing with many linguistic phenomena, but language is just a small part of human nature. The theory has not generated important contributions for child rearing or for education, in part because of its narrow focus (and in part because of its strongly endogenous position). Consequently, it is rated low for its versatility.

Availability.   Unlike other theories that have invaded the mainstream of public thought, Chomsky's remains highly technical and available primarily to linguists and philosophers. While many publications about generative grammar exist, they are found primarily in professional books and journals that occupy the shelves of university libraries. In short, there is little public visibility for Chomsky's theory, so it is rated low for its availability.

Guidance.   Chomsky provides virtually no advice in how adults should go about helping children progress from ungrammatical to grammatical speech. In fact, he is quite willing to designate the language faculty to account for this development without ever managing to describe how it actually works. In short, the theory is rated low for its guidance because it provides very little that is useful to parents or teachers, unless they happen to be educated linguists.

Summary Points

1. Chomsky is one of the twentieth century's most influential scholars, having published more than seven hundred articles and seventy books. He is the most cited living author in the world and ranks among the top ten authors ever cited, just behind Shakespeare, Plato, and Freud.
2. Chomsky's theory of generative grammar posits an innate language faculty that leads to the development of linguistic competence, the procedural rules for representing linguistic sounds and information about them, for generating and evaluating hypotheses about language, and for selecting these hypotheses.
3. The central problem of generative grammar is to explain linguistic knowledge: its nature, origins, and use. Language has two major components, syntax and semantics. To study language, Chomsky builds sentences and analyzes them for meaning. Although he does not study children directly, he is interested in their utterances.
4. The theory's internal principles consist of several important elements. *Competence* is a speaker's underlying (unconscious) knowledge of language, whereas *performance* is the actual production of language in concrete situations. Chomsky wants to analyze linguistic competence. While the original concepts of *deep structure* and *surface structure* referred to different aspects of language, they have given rise in more recent work to concepts of competence and performance, creativity, ambiguity, and synonymy. Language is both generative

and universal. It is generative in the hypothetical sense that linguistic competence can generate an infinite number of sentences and a sentence that is infinitely long. It is universal in the sense that linguistic competence underlies all human language.

5. Chomsky describes a number of key bridge principles. Among the most important are the following. He distinguishes between *principles,* the basic elements of universal grammar, and *parameters,* the categories within which variation in grammar occurs. In addition, he posits a *computation component* with its *attendant phase structure rewrite rules.* These rules codify the possible sentences, complete with phrases and clauses, that can be generated from universal grammar. Finally, Chomsky differentiates between *logical form,* which assigns meaning to an utterance, and *phonetic form,* which assigns sounds to the utterance.

6. The primary efficient cause of language development is the *language faculty,* an innate, biological change mechanism. The language environment provides supportive influences on speech facility and intonation and may even have a "triggering" effect on language functioning, but it has no effect on the language faculty's innate programming.

7. Chomsky's contributions to developmental psychology include his historical impact, his emphasis on the universal but species-specific characteristic of language, and the importance of his work as a reference mark for scholars. Criticisms of Chomsky's theory include his emphasis on formal linguistics rather than the study of children's language use, questions about the psychological reality of linguistic competence, and questions about the functioning of the language faculty.

8. Two points about Chomsky's generative grammar are important in evaluating the theory. First, in comparison to others in this text, it is a narrowly focused theory. Second, rather than empirical research with children, it relies on formal analysis of sentences presumably produced by linguistically competent children and adult speakers. These considerations lead to rather low ratings of the theory for its scientific worthiness, developmental adequacy, and pedagogical usefulness.

PROBLEMS AND EXERCISES

1. A new kindergarten teacher was telling her class about the things that had happened on her way to school. She described one event by saying, "This morning the little boy next door was bitten by a stray dog! Then the dog ran away. So you need to be very careful around strange dogs. They can be dangerous." Immediately, most of her kindergartners began to chuckle and laugh. Stunned by the students' reaction, the teacher asked what they found so funny. Finally, one boy remarked, "But Miss James, boys don't bite stray dogs."

What did the kindergartners learn about stray dogs?
Did the teacher's students hear what she had said?

How did her students understand what had happened?

How do young children understand passive constructions?

Why, according to Chomsky, might we expect young children to react as these kindergartners did?

2. During a throw and catch session with his 3-year-old daughter, a father gently tossed a beach ball back and forth. Each time the young girl tried her best to catch the ball, but it bounced off her arms and chest to the ground. Finally, after many gentle throws, the daughter caught the ball and exclaimed, "Daddy, Daddy, I catched it! I catched it!"

Surprised by his daughter's terminology, the father immediately corrected her with emphasis, "Yes, you *caught* the ball. That's terrific, the way you *caught* it." Immediately the daughter replied, "But Daddy, I caught it and I catched it." Try as he might, the poor father couldn't get his daughter to use *caught* instead of *catched*.

Several months later during another throw and catch episode, the father remarked on his daughter's improvement in catching the ball. After one throw, the daughter remarked, "Look Daddy. I *caught* it! But you didn't throw it very well. I can *catch* it almost every time."

Why did the young daughter originally use *catched* even when corrected by her father?

Why did the father's use of correct grammar have little initial effect on the daughter's use of *catched*?

Why do you think the daughter later substituted *caught* for *catched* in her spontaneous speech?

How would Chomsky explain this set of events?

3. Review Sandlot Seminar 6.2 about the absence of linguistic experiences for Victor and Genie. Note that each child was subjected to prolonged language training. Also note that these two children learned many words and phrases, but they did not learn syntax. In many ways, their language performance resembles that found for chimpanzees.

Why didn't intensive language training help Victor and Genie understand syntax?

Do children like Victor and Genie support or contradict Chomsky's notion of an innate language faculty? Why?

Do Victor and Genie support or contradict Chomsky's notion of "triggering" for the language faculty?

4. Parenting and language development. Study the two situations that follow and answer the questions after each one.

Situation 1

Two mothers were discussing their babies' development across the back fence when their discussion turned to language development of their 15-month-olds. One mother was proclaiming the virtues of pointing and naming things for her child, never missing the opportunity to attach language to an object. She wanted to hasten her daughter's language through an enriched environment in order to give her the best possible start. The other mother listened politely and responded, "We simply intend to let nature take its course. Our child's language will develop naturally, when she's ready. We don't feel a need to push her so hard." The first mother was a bit surprised at this mother's lack of interest in her child's language development.

> In comparing the two daughters, what do you predict will be the result of each mother's behavior toward language development?
>
> What would Chomsky say about the two mothers?
>
> Which mother's model of language development do you favor as a best fit for language development? Why? Classify your response as to the paradigm it represents.

Situation 2

Three years later the two mothers were again meeting over the back fence and noticing how much their children had grown. Now playmates, the two girls were actively engaged in the sandbox, playing with cars. The conversation between the girls, while somewhat disjointed, was nonetheless filled with requests, remarks, descriptions, and responses to each other's speech. One mother questioned the other, "Remember the discussion we had a few years ago about how we were going to help our children's language development?" "Why yes," replied the other mother. "I spent all that time with early language activities, even bought flash cards for Ginny. It seems funny now. Listening to the two girls talk, I can't tell their speech apart. Your "hands off" approach with Ivie hasn't done her any harm. Why do you suppose there's not more of a difference between the two girls' language?"

> Why was it, from Chomsky's point of view, that neither the language-enriched nor the naturalist approach was superior in helping the two girls develop language?

5. Use the Internet to search for sites related to Noam Chomsky and his theory. You can use his name as well as key words (internal and bridge principles). How do the Internet sites differ in terms of completeness and accuracy of information? What were the best sites you found? What problems did you encounter? What were some of the worst sites (and why)?

SUGGESTED READINGS

More about the Theory

Chomsky, N. (1975). *The logical structure of linguistic theory*. London: Plenum.

Chomsky, N. (1983). Noam Chomsky's views on the psychology of language and thought. In R. W. Rieber (Ed.), *Dialogues on the psychology of language and thought* (pp. 33–63). New York: Plenum.

Critical Reviews

G. Harmon (Ed.) (1974). *On Noam Chomsky: Critical essays*. Garden City, NY: Anchor Press.

Piaget, J. (1984). Schemes of action and language learning. In M. Piatelli-Palmarini (Ed.), *Language and learning: The debate between Jean Piaget and Noam Chomsky*. Cambridge, MA: Harvard University Press.

7 Ainsworth and Infant Attachment

Preview Questions

What assumptions underlie Ainsworth's theory?

What is her problem of study, and how do her research methods match the problem?

What are the theory's internal and bridge principles?

What change mechanism accounts for development?

Why is Ainsworth's theory a member of the endogenous paradigm?

What are the important contributions and criticisms of Ainsworth's theory?

How does Ainsworth's theory of infant attachment rate for scientific worthiness, developmental adequacy, and pedagogical usefulness?

Historical Sketch

From Past Roots, a New View of Infancy

The controversy that surrounded Darwin's *Origin of Species* intensified twelve years later with his publication of *The Descent of Man* (1871). But in academic circles, the dispute between science and religion had subsided by the beginning of the twentieth century. By that time, it was widely held in academic arenas that *Homo sapiens* had evolved from other species, and as a consequence was fundamentally animal in nature. Consequently, human infants were also viewed in biological terms, as sophisticated animals with inborn animal needs such as nourishment, fluids, and safety. Failure to meet any of these needs would result in injury and possibly death.

Mothers were considered essential to infants' health, because they were the ones who secured these biological needs. Deprive an infant of its mother, and it will suffer because its biological needs would go unmet. Whatever else mothers might contribute to their infants was viewed, at that time, as "nice" or perhaps even "helpful." But any contribution beyond biological needs was considered peripheral and unnecessary. No doubt mothers loved their babies as much then as now, but mother love was thought to fulfill their own motives, not the infants'.

This picture of infant needs remained unchanged until the middle of the twentieth century when two major breakthroughs occurred that irreversibly changed our understanding of human infants. Although each of these breakthroughs reflects complex and sometimes subtle issues, we summarize their important elements here.

Harry Harlow and Maternal Deprivation.   At Cornell University, Harry Harlow was conducting research in comparative psychology, the use of animal experiments to draw inferences about human nature. Harlow's specialty was infant rhesus monkeys, and his work during the 1950s and 1960s became landmark studies in developmental psychology. His findings were both surprising and unexpected. First, he discovered that infant monkeys exhibited a clear preference for a cloth-covered over a wire-mesh surrogate mother, even though both surrogates fed the infant through an artificial nipple embedded in the torso (Harlow, 1958). Moreover, when separated from its wire or cloth surrogate and placed in a strange situation, only the cloth-raised infants were comforted by the reappearance of their surrogate (Harlow & Zimmerman, 1959). Since both surrogates had provided food and nutrition (essential biological needs), there was no way at the time to explain these differences. After all, Harlow could not argue that rhesus monkeys have a "need" for cloth-covered surrogates.

Second, Harlow also raised infant monkeys in a metal isolation chamber so he could judge the effects of "motherless" rearing. Social isolation had profound effects. It produced highly unusual social behaviors, with severity correlated with the length of the infant's isolation. Infants isolated a short time quickly recovered and lived normal adult lives; those isolated for prolonged periods of time suffered lifelong difficulties in adjusting to the social life of the monkey colony. A few of the long-isolated females later became pregnant, but as mothers, their behavior was wholly abnormal and sometimes even abusive to their own infants (Harlow & Harlow, 1962). By the end of the decade, Harlow was convinced of the importance of some type of infant–mother connection, but his comparative data (monkeys to humans?) limited the claims he could make about the nature of that relationship (Harlow, 1971). The picture of infant needs could not be completed without the independent investigations of John Bowlby.

John Bowlby and Maternal Attachment.   John Bowlby was born in London in 1907 to a father who served as surgeon to King George V. As one of six children, young John was sent to boarding school at age 7. He later attended the Royal Naval College but served no military service before enrolling at Cambridge for premedical studies.

Renewed attention to the role of mothers came after World War II, when the World Health Organization was faced with developing a policy for the treatment and care of war orphans throughout the world. This organization turned to John Bowlby, the noted English psychoanalyst. Bowlby studied the problem, and with contributions from Mary Ainsworth and others, he published a report: *Maternal Care and Mental Health* (Bowlby, 1951). In it, he framed the origins of mental *ill* health this way:

. . . what is believed to be essential for mental health is that the infant and young child should experience a warm, intimate, and continuous relationship with his mother (or permanent mother-substitute) in which both find satisfaction and enjoyment (Bowlby, 1951, p. 11).

Bowlby underscored the debilitating effects of maternal deprivation, noting that in the extreme, it may "entirely cripple the capacity to make relationships" (1951, p. 12). To be clear, Bowlby's report challenged two important assumptions about infants' needs still widely held only half a century earlier. First, many were skeptical of his claim that young children need a continuous relationship with a permanent caretaker, since it was clear that others could easily ensure that children's basic biological needs were met. Second, many of his colleagues scoffed at the notion that infancy should be a time of fun and "enjoyment" (a nonbiological idea), and they criticized his notion that separation from a mother may have lasting consequences. Ironically, it was fairly typical in those days for a newborn to be separated from its mother at birth and cared for by a hospital's nursery staff for up to a week while the mother recuperated from the rigors of childbirth.

Nearly two decades later, Bowlby laid out a theory of attachment and its supporting evidence in three volumes, *Attachment and Loss* (1969, 1973, 1980). In this work he revolutionized our thinking about an infant's basic needs and showed that developmental disruption can occur through separation, deprivation, and bereavement. In retrospect we now understand that Bowlby had formulated an explanation for both Harlow's findings with rhesus monkeys (the importance of socialization) as well as a whole new body of data that had been compiled about infant–mother interactions. His explanation of *attachment* was received as both convincing and authoritative, so infant attachment was added to the "list" of *essential infant needs*.

Relatively late in his career Freud had recognized the importance of the mother to an infant's development. The attachment relationship, he believed, was unique because it established for a whole lifetime the very first and strongest love object and served as a prototype of all later love relationships (Freud, 1938). But while Bowlby argued against the Freudian "orality" (pleasure object) interpretation of attachment, he recognized its importance and attributed its source to an innate survival instinct.

Bowlby died in 1990 at age 83 and was buried on the Scottish island of Skye in a remote hillside grave (Holmes, 1995). While his first ideas about infant–mother "enjoyment" had been scorned, his death was followed by international conferences commemorating his contributions to developmental psychology (Goldberg, 1995). Where Freud had shown the importance of studying childhood, Bowlby had drawn our attention to the importance of infancy. Today, Mary Ainsworth occupies the fertile ground of infant attachment and is the world's leading authority on this aspect of development. She extended Bowlby's work by supplying new theoretical precision and carefully validated methods of collecting data.

Mary Ainsworth: Infant Attachment and Secure Bases

Mary D. Salter Ainsworth is recognized with Bowlby as the cofounder of attachment theory (Bretherton, 1995). Her research extends his into a well-defined research methodology matched to theoretical specifics about the infant's attachment formation. Ainsworth's theory of attachment represents one of the modern advances in developmental psychology and is summarized here as another example of the endogenous paradigm.

Mary D. Salter was born in 1913 and spent most of her youth in Toronto, Canada. She later attended the University of Toronto, where she earned her B.A., M.A., and Ph.D in developmental psychology in 1939. Following graduate school, she was commissioned in the Canadian Women's Army Corps and attained the rank of major. Following World War II, she flew to London to interview for a job that required special training in child development. Ironically, she was interviewed by John Bowlby, was awarded the position, and spent the next three years conducting home observations of infants and their mothers (Ainsworth & Marvin, 1995). But during this work, she remained unconvinced that Bowlby's ideas about attachment were fundamentally correct.

In 1953–1954, Ainsworth moved to Kampala, Uganda, to undertake the first longitudinal studies of mother–infant interaction during the first year of life. Observing infants and their mothers in a natural environment, she discovered that with different experiences, some babies organized their attachment behavior in different ways. As a result of this discovery, she experienced a total, irreversible paradigm shift, from thinking in psychoanalytic terms to viewing infant–mother interactions in terms of innate strategies suggested earlier by Bowlby. "It is the *presence* of the care giving figure rather than the care giving behavior that is essential for the attachment to develop" (Ainsworth & Marvin, 1995, p. 14).

Mary Ainsworth spent much of her later professional life teaching psychology at the University of Virginia. She died in 1999 at the age of 82.

Structural Components of Infant Attachment Theory

Assumptions

To a large extent, the assumptions underlying Ainsworth's theory of infant attachment can be traced to the work of John Bowlby. We recount them here because they are the underpinnings of her own work.

First, human infants exhibit an instinctive species "propensity" to seek proximity and contact. Attachment has been naturally selected in the evolution of humans because it serves a biological function: protection from predators and dangerous situations. The propensity is termed attachment, in contrast to "attachment behaviors," and refers to the actions that promote proximity, contact, and communication.

Second, attachment is a *social* rather than a biological phenomenon. Although the infant is motivated by instinct to form an attachment, its maintaining of close proximity to an attachment figure is not a derivative of feeding. Rather, attachment anchors curiosity and exploration to a secure base for extending oneself into the world. Establishing this base is a social instinct.

Third, attachment is instinctively proactive and needs no external motivation. "From birth onward an infant behaves in ways that promote proximity and contact with others" (Ainsworth, 1973, p. 2). A crying baby brings others to pick it up; smiling attracts others to come closer; and looking and searching bring others within the visual field. Such behaviors are precursors to attachment. But beginning at approximately 6 months of age, these precursors become organized into a behavior system: attachment to a primary caretaker. *The primary caretaker may or may not be the mother, and it may or may not be the person who spends the most time with the infant.* In addition, multiple caretakers may be recipients of the attachment bond. While external stimuli and people may "trigger" this instinct, much like events may "trigger" the language faculty in Chomsky's theory, such stimuli are not the motivating influence.

Fourth, the attachment behavior system is *goal corrected.* Just as a drivers monitor their position and turn the steering while when rounding a corner, so too do infants monitor the presence and proximity of an attachment figure. If crying, for example, does not produce a caretaker's return, an infant will try other behaviors in its system, such as crawling to find her. Sometimes, it will follow the mother or primary caretaker from room to room to maintain proximity.

Problems for Study

Phenomena to Be Explained. While Bowlby had studied the development of disorders that result from maternal separation, Ainsworth (1973) undertook a systematic study of variation among normal infants and their caretakers (usually but not always mothers). Central to her work (Ainsworth, 1973, 1979) was the idea that a sensitive, responsive caregiver is critically important to the development of a secure (versus insecure) attachment bond during infancy. Consequently, understanding the contributions of the caretaker, within the context of the infant's "propensity" to maintain proximity, became the primary problem of study.

Methods of Study. The Strange Situation (Ainsworth & Wittig, 1969) is a standardized, broadly validated method for studying infant–caretaker attachment patterns. It appears to work equally well whether caretakers are mothers, fathers, or other adults, but it is appropriate primarily for infants between 11 and 18 months of age.

The infant–caretaker dyad is brought into a novel environment, typically a strange playroom with several toys, and left alone for three minutes for exploration. Next comes a carefully orchestrated schedule of events. A stranger enters the room, speaks with the caretaker, then engages the baby in play. The caretaker leaves the room and returns after ten seconds to three minutes (depending on the infant's level of distress). The caretaker first greets the baby from the door, then proceeds to pick it up. The stranger leaves the room. After three more minutes, the caretaker leaves the baby alone, and the stranger returns. The caretaker then returns, greets the baby from the door, and picks it up.

Throughout the Strange Situation, the baby's responses are observed and recorded for later analysis. The Strange Situation has proven to be robust, and many replication studies of the theory have been carried out using this methodology (Colin, 1996). This situation produces a variety of infant responses. Some infants, for example, become upset with the disappearance of the caretaker. Others, initially upset, readily adapt and calm themselves. Still others display no outward signs of anxiety over the caretaker's disappearance.

The Strange Situation is a remarkable method of study that actually promoted theory development. The situation enabled Ainsworth to catalogue infant reactions, and these later served as the basis for classifying the types of attachment described in the section on Bridge Principles.

Internal Principles

Activators and Terminators.   Attachment defines our first social relationship, and because of this, it acts as an internal model for forming later relationships with others (Grossmann, 1995). In this way, all subsequent relationships adapt and extend from the original prototype: infant–caretaker attachment. To explain the development of attachment, Ainsworth incorporates two important internal principles. The first controls the *appearance* of attachment behaviors, while the second describes *four phases* in their development.

Attachment is linked to **activators** and **terminators** that control when the behavioral system is turned on and off (Colin, 1996). *Activators* for human infants include a variety of stimuli such as strange situations, frightening events, cold, distance, time lapse since the last contact with the attachment figure, and rebuffs from other children or adults. Note that situations such as these are associated with greater risk to the infant. If attachment is connected to protection, then it makes sense that the absence of the attachment figure would activate attachment behaviors.

Terminators are connected to the attachment figure. Proximity or contact typically terminates attachment behaviors. However, *the intensity of attachment behaviors varies according to the perceived threat,* so different terminators may be necessary in different situations. The two examples described in Sandlot Seminar 7.1 illustrate this point.

It is important to note here that while emotions may accompany activators and terminators, they are not the cause of attachment. Rather, it is the infant's cognitive appraisal of a situation that activates and terminates attachment.

Phases of Attachment.   Ainsworth (1973) maintains that attachment behaviors develop in four phases. The first two phases describe "precursors" of attachment behavior. In Phase 3 the infant becomes genuinely attached to the primary caretaker. In the fourth phase, the infant's attachment behaviors reflect the goal-correcting quality of mutual relationships. A time line showing these phases is displayed in Figure 7.1.

Sandlot Seminar 7.1

Baby Meets "Strangers"

Situation 1. Mrs. Brown sits in the waiting room of her pediatrician's office browsing through a magazine. Sitting on the floor nearby is 15-month-old Hillary playing with a toy. Periodically Hillary looks up to make visual contact with her mother. After a few minutes, a nurse opens a door and walks into the waiting room. She greets Mrs. Brown, smiles at Hillary, and walks over to chat briefly with the mother. Hillary continues playing with her toy while watching her mother talk with the nurse.

Hillary's attachment system has been activated, but the perceived threat has not been overwhelming. Visual contact with the mother has been a sufficient terminator for her in this situation.

Situation 2. That evening, Mr. and Mrs. Brown are all dressed up and sitting in their den. They are going out to dinner and awaiting the arrival of their baby-sitter, a teenage girl from up the street. Hillary is sitting on the floor near her mother examining her favorite picture book. The doorbell rings and Mr. Brown gets up to answer the door. Hillary immediately looks up, then rises and scrambles up the couch and onto Mrs. Brown's lap. Soon thereafter, Mr. Brown and the baby-sitter walk into the den. Mrs. Brown rises, puts Hillary on the floor, and begins to talk to the baby-sitter. Hillary clings to her mother's left leg, gripping her dress tightly with both hands.

Rather suddenly for Hillary's liking, the baby-sitter approaches, reaches down, and picks her up. Hillary immediately begins to kick and strike with her hands. The baby-sitter holds on tightly, and Hillary begins to cry. Mrs. Brown, all too familiar with this situation, talks soothingly to Hillary, but Hillary holds out her arms to her mother and continues crying. Mrs. Brown gives Hillary a kiss, and Hillary responds by grabbing her mother's hair. Untangling the tiny fingers, Mrs. Brown retreats to gather up her coat, retrieves Hillary's favorite "blankie," and together she and Mr. Brown head out the door.

Hillary continues crying and fussing until the baby-sitter sets her down on the floor. Then Hillary sets about walking through the house sobbing (perhaps searching for her mother?) and tightly clutching her "blankie."

All parents are familiar with this second situation. The intensity of Hillary's attachment behaviors are the result of the perceived threat of the "strange" baby-sitter. The sitter's approach was direct, and she restrained Hillary from maintaining contact with her mother. The "blankie," while soothing, was hardly an adequate substitute for the attachment figure.

Phase 1. Undiscriminating Social Responsiveness. Phase 1 occurs during the infant's first two to three months. Infants orient to prominent environmental features, particularly other people. They display various signaling and active proximity-promoting behaviors. However, they do not discriminate between different human adults who may respond to their overtures.

Phase 2. Discriminating Social Responsiveness. Between three and six months, infants continue to orient and signal, but they differentiate between familiar and unfamiliar

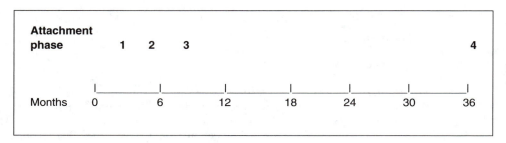

FIGURE 7.1   Time line of four phases of attachment.

adults. They also begin to differentiate their responses to adults depending on their familiarity.

Phase 3. Active Initiative in Seeking Proximity and Contact.   The median age for attaining Phase 3 is seven months (Ainsworth, 1973). Following, approaching, and clinging reveal active proximity and contact seeking by the infant. Infant signals are no longer merely expressive or reactive, but rather are intended to evoke a response from the primary caretaker. It is during this phase that an infant will display separation anxiety and attachment behaviors if temporarily abandoned in the Strange Situation.

Phase 4. Goal-Corrected Partnership.   This more-advanced form of attachment occurs sometime around 3 years of age and involves infant–caretaker reciprocity. Seen from the infant's point of view, behaviors that attempt to intervene with and modify the caregiver's plans are emitted. For example, when the phone rings, a toddler may glance up at the mother (or father) or even grasp her clothing in order to prevent her from leaving to answer the phone. In response, the mother may pick up her child or make a comment to redirect the child's attention.

With the formation of infant attachment, an important component of the personality has been established. Subsequent interactions with others will, to some extent, reflect the qualities of this first significant relationship. For example, once established, this level of attachment is remarkably persistent and can endure

> an extraordinary amount of absence, neglect, or abuse—although these adverse conditions are likely to affect both the quality of a child's attachment relationship and his subsequent personality development (Ainsworth, 1973, p. 13).

Bridge Principles

Ainsworth discovered that infant attachments differ in quality, not simply in amount. Moreover, attachment develops gradually (through the four phases) and only becomes clearly displayed as infants approach twelve months of age. Every attachment is driven by the same *instinctive* "program." However, the dynamics of infant–caretaker interactions can modify the program's output and result in different types of attachment display.

Secure Attachment.   Infants use caretakers as a secure base for exploration, both at home and in the Strange Situation. Securely attached infants explore freely in the caretaker's presence, check on her periodically, and restrict their activities in her absence. These infants exhibit varying degrees of stress during caretaker absence, but quickly revert to exploration following her return.

Avoidant Attachment.   Avoidant infants explore but display little interest in their caretaker's whereabouts and exhibit only slight distress over her departure. Significantly, they tend to "snub" and ignore the caretaker upon her return.

Ambivalent/Resistant Attachment.   These infants exhibit extreme distress when separated from their caretakers and display impoverished activity during their absence. When the caretaker returns, they seek immediate contact. However, they do not settle down easily or return to exploratory play.

Disorganized/Disoriented Attachment.   Subsequent research with the Strange Situation led Main and Solomon (1986, 1990) to discover a fourth category: *disorganized/ disoriented attachment*. Infants with this organization scheme do not appear to have any strategy for coping with caretaker absence or return. Often they will not even approach the caretaker upon her return, as if they are either frightened or confused.

Ironically, the *amount* of distress shown during separation (previously considered to reflect the strength of infant–caretaker relationships) is not related to secure attachments (Ainsworth, 1973). Infants in each of the four attachment categories range from mild to extreme distress during separation. Consequently, the critical factors in the quality of attachment are the infant's behaviors toward the caretaker prior to her absence and following her return.

The quality of babies' first relationships is a critical influence on their later social development. On the basis of their attachment bond, infants establish beliefs about themselves, models of expectation, and rules for organizing and accessing expectations. Equally important, they organize their behaviors around these models:

> The models based on the infant's actual experiences are then carried into new situations and new relationships. Unknowingly, the child helps recreate the blessings or woes of his or her first relationships (Colin, 1996, p. 16).

These early models establish a developmental "trajectory," a range of *flexible possibilities*, rather than a fixed, determined course for later social interactions. For example, a securely attached infant would typically feel secure in forming new friendships in later childhood and adolescence. Conversely, an insecurely attached infant might feel insecure in reaching out to others for new friendships over the same time span. However, the early attachment bond does not predetermine a later result. Some securely attached infants may still experience later childhood or adolescent anxiety, and some insecurely attached infants may grow into confident, outgoing individuals who readily make new friends in all types of situations.

Developmental theories typically take several decades to work their way into "modern" child-rearing practices. The "common sense" of one generation may not correspond with that of a later generation, at least in part because of the influence of new theories consumed by the public through media presentations and popular magazines. See if you can spot the theoretical underpinnings for the common sense described in Sandlot Seminar 7.2.

Sandlot Seminar 7.2

Bringing Up Baby

A young couple were expecting their first child. Amid their excitement about all the possibilities of parenthood, they were a little concerned about their abilities to handle the impending responsibilities and duties. It was with mixed feelings that they accepted an offer of help from their neighbor, a very experienced mother, Jill, who was also a bit too nosy. "Don't worry, kids; I'll only help out until you feel comfortable," Jill said.

After the happy couple brought their bundle of joy home, Jill pitched right in, even helping with occasional mundane chores such as cleaning, diapering, cooking, and sometimes bathing. The couple realized that they could never have made it without Jill's help. According to her, it was all a matter of "common sense," yet even with her expertise, things had begun to grow a little awkward. It had been two weeks now, and Jill was still spending a couple of hours each day "helping out." The couple wondered aloud to each other, "Don't you think she's starting to get in the way?"

Then one evening an event triggered the couple's liberation. The father, a graduate student at the university, had read several reports on infant attachment (Ainsworth, 1967, 1973) that emphasized the importance of responsiveness to infant's signals, and this information seemed to support the parents' habit of attending to their baby whenever it cried. Following dinner one night, as the baby began its evening "fussing," Jill barred the doorway to prevent the mother from attending to her infant. "Haven't you learned yet," she scolded the young mother, "that if you keep this up, you're only encouraging her to fuss more often! She'll never learn to sleep by herself if you start spoiling her so young! The only way to teach her not to fuss is to leave her alone. Just let her cry. She'll go back to sleep and learn that fussing will get her no attention. Believe me, you don't want to have a fussy baby, do you?"

The next day the young parents suggested that the neighbor read some of Ainsworth's studies, which were readily available in the father's study. After reading one article, the neighbor said, "I think you kids need to be on your own now. I don't know about these newfangled ideas, but I can sense that I'm not really helping any more. Just do what I've taught you, and you'll be fine." With that the young couple thanked the neighbor for all her sage advice, walked her to the door, and bid her goodbye. With a sigh of relief, they began their lives as parents.

1. Why did reading about Ainsworth's work help this couple convince Jill that it was time for her to leave?
2. Was Jill really helping with her advice about infant "fussing"? How can you tell?
3. Does consistently intervening with or picking up a crying infant increase the likelihood of producing a fussy child later on? How do you know? What would Ainsworth say?

Change Mechanisms

Instinct, one's innate genetic program, supplies the infant with a species "propensity" for "goal-corrected" behavior. This instinct is the origin of the infant's *need* for contact and proximity. There is no requirement of any additional motivating force to propel infant attachment, because the underlying genetic program makes the attachment behavioral system intrinsically *proactive*. Although environmental situations determine whether the behavioral system is activated or terminated, they do not in any way impact the genetic propensity underlying infant attachment. In short, attachment is a human characteristic, and given the appropriate nurturing, infants will bond with their primary caregiver.

Instinct is universal, but nurturance (caring) acts as a trigger mechanism that determines not whether attachment will occur, but what its qualities will be. The unique qualities of the permanent caregiver's nurturing style are the source of individual differences in quality of infant attachment.

Explaining Human Development: The Research

Because Ainsworth's theory of attachment is limited to such a restricted domain of human phenomena, the research base of support has likewise been restricted to various claims about attachment. A centerpiece of the theory is the role of the permanent caretaker (typically but not always the mother) in providing day-to-day care. Of particular importance is the "sensitivity" of the caretaker in responding to an infant's signals. Some caretakers, for example, respond primarily to verbal expressions, while others are equally well attuned to verbal, facial, and postural signals. Ratings of maternal sensitivity have been consistently linked to secure attachments in the Strange Situation for American families (Isabella, 1993), German families (Grossmann, Grossmann, Spangler, Suess, & Unzner, 1985), and economically disadvantaged, often single-parent families (Egeland & Farber, 1984). In addition, infantile security is associated with prompt responsiveness to distress (Del Carmen, Pedersen, Huffman, Bryan, 1993) and with warmth, involvement, and responsiveness (O'Connor, Sigman, & Kasasi, 1992). More recently, a review of thirty-four studies of infant attachment concluded that "the mother appears to play a more important role than the child in shaping the quality of the infant–mother attachment relationship" (van Ijzendoorn, Goldberg, Kroonenberg, & Frenkel, 1992, p. 840).

If sensitivity leads to secure attachments, do other variations consistently produce other types of infant attachments? Apparently so. For example, Sagi, van Ijzendoorn, Aviezer, Donnell, and Mayseless (1994) found that among Israeli kibbutz infants, those sleeping at home were much more likely to form secure attachments than infants who slept communally. In addition, disorganized attachments were more common on kibbutzim than they were among middle-class, North American families.

Infants who suffer documented maltreatment consistently develop "anxious" (disorganized/disoriented) attachments to their primary caregivers significantly more often than other infants (Carlson, Cicchetti, Barnett, & Braunwald, 1989;

Crittenden, 1985, 1988). At the extreme, Crittenden (1988) reports that abused and neglected infants were more likely to form avoidant/resistant attachments, but those who suffered only abuse were more than twice as likely as those who had been simply neglected to form this type of attachment. Finally, infants whose primary caretaker suffered from a chronic, severe psychiatric problem, such as schizophrenia or clinical depression, were also far more likely than others to exhibit disorganized/disoriented attachments (Teti, Nakagawa, Das, & Wirth, 1991).

Contributions and Criticisms of Attachment Theory

Contributions

New View of Infant Needs.   Ainsworth has irreversibly changed our view of infancy. Recall that a century ago, it was widely understood that infants were essentially animals whose biological needs must be met. In that regard, mothers were considered essential to infant development because it was they who secured these needs. At the turn of the twenty-first century, we have finally come to understand that the human infant also has genetically determined *social needs* that must be met for healthy development to occur. This progress in our understanding of infancy is due substantially to the precision of Mary Ainsworth's work in following the lead of John Bowlby.

Carefully Validated Methodology.   Ainsworth's design of the Strange Situation, together with its careful validation over the years, has provided developmental psychology with a new, robust research methodology. This robustness allows the Strange Situation to be adapted by investigators conducting research in different cultures without fear of invalidating their findings. Today, the Strange Situation is one of the most useful investigative strategies used in conducting infant research.

Beyond Infant Attachment.   Ainsworth's description of the scope and sequence of infant attachment formation has led some researchers to examine how the quality of early attachment influences later relationships over the course of the life span (Harris & Bifulco, 1991; Parkes, 1991).

Criticisms

Inadequate Theory.   T. G. R. Bower (1977) has argued that Ainsworth's theory of attachment overlooks important developmental phenomena, most particularly language development. Specifically, Bower views attachment not as a function of parental availability and warmth but as a function of communication rapport with *objects,* whether human or inanimate. He traces the rise in attachment to the absence of communication rapport with strangers, just as the decline in attachment intensity between two and four years of age corresponds to the infant's development of socialized language.

Rajecki and Lamb (1978) have made similar arguments in their criticism of Ainsworth's work. They note, for example, that infants of abusive parents still form attachments to their parents. Moreover, it is not at all unusual for animal young and human infants to form attachments with inanimate objects (e.g., blankets, plastic cups) that would fit within the four types described in Ainsworth's bridge principles.

Research Problems.   Reed and Liederman (1983) have attacked Ainsworth's work on methodological grounds. For example, the studies that originated her work were done on small, narrow samples of infants. Harwood, Miller, and Irizarry (1995) have shown, for example, that infant responses to the Strange Situation are subject to culturally specific shaping, and that some cultures may prefer "secure" forms of attachment while others prefer "insecure" forms. In addition, Kagan, Kearsley, and Zelazo (1978) maintain that Ainsworth's Strange Situation, the procedure used to assess infant attachment, is not as reliable a measure as originally thought. They wonder, for example, if infant temperament rather than attachment might be what the Strange Situation measures.

Evaluation of Attachment Theory

Scientific Worthiness

Ratings of the scientific worthiness of Ainsworth's theory are shown in Table 7.1. The basis for our judgments are described next.

Testability.   It is important to note that Ainsworth is not a mentalist to the same degree as Freud or Erikson. Her work emphasizes the measurement of infant behaviors in well-defined situations. At the same time, she does appeal to internal mechanisms, the *activators* and *terminators* discussed earlier, to explain her observations about the development of attachment, and some criticism of her methodology has occurred (e.g., see Eyer, 1992). These considerations lead us to rate her theory medium for its testability.

TABLE 7.1   **Ratings of Attachment Theory for Scientific Worthiness**

Criteria	High	Medium	Low
Testability		X	
External Validity	X		
Predictive Validity		X	
Internal Consistency	X		
Theoretical Economy			X

External Validity.   Ainsworth's theory is rated high for its external validity. This rating is based on three considerations. First, she limits her explanation of human development to the single domain of infant attachment, which is a small, though well-defined scope of study. Second, a substantial amount of empirical research supports her contentions. That is, in terms of the variety and formation of infant attachments, the theory provides a pretty good match with reality. Third, however, there is also some research (see Criticisms section) that suggests that Ainsworth's theory gives an incomplete account of infantile attachments.

Predictive Validity.   Only two decades old, Ainsworth's theory is relatively new in developmental psychology. While many confirmatory studies have been undertaken, the theory has seldom motivated the kinds of predictions that lead to new discoveries. Although our rating may well change in the future to reflect such discoveries, at this time we rate it medium for its predictive validity.

Internal Consistency.   Ainsworth's theory of infant attachment is a good example of the endogenous paradigm. Instinct is the fundamental mechanism underlying attachment. Instinct is triggered by the caretaker's nurturing, which in turn accounts for individual differences in infant attachment. This basic explanation is consistently applied by Ainsworth, so her theory is rated high for its internal consistency.

Theoretical Economy.   We rate the theory low for its theoretical economy. This rating is based on two considerations. First, the field of explanatory power is limited to the development of four types of infant attachment. To be sure, this is an important contribution, because attachment becomes the springboard for future social development. However, it is but a small part of the totality of human nature. Second, recall that four predisposing assumptions underlie the theory: the infant's instinct to seek proximity, its *social* nature, its proactive motivation, and its goal-correctedness. Overall, then, Ainsworth's theory explains a limited domain of human development, given her assumptions about the newborn.

Developmental Adequacy

Table 7.2 summarizes our ratings for the theory's developmental adequacy. An interesting comparison can be made between Ainsworth's ratings and those given to the endogenous theories of Freud and Erikson in earlier chapters.

Temporality.   Although limited in scope, Ainsworth's theory clearly explains the development of attachment as a function of time. Newborns display no attachment. One-year-olds display a significant degree of attachment. And, according to Ainsworth, our first attachment serves as a prototype for later social relationships. Consequently, attachment theory passes the criterion of temporality because it explains changes in development over time.

Cumulativity.   Reexamining the section on Phases of Attachment (an internal principle), we note that each phase builds on the previous one. In addition, some

TABLE 7.2   Ratings of Attachment Theory for Developmental Adequacy

Characteristic	Rating
Temporality	Yes
Cumulativity	Yes
Directionality	Yes
New Mode of Organization	No
Increased Capacity for Self-control	No

researchers (Harris & Bifulco, 1991; Parkes, 1991) have argued that relationships in adulthood and old age build on attachments formed during infancy. For these reasons, the theory passes the criterion of cumulativity.

Directionality.   Attachment develops over time, and later phases build on earlier ones. More importantly, the four phases of attachment form a fixed, irreversible *sequence,* an important quality of directionality. Infants simply can't go back to an earlier phase to revisit their social experiences, nor can they skip phases or travel through them in mixed order. This irreversibility implies that attachment is directional, so it passes this criterion.

New Mode of Organization.   With the acquisition of attachment, the infant establishes a base for exploration, and different infants exhibit different types of exploratory behavior depending on the quality of their attachment. At the same time, there appears to be no developmental milestone, universal among all infants, that suggests that new, unifying, holistic rules have come into being. In fact, there are few underlying similarities among infants who are securely attached, avoidant, or disorganized in their attachment. As used by biologists, there is little in Ainsworth's attachment theory that suggests that new mode of organization is a common outcome of the attachment process. Consequently, the theory fails this criterion.

Increased Capacity for Self-control.   There is a sense that increasing independence from caretakers is associated with the development of attachment. This consideration notwithstanding, the theory's primary change mechanism is instinct, which infants cannot control. So in the important sense of developing attachment, the theory does not pass this developmental criterion.

Pedagogical Usefulness

Table 7.3 on page 180 shows our ratings for the theory's pedagogical usefulness. Recall from Sandlot Seminar 7.2 that parents can and do use attachment theory to provide general guidance for their child-rearing practices. Ratings for specific elements of practicality are described next.

[handwritten margin note:] New mode of organization → But basis of other relationships

TABLE 7.3   Ratings of Attachment Theory for Pedagogical Usefulness

Criteria	High	Medium	Low
Interpretability	X		
Versatility			X
Availability		X	
Guidance		X	

Interpretability.   Attachment theory deals with infant development within the context of the Strange Situation and its extrapolations to real life. Given this limited scope, it should not be surprising that the theory introduces relatively modest amounts of theoretical jargon. In short, it uses few uniquely defined theoretical concepts, so we have rated the theory high for its interpretability.

Versatility.   A theory's versatility is directly proportional its scope and span of explanation. A broad theory that explains much about human nature over the life span will tend to have high versatility. In contrast, a more narrowly focused theory (its scope) covering a small range of years (its span) such as Ainsworth's will tend to have low versatility. Although recent initiatives reflect an interest in extrapolating from infant attachment to forms of attachment across the life span (e.g., Harris & Bifulco, 1991; Parkes, 1991), even these efforts are not intended to rewrite Ainsworth's theory about infants. Without belaboring the point, we have rated the theory low for its versatility.

Availability.   Parents are very interested in their infants' development, and pediatricians and developmental psychologists are well aware of that interest. Consequently, Ainsworth's work has often been translated and written about in popular magazines and parenting books readily available at the local library or bookstore. Most textbooks in developmental psychology provide at least some treatment of Ainsworth's theory, and professional journals have published empirical and theoretical studies of infant attachment dating back to the 1970s. All these sources support the medium ranking for availability we give Ainsworth's theory of attachment.

Guidance.   Although criticisms have been raised about the universality of "secure" forms of infant attachment, the theory does seem to provide helpful guidance for parents and nursery care workers. For example, recall the graduate student's experience with the neighbor in Sandlot Seminar 7.2. His interest in raising a securely attached infant led him to pick up and comfort a "fussing" baby instead of ignoring it as the neighbor had recommended. While Ainsworth does not suggest what parents should do in every situation, she is clear that qualities caretakers exhibit in nurturing will be reflected in the infant's quality of attachment. Consequently, we rate the theory medium for its guidance.

Summary Points

1. John Bowlby originated the idea of infant attachment and described it in broad, theoretical terms. Mary Ainsworth's research led to the discovery of different forms of attachment and specific phases in its development.

2. Ainsworth makes four basic assumptions about the newborn. The infant exhibits an (1) instinctive propensity to seek proximity and contact, and these actions reflect (2) social rather than biological needs. Because attachment is instinctively (3) proactive, it needs no external motivation. Finally, the infant's attachment behavior system is (4) goal-corrected.

3. The primary problem of study for Ainsworth is to understand the unique contributions of the caretaker in triggering the infant's attachment system. The Strange Situation, used for infants 11 to 18 months of age, is the preferred research method for studying attachment.

4. Ainsworth's theory utilizes two internal principles. First, activators and terminators control when the attachment behavioral system is turned on and off. Second, attachment is acquired through four phases, which begin with undiscriminating social responsiveness and end with goal-corrected infant–caretaker partnership.

5. There is one bridge principle in attachment theory, and it is the four distinct types of attachment: secure, avoidant, ambivalent/resistant, and disorganized/disoriented.

6. The change mechanism in Ainsworth's theory is instinct, the species' "propensity" for "goal-corrected" behavior. However, while instinct is universal, nurturance (caring) acts as a trigger mechanism that determines not whether attachment will occur, but what its qualities will be.

7. Because Ainsworth's theory is still relatively new in developmental psychology, it is difficult to gauge its enduring contributions. It is clear that Ainsworth has crafted an image of infant social needs that transcend the biological/animal needs model of humans prevalent at the start of the twentieth century. In addition, the Strange Situation is a unique research methodology that assesses infant development in ways that previously could only be surmised. In addition, new efforts have begun to examine implications of infant attachment on adult and later-life relationships. At the same time, however, the theory has been criticized for not explaining how infants attach to inanimate, nonnurturing objects. Recent concerns have also been raised about the theory's cultural relativism, perhaps an artifact of small samples and narrowly defined research strategy.

8. Ainsworth's theory was rated medium for its criteria of scientific worthiness and developmental adequacy. Except for the theory's low versatility (due to its narrow scope), it was judged moderately high for its practicality.

P R O B L E M S   A N D   E X E R C I S E S

1. Visit an airport, shopping mall, supermarket, park, or other busy place with lots of people. See if you can find young mothers or fathers with their infants. Observe them for a while. Note how the infant behaves if the caretaker disappears out of sight or if the distance between them suddenly increases. How frequently do infants move away from and glance back at their caretaker? How do infants act with the approach of strangers? If you observe enough infants, can you discern any age-related changes in behavior toward caregivers and strangers? Do your observations support or disagree with Ainsworth?

2. Spend an early morning and late afternoon at a local day-care center. Talk with your course instructor about the need to incorporate "informed consent" into your activity. Observe from a distance ten children whose parents drop them off in the morning and later return to pick them up after work. Did these children handle the separation from their parent in the same or different ways? Did some display greater separation anxiety than others? What types of anxious reactions did the children display? How did these same children handle the reappearance of a parent at the end of the day? Do your observations support or disagree with Ainsworth's theory of attachment?

3. With a group from your class, work as a team to study infant stranger anxiety. You will need to find a location where parents and infants (aged 4 to 12 months) are readily available, and you will need to do some planning to ensure "informed consent" for your study. Some possible locations to check out might be a neighborhood park, a pediatrician's waiting room, and a local day-care center that takes in infants. Record to the nearest whole month infants' ages. Then approach each infant (you are the stranger here) and attempt to pick it up and talk to it. Do some infants show no fear of strangers? What age is the youngest infant who shows stranger anxiety? What age is the oldest infant to show no stranger fear? Can you find an age-related pattern to the onset of stranger anxiety? Do your results support or disagree with Ainsworth's theory of infant attachment?

4. What is the best way to deal with a "fussy" baby? Using your understanding of Ainsworth's theory, write a one- or two-page essay describing how you would handle a fussing baby. Then, talk with your own mother. What was the conventional wisdom of her generation for dealing with fussy babies? Finally, talk with your grandmother. How did her generation deal with fussy babies? Do different generations have different approaches? If so, try to figure out why the common sense of dealing with fussy babies changes from one generation to another.

5. Use the Internet to search for sites related to Mary Ainsworth and her theory. You can use her name as well as key words (internal and bridge principles). How do the Internet sites differ in terms of completeness and accuracy of information? What were the best sites you found? What problems did you encounter? What were some of the worst sites (and why)?

SUGGESTED READINGS

More about the Theory

Ainsworth, M. D. S., & Wittig, B. A. (1969). Attachment and exploratory behavior of one-year-olds in a strange situation. In B. M. Foss (Ed.), *Determinants of infant behavior* (pp. 111–136). London: Methuen.

Colin, V. L. (1996). *Human attachment*. New York: McGraw–Hill.

Isabella, R. A. (1993). Origins of attachment: Maternal interactive behavior across the first year. *Child Development, 64,* 605–621.

Research Reviews

van Ijzendoorn, M., Goldberg, S., Kroonenberg, P., & Frenkel, O. (1992). The relative effects of maternal and child problems on the quality of attachment. *Child Development, 63,* 840–858.

Critical Reviews

Eyer, D. E. (1992). *Mother–infant bonding: A scientific fiction*. New Haven: Yale University Press.

PART THREE

The Exogenous Paradigm

Theories in the exogenous paradigm view development as the product of environmental causes. Theories in this paradigm vary in how much internal processes and states influence development, but they agree that external forces are the dominant causal influences to be taken into account. The primary focus of these theories is explaining how new behaviors are learned.

Skinner's impact on psychology is legend. Using laboratory animals, he attempted to derive laws of learning that were sufficiently accurate, robust, and generalizable to explain how new behaviors were learned. He led us far beyond S $\longrightarrow$ R (stimulus–response) reflex psychology in showing how organisms naturally emit behaviors with no controlling, eliciting stimulus. And he shows us how a behavior's future occurrence is controlled by the consequences it produces. These consequences may be reinforcing, in which case a behavior increases, or they may be aversive and cause the behavior to decrease. Since consequences, which are environmental events, are seen as the immediate, tangible causes of learning, Skinner's theory of operant conditioning is a good paradigm case for the exogenous perspective.

Building on Skinner's work, Albert Bandura has concentrated on the social determinants of learning. In his earlier work, he focused on the role of observational learning in which no overt reinforcement occurred. His later work provides an interesting contrast with Skinner's, because Bandura believes that both behaviors and the cognitive processes underlying them must be explained. Bandura's interest in cognitive processes has extended radical behaviorism into what today is termed "cognitive behaviorism." Chapter 9 describes his theory as an example of the exogenous paradigm because, in his view, cognition originates in society and in experience.

Over the past two decades, the work of Lev Vygotsky has received increased attention among developmentalists. This Russian psychologist did most of his work following the Russian Revolution, so Marxist ideas permeate his interpretation of development. Chapter 10 presents an introduction to Vygotsky's theory and the "zone of proximal development."

8 Skinner and Operant Conditioning

Preview Questions

What is the difference between operant and respondent conditioning; between methodological and radical behaviorism?

What assumptions underlie operant conditioning?

What types of phenomena does operant conditioning attempt to explain and what methods are used to study these phenomena? What important values of science are reflected in these methods?

What are the theory's internal and bridge principles?

What change mechanism accounts for learning?

Why is operant conditioning a member of the exogenous paradigm?

What are the most important contributions and criticisms of the theory?

How does the theory rate on scientific worthiness, developmental adequacy, and pedagogical usefulness?

Historical Sketch

Burrhus Frederic (B. F.) Skinner was born in 1904 in Susquehanna, Pennsylvania. His life began and ended with remarkable stability. In his childhood he built things, from wagons and sleds to gliders and perpetual motion machines (which did not work). He spent his whole childhood and adolescence in the house in which he was born and spent all twelve school years in the same building. After high school came Hamilton College in upstate New York, where young Skinner graduated Phi Beta Kappa in English literature. Two years of trying to write fiction and poetry with "nothing to say" prompted him to abandon the efforts (Skinner, 1976). In 1928 he enrolled at Harvard for graduate work in psychology, a field in which some momentous ideas were brewing.

Skinner (1967) recalls that upon entering this new field of study, he established for himself a rigorous daily schedule of study, meals, classes, laboratories, and library work beginning precisely at 6:00 A.M. and ending precisely at 9:00 P.M. He claims that this schedule was maintained for nearly two years, during which time it was seldom broken for movies, dates, or concerts. After completing his dissertation, Skinner spent a year working on the central nervous system at the Harvard Medical School, followed by a five-year stint of animal experiments in a subterranean laboratory.

Skinner moved to Minnesota to teach introductory psychology during World War II. During that time he worked on a program of training pigeons to guide missiles with far greater precision than was possible with "pilotless" missiles. In spite of the project's technical success, it never really got off the ground. Today the idea of using dolphins to deliver bombs to military targets is not so strange, but in Skinner's day, the idea of using pigeons in such a manner was dismissed.

Skinner had a first, then a second child, Deborah. Near the end of the war, Deborah's birth prompted Skinner to design a labor-saving device for his wife that would mechanize infant care. In addition, he also wanted to free up baby Deborah's movements without the restraining layers of diapers and clothing. Skinner described the invention of this Air Crib (*not* the same as a laboratory Skinner box) in a *Ladies Home Journal* article. The Air Crib was a large, oblong box with a cloth floor over wood. The cloth could be replaced to keep the child's environment clean. The Air Crib contained a panel for each entry and exit and a window for two-way viewing. It is perhaps with a touch of satisfied irony that he (Skinner, 1967) later reported his first daughter Julie's use of an Air Crib with her own first child.

In 1945, Skinner packed up his Air Crib, his *Walden Two* manuscript, and his family and moved to Indiana University to become chairman of the psychology department. Two years later he delivered the William James Lectures at Harvard, an occasion that prompted an invitation to become a permanent member of the psychology faculty there. Returning to Harvard the following year, Skinner maintained a prodigious pace of research and publication, always trying to advance the science of human behavior. When he retired in 1974, he was somewhat saddened that so many people still misunderstood operant conditioning as just another form of the stimulus–response behaviorism that reigned over academic psychology in the first half of the twentieth century. During his own lifetime Skinner became one of the giants in American psychology, and his death in 1990 left a rich legacy of innovative ideas about human nature.

Behaviorism

The central tenet of behaviorism is that individuals should be studied only in terms of observable characteristics. This attitude is displayed in two identifiable forms: **methodological behaviorism** and **radical behaviorism**. Methodological behaviorism assumes that inner experiences (thoughts, ideas, feelings) do not exist because they are unobservable. Radical behaviorism takes the position that mental entities may exist and may be studied with techniques such as introspection, but such techniques cannot lead to objective verification and thus cannot produce scientific knowledge. Skinner considers himself a radical behaviorist because his ideas about conditioning are very different from those of early behaviorists.

The Legacy of Ivan Pavlov

The experiments of Ivan Pavlov comprise one of psychology's founding landmarks. Pavlov distinguished between innate (unconditioned) and learned (conditioned) reflexes. Through a technique he called *conditioning*, he demonstrated a remarkable feat: that a dog's salivation response to food could be trained to occur in the presence of previously neutral stimuli—a bell, a light, and a whistle. He reasoned that unconditioned reflexes occur naturally as part of an organism's constitution; that is, a dog spontaneously salivates when food is placed near its mouth. The food acts as an unconditioned stimulus (*US*) since it automatically elicits salivation as an unconditioned response (*UR*). When a neutral stimulus, say a bell, is paired a number of times with the introduction of food, the bell itself will come to elicit the salivation response. In this manner, what was initially a neutral stimulus (the bell) becomes a conditioned stimulus (*CS*) that produces a conditioned response (*CR*). The key components of Pavlovian conditioning, termed *classical conditioning* today, are diagramed in Figure 8.1.

Pavlov advanced the scientific analysis of behavior through carefully documented experiments, and he demonstrated that some kinds of responses could be systematically trained to new stimuli. However, classical conditioning has an inherent shortcoming: It cannot explain how new, entirely novel behaviors are learned.

Note that with classical conditioning a conditioned response always originates in an unconditioned response. This means that the *UCR* and the *CR* are always very similar responses, differing primarily in amount rather than type. Potential *CR*s would have to already exist as *UCR*s, since entirely new *CR*s cannot emerge out of thin air. While classical conditioning accounts for the fact that already existing responses can be conditioned to new stimuli, it does not tell us how novel responses are acquired. Sandlot Seminar 8.1 on page 190 contains three examples of behavioral change, but only two reflect respondent (classical) conditioning.

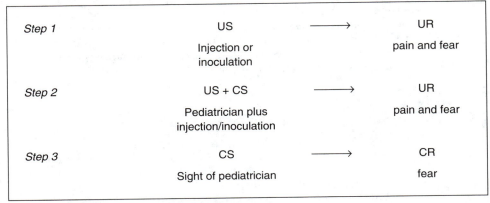

FIGURE 8.1   Elements of classical conditioning.

Sandlot Seminar 8.1

Examples of Conditioning

Episode 1. Mr. Thomas has a new puppy. Each morning he takes the eager and excited puppy for a brief walk outside while he gathers up his newspaper. Sometimes the puppy has "accidents" in the house. This makes Mr. Thomas angry, and he is determined to house-break the puppy. Whenever he spots an "accident," he grabs his puppy and a rolled-up newspaper. He holds the puppy near the "accident" while pounding the newspaper sharply on the floor and saying in a sharp voice, "No! Bad doggy!"

One morning Mr. Thomas notices his puppy happily scampering out the door in the morning. After retrieving his newspaper, Mr. Thomas walks back toward the house. The puppy interrupts her sniffing and suddenly begins to cringe and shake with fear. The closer Mr. Thomas approaches, the more his puppy cowers away from him. What has happened? Why?

Episode 2. Emma Howard is the proud mother of a brand new baby boy, Ethan. The morning following his birth, she attempts to breastfeed him, but he seems frustrated and fussy because he can't get much milk. Emma thought breastfeeding would be easy, since it was all a matter of simple biology. When released from the hospital two days later, Emma is surprised to learn that Ethan has lost weight. Concerned about his health, she talks to her pediatrician, who calms her with this advice, "Don't worry. This is very normal. Just keep trying. Every mother goes through this. You and Ethan will be just fine."

A month later, during Ethan's checkup, the pediatrician inquires about Emma's breastfeeding. She replies, "You were right. Ethan and I are doing great. But now it seems almost out of control. There's not a day goes by that something doesn't set off my milk flowing, and I end up leaking. Sometimes it's a little embarrassing. Why does this happen?"

What should the pediatrician tell Emma?

Episode 3. Tomiko Hakuta has learned how to answer the phone, and she runs to answer it whenever it rings. Her parents are pleased with her growing social skills, but they are troubled by unsolicited phone marketers who call during the evening meal and interrupt the family's conversation. One evening a new rule is instituted: No phone answering during dinner. At first, it is hard for Tomiko to ignore the phone. When it rings, she pleads to answer it, but her parents remain steadfast; no phone answering during dinner. To help Tomiko make this transition, the parents encourage her to ignore the phone and praise her when she continues the conversation while the phone is ringing.

A month later the phone rings during dinner, but no one notices. Conversation with Tomiko flows uninterrupted by the intrusion. What has happened?

Think About

All three examples describe a change in behavior. However, only two of the examples can be explained by classical conditioning.

1. Can you tell which ones? How can you tell?
2. In which example(s) does the individual actually control the target behavior? In which one(s) is the behavior automatic? Is this a hint about which kind of conditioning has occurred? Why?
3. Why can't respondent conditioning account for behavioral change in one of the examples? What key elements seem to control behavior that must be taken into account?

Roots of U.S. Behaviorism

After World War I, John B. Watson founded U.S. behaviorism when he argued that psychology, following on Pavlov's advances, would become truly scientific only by studying behavior that is objectively measurable, predictable, and controllable (Watson, 1919, 1924). A methodological behaviorist, Watson rejected such mentalistic concepts as motivation, will, intention, and thought because these internal states could never be objectively verified.

Watson initially took an extreme exogenous position in maintaining that he could train healthy infants to become whatever he might select for them.

> Give me a dozen healthy infants, well-formed, and my own specified world to bring them up in and I'll guarantee to take any one at random and train him to become any type of specialist I might select—doctor, lawyer, artist, merchant-chief and, yes, even beggar-man and thief, regardless of his talents, penchants, tendencies, abilities, vocations, and race of his ancestors. (Watson, 1928, p. 82)

In later years Watson softened this position somewhat but still maintained a strong behaviorist orientation. For example, his interest in emotional *behavior* led him to study the conditioning of fear in the now famous experiment with "little Albert," an 11-month-old infant he conditioned to fear a white rat (Watson & Raynor, 1920). Using classical conditioning, Watson paired a loud noise with the presentation of a white rat. After a number of paired presentations, Albert became afraid of the rat, and whenever he saw it, he cried and tried to crawl away. Watson later discovered that Albert also feared a rabbit, a dog, a tuft of cotton, and a Santa Claus mask—all furry objects that had not been previously feared. Watson's original and influential writings firmly established behaviorism as a central theme of U.S. psychology.

Following in Watson's footsteps, Edward Thorndike observed that a cat placed into a cage would learn how to undo a simple latch in order to retrieve a piece of fish placed outside its cage. This observation was remarkable primarily because of its implication. Thorndike argued that no conditioned response was involved in the cat's learning to escape, since there was no conditioned stimulus for that behavior. Rather, the cat appeared to "want" to get at the fish, and its goal-oriented behavior led to an efficient method of escape for procuring the fish. To explain this type of behavior, Thorndike (1933) proposed the *law of effect*, which holds that responses increase or decrease in likelihood as a function of the effects that they produce. Some effects make the previous response more likely to occur in the future; others make responses less likely.

Thorndike had discovered a new type of learning not accounted for by classical S———→ R (stimulus–response) conditioning. The law of effect explained how the *likelihood* of a previously existing response could change as a function of response consequences. However, even this novel idea could not explain how a new response not already part of an organism's repertoire could have been acquired. That breakthrough came in the work of B. F. Skinner.

Operant Conditioning

Skinner skillfully employed Thorndike's law of effect and showed how it could explain the acquisition of new behaviors. Skinner called his approach *operant* conditioning to emphasize that organisms operate on their environment, thereby producing consequences. Operant conditioning is *not* a form of classical $S \longrightarrow R$ conditioning. It is a fundamentally different view of behavior.

Skinner (1950) has claimed that he has not really written a "theory" at all; rather, he describes his own work as statements about empirical relationships or "laws." Notwithstanding this objection, Skinner's inclusion in this book is justified on at least three counts. First, he is opposed only to axiomatic theories that place their hypotheses and propositions in logical priority over the empirical facts needed to support them. He is not opposed to theories carefully built on descriptions and generalizations of empirical facts (Smith, 1994). In fact, it is this latter type of "theory" that he proposes. Second, operant conditioning contains all three of the components that define a developmental theory (see Chapter 1). Third, behavioral researchers have treated Skinner's work as if it were a theory, using the "laws" and methods of operant conditioning to test, predict, and control behavior change.

Historically, operant conditioning was the dominant theory in American psychology between World War II and 1970, but today behavior analysis exists alongside many other theoretical frameworks that occupy developmental psychologists. In retrospect, we understand today that well-known controversies surrounding some of Skinner's books (*Beyond Freedom and Dignity, Walden Two*) have been due more to misconceptions than to careful analyses of his beliefs. In Skinner's view, behavior is shaped by its effects. Human nature is *not* puppetlike in responding to stimuli (that is classical, not operant conditioning). Rather, Skinner sees the organism as acting on the environment; its actions produce consequences. Over time, consistent consequences come to control the behavior that produces them. Simply put, people behave in certain ways because those ways tend more often than not to produce favorable consequences. Skinner's operant conditioning reflects the exogenous paradigm because consequences that control behavior originate in the external environment.

Structural Components of Operant Conditioning

Assumptions

Operant conditioning makes three fundamental assumptions about the infant. First, it is born with a set of species-specific reflexes. Second, the infant is born with a *tabula rasa*, "blank slate" mind. The blank mind does not remain empty for long, because the infant immediately comes into contact with the world through direct perception and action. Third, and most important from Skinner's point of view, the infant is essentially active; that is, its nature is to emit or give out responses, *not* to simply react to specific stimuli. According to Skinner (1953), "Operant conditioning may be described without mentioning any stimulus which acts before the response is made . . . Operant behavior, in short, is *emitted*, rather than *elicited*" (p. 107).

Problems for Study

Phenomena to Be Explained. Skinner believes that the primary task of psychology is to discover laws that relate organismic behavior to environmental forces. More specifically, behavioral theory attempts to explain how behaviors are learned and how past experiences are related to future actions (Schwartz & Lacey, 1982). Ideally, such an explanation would include quantitative terms for predicting and controlling behavior. The theory does not attempt to account for mental or emotional phenomena unless expressed as behavior.

Skinner acknowledges four basic factors that are important in deriving the "laws of operant conditioning:" behavior, past learning (the habits and inhibitions already acquired), the present conditions, and genetic endowment. In the behaviorist's agenda, present conditions comprise a general category termed **stimulus variables** because they are the array of possible consequences that control behavior. Past learning encompasses the general category of **intervening variables**. Intervening variables cannot be directly observed or measured, but they can be controlled for in several ways: raising laboratory animals in identical environments from birth, keeping careful records of past behavioral acquisitions and their associated stimulus events, and conducting experiments that control situational elements in order to test predictions about causes and their effects on behavior change. Finally, genetic endowment defines restrictions on the range of possible behaviors that could be acquired (e.g., we cannot train humans to fly like a bird or smell like a bloodhound). This fourth factor generally does not figure into operant conditioning but rather functions as a "given" or fixed context within which research is carried out.

It is helpful to examine the behaviorist agenda in more detail in order to highlight the scientific values found in the study of human behavior. Operant conditioning attempts to describe, in precise quantitative terms, the relationship between independent (stimulus) variables and dependent (response) variables. In operant conditioning terms, *a stimulus is a consequence*, and stimulus variables are defined as *measurable* characteristics of physical consequences. A response, in turn, is measured in terms of its effect on the organism's environment. In Skinner's terminology, an **operant** is a general class of responses. For example, raising a hand to be recognized, saying "Yes, sir" in response to a question, and swimming laps in the nearby pool are all examples of operants. The general category is an operant. Each specific occurrence (every behavior) of an operant is a *response*.

The world of operant conditioning is a complex place. But researchers make the task of performing experiments considerably easier by assigning important elements to one of three categories of variables. Table 8.1 on page 194 shows how variables are classified. **Stimulus variables** are the independent variables manipulated by researchers in laboratory experiments to see what effects they produce on **response variables**, the dependent variables actually measured. **Organismic**

TABLE 8.1   Categories of Variables in Operant Conditioning

Stimulus Variables	Organismic Variables	Response Variables
Consequences manipulated by the researcher	Past learning "controlled for" in an experiment	Aspects of behavior measured by the researcher
Reinforcement schedule	Habits	Response rate
Number of reinforced trials	Drives	Amplitude (strength)
Type of reinforcement	Inhibitions	Latency
Length of deprivation	Motivation	Resistance to extinction
Type of deprivation		
Reinforcement delay		
Reinforcement amount		

variables are the results of previous learning. Because organismic variables cannot be directly controlled in an experiment, they are often "controlled for" by using laboratory animals whose previous experiences and genetics have been carefully controlled. When experimental manipulations of stimulus variables produce regular, predictable, and measurable effects on response variables, a quantitative relationship or "law" will have been discovered.

Methods of Study.   For ethical and social reasons, humans are only occasionally studied directly. Instead, researchers use operant conditioning to study animals, presuming that in the long run what they learn about animal behavior can ultimately be applied to human behavior. Skinner's specialty was pigeons, animals aplenty and cheap to raise. To study them in an experimental situation, Skinner designed a small, self-contained chamber (the "Skinner box"). The chamber allows an animal ample space for limited movement but is not so large that the animal spends much time exploring it. The sides of the chamber are opaque and contain few distracting stimuli. Each chamber contains a control panel with feed box, lever (for rats) or response key (for pigeons), and an on–off light to signal when a response will produce a consequence. The light does not "elicit" the response; it simply signals the availability of a consequence.

Initially, animals don't know what the light means, but because they are rewarded for responding only when the light is turned on, they learn to match their responses to the presence of the signal light. The lever or response key is connected to an electronic switch that records each response on a *cumulative record*. The cumulative record is a graphic display of some measurable element of responses (its strength, frequency, etc.) that has been emitted over a period of time. Figure 8.2 shows a cumulative record of a first-grader who has received verbal praise each time she raises her hand before speaking.

With the rat, the electrical switch in the Skinner box provides an objective way to record its behavior. Personal judgment and opinion are held strictly in

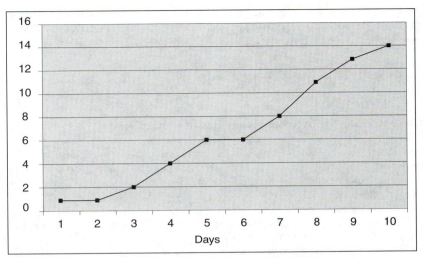

FIGURE 8.2 Cumulative record of hand raising (the target operant) in a first-grader over a ten-day period.

check, so the resulting cumulative record shows precisely the quantitative change in behavior for a given period of time. In the laboratory, it makes little difference to a behaviorist what response actually presses the lever; all that matters is that the lever is pressed and that this fact has been recorded on the cumulative record. All behaviors that result in lever pressing are equivalent; in this way they constitute an *operant* or general class of responses. In contrast, the classroom teacher's record of her first-grader's hand raising introduces the possibility of human error due to inattention or forgetting, but it will contain (presumably) only hand raising and not other extraneous behaviors.

In order for researchers to perform experiments efficiently, responses should ideally be relatively quick (so that many responses can be recorded) and require little expenditure of energy (so that the individual does not get fatigued). For scientific reasons, researchers attempt to control variables systematically. They determine which operants to reinforce, when to deliver reinforcement, and what type and amount of reinforcement to administer. Note that several qualities—objectivity, quantitative measurement, and controlled experiments—are built into the behaviorist's methods of study when carried out in the laboratory. These qualities are the hallmarks of modern science.

Internal Principles

Contingent Reinforcement. The principle of **contingent reinforcement** accounts for why some behaviors and not others are acquired. Infants, children, and adults emit behaviors, and some of these produce reinforcing consequences. The principle of *contingent reinforcement* holds that a reinforcing stimulus is contingent (dependent) on the individual emitting a particular operant. Sandlot Seminar 8.2 contains two scenarios that demonstrate how contingent reinforcement works.

Sandlot Seminar 8.2

Child Rearing, Clean Rooms, and Operant Conditioning

Scenario 1. Nine-year-old Caleb lives in a neighborhood filled with lots of other boys to play with, and these playmates enjoy the same kinds of games he does. After school, ten to twelve guys would meet him in a vacant lot next to one of their homes to plan the afternoon's activities.

Caleb's mother prides herself on a clean, well-ordered home. She is also tuned into Caleb's social network and understands how much enjoyment her son gets playing with his pals. Her immediate problem is getting Caleb to clean up his messy room, but long-term, she also wants to instill in him a sense of well-ordered cleanliness. After school one day, she and Caleb made a joint visit to his bedroom where she explained a new daily routine designed to make Caleb accountable for a clean room. The rule was simple. Each day after school, she would inspect his bedroom. If it was clean, he was allowed to play with his pals until dinner time.

The next few days were troublesome. Caleb was angry at having to stay indoors to clean his room. Moping around, he took so long to clean up and make his bed that by the time he finished, it was nearly dinner time. After several days spent grudgingly cleaning instead of playing, Caleb began a new strategy. After school, he hurried home, got a quick snack, and ran up to his room to pick up toys and dirty clothes, make his bed, and call for his mother's inspection. It worked! Within a few minutes, he was outside playing. In fact, Caleb found the new routine fairly painless. By keeping his room clean, there was only a few minutes' work to do on a day-to-day basis. Over time, the mother's bedroom inspections became less frequent and eventually disappeared altogether. Caleb's room stayed clean, and he was meeting his allies every afternoon in the vacant lot for play.

When Caleb was 11 years old, his family moved to a new neighborhood in the suburbs where homes were farther apart. Moreover, the only children his age were girls. It was not at all like his old neighborhood. This new one was boring. It didn't take Caleb long to figure out that there was no real need to keep his room clean. After all, what was the benefit? As his room began to deteriorate, Caleb's mother began to scold him about his untidy bedroom, but without play pals, Caleb seemed disinterested. It was clear to Caleb's mother that the new neighborhood situation called for a different strategy, but what was she to do? As a last resort, she sat Caleb down in a straight-back wooden chair at the dinner table and began to lecture him on the virtues of a clean room. The lecture went on . . . and on . . . and on, in a way only a mother can deliver. After what seemed like an eternity, the lecture finally ended, with the mother asking, "Now do you understand how important a clean room is?" An exhausted Caleb replied, "Yes, Mother. I do!" He immediately went to his bedroom. All during his cleaning, he kept thinking to himself, "Wow, I never want to go through that again."

Over the following weeks and months, Caleb's room would occasionally show signs of impending clutter. But all Mother had to do was ask, "Do we need to have the clean room lecture again?" Immediately Caleb would march to his room and clean it up.

1. In what way did Caleb's mother use contingent reinforcement? Can you identify elements such as a discriminative stimulus, positive reinforcement, and negative reinforcement?
2. What elements of Caleb's behavior reflect operant conditioning in action?
3. In Scenario 1, explain how positive and negative reinforcement had the same effect on Caleb's bedroom cleaning.

Scenario 2. Jeremy's mother, also desirous of an uncluttered home, has taken a different approach. When his room is not tidy, she gives Jeremy extra chores to do, which he hates. Then she confines him to his room where he must spend the afternoon doing extra homework, which he also hates. On these days, he cannot leave the house to play with friends. However, if his room is clean at inspection time after school, he can go outside and play.

It did not take Jeremy long to learn that a tidy bedroom avoids extra chores and the dreaded afternoon homework. His room is clean, clean, clean, and his mother is justifiably proud of her tidy home. There were occasional times when Jeremy accidentally forgot to empty his trash or pick up a wayward sock, and on such occasions, his mother would immediately remand him to an afternoon of sweeping, taking out garbage, and practicing multiplication facts. There were no excuses and no second chances, because Jeremy's mother believed that her child must learn and accept the consequences of his misbehavior. She was consistent in her use of extra chores and homework as punishment to ensure Jeremy's compliance with her clean-house expectations.

When Jeremy's mom and dad took a week's vacation to get away for some time to themselves, Grandma and Grandpa moved in to maintain the home. Everything seemed to go smoothly, except Jeremy's bedroom. It quickly became a mess. Grandma continually asked him to clean it up, and he promised that he would when he had time. When his mother returned from her vacation, she was aghast at Jeremy's room and asked, "What in the world happened in here? Your room was perfect when we left. Now it's a disaster!" She concluded that she was a better parent than her own parents, because Jeremy did what he was supposed to do when she was around.

1. How does Scenario 2 illustrate operant conditioning?
2. What are the immediate and long-term effects of punishment on controlling behavior?
3. If the punishing agent, Jeremy's mother, is viewed as a discriminative stimulus, what happens when that stimulus is no longer present? What are the long-term implications for Jeremy's cleaning habits?

Contingent reinforcement occurs *after* a behavior has been emitted. The consequence (stimulus variable) is contingent on the occurrence of an operant behavior, hence its name—contingent reinforcement. Contingent reinforcers account for a wide variety of learned behaviors—how we walk down the street, shopping and study habits, manners, dating and driving patterns, note-taking behaviors in college classrooms, and menu selections while dining out. We emit some operants and not others because of the consequences generated by past behaviors, not because specific stimuli elicit them. The mere sight of a telephone does not, for example, automatically elicit phone-calling behavior. Rather, whether or not we decide to phone someone is based on both the present circumstances and the past consequences of our phone-calling experience.

Some events, such as the presentation of food when we are hungry or the availability of fluids when we are thirsty, are reinforcing on their first presentation. These are called **primary reinforcers** because their effect is direct and need not be conditioned. However, primary reinforcers are not necessarily limited to food and water; they also include brain stimulation, the opportunity to exercise, and tactile stimulation.

A different order of stimulus, such as a mother's face, money, kissing, and watching television may initially be neutral, but with certain kinds of experiences, they may acquire their own reinforcing effects (Kling & Schrier, 1971). Events of this type, termed **secondary reinforcers,** are far more prevalent consequences of everyday behavior than are primary reinforcers. For example, the reinforcing effects associated with talking on the phone, reading a letter, and receiving public recognition are all acquired secondary reinforcers. Because secondary reinforcers acquired their effect during the individual's past experiences, their effects may be more limited than those primary reinforcers. For example, social approval and teacher praise are two effective secondary reinforcers for middle-class students, but they often do not have the same effect on some minority students.

Some people confuse Skinner's operant conditioning with earlier forms of behaviorism, such as respondent conditioning. As Table 8.2 illustrates, there are a number of fundamental differences between operant and respondent conditioning.

The Discriminative Stimulus.   Special attention should be paid to understanding the **discriminative stimulus** in operant conditioning. This stimulus signals the conditions under which some behaviors will be reinforced and others will not. This stimulus is *not* the reinforcing effect (the consequent stimulus) and thus cannot bring about changes in behavior. Nor is this stimulus the same stimulus found in classical conditioning. Unlike classical conditioning, a discriminative stimulus does *not* automatically prompt a response. Rather, when reinforcement occurs in the

TABLE 8.2   Differences between Operant and Respondent Conditioning

	Operant Conditioning	**Respondent Conditioning**
Also called	Instrumental	Pavlovian, classical
Symbolism	R ———→ S behaviorism	S ———→ R behaviorism
Type of behaviorism	Radical behaviorism	Methodological behaviorism
Organismic tendency	Proactive	Reactive, reflexive
Reinforcement	Follows operant	No reinforcement
New behaviors learned through	Shaping	Cannot explain
Responses	Emitted	Elicited

presence of or following its presentation, the discriminative stimulus will come to be associated with the behavior that produces the reinforcing effect (Skinner, 1953). Recall in the Methods of Study section that a Skinner box contains an on–off light. This light, when turned on, signals the availability of reinforcement. It is the discriminative stimulus in this situation. The relationship between a discriminative stimulus, an operant behavior, and a reinforcing stimulus is shown schematically in Figure 8.3. Note that in operant conditioning, the operant precedes the reinforcing stimulus. This type of R ——→ S behaviorism is very different from traditional S ——→ R behaviorism.

Over time and with repeated trials, an *association* is formed between the discriminative stimulus, an operant, and its reinforcing consequence. Associations among these three elements are built up over time, and that is why our behavior is so regular. We tend to act the same way in similar circumstances because we have a history of being reinforced for those operants.

Shaping. Even with contingent reinforcement and discriminative stimuli, new operant behaviors do not suddenly appear from nowhere. They must be learned through a process called *shaping*. This process has two components. The first is differential reinforcement, which means that some behaviors but not others are reinforced. The second component is successive approximation, which refers to the progression of reinforcement for operants that gradually and incrementally approximate the target behavior. For example, children do not automatically put their toys away after playing with them. In fact, if parents were to wait for that to happen in order to reinforce it, they'd have a very long wait indeed. Fortunately, such a behavior can be shaped. First, a discriminative stimulus needs to be established. This can be done by announcing, "It's time to put the toys away." Given that situation, reinforcement could be administered whenever the child approaches a toy. That increases the frequency of approaching toys after the verbal signal. Then reinforcement can be withheld until the child approaches and picks up a toy, after which reinforcement is administered. When picking up toys has been established, reinforcement may again be withheld until the child picks up a toy and turns toward the shelf where it goes. This routine may be repeated until the child learns successively to approach a toy, pick it up, turn toward its shelf, walk there, and place the toy in its place.

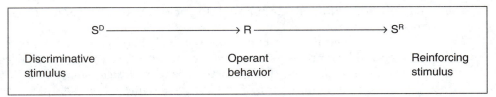

FIGURE 8.3 Relationship between discriminative stimulus, operant behavior, and reinforcing stimulus.

Megan's father taught her how to ride a bicycle by using shaping. Her past learning included mastery of the tricycle, so her dad wanted to use that behavior as a basis for teaching her the new behavior—bicycle riding. To do this he started with a set of training wheels on the bicycle so that its handling simulated her tricycle. By raising the training wheels a small amount every few weeks, Megan's dad gradually shaped her movements, balance, and coordination. By summer's end her bicycle riding behavior had become sufficiently competent to remove the training wheels.

Bridge Principles

Schedules of Reinforcement.   Consequences can be administered according to different patterns called **schedules** or **contingencies of reinforcement**. Each schedule has specific effects on the operant that is acquired. *Continuous* reinforcement is the administration of a stimulus after an operant, such as when a toddler is praised each time he uses the potty. Continuous reinforcement produces faster learning than any of the other schedules, but behaviors that are continuously reinforced are also the easiest to "forget."

Intermittent reinforcement occurs when stimuli are administered either on the basis of a ratio (reinforcing only a certain percentage of behaviors) or on the basis of a time interval (reinforcing only after a certain duration has elapsed). A *fixed ratio* schedule administers reinforcement every *nth* behavior, as when a fourth-grader receives one star on each fifth correct answer on her homework. Fixed ratio schedules produce high response rates. With *variable ratio* reinforcement, the stimulus is administered *on the average* of every *nth* behavior. For example, such a schedule might describe a toddler trying to hit a nail with a hammer. While missing most of the time, the child makes irregular contact with the nail (number of swings varies between reinforcements) *an average* of once every seventh swing.

Interval reinforcement parallels ratio schedules, except that it applies to elapsed time rather than number of behaviors. Interval reinforcement is typically used when long, continuous behavior is involved, such as jogging, studying for a test, or fishing. Interval schedules reinforce a response when a predetermined interval of time has elapsed (Kling, 1971). With a *fixed interval* schedule, reinforcing stimuli are administered every *nth* period of time during which a behavior is performed. For example, a teacher could reinforce his students once every five minutes that they spend "on task." With a *variable interval* schedule, time intervals vary from one reinforcement to the next according to *an average* of one reinforcer per time period. Figure 8.4 illustrates the technical differences between ratio and interval reinforcement schedules.

Ratio schedules tend to produce relatively high response rates when the ratio is small and lower responses rates when the ratio of rewards to behaviors becomes large (Ferster & Skinner, 1957). Exactly what constitutes "small" and "large" ratios is a function of both the organism and the situation. For example, a ratio of one hundred button presses for one dollar in reinforcement would likely produce many responses from a teenager hankering for video machine change. The same rein-

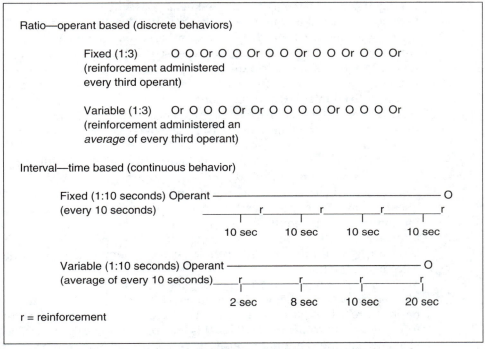

Ratio—operant based (discrete behaviors)

Fixed (1:3)   O O Or O O Or O O Or O O Or O O Or
(reinforcement administered
every third operant)

Variable (1:3)   Or O O O Or Or O O O O Or O O O Or
(reinforcement administered an
average of every third operant)

Interval—time based (continuous behavior)

Fixed (1:10 seconds) Operant ———————————————————— O
(every 10 seconds)
   10 sec   10 sec   10 sec   10 sec

Variable (1:10 seconds) Operant ————————————————— O
(average of every 10 seconds)
   2 sec   8 sec   10 sec   20 sec

r = reinforcement

FIGURE 8.4   Schematic of ratio and interval reinforcement schedules.

forcement and response ratio would produce virtually no responses from either a migrating pigeon on its way south or from a corporate executive fighting a takeover bid for her company. Additionally, fixed ratio schedules tend to produce post-reinforcement pauses as well as some complete interruptions in responding (Ferster & Skinner, 1957). This pattern can be avoided by using variable schedules that produce consistently high responding. Interval schedules produce a very steady, stable response rate with relatively few pauses or bursts of responses (Schwartz & Lacey, 1982) and are useful in maintaining continuous behaviors such as doing homework and raking leaves.

Random schedules administer reinforcement in a completely haphazard, inconsistent manner. It is relatively easy to get computers to generate completely random reinforcement schedules in today's modern experimental laboratory. Because there is no systematic pattern to administering reinforcement, the individual cannot anticipate when a particular behavior will result in a consequence. For this reason, behavior that has been acquired using random reinforcement is difficult to extinguish. This may explain why teachers sometimes find it so difficult to extinguish undesirable behaviors in their students and why some people become addicted to gambling.

When it is desirable that an individual acquire a new behavior, the schedules of reinforcement can be used to shape and maintain the desired behavior. One usually begins by shaping the desired behavior using continuous reinforcement to produce the fastest learning. When the behavior has been learned, it can be maintained with the least effort using intermittent reinforcement. One can establish complex routines in which two or more schedules operate simultaneously and independently, each tied to a different operant. Such procedures are called *concurrent schedules*. Children, for example, may receive a kiss each night from their mothers (fixed interval) and occasional gifts when they have been especially good (variable ratio). One's particular circumstances determines the schedule to be preferred. In the natural world, our lives are led in the context of concurrent reinforcement schedules.

Extinction is the administration of no reinforcement. Its effect is the elimination of a behavior because it disrupts the response–consequence association. Of course, some behaviors are more difficult to extinguish than others and, consequently, may require longer extinction. Ironically, the fact that an undesirable behavior continues to be emitted when a parent or a teacher steadfastly provides no reinforcing consequences is a sure signal that either (a) concurrent reinforcement is occurring or (b) the behavior was learned or maintained under a random reinforcement schedule.

Sandlot Seminar 8.3 illustrates real-life examples of how reinforcement schedules can be used. See if you can determine which schedule is being used in each scenario. In real life, parents are seldom aware that their behaviors may actually replicate a reinforcement schedule. This may be one reason that variable ratio, variable interval, and random (inconsistent) schedules are so common among parents.

Generalization.   Behavior that occurs in one situation will often occur in other similar situations. For example, children who are acquiring language often refer to their parents as "Daddy" or "Mommy," but they often use the same names to refer to other adults as well. Responding in this way to different discriminative stimuli (situational cues) with the same behavior is called **stimulus generalization;** different stimuli elicit the same behavior. Stimulus generalization accounts for many behaviors ranging from test and math anxieties to 5-year-old Sean's brandishing a fallen tree branch as a "sword." Stimulus generalization, the transfer of previous learning to new situations, is often a specific aim of education and a long-term goal of parents' independence training of their children.

In contrast, **response generalization** occurs when different responses occur in the presence of the same discriminative stimulus. This might be displayed, for example, when children learn to first pedal, then brake, then steer, then balance, then turn corners on a new bicycle. While the discriminative stimulus (bicycle) remains constant, these operant behaviors are learned generalizations essential to riding a bicycle. For some youth, response generalization expands to include tricks and bicycle competitions. Education also stresses response generalization as exemplified by homework lists of synonyms, homonyms, and antonyms that must be learned.

Chaining.   Discrete behaviors are often linked together into complex strings called *behavior chains*. To the delight of audiences, circus animals often display behavior

Sandlot Seminar 8.3

Identifying Reinforcement Schedules

Can you identify the reinforcement schedule used in each of the following scenarios?

Juanita's father is teaching her to play chess. She knows how the pieces move and has learned basic strategy, but her father wants her to improve. He tells her that for every game she completes with him, regardless of the outcome, she will receive $1 toward purchasing a CD in her new music club. After one month, Juanita has finished seventeen chess games with her father and received $17 from him.

Julia is an elementary school principal whose day-to-day schedule is always hectic. Still, it is important to her that her children learn to display good table manners so that they (and she) will not be embarrassed when eating out in public. While the children are generally not allowed candy, Julia keeps a ready supply of sugarless gum in her purse. This she uses for "dessert" when the children have exhibited good manners. The gum has worked well, but there are two problems. First, Julia is so busy and her schedule so erratic, she isn't always home to eat supper with her family. Second, her husband hates gum and refuses to participate in Julia's "manners building" scheme.

Sue Ellen is a freshman facing her first semester of college final exams. She wants to be very conscientious about her studying but dreads the long, uninterrupted hours of poring over her books and class notes. To break up the monotony of studying, she decides to take a snack break every ninety minutes. She is consistent in sticking to this schedule and ends up with four A's and two B's on her final exams.

Jill is a first-year, third-grade teacher. She thinks Josh, one of the students in her class, is a bit too assertive because he constantly shouts out answers without raising his hand or giving other students a chance to think of their own answers. She has talked with Josh about this behavior several times, but it appears to be beyond his control. After a short meeting with the school services specialist, Jill embarks on a new plan for Josh. Over the next three months, she studiously ignores all of his blurtings. But she also tries to call on him whenever he does remember to raise his hand. At the end of her first semester, Jill notices that Josh almost always raises his hand and seldom yells out any more.

Pebbles is a small, 2-month-old puppy that Matthew's parents have purchased under the condition that he train and take care of her. Matthew has watched dog-training videos and is attempting to mimic appropriate housebreaking procedures. In this vein, each morning before school and each afternoon upon his return, Matthew takes Pebbles outside to the backyard. He knows that she responds enthusiastically to "Good doggy! Good doggy!" by wagging her tail. So whenever Pebbles does her business in the backyard, Matthew tells her "Good doggy! Good doggy!" while stroking and petting her. After many weeks of this routine, Matthew has become lazy. Pebbles is sometimes ignored, resulting in an occasional indoor "accident." By the end of summer, Matthew is taking Pebbles outside for her morning and afternoon business only an average of five times per week, and on each of these occasions, Pebbles is reinforced with "Good doggy! Good doggy!" when she has finished.

chains, and these are among the most noticeable examples of chaining. But people also display behavior chains when they brush their teeth, take a walk in the neighborhood, change an infant's diaper, get dressed, or cook dinner. Because behaviors are linked together in almost automatic fashion, behavioral strings can be performed in a relatively smooth, integrated series of steps. However, it is the effect *produced by the last behavior in the sequence* that produces reinforcement for the chain. For example, the odor of a smelly diaper provides a discriminative stimulus for a father to pick up his son, take him to the changing table, remove his garments, take off his diaper, throw it in the waste basket, return and clean his son's bottom, pat on some powder, reach for a new diaper, put it on, reclothe the infant, and set him down off the changing table, thereby gaining reinforcement by removing a noxious odor. As Sandlot Seminar 8.4 illustrates, behavior chains may sometimes result in interpersonal conflict when reinforcers of one person's chain conflict with another's.

Sandlot Seminar 8.4

Frustration and Behavior Chains

Sometimes spouses frustrate each other because their behavior chains do not occur in the same way. Consider what might happen in such a simple task as backing a car out of the garage in order to drive to work each morning.

Husband	*Wife*
walks to garage (keys in hand) wearing sunglasses	walks to garage (purse in hand)
opens garage door	opens garage door
walks into garage	walks into garage
opens driver's car door	opens driver's car door
gets in and sits down	gets in and sits down
inserts keys and starts car	places purse beside driver's seat
places gear into reverse	opens purse to find keys
backs out while buckling seat belt	locates keys and removes from purse
turns car while pushing garage door mechanism (to close)	places keys into ignition
brakes	smoothes skirt or slacks
places gear into drive	puts on seat belt
pushes gas pedal and steers up driveway	starts car
	adjusts radio volume
Reinforcement: driving off	places gear into reverse
Elapsed time: 17 seconds	backs out of garage
	brakes
	pushes garage door closing button
	backs up while turning car
	brakes

Husband	*Wife*
	places gear into drive
	pushes gas pedal and steers
	up driveway
	stops
	reaches into purse to find
	sunglasses
	finds sunglasses and puts on
	pushes gas pedal
	stops
	changes radio station
	accelerates up driveway

Reinforcement: driving off
Elapsed time: 72 seconds

These behavior chains are rehearsed each weekday morning, and each is thoroughly ingrained. When first married, this couple used to go together on weekends to complete a list of chores. After twenty years of marriage, however, the couple seldom do chores together any more.

1. From the wife's point of view, explain why she would become frustrated if her husband drives? From the husband's point of view, explain why he would become frustrated if his wife drives.
2. Can you think of other examples of behavior chains that produce conflict between people?

Change Mechanisms

Skinner's operant conditioning provides psychology with an elegantly simple explanation for how consequences affect antecedent behaviors and how new behaviors are acquired through shaping. In this regard, the primary mechanism that propels these changes in behavior is reinforcement.

Skinner distinguishes between positive and negative reinforcement. The distinction is relatively simple: **positive reinforcement** consists of the administration of a stimulus that increases behavior, as when children are rewarded with praise, candy, or attention. **Negative reinforcement** also increases behavior but in a different manner. It denotes the release from a noxious or aversive stimulus (Skinner, 1953, p. 73). In both cases the effect is to strengthen the preceding operant behavior. For example, a child sitting in "time out" may apologize for hitting another and then be sent off to play. The cessation of "time out" acts as a negative reinforcer, the effect of which is to increase the likelihood that the child will apologize in the future when placed in "time out" for hitting. Note that with negative reinforcement, the child is already experiencing a noxious stimulus. Consequently, release from "time out" provides a favorable consequence—release from sitting alone. Sandlot Seminar 8.5 illustrates two examples of negative reinforcement.

Sandlot Seminar 8.5

Examples of Negative Reinforcement

Episode 1. Megan and Matthew's parents were pleased with themselves for creating a safe, happy, secure home in which two children had never lied, in part because there had never been any reason to. To understand the interaction that follows, it is important to know about two relevant family experiences.

First, when the children exhibited unsafe or severe antisocial behavior, they were immediately removed from the situation. Second, when these events did occur (e.g., wielding a kitchen knife, fighting), they were oftentimes followed by a loving "conversation" about the nature of the actions and why they would not be tolerated. It is significant that these conversations took place with the child sitting on the parent's lap, who, in turn, usually sat in the large, soft chair in the den.

One morning as Dad sat in his home office working, he realized that it had been quite a while since he actually heard the children. Naturally alarmed, he called out. No answer. He quickly checked the doors and bathrooms, but nothing was amiss. He called out again, but still the children didn't answer. Checking throughout the house, he found them on the screened porch playing. What he saw brought immense pride. Megan, 5 years old, was patiently teaching Matthew, $3\frac{1}{2}$ years old, how to stack blocks. Suddenly, Megan picked up a block and hit Matthew right on the side of his head. Matthew immediately burst into tears but wanted no consoling from Dad. Finding his pacifier nearby, he quickly resumed stacking blocks. But Dad had to deal with Megan.

DAD: Megan, please come with me. We need to have a conversation.

MEGAN: But, Daddy, I don't want to have a conversation now.

DAD: You must, Megan. Please come now.

MEGAN: No, Daddy. I want to play with Matthew.

(Dad picked up Megan and carried her into the den where the "conversation" chair was about to get some use.)

DAD: Megan, honey, did you hit Matthew with that block?

MEGAN (looking at her dad and saying with sincerity): Un unh, Daddy. I didn't do 'dat.

DAD (flabbergasted and realizing that dealing with this first lie would need to be discussed with Mom): Well, 'um, you need to go up to your room and play by yourself for a while.

MEGAN: OK, Daddy. Is that our conversation?

DAD (preoccupied with how to break this news to his wife): Uh, what? Yes. We're done for now.

MEGAN: OK, Daddy. (leaves humming and skipping happily out of the den)

Episode 2. Sean usually accompanies his mother to the supermarket, but today he's with his father who is helping out with the weekly grocery shopping. Moving into line at the checkout stand, Sean's father neatly positions the shopping cart midway between the magazine and candy racks. But Sean cries out from the cart as he stands up and tries to reach a brightly colored candy bar. The father quickly repositions the cart farther from the candy, but Sean reaches even farther, nearly falling out of the cart. What follows is a "full-blown" temper tantrum. Sean cries "real" tears, stamps his feet (trampling the vegetables and soup cans), and continues his precarious reaching. The father, mindful of the staring eyes of others waiting in checkout lines, eventually gives in and hands Sean a candy bar. Sean immediately ceases the tantrum and sits down quietly in the cart.

1. Who administered negative reinforcement in Episode 1? What precisely was the reinforcing stimulus?
2. Who administered negative reinforcement in Episode 2, Sean or his father? What was the reinforcing stimulus? What has Sean's father learned?
3. How do these episodes help us understand that reinforcement is defined solely by its effect rather than by a parent's intention?

Misconceptions sometimes occur in learning about positive and negative reinforcement. These are often due to our preconceived notions of what "positive" (something good) and "negative" (something bad) typically mean in social conversation. Misconceptions sometimes lead us to believe erroneously that positive (good) behaviors are positively reinforced while negative (bad) behaviors are negatively reinforced. But as used in operant conditioning, the terms *positive* and *negative* reinforcement denote logical rather than social meaning. Positive reinforcement occurs when a stimulus is added to a situation (e.g., saying "Good job!," giving a kiss, or awarding points). With negative reinforcement, an aversive stimulus, such as pain or stress, is *removed* or taken away. That is why negative reinforcement increases the likelihood of the preceding behavior, because it releases the individual from an aversive (painful) situation. Table 8.3 summarizes this situation somewhat differently.

Although it is a popular confusion, the reader should note carefully that punishment is *not* the same as negative reinforcement. These two consequences produce different effects. Negative reinforcement increases behavior; punishment temporarily suppresses it but does not eliminate the preceding operant (Skinner, 1971). Because its effects are only temporary, it would be incorrect to say that punishment produces the opposite effect of reinforcement. Punishment can consist of either the *administration* of an aversive stimulus or the *elimination* of a positive reinforcer (Skinner, 1953). For example, administration of an aversive stimulus could be used to punish misbehavior with a scolding, a scowl, or extra chores. Similarly,

TABLE 8.3   Differences between Reinforcement and Punishment

	Pleasant Stimulus	Noxious Stimulus
Added to subject's situation	Positive reinforcement	Punishment
Removed from subject's situation	Punishment	Negative reinforcement

removal of a positive reinforcer, such as taking away dating or driving privileges, could be used to punish a teenager for breaking curfew. It is important to recognize that *punishment and negative reinforcement are consequences rather than descriptions of the social value of a behavior.*

If punishment does not produce permanent cessation of behavior, why is it so widely used? There are really two answers to this question. The first reason, as Skinner has argued, is that it is actually reinforcing *to the punisher* because it produces "an immediate effect in reducing a tendency to act in a given way" (Skinner, 1953, p. 190). For example, if a parent stops a child's aversive behavior by punishing it, then he has removed an aversive stimulus, thereby providing negative reinforcement for the parent. The second reason punishment is so widely used is its immediacy, the temporary cessation of the preceding operant. Once the threat of punishment has been removed, however, the target behavior returns to its original level. That is, in the long run punishment does not actually eliminate operants (Skinner, 1953), and, consequently, it is an ineffective way to eliminate certain kinds of undesirable behavior. Moreover, it may produce unintended side effects such as fear, anxiety, awkwardness, timidity, aggression, and stuttering.

There are alternatives to using punishment that are effective in removing undesirable behaviors. One way is to reinforce a desirable behavior that is incompatible with the undesirable one. Young teachers, for example, quickly learn to reinforce walking as a way of eliminating running in the school hallways. A second way to remove undesirable behaviors is through extinction. A behavior is exhibited because it is maintained by some source of reinforcement. By locating and eliminating that reinforcement, one can extinguish any behavior.

It is important to note that reinforcement and punishment are defined solely by their effects on antecedent behaviors. Prime rib, for example, may be a positive reinforcer for some people, but a vegetarian (for whom the sight of red meat is noxious) might view the same entrée as punishment. Alcoholic beverages produce reinforcing effects for some but punitive effects in others. An author's son has grown up treating coffee beans as a rare delicacy (UGH!). The point here is that a stimulus is defined solely in terms of its effect on behavior rather than being a reflection of the administrator's intent. This is one of the points made earlier in Sandlot Seminar 8.5 wherein Megan received negative reinforcement *unintentionally* from her father for telling a lie.

Explaining Human Development: The Research

An extensive research literature on operant conditioning exists. Even a fairly short list of citations would exhaust the limits of this chapter. What follows then is only a brief outline of studies that provide a portion of the research base for operant conditioning. It should be noted that operant conditioning was in its zenith between 1940 and 1970, so in a historical sense, most of the research described in this section derives from that era. While behavior analysis still exists, it continues today in an academic arena fragmented by developmentalists working in such disparate fields as attachment theory, constructivism (see Part Four), information processing, and cognitive science.

Discrimination Learning

Discrimination learning is a general term that involves changing behavior in the presence of a discriminative stimulus. For example, learning the names of shapes requires one to discriminate between stimuli on the basis of their geometrical properties, and learning when it is safe to cross a street or drive through an intersection requires discriminating between the consequences implied by red and green traffic lights. Discrimination learning is one of the most pervasive types of learning, as evidenced by the following areas of research.

Concept Learning. Concept learning is a specific kind of discrimination learning. Concepts, like those taught in school, require us to learn associations between discriminative stimuli and behavior that are appropriate in their context. Cast in this light, considerable research has been undertaken to show how behavioral principles apply to learning academic content. Concept learning requires planning for both the stimulus material as well as the contingencies of reinforcement (Bijou, 1970). In turn, programming the stimulus materials may also include such necessary preparatory steps as (1) discrimination training on a sequence of progressively more difficult tasks; (2) the use of response errors to signal incomplete learning and the necessary return to earlier, less difficult tasks; and (3) *fading* or gradual changes in stimulus salience. Fading procedures require the gradual introduction or *fading in* of incorrect alternatives in discrimination tasks, as when students must choose between alternative answers on multiple choice tests. One may also *fade across* stimulus dimensions by transferring control from one stimulus to another. The gradual progression that takes many years to shift the toddler from "reading" picture books to reading word books is an example of fading across stimulus dimensions (Reese, Howard, & Rosenberger, 1977). A variety of studies have demonstrated the effectiveness of fading procedures in concept and skill acquisitions. For example, fading procedures have been used to teach handwriting (Skinner & Krakower, 1968), basic reading skills (Corey & Shamow, 1972), number concepts (Suppes & Ginsberg, 1962), right–left concepts (Jeffrey, 1958; Tochette, 1968), and form discrimination (Macht, 1971; Sidman & Stoddard, 1967).

Prosocial Behavior. Another area of children's discrimination learning is their acquisition of *prosocial behaviors,* defined generally as any cooperative, interpersonal behavior. Operant conditioning would predict that the frequency of children's helping and sharing would increase following reinforcement, and this prediction tends to hold up. For example, if preschoolers are reinforced for donating something (marbles given to them by an experimenter) to a classmate, they are likely to make future donations when the experimenter is in their room (Fischer, 1963). Moreover, behavior modification programs typically produce dramatic improvements in children's cooperative behavior (Mithaug & Burgess, 1968; Vogler, Masters,

& Merrill, 1970; Vogler, Masters, & Merrill, 1971). For example, in a typical study, children between 7 and 12 years of age were required to work together to solve a problem. They cooperated with each other much more readily when they were individually reinforced for working together, but their cooperation waned when the reinforcers were withdrawn (Azrin & Lindsley, 1956). While praise is often an effective reinforcer that increases sharing behavior in preschool children (Gelfand, Hartmann, Cromer, Smith, & Page, 1975), it seems to be more effective with middle-class preschoolers than those from lower socioeconomic groups (Doland & Adelberg, 1967).

Deviant Behaviors.   Deviant behaviors may be categorized as another type of discrimination learning, since the behaviors are assumed to have been acquired under some type of reinforcement contingency. Three techniques are typically employed to get rid of deviant behaviors: contingent reinforcement of incompatible behaviors, extinction, and punishment. The first two techniques are often used in tandem when undesirable behaviors are ignored (extinguished) and desirable behaviors are reinforced. For example, disruptive classroom behaviors have been eliminated and replaced by more desirable ones using differential teacher attention as a reinforcer (Becker, Madsen, Arnold, & Thomas, 1967; Hall, Lund, & Jackson, 1968; Ward & Baker, 1968). Increasing the frequency of behaviors *incompatible* with disruption, such as in-class studying, both reduces disruptive behavior and improves classroom productivity (Broden, Bruce, Mitchell, Carter, & Hall, 1970; Cossairt, Hall, & Hopkins, 1973; Madsen, Becker, & Thomas, 1968).

Differential social praise and attention are also useful in modifying behavior problems. For example, differential attention has been used to decrease inappropriate crying exhibited by two preschool children (Hart, Allen, Buell, Harris, & Wolf, 1964); to eliminate a nursery school girl's crawling around the nursery school floor (Harris, Johnston, Kelley, Wolf, 1964); to reduce excessive crying in infants (Etzel & Gewirtz, 1967); and to shape sitting still in a hyperactive preschooler (Twardosz & Sajwaj, 1972).

Learned Helplessness.   Some people act as though they have the world on a string; others act as if the world, in all its whimsical calamities, deliberately conspires to render them helpless. Psychologists believe such people have learned how to be helpless, a behavior pattern that can also be unlearned. *Learned helplessness* (Maier, 1970; Maier & Seligman, 1976; Seligman, 1975) has been demonstrated in both the laboratory and natural environments, with both humans and other species. This phenomenon can be clarified by a simple example. Suppose that parents are inconsistent with their children; sometimes they administer love and affection, other times abuse and punishment. However, neither type of consequence is consistently tied to their children's behavior. Sometimes the children will be reinforced and sometimes punished for the same behavior (e.g., asking permission to do something, requesting a snack). Such interactions may be fairly typical for children of alcoholic parents. The children learn they cannot effectively control their parent's administration of reinforcers. Couple this specific learning with stimulus generalization, and they may also learn that the larger environment is unresponsive to their efforts; consequences that they cannot control continue to befall them. Over time and with sufficient experiences like these, such children will learn a special kind of behavior called *helplessness*.

Contributions and Criticisms of Operant Conditioning

Contributions

Scientific Methodology. Operant conditioning has greatly advanced our understanding of the behavior of organisms, largely through the use of experimental procedures. The laboratory environment provides the scientist with (1) a means for systematically controlling an animal's environment and its experiences and (2) a situation for precisely measuring the quantitative relationship between independent (causes) and dependent (effects) variables. By concentrating their attention on the measurement of directly observable behaviors, behavioral scientists have avoided many of the problems inherent in mentalistic and introspective approaches to human nature.

Laws of Operant Conditioning. Skinner's approach to science represents the *inductive* method. Rather than postulate a theory and then proceed to test it (deductive method), he starts with his empirical observations and only gradually proceeds toward tentative generalizations or laws (Wolman, 1981, p. 124). His work has resulted in the discovery of a number of behavioral "laws" (Skinner, 1938). For example, the *law of compatibility* holds that two or more responses may occur simultaneously only if they do not overlap or interfere with one another. Accordingly, one could exhibit singing and bicycle riding at the same time, whereas studying and watching television cannot occur simultaneously because they are incompatible. The *law of conditioning of type R* holds that an operant is strengthened by the presentation of a reinforcing stimulus. Such laws represent an elegantly simple account of behavior.

Practical Applications. Because predictable effects are consistently produced by manipulating reinforcing or punishing stimuli, behavioral research has had widespread practical impact in a variety of arenas. Educators use behavioral principles to manage student learning and conduct; psychologists implement behavior modification programs in institutional settings; parents use reinforcers to shape children's toilet habits and manners. It is probably a reasonable claim to make that operant conditioning has had greater practical impact (in both number and variety of uses) than any other developmental theory.

Behavior Modification. A systematic plan for altering behavior is called *behavior modification* and is one of the most useful contributions of operant conditioning. Sandlot Seminar 8.6 on pages 212–213 summarizes the steps for developing an effective behavior modification plan.

Sandlot Seminar 8.6

Steps for Developing a Behavior Modification Plan

Step 1—Identify a Reinforcer. It is important to establish rather than assume that a consequence has reinforcing effects. To do this, one must first record a baseline or *operant level* of responding for some commonly occurring behavior (e.g., eye contact, smiling, uttering the word "I"). Typically, one would measure the frequency of an operant during a defined interval of time, say ten minutes. Next, administer continuous reinforcement whenever the operant occurs, and keep a cumulative record covering the defined period of time. If the response rate does not increase significantly, then the "reinforcement" you have selected is not producing reinforcing effects and is not, by definition, a reinforcer. It will not produce learning under the behavior modification plan. Try several other possible reinforcers and record their effect on response rates. Only when the operant rate increases significantly will we have confidence that an effective reinforcer has been identified. Before initiating the behavior modification plan, it is often advisable to identify several effective reinforcers. That way if the subject becomes satiated on one, another can be substituted.

Step 2—Establish the Final Form. The second step requires one to establish a specific description of the behavior to be learned, being sure to observe at least two rules. *First,* the final form must be observable and measurable. Specifying "a positive attitude toward school" would not constitute an observable behavior. However, "smiles when entering the classroom" is observable and might be taken as evidence of a positive attitude. *Second,* always specify the *presence* of a specific operant. The subject must act to receive reinforcement. Getting rid of a behavior can be accomplished through extinction; no behavior modification plan is needed, provided one has control over the reinforcers. Specifying that "Judy has to *stop* shouting in the hallway" would be inappropriate, since it describes the absence of behavior.

Step 3—Establish a Reinforcement Schedule. It is important to plan and follow an established reinforcement schedule. It is usually best to begin with continuous reinforcement, since it produces the fastest learning. Once a behavior has been acquired, one might switch to one of the intermittent schedules to maintain the behavior.

Step 4—Design a Learning Environment. You will need to design a situation, a learning environment, to maximize the opportunity to learn the target behavior specified in Step 2. Designing an effective environment may require a bit of creative behavior on your part, or it may be as simple as telling the subject what will be required to obtain reinforcement (e.g., "Each time you smile, I'll smile back"). In setting up an environment, it is often desirable to arrange conditions so that behaviors incompatible with the final form are eliminated. The learning environment contains the discriminative stimulus.

Step 5—Shape the Final Form. If the final form of behavior is not already part of the subject's repertoire, it will be necessary to shape it. To do that, first reinforce gross approximations to the final form. On successive occasions, reinforce only increasingly closer approximations to the final form. Using this "law of successive approximations" it should be possible to proceed with the behavior modification plan once the final form is emitted often enough to be reinforced. If the final form is already a part of the subject's behavioral repertoire, you may skip Step 5.

Step 6—Implement the Plan. Only when the first five steps have been carefully planned (including establishing rather than guessing at a reinforcer) is one in position to implement the behavior modification plan. It is important to keep cumulative records of responding and reinforcement, because revision of the plan may be necessary. Revisions should be made in the reinforcement, the reinforcement schedule, or the learning environment when data indicate that progress toward the final form of behavior is not being accomplished.

Token Economies. Token economies are another practical application of operant conditioning used in regular school classrooms, juvenile correction centers, and institutional settings. All token economies implicitly attempt to shape behavior by utilizing secondary reinforcers on an intermittent reinforcement schedule. Here's how it works. Individuals receive "tokens" (e.g., tally marks, chits, stars) for performing target operants in appropriate situations. For example, adolescents in a juvenile detention center may receive one token each time they make their bed before breakfast, scrape their plates following meals, and show up for work detail on time. The tokens are essentially worthless *except* that they may be accumulated and later traded for some valued prize. For example, an adolescent may be able to trade five tokens for watching one hour of TV or one hundred tokens for a day trip to a nearby amusement park. In some token economies, tokens earned cannot be taken away. In others, tokens can be both earned for "good" behavior and forfeited for "bad" behavior.

Criticisms

Reductionism. One of the most frequent criticisms made against operant conditioning is its inherent *reductionism*. In the classic sense, reductionism represents efforts to reduce higher-order processes to physiological or biochemical processes. In this classical sense, operant conditioning is not reductionist. However, there is a much broader sense in which operant conditioning is reductionist—namely in its assumption that complex behaviors can best be understood when they are broken down, differentiated, and separated into smaller units. By studying and testing the properties of each unit, behavioral scientists believe that a more accurate and detailed understanding of the complex behavior may be gained.

The problem with reductionism is that complex behaviors may not be adequately explained by simply piecing together the properties of its discrete elements. There is considerable debate, for example, about whether such complex behavior as talking, teaching, and programming a computer can be adequately explained in terms of their discrete elements.

Verbal Learning. Chomsky (1959) began the assault on Skinner's operant conditioning explanation of verbal learning. Chomsky pointed out that children create novel utterances they have never heard before (and which therefore could not have been reinforced), and he showed that language is infinitely generative. That is, a limited number of words in a language can be combined into an infinite number of sentences. Skinner's concepts of shaping and reinforcement simply cannot account for the complexity of language acquisition and performance.

Definition of Behavior.   Skinner shrewdly defines an operant behavior in terms of *its effect on the environment*. The advantage of such a definition is twofold. On the one hand, laboratory behavior can be objectively measured electronically in terms of its frequency, latency, or resistance to extinction. On the other hand, behavior can be conveniently segmented into discrete units. This is not a trivial point. Naturally occurring behavior tends to be like William James' consciousness: It seems to unfold as one long continuous stream of motion and activity, with one behavior sliding smoothly into another. How one goes about segmenting a continuous behavioral stream into separable units that can then be measured as repeatable events is a serious scientific issue. If, for example, behavioral events occur in different time spans (e.g., pressing a lever, turning off an irritating alarm clock, completing a triple gainer off a diving board), then a meaningful explanation of behavior must necessarily admit to different types of divisions of the behavioral stream (Zeiler, 1979, p. 79). Skinner was quite aware of this problem, and he hoped that future behavior analysis would be able to account for the fluidity of behavior (Evans, 1968).

The search for meaningful units of behavior reflects, in part, the extremely vital role "units" have played in the development of the sciences (Marr, 1979). Units allow measurement, and objective measurement is a vital element to scientific activity. The fact that natural behavior is artificially segmented in the laboratory (and it may well be artificially produced as well) reflects both a decision of convenience and an assumption about the orderliness of science. The gain for the behavioral psychologist is that such segmentation makes it simpler and hence easier to study behavior. The important question is, however, whether laws about conveniently segmented units of behavior can adequately account for the range of time spans (ranging from small to very large) over which natural behaviors occur.

Reinforcement Reconsidered.   One of the most vexing problems behaviorists face is explaining what makes a reinforcer reinforcing. Why do some stimuli and not others have reinforcing effects? A response which is reinforced will, by definition, increase in likelihood. If the response does not change, then there has been no reinforcement. But examine this issue carefully. Defining reinforcement in such a manner makes the concept of reinforcement irrefutable. The behaviorist cannot circumvent this problem easily, because such a definition is tautological (Smith, 1994). A stimulus is reinforcing if it increases behavior; increases in behavior are caused by a reinforcing stimulus. The tautology problem underscores the need for clear, thoughtful analyses by behavioral psychologists, especially since reinforcement plays such an important role in the explanation of operant behavior.

Evaluation of Operant Conditioning

Scientific Worthiness

Operant conditioning, with its strong empiricist tradition and its emphasis on control and prediction of observable, measurable behavior, garners very high ratings for its scientific worthiness (see Table 8.4).

TABLE 8.4 **Ratings of Operant Conditioning for Scientific Worthiness**

Criteria	High	Medium	Low
Testability	X		
External Validity	X		
Predictive Validity		X	
Internal Consistency	X		
Theoretical Economy	X		

Testability.   Many aspects of the theory, such as observable phenomena, experimental control, and measurable variables, all contribute to its high ranking for testability. For example, researchers can control and manipulate a wide variety of independent variables, and modern equipment makes possible the objective measurement and recording of behavior. The effects of different reinforcement schedules can be assessed with great accuracy across many individuals. While the theoretical failure to provide conceptual definitions for behavior and for reinforcement (see previous section) detracts from the theory's conceptual soundness, it does not diminish laboratory tests of the quantitative relations between stimulus and response variables. For these reasons, we have rated the theory high for its testability.

External Validity.   There is little doubt that at least some portion of children's behavior is acquired as the direct result of the administration of reinforcement. In actual life, reinforcement may be as much a matter of "hit-and-miss" inconsistency as of fully intentional planning. Nevertheless, it is probably true that the circumstances under which children receive reinforcement closely approximate several of the intermittent reinforcement schedules described earlier. The examples described earlier of discrimination and concept learning, learned helplessness, and control of deviant behaviors represent only a portion of the many published demonstrations of how behavior can be predicted and controlled by operant conditioning. Thus, the theory is given a high ranking for its external validity.

Predictive Validity.   Laboratory research has demonstrated that operant conditioning does quite well in predicting and controlling animal behavior. Some theoretical predictions can also be applied to humans in naturalistic settings. However, the theory's simplicity seems to be no match for the complexity of social and physical environments in which humans carry out their lives. Beyond the controls of a laboratory setting, human behavior is emitted in the context of multiple discriminative, reinforcing, and punishing stimuli that may occur according to different schedules. Teachers often complain, for example, that certain behaviors they are trying to extinguish in the classroom are being reinforced at home. The behaviorist's response to this type of complexity is to simplify—to place organisms in a laboratory where variables can be controlled. But we do not see how such simplification really advances our understanding of human behavior in natural settings. The fact that operant conditioning has fared well in laboratory studies but less well in the natural world leads us to judge the theory as medium in terms of its predictive validity.

Internal Consistency.   Ironically, the simplicity of operant conditioning, which led to a moderate rating for predictive validity, produces a high ranking for internal consistency. To explain behavior change, the theory relies on limited but simple internal and bridge principles with no need for recourse to other ad hoc concepts. Moreover, the small number and magnitude of exceptional findings (those unexplainable by the theory) have not been occasioned by many attempts to shore up the theory with revisions (there are, of course some exceptions to this point, such as those found in social cognitive theory in the next chapter). Overall, though, the simple mechanisms of operant conditioning provide clear, straightforward, and internally consistent explanatory principles.

Theoretical Economy.   From the foregoing discussion, it should be clear that the high rank of operant conditioning for theoretical economy also rests on the elegant simplicity of the theory. Relying on only three modest assumptions (inborn reflexes, active nature, *tabula rasa* mind), the theory proceeds to explain an incredible diversity of behavioral learning that applies to both humans and animals.

Developmental Adequacy

Temporality.   Shaping through reinforcement is the means by which new behaviors are acquired, and it necessarily implies a period of time during which a behavior is gradually learned. Consequently, the theory does account for how change takes place over time (see Table 8.5).

Cumulativity.   Shaping involves the learning of a new behavior from the starting point of previously learned behaviors. Later behavioral acquisitions are built incrementally, bit by bit, upon earlier acquisitions. Even complex behavior chains are comprised of the sequential addition of new elements to the behavior string. Thus, the theory passes this characteristic.

TABLE 8.5   Ratings of Operant Conditioning for Developmental Adequacy

Characteristic	Rating
Temporality	Yes
Cumulativity	Yes
Directionality	No
New Mode of Organization	No
Increased Capacity for Self-control	No

Directionality.   Directionality implies a certain sense of progress in the acquisition of new behaviors. In one sense, operant conditioning meets this condition—in the sense that adult behaviors are somehow different from infants' and children's behaviors, but the most important dimension of difference is quantity. Adults have simply acquired more behaviors and more behavior chains than children. Note, however, that acquiring more behaviors is characteristic of cumulativity, which has already been covered under that criterion. In a different vein, operant conditioning holds that behaviors that get acquired may also be extinguished through the removal of reinforcement. Since new behaviors are not necessarily permanent or enduring, the theory tends to imply that development is essentially nondirectional in nature. Put differently, the same principles that account for acquiring behaviors also account for losing them. There is nothing in the theory that places a priority or greater explanatory value on behavior acquisition over behavior extinction. For these reasons we believe the theory does not adequately explain developmental "progress" and judge it to fail this characteristic of human development.

New Mode of Organization.   This characteristic implies that accounts of development explain changes that result in new organizational rules or processes not previously present in the organism. In operant conditioning, the unit of organization is the *association* formed between a discriminative stimulus, a response, and a consequence. According to the theory, an adult's behaviors are organized no differently than the child's, although behaviors of each may be controlled by different discriminative and reinforcing stimuli. All of us learn specific associations that govern our behavior. But these new associations represent new additions (cumulativity) to the same mode of organizing behavior rather than differences in how our behaviors are organized. Since the association unit is the only unit of behavior organization described by operant conditioning, it fails this criterion.

Increased Capacity for Self-control.   The capacity for self-control is not recognized as a property of either human or animal nature. Skinner (1971) has argued that we are all controlled all of the time by the consequences of our actions. Even when we do *what we want to do,* we have been controlled through prior reinforcement to want to do certain things more than others. So, while Skinner views self-control and free will as both illusions and bad philosophy, there is one specific sense in which he would admit that individuals can acquire increasing self-control. Individuals can be trained to control their own reinforcement contingencies, as is the case with many institutionalized patients who are taught basic self-maintenance skills. However, self-control of one's own reinforcement contingencies must itself be controlled by other reinforcers. Simply put, operant conditioning recognizes no acquisitions in human nature that diminish the environment's control over our behavior. Consequently, the theory fails this criterion.

Pedagogical Usefulness

Table 8.6 on page 218 shows our ratings for the pedagogical usefulness of Skinner's operant conditioning. It is instructive to compare the majority of high ratings of

TABLE 8.6   Ratings of Operant Conditioning for Pedagogical Usefulness

Criteria	High	Medium	Low
Interpretability		X	
Versatility	X		
Availability	X		
Guidance	X		

this theory with those described earlier, which occupy the endogenous paradigm. By their very nature, one should expect exogenous theories to score higher than endogenous theories for their usefulness. This differential pattern of ratings reflects a fundamental tenet of the *nature versus nurture* controversy. There is only a limited range to what parents, teachers, and counselors can do to influence people's basic nature. Consequently, endogenous theories will tend to score relatively low on criteria of pedagogical usefulness. In contrast, nurture theories, which occupy the exogenous paradigm, have a real advantage. They concentrate on external factors and thereby provide parents, teachers, and counselors with specific implications and strategies for influencing development. As a consequence, they will tend to score higher for pedagogical usefulness than endogenous theories. Since operant conditioning is the paradigm case for the exogenous paradigm, we would expect it to rate uniformly high. In fact, it was John B. Watson (1928) who initiated what has today become a long history of pedagogical implications of behaviorism.

Interpretability.   The theoretical jargon of operant conditioning is, with two specific exceptions, easy to understand and not so technical as to be beyond the grasp of novices. The two exceptions are Skinner's unique definition of stimulus (a reinforcing *consequence*) and his logical rather than social use of the term *negative* in the concept of negative reinforcement. These exceptions aside, the theory reflects an elegant economy in the number of internal and bridge principles put forth to account for the prediction and control of behavior. For these reasons, we have rated operant conditioning medium for its interpretability.

Versatility.   A good measure of a theory's versatility is the variety of uses to which it has been put. Few twentieth-century theories have generated the diversity of uses accorded operant conditioning. Skinner's *Technology of Teaching,* for example, describes in good detail direct instructional applications of operant conditioning principles. Skinner's teaching machine is the forerunner of today's individually paced instruction strategies. Behavior modification programs and token economies (described earlier) are used in many educational and clinical settings, and teachers' classroom management techniques often reflect underlying principles derived from operant conditioning. Although often implemented inconsistently, parents intuitively use consequences to alter and maintain their children's behavior. Even state and national governments, through monetary and tax policies, directly shape the financial behaviors of their citizens. Without belaboring the point, few theories in developmental psychology have demonstrated the versatility of operant conditioning, so it is rated high on this criterion.

Availability.   Standard textbooks in developmental psychology provide at least an introductory treatment of Skinner's theory of operant conditioning. In addition, numerous books have been written about the theory and many of its specialized applications. Specialized journals in behavior analysis contain ongoing research about the theory and its uses in laboratory, social, and institutional settings. Finally, few theorists can match Skinner's attempt to put theoretical principles before the public in the form of popular books (e.g., *Walden Two, Beyond Freedom and Dignity*). All these sources lend support to our high ranking of the theory's availability.

Guidance.   Although Skinner's operant conditioning does not tell us which behaviors are socially desirable and should be candidates for shaping children's development, his theory does a good job dealing with controlling and predicting behavior. In addition, the change mechanism of reinforcement can easily be controlled by counselors, teachers, and parents. Once learned, the principles of behavior modification can be consistently employed with considerable success. In fact, a number of works dealing with pedagogy have been published. Two relevant examples are classroom applications of operant conditioning and the use of behavior modification to teach personal hygiene skills to institutionalized patients. These considerations, and many more like them, lead us to a high rating of operant conditioning for its guidance.

Summary Points

1. Pavlovian (classical or respondent) conditioning *elicits* responses because the controlling stimulus (UCS or CS) precedes the behavioral response. Operant conditioning views the organism as active and instrumental in producing consequences from its actions.
2. The theory of operant conditioning assumes that infants begin their learning with a species-determined set of reflexes, a *tabula rasa* mind, and a naturally active disposition.
3. Operant conditioning attempts to explain the cause–effect relationship between the class of stimulus variables and the class of response variables. Stimulus variables are uniquely defined as measurable *consequences* of an individual's behavior. The theory fosters scientific attitudes toward research in its collection of data, which is observable, objective, and measurable.
4. The theory's internal principles are discriminative stimulus, reinforcement, and shaping. A discriminative stimulus controls behavior by signaling the *availability* of reinforcement. However, this type of stimulus has no reinforcing power of its own. Behaviors that produce consequences are learned because they are contingently reinforced. Consequences are called primary reinforcers

if they are effective on their first presentation. Secondary reinforcers, such as money or social praise, must be learned. New behaviors are acquired through shaping, the reinforcement of successive approximations.

5. Positive reinforcement is the administration of a consequence that increases behavior. Negative reinforcement, the release from an aversive stimulus, also *increases* behavior. Punishment is the administration of an aversive stimulus; its effect is to decrease behavior.

6. Reinforcement schedules describe the arrangement or timing of consequences. These include contingencies for continuous, intermittent, and random timing, as well as extinction.

7. Individual operants may be conditioned to occur in a sequential string of behavior events. This string is called a behavior chain. The last behavior in a chain produces reinforcing consequences.

8. The theory's contributions to developmental psychology include its scientific methodology, laws of conditioning, and practical applications. It has been criticized for its reductionism, definitions of behavior and reinforcement, and presumption that general laws independent of built-in species biases can be found.

9. Operant conditioning rates high on criteria of scientific worthiness but relatively low on developmental adequacy. As the paradigm case for the exogenous paradigm, the theory is rated high for its pedagogical usefulness.

PROBLEMS AND EXERCISES

1. At the end of the chapter on Freud's theory, you were asked to provide a psychoanalytic explanation for *infantile amnesia,* the well-documented phenomenon in which adults fail to remember any infantile experiences. You probably responded in terms of the developing ego and its mechanism of repression or its secondary process thought. Now describe how operant conditioning would explain infantile amnesia.

2. In a general way, sketch out the primary factors operant conditioning would use to explain how children acquire language. Among the first nouns children acquire are the names for body parts, particularly the features of the face (e.g., nose, mouth, ear). Using operant conditioning, explain how children learn to name facial features.

3. *Separation anxiety* is a universal experience that occurs during the second half of the first year of life. During the first six months, infants are not particularly bothered when their primary caretaker leaves them alone in a strange situation. However, between 6 and 12 months, infants become distressed and anxious when temporarily abandoned by a caretaker who leaves the room. Describe how Skinner might explain the infant's stranger anxiety.

4. Design a behavior modification program to teach a puppy how to "shake hands" with its paw.

5. Describe how you would set up a controlled experiment to analyze the effects of reinforcement delay on learning.

6. A father institutes a behavior modification program to teach his 2-year-old son how to put on his own socks.

   a. Identify the relevant theoretical principles that must be taken into account.

   b. Assume that some degree of chaining will be required. Specify the order in which you would condition the individual behaviors that comprise the chain.

   c. Describe in observable, measurable terms the final form your behavioral chain would take to get reinforced.

7. Using principles of operant conditioning design a plan to rid a friend of an unwanted behavior, and describe how you would evaluate your success. Do you need a behavior modification plan to accomplish your goal? Why or why not?

8. College freshmen, typically housed in dorms with complete strangers, sometimes experience "personality clashes" with their new dorm mates. Explain how these clashes can be interpreted using operant conditioning. How is it that some dorm mates become lifelong friends?

9. Use the Internet to search for sites related to B. F. Skinner and his theory. You can use his name as well as key words (internal and bridge principles). How do the Internet sites differ in terms of completeness and accuracy of information? What were the best sites you found? What problems did you encounter? What were some of the worst sites (and why)?

SUGGESTED READINGS

More about the Theory

Schwartz, B., & Lacey, H. (1982). *Behaviorism, science, and human nature.* New York: Norton.
Skinner, B. F. (1953). *Science and human behavior.* New York: Free Press.
Skinner, B. F. (1974). *About behaviorism.* New York: Knopf.
Skinner, B. F. (1983). Origins of a behaviorist. *Psychology Today,* September, 22–33.

Research Reviews

Kling, J. W., & Riggs, L. A. (Eds). (1971). *Experimental psychology* (3rd ed.). New York: Holt, Rinehart and Winston. (*Note:* Only Chapters 14 through 19 are relevant.)
Stevenson, H. W. (1970). Learning in children. In P. Mussen (Ed.), *Carmichael's manual of child psychology. Vol. 1* (3rd ed.). New York: John Wiley & Sons.

Critical Reviews

Chomsky, N. (1959). Review of *verbal behavior* by B. F. Skinner. *Language, 35,* 26–58.
Modgil, S., & Modgil, C. (Eds.). (1987). *B. F. Skinner: Consensus and controversy.* London: Falmer Press.
Wessels, M. G. (1982). A critique of Skinner's views on the obstructive character of cognitive theories. *Behaviorism, 10,* 65–84.

CHAPTER

9 Bandura and Social Cognitive Theory

Preview Questions

What significant problem left unsolved by operant conditioning is solved by social cognitive theory? In what important ways does Bandura's theory differ from Skinner's theory of operant conditioning?

What assumptions does Bandura make, and in what way might they be considered unusual?

What are the theory's problems of study and research methods?

What are social cognitive theory's internal and bridge principles?

What change mechanism does the theory propose to explain development?

Why does Bandura's theory belong to the exogenous paradigm?

What are the important contributions and criticisms of the theory?

How does the theory rate for scientific worthiness, developmental adequacy, and pedagogical usefulness?

Historical Sketch

Social cognitive theory is a "radical" departure from Skinner's radical behaviorism in that cognitive processes are directly inferred through the study of behavior. In addition, the theory attempts to explain a particular type of behavior learning not addressed by Skinner's theory of operant conditioning. Recall that with operant conditioning Skinner explained how novel behaviors were acquired through shaping and thereby solved an important problem left unsolved by classical conditioning. However, an important class of behaviors that cannot be accounted for by operant conditioning consists of *behaviors that are learned without any reinforcement.* Consider an example. After watching Mr. Rogers demonstrate on television how to make artificial flowers using scissors, tape, and old hosiery, 6-year-old Megan proceeded to gather up a butter knife, some cellophane tape, and some socks from her bureau drawer. She first taped her socks together and then tried to cut them with the butter knife. When her father asked her what she was doing, she told him, "I'm making some flowers for Mommy, just like Mr. Rogers did." This sequence of activities had never before occurred, although Megan had used a knife at meal times. The novelty of this behavior chain and the uniqueness of the Megan's utterance, after watching Mr. Rogers make artificial flowers, cannot be explained by operant conditioning because Megan's behaviors and her utterance had not been previously reinforced.

The theoretical problem with Megan's actions is how to explain behaviors acquired all at once without gradual shaping and without the administration of previous reinforcers. One solution to this problem, and others like it, is provided by Albert Bandura's theory of social cognitive development.

In this chapter, Bandura's theory, the most prominent among social learning theories, will be described. His emphasis on the social basis of cognitive processes is why his work falls within the exogenous paradigm of developmental theories. In short, he argues that individuals learn both behaviors and cognitive strategies by observing the behavior of others, and these acquisitions can be learned without being directly reinforced.

Albert Bandura was born in 1925 in a small hamlet in northern Alberta, Canada. He attended the town's only school until college where he studied psychology and graduated from the University of British Columbia in 1949. While in graduate school at the University of Iowa, his interest in learning theory was supported by a faculty of vigorous and active researchers, including Robert Sears, who was pioneering an effort to recast psychoanalytic theory in terms of social learning.

Bandura was a bright and able student. He completed his PhD in only three years, did a clinical internship at the Wichita Guidance Center, and then become a psychology instructor at Stanford. His productivity there was rewarded when he rose through the professorial ranks to become a full professor in only nine years. Following the impetus of his mentor Robert Sears, Bandura's early investigations focused on social learning and aggression. In collaboration with his first doctoral student, Richard Walters, he spent several years studying observational learning. Much of this work was described in an early formulation of what became known as *social learning theory* (Bandura & Walters, 1963). Recognizing the inherent limitations of operant conditioning and tempered by the 1970s surge of interest in cognitive processes, Bandura began to examine how individuals acquire abstract, rule-governed behavior and the function of cognitive mechanisms in mediating observational learning.

Extending Skinner's Legacy

Social learning theorists agree to a large extent with Skinner's analysis of operant learning, and they attempt to build on rather than dismantle his basic theory. Foremost in Bandura's earlier analysis of learning was the role of imitation, which has its conceptual foundation in operant conditioning. In an early publication, Bandura (Bandura & Walters, 1959, pp. 253–254) argued that imitation often leads to the reinforcers children seek. For example, they learn to reproduce parents' behaviors because those behaviors produce reinforcement for the parents, and soon the repetition of similar behaviors becomes self-reinforcing because the behaviors are valued by the parents. At the same time, children do not haphazardly imitate everything in sight. Bandura and Walters (1963) contend that behaviors are imitated more often when models are of the same sex, well respected, receive tangible rewards for their actions, and are perceived as similar to the observer. Models are less likely to be imitated when their actions are punished and when the model is perceived as different by an observer.

Carrying the analysis a step further, Bandura and Walters (1963) argued that new behaviors could be acquired by simply *observing* a model; it is not necessary that the observer actually produce an overt behavior or even be reinforced. Rather, the reinforcement the model obtains is itself sufficient to reinforce the observer. Bandura and Walters termed this process *vicarious reinforcement*. They argued that the concept of vicarious reinforcement explained "no trial learning," a widely recognized phenomenon in which learning occurs in the absence of shaping. Vicarious reinforcement involves conceptual reasoning since it requires observers to judge expected outcomes about their own behavior on the basis of outcomes produced by models.

In recent years, Bandura (1992, 1993, 1995, 1997) has turned his attention to exploring how the development of self-efficacy influences addiction, anxiety, athletic prowess, career choice, family dynamics, education, life transitions, and risk avoidance. Moreover, his analysis of social learning has become an important influence on developmental psychology in the past quarter-century, during which time it motivated numerous laboratory studies of altruism, aggression, sex-role learning, and empathy. His social cognitive theory attempts to explain how individuals acquire information, behaviors, and internal standards and values by observing the conduct of others. A fundamental element of Bandura's theory is the role of cognition in development, and this consideration defines the framework for what today is termed "cognitive behaviorism." Bandura's model of cognition is not well defined, but we can glean some basic properties. Cognition consists of image, symbol, and linguistic encodings. These encodings may interact with one another and produce new meanings. The most fundamental difference between an infant and an adult is quantitative, how much learning has occurred and how many new meanings have been derived.

Structural Components of Social Cognitive Theory

Assumptions

Bandura (1986, pp. 18–22) describes five prerequisite capabilities for observational learning. He is not specific about when these capabilities appear, but he suggests that infants engage in some forms of simple observational learning.

First, infants possess *innately organized reflexes* and biological tendencies. But the infant's biological programming also implies a potential for learning that reflects both a high degree of behavioral plasticity and inborn, physiological constraints that limit the flexibility of human nature.

Second, Bandura assumes that a *symbolizing capacity* gives humans a powerful tool for processing and transforming their experiences into internal models that guide future actions. This symbolizing capacity includes the ability to formulate both rational judgments and irrational beliefs.

Third, the capacity for *forethought* influences our present actions. Forethought is the ability to anticipate specific actions, consequences, or events that have not yet occurred and which, therefore, cannot have become a part of our personal history. Desirable goals (symbolically represented) often motivate behaviors that are most likely to bring about their actualization.

Fourth, Bandura assumes the capacity for *vicarious learning,* that is, learning by observation. Moreover, he assumes that individuals can imitate activities that vary considerably depending on who the models are and how they perform. For example, a child but not an adolescent would be more likely to mimic a cartoon character's heroic actions. Conversely, the adolescent but not the child would be more likely to mimic a rock star's clothing. The capacity for vicarious learning is an important assumption because it presumes that people are capable of learning rules that generate and regulate their actions without having to go through a lengthy trial-and-error process of discovery. Bandura notes, for example, that the power of observational learning is found in the fact that children do not learn to swim and medical students do not learn to perform surgery by discovering through trial and error the personal effects of their efforts (which theoretically would be required with the theory of operant conditioning).

Fifth, *reflective self-consciousness* enables individuals to think about their own thoughts and attribute meaning to their experiences. Self-reflection not only improves understanding, it also provides a means for evaluating and altering one's thinking. The capacity for self-reflection influences individuals' self-concepts in terms of verifying beliefs, monitoring ideas, and deciding how much effort to invest in certain activities and whether to approach the activities anxiously or with confidence.

Problems for Study

Phenomena to Be Explained.   Social cognitive theory attempts to explain socialization broadly, including processes whereby individuals acquire their society's norms of thought and action. Within this broad agenda, Bandura attempts to explain four types of learning effects.

Observational Learning Effects.   The theory attempts to explain how individuals acquire the ability to perform *novel* physical and cognitive behaviors, including standards of judgment, thinking skills, and rules for generating behavior that have no reinforcement history. Novel performance in this sense includes both new behaviors as well as new organizational patterns that combine and recombine simpler, previously learned behaviors into more complex ones. For example, when a child utters a novel sentence, it contains individual, previously learned words organized into a new, original sequence. Similarly, when a young couple moves into a new house, they reorganize previously acquired furniture, appliances, and decorations in a unique and distinctive manner.

Inhibitory and Disinhibitory Effects.   Behaviors that have already been acquired may also be strengthened or weakened under certain circumstances, or they may not occur at all. For example, most people decelerate when driving past a police or highway patrol car, and parents dining together at an expensive restaurant tend to eat more slowly than when dining with their children at a fast-food restaurant. In other situations, behavior may be accelerated, as when children learn to become more talkative as bedtime approaches or when some college professors learn to grade final exams more rapidly than midterms. Yet other situations may inhibit behavior altogether. People are far more likely to obey "no smoking" signs in hospitals and churches than in bus stations or at outdoor concerts. One task of the theory is to explain how people learn these inhibitions and disinhibitions.

Response Facilitation Effects.   Whereas the term *disinhibition effects* refers to situational variables, *response facilitation effects* refers to a function of the behavior of others, which may instigate one's behavior when other cues are absent. Response facilitation can occur when models function to activate, direct, or support specific behaviors of other individuals in a particular situation. This type of learning may be found in peer group pressure or Sunday church when individuals are likely to follow the leads of others in how they behave. No new behaviors are involved here. Rather, it is a matter of initiating a previously acquired behavior in the presence of others who are exhibiting that behavior. A father is more likely to spend Saturday raking leaves than watching TV if he sees his neighbors outside engaging in this fall ritual.

Environmental Enhancement Effects.   According to Bandura some behaviors direct our attention to environmental prompts or settings rather than cue behavior. Behavior that is directed in this manner must be explained as much as behavior that is cued. Even similarities in behavior may result from attention-directing rather than behavior-cuing models. For example, children will typically eat more when fed in pairs than when fed alone. Even those who are full may ask for more food if they observe parents snacking. In these cases, their attention is directed at the food rather than at others' eating behaviors. Sandlot Seminar 9.1 on pages 228–229 helps readers differentiate between response facilitation and environmental enhancement effects.

Methods of Study.   The influence of U.S. behaviorism on social cognitive theory is perhaps most clearly seen in two aspects of conducting research. First, social cognitive theorists concentrate on observable, measurable behavior. However, in contrast to radical behaviorists, social cognitive researchers use their observations to draw direct inferences about learning and the presence of cognitive processes. Second, working within the strong empirical tradition of behaviorism, social cognitive

Sandlot Seminar 9.1

Response Facilitation and Environment Enhancement Effects

Response Facilitation Effects

1. A young man is walking down the sidewalk in the middle of town. He notices an attractive woman approaching who looks at him and then smiles. The man smiles in return.
2. A second-grader is learning how to use the computer. She notices that the girl next to her clicks her computer mouse, and suddenly the computer screen changes to show a picture of a dog. "Show me how you did that," says the first girl.
3. During parallel play, young Rolanda is playing dolls with her best friend Rhaji. Rhaji dresses her doll, then uses her doll to pretend to cook a meal. Rolanda, who had been playing "dress up," watches Rhaji play cooking, and then follows her lead with her own doll.

Note: All examples of response facilitation effects show how a previously acquired behavior was initiated in the context of another behavior that was already occurring.

Environment Enhancement Effects

1. While competing in a high school track meet, Miriam notices a runner coming up on her outside shoulder during the third lap of the mile run. Miriam naturally speeds up. (Miriam is already running, but runs faster when another runner threatens to pass her.)
2. Sixteen-year-old Megan thinks of herself as a safe driver. One morning on her way to school, a car passes her in the fast lane. Megan turns her head just in time to see Jason, an attractive senior at her school, speed by. Megan accelerates to keep up with Jason.
3. Amy is on her way home from work in rush-hour traffic. As she approaches an intersection, the light turns yellow. Cars to her left and right immediately speed up. Amy speeds up, too, and makes it through the intersection before the light turns red.

Note: All examples of environment enhancement effects show changes in an ongoing behavior.

Classify the following examples as **RF** (response facilitation) or **EE** (environmental enhancement).

_____ Matthew and his father visit an ice cream shop. The father orders a chocolate chip sundae. Matthew says, "I'll have one of those too."

_____ Wendy rents an apartment in the inner city. One morning while she is eating breakfast, her landlord walks outside and waters plants spread about his deck. Wendy watches her landlord's actions, and then interrupts her breakfast, goes inside, and returns with a watering can in her hand. She then proceeds to water the plants on her own deck.

_____ Amanda, on request from her mother, interrupts her TV viewing to feed the family puppy. Abby, watching the same TV program, notices what Amanda does. Then Abby gets up and fixes some food for the family cat.

_____ Chris and his father are gathering firewood for their campfire. With arms full, Chris heads toward camp when he notices that his father, with his arms full, balances all the firewood on his left arm, then reaches down for an extra piece of firewood with his right hand. Chris immediately switches all his firewood to his left arm and heads back to camp. On the way, he reaches down with his right hand to pick up an extra log.

theorists tend to favor experimental research designs. In particular, studies often utilize a controlled situation in which a single behavior or aspect of behavior is isolated and manipulated for the purpose of measuring its influence on observers' behavior. For example, in a typical study one might find three groups of children. The first group may observe a real model, the second a video recording of the same model, and the third a televised scenario of the same model. Consequently, the study may compare the three groups to determine which contains the most frequent displays of the model's behavior. In a different study, an experimental group of children may watch a television clip of an actress helping someone in distress. A control group may watch a similar clip in which the actress ignores the person in distress. During a simulation later on, the study may compare the two groups of children to see how frequently they engage in altruistic helping.

Internal Principles

Triadic Reciprocality.   People are only partial products of their environments. Just as important is the fact that we create beneficial environments and then proceed to exercise control over them. By selecting environments carefully, we can influence what we become. Our choices are influenced by our beliefs as well as our capabilities (Bandura, 1997, p. 160).

Bandura proposes only a single internal principle comprised of three interacting elements. This principle is termed **triadic reciprocal determinism** or **triadic reciprocality** for short. Triadic reciprocality attempts to reflect a genuinely causal–interactional view of human development. From this view, learning results from interaction among three types of causes that commingle with one another and jointly determine what, where, and when learning occurs. These three factors, shown schematically in Figure 9.1 on page 230, are *observed behavior, cognition and other personal factors*, and *environmental factors*.

The first determinant, observed behavior, includes important considerations such as its complexity, duration, and the skill involved. The second determinant, cognition and other personal factors, refers to the individual's past learning because these elements are brought to the observation. This determinant includes acquired

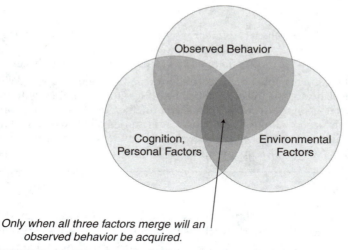

*Only when all three factors merge will an
observed behavior be acquired.*

FIGURE 9.1   Diagram of triadic reciprocality.

concepts and beliefs, motives, intentions, and personality characteristics. Finally, the third determinant, environmental factors, refers to the situation in which the observation takes place. It includes the roles and relationships of model and observer as well as personal characteristics of the model.

Sandlot Seminar 9.2 illustrates some examples of how these factors might interact. See if you can identify which factor is the most relevant in each situation.

A second-grade teacher has just asked Jillian a history question. According to Bandura, the three factors of triadic reciprocality will interact to determine how Jillian responds to her teacher's question. One important factor would be the child's vocabulary and ability to pronounce the words (the behavioral determinant). A second factor, of course, would be her knowledge of the correct answer and her current motivation (cognitive determinants), or how meaningful Jillian thinks this question is or how well she likes this teacher (personal factors). Finally, Jillian's response will be influenced in part by the current classroom conditions (environmental determinants), such as previous responses by other students, her teacher's demeanor, and temporal proximity to lunch or recess. According to Bandura, all these factors will enter into a complex but causal solution that results in (1) whether or not Jillian tries to answer the question, (2) what answer she gives (if she does), and (3) how she phrases her answer.

The most interesting element of this triad is cognition, because Bandura's efforts to explain its role in learning differentiate him from other radical behaviorists that preceded him. In his thinking, cognition plays a specialized role in learning because it brings into play particular functions that cannot be accounted for with the other two elements of triadic reciprocality. However, cognition is not a transcendental influence; it is simply one of three important causal factors. In this context, it is important to note that Bandura's concept of cognition resides in the *types* of functions he presumes at birth: a symbolizing capacity, forethought, self-

Sandlot Seminar 9.2

Understanding Elements of Triadic Reciprocality

According to Bandura, every situation involves all three elements of triadic reciprocality. But in some situations, one element ends up being more important than other elements. In the following examples, see if you can identify the most influential element of triadic reciprocality. Remember, all elements enter into every interaction to some degree. However, in many (if not most) interactions, one element more than others is a determining factor in acquiring a new behavior. Use the following rules.

1. If anyone, under the same conditions, would imitate the behavior, select *behavior* as the most important determinant.
2. If a given behavior or situation affects some people more than others, select *cognition and personal factors* as the most important determinant.
3. If the situation or model is so compelling that anyone would imitate it, regardless of the behavior, select *environment* as the most important determinant.
4. When the preceding three rules don't help, use your best judgment about the most important factor.

Task: Decide the most important determinant (behavior, environment, or cognition) in each of the following situations.

_____ Fourteen-year-old Matthew watches MTV every afternoon following soccer practice. One evening he is called into the kitchen to eat supper. He enters the kitchen playing "air guitar" to the tune of the previous MTV hit he was just watching.

_____ Sophie goes to day care each day. The most popular girl in her class, Jennifer, always wears a ribbon in her hair. One morning Sophie demands that her mother put a ribbon in her hair before taking her to day care.

_____ John is a junior at State University. In a psychology course, he gets a "D" on his first exam. The nice but unattractive girl next to him gets an "A." After class, John asks the girl what she does to study for exams. She replies, "I spend all my spare time in the library reading and studying." Later that afternoon, John's psychology professor notices that John is walking into the library instead of the cafeteria, where John usually hangs out after class.

_____ Lance Armstrong is pedaling up the mountains in France. He is racing in the Tour de France. From time to time he notices riders trying to overtake him on the left and right. Each time, he immediately pedals faster to keep ahead of them. Lance wins this stage of the Tour de France.

_____ Jan is a high school soccer player. She plays midfield adequately, but her coach tells her she should pass the ball more rather than try to dribble it up field. After watching the USA Women win the World Cup Soccer Championship, Jan scores five assists (passes) in the next four games.

_____ Jim walks into a casino in Las Vegas and notices the woman at the third slot machine on the right pull off a jackpot. When exiting three hours later, Jim notices an older gentleman pull off a jackpot on the same slot machine. Jim tells the people he is with to wait a few minutes. He walks over to the "lucky" slot machine and begins to play it.

reflection, and the ability to learn through observation (Bandura, 1986, pp. 18–31). Given these assumed abilities, his theory is not so much about the development of cognitive processes as it is about how such processes are used in observational learning. It is a theory about the outcomes that are produced (observational learning) through the operation of cognitive factors rather than a theory about the development of those cognitive factors. Certainly Bandura recognizes that cognitive factors change over time, but he attributes these changes to observational learning rather than to independent changes in the factors themselves.

Bandura (1986) points out that even a supposedly simple act is determined by multiple, interacting determinants, and most courses of action are initially shaped in thought (Bandura, 1997, p. 116). When watching TV, for example, personal preferences (cognition) partially determine at what times and which programs we watch. Some people prefer their news in the morning while dressing and eating breakfast and reserve evening viewing for pure entertainment (personal factors). At the "big picture" level, our viewing patterns (behavior) partially determine which programs are available for future viewing, while advertising and production costs (environment) partially determine what viewers are shown and thus constrain their possible choices.

While behaviors and personal factors are important, environmental influences are often structurally organized by society and can produce profound influences on observational learning. For example, U.S. society is often socially differentiated along age, gender, ethnic, and socioeconomic lines, and these organizational structures largely determine what models and what behaviors we are exposed to (Bandura, 1997). Consider, for example, the social organization of elementary schools staffed primarily by adult females, and contrast that with the social organization of Marine boot camp. We can find socially imposed patterns of organization all the way from the first-grade classroom to the scientific laboratory and corporate boardroom. Bandura's point here is that some of our values, attitudes, beliefs, and even prejudices are developed not so much through watching models as they are through our exposure to the structural characteristics of the setting.

Bridge Principles

The concept of triadic reciprocality implies the operation of several subordinate factors that constitute the theory's bridge principles. **Differential contributions** consist of the relative influence associated with each of the individual components of reciprocal causation. **Temporal dynamics** of interacting components refers to the timing of behavioral, environmental, and personal events. **Fortuitous determinants,** the role played by chance events, give unexpected opportunities and impose unforeseen constraints on behavior. Each bridge principle is described in turn.

Differential contributions of the triadic factors means that the impact of behavior, environment, and personal factors on social learning varies according to circumstances, individuals, and activities. For example, when environmental conditions are the primary influence, individuals would be expected to behave pretty much the same, much like children eating a meal or teenagers at a rock concert. If environmental constraints are weak, personal factors may dominate a situation, as when, for example, students decide what they will do on their first free day of summer vacation. Some personal factors such as false beliefs, defensive behavior, unusual habits, and unconventional values may be so strong that they partially insulate individuals from corrective environmental influences (Bandura, 1986). For example, very bright but equally shy students may feel inhibited from speaking out in class, even when praised by their teacher and other students.

Temporal dynamics means that the triadic factors exert their influence over time and often in different amounts. People everyday choose between activities that produce short-term and long-term results. More importantly, some choices made during formative periods carry special weight because they lead to enduring or life-altering events (Bandura, 1997, p. 161). When an elementary school child, for example, makes a decision to attend a particular college, we understand that, given the child's immaturity, such a decision may be revisited many times. In contrast, when a high school senior announces a decision to attend the state university the following year, we give much more credence to the selection and accord it customary expectations for the adolescent's future.

Temporal dynamics also refers to the variation in time between causes and effects. For example, dedicated athletic training typically produces effects that occur gradually. An ardent kiss produces a more immediate reciprocal effect than does mailing a friendship card. A steady diet produces less-immediate but more-enduring and beneficial health effects than fasting.

The principle of *fortuitous determinants* refers to the entire class of unforeseen chance events that alter individuals' life courses in enduring and important ways. Bandura notes that most developmentalists avoid trying to explain how chance events influence learning because their effects are so unsystematic. In contrast, social cognitive theory recognizes that chance plays a more important and enduring role in determining "life paths" than is often recognized. The effects of chance events lie in the kinds of interactive processes they initiate rather than in qualities of the events themselves. For example, an unintended meeting between two children may have little consequence, whereas for two adults, a chance encounter may lead to marriage. Even traffic accidents can inalterably modify one's driving behavior.

Change Mechanisms

While the three elements of triadic reciprocality determine what, where, and when observational learning will occur, they do not explain the "how" of behavior acquisition. To explain the mechanisms of observational learning, Bandura differentiates between an **acquisition phase** and a **performance phase**. It is during the acquisition phase that new behavior is actually learned. However, once acquired, a behavior may or may not be performed. It is the performance phase that determines when a previously acquired behavior will be displayed. The relationship between acquisition and performances phases and their attendant components is shown in Figure 9.2 on page 234.

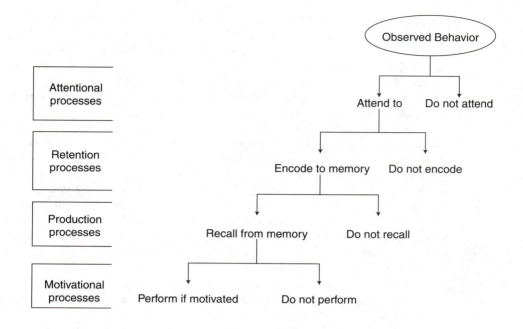

Only some behaviors that have been observed and encoded to
memory will later be recalled and actually performed.

FIGURE 9.2   Subprocesses governing observational learning.

Bandura emphasizes the cognitive components of how we learn from models
and thus might be expected to be more closely aligned with Piaget's cognitive theory than with behavioral theory, but there is a critical distinction between the two.
For Bandura, the components of cognition originate in the external world. Observational learning teaches us what, how, when, and where to activate a specific memory of a model's behavior. Consequently, his theory, which locates in external
models the source of learning (both cognitive and behavioral), is an example of an
exogenous theory even though it utilizes mental constructs such as cognitive
processes. Piaget, in contrast, views cognition as the result of synthetic construction,
which is why his theory is taken up in the constructivist paradigm.

Acquisition Phase

Attentional Processes.   In order for observational learning to occur, individuals must
do more than be passive sponges to experience. They must pay attention to and
accurately perceive the important characteristics of the behavior to be learned. *Atten-*

tional processes govern which aspects of a model are ignored, which are attended to, and which are selected from the multitude of ongoing model behaviors. For example, teachers and parents both attempt to make complex tasks a bit easier for children by supplementing them with attention-directing aids—decomposing them into discernable steps, amplifying them with verbal descriptions, or giving concrete examples. Observer characteristics also play a part in observational learning to the extent that prior learning, familiarity, and training can prepare the perceiver to attend to more subtleties than might otherwise be possible. In addition, models can attract attention by their distinctiveness, prestige, power, and success (Bandura, 1986). In this regard it should not be surprising that the authors' spouses would rather receive a golf lesson from Arnold Palmer or Jack Nicklaus than from their husbands.

Another component of attention is the functional value or utility of the observed activity. Activities that produce desirable rewards *for the model* are more likely to be imitated by an observer, and models whose personal attributes are desired by observers (e.g., professional athletes, rich people, Nobel prize winners) are more likely to be imitated. In short, individuals tend to pay more attention to effective and influential models than to those who are not (Bandura, 1986).

Retention Processes.   People cannot be influenced by models they do not remember. Remembering modeled behaviors requires that we encode their critical features into our memory. Active memory involves the transformation and reorganization of events into mental representations (symbols, rules, and concepts) that facilitate retention of events for later recall. *Retention processes* include symbolic transformations, representational systems, and rehearsal.

The two most important representational systems involve mental images and language. Sometimes observed activities are encoded in terms of symbolic mental images. For example, many of us know how to drive to our best friend's residence using a "mental map," even though we may not know the precise address or apartment number. The second mode of representation, language, involves encoding observed activities into words, rules, or phrases. This mode is often found in primary grades where children are specifically taught the alphabet song and even a simple rhyme for counting ("one, two, buckle my shoe . . ."). The fact that words often evoke corresponding images implies that the two representational systems function in an integrated rather than mutually exclusive manner.

According to Bandura (1986, 1997), symbolic transformations are not simply mental copies. Instead, they are cognitive manipulations that confer personal meaning on events while also preserving important information that allows later decoding of that symbol into actions. In this respect, rehearsal (mental practice) may serve as an important memory aid. By rehearsing or actively practicing observed activities, values, or attitudes, people are simply less likely to forget. In fact, some behaviors become so routine they can be performed almost automatically with only minimal representational guidance (e.g., counting, tying shoelaces, dialing a good friend's phone number).

Performance Phase

Production Processes.   The second phase of observational learning involves *production processes* that transform memories and encodings into courses of action appropriate for a situation, place, and time. Overall, these processes function to match behavior to one's representation of it by initiating, organizing, guiding, monitoring, and correcting one's behavior. For example, one evening a parent discovers her daughter trying to shave her leg. She wasn't very adept at it, and while she didn't cut herself, she did push and pull the razor up and down her leg. This mimicry doesn't represent so much a new behavior as it does a new organization of already learned component responses such as grasping, pushing, and pulling. Moreover, the fact that the daughter watched herself "shaving" in front of the bathroom mirror indicates her interest in monitoring her own performance.

The extent to which individuals benefit from observing models depends in part on the timing of feedback (consequences), its informational content, and the person who gives it. For example, to enhance student learning, most teachers learn to display precise behaviors that can be emulated by students, to carefully monitor student performance, and to provide evaluative feedback with as much detail as possible.

The ability to reproduce behaviors is also affected by maturation. For example, infants are unable to imitate adult speech, and although toddlers can imitate some speech, they have difficulty imitating a two- or three-step sequence of behaviors. Young children are also unable to retell a story in the proper sequence of events even though they may pay great attention to its reading.

Motivational Processes.   Social cognitive theory recognizes that while people may learn new behaviors, they do not perform everything they learn. *Motivational processes* explain the discrepancy between acquisition and actual performance. Motivation is an important determinant of when, under what circumstances, and how often learned behavior will be displayed. But performance is influenced by three types of motivators: direct, vicarious, and self-produced (Bandura, 1997).

Direct incentives occur when imitated behaviors are followed by external consequences to the observer rather than the model, as when an observer receives a reprimand, a kiss, or a special treat. In contrast, vicarious motivation occurs when a model receives reinforcement whether or not the observer is reinforced. For example, newspapers, magazines, and television media often recount acts of heroism by our nation's men and women. Although we receive no reinforcement, we may be vicariously motivated as observers to emulate heroic acts, because heroes have been reinforced for their deeds with public acclaim and adulation. Individuals' unique prior learning and experience will also influence what has incentive value when they observe models. For example, a model who receives candy may provide sufficient incentive for children, but a model who receives money is far more likely to be motivating for adults.

Self-produced motivation also determines how people react to their own behaviors and influences which ones they are most likely to display in a particular situation. For example, a son's first attempts at dressing himself and tying his own shoelaces support his self-conception as behaving like a "big boy." Subsequently, he may insist on performing these same behaviors himself even though his tedious, time-consuming skills cause him to miss valuable playtime.

It is important at this point to compare Bandura's concept of vicarious reinforcement with Skinner's belief that reinforcement operates to condition operant behavior by building associations. Bandura maintains that reinforcement works because it is primarily informative and motivational, not because it builds associations. In other words, the consequences of a model's behavior inform observers of what can reasonably be expected to occur should they perform the same (or a similar) behavior under the same conditions.

The reader may be left with the impression that Bandura's change mechanism, invoking two phases and four cognitive processes, is very complicated. However, the theory's technical jargon disguises some relatively simple, straightforward ideas about observational learning that many people take for granted. These are described more fully in Sandlot Seminar 9.3.

Sandlot Seminar 9.3

Bandura's Two Phases and Four Cognitive Processes

Bandura's change mechanism involves two phases and four cognitive processes. While these elements have technical names, they typically reflect intuitive notions many people have about how learning occurs. Examine carefully the following columns, and then answer the questions that follow them.

Technical Jargon	*Translated Meaning*
ACQUISITION PHASE	*Observing and learning something new*
Attentional processes	You have to look at or hear a model in order to learn something new.
Retention processes	You have to encode or mentally represent what it is you intend to learn.
PERFORMANCE PHASE	*Remembering and deciding whether to do something you've learned*
Production processes	You have to remember your encoding or mental representation in order to initiate and guide your modeled behaviors.
Motivational processes	There's no good reason to perform what you've learned from another unless you want to. "Wanting to" means that you expect some payoff (no matter how small), which is what motivates you to display a learned behavior, value, or attitude.

(continued)

Sandlot Seminar 9.3   Continued

1. Which column is easier to understand? Why?
2. Which column contains a more *efficient* linguistic means of communicating about the meaning involved? How did you decide?
3. What is the purpose of theoretical jargon (see Chapter 1)?
4. Does Bandura abuse or take advantage of theoretical jargon? (Answer this question only after reviewing the section on Bridge Principles in Chapter 1.) How did you decide?

Explaining Human Development: The Research

The most supportive research for social cognitive theory is found in the literature on children's socialization. Described here are samples of studies of aggression, altruism, sex roles, and self-efficacy.

Aggression

Research on aggression provides one of the most clear-cut examples of children's observational learning. Early studies established the presence of a relationship between parents' and children's behavior. For example, very aggressive children tend to come from families in which parents often fight, commit violent crimes, or exercise severe and erratic punishment (Bandura & Walters, 1959; McCord, 1979). Moreover, a steady diet of aggressive cartoons has been shown to be associated with increases in aggressive displays—hitting, kicking, and throwing things—in preschool children (e.g., Friedrich & Stein, 1973; Steuer, Applefield, & Smith, 1971), and these effects seem to be cumulative in that children who consistently prefer violent television are more likely to become aggressive as adults (Eron, Lefkowitz, Huesmann, & Walder, 1972). In one series of typical experiments, institutionalized male delinquents were exposed to either an aggressive or a nonaggressive movie for each of five consecutive nights (Parke, Berkowitz, Leyens, West, & Sebastian, 1977) and were prevented from watching television during the week. Boys exposed to aggressive movies displayed more restlessness, foot stamping, yelling, and shouting than those exposed to nonaggressive movies. In addition, the boys who watched aggressive movies behaved more violently toward one another following the movies than did the other boys, and this aggressive pattern was most pronounced among the more dominant males.

Certain characteristics of models and situations are associated with the frequency of imitated aggression. For example, children are more likely to model aggression when the model is rewarded or escapes punishment for the aggressive act than when the model is punished (Bandura, 1986). This tendency applies to children even when the aggressive act is fictional rather than real-life, whether it depicts cartoon or real-life characters, and whether presented in live, television, or film format (Meyer, 1972; Stein & Friedrich, 1975). Findings like these suggest that widespread concern over children's viewing of television violence might be justified, although they do not clearly delineate between conditions that promote acquisition versus performance.

However, merely observing aggressive models does not in itself produce imitative aggression. It can result in reduced altruism (Drabman & Thomas, 1974; Hapkiewicz & Roden, 1971), reduced emotional sensitivity to violence (Cline, Croft, & Courrier, 1973; Thomas, Horton, Lippincott, & Drabman, 1977), and a distorted view of social reality (Stein & Friedrich, 1975).

Altruism

While children clearly learn aggressive forms of behavior by observing models, they also learn altruism—acts of concern directed at the welfare of others. In a recent review of this research literature, Bryan (1975) concluded that a wide variety of prosocial behaviors—exhibiting sympathy, rewarding others, rescuing, and sharing—can be taught through observational learning. In fact, children learn to behave altruistically even in situations in which adults are not present, and they generalize altruistic behavior to situations unrelated to that in which an altruistic model was originally observed (Rice & Grusec, 1975; Rushton, 1975).

The acquisition of altruism through observational learning takes many forms. Nursery school children whose parents are frequently affectionate exhibit hugging, kissing, and friendly greetings to others (Hoffman & Saltzstein, 1967). Children's television programs such as "Mr. Roger's Neighborhood" and "Sesame Street" often develop themes that demonstrate altruistic relationships between characters, and when entire classrooms of nursery school children watch either of these programs as a part of their daily routines, there is a significant increase in their prosocial behaviors within the classroom environment (Friedrich-Cofer, Huston-Stein, Kipnis, Susman, & Clewett, 1979). Young children in particular seem to benefit more from watching models than from verbal instructions (Grusec, 1972; Grusec & Skubiski, 1970). Finally, models who are warm and attentive toward children (Bryan, 1975; Weissbrod, 1976) or are perceived to have power over them (Bryan, 1975) are more likely to be imitated than models lacking these qualities.

In a different vein, the concept of triadic reciprocality posits a crucial role in social learning for situational factors, and a number of studies have examined the manner in which these contextual parameters influence observational learning. For example, the presence of bystanders has been shown to inhibit altruism toward others in distress (Darley & Latane, 1968; Latane & Rodin, 1969), and this inhibiting effect seems to begin in the mid-elementary years (Staub, 1970). Mood may also play an important situational role in observational learning. For example, children asked to think of something that makes them happy are more likely to share money they have been given than children asked to think about other things (Moore, Underwood, & Rosenhan, 1973; Rosenhan, Underwood, & Moore, 1974), and college students who happen (by experimenter design) to experience a positive event (receiving cookies or a gift, finding money) are more willing to help someone with a phone call or by mailing a letter they find (Isen, Clark, & Schwartz, 1976; Levin & Isen, 1975).

Sex Roles

Sex-role development, in terms of behaviors, values, and motivations, has often been associated with observational learning. By the time children are 2 years old, they already show considerable sex typing in toy and activity preferences (Blakemore, Larue, & Olejnik, 1979; Etaugh, Collins, & Gerson, 1975). Knowledge of sex-role stereotypes comes later, around 3 years of age (Blakemore et al., 1979; Kuhn, Nash, & Brucken, 1978), by which time preschool and early elementary school children hold fairly rigid, though concrete, stereotypes. For example, they tend to believe, in spite of parental claims to the contrary, that doctors must be men, and nurses must be women. Later in childhood such stereotypes become more relaxed as children realize that many activities are not the exclusive province of one sex, although some behaviors may be more typical of one sex than the other (Garrett, Ein, & Tremaine, 1977; Meyer, 1980). In turn, high school students hold to more rigid stereotypes than adults (Urberg, 1979).

Sex-role stereotypes consist of mental images of and beliefs about how males and females are "supposed to" behave. These cognitive representations often provide important guides for memory and forethought and may affect the manner in which children attribute meaning to their perceptions. Most people, for example, are prone to ignore or forget information that is incongruent with their beliefs (Martin & Halverson, 1981). Applying this principle to sex-role stereotypes, Koblinsky, Cruse, and Sugawara (1978) read stories to a group of fifth-graders in which male and female characters engaged in both sex-appropriate and sex-inappropriate activities. When asked to retell the stories later on, the children remembered the sex-appropriate activities much better than the sex-inappropriate activities. Even more striking findings were reported by Cordua, McGraw, and Drabman (1979) who showed 5- and 6-year-old children a short movie about a male nurse and a female doctor. After the film, the children reported that the doctor had been male and the nurse female. Interestingly, children have a harder time remembering a male performing a stereotypical female activity than a female performing a traditional male activity (Cordua et al., 1979; Liben & Signorella, 1980).

Self-efficacy

A more complex form of observational learning comes in the beliefs and values we learn about how well we can control our own lives; this construct is called self-efficacy. Studies of children burdened by unrelenting adversity provide insight into the origins and growth of self-efficacy. Such children grow up in families plagued by chronic poverty, physical neglect or abuse, divorce, or parental alcoholism or mental disorders. Children who are resilient under such circumstances have learned proactive, resourceful behaviors for shaping their lives (Werner & Smith, 1992). In contrast, children with low social efficacy encounter many obstacles to good peer relationships (Connolly, 1989). In some families, parents and siblings learn to control each other by coercion and aggression, and self-efficacy associated with aggressive control is associated with later delinquency (Paterson, DeBaryshe, & Ramsey, 1989). Children's self-efficacy beliefs are correlated with their social goals and their likely behavior in different social situations (Erdley & Asher, 1996).

School environments foster self-efficacy in different ways than families. Children with high self-efficacy exhibit higher academic goals and engage in more out-of-school learning than do similar students with low self-efficacy (Zimmerman, Bandura, & Martinez-Pons, 1992). Even teachers may have their own self-efficacy eroded when they experience recurring difficulties with low-performing students (Bandura, 1993).

Adolescents experience simultaneous transitions in puberty, schooling, and social groups that challenge their ability to navigate important life changes. Their sense of self-efficacy plays a vital role in the success of the journey. For example, low self-efficacy leads boys to become despondent over social relations, and a sense of low academic efficacy leads to problem behaviors, low prosocialness, and deficient academic performance (Pastorelli, Barbaranelli, Bandura, & Caprara, 1996). Adolescent girls, in contrast, tend to experience depression about their academic performance no matter how well they do in school, and they get depressed more than boys over many aspects of their lives that impinge on social relations. For both boys and girls, however, supportive family and peer relationships mitigate against depression (McFarlane, Bellissimo, & Norman, 1995).

Managing new pressures of sexuality should be influenced by teenagers' beliefs about their self-efficacy. Research by Kasen, Vaughan, and Walter (1992) shows that this is the case. High self-efficacy is associated with effective contraceptive use. Moreover, even among women who are knowledgeable about contraceptives and intend to use them, self-efficacy consistently differentiates between those who put their intentions into practice and those who do not (Heinrich, 1993; Basen-Engquist & Parcel, 1992). Unprotected sex puts teens at risk of pregnancy and sexually transmitted diseases. Yet teen programs that incorporate self-efficacy training produce significant reductions in risky sexual behavior for both male and female adolescents (Jemmott, Jemmott, & Fong, 1992; Jemmott, Jemmott, Spears, Hewitt, & Cruz-Collins, 1992).

Engaging in risky behaviors and life-styles is also influenced by self-efficacy. Insecure adolescents with low self-efficacy are more involved with drugs, unprotected sex, and delinquent conduct than those who have a strong sense of self-efficacy (Allen, Leadbeater, & Aber, 1990).

Contributions and Criticisms of Social Cognitive Theory

Contributions

Observational Learning. Observational learning is an important explanatory concept that accounts for the acquisition of novel behaviors that have not been directly reinforced. This concept is a more direct explanation of how, for example, children might imitate something they have seen on television or read in a book than

Skinner's account, which posits that novel behaviors must be gradually shaped through reinforcement of successive approximations. The concept of observational learning also has a certain elegant simplicity as a theoretical construct that is immensely useful to our understanding of how children learn.

Cognitive Processes.   Social cognitive theory presents an account of learning and development that, unlike Skinner, makes a strong appeal to the influence of mental processes in learning. These processes help us understand two important things: (1) how a behavior can be acquired without being displayed and (2) how individuals behave not in terms of reality as it actually is, but in terms of how they perceive it to be.

Bandura is also different from Skinner in the kind of data deemed to be important to a theory of human learning. Where Skinner relied on animal experiments to derive general laws of learning, Bandura studied children directly. His choice of humans as objects of investigation is as closely connected to the claims he makes about social learning as are generalizations to humans from animal learning experiments. After all, Bandura assumes certain cognitive processes that enable humans to learn through observation; Skinner made no such assumption. That difference is what motivated Bandura and Skinner to study different creatures.

Criticisms

Developmental Differences.   Bandura emphasizes the role of three factors—environment, behavior, and cognitive processes—in explaining development. However, he gives virtually no attention to developmental differences between infants, children, and adults in terms of the cognitive processes available to them or their ability to profit from models. It seems reasonable to suspect that an infant's social smile in response to a father's face reflects vastly different cognitive processes than those underlying a 12-year-old's computation of the area of his backyard after reading the school's mathematics book. The unanswered question here is, do the processes underlying observational learning change during development and, if so, how?

Cognitive Processes.   In establishing the importance of observational learning, Bandura seems to subscribe to a "copy" theory of knowledge even though he doesn't want to. Recall that he believes symbolic encodings are constructive in the sense that they are not exact copies of a model's behavior. However, his work emphasizes how experience may be represented (and sometimes misrepresented) and stored for later recall. In this way, selective attention, symbolic representations, abstract modeling, and vicarious motivation are all believed to derive from social origins. That is, they derive from external reality and are acquired through observational learning. But social cognitive theory does not explain how symbolic representations of specific events come to organize themselves spontaneously into complex belief structures, personal attitudes and interests, or problem-solving strategies not directly observable in the activities of models.

Social Conformity.   Hoffman (1971) argues that social learning theory is limited to explaining how learning leads to similarity between children's behavior and that of adults. Social norms and adult social behavior are implicitly held as targets toward which children should strive, and conformity to such norms is considered a mature state of social learning. The problem Hoffman sees is that unconventional behavior is by implication considered to be "less developed" than conforming behavior. Yet, individuals who display unconventional behavior sometimes lead the way to widespread social reforms in the definition of conventional behavior (e.g., the sexual revolution, the women's movement, the civil rights movement). A theory that assumes that development naturally progresses toward increasing social conformity cannot at the same time explain the development of truly novel forms of behavior that entail new ways of adapting to the world.

Evaluation of Social Cognitive Theory

Before reading the following section, test your reasoning. Sandlot Seminar 9.4 asks you to evaluate Bandura's theory. Recall that you have already read evaluations of theories in the endogenous and exogenous paradigms.

Sandlot Seminar 9.4

How Would You Evaluate Bandura's Theory?
Use your own understanding to evaluate Bandura's theory of social cognitive development on each of the three sets of criteria. It may be useful to review Chapter 2 before proceeding. Compare your evaluations and reasons with those given by the authors.

Scientific Worthiness
Testability   _____
External validity   _____
Predictive validity   _____
Internal consistency   _____
Theoretical economy   _____

Developmental Adequacy
Temporality   _____
Cumulativity   _____
Directionality   _____
New mode of organization   _____
Increased capacity for self-control _____

Pedagogical Usefulness
Intrepretability   _____
Versatility   _____
Availability   _____
Guidance   _____

Scientific Worthiness

Testability.   There are several reasons social cognitive theory is rated high for its testability (see Table 9.1). As an example of the exogenous paradigm, the theory has much in common with Skinner's operant conditioning. It concentrates on measurements of observable behavior, and the extensive use of experimental situations advances the search for cause–effect relationships. Recall the description of typical research methods employed by Bandura in the Problems for Study section. Using such methods, researchers can clearly test their hypotheses about observational learning because behavioral performance is easily observed. However, while Bandura does differentiate between an acquisition phase and a performance phase in observational learning, the two cannot always be separated empirically. For example, a problem occurs in attempting to disprove observational learning; that is, if an observed behavior is not performed, it is difficult to determine whether its absence is due to a failure of acquisition or performance processes. There is no straightforward, objective means for resolving this problem within the social cognitive framework. Still, the theory's general emphasis on observable behavior, coupled with theoretical relationships that are frequently amenable to experimental study, support the high rating given the theory on this criterion.

External Validity.   The theory also gets a high rating for its external validity because of the well-established claim that individuals do acquire new behaviors through observational learning. There exists no compelling evidence that learning cannot occur by observing the activities of models, providing one takes into account the influence of mitigating variables (age of observer, conditions under which observation occurs, motivation, etc.). In fact, the importance of imitation in children's learning is recognized by many developmental theorists. For example, Piaget (1962) has devoted explicit attention to the role played by imitation in the development of thought. In addition, Freud's concept of identification, an unconscious process that resolves the Oedipus/Electra complex, implies (but does not state explicitly) that *something like* imitation may occur when boys incorporate masculine characteristics from their fathers and girls incorporate feminine characteristics from their mothers. On a different note, research has clearly demonstrated that imitation of a model is more likely under some circumstances than under others, is influenced by

TABLE 9.1   Ratings of Social Cognitive Theory for Scientific Worthiness

Criteria	High	Medium	Low
Testability	X		
External Validity	X		
Predictive Validity		X	
Internal Consistency	X		
Theoretical Economy			X

personal values and attitudes, and is mitigated by qualities of the model and characteristics of the behavior that are observed—all of which are elements of triadic reciprocality.

Predictive Validity.   Bandura's theory is rated medium for its predictive validity, primarily because there are so many possible variations within triadic reciprocality that predicting an effect is quite difficult. The theory does not, for example, specify why television violence may be imitated by some individuals but not others or why some people display socially conforming behaviors while others are stridently nonconforming. The inadequate account of the disparity between (1) a general tendency to learn through observation and (2) observational learning in some specific situations but not others is the basis for the medium rating given on this criterion.

Internal Consistency.   The theory garners a high ranking for its internal consistency. Three variables—behavior, environment, and personal cognition—are consistently used to explain observational learning. Ironically, the failure to acquire new behaviors through observational learning is also attributable to different interactional patterns among the same three kinds of variables. For this reason, social cognitive theory attempts to explain all observational learning as a function of triadic reciprocality. There are virtually no exceptions needed to account for the variety of observational learning effects. Given a specific mixture of interactive causes, only one possible outcome would be expected to occur. Future research will need to be conducted under many different controlled mixtures of these variables and will ultimately determine the internal consistency of the theory. At this time social cognitive theory has not been challenged on grounds of incompatible principles.

Theoretical Economy.   The theoretical economy of social cognitive theory is rated low because of two competing considerations. On the one hand, Bandura does attempt to account for an extremely broad array of social behaviors—altruism, creativity, empathy, conformity, aggression, friendship, helplessness, delinquency, and much more. On the other hand, a relatively large number of major assumptions are made about inborn cognitive capacities. Many developmental psychologists would question these assumptions, and some would contend that the cognitive capacities are themselves subject to developmental change rather than being inborn. In addition, one of Bandura's assumptions, that infants are innately predisposed to profit from vicarious reinforcement, is tantamount to saying that a tendency to imitate is an inborn quality. If such a predisposition is an inborn trait, then a theoretical explanation of observational learning, which itself is predicated on vicarious reinforcement, may be little more than a tautology—infants imitate because they are born to imitate. While Bandura's entire theory is not really so simplistic, the various cognitive processes he attributes to birthright play a prominent role in the concept of triadic reciprocality. In sum, Bandura attempts to explain a number of phenomena within a limited developmental domain, and he does it with preliminary assumptions that may be questionable. Moreover, at least one of the assumptions is used as the basis of the social learning argument that many behaviors can be acquired without direct reinforcement. Because of these problems, we have judged the theory to be low in terms of its theoretical economy.

Developmental Adequacy

Temporality.   Recall that for Bandura temporal dynamics explains the influence of time on how the triadic factors exert their influence (e.g., weight lifting takes months to build muscle mass, but a "crash" diet can produce several pounds of weight loss in only a few days). With this concept, Bandura specifically addresses the issue of how development occurs over time, so we have judged the theory to pass this criterion (see Table 9.2).

Cumulativity.   According to the theory, development occurs through the acquisition of new social behaviors. Some behaviors are acquired later in life because they are built upon or added to previously existing behaviors. In this manner certain behaviors (e.g., giving, pushing) may be prerequisite to other behaviors (e.g., altruism, aggression). Adolescents, for example, are generally considered to be "more developed" than children in part because they have more social behaviors and cognitive strategies available to them in any given social situation. Consequently, the theory passes this criterion.

Directionality.   Bandura contends that there is a progressive aspect to development, and it can be found in the movement toward increasing socialization. Older children are more mature because they display more adultlike social behaviors, in more situations, and more consistently than do younger children. For example, in the development of sex roles, there is a gradual progression from infancy into adolescence toward greater rigidity and conformance to sex-role stereotypes. Because youngsters are more likely to imitate older than younger models, advertisers spend billions of dollars each year portraying various images of more "mature" and desirable models. Finally, the fundamental question at issue here is: Does the theory account for how people develop from less socialized to more socialized states? The answer is "yes," and the mechanism is observational learning. For these reasons, the theory is judged to pass this criterion.

TABLE 9.2   **Ratings of Social Cognitive Theory for Developmental Adequacy**

Characteristic	Rating
Temporality	Yes
Cumulativity	Yes
Directionality	Yes
New Mode of Organization	No
Increased Capacity for Self-control	Yes

New Mode of Organization. Models may be imitated when individuals selectively attend to certain informational cues, encode relevant information for memory, remember the symbolic code, and rehearse the behavior to be modeled. Infants and toddlers are believed to learn new social behaviors in basically the same ways that adults do. More mature individuals organize their behaviors around the same principles as youngsters—motivation, selective attention, environmental situation, and model characteristics. At the same time, individuals are believed to modify their memories to correspond to past experiences, and such memories and symbolic encodings of information may be revised and given new meanings in light of new experiences. Modifications of encoded information consist of realigning and correcting one's conceptions in order to bring them into a closer match with actual or expected experiences. However, nothing in this account suggests that individuals evolve new organizational rules or new principles of learning that are not already found in experience. While Bandura attempts to account for learning abstract concepts, such learning is explained in terms of inductive generalizations from specific experiences. The theory does not view development in terms of the kinds of structural reorganizations found in Piaget's and portions of Freud's theories. Nor does it depict social learning at one age as the result of qualitatively different principles than at any other age. Consequently, the theory is judged to fail this criterion.

Increased Capacity for Self-control. Note that Bandura assumes the capacity for self-reflective consciousness as prerequisite to observational learning. Given this inborn capability, how does the capacity for self-control improve? Two of the three elements of triadic reciprocality lie outside direct personal control. Still, Bandura argues that forethought and personal motivation are important determinants of observational learning. Through social learning, individuals become more adept at anticipating social situations and matching their behaviors to expected outcomes. They learn certain expectations for conduct and standards for valuing behaviors by watching others. They learn to varying degrees self-efficacy. These acquisitions do not come from an automatic stamping in of associations between behavior and consequences; they involve judgments about which behaviors displayed by which models under which circumstances will be activated for display at a particular time and for a particular purpose. All of these considerations reflect elements of increasing self-control, which is why social cognitive theory passes this criterion.

Pedagogical Usefulness

Table 9.3 on page 248 shows our ratings for the pedagogical usefulness of Bandura's social cognitive theory of development. Like Skinner's theory, Bandura's tends to score well on these criteria. By their very nature, one should expect exogenous theories that emphasize environmental influences to score higher for their usefulness than those that do not.

Interpretability. As described earlier, Bandura's theory is weighted down with an abundance of theoretical jargon, and while most of his terminology is familiar

TABLE 9.3   Ratings of Social Cognitive Theory for Pedagogical Usefulness

Criteria	High	Medium	Low
Interpretability	X		
Versatility	X		
Availability		X	
Guidance	X		

ground to psychologists, it does produce a degree of dismay among novices. At the same time, recall from Sandlot Seminar 9.3 that much of the technical jargon is just a more precise way of communicating about ideas that really reflect some of our most basic intuitions about how children learn. In our opinion, Bandura's work is very interpretable, and his own writings contain far more specific examples of his meaning than one would normally encounter in theoretical presentations. This is why we rate his theory high for its interpretability.

Versatility.   Bandura's theory applies to virtually any learning (e.g., values, attitudes, behaviors) that occurs without reinforcement. This covers a huge range of learning possibilities, all the way from learning to crawl in infancy to learning values about the importance of voting in adulthood. For example, Bandura's ideas about the "salience" and "functional value" of models can be used by parents, counselors, and teachers to influence the behaviors of children, adolescents, and adults. Children's Television Network takes advantage of children's tendencies to learn from generous, kind-hearted models found on "Sesame Street." Adolescents reject such models but are quickly drawn to music stars and highly successful athletes. Young adults reject adolescent models in favor of others who demonstrate financial success or sexual prowess. Middle-aged and older adults reject earlier models and pay more attention to those who are successful in child rearing, family relations, and paying for college. In these situations and many more like them, Bandura's social cognitive theory does a good job showing how models, the situation, and one's past experiences (triadic reciprocality) interact to influence learning. Consequently, we rate the theory high for its versatility.

Availability.   Standard textbooks in developmental psychology provide at least an introductory treatment of Bandura's theory of social cognitive development. However, Bandura is not quite a "household" name like Skinner. His work tends to be highly academic, and his writings appear primarily in psychological journals and books. His theory is also relatively new. Few popular magazines have attempted to make the theory accessible for the population at large. Still, Bandura is one of the most readable modern theorists, and his work is filled with everyday examples of the theory at work. While we may upgrade this rating a decade from now, we currently rate social cognitive theory as medium for its availability.

Guidance. Bandura's theory does nearly as good a job in guiding professionals and parents as did behavior modification programs emanating from Skinner's theory of operant conditioning, so it receives a high rating for guidance. The most important element for influencing learning is knowing what motivates the learner, because it is motivation that determines whether a learned behavior will actually be performed. A very basic but powerful lesson is, when trying to teach a new behavior, provide a model.

Summary Points

1. Social cognitive theory has its roots in American behaviorism, but Bandura extends radical behaviorism to include cognitive factors in his account of social learning. Social cognitive theory attempts to explain how novel behaviors can be acquired in the absence of observable reinforcement.

2. In addition to innate reflexes, Bandura assumes that neonates possess a number of cognitive functions, including capacities of symbol formation, forethought, self-consciousness, and a capacity for vicarious learning.

3. The theory attempts to explain the acquisition of society's norms of thought and action. More specifically, the phenomena to be explained include the effects of observational learning, inhibition and disinhibition, response facilitation, and environmental enhancement. Researchers tend to operate within the American behaviorist tradition in their preference for experimental designs and observational methods.

4. The theory's internal principle is triadic reciprocal determinism. This principle is often called triadic reciprocality, and it refers to the interaction between three kinds of causal influences: behavior, cognitive and personal factors, and situational context.

5. The theory has three bridge principles: the differential contributions of the elements of triadic reciprocality, temporal dynamics or timing of events, and fortuitous determinants or chance interventions.

6. The mechanism of social learning occurs in two phases—acquisition and performance. The acquisition phase reflects the functioning of attentional and retention processes. The performance phase is governed by production and motivation processes.

7. Bandura's most important theoretical contributions are his account of (1) observational learning (acquisition of novel behaviors in the absence of shaping and observable reinforcement), (2) the influence of cognitive processes on behavioral acquisition and performance, and (3) the interaction of mind and society in individual development.

8. Social cognitive theory has been criticized for its inadequate account of age-related developmental differences, inadequate specificity of cognitive processes, inability to clearly explain differences between behavioral competence and performance, and implications that social conformity is a developmentally mature achievement.

9. The theory was rated medium high for both its scientific worthiness and its account of characteristics of development and medium high for its pedagogical usefulness.

PROBLEMS AND EXERCISES

1. Perform a simple exercise by comparing children's and adults' capacity to imitate an unusual, complex behavior. Using social cognitive theory, attempt to explain the similarities and differences in their learning.

2. Children and adolescents often sing or hum songs derived from television show themes. Explain the difference in theme songs displayed by these two groups in terms of the theory's internal and bridge principles.

3. Explain the impact "fortuitous determinants" have had on your development by describing a specific chance encounter or event you've experienced. Also describe what you learned and how it affected your life. In your opinion, should a developmental theory account for the role of chance? Why or why not?

4. Many instances of imitation in animals have been published. Do you think Bandura would rely on the same cognitive processes to explain animal imitation as he does human imitation? Why or why not?

5. Use the Internet to search for sites related to Albert Bandura and his theory. You can use his name as well as key words (internal and bridge principles). How do the Internet sites differ in terms of completeness and accuracy of information? What were the best sites you found? What problems did you encounter? What were some of the worst sites (and why)?

SUGGESTED READINGS

More about the Theory

Bandura, A. (1986). *Social foundations of thought and action.* Englewood Cliffs, NJ: Prentice-Hall.
Bandura, A. (1997). *Self-efficacy: The exercise of control.* New York: W. H. Freeman.
Wishart, J. G. (1986). Siblings as models in early infant learning. *Child Development, 57,* 1232–1240.

Research Reviews

Akamatsu, T. J., & Thelen, M. H. (1974). A review of the literature on observer characteristics and imitation. *Developmental Psychology, 10,* 38–47.
Mcall, R. B., Parke, R. D., & Kavanaugh, R. D. (1977). Imitation of live and televised models by children one to three years of age. *Monographs of the Society for Research in Child Development, 42* (No. 5).
Mischel, W. (1970). A social learning view of sex differences in behavior. In P. H. Mussen (Ed.), *Carmichael's manual of child psychology* (3rd ed., Vol. 2). New York: Wiley.

Critical Reviews

Kuhn, D. (1973). Imitation theory and research from a cognitive perspective. *Human Development, 16,* 157–180.

10 Vygotsky and Zones of Development

Preview Questions

What historical influences contributed to Vygotsky's theory of development?

What assumptions underlie his theory?

What is the problem of study, and how do the research methods match the problem?

What are the theory's internal and bridge principles?

What change mechanism accounts for development?

What differences can you find between Vygotsky's and Bandura's accounts of cognition?

Why is Vygotsky's theory a member of the exogenous paradigm?

What are the important contributions and criticisms of the theory?

How does Vygotsky's developmental theory rate for scientific worthiness, developmental adequacy, and pedagogical usefulness?

Historical Sketch

Lev Semyonovich Vygodsky was born November 5, 1896, in Gomel, a provincial town in Belarus several hundred miles from the Polish border. Little is known about his childhood except what derives from conversations with his childhood friend Dobkin and his daughter Gita (van der Veer & Valsiner, 1991). His Jewish parents were highly educated and enjoyed favorable financial conditions. They could afford to give their children an excellent education, so all the young Vygodskys were tutored at home instead of attending school. Young Lev was fortunate in that his tutor believed that learning involved more than simply filling a child's empty mind with memorized facts. The tutor taught Lev to be fully engaged in learning by answering questions, posing questions, processing answers, and thinking about how one piece of knowledge was integrated with other knowledge (Daniels, 1996). Although his parents were not very religious, Lev identified somewhat with traditional Jewish values (reading the Torah in Hebrew, giving a speech at his bar mitzvah). Under the Czarist government, Jews were subjected to periodic *pogroms* (ethnic exterminations). Still, Vygodsky and his family survived, and the young Lev probably led as normal a life as the conditions would allow, collecting stamps, studying, and playing chess (van der Veer & Valsiner, 1991).

Czarist Russia used a 3 percent quota system for admitting only the most qualified Jews to university. Lev was among those admitted to the University of Moscow, where he studied law and continued to spell his name with a "d." By the time he graduated in 1917, Vygodsky had become Vygotsky, Marxism was rampant, and the Bolsheviks controlled Russia. Into this cultural "stew," Lev returned to his hometown Gomel to teach in what had become "state" schools.

During the next ten years, his life deteriorated along with the general state of Russia. In 1920, Vygotsky contracted tuberculosis and fell seriously ill. Although he recovered, the disease plagued him throughout his short life. In 1924, the year Stalin took power after Lenin's death, Vygotsky fell in love, married, and promptly moved to Moscow. Life conditions did not improve, and in the upheaval of the revolution, Vygotsky shared miserable conditions with his fellow Muscovites. For example, he lived with his wife and two daughters in one room of an overcrowded apartment, and he undertook a weighty work schedule that included editorial work for a publishing house and a heavy teaching schedule of traveling back and forth between Moscow and Leningrad and Kharkov. He also worked for the Institute of Psychology and founded the Institute of Defectology, in which he directed the department of education for physically defective and mentally retarded children. And he continued periodic treatments for his tuberculosis.

Having withstood the Czar's Jewish pogroms, the Bolshevik Revolution, World War I, and tuberculosis, Vygotsky quickly gained influence in Moscow. He gathered together a large group of young, able scientists interested in psychology, defectology, and mental abnormality. Through them, his ideas gained power and influence, and some of his students later became paragons of Soviet psychology. Within a decade he had become the intellectual leader of Soviet psychology by championing a "new science." This "science" stood in sharp contrast to two ideas prominent in early twentieth-century psychology. First, both Soviet and American psychology presumed psychology to be a science of *behavior*. Second, American psychology reflected its national history of "rugged individualism" in pursuing explanations of *individual* development. Vygotsky railed against both of these traditions, and like many other theorists in this text, events in his personal life exerted an identifiable influence on his theoretical formulations.

Vygotsky and his followers reinvented Soviet psychology. They studied education, illiteracy, and remediation; cultural differences among hundreds of ethnic groups comprising the new nation; and those who where underserved by the new society. He was a Marxist and a psychologist (Newman & Holzman, 1993), and his agenda was to understand how individuals incorporate social (collective) consciousness into their own activities.

In 1934 Lev Vygotsky died after fourteen years of suffering from tuberculosis. Although tragically short, his professional life was very productive; he left behind several books, many articles, and drawers full of unpublished manuscripts (van der Veer & Valsiner, 1991). Still, he did not have the long-term opportunity for continued research, reflection, and theory refinement as other great theorists such as Freud, Skinner, and Piaget. Today, well over half a century after his death, Vygotsky's ideas are reinvigorating developmental psychology.

Why does Vygotsky's theory garner so much interest today? One major reason is that since the 1960s, both developmental psychology and education have shifted attention away from behavior and into investigations about children's cognitive processes and abilities. This shift from behavior to cognition has been accompanied by two other historical changes. First, according to Wertsch and Tulviste (1996), current interest in Vygotsky can also be traced to a relatively modern understanding (1) that the child is not an independent operating agent and (2) that cognitive development derives from an *interaction* between innate abilities and social experiences. Second, at the present time in developmental psychology, there seems to be a natural marriage between the importance of language, the influence of culture, and social interaction, all of which are given prominent roles in Vygotsky's theory of cognitive development.

Vygotsky's works most often cited in Western literature are *Thought and Language* and *Mind in Society,* both of which suffer from translation difficulties. For example, virtually all references to Marx were expunged from the first English translation of *Thought and Language* (Daniels, 1996). Consequently, the Vygotsky of Western academics was almost certainly not the Vygotsky of the 1920s and 1930s in postrevolutionary Russia. To understand Vygotsky properly, one simply must have some understanding of the ideological, political, historical, and social forces that pervaded Soviet culture after the revolution and before the end of the cold war.

Structural Components of Zones of Development

Assumptions

Vygotsky's theory makes three indispensable assumptions. The first two concern capacities and tendencies of the newborn. The third is concerned with the very nature of psychology, a predisposition to view child development in terms of Marxist historical materialism.

First, children are born with fundamental cognitive and perceptual abilities, including capacities for memory and for attention. Humans share these primitive abilities with other animals. During the first two years, these abilities develop and mature according to an inborn biological calendar and in response to the child's primitive contacts with the environment. Given these presumptions, Vygotsky's theory then begins when a child becomes capable of mentally representing the environment.

Second, the infant is an active agent in its quest for understanding and knowledge about the world. Interactions with the environment are purposeful and are aimed at adapting the individual to culture and to people such as parents, siblings, and others.

Third, Cole and Scribner (1978) describe Vygotsky's approach to child development as a "psychologically relevant application of dialectical and historical materialism" (p. 6). Their point is that Vygotsky didn't merely reflect the dominant Marxist political philosophy, he considered it endemic to the problems, methods, and explanatory mechanisms of psychology. Given the historical moment of postrevolutionary Russia, it should not be surprising that Vygotsky presumes the individual to be both a product and a servant of the culture.

Problems for Study

Phenomena to Be Explained.   In the broadest sense, Vygotsky's primary objective was to explain the development of thought. In his early works, he attempted to trace the evolutionary history of symbol use from apes to primitive tribes to modern humans (Vygotsky & Luria, 1993). Although he wrote extensively about language, those writings were almost always directed at deciphering its role in the formation of thinking.

A central idea of Vygotsky's theory is that lower psychological processes such as attention and arousal would be the same for all living people, while the higher psychological processes such as thought and language would differ between persons belonging to different cultures. In contrast to the influence of Pavlov in Soviet psychology, Vygotsky aimed to show that the structure and origin of these higher mental functions could not be attributed to instinct or to conditioned reflexes. He believed that a researcher must observe children at play, assess their efforts at learning, and measure their responses to teaching. By the time of his death, he had narrowed his investigations to two general problems of study: (1) explaining the social situations that define the child's life and (2) explaining the origin and development of thought.

Methods of Study.   In his early Moscow years, Vygotsky and his colleagues concentrated on two types of research. First, they studied rudimentary sign systems that mediate behavior, such as using fingers when counting, notching sticks as memory aids, or drawing straws to aid decision making. Second, they attempted to study how the child's behavior is internalized and restructured through the introduction of external signs during social interactions.

Later, however, Vygotsky turned his attention to the role speech plays, first in regulating social interactions, and then in directing individual behavior. More specifically, he initiated new work into the development of word meaning, its evolution from social interaction to the psychological mediation of individual behavior. To study the role of speech in regulating social behavior, for example, he set up a situation that required normal children to engage in cooperative activity with others who did not share their language (either deaf or foreign-speaking children). In another study, he provided different types of materials that children could use to solve a problem and then noted the various uses children make of these materials. A third technique, used to study the origin of new skills, involved a task that exceeded children's knowledge and abilities.

In general, Vygotsky employed various types of cognitive tasks to study concept formation and thinking strategies. In one such task, for example, a collection of wooden blocks varying in size, shape, height, and color were mixed up and laid out on a tabletop (Vygotsky, 1962). On the underside of each block was written one of four nonsense words: *lag, bik, mur,* and *cev.* These words were found only on the bottoms of certain blocks. For instance, regardless of color or shape, *lag* was found only on tall, large figures and *bik* only on large, flat ones. The researcher selected a "sample" block, turned it over, and read the word underneath. Then the subject was asked to pick out all the blocks that he thought contain the same word. When the subject was finished, the researcher turned over one of the *wrongly selected* blocks and revealed its hidden word. The subject was then asked to continue trying. After each attempt, another wrongly selected block was turned over. This process continued until the subject discovered that each nonsense word was associated with a particular type of block. The extent to which a subject used conceptual understanding could be inferred from the sequence of groupings he built. Every step of the experiment, from initial attack on the problem to handling the blocks to response correction to finding a complete solution, provided information about the subject's level of thinking.

Vygotsky's "experiments" are more reminiscent of Piaget's cognitive tasks than the carefully controlled environments of Skinner boxes. His data could be either qualitative or quantitative; sometimes an experiment yielded both. Detailed descriptions were often employed as substitutes for records of children's performance (Cole & Scribner, 1978). Finally, because he believed in the influence of culture, Vygotsky's experiments were often conducted in the "field" (e.g., in schools, home play, clinical settings) instead of in a laboratory.

Internal Principles

The Flow of Speech into Thought.   One of Vygotsky's most important theoretical contributions concerns the influence of speech, a social instrument, on the development of thought. Attempts to relate social events and situations to individual psychological processes have occurred throughout the twentieth century (Daniels, 1996). Yet few have taken a more direct route than Vygotsky, with speech being the key ingredient. More specifically, he contends that speech gradually turns into thought: "Thought is not merely expressed in words; it comes into existence through them" (Vygotsky, 1962, p. 125). In this view, speech is not simply a tool used to express thought; it is the reality and the form of thought as well. Consequently, speech organizes perception and creates new relations among psychological functions involved in such enterprises as remembering, drawing, writing, reading, and using number systems (Vygotsky, 1978). In other words, the memory of older children is not only different from younger children's memory, it also plays a different role in older children's cognitive activities. For example, *"For the young child, to think means to recall; but for the adolescent, to recall means to think"* (Vygotsky, 1978, p. 51 [original emphasis]).

For Vygotsky, the essential unit of thought is **word meaning,** because meaning has connections to both speech and thought. A word is simply an empty sound unless it means something, so meaning is indispensable. At the same time, Vygotsky contends that the meaning of every word is a generalization. This generalization or concept is instrumentally an act of thought. That is, word meaning is an instrument of psychological activity, analogous to a hammer or screwdriver as an instrument of labor. In this sense, meaning is intrinsically connected to both words and thought; meaning is both the form and the substance of thinking.

By way of overview, thought develops from preconcepts, through complexes or bundles of related ideas, and matures with pure concepts. Similarly, language influences thought through its own developmental phases: **social speech, egocentric speech,** and **inner speech**.

> The earliest speech of the child is . . . essentially social. At first it is global and multifunctional; later its functions become differentiated. At a certain age the social speech of the child is quite sharply divided into egocentric and communicative speech . . . Egocentric speech emerges when the child transfers social, collaborative forms of behavior to the sphere of inner-personal psychic functions. (Vygotsky, 1962, p. 19)

Types of Speech.   *Social speech* is external, communicative speech. Its signs and words serve children first and foremost as a means of social contact with other people (Vygotsky, 1978). Moreover, the

> human capacity for language enables children to provide for auxiliary tools in the solution of difficult tasks, to overcome impulsive action, to plan a solution to a problem prior to its execution and to master their own behavior . . . The cognitive and communicative functions of language then become the basis of a new and superior form of activity in children. (Vygotsky, 1978, pp. 28–29)

Egocentric speech is a transitional form between social and inner speech. While it is the basis for later inner speech, it is still embedded in external, communicative speech (Vygotsky, 1978). Egocentric speech reflects a new and superior form of activity in children and distinguishes them from the tool use of other animals.

Vygotsky (1978) claims that children's egocentric speech is as important as their physical actions when they are trying to solve a problem. According to him, they not only speak about what they are doing, their speech and actions are part of "one and the same complex psychological function" (Vygotsky, 1978, p. 24). Moreover, the more complex a problem is, the more the amount and the greater the role played by speech in achieving a solution. Speech is one among several other tools available to the child (e.g., vision, hearing, prehension) to help solve practical tasks. In addition, egocentric speech is pliable. Sometimes it simply expresses emotions; other times it seems to substitute for achieving a goal (Vygotsky, 1978). Egocentric speech lessens as children begin to think words instead of pronouncing them aloud, a sure sign that inner speech has begun to develop (Vygotsky, 1962).

The relationship between speech and action shifts during the period of ego-centric speech. In its early stage, speech accompanies a child's actions, while later it precedes action by functioning as an aid to a plan that has not yet been realized in behavior. By way of analogy, Vygotsky describes the drawings of young children, which can be named only after they have been completed. Children must first see what they have drawn to know what it is. As they get older, however, they begin to name in advance what they are going to draw. This naming displacement reflects a change in the function of speech, away from a description of action toward a planning function of the intellect. There are many examples in everyday life for how we use and sometimes even teach through the mechanism of speech. Sandlot Seminar 10.1 provides some examples.

Sandlot Seminar 10.1

Using Speech to Generate Thought
We often rely on the power of language and, in particular, words to learn new information and skills. We may memorize steps in a sequence, such as the long division algorithm: "estimate, multiply, subtract, bring down, ..." We may memorize concept definitions, as if the words in the definition will actually help us understand the concepts themselves. In learning a new athletic skill, we memorize key words that evoke images. Here are two well-known examples of how we rely on outer and inner speech to help us remember.

1. Can you name the planets in their order from the sun? We often use a simple memory device. The first letter of each word in the following sentence is also the first letter of each planet: "Mary's violet eyes make John stay up nights playing."

   Can you name the planets in order now?

   Mary's _____
   Violet _____
   Eyes _____
   Make _____
   John _____
   Stay _____
   Up _____
   Nights _____
   Playing _____

2. Teachers and parents use rhyming songs to teaching children simple facts.

   Counting: "One, two, buckle my shoe; three, four, open the door; five, six, _____"

   The Alphabet Song

Can you think of other examples?

Inner speech, according to Vygotsky (1962), ". . . is speech almost without words" (p. 145). That means that syntactic and phonetic elements of speech have been reduced to a minimum, thereby elevating pure semantic meaning into the forefront. In this way, inner speech uses word meanings stripped of their symbolic properties. Put differently, with inner speech we are no longer talking to ourselves inside our head (as with egocentric speech). Since inner speech depends heavily on the semantic meaning of words, Vygotsky (1962) chose to differentiate between three types of semantic properties. First, there is the "preponderance of the sense of the word" (p. 146). This means that words produce a variety of psychological events. Think of the word *race,* for example. Monitor your thoughts carefully. You may be generating images of race cars, Olympic track events, a high school race you won, faces of your college friends, or any number of other possibilities. All these thoughts taken together constitute the "preponderance" of sense given the word *race.* According to Vygotsky, this preponderance is the most stable semantic meaning of a word.

The second semantic property is *agglutination,* a way of combining several words into a new, more complex single word (Vygotsky, 1962). A young child growing up in New York City, for example, may first acquire separate meanings for *tall, office,* and *building.* But these separate meanings eventually become *agglutinated* into a single new word, *skyscraper.* As inner speech develops, children use agglutination to form compound words (e.g., *outside, eyebrow, textbook*) and express complex ideas such as society, justice, and health.

The third property of inner speech is the manner in which senses of words *combine and unite.* The word sense of *honor,* for example, may give rise to related but entirely different details of thought for a marine, a Japanese banker, a high school jock, and a city gang member. Each individual would find this single word "so saturated with sense that many words would be required to explain it in external speech" (Vygotsky, 1962, p. 148).

Inner speech is not the interior aspect of social speech; it is a function in itself. It still remains speech in the sense that thought is connected *with* words, but to a large degree, inner speech is thinking in pure meanings. It is dynamic and unstable, shifting back and forth between word and thought.

Pure thought is the highest plane of inner speech. But communicating thoughts can only be achieved in a roundabout way. "Thought must first pass through meanings and then through words" (Vygotsky, 1962, p. 150). Consequently, pure thought, meaning, and words interact at this level in complex ways. Thought and speech are not identical, and there is no fixed rule for their varied and possible interrelationships. As Vygotsky (1962) puts it, a single sentence can be used by different individuals in different contexts to convey different thoughts, but so also can a single thought be expressed using different sentences.

Zone of Proximal Development

According to Vygotsky (1978), there is a psychological distance between children's individual performance in solving problems and their potential for higher levels of performance when guided by more capable peers or adults. This psychological distance is called the **zone of proximal development**.

To take an example from Vygotsky, imagine the following situation. Two 6-year-olds enter the first grade with a mental age of 6. Are they the same? To a point, yes. Both have been tested, and their performance places them squarely on the average for 6-year-old children. During their first week of class, their teacher works independently with each child. She discovers that the first child can solve tasks normally solved by 9-year-old children, provided she gives supportive hints and asks leading questions during the activity. Using the same hints and questions, the second child cannot solve problems beyond the 7-year-old level. Are these two children at the same mental level? Vygotsky would say no. He would explain that their subsequent ability to learn would be markedly different because they possess different *zones of proximal development*, the psychological distance between children's actual performance and their level of assisted or potential performance. The first child's zone is three years; the second child's is one year.

The zone of proximal development defines the psychological functions that are in the process of maturing. From a developmental point of view, this zone foretells the child's immediate future. What is in the zone one week may well become a child's actual developmental level the next. By way of analogy, the developing functions might be likened to "buds" or "flowers" rather than fully mature fruit (Vygotsky, 1978).

The zone of proximal development is a powerful idea that has clear parenting and educational implications. According to Vygotsky (1978), when learning is properly organized, it results in mental development and sets into motion a whole variety of developmental processes. Learning, in the context of this zone, is a universal aspect of developing culturally organized psychological functions. Sandlot

Sandlot Seminar 10.2

Changing the Oil in Two Cars
One Saturday morning, a father decides to teach his 14-year-old son how to change the oil in the two family cars. After explaining to the son that the dirt and oil on the garage floor requires them to wear old clothes, both appear in the garage ready for the task.

First Car

DAD: Here's the socket and ratchet. Slide on under there and loosen up the oil plug.

SON: What does it look like?

DAD: It's the screw top sticking out of the back of the oil pan.

SON: Where's the oil pan? What does it look like?

DAD (crawls under the car): Here it is. This whole housing is the oil pan. See that screw (pointing)? That's what you have to unscrew.

SON: Which way do I unscrew it?

(continued)

Sandlot Seminar 10.2   Continued

DAD: It works like all screws. Clockwise to screw it in; counterclockwise to take it out.

SON (after trying for a while):   Dad, I think it's stuck.

DAD: It probably is very tight. Here, use this hammer to hit it. That should loosen it up a bit.

SON (after using the hammer to loosen the oil plug):   I think I got it. Now what?

DAD: OK. Now take it out slowly. You don't want the oil pouring out all over the floor. So before you unscrew it, slide this pan underneath to catch the oil.

SON: I think it's almost out. Now what should I do?

DAD: Go very slowly. The oil is under pressure, so it will spurt out backward. Set the pan slightly back but underneath the outlet.

SON (a minute later, when the oil slows to a drip):   What's next?

DAD: Did you get it?

SON: Yeah, it's pretty much done now.

DAD: Is it spilling on the garage floor?

SON: Dad, I got it, OK? Now what?

DAD (slides under car and finds no oil spilled on the garage floor):   That was good. Now before we put in the new oil, we have to replace the plug and tighten it.

(Dad and son then change the oil filter and replace oil.)

Elapsed time: 36 minutes

Second Car

DAD: Here's the socket and ratchet. Slide on under there and loosen up the oil plug. The oil pan looks just like . . .

SON (sliding under the car):   Dad I know! Just let me do it, OK?

DAD: OK, you do it.

SON: I got it. Do you want to check it out?

DAD: Not if you have it right.

SON: I got it.

DAD: Do you need a hammer to loosen it up?

SON: I don't think so. Just a minute. (After a short period of time) Dad, give me the drain pan.

DAD (pushing it under the car): Here

SON (sliding out from under the car with a big smile):   That was easy.

(The son then changes the oil filter and replaces the oil.)

Elapsed time: 19 minutes

1. Why did the second car take so much less time than the first?
2. How did the father's role change between the first and second car?
3. How does Vygotsky's zone of proximal development explain the time difference?
4. Would you expect a similar "zone" if the son had been 8 years old instead of 14? Why?

Seminar 10.2 exemplifies how the zone of proximal development occurs in the rather ordinary life of a teenage boy.

When young children begin to talk to themselves, often using words to accompany their actions, they cross an important threshold in their cognitive development (Vygotsky & Luria, 1994). From this point on, they will use language to direct their actions and to learn how to get things done (Wertsch & Tulviste, 1992). Moreover, it is at this point that language begins to shape children's mental abilities into higher-order cognitive processes (e.g., performing arithmetic, forming a hypothesis, planning a vacation) not found in other animals. The following example of a young child learning how to tie his shoe should clarify how this kind of language directs thought and action. The child is simply talking to himself, not directing his language to anyone in particular. "Okay, let's see, first we make a bow, there that's a bow, and then we follow the bunny around the bow, yes, that looks good. Then we take the bunny and put him in the hole, hmmmmmmm, where's the hole? Oh, there it is, and then pull it tight! Is that tight enough? Yes, I think it is!"

While each child progresses through the same sequence, these progressive changes are continuous rather than stage by stage. Moreover, cognitive development is strongly influenced by important adults and peers and by the experiences unique to one's culture. And while developmental changes are generally systematic between infancy and adulthood, their precise character varies from culture to culture because different types of social interactions occur. Imagine, for example, the child–adult interactions that occur on Israeli kibbutzim where multiple caretakers provide child rearing versus *monomatric* societies in which the mother provides virtually all child care. Also, the tasks around which learning occurs differ from one culture to another. For example, in some cultures young boys are expected to learn how to hunt, farm, or fish. But in many industrialized cultures, children are freed from such chores by a prolonged period of playing sports, having fun, and watching television. In short, children who must learn how to farm or forage in order to eat will have radically different social experiences and communicative exchanges than children who, at the same age, are learning how to ride a bicycle, put together a puzzle, or color in a coloring book. Moreover, children who live in cultures that place a premium on written language will face different cognitive challenges and will experience different social and communicative interactions than those which depend solely on spoken language.

Vygotsky differentiates between public and private speech. Public speech is communicative and social. It is a mainstay of adult social interaction. In contrast, young children engage in private speech, which is not communicative because it serves a different function. Anyone who has watched young children play has overheard how their private speech accompanies their activities. Sandlot Seminar 10.3 illustrates an example of private speech.

General Genetic Law of Cultural Development

A general "law" that connects culture with individuals lies at the heart of Vygotsky's (1981) theory of mind. This **genetic law** holds that any function in the child's cultural development appears on two different planes. First, it appears on the social plane in interactions with others. Only later does it appear within the psychological processes of the individual.

> This is equally true with regard to voluntary attention, logical memory, the formation of concepts, and the development of volition. We may consider this position as a law in the full sense of the word, but it goes without saying that internalization transforms the process itself and changes its structure and functions. Social relations or relations among people genetically underlie all higher functions and their relationships. (Vygotsky, 1981, p. 163)

Sandlot Seminar 10.3

Young Children's Private Speech

CHRIS (5 years old, putting together a dinosaur puzzle on the dining room table at home): "Tyranna . . . Tyraaaaaaaanna . . . Tyrannosaurus Rex. You can't hide from me. Where is your head? Head, Fred (giggling). I never heard of a dinosaur named Fred. Where is your head, Fred? (giggling). Turn over all the pieces first. Ah! Got you now. Hmm. Where is your mouth? Mouth . . . Mouth . . . Mouth . . . Come on out mouth. Gotcha! Now what (picking up the puzzle box and glancing at the picture)? I know. Look for the neck. Neck . . . Neck . . . Neck is heck. Oh Oh. This one looks like a neck and a tail. So Tyrannosaurus had two tails, only it had a head at the end of one tail and a tail at the end of the other tail. (Calling out) Daddy! Come here. I can't tell which ones are the tail and the neck." (Picks up puzzle box with picture but no pieces and goes searching for Dad.)

1. Is Chris's speech expressive, communicative, or some of both? Which parts?
2. Does the speech direct Chris's action or follow it?
3. Is all the speech in the example "private" speech? How can you tell?
4. In Vygotsky's scheme, how would you interpret Chris's word play at the beginning of the episode?

What Vygotsky is saying is that the individual develops not only new means of carrying out actions, but also qualitatively new kinds of mental functions. These actions and functions originate in social behavior, and through incorporation, they become changed into mental processes (Minick, 1996).

Imagine a young preschooler who is crying because she has had her feelings hurt. Retrieving a teddy bear from her supply box, Mrs. Johnson, her teacher, approaches and says, "Here's Teddy for you to hold, Samantha. He will make you feel better." Samantha reaches out to clutch the teddy bear, and rocking him in her arms, slowly stifles her sobs. Later she rejoins a group of children working a simple puzzle. The next day while watching a video, Samantha notices a tear in Mrs. Johnson's eye. Immediately she retrieves Teddy from the supply box and offers it to Mrs. Johnson saying, "Here's Teddy. You can hold him. He will make you feel better." It is this kind of scenario Vygotsky envisions when he theorizes that social actions change mental processes. He does not tell us how the act of transforming social into personal processes actually occurs. But he clearly underscores the importance of this general principle.

To look at it a different way, the *general genetic law* of cultural development generates the landscape upon which the individual's conceptual map gets laid out. Within that landscape, the zone of proximal development provides the settings in which culture and the individual are brought together.

Vygotsky contends that humans "master" themselves from outside in, and they do this through symbolic, cultural systems, the most systematic and powerful of which is language. However, it is not the linguistic tools or signs themselves that are important. What matters is the meanings encoded in them. It is the attachment of meaning to social symbols that children internalize. In this way, language functions as the basis for higher order mental processes (Knox & Stevens, 1993).

In somewhat cruder terms, Vygotsky sought to argue that collective activity gives rise to collectivist consciousness. This notion suggested, in the context of Marxist–Stalinist Russia, that the state could organize labor activities that would give rise to specific forms of individual consciousness (Daniels, Lucas, Totterdell, & Fomina, 1995). However, this is not to say that the social becomes individual by a process of direct transmission. Rather, individuals assemble their own sense and personal meanings from those that are socially available (recall Samantha and the teddy bear). The social voice becomes the inner voice as changes in social circumstances and patterns of communication give rise to changes in the patterns of personal meaning (Daniels, 1996). For example, a child's meaning for the word *mother* would be expected to differ markedly from the meaning that same word has for an adolescent or even a middle-aged woman. The differences in meaning arise from differences in the number and variety of social experiences with one's mother and with the word *mother*. Using an educational example, Vogotsky's approach would be heavily involved with collaborative learning and group problem-solving approaches, because he placed a great deal of emphasis on social interactions in the cognitive development process.

Bridge Principles

Phases and Stages.   Speech and behavior interact in the child's development. Speech first accompanies action, then precedes it, and finally displaces it by taking over the planning function so essential to complex thinking. According to Vygotsky, thought develops in the opposite direction posited by Piaget. That is, the Vygotskyian child internalizes external verbalizations to create thought, whereas the Piagetian child externalizes his internal thoughts through speech (Emerson, 1996). In other words, "development in thinking is not from the individual to the socialized, but from the social to the individual" (Vygotsky, 1962, p. 20).

But how, precisely does this development occur? Review the description of an experimental task with wooden blocks and nonsense words described in the Methods of Study section earlier in the chapter. From experiments like that, Vygotsky discerned that concept development occurs in three basic phases between early childhood and adolescence. Each phase entails corresponding "stages." These are described in Table 10.1.

For Vygotsky, word meaning carries the burden of generating thought because its essence unifies thinking and speech like a cognitive "glue." All thinking attempts to unify itself by establishing relationships between things, and word meaning supplies the force underlying this unifying process (Newman & Holzman, 1993).

Functional Activities within the Zone of Proximal Development.   Although Vygotsky seldom discussed theoretical applications of his work, Gallimore and Tharp (1990) and Tharp (1993) explicitly describe seven types of activities that teachers might employ to facilitate children's learning in the zone of proximal development. These activities include:

Modeling behavior for imitation gives the learner information and an image to remember as a later performance standard.

Feedback assists performance by giving a standard that can later be used for self-correction.

Contingency management applies reinforcement and punishment to control behavior.

Direct instruction provides clarity, information, and decision making about correct responses and solutions to tasks.

Questioning prompts a verbal response and mental operation that the learner would not produce alone and gives information about the learner's level of understanding.

Task structuring involves organizing a task into or from its components so that an overwhelming task is presented in understandable components within the zone of proximal development.

Cognitive structuring assists learning in the zone of proximal development by having students explain their reasoning. Knowing how students reason helps teachers and adults structure new learning situations.

It is instructive to note the similarity between the activities just described and the theoretical concepts introduced earlier in the Skinner and Bandura chap-

TABLE 10.1   Vygotsky's Stages and Phases of Concept Formation

Phase	Stage	Defining Characteristic	Child's Speech
1		Egocentric, unorganized conglomerations	
	1	Trial and error—grouping by guessing	Is that a dog?
	2	Visual organization—syncretic image, how things look	Four legs and furry with a tail means that is a dog.
	3	Two-step operations—comparing new objects to previous groupings	Wait. Some are cows. They have fur too.
2		Thinking in complexes; recognizing concrete similarities and differences (relationships) among objects	
	1	Associative complexes—a single property is shared by two or more objects in a group	Dogs and cows both have fur.
	2	Collections—a single property is shared or differentiated by members in a group	Dogs don't have horns. Cows do.
	3	Chain complexes—consecutive joining of new elements preserving one property from one object to the next	Cows have horns. So do deer and elk.
	4	Diffuse complexes—attribute fluidity	Dogs don't have horns; neither do horses. Horses are bigger.
	5	Pseudoconcepts—objects grouped by perceptual attribute rather than abstract concept	Those big ones are horses. But their feet look like a dog's with toenails.
3		Concepts—abstract generalizations, class inclusion	
	1	Part–whole relationships—unifying parts and separate members of a whole	A mammal has fur.
	2	Potential concepts—using concrete examples that lack generality or abstractness	A dog and a horse have fur, so they must be mammals.
	3	Concepts—abstract, rule-governed generalizations	All furry animals are mammals.

ters. For example, note how the first two and last activities in the list imply the kind of modeling from external models and monitoring of performance described by Bandura in social cognitive theory. Contingency management and direct instruction may even sound like Skinner's operant conditioning. Why do Gallimore and Tharp's proposals for using Vygotsky's theory sound so familiar? Perhaps one reason is that all three theories reflect the exogenous paradigm in that they naturally seek external methods, agents, and influences that produce changes in children's behavior.

Change Mechanisms

Vygotsky exemplifies the exogenous paradigm because he considered language, an environmental factor, to be the origin and influence underlying mental development. It is true that he took into account a certain degree of maturation for inborn cognitive and perceptual processes, but the primary mechanism governing cognitive development is a process called **internalization** (Vygotsky, 1978).

Thinking is determined by language and by the sociocultural experience of the child. Ultimately, children's inner speech depends on internalizing external, social speech. Consequently, intellectual growth is contingent on mastering the means of thought—language (Vygotsky, 1962).

Development continues from childhood to adolescence, and Vygotsky was very much aware of the adolescent's dynamic social and cultural growth. Even here, speech, through the power of *words,* was viewed as the primary, efficient cause of this rapid mental development:

> The . . . word, its use as a means of concept formation, is the immediate psychological cause of the radical change in the intellectual process that occurs on the threshold of adolescence . . . Learning to direct one's own mental processes with the aid of words or signs is an integral part of the process of concept formation. (Vygotsky, 1962, p. 59)

Explaining Human Development: The Research

While increasing attention to Vygotsky's work has been evidenced in the past two decades, a significant amount has been devoted to general conceptual and theoretical discussions. Relatively less attention has been given to empirical research that tests elements of Vygotsky's theory. In this section we review relevant research on two topics, private speech and the zone of proximal development.

Egocentric Speech

Recall that in Vygotsky's theory egocentric speech marks a transition between external, public speech and inner, thoughtful speech. Berk (1992) has examined situational and developmental aspects of egocentric speech. She has reported, for example, that children tend to use more egocentric speech when engaged in difficult tasks, after they have made errors, or in situations where they are not sure about how to proceed (Berk, 1992). Moreover, children who use egocentric speech while engaged in solving a puzzle exhibit greater engagement, more attention, and more improvement in subsequent tasks than their less-talkative age mates (Behrend, Rosengren, & Perlmutter, 1992; Berk & Spuhl, 1995; Bivens & Berk, 1990). In contrast, children who have learning difficulties tend to develop egocentric speech more slowly and to use it less (Diaz, 1987).

Does egocentric speech give rise to inner speech and thought? According to Berk and her colleagues, speech seems to move "underground" with age. More specifically, egocentric speech gives way first to whispers and then to silent lip movements (Berk & Landau, 1993; Bivens & Berk, 1990). In addition, there is a general pattern of diminishing egocentric speech as children mature (Berk & Landau, 1993; Frauenglass & Diaz, 1985).

Zone of Proximal Development

The literature on child pedagogy and child language refers to "scaffolding," the activities parents, teachers, and other adults engage in to support and extend children's development (see, for example, Plumert & Nichols-Whitehead, 1996). The concept of scaffolding is a very close cousin to Vygotsky's zone of proximal development, and as such, much of the literature on scaffolding can, by reasonable inference, also be applied to Vygotsky's theory.

One line of research in this vein concerns studies of "reciprocal teaching" aimed at understanding how adults help children solve problems or use strategies that are initially beyond their individual abilities (Valsiner, 1984). In one study (Brown & Palincsar, 1989), a teacher showed children how to summarize and clarify reading passages. Then later, through reciprocal teaching, the children took turns "being the teacher" in helping their classmates learn the strategies. This method led to improved reading among the reciprocal teachers (Radsiszewska & Rogoff, 1988). As Rogoff (1990) notes, "Children appear to benefit from participation in problem solving with the guidance of partners who are skilled in accomplishing the task at hand" (p. 169).

In another approach, children have been paired with adults or expert or naive peers to work on a problem. The results indicate that children benefit from cooperative learning, even when paired with a naive peer. However, their planning and problem solving improved significantly only when paired with an adult or expert peer (Azmitia, 1988; Radziszewska & Rogoff, 1988). According to Pressley (1995), children also tend to internalize difficult procedural knowledge when adults ask them questions and help them monitor their own behaviors.

In a different study Adams (1987) compared mothers who read stories to their 3-year-olds using class inclusion and taxonomy information about the story with mothers who did not. Two weeks later, the children who experienced those advanced conceptual strategies showed advances in their categorization of animals to a level approaching adult usage compared to the other children. Experiments also indicate that children learn memory strategies from parents who help them learn a list of items (Rogoff & Gauvain, 1986).

Vygotsky's fundamental concept of the zone of proximal development has been successfully applied by therapists to help victims of abuse develop a sense of self-control over their lives (Mittenburg & Singer, 1999). Tharp (1999) also has adapted the concept for effective implementation in therapeutic situations (Tharp, 1999).

Contributions and Criticisms of Zones of Development

Contributions

Zone of Proximal Development.   Vygotsky's most practical idea, the zone of proximal development, has been used to successfully design effective teaching situations. For example, Hedegaard (1996) taught young Danish students about the evolution of species using lesson plans derived from how the zone should function. Earlier, we described Gallimore and Tharp's (1990) educational practices they believe this concept implies. The Goodmans have argued that the zone of proximal development supports the use of the "whole language" instruction in elementary language arts (Goodman & Goodman, 1990). Finally, Moll and Greenberg (1990) have translated the zone of proximal development into "zones of possibilities" in describing how social contexts can be overlapped and combined for instructional purposes. More than any other Vygotsky concept, this one has invigorated educators with new ideas about how to structure classroom experiences that promote mental development and critical thinking, in contrast to more traditional aims such as skill acquisition or memorization of basic facts.

Societal Influence.   Vygotsky, at least as much as any other modern theorist, attempts to show us the power and impact of social influences on development. This should not be surprising, particularly in light of the sweeping changes that surrounded him in Russia. Even Erikson's (Chapter 4) view of society pales in comparison to the fundamental power society imposes on individual development in Vygotsky's theory. Society exerts its will on child development primarily through its language, and in Vygotsky's view, language becomes the essence of thought. So we have a direct connection between society → language → thought that instills the individual with a sense of self and purpose defined by social obligations and constraints: Preserve and extend one's culture through language.

Cognitive Science.   Vygotsky contends that language is the vehicle of thought, and that language is a rule-governed symbol system. Consequently, it should be possible to study language rules as vehicles for thinking rules. Such an approach has been taken by Frawley (1997), who attempted to show how modern "cognitive science" could be extracted from Vygotsky's theory. To be sure, Frawley's analysis reflects extractions from Vygotsky, and few others have followed his line of thinking. Still, the fact that Vygotsky's theory can be connected with modern cognitive science must be considered a contribution for a theory prepared over half a century ago.

Criticisms

Anchoring the Zone of Proximal Development.   Rogoff (1990) has argued that all attempts to augment a child's thinking must begin with the child's understanding. This is an important point that is often overlooked by parents, teachers, and researchers in their pursuit of improving children's performance. Virtually all empirical attempts to improve children's performance using the zone of proximal development begin with a pretest of information, strategy, or skill, and then invoke an adult or expert peer in teaching more-advanced performance. Subsequently, children exposed to the treatment typically improve their performance. What is missing here is any account of children's level or "stage" of development. Are they learning specific information, or is genuine cognitive development involved in the improvement? We simply cannot tell. Without anchoring children's preliminary performance in the larger arena of their development, one has no way of knowing whether the teaching results in improvements of specific information or more general cognitive development.

Societal Influence.   The astute reader will quickly note that this heading also appeared under Contributions. Unfortunately, the broad power of society and language in Vygotsky's theory is also a drawback in American psychology. Consider this: Bandura also attributes to society a variety of specific roles in determining the scope, shape, and details of acquiring increasingly mature forms of cognition and behavior. The detail found in Bandura's theory contrasts sharply with a far more general appraisal presented by Vygotsky. This is perhaps ironic. Vygotsky, his life cut short, could not possibly have carried out sufficient research to invigorate his formulations with the kinds of details Bandura gives us for social influences. Such a shortcoming—missing details about the how, when, and why of social influences—leaves psychologists grappling with only general principles from which to derive their research hypotheses (see Moll, 1990). As we will see later, this relative absence of details has additional implications for the theory's predictive validity.

Evaluation of Zones of Development

Before reading the rest of this chapter, pause to reflect and think about what you have learned. Use your learning to complete Sandlot Seminar 10.4 on page 270.

Although Vygotsky's ideas originated over half a century ago, they have begun to generate significant attention in the United States during the past two decades. The primary reason for such a long delay is that only two pieces of work, *Thought and Language* and *Mind in Society*, had been translated into English. The planned completion of Vygotsky's *Collected Works* will make the entire range of his interests and formulations available for the first time. The point here is that we have attempted to be conservative and cautious in rendering our evaluation of Vygotsky's theory. As researchers gain more experience in working out the theory's implications, we may well want to revise our currently tentative thinking about its merits.

Scientific Worthiness

Table 10.2 on page 270 shows a summary of our ratings for the scientific worthiness of Vygotsky's theory. Details of these ratings are described next.

Sandlot Seminar 10.4

How Would You Evaluate Vygotsky's Theory?

Use your own understanding to evaluate Vygotsky's theory of social cognitive development on each of the three sets of criteria. Compare your evaluations and reasons with those given by the authors.

Scientific Worthiness
Testability   _____
External validity   _____
Predictive validity   _____
Internal consistency   _____
Theoretical economy   _____

Developmental Adequacy
Temporality   _____
Cumulativity   _____
Directionality   _____
New mode of organization   _____
Increased capacity for self-control   _____

Pedagogical Usefulness
Intrepretability   _____
Versatility   _____
Availability   _____
Guidance   _____

Testability.   A central tenet of the theory, the zone of proximal development, comes with a degree of conceptual clarity and a general methodology for appraising its range (see Internal Principles). One could clearly test this basic idea for a wide variety of problems and relevant cognitive skills and processes. In addition, a range of escalating hints and guiding strategies that determine the zone could

**TABLE 10.2   Ratings of Vygotsky's Theory of Zones of Development
for Scientific Worthiness**

Criteria	High	Medium	Low
Testability		X	
External Validity		X	
Predictive Validity		X	
Internal Consistency	X		
Theoretical Economy			X

also be tested. At the same time, however, Vygotsky's claim that social speech becomes internalized to direct thought is far less testable, even though it is a central tenet and primary change mechanism of the theory. While there is implicit sense in relating anecdotal evidence about the influence of culture on individual development, it is not at all clear how researchers would test specific cultural causes of psychological processes. For these reasons, we have tentatively rated the theory as medium for its testability.

External Validity.   Review Sandlot Seminar 10.2 about the son who, under his father's guidance, learned to change the oil in his family's cars. Such an everyday example of the zone of proximal development can be generalized easily to many instances when teachers and parents support children's efforts to solve problems. In this light, the zone of proximal development makes a strong appeal to common sense about children's developing abilities. Moreover, learning within the zone bears close resemblance to concepts in other theories, such as Skinner's "organismic variables" (which includes previously acquired habits and inhibitions) as well as Bandura's "cognition and personal factors" (like previously acquired behaviors, concepts, beliefs, and motives). In addition, most parents, teachers, and developmental psychologists would probably agree with Vygotsky's general description of egocentric speech in terms of its onset, accompaniment to actions, and gradual disappearance. In these respects, the theory seems to reflect external validity about the real world of childhood.

But recall that Vygotsky's primary thesis is that speech functions as the vehicle for thought. Thinking progresses only to the extent that speech has become internalized. This is a rather radical claim about how thinking develops. While it is one thing to claim that language and thought are related, perhaps even interdependent in important functional ways, it is quite another to argue that language is the ultimate cause of thought. Simply put, we remain skeptical about this aspect of Vygotsky's account of cognitive development. For example, deaf children obviously think and will invent their own system of communicative gestures long before sign language is imposed on them as a social symbol system. Second, even Chomsky's search for robust linguistic rules has shown a marked shortcoming in helping us understand thought. We think these considerations mitigate somewhat the previously mentioned arguments. Consequently, we have attempted to balance our appraisal of the theory's external validity with a medium rating.

Predictive Validity.   Recall that predictive validity tells us how well a theory produces new facts about child development. This aspect of scientific worthiness is to some degree influenced by the number of researchers interested in a theory as well as the type of research they conduct. In comparison to other theories presented in this text, limited research has been conducted using Vygotsky's theory. In addition, his theory is, by modern standards, lacking in specifics. This alone means that theoretical predictions will not reflect the precision characteristic of modern psychology. This situation will probably change over the next decade as more Vygotsky theorists expand on his seminal work. Still, as this text is being published, the predictive validity of the theory is rather meager, and we have given it a medium rating.

Internal Consistency. The primary role of speech in cognitive development appears to fit hand in hand with the zone of proximal development. After all, most adults guide and direct children's problem solving by using language. We use speech to direct attention to overlooked clues, to identify new strategies, and to describe relevant aspects of a situation. In addition to conveying factual information, language also functions as an important device for organizing, cuing, and focusing children's thought. These are important elements at work in the zone of proximal development. Consequently, because these two internal principles fit so well together, we have rated the theory high for its internal consistency.

Theoretical Economy. Without a doubt Vygotsky's contributions to developmental psychology were cut short by his untimely death at age 38. And while his general ideas about cognitive development and the role of language in directing thought were unique, his short life limited the range and variety of cognitive processes he could explore. Compare, for example, the richness, range, and specificity of Bandura's and Piaget's examination of cognitive processes, and it is easy to see that Vygotsky's theory covers only a small range of the cognitive landscape. Moreover, his explanation is purchased with four predisposing assumptions (fewer than Bandura, more than Piaget). Given this ratio of assumptions to explanatory power, we have rated the theory low for its theoretical economy.

Developmental Adequacy

Table 10.3 summarizes our ratings of the theory's developmental adequacy.

Temporality. Vygotsky's account of the role of speech in cognitive development reveals three phases, which he calls social, egocentric, and inner speech. These phases are time-dependent and reflect qualities of culture experienced over time. Consequently, the theory meets the criterion of temporality.

TABLE 10.3   Ratings of Vygotsky's Theory of Zones of Development for Developmental Adequacy

Characteristic	Rating
Temporality	Yes
Cumulativity	Yes
Directionality	Yes
New Mode of Organization	Yes
Increased Capacity for Self-control	Yes

Cumulativity.   Developmental changes are cumulative in the sense that egocentric speech builds from social speech, and inner speech builds from egocentric speech. Within the zone of proximal development, we also see guided problem solving as most effective when it builds on and expands the child's use of tools and strategies already acquired. Both of these aspects of the theory reflect cumulativity and prompt us to give it a "pass" for this criterion.

Directionality.   In Vygotsky's theory, we can detect several patterns of directionality from birth to intellectual maturity. For example, thinking evolves from concrete to abstract and from the external to the internal, gradually becoming more generalized in scope and rule use. Thought becomes increasingly systematic, beginning with merely personal intuitions about things in the world and ending with scientific concepts and systems of reasoning. Language itself undergoes a transformation from social function to an egocentric accompaniment to action on its way to inner speech, which eventually both directs and embodies thought processes. All these aspects of the theory describe specific types of enduring progress from birth to maturity and support a passing judgment for its directionality.

New Mode of Organization.   For Vygotsky, the primary organizing agent in cognitive development is speech. In one sense, the different phases of speech reflect the same speech, but speech serving a new role or function. Each new function entails a different way of using speech to organize one's activities (both intellectual and physical). In this sense, the theory accounts for new modes of organization in development. In a different light, however, the speech itself which children acquire from peers and adults is still the same speech. While older children acquire more complex speech than younger children, the difference in complexity properly falls under the criterion of cumulativity and cannot be justification for passing the new mode of organization criterion. Given this dilemma, we have elected here to credit Vygotsky for his emphasis on the *function* of speech rather than its content. That is why we have judged the theory to pass this important criterion of developmental adequacy.

Increased Capacity for Self-control.   Vygotsky and Bandura share important theoretical ground in that both believe that the environment is the ultimate source of cognitive processes. Moreover, through acquisition (Bandura) or internalization (Vygotsky), innate cognitive capacities become enriched and organized. Ultimately, cognitive maturity is reached when our intellectual and physical activities become self-directed. Environmental control has been supplanted by self-control. This is not to say the environment doesn't matter anymore. Rather, it means that self-control is exerted in the selection of and in the context of both the physical and the social environments. Vygotsky's theory clearly passes this criterion.

It is interesting to note here that Vygotsky's theory is the only representative of the exogenous paradigm to pass all the criteria of developmental adequacy. We think this is important because the resurgence of interest in his work by English-speaking developmentalists reflects a recognition that he has captured important aspects of child development not adequately addressed by other theories. We are not claiming that developmentalists set out by asking, "How many characteristics of development does Vygotsky account for?" However, perhaps their interest comes at least in part from the fact that his theory is a better *developmental* theory than others in the exogenous paradigm.

Pedagogical Usefulness

Between 1921 and 1923, Vygotsky delivered a series of lectures at Gomel's teacher's college. Those lectures were translated and recently published in book form as *Educational Psychology* (Vygotsky, 1997). However, much of that work is far too general (the popular writing style of the day) to be read by teachers or parents. For example, Vygotsky suggests that teachers create obstacles for children, as these are what lead to learning. Such obstacles accord generally with the zone of proximal development, but Vygotsky provides little guidance for helping teachers or parents understand what types of "obstacles" best promote learning. Our specific ratings of the theory are shown in Table 10.4.

Interpretability.   We have rated Vygotsky's theory high for its interpretability. Key concepts such as inner speech, zone of proximal development, and internalization are relatively easy to understand. Put differently, Vygotsky's theory is conceptually rich without the burden of an extensive, specialized vocabulary. Compare, for example, the relatively few new terms introduced in this chapter with terminology introduced for Wilson's sociobiology, Chomsky's theory of generative grammar, and Bandura's social cognitive theory.

Versatility.   Vygotsky's concept of zone of proximal development and his ideas about the critical role of language in the formation of thought offer tremendous possibilities for researchers. However, Vygotsky sees the primary applications of these seminal ideas as teaching children about scientific concepts. Others have enlarged Vygotsky's vision by using his ideas to teach memory strategies and to treat the trauma of child abuse. These are important extensions of the theory, which derive from the power of its broad concepts. In short, Vygotsky's theory seems to

TABLE 10.4 **Ratings of Vygotsky's Theory of Zones of Development for Pedagogical Usefulness**

Criteria	High	Medium	Low
Interpretability	X		
Versatility	X		
Availability			X
Guidance		X	

have very broad applications beyond teaching and beyond scientific concept formation. For this reason, his theory is rated high for its versatility.

Availability. Vygotsky's work is primarily available in university libraries and professional journals. Virtually none of his work can be obtained in city libraries or through popular magazines. Although students in education and psychology programs can learn about the theory in selected course work, there is no evidence that important ideas are drifting into public view. Consequently, we rate the theory low for its availability.

Guidance. Vygotsky's concepts of language and the zone of proximal development have given many researchers ideas about how to promote children's development, and, indeed, educational applications were cited earlier as a contribution of the theory. With increasing interest in Vygotsky, we anticipate even more work in promoting education and parenting skills than has been reported to date. However, little specific guidance for parents or teachers can be found outside university libraries or professional journals. For example, Vygotsky's *Educational Psychology* suggests that writing be introduced in preschool years because young children are capable of discovering the symbolic function of writing. He also recommends that we get past a "motor skill" orientation to writing and treat it as a complex social phenomenon that is "relevant to life." These two recommendations suggest a something like a "whole language" approach to writing, something that garners controversial support in educational thought today. However, Vygotsky's recommendation that writing begin in preschool is something that most educators would reject, in part because children are not as developmentally ready as Vygotsky thought them to be. For these various reasons we have rated Vygotsky's theory medium for its guidance.

Summary Points

1. Lev Vygotsky created a sociocultural theory of development that very much reflected the historical influences of communist Russia. In that vein, he attempted to show how society, through speech, exerts a powerful influence on the development of thought.
2. Vygotsky's theory rests on three assumptions. First, humans are born with essential cognitive and perceptual abilities that mature over time. Second, like Skinner, Vygotsky assumes the newborn is essentially active in engaging the environment, including social agents (i.e., parents, siblings, others). Third, Vygotsky attempts to incorporate communist assumptions about the importance of social order in explaining individual development.
3. Vygotsky attempts to explain the development of thinking and, in particular, how social situations are both the origins and the determinants of a child's development. To study this problem, he used various types of cognitive tasks to study concept formation and thinking strategies. And because culture was

thought to be so important, he collected data from individuals "in the field" rather than in a controlled laboratory.

4. Vygotsky's theory contains four internal principles. These are: (1) the flow of speech into thought, (2) the types of speech (social, egocentric, inner, pure thought), (3) the zone of proximal development, and (4) the general genetic law of cultural development. These are the theory's most basic core concepts, and they cannot be derived from other more fundamental principles.

5. The theory incorporates two bridge principles to connect the basic concepts with children's actual behavior. The "phases and stages" bridge principle describes various developmental states in children's cognitive development. The functional activities within the zone of proximal development, activities that promote cognitive development, were not part of Vygotsky's original writings. However, given his early death, their incorporation here reflects a degree of "completeness" unavailable in the primary sources.

5. Vygotsky admitted to a degree of maturation for inborn cognitive and perceptual processes. However, it is clear that children's cognitive development was fundamentally the result of *internalization*, the change mechanism that accounts for how social origins are transformed into thinking.

6. Most of the research base for Vygotsky's theory is concerned with assessing his concepts of egocentric speech and the zone of proximal development. There is empirical evidence that children's egocentric speech precedes certain types of thinking. And, empirical studies have demonstrated the effectiveness of the zone of proximal development as a concept for designing both educational and clinical programs.

7. Vygotsky's theory has contributed important ideas to developmental psychology. Among the contributions are the zone of proximal development, the importance of social and cultural influences on thought, and an early version of what today would be called cognitive science. But the theory has also been criticized for failing to specify "anchors" for the zone of proximal development and for not including adequate details about social influences on the development of thought.

8. In evaluating the theory, we rated it medium for its scientific worthiness, considered it a strong example of developmental adequacy, and gave it an overall medium rating for its pedagogical usefulness.

PROBLEMS AND EXERCISES

1. Reread the description of Genie and Victor's language development in Chapter 6 on Chomsky. According to Vygotsky's theory, what do their language experiences and subsequent learning suggest about their cognitive development?

2. Review Sandlot Seminar 10.2 in which the father and son are changing oil in the family cars. Note how much of the son's actions are directed by the father's speech. At that time, the son was 14 years old. Given that interaction, how would you

describe the son's zone of proximal development? How do you think the father–son interaction would have been different if the son had been only 8 years old?

3. Vygotsky's theory teaches us that social context is immensely important in determining language and cognitive development. Think about different social contexts in your life (Internet chat groups, church groups, youth groups, classmates at school, sports teams, peers at work). How does language differ among the different groups? How does it direct specialized learning unique to each group? Do these different groups provide a context for your personal zone of proximal development? How or how not?

4. If you were a third-grade teacher, how would you use Vygotsky's theory to structure your classroom to maximize student learning? What types of activities would you use? How much would you use "whole class" instruction? If you were a parent of a third-grader, how would you structure homework to maximize your child's learning?

5. Use the Internet to search for sites related to Lev Vygotsky and his theory. You can use his name as well as key words (internal and bridge principles). How do the Internet sites differ in terms of completeness and accuracy of information? What were the best sites you found? What problems did you encounter? What were some of the worst sites (and why)?

SUGGESTED READINGS

More about the Theory

Emerson, C. (1996) The outer word and inner speech: Bakhtin, Vygotsky, and the internalization of language. In H. Daniels (Ed.), *An introduction to Vygotsky,* (123–142). New York: Routledge.

Vygotsky, L. S. (1962). *Thought and language.* E. Hanfmann & G. Vakar (Eds. & translators). Cambridge, MA: MIT Press.

Vygotsky, L. S. (1978). *Mind in society: The development of higher psychological processes.* Cambridge, MA: Harvard University Press.

Critical Reviews

Wertsch, J. V. (1985). *Vygotsky and social formation of mind.* Cambridge, MA: Harvard University Press.

PART FOUR

The Constructivist Paradigm

Constructivist theories uniformly reject endogenous and exogenous explanations of human nature. Instead, constructivists view development as a *synthetic construction* made by individuals within the context of their experiences (review Kant in Chapter 1) rather than a product of either nature or nurture dominating the other. Jean Piaget's cognitive–developmental theory is the paradigm case for constructivism. The most influential American in this paradigm is Lawrence Kohlberg, whose constructivism pervades his theory of moral development.

Piaget's cognitive–developmental theory is both a philosophy of knowledge that addresses philosophical questions about the nature and origins of scientific knowledge and a theory of mental development in individuals. He believes that children adapt their ideas to the world by inventing mathematical and scientific concepts in their commerce with the environment. Piaget's theory, described in Chapter 11, views children are seen as natural philosopher–scientists whose spontaneous curiosity motivates them to fabricate ideas that make sense of their experience.

Kohlberg builds upon Piaget's ideas about the formation of cognitive stages, and he attempts to utilize Piaget's own constructivism to explain the development of universal stages in moral reasoning. Kohlberg argues that moral judgment reflects rational thinking that cannot be attributed to innate predispositions or learned rules. Rather, moral development originates from the synthesis that occurs when an individual's beliefs about moral principles are applied and adapted to one's social interactions and moral problems. Chapter 12 reviews Kohlberg's theory of moral development.

CHAPTER 11

Piaget and Cognitive-Develop Theory

Preview Questions

How did the ideas of Kant and Spencer influence Piaget?

What two assumptions underlie Piaget's theory?

What problems of study does Piaget pose?

What methods does Piaget employ?

What internal and bridge principles does Piaget use in his theory?

What is the difference between operative and figurative knowledge, and why is that distinction important for Piaget?

What factors influence development, according to Piaget? Among these factors, which is posited as the primary mechanism of development?

Why does Piaget's theory belong in the constructivist paradigm?

What are the major contributions and criticisms of Piaget's theory?

How does the theory rate for its scientific worthiness, developmental adequacy, and pedagogical usefulness?

Historical Sketch

Jean Piaget was born August 9, 1896, in Switzerland, and from his own accounts (Piaget, 1952), he devoted considerable study to biology and philosophy. At the age of 10 he published his first scientific paper, a one-page observation of an albino sparrow. Shortly thereafter Piaget was introduced to philosophy and Kant's constructivism by his godfather, Samuel Cornut, thereby sparking a lifelong interest. His mother's psychological ailments and psychoanalytic treatment prompted young Piaget's first interest in psychology. But his passion for biology dominated, and he continued publishing at a pace that brought him early recognition and an invitation for the position of curator of the mollusk collection at the Museum of Natural History in Geneva. Young Piaget declined the invitation, informing his interviewers that he thought it better to finish high school first. By his twenty-first birthday he had already published over twenty articles. He completed both a bachelor's degree and a doctorate at the University of Geneva, where he studied natural science. Ironically, his dissertation was a comparative study of freshwater mollusks.

After receiving his doctorate, Piaget spent several years working in France for Alfred Binet, who was himself constructing the first intelligence tests. Piaget's job was to help administer reasoning tests to Parisian schoolchildren. In that work, he became intrigued by children's *wrong answers,* and he began to use diagnostic interviews to better understand their reasoning errors.

In 1921, Piaget became the director of research at the Jean Jacques Rousseau Institute in Geneva, where he proceeded to launch a series of investigations on the development of children's thought. This work made him famous throughout Europe before he was 30 years old. In the ensuing years he held many prestigious positions and wrote extensively about psychology, epistemology, and education. Piaget, together with Freud and Skinner, is widely considered to be one of the "big three" shapers of developmental psychology.

The Stimulus of Kant

Recall from Chapter 1 that Immanuel Kant was the architect of constructivist epistemology. Piaget's (1952) autobiography acknowledges his early philosophical indebtedness to Kant, particularly the Kantian ideas of *categories, schemata,* and *constructivism.* Kant believed that general *categories* of experience such as space, time, causality, and number were inborn structures that filter, shape, and interpret all experience. Piaget turned Kant's categories into topics of investigation and showed that they evolve through developmental stages rather than being innate as Kant had claimed. Kant also proposed that knowledge derives from the application of inborn *schemata* to experience. In this view, a schema is a capacity to form concepts or images that produces meaning when applied to sensations. Using Kant's idea of "schemata," Piaget showed that they begin with infantile patterns of organized actions that function as the "building blocks" of knowledge. Finally, Kant's epistemology rejected both rationalist and empiricist explanations of knowledge, a position Piaget (1963, 1971b, 1972) echoes in arguing that cognitive development results from a constructive synthesis between innate organizers and personal experience. In the Piagetian sense, knowledge is invented; it can originate neither in innate programming nor in discoveries of things given in reality (von Glasersfeld, 1979).

Spencer's Principles of Psychology

Herbert Spencer, a cousin of Charles Darwin, believed that evolution was such a powerful natural force that it could explain many natural phenomena. In setting out to popularize Darwin's theory of evolution, Spencer proposed a universal law called the *synthetic principle.* In Spencer's hands, this principle undergirded both biological and psychological development. Half a century before Piaget, Spencer developed several themes that Piaget incorporated freely and virtually unedited into his own theory of cognitive development (Green, 1990).

Piaget borrows, for example, Spencer's theme that *ontogeny recapitulates phylogeny* (individual development follows the same pattern as the development of the species). We find this idea in Piaget's (1971a) view that children's cognitive development parallels the historical development of scientific thought. A second theme in Spencer's work comprises one of Piaget's most important internal principles: *equilibration is a balance between opposing tendencies of assimilation and accommodation* (more about what this means later). In fact, not only is this general idea incorporated, Piaget also uses Spencer's terminology and definitions. Finally, Spencer proposed a four-stage theory of intellectual development. While Piaget's four stages are far more specific and detailed than Spencer's general description, Spencer's footprints are clearly evident in Piaget's cognitive–developmental stages.

Heinz Werner and John Flavell

The first English translations of Piaget's research appeared in the 1940s, but they had little influence in America because behaviorism dominated academic psychology. Heinz Werner and John Flavell played unanticipated roles in popularizing Piaget in the United States.

Heinz Werner (1948) introduced his *organismic* theory of mental development more than a decade before Chomsky's (1959) scathing review of B. F. Skinner's *Verbal Behavior* (see Chapter 6). Werner's organicism challenged the inherent reductionism of behavioral theory (see critique of Skinner's theory in Chapter 8). Where behaviorism attempted to reduce complex behavior into simpler more analyzable units, organicism countered by arguing that behavior could only be understood holistically. While organismic theory never attracted a sufficient number of followers, it offered a new framework for developmental psychology at a time when behaviorism began to wane, and it helped establish an academic climate receptive to Piaget's theory.

Given this change of climate, one of Werner's graduate students, John Flavell, traveled to Geneva, Switzerland, to work in Piaget's laboratories. In 1963 Flavell introduced American psychologists to *The Developmental Psychology of Jean Piaget,* an encyclopedic summary in English of Piaget's methodology, research investigations, developmental theory, and philosophical ideas. Since that influential publication, many of Piaget's books and papers have been translated into English, and his theory has generated a vast amount of research in developmental psychology. Some older developmentalists who remember those days refer to the 1960s and 1970s, following Flavell's translation of Piaget's work, as a "Piagetian boomlet!" in developmental psychology.

Structural Components of Cognitive-Developmental Theory

Assumptions

Piaget's theory makes two important assumptions. First, he assumes that we are born with a species-specific set of biological reflexes that, in typical Piagetian fashion, he terms "hereditary organic reactions" (Piaget, 1963). These reflexes are biologically programmed behaviors that produce consequences (very much like Skinner's concept of operant behavior). Second, Piaget assumes that infants are naturally proactive; they spontaneously initiate encounters with the environment.

Equally important here is what Piaget does not assume. Where Freud assumed the presence of an irrational mind (the id), and where Skinner assumed a *tabula rasa* mind ready-made to begin accumulating associations, *Piaget assumes no mind at all*. The irony of this situation should not be overlooked. Piaget's position poses an interesting problem whose solution reflects some philosophical sophistication. On the one hand, Piaget knew that if he assumed some primitive mental capacity at birth, he was relieved of the problem of explaining the origin of mind. But since that was precisely what he wanted to do, he recognized that he could not assume its presence at birth. Rather, his task was to explain how the mind evolves as a natural consequence of his two prior assumptions.

Problems for Study

The purpose of cognitive-developmental theory is to explain the origin and genesis of knowledge. Like other theories, Piaget's can be viewed in terms of the phenomena it attempts to explain and its primary research methods.

Phenomena to Be Explained.   Piaget attempts to explain the ontogenesis or individual development of scientific and mathematical knowledge. More specifically, he attempts to show how we come to understand space and geometry, movement and speed, time, causality, number, weight, volume, probability, chance, logic, and many other scientific, mathematical, and logical concepts. In addition, he examines the relationship between the development of knowledge and specialized cognitive functions, such as memory, perception, and language (Piaget, 1983). Finally, he proposes a unique theory of knowledge, termed *genetic epistemology,* in response to philosophical questions about the nature and origin of knowledge.

Methods.   Piaget utilizes two complementary methods in collecting his developmental data: observations and clinical interviews. When his three children were infants, he recorded copious and detailed observations of their spontaneous activities and their reactions to stimuli he would produce. These notes provided the basis for several books published in the 1920s about infant intellectual development.

While working with Binet on children's reasoning tests, Piaget developed the *clinical interview*. This method uses an open-ended collection of questions in the context of a cognitive task or problem children attempt to solve. The interview is designed to get children to talk about their strategies, plans, possible solutions, and the meaning of their manipulations. It is worth noting here that from Piaget's point of view, a flexible interview specially attuned to each subject (and therefore not standardized) does not invalidate his data. His aim is to ensure that subjects are given an opportunity to fully divulge their thought capabilities. This "Genevan" notion of standardization is quite different from the American version of test standardization. Where the Genevans emphasize the importance of standardizing the *relationship* between subject and problem (i.e., ensuring that every subject was given an opportunity to demonstrate optimum performance), the classical American concept of standardization refers to the sameness of task instructions for each subject.

Internal Principles

Assimilation, Accommodation, and Equilibration.   According to Piaget, all activity is characterized by two opposing tendencies—**assimilation** and **accommodation**. *Assimilation* is the tendency toward self-preservation and the incorporation of environmental sensations into the activities and systems already possessed by an individual (Piaget, 1963). Every interaction between individual and environment requires some degree of modification in order to give reality meaning and make it "fit" with previous understanding. For example, one author of this text once used the phrase *window of vulnerability* to describe in a human development class the time span both before and after ovulation when intercourse can lead to pregnancy. That phrase was recorded in one student's notes as "winoverability," a like-sounding, but different notion. When the student was later asked what her notation meant, she said, "Well, if a really hot guy has a lot of winoverabilty, then you have to be careful. Because if you're not, you might have sex with him, and then you could get pregnant." This example of assimilation shows how the new concept *window of vulnerability* was distorted, both phonetically and conceptually, in order to make sense to a young college student's preexisting beliefs about getting pregnant.

Assimilation exists in many forms (Piaget, 1962). When, for example, toddlers make trains from wooden blocks, "read" stories from dad's newspaper, and "eat" make-believe food from empty pots on the kitchen floor, they are distorting certain qualities of reality by inventing their own meanings. Assimilation confers meaning on experience by making new experiences "fit" into previously constructed understandings of prior experiences.

Accommodation is the complement to assimilation; it entails adjustments the individual makes to the real world (Piaget, 1966). The student in the above example adjusted her previous understanding of pregnancy to what she thought was a new technical term introduced by her professor—"winoverability." While this student clearly understood that sex can lead to pregnancy, she also expanded her understanding to take account of "hot guys" who have a lot of "winoverability." As with this student, everyone is constantly adjusting prior information in order to adapt to new information. Readers of this textbook will have to make many accommodations to new material, and some ideas like Freud's "infantile sexuality" and Skinner's "negative reinforcement" may require serious, concentrated effort.

All interactions contain a mixture of these complementary tendencies. That is, one action does not assimilate reality while a different action accommodates reality. Rather, every interaction involves some degree of incorporating external information while simultaneously adjusting one's understanding to account for new features of the environment.

Five-year-old Matthew illustrates how assimilation and accommodation are interrelated. During dinner one evening, 6½-year-old Megan proclaimed that she had learned how to count backward, and she proceeded to demonstrate: "Five, four, three, two, one." Following the customary parental praise, Matthew announced that he too could count backward, whereupon he turned around on his chair and *with his back to the table* proceeded to count: "One, two, three, six, eleven." Matthew's action reflects accommodation in his adjustment to the situation of counting backward. However, assimilation also occurred in that he incorporated Megan's meaning to his own understanding—to count backward, one turns backward and counts!

Equilibration is one of Piaget's most important concepts, and it is the primary reason his theory belongs in the constructivist paradigm. Following Spencer's lead, Piaget viewed equilibration as the most fundamental process of adaptation, a process in which assimilation and accommodation are brought into balance. Equilibration is a dynamic process that regulates all adaptive activities. By adapting to social and physical environments, individuals tend toward a balance or *equilibrium* between knowledge they have already acquired (assimilation) and new information (accommodation). Moreover, it is equilibration that motivates the intellect to move from the equilibrium of one stage, through a transition, and onto a new type of equilibrium at the next stage.

Intellectual equilibration is like biological *self-regulation*. Body temperature and digestion, for example, are automatically maintained and adjusted to different conditions. Similarly, intelligence is also at work self-correcting and self-coordinating assimilation and accommodation. In this way, equilibration directs mental development toward increasingly general, more flexible cognitive organizations for adapting to novelty and unpredictability in the world (Flavell, 1963). More will be said about equilibration in the section on change mechanisms.

The Functional Invariants: Organization and Adaptation.   All creatures possess certain invariant processes that function across time and situations to control reproduction, eating, digestion, circulation, and metabolism. Analogously, Piaget believes that intelligence is also governed by two invariant functions—**organization** and **adaptation**. *Organization is an intellectual predisposition to interrelate, order, and arrange elements of personal experience* (e.g., activities, ideas, sensations) *into a systematic whole.* When Matthew demonstrated his prowess at counting backward, he was displaying his own spontaneous arrangement of how "backward" and "counting" were related. In contrast, Megan had learned a different way to organize two concepts (counting, backward) into a single idea (counting backward). Like Matthew and Megan, individuals organize their intellect to make sense of their experiences.

In contrast to organization, *adaptation is the process of adjusting one's intellect to the external world*. In any active encounter between the self and external events, individuals adjust their knowledge to account for new information. These adjustments usually ensure more efficient future encounters with external events.

The tendency for thought to structure itself while adjusting to and comprehending reality implies that organization and adaptation are complementary, interrelated processes. "It is by adapting to things that thought organizes itself and it is by organizing itself that it structures things" (Piaget, 1963, p. 8). Sandlot Seminar 11.1 illustrates typical ways young children exhibit these principles.

Sandlot Seminar 11.1

Examples of Children's Organization and Adaptation

Example 1. At age 5, Megan went with her family to see "Peter Pan," presented as a play. It was an enjoyable time for all, followed by a "fancy" lunch at a local fast-food restaurant. Later that evening, on the way to bed, Megan asked her dad to read one of the chapters from the *Peter Pan* book. About 2:00 A.M., Megan's dad awoke to screams from Megan's bedroom: "Get away! No! Daddy!" Like a shot, and fearing the worst, her dad went running to Megan's bedroom. What he found was Megan standing on her bed saying, "No! Get away!" Megan was having a nightmare about the crocodile in "Peter Pan" coming to visit her during her sleep. At her age, however, Megan could not differentiate between what her eyes see during sleep (inside the mind) and what her eyes see when she is awake (outside in the world). Megan's organization followed the rule, "If you can see it, it is real." This organization applied to both dreams and real-world experiences.

Years later Megan fell asleep on the couch while watching a video. Shortly after falling asleep, her parents noticed her arms and legs twitching and slight murmurs of "Un unh. Call Dad. I . . . uh . . . no." Megan's mother shook her awake and asked, "Are you OK, Megan?" Megan opened her eyes, looked up, and said, "Mom. What are you doing . . . Oh, sorry. I must have been dreaming." It turns out Megan's dream was about going to a party and not being able to get home. She dreamt about calling home for her dad to come get her.

Note the contrast in adaptation between Megan's two dreams. In her first dream of "Peter Pan's" crocodile, she was organizing her perceptual experiences into a single, unitary construction. Pictures seen with the eyes and pictures seen with the mind were both real to her. However, the older Megan clearly differentiated between dream images (not real) and her perceptions of the real world. She had adapted her understanding of how mental images work and organized it into differentiated functions: Mental pictures are not part of external reality, but visual perceptions are.

Example 2. Six-year-old Sophie and her father are looking at a world atlas. Using the world map, her father is patiently pointing to different countries (depicted in various colors) and explaining some of their characteristics. The father begins by pointing to the United States (green colored) and telling young Sophie, "This is the United States. This is where we live." "I know," says Sophie. "It's the same color as our grass outside." "That's right," replies her father.

After watching and listening attentively to her father, Sophie suddenly interrupts and points to Siberia saying, "This is where I want to live." Her father vainly tries to explain that Siberia is very cold, lonely, and dark much of the year. Still Sophie insists she wants to live there. Somewhat perplexed, the father finally asks, "Why in the world would you want to live in a country like that?" Sophie replies matter-of-factly, "Because it is my favorite color, pink!"

1. How do Sophie's responses give clues about her organization of knowledge?
2. How much of her father's explanation of different countries do you think Sophie actually understood?
3. How has Sophie adapted her understanding of countries to her father's lessons with the atlas?

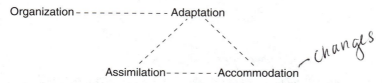

FIGURE 11.1   Relationship between four key Piagetian concepts.

Adaptation itself has two components: assimilation and accommodation. Figure 11.1 illustrates the relationship between organization, adaptation, assimilation, and accommodation.

Bridge Principles

Schemata.   Following Kant's lead, Piaget defines **schema** as *an organized, generalizable action pattern* that evolves naturally from the infant's inborn reflexes. It is through repetition of the infant's proactive reflexes that they become generalized and differentiated into organized action patterns—schemata. Experience is always assimilated into an individual's schemata, but at the same time these schemata become elaborated, generalized, and differentiated to accommodate different features of reality. The concept of schema gives Piaget a way to directly apply his internal principles to the development of thought, since schemata are the infant's means of constructing reality through assimilation and accommodation of their actions on objects.

Between 4 and 6 months of age, infants typically assimilate very different types of objects to one or more simple action patterns (schemata) that are generalized to all sorts of objects. For example, they may reach out to grasp an object, look at it, bring it to the mouth, then mouth it, hit the object against their leg, mouth it again, look at it, change it to the other hand, mouth it again, and finally discard the object on the floor and crawl away. These typical schemata (reaching to grasp, mouthing, hitting, looking) confer meaning on objects. That is, *objects* are understood in terms of what the infant *can do to* them, much like *ideas* for adults are understood in terms of what we *can do with* them. One reason parents must "childproof" their home is because young infants utilize their schemata indiscriminately. It does not matter to them that an object may be a knife, a pen, a cotton ball, or a glass. They actively explore the object with the schemata they have constructed, and they fail to attend to important differences in object features (e.g., a knife versus a cotton ball) until the second half of the first year of life.

Schemata are constructed throughout life for conferring meaning on experience. They vary widely in their onset, complexity, relationship to one another, and the objects toward which they are directed. For example, children who recognize their mothers in a crowd of picnicking families, teenagers who avoid faddish hairstyles solely because of anticipated maternal hassles, and middle-aged adults who call their mothers long distance every Sunday can all be said to have a "mother" schema. Each has a generalizable action pattern for relating to "mother."

Cognitive Operations. **Cognitive operations** *are reversible mental action patterns,* and they make their first appearance between 7 and 8 years of age. The significance of operations in Piaget's theory can be found in the names he gives to three developmental stages: *preoperational, concrete operational,* and *formal operational.*

There are many kinds of cognitive operations. Arithmetic operations such as addition, subtraction, multiplication, and division have corresponding cognitive operations. Other cognitive operations involve one-to-one and many-to-one correspondences. These somewhat foreboding terms are really quite manageable when one understands the rather ordinary activities to which they apply. For example, a child could perform mental operations to figure out that Matt is the tallest of three boys, provided that Matt is taller than Samuel, and Samuel is taller than Adam. In reaching that conclusion, the child would simply perform the operation of *asymmetrical, transitive inference* (Matt > Samuel, Samuel > Adam, therefore Matt > Adam).

Operative and Figurative Aspects of Knowledge. Piaget (1983) differentiates between two aspects of knowledge: the **figurative** aspect and the **operative** aspect. Figurative knowing is oriented toward organizing sensory data by grasping reality as it appears without attempting to transform it. When we touch, listen to, see, or taste something we receive sensory information—figurative knowing. When we see objects and know what they are—cars, fire trucks, circles, forests—that is figurative knowledge. When we learn language, particularly naming words, we are acquiring figurative knowledge. Much of our early socialization and schooling concentrates on figurative knowledge by learning *names:* word names, object names, color and shape names, counting and number names, people's first and last names, story and song names, food names, tool and toy names, rule names, game names, state names, calendar and temperature names, geographic names and date names, and even cereal names. Learning the names of things, as does all language, reflects figurative knowledge about our world.

Operative aspects of knowledge constitute what Piaget calls *logico-mathematical* knowledge, which is really what his theory is all about. Operative knowledge derives from mental and physical activities that transform an object with properties or new relationships of classification, order, composition, and arrangement (much like Kant's categories). For example, number value is not a property we derive from an object; it is a property of our counting activity. So, when we count the number of objects in a collection, the number we derive represents operative, or logico-mathematical knowledge. Similarly, when we arrange a set of objects from smallest to largest, we confer ordinal arrangement onto those objects. Order is something we bestow by our physical and intellectual actions; it is not a property objects transmit to our sensations. When examining a restaurant menu, for example, we may spontaneously order entrées from least to most expensive, thereby conferring operative meaning on those items. Some examples of figurative and operative knowledge are described in Sandlot Seminar 11.2 to help you understand differences between these two types of knowledge.

Sandlot Seminar 11.2

Figurative and Operative Knowledge
For each of the following examples, decide which reflect **F**igurative and which reflect **O**perative aspects of knowledge. The first six examples have been completed for you. If you have a question, think of the difference between sensation or language (figurative knowledge) versus your own actions that confer meaning (operative knowledge).

__F__	Sarah knows the capital of Washington is Olympia.
__O__	Billy Joe is counting pennies from his piggy bank.
__O__	Mr. Shoreham knows that really fresh fish have very little odor.
__O__	Terri is tying her shoelaces.
__F__	Matthew has memorized his "times" tables through six.
__F__	Matthew imagines himself as a superhero with a super dog.
_____	Henry looks out the window and sees a bird eat seed from the bird feeder.
_____	Morgan knows the state bird of Maine is the chickadee.
_____	Jack knows how to read a restaurant menu.
_____	Billy has a quarter, two dimes, and three nickels. Counting from the largest to smallest denomination, he figures out he has sixty cents. Then, counting in reverse order from smallest to largest denomination, he discovers he still has sixty cents.
_____	Cathy knows a "shortcut" for avoiding rush-hour traffic.
_____	Cathy knows that blue fish is really gray and fresh cod is white.
_____	Charlie knows that John Steinbeck wrote *The Grapes of Wrath*.
_____	William knows that telephone is spelled t–e–l–e–p–h–o–n–e.
_____	Jessica knows that some brands of paper towels are more absorbent than others.
_____	Samantha, having just traveled throughout Europe, now appreciates more fully some of her family's customs.
_____	Fred knows when to get up in the morning.
_____	Fred knows how to play chess.
_____	Fred knows how much his parents earn.
_____	Fred knows that three peanuts are the same number as three elephants, even though the elephants are so much larger.

Cognitive Structures.   The part of Piaget's theory that has received the most widespread attention is the sequence of cognitive-developmental structures or "stages." The concept of "stage" in Piaget's theory differs in important ways from Freud's and Erikson's use of the "stage" idea.

Piaget's Concept of "Stage."   Piaget's stages reflect three general properties that differentiate them from the kinds of stages proposed by Freud and Erikson. First, Piaget views stages as stable, cohesive, organized systems of interrelated actions called *structures*. In this sense, a stage is a holistic, generalized way of acting and thinking, not a collection of specific facts and behaviors (Freud and Erikson would agree with this property). Second, stages occur in a universal sequence; they cannot be rearranged or skipped (Freud and Erikson would also agree with this property). Third, later stages are transformations of earlier stages. This means that when one stage changes into another, it gets reorganized into a hierarchically inclusive new stage. Once this reorganization has occurred, the previous stage no longer exists. Unlike Freud and Erikson, Piaget contends that there can be no developmental regression once earlier stages have been irreversibly transformed into new cognitive structures.

The foregoing discussion has prepared us for an examination of Piaget's four cognitive–developmental stages. Note that in Piaget's theory, stages are bridge principles. Even though they have received more attention than the internal principles, Piaget's stages are derived from his theory's internal principles. They are general organizations of actions (operative knowledge and schemata) that reflect a balance between assimilation and accommodation.

The *sensorimotor* stage consists of six substages that comprise practical intelligence, or action knowledge. The *preoperational* stage marks the beginning of thought and the prelogical mental frolic of early childhood. The *concrete operational* stage heralds the onset of mental abilities that enable children to genuinely classify, quantify, and arrange objects. The last stage, *formal operations,* brings a new cognitive ability to operate on ideas themselves, including some ideas that may be contrary to fact.

The Sensorimotor Stage.   Piaget describes six substages in the sensorimotor stage, which lasts from birth to approximately 2 years of age. Recall that Piaget does not assume a mind at birth. His explanation of how the mind originates is found in the sensorimotor stage where infants construct knowledge through action. The development of generalizable action patterns called *schemata* reflects the infant's evolution from a biological, proactive organism into a truly psychological being capable of thinking. Sensorimotor knowledge, constructed through assimilation of and accommodation to the external world, is not contemplative; rather, it is a *pragmatic knowledge in action* that consists of increasingly complex and differentiated coordinations of schemata for relating to objects.

Newborn infants do not understand objects unless they are acting on them. In this sense we can say that newborns understand only their own activities, their schemata, before they understand the objects of their actions. Only later does their action knowledge extend to include the properties of objects themselves. With infant–environment interactions, schemata become differentiated according to object characteristics and more specialized in eliciting information from objects. For example, the sucking schema, prevalent in early infancy, is both global and undifferentiated. Infants can tell only so much from sucking objects. But the sucking schema gradually gives way to examination, looking mixed with manipulation.

Infants can tell much more about objects by examining them. During the second half of the first year, infants construct an important understanding about objects in the world: They continue to exist independent of actions performed on them. This important construction is called *object permanence*. Later, by the end of the sensorimotor period, infants become capable of mentally representing objects, a sign that infancy has been completed.

The infant's progression through the six substages of sensorimotor intelligence is governed by equilibration rather than being the product of either maturation or experience acting alone. During the first three substages, the infant begins with proactive, inborn reflexes. Through repetition, the reflexes become generalized and differentiated, giving rise to schemata, the organized action patterns. Gradually these schemata become increasingly coordinated with objects and with each other, leading the infant to perform actions that reproduce interesting events in the environment (e.g., kicking a mobile hanging over the crib, reaching to grasp an object, sucking and mouthing an object). In the early subperiods, assimilation dominates accommodation, although both occur in every interaction. Put differently, during the first half year of life, infants tend to pay more attention to their action patterns (schemata) than they do to objects and their characteristics. In addition, young infants fail to understand that objects continue to exist independent of their actions performed on them. For the young infant, "out of sight is out of mind."

Beginning at substage IV (about 8 to 12 months), important developmental changes begin to occur. The first is *object permanence*. Infants begin to retrieve objects that are momentarily "out of sight," which tells us that they are beginning to understand that objects have an existence of their own, independent of actions that can be performed on them. A second important change, the onset of intention, also occurs at this substage. Piaget (1963, p. 211) defines intention as the differentiation between means and ends, between procedures and objects, and he argues that this critical differentiation is the *creation of intention* only in sensorimotor *actions*. Mental intention will not be developed until the end of the sensorimotor stage. For example, when we hide an object underneath a towel, an infant reaches out, removes the towel, and retrieves the object. According to Piaget, this action is intentional not because the infant used thinking to imagine the invisible object, but because *the actions of removing the towel and retrieving the object were differentiated from the object itself*. This kind of differentiation is the essence of intention.

Substage IV is also the first time infants begin to use different schemata with different objects instead of using the same schemata over and over again. These refinements reflect active reorganizations of schemata and lead to the construction of an objective universe of objects whose permanence is detached from the self precisely because objects have become independent of personal action schemata (Piaget, 1963, p. 211).

During the remainder of the sensorimotor stage, infants continue assimilating and accommodating their action schemata to objects. As the end of the sensorimotor stage nears, infants begin to engage in *groping* when they actively experiment with their schemata to see what different effects are produced. They adapt themselves to unfamiliar situations not only by applying schemata already acquired, but also by trying to fashion or construct entirely new schemata in the act of solving problems.

The end of the sensorimotor period, substage VI, is marked by the transition from sensorimotor action to mental representation and the beginning of thought. The most important advance in this transition is the onset of mental *representation*. In its interactions, the infant begins to anticipate the results of its schemata, and these anticipations occur mentally before the fact rather than physically after the fact. That is, the infant's own schemata become *internalized* and thereby give rise to mental representations of themselves *before* the schemata are actually activated (Piaget, 1963, p. 341). Through this internalization, the infant begins to anticipate by mentally combining schemata designed to produce certain results.

Here is the heart of Piaget's constructivism. Born with no mental capability, the infant gradually constructs schemata during the sensorimotor stage. These schemata, by becoming increasingly generalized, differentiated, and automated, gradually become internalized. **Internalization** produces mental images of schemata that had previously been carried out only in action, thereby enabling infants to invent mentally and before the fact new relationships between schemata that had previously been discovered only on the physical plane and only during or after the activity itself. In short, the end of the sensorimotor stage occurs when the toddler begins to form mental representations. But the first mental representations are images of *the infant's own schemata*. Later, as mental capacity becomes more differentiated and efficient, it generates images of objects as distinct from action schemata. Sandlot Seminar 11.3 illustrates one type of experience everyone has had that helps us understand Piaget's concept of internalization.

Sandlot Seminar 11.3

Understanding Piaget's Concept of Internalization

Most people have routine memory lapses that are analogous to the action-to-thought pattern of development posited by Piaget. For example, we sometimes begin to do something (e.g., fetch a drink from the kitchen) only to be distracted along the way and end up forgetting what we set out to do. When that happens, we typically attempt to retrace our steps by repeating the same activities we were engaged in when we had the original idea. According to Piaget, the reason this strategy works is that our actions are the original source of mental representations. Our natural expectation is that by reproducing the original activities we will reproduce the original ideas.

According to Piaget, why do we *retrace our steps* when we can't remember something? According to Piaget, why does this strategy work? Do actions precede thoughts? Is there a developmental relationship between acting and thinking?

Piaget's account of sensorimotor intelligence contrasts sharply with endogenous theories that view mental functioning as a product of biological maturation and with exogenous theories that posit sensation and perceptual experience as the source of thought. Piaget sees individuals as biological creatures that are inherently proactive. Infantile actions incorporate reality (assimilation) while adjusting to it (accommodation). Through repetition, generalization, and differentiation, actions become organized and adapted to reality and give rise to intention when schemata (means) become differentiated from objects (ends). Finally, thinking begins when schemata become internalized and begin to evoke mental images. Such images gradually become extended to the world of objects during the next stage of cognitive development. In short, schemata construct knowledge of objects through assimilation and accommodation. Sandlot Seminar 11.4 compares two of Piaget's sensorimotor concepts with similar-sounding ideas introduced in earlier chapters.

The Preoperational Stage.   The end of the sensorimotor stage is also the beginning of the *preoperational* stage, which lasts from approximately 2 to 7 or 8 years of age. The most important new ability of this stage is the *semiotic* or mental function that enables the child to perform mental actions (e.g., imagination, memory, symbolic encoding) and mental manipulations of objects that replace the previous stage's physical activities. Preoperational children still perform actions on objects, but now their actions are directed by anticipation and coordination. Even the toddler who hits his sister anticipates the action of hitting, though the resulting screams and maternal scolding could not yet be anticipated. The most powerful of the semiotic functions is language, which provides the user with a ready-made system of symbols for relating to objects and for socializing thought through communicative interactions with others.

Operative knowledge in this stage consists of egocentric intuitions and preconcepts that are not yet logical but are semisocialized patterns of thinking (Piaget, 1966). Figurative knowledge in this stage consists of the specific mental images, memories, symbols, and language actually used by the child. The most notable characteristics of the preoperational stage are the following.

Narrow Field of Attention.   The preoperational child centers on only one element of a situation at a time, though many details may be noticed in rapid succession. This cognitive *centration* limits thought to only one idea at a time, a serious constraint that is sometime the source of misjudgments, as when for example, a youngster sees a penguin swimming at the zoo and decides it must be a fish or when another notices that the water in one container is higher than in a second and judges the first to have "more water" without taking into account the width of the containers. While ideas may occur in rapid sequence, true comparisons are not possible since they require simultaneous evaluation of two or more pieces of information. Children's *narrow field of attention* often leads them to notice situational details missed by adults who are more concerned with the "big picture" than the minutiae of details. Finally, it is the narrow field of attention that prevents young children from using hindsight or foresight in a systematic manner.

Sandlot Seminar 11.4

Piaget's Concepts of Schemata and Internalization

It is useful to highlight two comparisons between Piaget's description of sensorimotor development and theoretical concepts introduced in other theories. First, how does Piaget's idea of *schema* compare with Skinner's concept of *operant*? Second, is there any difference between Piaget's and Vygotsky's concepts of *internalization*?

Schema and Operant. Recall that Piaget defined *schema* as an organized action pattern, whereas Skinner defined *operant* as a class of behaviors. If one directly observes in action both a schema and an operant behavior, one might well be looking at the same event. At first glance, there is no apparent or theoretically meaningful difference between the two concepts. First glances, however, are often misleading, and that is the case here. A critical distinction between the two concepts is found in answering the question, "What happens to schemata and operant behaviors once they have been acquired?"

An operant behavior remains a relatively permanent, stable operant behavior. It can be associated with various discriminative stimuli and reinforcers, but it still remains an operant. Operants can be combined into complex sequences called chains, but each operant remains a discrete contribution to that chain. In contrast, Piaget's schemata are the building blocks of understanding. These action patterns evolve, through internalization, into mental representations. In turn, mental representations, through equilibration, are transformed into reversible operations. We can see then that the two concepts play strikingly different theoretical roles. Skinner's operant is an end in itself. Piaget's schema is a means to an end; it is the building block for later mental development.

Internalization. Both Piaget and Vygotsky invoke the theoretical concept of *internalization*. Is it the same concept, or are they endowing this terminology with different theoretical meanings? To answer this question, we must examine two considerations. First, what gets internalized? Second, what is the nature of the internalization process?

What gets internalized? In Vygotsky's theory, internalization is the process of acquiring public speech. In Vygotsky's sense internalization means to "take in" or "to incorporate." Words and meanings are simply acquired through learning and become the individual's own words for guiding thought. In contrast, Piaget's concept of internalization takes as its objects the individual's own schemata. Understanding what gets internalized leads us to a more important consideration about the essence of internalization.

What is the nature of the internalization process? For Vygotsky, internalization is a process of learning or appropriation. Neither the words nor their meaning are substantially changed or transformed. Individuals simply take another's words and their public meanings and begin using public speech as their own. In this sense, speech is both shared and borrowed. In contrast, Piaget's concept of internalization confers new meaning on schemata by transforming them into something that did not previously exist—mental representations. For Piaget, transformation involves the construction of new meanings, and it is the essence of internalization.

Seeing Is Believing.   Preoperational children believe that what they "see" is real and true by virtue of their vision. They often fail to differentiate between the apparent and the real (recall Megan's crocodile dream after seeing "Peter Pan"), and they tend to believe that something is real even if it is only imagined. For example, they may believe that the moon follows them while they are riding in a car or walking down the street simply because it looks that way to them. Advertisers are very much aware of this characteristic of preoperational thinking. Television images and toy packages targeted to young children often contain visual displays that capitalize on this "seeing is believing" aspect of thought. In fact, one of the authors' sons at 4 years of age insisted on buying a box of cereal because it had a picture of strawberries on the front. When the son found no strawberries in the package, he cried but made sense of the situation by explaining, "They forgot to put any strawberries in this one." Three cereal boxes later, the son announced a hard lesson: "They put strawberries in the picture so kids who like strawberries will buy it."

Subjective Egocentrism.   This aspect of thinking derives from, is directed by, and aims toward ends determined by the child's own point of view. While thinking is socialized to the point where it can be communicated, it is not yet cooperative since it cannot take others' points of view into consideration. Thus, children talking on a phone may simply nod their heads in response to Grandpa's questions, or they may suggest getting Mommy some bubble gum for Mother's Day. Without any awkwardness, 4-year-old Megan used to start hide-and-seek games with her father by warning, *"Don't* look under my bed." Of course, you know where she went to hide.

Animism and Artificialism.   The subjective egocentrism of preoperational thought is associated with two well-defined tendencies in this stage. The first is animism, a childlike belief that inanimate objects are endowed with human qualities. Preoperational children, for example, often think that movement or appearance determines "life." They may believe, for example, that clouds, the wind, and flowing rivers are alive because they move. Similarly, cartoon characters and stuffed toys are believed to think and have feelings simply because they look real or are animated.

  Artificialism is less frequently encountered. It is found in children's belief that natural features were created by people "long ago" for their own purposes. In this vein, mountains result from piling up the dirt from digging holes for lakes, and rivers result from digging channels.

One-Way Thinking.   Preoperational thought simply unfolds in one direction without an accompanying ability to reverse itself, self-correct, or be sensitive to contradiction. A child's recounting of an event, for example, is held together more by the order in which memories are evoked than by the original logic of order in which the events occurred. Most parents have heard young children's "and then" stories retold out of sequence, their recollections merely a fractured mosaic of time. This one-way thinking, also called *transductive reasoning,* simply unfolds because it lacks the self-correcting reversibility of the next stage. See if you can correctly identify the various preoperational characteristics in Sandlot Seminar 11.5.

Piaget believed that the most important quality of each stage was the structure of reasoning rather than how many facts one knew. Consequently, he developed a number of tasks to elicit reasoning about scientific concepts.

Sandlot Seminar 11.5

Understanding Preoperational Children

See if you can correctly identify the characteristic of preoperational thought represented in each of the following examples. Use the following key to mark your selections:

NFA = narrow field of attention
SIB = seeing is believing
SE = subjective egocentrism
AA = animism or artificialism
UT = unidirectional thought

_____ Five-year-old Megan is being interviewed by her father about babies. Near the end of the interview, she is explaining that they are covered with blood when they are born (an understanding that derives from pictures of her own birth). She explains the blood saying, "Because babies are people, and people always have blood, except the bad witch. She doesn't have any." "Huh?" asks her father. Megan continues, "Well, she doesn't! You know, the bad witch in *The Lion, the Witch, and the Wardrobe* [a children's book]. She doesn't have any blood!"

_____ Six-year-old Chris is excited about his family's trip to Discovery Place to visit the new "life-size" dinosaur exhibit. Chris loves dinosaurs and can hardly wait. When the family finally reaches the exhibit hall, Chris runs inside and quickly comes running back out saying that he wants to go home and watch cartoons. When his dad picks him up to carry him inside, Chris begins to scream and kick. "Please, Daddy, no! I don't want to," cries Chris.

_____ Six-year-old Matthew is celebrating his birthday by playing catch with Dad using his new baseball and mitt. When Grandpa calls on the phone, Matthew runs inside still wearing his mitt. Talking to Grandpa, Matthew says "Yes . . . Yes . . . Yes . . . I got it for my birthday. See!" (holding up his mitt for Grandpa)

_____ June is a smart first-grader practicing her numbers. The teacher says, "Tell me a number that is bigger than four." June answers "Seven." "Good," says the teacher. Now June, tell me a number that is *bigger* than four *but smaller* than six. "Seven," answers June.

_____ Sherri insists on taking Strawberry Shortcake, her favorite doll, with her to the movies so Strawberry won't get lonely.

Problem: To understand that liquid quantities are not changed when they move to differently shaped containers

Initial Presentation: Two containers, same size and shape (S 1 = S 2), containing equal amounts of water. Proceed only when child indicates that each container contains the same amount of liquid.

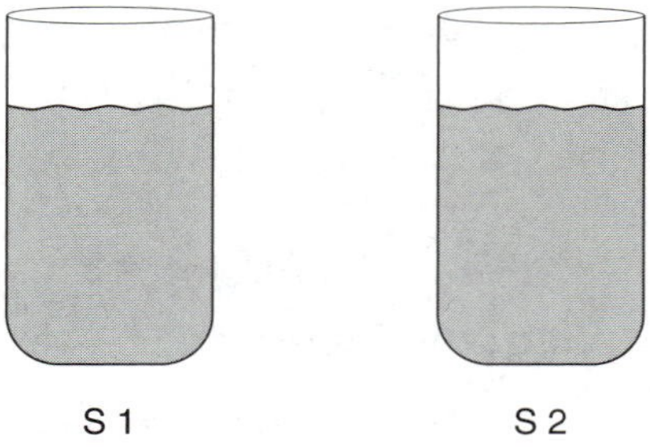

S 1   S 2

Change 1: Pour liquid from one container into taller, narrower container. *Question: Now does each glass have the same amount to drink, or does one have more than the other? How can you tell?*

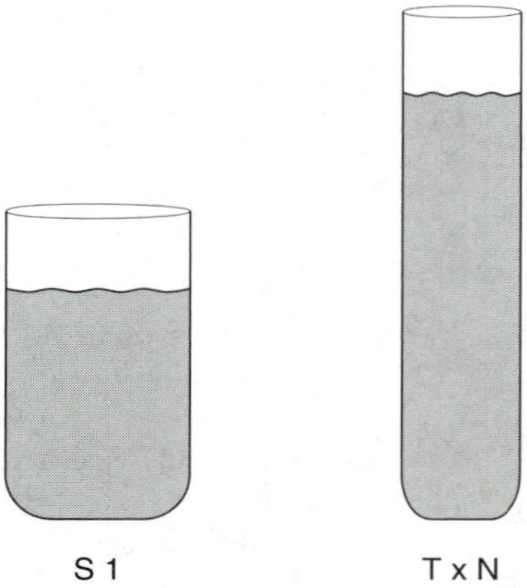

S 1   T x N

Change 2: Return liquid to original container, ascertain its equivalence, then pour one container into shorter, wider container. *Question: Now does each container have the same amount to drink, or does one have more than the other? Can you tell me how you know that for sure?*

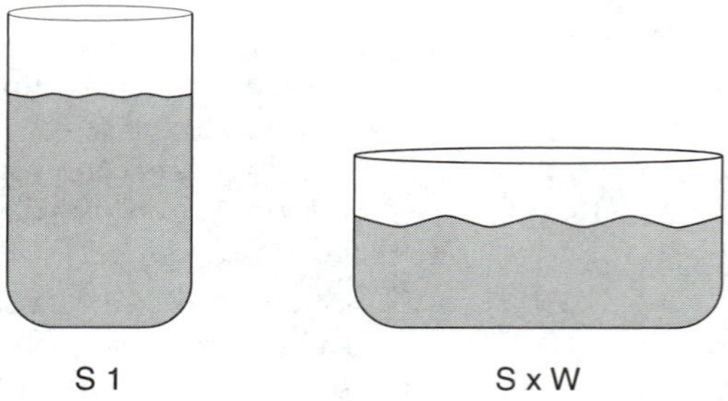

S 1   S x W

FIGURE 11.2   The conservation of liquid task.

Figure 11.2 illustrates the classical conservation of liquid task and summarizes both preoperational and concrete operational responses.

Concrete Operational Stage.   The concrete operational stage is the beginning of cognitive operations on concrete objects. It begins at 6 to 7 years of age and lasts until early adolescence for some and *for the rest of their lives for others*. In Piaget's lex-

Change 3: Return liquid to original container, ascertain its equivalence, then pour one container into several small cups. *Question: Now does this (point to original container) have the same amount to drink as these (point to small cups) or does one have more than the other? How can you tell that they are the same/are different?*

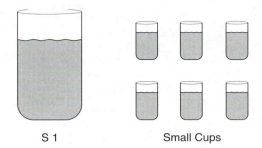

S 1   Small Cups

Analysis

Preoperational children typically reason that the amount of liquid changes with each transformation and in correspondence to one of the dimensions of the containers. The examples of reasoning that follow are typical of reasons used to justify nonconserving responses.

Concrete operational children conserve the liquid quantities due to the presence of reversible operations of classification and relation. Examples of their reasoning and the underlying cognitive operations can be found on the right.

Preoperational Reasons	*Concrete Operational Reasons*
The water is higher/taller. (narrow field of attention)	If I pour it back it will be the same. (inversion–negation)
It looks like more. (seeing is believing)	It's taller but narrower, so it's the same. (reciprocity, compensation)
It's more spread out. (seeing is believing)	It started out the same, so it has to stay the same. (transitivity)
I can just tell. (egocentrism)	It looks like more, but it isn't. (identity)
	None was added or taken away, so it's still the same amount. (identity)

FIGURE 11.2   Continued

icon, *an operation is a reversible mental action*. The term *concrete* refers to the child's ability to think about and mentally transform elements of physical reality. These elements need not be physically present and manipulated; what is important is that the elements be capable of being physically experienced *or imagined*. The current rage among many elementary teachers to provide their students with Piaget-inspired concrete "manipulatives" reflects a misreading of Piaget, who contends that concrete operational thought applies itself to physically present objects and to *mental images* that derive from physical experience.

Piaget uses the term *operational* to describe the child's cognitive ability to perform reversible logical and mathematical transformations on concrete entities. These transformations are called *logico-mathematical* (Piaget, 1966, 1983).

Conservation and class inclusion tasks, because they require logical and mathematical operations for their solutions, are most often employed to assess the

Problem: To maintain the relationship of equality across irrelevant changes that perceptually distort the equality.

Initial Presentation: Two rows of seven and eight chips, all the same color.

Row 1 ◯ ◯ ◯ ◯ ◯ ◯ ◯ ◯

Question: Does each row have the same number of chips or does one have more than the other?

Row 2 ◯ ◯ ◯ ◯ ◯ ◯

Responses: Both preoperational and concrete children typically give the same response: The top row has more because there are more chips.

Change 1: Space out chips in Row 2 so that it begins and ends in alignment with Row 1.

Row 1 ◯ ◯ ◯ ◯ ◯ ◯ ◯ ◯

Question: Now does each row have the same number of chips or does one have more than the other? How can you tell?

Row 2 ◯ ◯ ◯ ◯ ◯ ◯ ◯

Response: Concrete operational children continue to say that the top row has more chips because it has eight, whereas the bottom row has seven. Preoperational children, however,

FIGURE 11.3   The conservation of number task.

presence or absence of children's underlying cognitive operations. In that vein, it is instructive to take a closer look at conservation of liquid, or in Piaget's (1965a) lexicon, the *conservation of continuous quantity*. Figure 11.2 shows the structure of the task, preoperational and concrete operational responses, and an analysis of children's reasoning in terms of their underlying cognitive operations.

While preoperational reasoning involves characteristics such as seeing is believing and egocentrism, concrete operations are given logico-mathematical names such as *identity, transitivity, inversion–negation,* and *reciprocity*. Piaget (1965a) contends that it is the invention of concrete operations that marks the difference between preoperational and concrete operational responses on the liquid conservation task. In other words, the difference between one cognitive stage and another is not a matter of knowing more; it is a difference in cognitive structure that a child applies to making sense of the world.

Similar differences consistently show up in other cognitive tasks. Figure 11.3 illustrates how preoperational and concrete operational children respond to a task involving conservation of number.

now assert that the top and bottom rows have the same number, because they are both the same length (narrow field of attention) or because they both begin and end at the same places (seeing is believing).

Change 2: Space out chips in Row 2 so that it begins and ends in alignment with Row 1.

Row 1 ◯ ◯ ◯ ◯ ◯ ◯ ◯ ◯

Question: Now does each row have the same number of chips or does one have more than the other? How can you tell?

Row 2 ◯ ◯ ◯ ◯ ◯ ◯ ◯

Responses: Concrete operational children say that the top row has more because it has eight chips, and the bottom row only has seven. Preoperational children tend to assert that there are now more chips in the bottom row because "they are spread out," "they look like more," or "there are more chips" (seeing is believing).

Analysis of Reasoning
Preoperational children believe that the number of chips is a function of the length of the row, in spite of how many chips the row has and in spite of attempts to count the number of chips. Concrete operational children argue that just changing the length of the rows does not alter the quantity of chips. They believe that counting with one-to-one corrospondence between rows is a better way to determine quantity than simply looking at the length of the row. Their counting is quantitive and numerical.

FIGURE 11.3   Continued

Cognitive Reversibility.   One of the most important achievements of the concrete operational stage is the construction of logico-mathematical operations that are *reversible*. Reversibility is the cognitive ability to mentally perform a cognitive action coupled with the ability to mentally undo that action. This aspect of thought implies a degree of cognitive *decentration,* the ability to simultaneously think about two or more aspects of a situation at the same time, which makes true comparisons possible. For example, in the liquid conservation task, the concrete operational child evaluates the increase in height, compares it with the decrease in width, and concludes that the two physical changes in dimension *compensate* each other.

Reversibility makes the concrete operational child's thinking bidirectional in contrast to the unidirectional thought of the preoperational child. Each of the logico-mathematical operations Piaget attributes to this stage is a particular kind of reversible, mental transformation.

Logical Operations of Classification and Relation.   The operations of classification and relation reflect Piaget's view that the child is a natural logician and mathematician. The concrete operations form a tightly knit group of interconnected mental actions that comprise the child's operative knowledge at this stage. While a detailed description of the concrete operations is beyond the scope of this book, a brief look at a few examples may be instructive. Interested readers may wish to examine Flavell's (1963, pp. 172–201) more comprehensive treatment of these operations.

Logical classification implies operations such as *inversion–negation, resorption,* and *closure.* The *inversion–negation* operation means that classes can be composed and decomposed through opposing transformations that cancel each other. For example, beginning with the class of sons, we can add the class of daughters to produce the class of children. This transformation can be undone by subtracting the class of daughters from the class of children to arrive at the original class of sons. The operation of *resorption* holds that every class plays an identity element to subordinate classes. For example, if one adds tulips and daisies to the superordinate class of flowers, one obtains the original class of flowers rather than more flowers. *Closure* implies that elements of a class can be combined to form a new class and that classes can be combined to form superordinate classes. For example, this operation gives concrete operational children the capacity to understand that the addition of two classes, say dogs and cats, yields a new class—popular four-legged pets. Moreover, four-legged pets plus other pets produces the superordinate class of pets.

There are also logical operations that transform relationships. *Reciprocity* is the reciprocal of a logical relationship. For example, if Susan is older than Jane, then Jane is younger than Susan. *Transitivity* implies that if A is related to B in the same way that B is related to C, then A is related to C in the same manner. For example, if Sol and Kenji are the same weight, and Kenji weighs the same as Jack, then Sol and Jack must also be the same weight.

The various concrete operations constitute the rules for assimilating the real world in terms of logical classifications and relationships. However, this is not to say that children perform every mental operation whenever they encounter a new problem or experience. At the same time, since these operations are interdependent, children are believed to have the competence to perform all of them if needed. These operations are important in child development because they in large part define what is meant by "rational" thought. Yet rational thought requires one more characteristic, numerical quantification, to become genuinely scientific.

The Concept of Number.   Piaget (1965a) believes that children's understanding of number is a construction implied by the joint operations of classification and operations of relationship. Put differently, when children spontaneously begin to classify relationships and order classifications, they are inventing numerical quantity. In Piaget's terms, the concept of number reflects the mental ability to "unite parts into a whole, to divide a whole into parts, to coordinate equivalences and to multiply relationships" (Piaget, 1965a, p. 240). The number system acts as powerful cognitive "glue" that binds into a single, holistic system the concrete operations of classification and relationship (the cardinal and ordinal values, respectively).

It is often instructive to compare and contrast children's reasoning when they are similar ages but in different stages of cognitive development. Look at Sandlot Seminar 11.6 to see whether you can use your learning to compare Megan's and Matthew's strategies for playing "Twenty Questions."

Formal Operational Stage (approximately 12 to 14 years through adulthood). The stage of formal operations extends concrete thought to propositional logic

---

Sandlot Seminar 11.6

Twenty Questions with Megan and Matthew

Megan *(age 7½)*	*Matthew* *(age 6)*	*Author's* *Answers*
1. Does it have fur?		Yes.
	Is it a dog?	No.
2. Does it have four legs?		Yes.
	A lion?	No.
3. Does it live in a zoo?		No.
	I know! A shark! Sharks don't live in zoos. They live in 'quariums.	No. Yes.
4. Have I seen it?		
	A monkey? They live in zoos.	No, it doesn't live in a zoo.
5. Is it a mammal?		Yes.
	A whale? A whale's a mammal!	No.
6. Does it live in North Carolina?		Yes.
	I know, people. People live in North Carolina.	No, it's not a person.
7. Does it eat meat?		Sometimes.
	Is it a tiger? I know, a tiger shark!	No.
8. Is it wild?		No.
	A dog?	No.
9. Is it a pet?		Yes.
	Is it Mishi (family cat)?	Yes!

(continued)

Sandlot Seminar 11.6   Continued

Using what you have read about preoperational and concrete operational stages, see if you can answer the following questions about Megan and Matthew.

1. How do Matthew and Megan differ in their hindsight?
2. How do the two children differ in their foresight?
3. What strategy is Matthew using? How long would he take to play this game if he were by himself (no help from Megan)?
4. What strategy is Megan using?
5. Which child uses operative knowledge about class inclusion? How can you tell?
6. Which stage of development do you think each child is in? Why?

through the construction of more abstract, higher-order operations (Inhelder & Piaget, 1958). Some never achieve this stage. To assess these operations, Piaget has designed various tasks that represent complex scientific phenomena.

In one problem, for example, subjects are asked to determine what controls how fast a pendulum swings. Subjects are provided a simple pendulum apparatus for measuring the effect of several possible variables: *weight* (several weights differ from light to heavy), pendulum *length* (ranging from short to long), *impetus* or force imparted at the start of the pendulum's swing (ranging from small to large), and *height* at which the pendulum's swing is initiated (ranging from low to high). Subjects are asked to conduct several experiments in order to assess the influence of the four variables. To solve this problem effectively, they must isolate the effects of one variable from the effects of the other three. This task is useful in differentiating concrete operational solutions involving classification and arranging of variables, from formal operational solutions that effectively isolate the influence of the four variables one at a time (Inhelder & Piaget, 1958). Tasks such as this one reveal several cognitive qualities not found in earlier stages.

Hypothetico-deductive Reasoning.   Formal operational thought is said to be *hypothetico-deductive* because the mind is capable of formulating hypotheses and deducing their logical implications. Whereas the concrete operational thinker reasons in terms of concrete experiences, the formal operational thinker reasons in terms of possibilities and their logical implications. These possibilities are not arbitrary imaginings or fantasies freed of cognitive constraints or objectivity (Inhelder & Piaget, 1958). Rather, such possibilities entail the logical permutation of potential realities and the consideration of "if . . . then" logical relationships. The advantage of hypotheses over reality-states is that hypotheses can be contrary to fact, and yet their logical implications will still be valid (though not necessarily true). Two examples are instructive.

1. *Premises:* If grapes are larger than oranges, and
   if oranges are larger than watermelons,
   Conclude: then grapes are larger than watermelons.
2. *Premises:* If children are older than babies,
   and adults are older than babies,
   Conclude: then adults are older than children.

The first conclusion is untrue in the real world, but it is valid because it follows by deductive inference from its premises. The second conclusion is true in the real world, but it is invalid because it does not follow logically from its premises.

Multivariate Thinking.   Hypothetico-deductive thinking elevates thinking to the level of scientific explanation. For example, scientific phenomena consist of both simple and complex events. Simple, single-cause events are fully comprehensible with concrete operationals. However, whenever variables interact to produce complex events (e.g., weather, corrosion, combustion, the pendulum), then sorting out their individual and interactional effects requires a system like formal operations that can generate all their possible combinations.

Thinking about Thinking.   Formal operational thought can be turned inward on itself; adolescents can contemplate their own thoughts and take those thoughts as objects of thinking itself. This characteristic is called *recursive* thought.

Imagine Samuel, a young engineer, who has landed a job interview with another company. He is hopeful that a job offer with more pay will help him leave his current, unsatisfying job. In preparing for the interview, Samuel paces around his kitchen imagining the kinds of questions that will be asked and generating what he hopes will be the "right" answers. After a few minutes, Samuel stops pacing and thinks to himself "Why am I even worried about this? There's nothing to lose. I already have a job, so why don't I just tell them what I really think?" Then Samuel abruptly sits down at the kitchen table to consider his next thought. "Hold on here. Why am I even wondering about why I am worried? Should I even be thinking about why I am thinking about this interview? Maybe I should just go do it and not try to second-guess myself." Samuel is engaging in recursive thought; he is thinking about thinking.

When teenagers first begin thinking about thinking, we see a rise in adolescent egocentrism. It is because they can think about their own thoughts that they realize others can do the same thing. The egocentric aspect here is that adolescents often believe others are as preoccupied with them as they are themselves. In thinking about the thoughts of others, they often attribute to others (especially parents) motives thought to be highly critical of themselves. Elkind (1974) refers to this as *the imaginary audience* because adolescents often seem to imagine themselves performing before an audience of critics who are as interested in teenagers' shortcomings as are the teenagers themselves. A second aspect of adolescent egocentrism is the *personal fable,* a glorified self-image in which teenagers view themselves as so unique that they are somehow immune to natural forces such as aging, death, disaster, and pregnancy (about which many adolescents say, "I didn't think it would happen to me").

Subordination of Reality to Possibility.   In the previous stage, concrete operational children thought that what was real determined what was possible. At the formal operational stage, thought frees itself from reality and subordinates the real world as simply one example of possible worlds. Parents are all too familiar with this new ability. Family tensions often occur when teenagers use their new cognitive abilities to generate hypothetical "perfect" parents. Unfortunately when real parents are compared to their imagined perfections, the real ones nearly always come up short.

Change Mechanisms

Piaget (1983) identifies four factors that work together to produce cognitive development. The first three he terms the "classical factors" because they are widely recognized as influences on development. These include biological maturation, physical experience, and social transmission. The fourth factor, *equilibration,* is the most important because it regulates the other three and is the primary reason his theory is classified in the constructivist paradigm.

Biological Maturation.   Biological maturation, especially the growth of the nervous system, sets the maximum limits of development. It produces new possibilities for cognitive construction but does not predetermine intellectual abilities per se (note in the previous section that not everyone reaches the formal operational stage of development). Consequently, maturation provides a necessary but not sufficient condition for cognitive progress. In other words, development could not occur in the absence of maturation, but neither can it be wholly explained by maturation.

Physical Experience.   Experience contributes a worldly context of sensations within which cognitive constructions become adapted. But, according to Piaget, there are two kinds of experience, analogous to the operative–figurative distinction described earlier. *Physical experience* consists of behavioral or perceptual sensations we derive from objects and events, and these sensations result in figurative knowledge. It is important to note that children do not obtain physical experience by simply reading their sensory impressions like a camera. Rather, all actions are accompanied by some degree of assimilation (distortion and meaning making) to prior cognitive structuring. Object permanence, for example, is dependent on the schemata previously constructed by the infant, and lacking a schema of the permanent object, an infant will be unable to derive "permanence" from its own physical experiences.

   In contrast, *logico-mathematical experience* is produced by the coordination of one's actions (whether mental or physical) on objects or events. This kind of experience gives rise to operative knowledge, which occurs, for example, when a child discovers that the sum of a group of items is the same in spite of their arrangement or the order in which they are counted. With logico-mathematical experience it is the individual's coordinations rather than the objects themselves that constitute the source of operative knowledge. Piaget believes that it is not the quantity of experience that determines cognitive development—rather, it is the fact of experience. For example, it does not matter whether children have brightly colored toys and laser guns in America or twigs and stones in Argentina. What matters is that they have experience with objects, because objects provide opportunities for physical and mental manipulation, the foundation of operative knowledge.

Social Transmission.   Society provides the cultural milieu that transmits to individuals the "social facts"—names, expectations, rules, and events. These facts are often somewhat arbitrary but are still necessary for orderly interpersonal conduct. Learning to count to twenty, for example, is a fact of social transmission. Learning that twenty cows and twenty marbles are equivalent amounts (in spite of their size difference) is a matter of operative knowledge. Socialization leads to cooperation, and Piaget (1966) is fond of pointing out that social cooperation is a necessary condition for the evolution of cognitive operations. Social transmission, through child rearing, schooling, and especially language learning, arms the child with the social "facts" for getting along with other people. But social transmission is like the other "classical factors" in that it is a necessary but not sufficient condition for cognitive development.

Equilibration.   Equilibration regulates the interplay between the three "classical" factors. In fact, Piaget believes that cognitive development is primarily the work of equilibration (1983), and this makes it the most important of the four factors.

Equilibration is a dynamic process of intellectual self- regulation that may be either retroactive (using feedback derived after the fact from hindsight) or proactive (using feedback derived before the fact from anticipation). Following Piaget's lead, Langer (1969, 1974) has noted that *cognitive conflict* may be induced from either intrinsic (*intra*psychic) or from extrinsic (interpersonal, self–other) sources. It is cognitive conflict, which produces the disequilibrium between assimilation and accommodation, that promotes cognitive development. For example, when an individual has two logically inconsistent ideas or beliefs (intrapsychic conflict), self-reflection may result in modification of one, the other, or both ideas into a better-adjusted, more general idea. Similarly, when an individual recognizes that personal beliefs conflict with those of others, self-reflection may also produce changes in one's own beliefs. Sandlot Seminar 11.7 on page 308 helps clarify the difference between internal and external sources of cognitive conflict.

From time to time the process of equilibration achieves a state of cognitive *equilibrium* or balance between assimilation and accommodation. This equilibrium is one of the "structured wholes" that comprise a Piagetian stage.

Sandlot Seminar 11.7

Understanding Sources of Disequilibrium
See if you can identify the source of the following cognitive conflicts. Use the following key to identify the source.

> I = internal source (intrapsychic, within the same mind)
> E = external source (interpsychic, between minds)

_____ Jill is an English major at a state university. She believes that astronauts practice their space walks by entering a large tank at the Houston Space Center, and when all the air is pumped out, the astronauts begin floating. Jill's boyfriend points out that astronauts practice weightlessness in a large pool of water that gives them "buoyancy." He also tells Jill that the "airless" tank in Houston is used to test the integrity of space suits, not weightlessness. Jill begins to rethink her belief that gravity comes from air.

_____ Coming from a very conservative family, Chad hates "liberal" Democrats who he thinks want to take over the government and ruin our lives. While grieving for his grandfather who has recently died, Chad is surprised to learn that his congressman, a "liberal Democrat," has arranged for a burial in Arlington Cemetery (the national cemetery for members of the armed forces). Chad begins to rethink his beliefs about "liberal Democrats."

_____ Seth enters sixth-grade math class firmly convinced that numbers are values like 1, 2. . . , 14. . . , 156. In this class he is introduced to integers, which may be positive or negative values. Seth realizes that numbers always have a value, but that value may lie either to the positive or the negative side of zero.

_____ Twelve-year-old Mary is a very nice girl from a very nice family. She has a secret crush on Bubba, the class bully. She loves his size, his strength, and his ability to control smaller children. But she also recognizes that Bubba is not nice, is not fair, and doesn't like her. Mary thinks about what it might be like to date Bubba. She thinks it might not be very nice. She also wonders if she might be able to make Bubba nice.

Explaining Human Development: The Research

As with other paradigm cases, Piaget's theory has generated considerable research. Excluding his own work, which originated in the 1920s, most of the modern research base for the theory was established between the late 1960s and the mid 1980s. After that, Piaget's research waned in the wake of groundbreaking work in the field of information processing and artificial intelligence.

Sensorimotor Stage

There are two general types of research studies associated with the sensorimotor stage. These are studies of the sequentiality of the six substages and object permanence studies.

Sequentiality Studies. Uzgiris and Hunt (1974), using a number of behavioral indices, have performed the most extensive studies of the sensorimotor sequence of substages in such areas as object permanence, schemata, imitation, space, and causality. In another large study of 295 infants, Corman and Escalona (1969) tested the sequentiality of sensorimotor developments related only to object permanence and space. The results of both of these studies were supportive of Piaget's description of sensorimotor development. Finally, Glick (1975) reviewed a large body of research and concluded that in spite of cultural differences in child-rearing practices, there is little variation in the sequence of sensorimotor substages.

Object Permanence. The development of *object permanence* has been studied in human as well as nonhuman (monkey and cat) infants. The picture here is less uniform than for the sequentiality research. Many studies in the early 1970s generally confirmed Piaget's claim that object permanence occurs in substage IV (Gratch, 1972; Gratch & Landers, 1971; Harris, 1973, 1974). Subsequent work, however, revealed that primitive forms of object permanence emerged earlier, depending on memory requirements (Harris, 1973, 1974), task difficulty (Bower & Wishart, 1972), and performance criteria (Bower, 1974).

Concrete Operational Stage

Research on this stage was quite extensive during the 1960s and 1970s. A number of studies have attempted to replicate Piaget's (1965a) two major claims about conservation: First, that it develops in three phases (absence of conservation, followed by a mixture of conservation and nonconservation reasoning, and finally complete conservation reasoning), and second that conservation of number develops before conservation of weight, which develops before conservation of volume.

Brainerd and Brainerd (1972) devised independent tests of the three phases and administered them to children between 5 and 7 years of age. The Brainerds reported that not a single subject deviated from the predicted order. Many other studies have reported substantially the same results (Barrouillet & Poirier, 1997; Brainerd, 1976; Curcio, Kattef, Levine, & Robbins, 1977).

Many training studies have been reported in the literature. Some of these have examined the use of cognitive conflict to induce disequilibrium (Piaget's primary change mechanism) and subsequent cognitive development. These studies have been more successful with children who were already transitional between preoperational and concrete operational stages than with purely preoperational children (Inhelder, Bovet, Sinclair, & Smock, 1966; Inhelder & Sinclair, 1969; Langer, 1969; Murray, 1972; Murray, Ames, & Botvin, 1977). Training studies with preoperational children may not be successful because they attempted to teach specific rules (figurative knowledge) that should have little effect on operative aspects of knowledge.

Finally, some researchers have reported success at teaching nonconservers how to use the identity operation to improve conservation performance (Hamel & Riksen, 1973; Siegler & Liebert, 1972). Similarly, Halford and Fullerton (1970) found that training nonconservers on the use of the compensation rule was an effective means of producing conservation responses in later tests. Other training studies have attempted to elicit conservation performance by directly teaching the inversion–negation operation. It is important to note here, however, that attempts to teach conservation either directly or indirectly have themselves been criticized as a misguided endeavor to speed up rather than understand development (Voyat, 1977).

Formal Operational Stage

Using one of the largest samples in a study of its kind, Kuhn, Kohlberg, Langer, and Haan (1977) individually tested 256 subjects, aged 10 to 50 years. Subjects were given two formal operational tasks. These researchers reported: (1) approximately 70 percent exhibited predominantly formal operational reasoning and (2) only 30 percent exhibited exclusively formal operational reasoning. These findings are consistent with those obtained earlier by Nadel and Schoeppe (1973), Tomlinson-Keasey (1972), and Schwebel (1975). Those researchers had reported that only about 30 percent of 13-year-olds show formal reasoning, whereas about 60 percent of college students exhibit formal reasoning.

Other Validation Studies

Invariant Sequence.   Perhaps the most impressive evidence marshaled to date concerns Piaget's hypothesized universal sequence of stages. Piaget claims that children develop through the same stages in the same order in spite of vast differences in their cultural milieu, educational training, and personal experiences. Focusing primarily on the childhood and adolescent stages, many researchers have used Piagetian tasks to test the sequence of stages. Consistent support for the stage sequence has been found in many different cultures. They include Aborigines (Dasen, 1972), Costa Ricans and Koreans (Youniss & Dean, 1974), French-speaking Canadians (Pinard & Lavoie, 1974), Hungarians (Hollos, 1975), Mexicans (Price-Williams, Gordon, & Ramirez, 1969), North Slope Eskimos of Alaska (Feldman, Lee, McLean, Pillemer, & Murray, 1974), Norwegians (Hollos, 1975; Hollos & Cowan, 1973), and Rwandese (Pinard & Lavoie, 1974).

Metacognition.   Piagetian theory has inspired a relatively new field of study in child development, *meta-*. *Meta*research is concerned with how children think about and understand language (*meta*linguistics or *meta*communication), memory (*meta*memory), and their own thinking processes and strategies (*meta*cognition). Metaresearch is not so much a test of Piaget's theory as it is an extension of it. In this context, such research can be viewed as one measure of the theory's predictive validity.

For more than a decade, John Flavell and his colleagues have been studying children's metacognitive development (Flavell, 1993; Flavell, Green, & Flavell, 1990, 1993, 1995). Broadly speaking, they have discovered rapid development in children's understanding of their own and others' minds at approximately the same time that children undergo the change from preoperational to concrete operational thinking. Other work in metalinguistics has shown that children's understanding of both reading (Huffman, Edwards, & Green, 1982) and oral language (Green, 1985; Seitz, 1997) develops in stagelike correspondence with their movement from one cognitive stage to the next. Finally, some researchers have argued that children construct a personal theory of mind in much the same way as their own mind constructs knowledge of the physical and social world (see Schwanenflugel, Fabricius, & Noyes, 1996).

Contributions and Criticisms of the Cognitive-Developmental Theory

Contributions

Scientist–philosophers. To Piaget, children are little scientist–philosophers whose curiosity spontaneously motivates them to investigate nature and make sense of their experiences. Children organize their knowledge to make sense and adapt their sense making to reality. They do this by constructing knowledge that is logically consistent. Piaget's portrait of youth challenges exogenous views of children as recipients of learning (*tabula rasa* minds to be filled with factual information) and endogenous views of children as slaves to their own genes.

Stages. Piaget's cognitive-developmental stages have concentrated psychologists' attention on *how* children understand their experiences rather than on how many facts they know. Moreover, the widespread belief that humans are rational animals finds its most exalted expression in the logico-mathematical operations Piaget uses to describe cognitive structures. What makes Piagetian stages different from those of other theorists is that they represent transformations of earlier modes of understanding into qualitatively different organizations of knowledge. These stages have provided educators with many insights into children's readiness for certain kinds of instructional content and have led to innovations in curriculum design.

Methodology. Piaget revolutionized child study. His methods, incorporating tasks and clinical interviews that assess scientific and mathematical concepts, challenged the assumption that experimental control and quantifiable measurement were the pinnacle of psychology. The numerous Piagetian-style studies published in the 1960s and 1970s have left in their wake a heightened appreciation among developmental psychologists for the kind of discoveries Piaget's methodology can lead to.

Philosophy–Psychology.   Piaget's genetic epistemology represents a unique blend of psychology and philosophy. He uses his research to argue that rationalist and empiricist interpretations of knowledge are neither psychologically redeemable nor philosophically tenable. In an age when psychologists tend to forget their historical symbiosis with philosophy, Piaget forged a new relationship between questions of fact (psychology) and questions of meaning (philosophy). For example, Piaget's distinction between operative and figurate aspects of knowledge corresponds to philosophers' questions about ontology (what is fact) and epistemology (how are facts known), and his theory addresses the development of both aspects.

Criticisms

Operation.   One of the most important concepts of Piagetian theory is the cognitive *operation*. But because operations are a mentalist construct, they tend to be difficult to verify empirically. Tests of the mental operations hypothesized for concrete and formal operational stages have reported that some but not all operators are present in a given situation. Such findings call into question Piaget's contention that cognitive stages are holistic structures whereby the presence of one mental operation implies the presence of many others.

Formal Operations.   A minor controversy has arisen around the contention that the formal operational stage is the terminus of cognitive development. As noted earlier, some researchers have reported that a significant portion of the adolescent and adult population fails to achieve formal reasoning (Kuhn, Langer, Kohlberg & Haan, 1977; Nadel & Schoeppe, 1973; Schwebel, 1975; Tomlinson-Keasey, 1972). In addition, other researchers have argued that cognitive development continues beyond the formal operational stage (Commons, Richards, & Kuhn, 1982).

Three kinds of responses have been made to these criticisms. First, Piaget (1972) has acknowledged that some people do not achieve the stage of formal operations, and he contends that adolescent aptitudes and interests sometimes lead to vocational choices in which formal reasoning is not developmentally adaptive. He also believes that a number of people may reason formally in their chosen professions but still fail to show formal operations on tests of science and logic. Second, the theory emphasizes the sequence of cognitive-developmental stages rather than their terminus. Studies cited earlier lend strong support to the sequentiality claim of Piaget's stages. Third, Piaget does not discount the possibility of postformal stages of reasoning (although he had no interest in pursuing adult thought himself). In fact, the internal principles of organization and adaptation imply the possibility of increasingly more adequate cognitive structures.

The Concept of Stage.   Piaget's concept of a stage has been criticized on three counts by Brainerd (1973, 1977, 1978a, 1978b), a well-known critic of Piaget. He contends (1) that developmental changes Piaget attributes to equilibration can be explained by simpler principles of learning; (2) that qualitative changes from one stage to the next can be reduced to quantitative accumulations of learning; and (3) that Piaget's developmental stages can be explained by an endogenous, maturational account of development. While Piagetian theorists allow that the origin of qualitative changes must ultimately reside in small developmental changes, they disagree with Brainerd in their belief that cognitive development is best conceptualized in constructivist, stagelike rather than maturational or learning terms.

Evaluation of Cognitive-Developmental Theory

In the previous two chapters, you have been asked to evaluate theories on your own, using the three sets of criteria given in Chapter 2. Keeping in mind that Piaget's theory is the paradigm case for the constructivist paradigm, see if you can complete Sandlot Seminar 11.8.

Sandlot Seminar 11.8

How Would You Evaluate Piaget's Theory?
Use your own understanding to evaluate Piaget's theory of cognitive development on each of the three sets of criteria. Compare your evaluations and reasons with those given by the authors.

Scientific Worthiness
Testability   _____
External validity   _____
Predictive validity   _____
Internal consistency   _____
Theoretical economy   _____

Developmental Adequacy
Temporality   _____
Cumulativity   _____
Directionality   _____
New mode of organization   _____
Increased capacity for self-control _____

Pedagogical Usefulness
Intrepretability   _____
Versatility   _____
Availability   _____
Guidance   _____

Scientific Worthiness

Testability.   Because Piaget is a mentalist, his theory is rated only medium for testability (see Table 11.1). Concepts such as equilibration, mental operations, and cognitive structures are not directly observable and therefore cannot easily be tested. Nevertheless, other Piagetian concepts such as schema can be more directly tested, and *inferences* drawn from the Piaget's concepts can be assessed with both verbal and behavioral data. On balance, Piaget's theory seems to be more testable than Freud's but less testable than Skinner's.

External Validity.   The theory is rated high for its external validity. What is interesting from a historical point of view is that so many of Piaget's discoveries about child development went undiscovered for so long: object permanence, cognitive egocentrism, conservation, the concept of number, hypothetical reasoning. The evidence supporting Piaget's theory is substantial, and the cross-cultural component of the validation research is impressive. Piaget's most important major contentions—the theory of stages, as well as the cognitive capabilities theorized for each stage—accord fairly well with what is known about infant, child, and adolescent cognition. In fact, the field of social cognitive development often relies on cognitive-developmental principles to analyze children's social knowledge and relationships.

The above considerations notwithstanding, it is important to note that a number of researchers have challenged the external validity of Piaget's work. While a full discussion of that work is beyond the scope of this book, two general patterns are relevant here. First, it appears that children understand substantially more and at earlier ages than Piaget has theorized. Second, such findings nearly always result from research methods that do not require children to explain or justify their reasoning. Balancing these results and methods with our earlier considerations, we have nonetheless given the theory a high rating for its external validity.

Predictive Validity.   The theory's predictive validity reflects a large body of empirical research that has attempted to test theoretically derived predictions, many about specific interrelationships between two or more cognitive functions. For example, Piaget's prediction that intellectual functioning in large part determines

TABLE 11.1   **Ratings of Cognitive-Developmental Theory for Scientific Worthiness**

Criteria	High	Medium	Low
Testability		X	
External Validity	X		
Predictive Validity	X		
Internal Consistency		X	
Theoretical Economy	X		

linguistic development has received considerable empirical support (e.g., Green, 1979, 1985; Templeton & Spivey, 1980). Although exceptions exist, many other attempts to verify theoretical predictions indicate that this theory's predictive validity is high.

Internal Consistency. On the one hand, Piaget maintains a steadfast constructivist interpretation of development that is unswerving in its antiendogenous and antiexogenous orientation. It would be difficult to argue that Piaget at any time poses an inconsistent plot in his message that intellectual development is dynamic, organized, adaptive, and constructivist in nature. There is, on the other hand, a major inconsistency in Piaget's theory. Piaget maintains that a cognitive stage is a holistic structure, a general mode of action or operation. If a cognitive stage fits this conception, then one would expect that when one stage is transformed into the next, the new stage becomes operational in a relatively complete way and should therefore permeate the thought of the child. Yet considerable evidence indicates that what happens is that the new stage, rather than exhibiting a general mode of operation, only gradually gets applied to the field of experience. To account for this gradual elaboration, Piaget invokes a principle he calls *de calage,* or small differences in development. The concept of *de calage* seems to be a contradiction to the concept of a holistic, structured stage. The importance of this problem for Piaget's stage concept is sufficient to result in a medium rating for internal consistency.

Theoretical Economy. Piaget's theory ranks high on theoretical economy for two reasons. First, his theory makes only two assumptions about the nature of the child at birth, fewer than any other theory in the text. Moreover, he does not make the mistake of assuming qualities of mind when he knows that those qualities are the very elements he must explain. Second, his theory attempts to account for the development of a broad range of cognitive phenomena from birth to adulthood.

Developmental Adequacy

Overall, Piaget's theory is rated high for its developmental adequacy. Individual ratings are shown in Table 11.2.

TABLE 11.2   Ratings of Cognitive-Developmental Theory for Developmental Adequacy

Characteristics	Rating
Temporality	Yes
Cumulativity	Yes
Directionality	Yes
New Mode of Organization	Yes
Increased Capacity for Self-control	Yes

Temporality.   Since Piaget explains development as a gradual process of organization and adaptation that occurs between birth and maturity, his theory passes this criterion.

Cumulativity.   Earlier developmental stages function as cognitive preparation for later stages. Moreover, later stages build upon, expand, and transform cognitive capacities acquired in earlier stages. Consequently, his theory passes this criterion.

Directionality.   The inherent directionality of Piaget's theory is best captured by his concept of equilibration which regulates cognitive development toward increasing logical adequacy. Later stages are logically more adequate than earlier stages because individuals can solve all the problems solved at earlier stages while simultaneously solving new kinds of problems not previously solvable. For example, concrete operational children retain the representational capacities of preoperational children, but their capabilities are organized into a cognitive structure of reversible operations capable of classification and relation that cannot be performed at the preoperational stage. Piaget's theory passes this criterion because his theory represents human cognitive development as a gradual evolution toward progressively more adequate structures of knowledge.

Increased Complexity.   Piaget's theory passes this criterion because it depicts developmental change in terms of increased differentiation and hierarchic integration. Examples of changes that result in increasingly complex cognitions include the differentiation of means from ends and the accompanying construction of object permanence, the internalization of schemata and accompanying formation of mental representations, the change from unidirectional to reversible thinking, and the objectification and then the hypothesizing of reality.

New Mode of Organization.   Piaget's cognitive-developmental stages are transformations of earlier modes of knowing into new, more adequate structures. In all his work, Piaget's depiction of a cognitive structure is as an organized system of mutually implied cognitive abilities that comprise a structured whole. In this sense, each of Piaget's stages is conceived as a new mode of organization vis-à-vis the previous stage. For this reason, the theory passes this criterion.

Increased Capacity for Self-control.   In contrast to sensorimotor actions, the beginning of mental representation at the onset of the preoperational stage allows children to cognize symbolic realities without actually having objects physically present. In addition, formal operational thought is able to anticipate *possible circumstances* and thereby adjust itself ahead of time. Such "feedforward" is more than being able to anticipate what in fact will be the result of one's actions; it is the ability to cognize possible results and adjust planned activities to maximize certain potential effects while minimizing other possible effects. This process indicates how thought first transcends objects and eventually transcends reality and even controls it to some extent. Consequently, Piaget's theory does explain how development reflects an increased self-control, so it passes this criterion.

Pedagogical Usefulness

Piaget's theory has become one of the more useful twentieth-century theories provided by developmental psychology. Summary ratings for its pedagogical usefulness are shown in Table 11.3.

Interpretability.   On balance, we have rated Piaget's theory medium for its interpretability for several reasons. First, its high external validity implies that it does a fairly good job of accounting for children's and adolescents' thinking. Second, most of Piaget's concepts (e.g., assimilation, accommodation, stages, schema, operation) can be readily interpreted through real-life examples of children. To be sure, the concept of equilibration is more complex and difficult, but on balance, much of Piaget's theoretical jargon has become relatively commonplace in educational and psychological arenas. Third, the theory helps educators, counselors, social workers, and parents interpret children's experiences and understandings from a child's point of view. Today, for example, teachers often introduce mathematics to elementary students with concrete manipulatives they can see and arrange directly with their hands. Such a practice reflects educational interpretations of Piaget's theory and signals a change away from more traditional teaching methods, which began with counting and paper-and-pencil activities. Fourth, Piaget's theory has motivated many developmental psychologists and educators to write various interpretations of his work. Nearly always, these interpretive essays have been easier to understand than Piaget's own writings.

In contrast to the foregoing considerations, we must point out that Piaget's writings tend to be quite dense and difficult to read. This "academic" writing style may be a function of translators or the complexity and subtlety of his ideas. Whatever the case, his writing does not lend itself to easy interpretation, and this factor prevents us from rating his interpretability better than medium.

TABLE 11.3   Ratings of Cognitive-Developmental Theory for Pedagogical Usefulness

Criteria	High	Medium	Low
Interpretability		X	
Versatility		X	
Availability		X	
Guidance		X	

Versatility.   Recall that versatility is a reflection of variety or generality. We believe Piaget's theory is medium in its versatility. For example, it is useful in helping parents deal with a variety of developmental phenomena: infantile schemata such as mouthing, dropping, and throwing (often exercised when learning to eat solid food); age-related differences in children's responses to nightmares; childhood misconceptions about death being just another form of sleep; unrealistic fears that originate in imagination or cartoons; the onset of adultlike thought and understanding during middle childhood; and even the linguistic battles with adolescents about words and their meanings. Teachers use Piaget's theory to plan when and how to teach new science and mathematics material. Counselors and social workers use the theory in carrying out therapeutic treatments for children who have experienced traumatic events or abuse. Even pediatric nurses and physicians use their understanding of children's cognitive development to help them explain disease and treatment to children of different ages. But Piaget's theory is not universally versatile. It does not help us understand children's emotional, physical, or perceptual development. It does little to help parents plan better meals, summer camps, or daily routines for their children. What it does best is help adults view the world from a child's point of view.

Availability.   Piaget's own and others' derivative writings about the theory are found primarily in academic libraries in books and professional journals. Extensive treatment of his theory can also be found in virtually any textbook about child development or developmental psychology. Other presentations can be found in educational journals and magazines, particularly during the 1970s and 1980s. However, ideas derived from Piaget's theory have simply not made their way into the mainstream of public consciousness to the same degree as Freud's and Skinner's ideas have. While many nonpsychologists have heard the name "Piaget," and some even associate the name with "stages" of development, few know any particulars about Piagetian theory. For these reasons, we have judged theory to be medium for its availability.

Guidance.   If one assumes that any intervention (e.g., counseling, schooling, parenting) should begin with a child's eye view of the world, then few theories offer as much guidance as does Piaget's. After all, in its most basic form, his theory is about how children construct their own understandings of the physical and social world they inhabit. Armed with such knowledge, parents can understand that infants throw food not out of spite or anger but as a way of using their "throwing" schema to explore objects, that toddlers awake crying with nightmares that appear real, and that childhood egocentrism is a cognitive constraint on taking another's point of view rather than the result of selfishness. Parents and teachers both can use Piaget's theory to understand and plan optimum experiences for early and middle childhood (see McGilly, 1996), a time when thinking becomes more logical, objective, and rational. We can also understand that parent–adolescent conflict is a natural consequence of using hypothetico-deductive thought to examine and explore the implications of parental values and standards; it is not the project of irrational rejection of parental authority. In these ways and more, Piaget's theory provides a basis for developmentally appropriate pedagogy and would be ranked high for its guidance were it not for one mitigating factor that leads us to a medium rating for this criterion.

Recall from Chapter 2 that the primary evidence of a theory's guidance will be found in its *change mechanism,* which in Piaget's theory is equilibration. Unfortunately, we do not know how to control equilibration to systematically invoke cognitive conflict and enhance cognitive development. The primary problem here is that equilibration is a quite general concept that gives little pedagogical guidance in specific situations.

Summary Points

1. Piaget's theory draws on ideas first set forth in Kant's epistemology and Spencer's developmental psychology. Heinz Werner's organismic psychology, followed by John Flavell's English summary of Piaget's work, both contributed to making Piagetian theory accessible to American developmental psychology.

2. Piaget makes two assumptions about the newborn: that it has innate, biological reflexes and that it is inherently proactive.

3. The problem of study for cognitive-developmental theory is to explain the origin and genesis of scientific and mathematical knowledge. Applied to individual development, this problem amounts to explaining the development of logico-mathematical thought. Piaget's methods include observations for infants and clinical interviews for children and adolescents.

4. The theory's internal principles are assimilation and accommodation, equilibration, and the functional invariants of organization and adaptation.

5. Piaget's theory incorporates three bridge principles: schemata, the building blocks of knowledge; cognitive operations, reversible mental actions; and cognitive structures, stagelike organized systems of mental actions. These cognitive structures define four stages of cognitive development: sensorimotor stage, preoperational, concrete operational, and formal operational stages.

6. The four mechanisms of development include the three classical factors—biological maturation, physical experience, and social experience—which are regulated by the most important factor, equilibration. It is equilibration that reflects constructivism in Piaget's theory.

7. Piaget's most important contributions are a conception of children as inquiring scientist–philosophers, a conception of psychological stages irreducible to maturational timetables, a methodology that combines cognitive problems with clinical interviews, and the application of psychological data to long-standing philosophical questions. The three most prevalent criticisms of his theory concern his concepts of operation and stage and his description of formal operations as the terminus of cognitive development.

8. Piaget's theory is rated medium for its scientific worthiness, high for its developmental adequacy, and medium for its pedagogical usefulness.

PROBLEMS AND EXERCISES

1. Most people cannot remember any specific events from their infancy (before about 2 years of age). This widely acknowledged phenomenon is called infantile amnesia. Freud would explain infantile amnesia as due to the defense mechanism of repression; memories are retained in the unconscious, but they are repressed by the ego. Skinner would explain the same phenomenon as the result of extinction; infantile behavior does not continue to be reinforced once we reach childhood, so it is extinguished. How would Piaget explain infantile amnesia?

2. Piaget (1962, p. 63) describes the following observation. One afternoon his daughter (16 months old) observed another youngster throw a temper tantrum. The daughter had never before seen a temper tantrum. The following afternoon she proceeded to scream and stamp her feet several times in succession while in her playpen. The problem is to explain how Piaget's daughter could have performed such a "deferred imitation." It is important to follow Piaget's lead. He cannot attribute his daughter's actions to memory, since no mind exists to remember. Another explanation must be sought. Compare your answer with the explanation Piaget gives in *Play, Dreams and Imitation in Childhood* (1962, pp. 67–86).

3. Administer one of the conservation tasks described in this chapter to three children, each between 6 and 7 years of age. Be sure to ask the children to justify their responses with reasons. Are all three children in the same cognitive stage? Why or why not? How can you tell?

4. A father wanted to convey a sense of family history to his two young children. He did this through a series of letters he wrote to them about his own childhood experiences and memories. One such letter described a camping trip and a hike along a streambed during the summer. Near the end of this letter, things got dramatic as the father described nearly stepping on a rattlesnake sunning itself in the hiking trail. The letter ended with a question for the children, "What's the most important thing to learn from this letter?" Matthew (aged 6½ years) responded, "Don't step on rattlesnakes because they'll bite you, and you'll die." Megan (aged 8 years) said, "The most important thing is to look where you're going, so you won't have an accident." Consider your learning about cognitive development in this chapter and describe the thinking characteristics of the two children that underlie their responses.

5. Use the Internet to search for sites related to Jean Piaget and his theory. You can use his name as well as key words (internal and bridge principles). How do the Internet sites differ in terms of completeness and accuracy of information? What were the best sites you found? What problems did you encounter? What were some of the worst sites (and why)?

SUGGESTED READINGS

More about the Theory

Gallagher, J. M., & Reid, D. K. (1981). *The learning theory of Piaget and Inhelder.* Monterey, CA: Brooks/Cole.

Piaget, J. (1960). *The child's conception of the world.* New Jersey: Littlefield, Adams.

Piaget, J., & Inhelder, B. (1969). *The psychology of the child.* New York: Basic Books.

Research Reviews

Ashton, P. T. (1975). Cross-cultural Piagetian research: An experimental perspective. *Harvard Educational Review, 45,* 475–506.

Dasen, P. R. (1972). Cross-cultural Piagetian research: A summary. *Journal of Cross-Cultural Psychology, 3,* 23–29.

Gratch, G. (1977). Review of Piagetian infancy research: Object concept development. In W. F. Overton & J. M. Gallagher (Eds.), *Knowledge and development.* New York: Plenum Press.

Mogdil, S., & Mogdil, C. (1976). *Piagetian research: Compilation and commentary,* Vol. 7. Rochester, UK: NFER Publishing Co.

Critical Reviews

Brainerd, C. J. (1978). The stage question in cognitive–developmental theory. *The Behavioral and Brain Sciences, 2,* 173–213.

Brown, G., & Desforges, C. (1979). *Piaget's theory: A psychological critique.* London: Routledge & Kegan Paul.

Mogdil, S., Modgil, C., & Brown, G. (Eds.) (1983). *Jean Piaget: An interdisciplinary critique.* London: Routledge & Kegan Paul.

Vuyk, R. (1981). *Overview and critique of Piaget's genetic epistemology: 1965–1980,* Vol. 1. London: Academic Press.

12 Kohlberg and Moral Development Theory

Preview Questions

> What are the general similarities and differences between Piaget's theory and Kohlberg's theory?
>
> What problem does Kohlberg address, and what methods are used to collect data?
>
> What are Kohlberg's internal and bridge principles? How do these compare with Piaget's?
>
> What change mechanism does Kohlberg propose?
>
> Why is Kohlberg's theory a member of the constructivist paradigm?
>
> What are the major contributions and criticisms of Kohlberg's theory?
>
> How does Kohlberg's theory rate for its scientific worthiness, developmental adequacy, and pedagogical usefulness?

Historical Sketch

Lawrence Kohlberg's affinity for Piaget's theory of cognitive development is evident in his philosophically grounded theory of moral development. In fact, in describing children as natural moral philosophers, Kohlberg (Kohlberg & Gilligan, 1971) parallels Piaget's contention that children are natural scientists and mathematicians. It is no surprise, then, that we find Kohlberg relying extensively on Piaget's constructivism to explain moral development.

Lawrence Kohlberg, born in 1927, grew up in a suburb of New York City and later attended an elite prep school. Before going on to college, however, he worked on a freighter that ran the British blockade in transporting Jewish refugees from war-torn Europe to Israel. In 1948 he enrolled at the University of Chicago. His admission test scores were so high that a number of courses were waived, allowing him to complete his undergraduate degree in only one year (the authors know of no one else who has ever done this). He continued his graduate work there and focused on moral thinking in adolescent males. He had the good fortune to be trained by outstanding academicians—Charles Morris in philosophy, Bruno Bettle-heim and Carl Rogers in clinical psychology, and Bernice Neugarten and Robert Havighurst in developmental psychology (Kohlberg, 1984, p. vii).

Following the completion of his dissertation, Kohlberg continued a longitu-dinal study of the moral development of his dissertation subjects as they grew into adulthood and middle age. In 1968 he moved to Harvard University as a professor of education and social psychology where he founded the Center for Moral Edu-cation. The Center was a world-renowned hotbed of research and educational inter-vention activity for two decades until it closed after Kohlberg's death. Together with a number of colleagues, he began to investigate the universality of moral devel-opment in different cultures. During the 1970s, he worked with a group of Cam-bridge teachers to found the Cluster School, an alternative school that incorporated his philosophy of the "just community." At the Cluster School, students were chal-lenged to participate with their teachers in defining their own educational goals and values. In later years, Kohlberg was involved in refining his theory, working on practical applications for education and penal reform, and teaching his classes on moral development. He died in 1987.

From Piagetian Roots

Early in his career, Kohlberg developed the conviction that Piaget's account of cognitive development was basically sound, but his own analysis of moral devel-opment did not square with Piaget's formulation. To understand Kohlberg's con-structivist theory, it is important to recognize the exogenous elements found in Piaget's account of moral development.

First, in one of his earliest books Piaget (1965b) had defined morality as a sys-tem of rules and located its origin in children's learning of and respect for rules that are culturally specific conventions, habits, and modes of conduct. The irony here is that while Piaget himself proposed universal stages of cognitive development, he maintained that moral judgment reflected only culturally specific learning. Kohlberg recognized that Piaget had set forth an exogenous rather than a constructivist account of moral development.

A second irony is found in Piaget's contention that motives underlying moral behavior were derived from respect and other moral feelings. So it is again ironic that Piaget accounted for moral development in terms of figurative knowledge (moral feelings, elements of respect, and specific rule learning) when his account of cognitive development concentrates so heavily on rational constructions and reor-ganizations of operative knowledge (Kohlberg, 1969, 1972, 1974).

Beginning with his dissertation, Kohlberg has consistently espoused a theory of moral development that addresses the problems with Piaget's analysis. For exam-ple, Kohlberg developed a methodology, the moral dilemma, derived from Piaget's clinical interview technique and focusing not on consequences or rules but on rea-soning and judgment. Moreover, by rooting his conception of morality in philo-sophical conceptions of justice and fairness (see Rawls, 1971), Kohlberg avoided problems inherent in equating morality with the amount of respect one holds for people and rules. In the end, Kohlberg's theory is structurally similar to Piaget's theory of cognitive development, and in that regard, it seems to be a more of a constructivist account of moral development than Piaget's own.

As noted in the previous chapter, simply positing a sequence of developmental stages does not in itself classify a theory as constructivist in nature. Stage theories may, after all, embody markedly different notions about how stages develop or even what constitutes a "stage." Kohlberg's theory is an example of the constructivist paradigm because he, like Piaget, contends that later stages are hierarchic reorganizations of earlier stages. As a constructivist, Kohlberg also argues that moral reasoning derives from adaptive resolutions of interpersonal conflicts.

Structural Components of Moral Development Theory

Assumptions

Most developmental psychologists view birth as the beginning of psychological development. Kohlberg makes a radical departure from such a traditional starting point. He makes no attempt to root his theory in the early years of infancy. Instead, he assumes that a critical amount of cognitive and social development has already occurred as a necessary condition for the later development of moral judgment.

First, Kohlberg defines morality as *justice* and *fairness*, and he believes that individuals' moral judgments reflect cognitive rather than emotional processes. In this sense, moral development is viewed as the *rational, cognitive construction* of ethical premises, rules, and conclusions that motivate moral judgments. The importance of this assumption is that it leads Kohlberg to seek the roots of moral reasoning in the intellectual constructions of youth rather than in such other processes as reinforcement, modeling, and identification (Kohlberg, 1971, p. 155). His theory provides a framework for understanding how moral reasoning develops from stages of less adequate to more adequate conceptions of justice (Levine, Kohlberg & Hewer, 1985, p. 95). His primary concern is with moral thinking and justification rather than moral behavior. The reason here is that there is nothing in the behavior itself that is necessarily moral or immoral; the only element of morality lies in an actor's intent, not in the behavior. We can imagine, for example, two situations involving the same behavior. In the first, one person pushes another down a flight of stairs *in order to* extract revenge for a previous transgression. In our second example, the same pushing occurs, but this time it was initiated *in order to* save the second person from a bomb set to explode near the top of the stairs. The only difference between the two scenarios is the underlying intention, not the manifest behaviors. In order to avoid problems with analyzing behavior, Kohlberg elects to limit his work to rational *judgments* about justice and fairness.

Reminiscent of Piaget's distinction between figurative and operative knowledge, Kohlberg also differentiates between content and structure in moral reasoning. This distinction leads to the search for how individuals use operations of justice involving equality, reciprocity, and equity in their thinking rather than which social rules and values they have learned.

Second, in order for rational judgments of justice and fairness to occur, Kohlberg requires that a sufficient degree of cognitive development in infancy and early childhood has already occurred. For example, he assumes that children cognitively differentiate between social and physical objects and that they understand that social objects (people) act intentionally. More specifically, people engage one another in social interactions, and through their interpersonal commerce, they construct patterns of expectations that proscribe and regulate social behavior. Social interactions are important precisely because they create conflicts that must be resolved, not because they result in learning social norms and values.

Third, Kohlberg assumes that individuals differentiate between (1) manifest behavior, (2) the underlying intentions that motivate behavior, and (3) the overt consequences of individuals' actions. This assumption is reflected in his methodology where he elicits from subjects their reasoning about how these three factors interrelate and influence moral judgments. The importance of this assumption is shown in Sandlot Seminar 12.1.

Sandlot Seminar 12.1

Consider This

Scenario 1. Six-year-old Gima wants to help her mom set the table for a "special" dinner. Trying to be helpful, she climbs on the counter and retrieves four dinner plates, which she then sets on place mats already located on the kitchen table. Next, she gets the forks and knives and sets each pair on a place mat. Finally, she climbs up onto the kitchen counter, reaches up to the highest shelf, and tries to grab the crystal glasses she knows her mother loves. Retrieving four of these fine glasses, Gima carefully sets them on the counter. Then, while climbing down, her knee swings forward and hits the glasses. They bounce off the counter, onto the kitchen floor, and shatter into tiny pieces. Four fine crystal glasses are all broken.

Scenario 2. Seth's mother has just baked a batch of chocolate chip cookies for an afternoon snack. After cooling them, she gives three cookies and a glass of milk to Seth and says, "No more cookies until tomorrow. Understood?" Seth nods his head in agreement.

Before going to bed Seth notices that the kitchen is empty and the light is turned off. Sneaking quietly, he decides to steal a couple of cookies before bed. Knowing how good cookies are with milk, Seth gets a glass from the kitchen cupboard. As he turns around, the glass slips from his hand and breaks on the floor.

1. Gima broke four expensive crystal glasses trying to help her mom set the dinner table. Seth broke one ordinary glass trying to steal cookies. Which child has committed the more serious error? Why?
2. Young children typically say Gima should receive more punishment than Seth. Why would they say that?

3. Do young children typically consider another's intentions in making moral judgments? Why or why not? (Think about what your learned about cognitive development in Chapter 11.)

4. Why are intentions important in considering the moral worth of another person's actions?

Scenario 3. A 43-year-old homeless man has twice been convicted of felonies (defined in his state as stealing more than $50 in cash or material). On these occasions, he was attempting to steal more than $50 worth of goods (mostly food and clothing) from local stores. A third felony under the "three strikes" law means that he will spend the rest of his life in jail. That's the law in his state.

In a state of hunger, the man breaks into a church to steal some money. Once inside, he quickly finds nearly $100 in cash hidden in a coffee tin in the church kitchen. Noticing the abundance of food that has already been prepared for the next morning's congregation, he remembers the "three strikes" law and decides to leave the money alone and take some food instead. What he doesn't know is that he has tripped a silent alarm. The local police are already on the way. A few minutes later, he is caught outside the church with food stuffed in his clothes and in two grocery bags. The police estimate the cost of food at $60. The next morning they verify their estimate with a local food market and learn that the prepared food the man stole would retail for $100.

1. Is the homeless man guilty of breaking his state's felony law against stealing more than $50 worth of cash or material?

2. The man admits taking the prepared food from the church kitchen. Does that make any difference?

3. What is this man's intention? In your opinion, should his intention make any difference in this case? Why or why not?

4. In this man's state, his crime is punishable by life imprisonment. Should the man be sent to prison for life? Why or why not?

5. What does this man "owe" society for breaking its law?

Problem for Study

Phenomena to Be Explained. Kohlberg attempts to study how individuals develop increasingly complex moral reasoning. Note that this theoretical problem is quite limited in scope. In fact, Kohlberg declines any attempt to explain the entirety of morality, preferring instead to concentrate on the rational foundations of moral judgments. He does not, for example, attempt to explain other forms of morality as might be found in legal jurisprudence (courts-martial, trials by jury), types of litigation (criminal, civil), or even immorality (sadism, cheating, aggression). Nor does he attempt to account for superficial forms of social conformity—obedience, honesty, manners, or other social virtues.

Methods of Study.   Kohlberg has developed a series of *moral dilemmas* that place into conflict competing moral claims and personal rights of hypothetical individuals. The individual's task is to resolve the dilemmas and provide appropriate moral justifications. Individuals are told a moral dilemma then interviewed extensively by an extensive open-ended interview that probes their resolutions and rationalizations. The most famous Kohlberg dilemma is the story of Heinz, which has appeared in many variations.

> A woman was dying from a rare form of cancer. A local druggist had concocted a cure, but it was very expensive to make. The woman's husband, Heinz, went to the druggist to buy the cure, but the druggist wanted too much money for it. The druggist declined to negotiate a loan or to sell it for a lower price. The husband was desperate, so he thought about stealing the drug. (after Kohlberg, 1971, p. 156)

In the Piagetian constructivist tradition, Kohlberg probes individual reasoning on a person-by-person basis, with each subsequent question in the clinical interview dependent on what has been said so far. In the Heinz dilemma, subjects would be asked if Heinz should steal the drug (and why or why not), if the druggist is entitled to set a price for the cure (why or why not), and if caught stealing, whether or not Heinz should go to jail (why or why not). In Kohlberg's wake, other more direct methods have been developed for measuring moral development. One of the most popular is the Defining Issues Test, a paper and pencil test developed by James Rest. This test has been shown to have high validity and reliability in terms of yielding results similar to those obtained by Kohlberg (Rest, 1975, 1979).

Internal Principles

Cognitive Conflict and Equilibration.   **Cognitive conflict** is Kohlberg's term for Piaget's concept of equilibration. Cognitive conflict occurs when an individual has two beliefs that may be contradictory (e.g., never lie—don't get in trouble) or when a belief conflicts with external information (e.g., liars are punished—my friends lie and don't get caught). Cognitive conflict leads to the invention of moral principles and beliefs that reflect resolutions of these conflicts. The ultimate result of accumulated conflicts and resolutions is a sequence of stages that embody differentiation and hierarchic integration of moral concepts. In other words, cognitive conflict is a natural byproduct of interpersonal interactions and self-reflection (Kohlberg, 1971, p. 183), and it leads to increasingly adequate reasoning about justice and fairness. Later stages of moral reasoning are capable of resolving more moral conflicts and more interpersonal points of view in a more self-consistent way than earlier moral stages. Cognitive conflict is constructive in the sense that individuals invent moral rationalizations to make sense out of and to solve moral problems and inconsistencies. These rationalizations, in turn, become increasingly organized and adaptive as more complex moral problems are recognized and resolved. The theoretical relationship between cognitive conflict and the other two internal principles is shown in Figure 12.1.

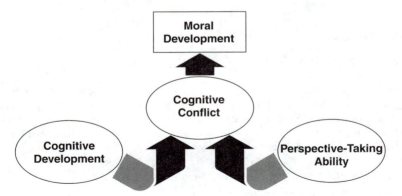

FIGURE 12.1 Schematic of the relationship between Kohlberg's internal principles.

Cognitive Development. Kohlberg employs Piaget's cognitive developmental stages as a second internal principle. He explicitly argues that Piaget's stages provide the psychological apparatus required for increasingly complex moral judgments (Kuhn, Langer, Kohlberg, & Haan, 1977). In this way moral judgments are viewed as the application of underlying cognitive operations toward the regulation of interpersonal relations and social conduct. Kohlberg contends that moral reasoning is constrained but not solely determined by one's stage of cognitive development. In other words, a child's stage of cognitive development may support several stages of moral reasoning, but the most complex moral reasoning possible is limited by the child's cognitive operations. This relationship between cognitive and moral development stages provides a constructivist explanation for why adolescents who are formal operational would exhibit higher stages of moral reasoning than other adolescents or younger children who are concrete operational. Such an explanation of moral reasoning differentiates Kohlberg's constructivist position from endogenous (age-specific) and exogenous (learning and experience) theories that preceded him.

Perspective-taking Ability. Kohlberg's third internal principle is perspective-taking ability. Moral judgments require the mental ability to assess and evaluate multiple points of view. Since interpersonal conflicts are comprised of clashes between different points of view and different interests, one's adaptation to these encounters must to some extent rely on perspective-taking ability. Perspective taking, in Kohlberg's sense, is the ability to take the point of view of another person, to see things from others' points of view, and to understand the interests, intentions, and claims others bring to a particular situation. Opportunities for perspective taking, for looking at situations from multiple points of view, and for examining the consequences of each viewpoint, are prerequisites to having genuinely social experiences and the development of moral reasoning. For example, imagine a toddler who is developmentally incapable of taking another's point of view. The importance of perspective taking is shown in Sandlot Seminar 12.2 on pages 330–332.

Sandlot Seminar 12.2

Perspective Taking and Moral Development

Scenario 1. On a warm fall evening a typical toddler demands, before supper time, to be swung on the outdoor swing by Dad. Dad has just finished a day-long spring cleanup of mowing the lawn, trimming the shrubs, changing oil in the cars, erecting ladders to clean fall leaves out of the rain gutters, and cutting the vines off the backyard fence. Dad is tired. But the toddler persists.

> TODDLER: Daddy, I want to swing. Swing me.
>
> DAD: I can't, sweetie. I'm too tired.
>
> TODDLER: But, Daddy, I REALLY want to swing.
>
> DAD: I know, but can't you have Mom do it?
>
> TODDLER: I don't want Mommy to swing me. I want you to swing me.
>
> DAD: But, sweetie, listen to me. I'm too tired to swing you. Get Mom. OK?
>
> TODDLER: Daddy, PLEASE. I want YOU to swing me, not Mom.
>
> DAD: I'm too tired. I just can't do it right now. Maybe later.
>
> TODDLER (with tears): But Daddy, I REALLY WANT YOU TO SWING ME RIGHT NOW! DADDY, come back. I want YOU to swing me.
>
> DAD: Sorry, sweetie. (disappears indoors leaving his daughter in tears on the family's back lawn)

1. Does this scenario involve a moral dilemma?
2. For whom?
3. What (if anything) is the dilemma?
4. What role-taking ability does the daughter exhibit?
5. Is the daughter experiencing cognitive conflict? If so, does she have the capacity to make a moral decision? If not, is moral decision making possible for her?

Scenario 2. Lakisha and Towanda live on the same street and are best friends. One day Lakisha tells Towanda that she doesn't like her any more because Towanda didn't invite her to a Christmas party. Towanda talks to Lakisha later and explains that the Christmas party was only for family relatives.

> LAKISHA: I didn't know that. You could have told me.
>
> TOWANDA: I just didn't think about it, since it was only my own family.
>
> LAKISHA: I know. But you hurt my feelings. That's not nice.
>
> TOWANDA: I'm sorry. I didn't mean to. You're still my best friend.
>
> LAKISHA: OK, so let's do something fun.
>
> TOWANDA: OK.

1. Do Lakisha and Towanda display the same perspective-taking ability as the daughter in the previous scenario?

2. What are the differences in perspective-taking ability?
3. How might Lakisha and Towanda's friendship involve an element of morality that was not involved in the toddler dilemma?

Scenario 3. Kenji and Diego are playing soccer. Kenji dribbles the ball down the field past Diego and kicks the ball into the goal.

> KENJI: I scored! Yeah!
>
> DIEGO: That's not fair. You cheated.
>
> KENJI: No, I didn't.
>
> DIEGO: Yes, you did.
>
> KENJI: No, I didn't.
>
> DIEGO: Yes, you did.
>
> KENJI (louder): NO, I DIDN'T!
>
> DIEGO (also louder): YOU DID TOO!
>
> KENJI: I DID NOT!
>
> DIEGO: DID TOO!
>
> KENJI: DID NOT!
>
> DIEGO: DID TOO!
>
> (so it goes on)

1. Do either Kenji or Diego exhibit perspective-taking ability?
2. Can either of them, according to Kohlberg, make moral judgments?
3. Why or why not?

Scenario 4. Megan, a high school junior, completed a math quiz yesterday. Getting her paper back today, she sees that it has been scored 100, but the 100 has been crossed through, and next to it is a zero.

> MEGAN: Mr. Whiznot, did I get a hundred or a zero on this quiz?
>
> MR. WHIZNOT: Well, Megan. You got all the answers right, but your quiz was done in pen rather than pencil, so you got a zero.
>
> MEGAN: So I got all the answers right?
>
> MR. WHIZNOT: Yes, you did.
>
> MEGAN: But you gave me a zero?
>
> MR. WHIZNOT: I didn't give you a zero. You gave it to yourself.
>
> MEGAN: I don't understand. How did I give myself a zero by getting all the answers right?
>
> MR. WHIZNOT: You know the rule. *Always* use a pencil. You know that if it's not in pencil, any work gets a zero.
>
> MEGAN: But, Mr. Whiznot, I didn't have a pencil yesterday. All I had was a pen. Then we had this pop quiz.

(continued)

Sandlot Seminar 12.2   Continued

MR. WHIZNOT: But, Megan, I have plenty of pencils. I could have given you one.

MEGAN: I didn't know that.

MR. WHIZNOT: Did you ask?

MEGAN: No, but I still don't see why I should get a zero. It shows that I didn't learn anything, and I really learned everything.

MR. WHIZNOT: Megan, you're a good student, but you need to follow the rules.

MEGAN: I know, but I didn't have a pencil. I didn't know there was going to be a pop quiz, and I didn't know we could ask you for a pencil. I just did the quiz.

MR. WHIZNOT: That's enough, Megan. I don't think it will make any difference in your grade for this course, but everyone needs to follow the rules.

1. Does Megan show any perspective-taking ability? How can you tell?
2. Does Mr. Whiznot exhibit any perspective-taking ability? How can you tell?
3. What is the moral dilemma in this scenario?
4. Should students be expected to follow "rules"? Why or why not?
5. Megan seems to believe that "rules" should be fair. What do you think?
6. Are rules (e.g., chess, checkers, cards, or dominoes) "fair" or are they simply rules to play by?
7. What is the difference between game rules and society's rules?
8. Does Mr. Whiznot's "pencil rule" seem to be at the same level as society's rules (e.g., don't speed in a school zone, pay your bills, be a good sport).
9. Are all rules created equally? Why or why not?

Individuals capable of perspective taking and understanding competing points of view have a higher potential for moral development than those whose perspective-taking abilities are more limited.

A final point of clarification is important here. Cognitive and perspective-taking abilities constrain and regulate moral judgments. In this sense, they determine the maximum potential (necessary but not sufficient conditions) for moral reasoning (Kuhn, Langer, Kohlberg, & Haan, 1977). But two individuals with the same cognitive and perspective-taking abilities may have experienced dissimilar social interactions and interpersonal problems that lead to different constructions of moral reasoning. For example, of two 12-year-old concrete operational sixth-graders, one may be in stage 2 moral development, while the other is in stage 3.

Bridge Principles

Stage Concept. Stages of moral development are the single bridge principle in Kohlberg's theory. Reflecting a close affinity for Piaget's constructivism, these stages exhibit four essential qualities:

1. An invariant sequence under varying cultural conditions.
2. "Structured wholes" or psychological organizations that unify superficially different behaviors.
3. Qualitative differences in the general mode of reasoning (rather than quantitative differences in how much information one knows).
4. Hierarchical integrations and reconstructions of lower stages.

These qualities are general properties of the moral development stages proposed by Kohlberg. Sandlot Seminar 12.3 on page 334 illustrates how the notion of universality is addressed by Kohlberg in the sense that children from very different cultures all reference cultural norms (stage 3) as a basis for their judgment.

Moral Development Levels and Stages. Kohlberg's theory differentiates between **levels** and **stages**. There are three levels and six stages. The *preconventional* level, which incorporates stages 1 and 2, consists of moral reasoning that is individualistic and which predates genuinely social considerations. The *conventional* level, consisting of stages 3 and 4, reflects concepts of societal need and value. The *postconventional* level, stages 5 and 6, transcends societal interests and motivates moral decision making based on universal principles of justice and fairness. Different stages reflect different underlying structures of moral reasoning. Behaviors are not necessarily indicative of an individual's moral stage. In fact, the same behavior can occur at different stages because it is the reasoning that indicates moral stage, not the behavior itself. Stages of moral development can be summarized as follows (see Kohlberg, 1984, pp. 174–176).

Level I: Preconventional Morality. At Level I, moral judgments are subordinated to personal interests in terms of what is good for the individual.

Stage 1: Heteronomous Morality—Punishment and Obedience Orientation.
Regarding something as good or bad depends on whether the act is rewarded or punished. Punished acts are bad, and rewarded acts are good, both regardless of an individual's intentions. The power of authority determines right and wrong. Moral right means not breaking rules to avoid punishment, obeying authorities because of their superior power, and avoiding physical damage to persons and property. This stage is presocial and egocentric because others' points of view are not differentiated from the self's.

Stage 2: Individualistic Morality—Instrumental Purpose and Exchange.
Moral actions and decisions are cast in terms of the self's wants and needs, which,

Sandlot Seminar 12.3

Being "Nice" in Different Cultures

Twelve-year-old children in each of the following cultures were asked whether Heinz should steal the drug to save his wife. Whether or not they say he should, the subjects gave the following justifications.

Rwanda. If a man steals, his neighbors and friends will no longer honor his judgment. He will become an outcast.

Guatemala. Marriage is an important sacrament. There is nothing more important than the bond between a man and wife. Everyone would expect him to do what he did.

United States. Stealing is wrong, no matter what. It's sad that his wife might die, but we all know stealing is wrong. If you let one person get away with it, you would have to let others.

Russia. You steal. You go to jail. It's that simple. But people would respect him.

Italy. My friends and I all agree that he should steal the drug. If he didn't, none of us would understand.

China. We are taught that stealing is wrong. But sometimes honor is more important. If he refused to steal the drug, he would bring dishonor on himself. Everyone would see and know. I do not see how he could dishonor himself so much.

1. What are the cultural differences in the responses?
2. Are there any common themes across cultures?
3. Kohlberg differentiates between content and structure. Given that the 12-year-olds say different things, can you find any structural similarities in their reasoning?
4. Do the responses refer to social expectations as a frame of reference for moral judgments?
5. Can you classify these explanations as (1) preconventional, (2) conventional, or (3) postconvenvional?

---

to be met, may also satisfy the needs of others. Justice is dictated by arrangement and mutual consent, not power, because people follow the "cosmic law" of mutual back scratch: "You help me, and I'll help you." Thus, moral right means acting in ways that meet one's own needs and letting others do the same; right includes living up to interpersonal agreements. The social perspective is concrete and individualistic. All people have their own perspectives and interests. These may sometimes come into conflict, thus making morality relative to the individual.

Level II: Conventional Morality. At Level II, justice is determined by society's needs, as cast in the expectations and laws of cultural *groups* such as families, peer groups, churches, clubs, states, and nations.

Stage 3: Morality of Interpersonal Expectations, Relations, and Interpersonal Conformity—Good-Boy, Good-Girl Intuitions. Justice is determined by one's peers' and social group's expectations as well as by one's desire to please important others. One attempts to be helpful in terms of peer group and social group needs. Intention becomes more important than the consequences of a well-intended action. Being good is important because it affirms stereotypical virtues (e.g., trust, loyalty, respect, empathy, gratitude). Socially, this perspective involves an understanding of relationships, including an awareness of shared feelings, agreements, and expectations that take precedence over personal interests.

Stage 4: Morality of Social Systems and Conscience—Law-and-Order Orientation. Justice is defined as fulfilling one's contractual obligations. Laws are to be upheld because they keep the social system orderly. Moral right means contributing to society and following one's conscience in living up to defined obligations. Doing what is moral means doing one's duty, respecting social authorities, and acting to maintain the established social order simply for the greater benefit of society vis-à-vis the individual, since individuals also benefit from society's order. The social perspective of this stage differentiates society's point of view from the perspective of interpersonal agreements and motives.

Level III: Postconventional Morality. Level III consists of reasoning in terms of principles of justice that are independent of personal authority, social status, or society's rules. Justice is independent of any particular authority, social group, or cultural expectation, which is not to say that morality is egocentric.

Stage 5: Morality of Social-Contract, Utility, and Individual Rights. Society's values, rules, and expectations should generally be followed because they comprise an implicit social contract. Some nonrelative values and rights, such as *life* and *liberty*, however, must be upheld in any society regardless of majority opinion. One is obliged to obey society's rules in order to provide the greatest good for the most people. Thus, laws are made for public welfare and to protect all people's rights. The social perspective is defined as *prior-to-society*, which means that concerns for values, rights, and due process underlie the making of social rules. Morality may occasionally conflict with legality.

Stage 6: Morality of Universal Ethical Principles. Justice is based on self-chosen but not egocentric ethical principles. Society's laws are to be followed because they usually rest on such principles. When laws violate these principles, one acts in accordance with the moral principle. Moral reasoning appeals to comprehensiveness, reciprocity, universality, and consistency, which are abstractions (like the Golden Rule) rather than concrete moral rules like the Ten Commandments. Such moral concepts consist of principles that all humanity should follow in order to protect the rights of individuals. Moral right involves the rational validity of moral principles and a sense of personal commitment to them. The social perspective of this stage views morality (rather than power or need) as the foundation from which social arrangements derive.

Table 12.1 on page 336 contains examples of how individuals at different stages might resolve the Heinz dilemma. Note that each stage may embody reasons both

TABLE 12.1   Examples of Moral Reasoning

Stage 1   Heteronomous Morality—Punishment and Obedience Orientation

---

Do steal: If you let your wife die, you will get into trouble.
Don't steal: You shouldn't steal the drug so you won't go to jail.

Stage 2   Individualistic Morality—Instrumental Purpose and Exchange

---

Do steal: He promised his wife he'd stick by her. So he has to steal the drug to keep his promise.
Don't steal: If he doesn't steal the drug, his wife will die. But she knew this might happen; it isn't
                 his fault his wife has cancer.

**Stage 3   Morality of Interpersonal Expectations, Relations, and Interpersonal Conformity—
Good-Boy, Good-Girl Intuitions**

Do steal: No one will think you're bad if you steal the drug, but everyone will hate you if you
                 don't. He owes her that much.
Don't steal: You'll be a criminal. Who could ever trust you after that? You wouldn't have any
                 friends.

Stage 4   Morality of Social Systems and Conscience—Law-and-Order Orientation

---

Do steal: Its your duty. That's what husbands and wives are. If husbands and wives don't do this
                 for each other, there wouldn't be a society for generations to come.
Don't steal: If you steal the drug, you'll always feel bad that you broke the law, even though you're
                 desperate.

Stage 5   Morality of Social-Contract, Utility, and Individual Rights

---

Do steal: You would lose respect, not gain it, if you don't steal. How could anyone trust you
                 anymore?
Don't steal: His wife will understand that you can't just go around stealing, because it would mean
                 people could steal from her too, and she wouldn't want that.

Stage 6   Morality of Universal Ethical Principles

Do steal: Everyone would understand if you stole the drug to save a life.
Don't steal: If you stole it, everyone would understand but they'd wonder what to do with other
                 people who thought they had a good reason for stealing. They'd put themselves in your
                 place and think that maybe they'd do the same thing.

---

for and *against* Heinz stealing the drug for his wife. That is because reasoning is categorized according to its underlying rationale and not whether an individual
accepts or rejects Heinz stealing the drug.

   Sandlot Seminar 12.4 shows how everyday events may invoke some type of
moral reasoning.

Sandlot Seminar 12.4

Everyday Moral Dilemmas

1.a. While walking from her house to her garage, a woman drops a cigarette on her driveway, stamps it with her heel, and walks on to her car. Is this a moral dilemma? Why?

 b. While hiking in the pristine Rocky Mountains, a woman drops a cigarette on the hiking path, stamps it with her heel, and walks on. Is this a moral dilemma? Why?

 c. Explain why your response is different or the same for the two situations described.

2.a. In a checkout line at the supermarket, a child in front of you throws a temper tantrum over some candy, which the mother refuses to buy. The mother spanks the child into submission, pays her bill, and quickly leaves the store with a sobbing child.

 b. In a checkout line at the supermarket, a child in front of you throws a temper tantrum over some candy, which the mother addresses with a prolonged conversation about the detriments of candy for children. The child continues the tantrum, but the mother maintains her calm explanation while the line behind her is stalled. As you watch the situation, you notice that others behind you have moved to other lines moving faster than yours. You think about moving to another line yourself, because the mother is in no hurry. She is calmly explaining to her whining child why she will not buy candy.

 c. From your observations, which approach would you use if your child had a temper tantrum at a supermarket checkout?

 d. These children grow up to be teenagers. Assuming each mother was consistent during the child's youth, which teenage child would you prefer to work with? Why?

 e. What would Kohlberg say about the trade-off between short-term and long-term results?

3.a. You hear a news report of an urgent need for blood following a devastating hurricane in Cuba. The Red Cross is asking for donations of your blood type. What will you do? Why?

 b. You hear from a neighbor that the kindly old woman down the street urgently needs blood donations for major surgery. What will you do? Why?

 c. You learn that your father is in the hospital and needs a blood transfusion of your type of blood. What will you do? Why?

 d. Examine your responses to *3.a, b,* and *c.* Why are they similar or different?

4. Does your reasoning concerning the scenarios in *3.a, b,* and *c* reflect Kohlberg's contention that moral development is a matter of rational judgments about fairness and justice? Do the situations involve moral judgments? What is the moral component of each situation?

Moral Types. In his later years, Kohlberg (1984, pp. 252–257) added to his theory a distinction between *A* and *B* substages. Individuals whose moral reasoning is type *A* tend toward a moral orientation involving rules and authority. *B*-type individuals orient toward moral concepts of fairness, equality, and reciprocity. Kohlberg proposed this distinction to help account for the relationship between moral judgment and moral action, a problem that has long perplexed those interested in figuring out why some individuals act on their moral principles and others don't. In his view, individuals at the same stage of moral development use similar moral principles to justify their responses to moral dilemmas. However, B-type individuals are far more likely to actually engage in moral actions consistent with their beliefs than are A-type individuals. Moreover, when moral development occurs, movement from type A to type B is more likely than from B to A. However, there is also a tendency for both A- and B-type individuals to remain the same type while they progress through the moral development stages.

Following Kohlberg's lead, others have attempted to examine the discrepancy between moral judgment and motivation to behave in accord with one's conscience. Oser (1996), for example, has hypothesized dimensions of moral motivation that correspond closely with Kohlberg's stages of moral reasoning. Yet others have questioned whether any theoretical construct is sufficiently robust but differentiated to account for the difference between moral thought and moral behavior (Park & Johnson, 1984).

Unlike Piaget, Kohlberg does not suggest age ranges for each stage. The reason for this is that, at the upper end, adults may vary widely in their moral development stage. For example, Kohlberg has suggested that only about 5 percent of adults reach stage 5 or 6 (postconventional reasoning). But at the lower end, children cannot be moral before they are able to understand punishment as an outcome for a moral transgression. This means that adults could be at any stage from 1 to 6, and children could be no more than stage 1 or 2. Because Kohlberg considers only reasoning, rather than age, no age approximations are given for his stages.

Change Mechanisms

As described in the section on Internal Principles, Kohlberg believes that moral development is a function of *cognitive conflict* in the same sense that Piaget's process of equilibration controls cognitive development. Cognitive conflict naturally occurs when individuals interact from different points of view (e.g., I want something; you want something else). Perspective taking, through opportunities to take the point of view of another, provides experiential discrepancies between one's own point of view and that of another person. For example, through perspective taking one may discover a conflict between one's own wishes and the wishes of others, as occurs when one group believes in busing to achieve school integration while another group believes in neighborhood schools to achieve educational choice. Perspective-taking ability applies to moral judgment when one's own reasoning takes into account and adapts to the reasoning of others.

Cognitive conflict is the "motor" that drives moral development. More specifically, Kohlberg believes that an *optimum mismatch* between the moral systems of two individuals who differ by only one stage can produce an ideal level of cognitive conflict for the lower-staged individual. Through cognitive conflict, individuals synthesize competing claims, expectations, and principles in order to construct a principle that resolves or at least minimizes the conflict. Turiel (1966), one of

Kohlberg's early colleagues, has attempted to apply the concept of cognitive conflict and optimal mismatch in order to determine whether it is effective in promoting moral development. This attempt and Kohlberg's own attempts to induce moral development are described in the following section.

Explaining Human Development: The Research

A number of Kohlberg's claims about moral development have been studied empirically. Several of the most important claims are examined in this section: universality of the stage sequence, cognitive and role-taking prerequisites for moral development, and attempts to promote development of moral reasoning.

Stage Sequence

Kohlberg claims that his stages are rational constructions of moral principles and not culturally specific learning of social norms and rules. If this claim is correct, then stages of moral development should follow a universal sequence that is independent of varying cultural experiences.

In the most comprehensive review to date, Snarey (1985, 1987) examined forty-five cross-cultural studies that tested Kohlberg's claim for universality. These studies included both cross-aged and twenty-year longitudinal studies ranging from India to Israel and from New Guinea to Taiwan. Some researchers used standard Kohlberg dilemmas, while others created completely new dilemmas. In spite of the variety of cultures studied and the differences in methodology used by various researchers, Snarey concluded that the available evidence provides strong support for the universal sequence and presence of Kohlberg's first four stages. However, Snarey found little evidence in those studies to support Kohlberg's postconventional stages among non-Western cultures. At the same time, sequential moral development stages have been found across the life span (Armon, 1998; Armon & Dawson, 1997) and through longitudinal studies (Walker, 1989).

The failure of many researchers to find evidence of postconventional moral reasoning has been examined by Vasudev and Hummel (1987), who cite Snarey (1985) in arguing that the absence of principled moral reasoning in non-Western cultures may be more attributable to degree of urbanization than to Western culture per se. Specifically, cross-cultural studies of Kohlberg's theory have tended to use subjects from small tribes and villages. Such subjects typically have not experienced the kinds of complex interpersonal relationships and conceptual issues that are associated with higher education and urban societies. As a test of their reasoning, Vasudev and Hummel (1987) sampled 112 middle- and upper-class residents in an urbanized region of India and reported finding that 11 percent of the adults used Level III moral judgments to resolve moral dilemmas.

Other studies bear on the invariant sequence issue. In a ten-year longitudinal study, Snarey, Reimer, and Kohlberg (1983) examined Israeli children and adolescents. The results showed that subjects who developed through the first five stages did so in the invariant sequence proposed by Kohlberg. Moreover, no sex differences in moral development were found. In a similar study, Nisan and Kohlberg (1982) conducted a ten-year longitudinal study of moral development in Turkish city and village males. Their results indicated an invariant sequence through stage 4 and the presence of some stage 5 reasoning among city but not village males. A more recent study by Czyzowska and Niemczynski (1996) of 15- to 80-year-old Polish citizens found general support for Kohlberg's claim of cultural universality. Finally, Thoma and Rest (1999) reported evidence that the movement from one stage to the next is accompanied by the types of consolidation and transition one would expect in Kohlberg's stages.

Research findings such as these are consistent with Kohlberg's claim of a universal sequence of stages. The importance of this empirical support should not be overlooked, because it is difficult to imagine how other theoretical perspectives might account for the cross-cultural data. For example, endogenous theories that posit age-specific development have difficulty accounting for the age variation associated with each moral stage and the fact that some individuals fail to achieve higher moral stages. At the same time, exogenous theories do not explain how learning of culture-specific norms and rules could result in a universal sequence of stages.

Cognitive and Perspective-taking Development

Kohlberg claims that the development of moral reasoning at a particular stage is predicated on the presence of (1) specific underlying cognitive operations and (2) related perspective-taking abilities. Evidence bearing on each of these claims is examined next.

The most extensive study of the relationship between cognition and moral reasoning was conducted by Kuhn, Langer, Kohlberg, and Haan (1977), who tested 265 individuals from two generations: 130 parents averaging about 50 years of age and 135 of their children between the ages of 10 and 30 years. Subjects were individually administered two Piagetian tasks in order to determine their stage of cognitive development and four of Kohlberg's moral dilemmas to assess their stage of moral reasoning. This study revealed several noteworthy patterns of development. First, regardless of age, 94 subjects who showed no evidence of formal operational reasoning also showed no principled (stages 5 or 6) moral reasoning. In contrast, 96 percent of those who showed Level III moral reasoning showed evidence of formal operational thinking. Second, 76 percent of subjects who showed formal operational thought were scored at Level II of moral development. Third, the higher a subject's cognitive performance, the more likely that subject was to use Level III moral reasoning in the Kohlberg dilemmas. In a similar study, Smith (1979) reported that in a sample of 100 children aged 8 to 14 years, concrete operational thinking and the transition to formal operational thought were associated with stages 2 and 3 of moral development, respectively. Such data provides modest correlational support for Kohlberg's claim that specific levels of cognitive development may be necessary but are not themselves sufficient prerequisites to achieving particular moral development stages.

Several studies have examined the claim that perspective-taking ability underlies the ability to reason at particular moral stages. For example, Selman (1971) found that perspective taking was significantly correlated with stage of moral reasoning in a sample of 60 children aged 8 to 10 years. In a one-year follow-up of ten children who had been previously categorized as Level I in moral reasoning and who lacked perspective-taking ability, Selman found that the only ones who achieved conventional morality were the ones who also displayed perspective-taking ability at the follow-up. Similarly, Kuhn (1972) examined this relationship in sixty-eight kindergarten through sixth-grade children. She found that her subjects achieved stage 2 of moral reasoning only if they demonstrated the perspective-taking ability to attribute intention to another person. Finally, Smith (1979) concluded from her study of moral reasoning and perspective taking in one hundred 8- to 14-year-olds that the level of complexity in perspective-taking ability precedes corresponding levels of moral reasoning.

Although the evidence suggests support for Kohlberg's claims of cognitive and perspective-taking prerequisites to moral development, it is still not conclusive because most studies have used cross-sectional (different subjects tested at the same time) rather than longitudinal (same subjects tested at different times) research designs. These correlations between cognition, perspective taking, and morality are important, but they do not directly test the developmental priority for each person (in what order the three domains develop), which can only be addressed with careful longitudinal studies (Kurdek, 1978).

Promoting the Development of Moral Reasoning

Kohlberg believes that cognitive conflict is the source of moral development. Cognitive conflict occurs when individuals recognize (1) that their moral values provide inadequate solutions to a moral problem or (2) that the moral reasoning of others provides better solutions to moral problems than their own.

One attempt to induce moral development was undertaken by Turiel (1966), whose classic study tested the hypothesis that exposure to higher levels of moral reasoning would produce greater stage change than exposure to any other stage of moral reasoning. Turiel reasoned that if stages of moral reasoning consist of increasingly complex, hierarchic reorganizations of earlier reasoning, then individuals should prefer moral reasoning one stage higher than their own (moderately more complex organization). To test his hypothesis, Turiel exposed a sample of 12- to 13-year-old boys to one of three conditions: reasoning at one stage above their moral stage (+1), reasoning two stages above their own (+2), and reasoning one stage below their own (–1). A fourth group provided a control sample. A moral dilemma was administered to determine pre- to post-test gains.

Turiel found that his subjects virtually always understood levels of moral reasoning lower than their own, almost never understood reasoning at +2 stages above their own, and sometimes understood reasoning at +1 stage above their own. More important, only the +1 stage reasoning condition produced significant progress in subjects' moral reasoning. The −1 group regressed slightly, but the regression was much less than the progress of the +1 group. Turiel argued that his subjects could not have memorized the moral reasoning presented to them. Rather, he concluded that the progress of the +1 group is attributable to cognitive conflict brought about by an optimum mismatch between subjects' own level of moral reasoning and the organizational adequacy of the next higher stage. In a test of Turiel's study and Kohlberg's stage-sequentiality claim, Walker (1982) replicated Turiel's results except that his +2 stage condition was more effective than the +1 stage condition in motivating moral development.

In a moral naturalistic vein, Turiel (1974, 1977) interviewed college students to determine both their moral stage and their reasoning strategies for novel moral problems. Following the same subjects over several years, he found that these adolescents exhibited both the logical contradictions and the cognitive confusion during transition from one moral stage to the next that would have been predicted if these subjects had been experiencing cognitive conflict.

To assess direct interventions, Blatt and Kohlberg (1975) instituted a program of moral education using 10-, 11-, and 16-year-olds' school classrooms. They found that class discussions of moral conflicts and moral problems resulted in a significant improvement in moral reasoning. In a replication of the Blatt and Kohlberg study, Hayden and Pickar (1981) engaged seventh-grade girls in ten weeks of discussions about moral dilemmas. The program produced an average 10 percent gain in students' moral development. Others have also reported success in using discussions to induce cognitive conflict and promote moral development (Clare, Gallimore, & Patthew-Chavez, 1996; Taylor & Walker, 1997). Still others have utilized training in personal reflection to promote moral development (Lopez & Lopez, 1998).

Contributions and Criticisms of Kohlberg's Theory

Contributions

Individuals as Moral Philosophers.   Analogous to Piaget's portrait of children as natural scientists, Kohlberg believes that it is the nature of individuals to be moral philosophers (Kohlberg, 1968a; Kohlberg & Gilligan, 1971). This claim is noteworthy because it implies that individuals ask questions about the nature of morality (e.g., "What does moral mean?" "What is it to be moral?" and "What is the moral thing to do in this situation?"). In arriving at answers to these questions, people consider relevant evidence and reasons. The point Kohlberg makes is that children, adolescents, and adults quite naturally and without benefit of formal training attempt to solve moral problems by inventing solutions, trying them out, and adapting them to interpersonal situations.

Morality as Rational Intelligence. One of the most important points Kohlberg makes is that morality is more a matter of intellect than emotion. This view is considered an important contribution because it is strikingly different from and challenges common sense notions of morality. Many people intuitively believe that morality is a matter of one's emotional state. Such concepts of morality have been soundly rocked by Kohlberg's analysis of moral development.

The argument against emotionality and specific instruction has been most succinctly conceptualized by Bailey (1980), who notes that morality must invoke a system of rational principles or else there can be no morality at all. The reason is that all appeals to nonrational processes, such as one's feelings or emotions, lead to indefensible solutions to moral problems. For example, consider the case for morality by *feelings* and morality by *sympathy*. One might argue that we do moral deeds because they feel right. However, in order to relate one's feelings to an "appropriate" moral action requires a rational judgment; otherwise the perception of a feeling and its associated need to act would remain unconnected with each other.

In arguing for the priority of rationality over emotion, Kohlberg does not mean to convey the impression that personal feelings are irrelevant to moral problems. Hoffman (1975, 1983), for example, has shown that empathy plays a powerful role in the internalization of moral conduct, and empathy is an important influence of altruistic motives. Kohlberg does not dispute Hoffman's claims. Instead, he contends that emotions such as empathy are in themselves insufficient grounds for making moral judgments. In support of Kohlberg's position on this issue, Bailey (1980) contends that acting out of sympathy for another is simply inadequate to sustain a claim that an act is "moral"; that is, one cannot claim to be acting morally when one acts out of sympathy. The real test of morality is determined by how one acts toward those for whom indifferent or hostile feelings are held. In fact, we often judge ourselves high on the moral scale (because there is no other justification for our deeds) precisely when we do act to assist those for whom we have no sympathy at all.

Kohlberg has significantly advanced the psychological understanding of morality by demonstrating its connections to rational thought. In this way, his constructivist theory gives us an explanation of moral development that is not susceptible to the same theoretical and empirical problems as explanations that posit morality as a quality of feeling states (endogenous explanation) or as culturally learned values (exogenous explanation).

Cultural Universals. Kohlberg's theory suggests that there is something about social interaction between individuals (e.g., cognitive conflict) that produces increasingly adequate thinking about ethical issues, in spite of diverse cultural traditions, customs, and values. Up until the 1970s, when Kohlberg's theory began receiving widespread attention among developmental psychologists, it was widely believed that morality was a matter of learning norms and values promulgated by society. At that time, such learning could be explained by both operant conditioning (through shaping and reinforcement) and by Piaget's (1965b) early work on morality as a function of learning social rules. In that historical context, Kohlberg changed the entire theoretical map of developmental psychology by concentrating on the structures of moral reasoning rather than its content. His claim that individuals in very different cultures develop through the same *sequence* of moral stages was a revolutionary idea. It concentrated on the increasing complexity of moral thought rather than on the cultural content of moral values, and that theoretical contribution shifted forever the study of moral development.

Education for Moral Development.   The Center for Moral Education at Harvard has for nearly two decades attempted to devise strategies for using Kohlberg's theory to promote moral development. Unlike Piaget, Kohlberg had actively promoted techniques and ideas directed at improving education. Some of his early publications are related to enhancing cognitive development in general (Kohlberg, 1966, 1968b; Kohlberg & Mayer, 1972), but many of his later publications report educational strategies designed to improve moral reasoning (Kohlberg 1972, 1973, 1974, 1975a, 1975b, 1977). For Kohlberg, moral education is designed for the purpose of improving students' moral reasoning and thus does not constitute indoctrination or learning socially sanctioned virtues and conventions. What makes this work so important is its radically different, constructivist approach to moral development without invoking more traditional strategies such as imitation and factual learning.

Criticisms

Reliability and Validity.   Kohlberg's theory has been challenged on a number of grounds for its purported lack of reliability and validity. One problem with empirical validity is his claim that stage 6 completes the hierarchy of moral development stages. The evidence to support that claim is scanty at best. Other than some literary references about the moral reasoning of Socrates, Jesus, and Martin Luther King, there is little evidence that real people actually reach stage 6 (Locke, 1979, 1980).

A second criticism is that because the original theory derived from interviews with males, it inherently misrepresents women's moral development. This problem has been noted most eloquently by Gilligan (1977, 1982), who contends that, much like the psychological tradition that spawned it, Kohlberg's theory tends to rely heavily on rational justifications for hypothetical moral dilemmas. Based on her own interviews with women facing *real-life* moral dilemmas, Gilligan believes that Kohlberg's theory was insensitive to some of the most dominant female moral concerns such as the power of mercy and the wisdom of interpersonal caring, each of which would be categorized by Kohlberg as emotional rather than rational criteria. Kohlberg denied any sex bias in his methodology because subsequent research has shown that same-aged females and males typically score about the same on moral dilemmas. However, he also believed that Gilligan made a significant contribution to the theory by enlarging the domain of moral judgment to include orientations toward personal responsibility and care (Levine, Kohlberg, & Hewer, 1985).

Among the most frequently cited criticisms are those outlined by Kurtines and Greif (1974), who have systematically evaluated Kohlberg's work from a psychometric (measurement) point of view. They argue that his methodology has both low reliability (consistency) and low validity (accurately measuring moral thinking). There is nothing, for example, which guarantees that subjects will give honest (as opposed to socially acceptable) answers about their own reasoning. Moreover, Kurtines and Greif note that two raters who read the same interview material may judge a subject at entirely different moral development stages (a problem with reliability). They also note that individuals may often behave in ways different from the motivations and justifications they describe in hypothetical, moral reasoning interviews (a possible problem with validity). Finally, they believe that Kohlberg's measurement of moral development does not distinguish between moral reasoning per se and the complexity of vocabulary used. For example, they suggest that individuals who use complex vocabularies are scored at higher stages than those with more basic vocabularies. Such criticisms are important, and in response to them, Kohlberg and his colleagues attempted to improve the precision of scoring moral-judgment interviews (see Colby & Kohlberg, 1987).

Thought and Action. A recurring criticism of Kohlberg's early work was that little effort had been made to determine how moral reasoning actually translated into behavior. That is, if stages of moral development reflect qualitative differences in rational judgments, then they should affect the behaviors exhibited by individuals in different moral stages. This fundamental issue, the relationship between thought and action, is ultimately faced by all constructivists. In his early work, Kohlberg (1971) had addressed the issue by pointing out that intentions that underlie behavior were the relevant dimension of morality. Two identical behaviors, for example, each motivated by different intentions, could best be understood by examining the motivating rational judgments of each individual rather than the overt behavior. Consequently, Kohlberg attempted to explain the development of moral reasoning and *not* moral behavior. At the same time, however, the intuitive appeal of such an approach has shortcomings. Critics wondered if criminals might invoke morally sophisticated arguments to justify their crimes. More importantly, there seemed to be nothing in the theory to account for why some individuals acted on their beliefs while other did not.

Recall from the earlier section on Bridge Principles that Kohlberg's (1984) later work addressed the thought and action problem by differentiating between type *A* and type *B* moral reasoning. At each stage, type *A* moral reasoning reflects concerns with rules and authority, whereas type *B* reasoning is oriented toward concepts of fairness, equality, and reciprocity. Furthermore, at the same stage, *B*-type individuals were more likely to actually engage in moral actions consistent with their beliefs than were *A*-type individuals.

Why Be Moral? A theory of moral development should answer the most fundamental question of all: Why be moral? Kohlberg would probably attempt to answer the query by stating, "Because it is the right thing to do." However, such a retort will not do because it does not fully answer the question. The difficulty of the question has been underscored by Hare (1960) and Hyland (1979), who argue that no deductive justification of moral principles is possible. It is not a matter of whether this or that moral principle should hold in a given situation, but rather why hold or apply any moral principles at all . . . ever? Such questions are bothersome because if morality cannot be derived from a logical justification, then some other kind of justification not found in Kohlberg's theory must be provided.

Evaluation of Moral Development Theory

Having taken an active role in using evaluation criteria to evaluate theories in earlier chapters, you are now prepared to evaluate Kohlberg's theory of moral development. Complete Sandlot Seminar 12.5 and then see how your evaluation compares with the authors'.

Sandlot Seminar 12.5

How Would You Evaluate Kohlberg's Theory?
Use your own understanding to evaluate Kohlberg's theory of moral development on each of the three sets of criteria. Compare your evaluations and reasons with those given by the authors.

Scientific Worthiness
Testability   _____
External validity   _____
Predictive validity   _____
Internal consistency   _____
Theoretical economy   _____

Developmental Adequacy
Temporality   _____
Cumulativity   _____
Directionality   _____
New mode of organization   _____
Increased capacity for self-control _____

Pedagogical Usefulness
Intrepretability   _____
Versatility   _____
Availability   _____
Guidance   _____

Scientific Worthiness

Testability. Kohlberg measures moral judgment by presenting moral dilemmas to subjects and inquiring of them both their resolution of the dilemmas and their justification for the resolution. Subjects, in turn, put into words their solutions and the kinds of cognitive concerns they considered in formulating their responses. In this way, Kohlberg is a mentalist (stages, rational judgment, *A*- versus *B*-type moral reasoning, and cognitive conflict). He commits himself to the inferential leap required to move from verbal self-reports to claims about the presence of these theoretical constructs. He claims that his theory reflects patterns in his data that are natural, personal formulations of moral principles. In all fairness to Kohlberg, his theory does seem to reflect reasonable inferences about the data he reports. Still, inferences such as Kohlberg's, which appeal to mentalist constructs, are not based on direct observation. Consequently, Table 12.2 shows our medium rating for the theory's testability.

External Validity. Kohlberg and his colleagues have marshaled a large body of cross-cultural data that they argue support the theory of a universal sequence of moral development stages. While criticisms of technical difficulties with such data should not be ignored, one cannot easily overlook the general patterns of moral development stages across quite diverse cultures. Moreover, the theory seems to accord well with parents' and teachers' intuitions about children's moral integrity. Young children seem naturally to be more attuned to obedience and authority (stage 1) than to other kinds of moral invocations. In contrast, many adolescents rebel against obedience to authority in order to live up to the expectations of others (stage 3). Finally, if we consider important historical figures who contributed greatly to the advancement of social morality (e.g., Socrates, Jesus, Martin Luther King), we would probably agree that they exemplified what Kohlberg terms principled moral reasoning. For these reasons, Kohlberg's theory is judged high in terms of its external validity.

Predictive Validity. Most of the evidence for the predictive validity of Kohlberg's theory derives from experimental tests of the logical adequacy of later stages vis-à-vis earlier stages and from attempts to educationally induce development of moral

TABLE 12.2 **Ratings of Moral Development Theory for Scientific Worthiness**

Criteria	High	Medium	Low
Testability		X	
External Validity	X		
Predictive Validity		X	
Internal Consistency	X		
Theoretical Economy			X

reasoning. The Turiel (1966) and Walker (1982) studies, for example, demonstrated that subjects at a given moral development stage understood earlier but not later stages of moral reasoning. Also, attempts by Kohlberg and his cohorts to induce moral development through educational programs have met with moderate success. Such attempts to draw out and evaluate the implications of Kohlberg's theory reflect a moderately good degree of predictive validity. At the same time, however, these efforts must be balanced against the findings of non-Kohlbergians who have failed to replicate his results. A rating of medium for Kohlberg's predictive validity represents a conservative estimate of this complex situation.

Internal Consistency.   The theory is rated high for its internal consistency because it does not deviate from the constructivist paradigm and because it parallels Piaget's cognitive developmental theory. Nonconstructivist views are consistently rejected. Kohlberg discards both maturationist (endogenous) and learning (exogenous) explanations of moral development in favor of a constructivist interpretation.

Theoretical Economy.   Morality is a complex phenomenon. As such, its explanation should be comparably complex, and Kohlberg's theory is faithful to that expectation. He attempts to explain only the relatively small portion of human conduct called moral judgment. To accomplish that goal, he makes three major assumptions. However, Kohlberg's assumptions are far more complex than most others introduced in this text, and what is accomplished with those assumptions is a relatively narrow field of explanation—the development of moral reasoning. For these reasons, the theory garners a low rating for theoretical economy.

Developmental Adequacy

Temporality.   Kohlberg's account of moral development clearly passes this criterion (see Table 12.3). Children's moral judgments reflect increasingly complex moral principles, which they construct as they experience cognitive conflict. These experiences take place as they grow older, so their moral reasoning evolves through many years of social interaction.

Cumulativity.   The theory is cumulative in the sense that later stages of moral reasoning build on and replace moral concepts from earlier stages. Moreover, Kohlberg

TABLE 12.3   Ratings of Moral Development Theory for Developmental Adequacy

Characteristic	Criteria
Temporality	Yes
Cumulativity	Yes
Directionality	Yes
New Mode of Organization	Yes
Increased Capacity for Self-control	Yes

argues that stages occur in the same sequence regardless of culture. In this way, for example, we cannot get to stage 3 moral reasoning unless we have first developed through stages 1 and 2. Thus, it passes this criterion.

Directionality. Kohlberg believes that moral development evolves from less-adequate to more-adequate forms of reasoning. That is, moral reasoning of later stages resolves not only more moral problems but also moral problems of a different kind than earlier stages. For example, an individual at stage 4 is able to resolve all the moral dilemmas a stage 3 individual could resolve. However, the stage 4 person could also resolve more-complex moral dilemmas that the stage 3 person could not resolve. For this reason, stage 4 is said to be more adequate than stage 3 in resolving moral dilemmas. Kohlberg's notion of "increasing adequacy" holds that moral development is directed toward increasing moral equilibrium, and thus it passes this criterion.

New Mode of Organization. Like Piaget's theory of cognitive development, Kohlberg argues that a stage of moral development becomes reorganized into a new rational structure (the next stage) that involves moral values and principles not present at the earlier stage. Structural reorganizations of this type represent precisely what is meant by the concept of a "new mode of organization." Later stages entail moral structures applied to solving moral situations that are not exhibited at earlier stages. Consequently, the theory passes this criterion.

Increased Capacity for Self-control. Moral development evolves toward a state of increasingly autonomous moral reasoning. Level I moral stages are defined by concepts of fairness that are personal and situation-specific. At Level II, reasoning shifts toward more socially defined, increasingly objective moral principles. This shift, due to its social objectification, results in moral reasoning that is more stable and less situation- or person-specific. This element of stability reflects an increase in self-regulation because society's values have been incorporated into individuals' own reasoning. Finally, Level III involves universal moral principles that overcome the cultural egocentrism of Level II. Presumably, if everyone were developed to stage 6, all moral difficulties and problems would be solvable in ways that were universally acknowledged to be fair and just. At each stage and level of moral reasoning, individuals construct increasingly abstract, generalizable principles of justice and fairness as their own personal basis for making moral judgments. Such a pattern reflects an increased capacity for self-control because the individual is increasingly freed from personal and societal motives for making moral judgments. Given these considerations, Kohlberg's theory is judged to pass this criterion.

Pedagogical Usefulness

Table 12.4 on page 350 shows our ratings for the pedagogical usefulness of Kohlberg's theory. In comparison to previous chapters, we find the theory slightly less useful than Piaget's constructivist theory and the endogenous theories and significantly less useful than the exogenous theories.

TABLE 12.4   Ratings of Moral Development Theory for Pedagogical Usefulness

	High	Medium	Low
Interpretability			X
Versatility			X
Availability		X	
Guidance		X	

Interpretability.   Kohlberg's theory is among the more subtle in developmental psychology. Most of this subtlety derives from two structural components: assumptions and bridge principles. First, Kohlberg assumes an important distinction between moral content (facts) and structure (reasoning). Only reasoning is used to determine an individual's stage of development. Unknowingly, novices would find it difficult to distinguish between these two elements of an individual's arguments about any moral dilemma. Second, Kohlberg's stages are based on reasoning that underlies a moral judgment. Given the Heinz dilemma, for example, one individual might say "Heinz should steal the drug to save his wife's life." Such a judgment, however, involves no reasoning. So we might think saving the wife's life is laudable, but there is no basis for determining the individual's stage of moral development. Again, novices often confuse the moral judgment with the structure of reasoning that underlies it. For these reasons, it is often difficult for parents, counselors, and other child-centered adults to interpret children's behavior using Kohlberg's theory. While the general stages do make sense, using them to guide children's development is actually quite difficult. For this reason, the theory is rated low for its interpretability.

Versatility.   Like Ainsworth's theory of attachment, the scope of Kohlberg's theory is narrowly defined as moral development. In contrast to Ainsworth, however, Kohlberg's theory spans many years, from childhood to old age. But the theory cannot be used to influence personality, cognitive development, language development, or math performance of children. Its versatility is limited to the scope of moral development. Without belaboring the point, we have rated the theory low for its versatility.

Availability.   Original writings about Kohlberg's theory are available primarily in academic and university libraries. However, virtually all high school social studies teachers and most elementary teachers learn about the theory in their licensure course work. Most textbooks in developmental psychology provide at least some treatment of Kohlberg's theory. So teachers and psychology majors who become parents may attempt to use their learning in raising their own children. But Kohlberg's theory is not available to most citizens. It has not made its way into popular magazines or media interpretations of human behavior. And even media presentations with "experts" about youth violence make no mention of Kohlberg's theory of moral development. For these reasons, we rate the theory as medium for its availability.

Guidance.   Many parents and teachers are concerned about the moral development of children. If they all read Kohlberg's theory, what would they learn? They would learn that children naturally engage in cognitive conflict in working out solutions to interpersonal engagements. They would learn that children's development could be promoted by engaging them in discussions that produce cognitive conflict. And they'd learn that, over time, children get better at solving interpersonal conflicts. But if parents and teachers knew all this, how would they use Kohlberg's theory? And if they really did use it, would children behave any differently? Probably not.

   The reason is that Kolberg does not believe behavior itself involves any moral dimension. He believes moral judgment is properly located in rational thought. Consequently, his theory provides only limited guidance to parents and teachers—invoke cognitive conflict. Using that principle, adults should ask children to think about and reason through their moral conflicts. This can be done through children's discussions of literature (Clare, Gallimore, & Patthew-Chavez, 1996). But recently, Berkowitz and Grych (1998) have argued that this approach omits other important elements, such as social orientation, self-control, compliance, and self-esteem. Consequently, aside from trying to induce cognitive conflict, Kohlberg's theory gives only limited advice in raising children. Consequently, we rate the theory medium for its guidance.

Summary Points

1. Kohlberg's theory is basically a cognitive developmental theory applied to the specific area of moral judgment.
2. The theory assumes that morality is (1) justice and fairness; (2) a matter of rational, constructive thinking that depends on prerequisite cognitive and perspective-taking stages, and (3) reflected in one's ability to differentiate between motives, behaviors, and consequences.
3. Kohlberg attempts to explain the development of moral reasoning by using moral dilemmas coupled with extensive clinical interviews.
4. Internal principles of Kohlberg's theory are equilibration or cognitive conflict, Piaget's cognitive development, and perspective-taking ability.
5. The theory's bridge principle is the universal sequence of moral development stages and the relationship between moral stages and moral behavior.
6. The change mechanism in Kohlberg's theory is cognitive conflict, his preferred term for Piaget's concept of equilibration.
7. Kohlberg's most enduring contributions include his image of people as natural moral philosophers, the notion that morality reflects rational rather than emotional considerations, his view of moral development as following a universal sequence of stages, and his work in moral education.

8. Criticisms of Kohlberg's theory often refer to serious questions about its reliability, validity, and philosophical concerns about "why be moral?"

9. The theory gets a medium rating overall for its scientific worthiness, a high rating for its developmental adequacy, and a low rating for its pedagogical usefulness.

PROBLEMS AND EXERCISES

1. Reread the moral dilemma about Heinz described earlier in this chapter; then answer the following questions.

   Should Heinz have stolen the drug to save his wife? Why?

   What if he didn't love her; should he have stolen it anyway? Why?

   Should he steal the drug to save another relative? Why?

   Should he steal the drug to save a stranger? Why?

   If Heinz gets caught and admits he stole the drug, how should the judge sentence him? Why?

   Examine your answers to the "Why?" questions (these are your moral rationales) and try to distill the common, underlying moral principles that recur in your reasoning. See if you can determine your stage of moral development for this dilemma.

2. Administer the Heinz moral dilemma and accompanying questions to a child, a teenager, an adult, and a retired person. Try to figure out their stage of moral reasoning by gleaning the moral principles of their judgments from their responses. Does moral development appear to increase with age in your limited sample? If so, why? If not, why not? In either case, have you evidence that supports or contradicts Kohlberg's theory?

3. Look up and review the series of experiments described by Milgram (1974) to test obedience to authority. Identify the moral issues and problems in these studies. How would Kohlberg analyze Milgram's results?

4. Use the Internet to search for sites related to Lawrence Kohlberg and his theory. You can use his name as well as key words (internal and bridge principles). How do the Internet sites differ in terms of completeness and accuracy of information? What were the best sites you found? What problems did you encounter? What were some of the worst sites (and why?).

SUGGESTED READINGS

More about the Theory

Kohlberg, L. (1973). Contributions of developmental psychology to education: Examples from moral education. *Educational Psychologist, 10,* 2–14.

Kohlberg, L., & Gilligan, C. (1971). The adolescent as a philosopher: The discovery of self in a post-conventional world. *Daedalus, 100,* 1051–1086.

Levine, C., Kohlberg, L., & Hewer, A. (1985). The current formulation of Kohlberg's theory and a response to critics. *Human Development, 28,* 94–100.

Research Reviews

Schlaefli, A., Rest, J. R., & Thoma, S. J. (1985). Does moral education improve moral judgment? A meta-analysis of intervention studies using the Defining Issues Test. *Review of Educational Research, 55,* 319–352.
Snarey, J. R. (1985). Cross-cultural universality of social–moral development: A critical review of Kohlbergian research. *Psychological Bulletin, 97,* 202–232.

Critical Reviews

Aron, I. E. (1977). Moral philosophy and moral education: A critique of Kohlberg's theory. *School Review, 85,* 197–217.
Kurtines, W., & Grief, E. B. (1974). The development of moral thought: Review and evaluation of Kohlberg's approach. *Psychological Bulletin, 8,* 453–470.
Simpson, E. L. (1974). Moral development research. A case study of scientific cultural bias. *Human Development, 17,* 81–106.
Sullivan, E. V. (1977). *Kohlberg's structuralism: A critical appraisal.* Toronto: Ontario Institute for Studies in Education.

PART FIVE

Summing Up

Within the field of applied psychology, professionals such as counselors and teachers make many decisions that affect the individuals they serve. In the best light, these decisions require the selection, evaluation, and application of theoretical principles. Without a theoretical basis, such decisions would result more often from personal whims than from objective analysis.

The purpose of Chapter 13 is to examine one of the most pervasive and perplexing issues in developmental psychology—the controversy between theoretical eclectics and theoretical purists. The controversy centers on which of two mutually exclusive positions serves the best interests of our clients. On the one hand, theoretical eclectics argue that picking and choosing the most viable components from a variety of theories makes them more flexible in meeting individual needs. On the other hand, theoretical purists contend that individuals are best served by adhering to consistent interpretations derived from principles of a single theory or a single paradigm.

All professionals take a position on this eclectic–purist controversy, whether they know it or not. Very often, their position is not consciously decided but is implicit in the kinds of professional decisions they make. In Part Five we encounter this debate to understand why psychology, more than most other disciplines, is plagued by controversies and why they will continue into the foreseeable future. In addition, many of the implicit assumptions of the eclectic and purist positions are explicitly examined, together with their strongest arguments and weakest points. These discussions are designed to give readers sufficient grounds for examining their own professional responsibilities and commitments vis-à-vis the eclectic–purist controversy.

Chapter 14 attempts to look ahead to see what developmental psychology might look like in the future. While all of the preceding material has been carefully grounded in published work, predicting the future is decidedly speculative, so a word of caution is advised. While we identify a number of current trends and initiatives, our discussion about where they might take us is based solely on our own speculation. Given that, it will be helpful to consider how the issues raised in Chapter 13 might influence the future of developmental psychology (Chapter 14).

13 Are Theories Compatible?

Preview Questions

What does it mean to be a theoretical eclectic?
What does a theoretical purist contend?
What is the eclectic–purist controversy?
What pragmatic arguments support the theoretical eclectic?
What logical arguments support the theoretical purist?
Why is psychology plagued by theoretical "controversies?"
What implications does the eclectic–purist controversy have for you?

The Case for Theoretical Eclecticism

Some professionals take pride in calling themselves **eclectic,** by which they mean that they select elements from different theories to suit their needs. Eclectics may reject some theories in their entirety, others in part, and accept still others in their entirety. This decision is typically made on the basis of personal intuition, needs, or sense of value.

A number of arguments support the eclectic's position. These are outlined in Table 13.1 on page 358 and described in more detail in the following paragraphs.

Eclectics see human nature as extremely complex, and they recognize that no single theory can account for all this complexity. Eclectics argue that people are like pieces of a complex puzzle. Since individual theories attempt to account for only a portion of human nature (see Chapter 1), a complex mosaic can be constructed only by gleaning various pieces from different theories to produce a more complete picture than any single theory can accomplish.

The puzzle analogy appeals to common sense. But the analogy can be extended another step. People are not just complex, they also display tremendous variation. The eclectic believes that since people differ so much from one another, different theories are needed to account for different kinds of people or different types of issues and problems. If one theory isn't appropriate for a particular person or situation, then another theory might do a better job. In addition to selecting among possible theories, eclectics may also select among one or more principles that

TABLE 13.1   Basic Tenets of Theoretical Eclecticism

- Theories are basically compatible, so pieces of one theory can be combined with pieces of another theory.
- Matching any theory to specific humans and needs allows for individualization.
- Benefits to students and clients are maximized.
- Assumption-free means one can view reality as it really is.
- Dogma-free means no distortion by making people fit a single theory.
- Greater efficiency and less error implies no distortion.

derive from very different theories. These principles may be employed singly or in virtually limitless combinations with one another.

Regardless of the profession involved, eclectics tend to subscribe to a *matching* strategy wherein the professional relies on matching up a theory with the kind of person or problem to be treated. If one can identify the proper match between person/problem and theory, then the treatment or education plan should be straightforward. For example, if a student displays a behavior problem, then principles of operant conditioning and behavior modification would be indicated. If the same or another student shows signs of cognitive misunderstanding, then some plan for cognitive development might be devised. Accordingly, eclectics could argue that excellent professionals earn their reputation because they do a careful job of *matching* and thus produce a high number of educational or therapeutic successes.

In their strong appeal to common-sense considerations, eclectics believe they are in a position to freely select from any theory the one that is most appropriate for a particular problem or individual. Teachers, for example, can select from many educational methods only those they believe most useful in teaching different material, and counselors can adopt whatever concepts or theory they believe can most adequately help resolve their clients' particular problems.

Eclectic teachers may use principles of operant conditioning to set up skill-and-drill exercises where memorization of factual material is important, but they can also utilize Piagetian concepts in their mathematics and science lessons in which conceptual understanding is more important than memorization. They may even call on their understanding of psychoanalysis to select therapeutic reading materials for students experiencing parental divorce or exhibiting certain phobias (see, for example, Bettleheim, 1976). Psychologists and counselors may involve a similar collection of theories to treat their clients' varied problems. The point here is that eclectics are firm believers in individualization. They can best individualize and specialize their work by using whatever theory or whatever concepts are most relevant to an individual's needs.

It would be unfair to characterize an eclectic as a proverbial "jack of all trades, master of none." Eclectic teachers and counselors take their professional work seriously, and they understand the difficult responsibility of having to learn many different theories in order to understand the kinds of choices these theories enable them to make. To be effective eclectics, practitioners have to become experts or near experts in each theory so that appropriate matches between theory and situation can be made. There is nothing, however, in being an eclectic that guarantees that a teacher or counselor will actually learn each theory well, or once learned, will actually use it in a manner consistent with its original design.

In essence, the arguments that favor eclecticism rest primarily on pragmatic grounds. Using concepts derived from many theories is believed to be maximally beneficial because programs can be individualized to a particular person and specialized to a specific need. Eclecticism offers an approach to the many varied problems encountered by human service professionals, and teachers and counselors are more often than not trained in an eclectic approach. However, when eclecticism is carefully examined, a number of hidden difficulties become apparent.

Because they are free of the dogma of any single theory or paradigm, eclectics believe that their position allows them to view human nature pretty much as it really is. Underlying this belief is the assumption that problems can somehow define themselves and that theories distort rather than clarify our understanding of human nature. Ultimately, the eclectic's position is credible only if it makes no predisposing assumptions, new situations are viewed more clearly, information is gathered more objectively, and decisions about the nature of the problem and the solution required are made with more efficiency and less error than would be possible with noneclectics. The trouble here is that problems are never self-evident; they do not spontaneously identify themselves to teachers or therapists. Professionals, like scientists, cannot simply read off a body of data and thereby know what it means. Often the most difficult professional task is figuring out how to organize data and thus arrive at an interpretation of what "the problem" is. If it is true that theories give facts meaning (see Chapter 1), then by implication both educational and clinical problems are observer-defined rather than reality-defined.

Consider an example. Two eclectic counselors have an individual suffering from anorexia nervosa, an eating disorder that leads to rapid, sustained weight loss and sometimes death. The first counselor may decide that the anorexic is suffering from a weak ego and unconscious fear of sexual maturity; consequently, psychoanalytic treatment is in order. The second counselor may decide that the disorder is due to eating habits that have somehow been reinforced by members of the client's family. Consequently, a behavior modification plan is needed. The ultimate problem is to determine which therapist is right. Is it simply a matter of each one being entitled to an opinion? If so, then there is no reasonable way to hold professionals accountable for their work. If not, then something must intervene to help us decide the proper identification of a problem. That "something" usually comes in the form of predisposing assumptions that guide the collection and interpretation of data. These assumptions, in turn, are found in theory. But if an eclectic makes the decision to begin with a theory instead of a problem, then how is one to decide which theory to start with? No obvious answer comes to mind.

The analogy that theories are like pieces of a puzzle, and that by fitting them together one gets a more complete view of human nature than would be possible with a single theory, is powerful. Perhaps the reader can almost picture the pieces falling into place: get enough theories, put them together, and you're bound to get a better picture of human nature than any single theory can give.

In fact, one of the strongest cases for theoretical eclecticism can be found in attempts to synthesize the concepts of one theory with those of another, because this kind of work produces new knowledge. Such eclectic syntheses generally take one of two forms. In the first form, the job of synthesizing two concepts is accomplished by assimilating the meaning of one to the meaning of another, often attempted by showing that one concept actually contains the other as a special case. For example, Bereiter and Engelman (1966) have designed a preschool educational program derived from learning theory and emphasizing daily drills on concepts and definitions. They believe that didactic instruction is an effective means for directly training kindergarten children to perform Piagetian formal operational tasks. More specifically, they attempt to incorporate Piaget's theory of cognitive development into learning theory. In this case, Piaget's stage of formal operations is assimilated to a specific case of learning.

A classic and comprehensive effort at synthetic assimilation in developmental psychology was undertaken by Sears (Sears, Maccoby, & Levin, 1957; Sears, Rau, & Alpert, 1965; Sears, Whiting, Nowling, & Sears, 1953), who spent many years attempting to incorporate psychoanalytic concepts into a systematic analysis of behavior. In the main, Sears has been concerned with understanding childhood dependency and aggression. For example, where dependency for Freud was viewed in terms of maturation and psychosexual conflict, Sears recast it as learned behavior, shaped by secondary reinforcement processes that arise because the parent is instrumental to the reduction of primary drives in the child.

Interested readers may find it helpful here to examine some other attempts at synthetic assimilation. Attempts have been made to assimilate some of Piaget's concepts into Skinnerian principles of operant conditioning (Berlyne, 1960, 1965) and to assimilate certain Freudian concepts into Piaget's (Decarie, 1965; Wolff, 1960).

In the second form of synthesis, concepts from different theories are incorporated into a new, hierarchically inclusive concept not specific to the original theories. For example, Brainerd (1981) has proposed a synthesis of Piagetian and learning theory accounts of how children acquire probability concepts. He argues that what develops is not cognitive stages or specific learning, but rather a working-system memory containing three kinds of storage operations and three types of processing operations.

Both forms of eclectic synthesis have in common the assumption that theory concepts are compatible either with each other or with some hierarchical unifying concept. However, a significant problem encountered in these and other theoretical integrations is that they often entail only theoretical parts isolated from the context of the whole theory. Isolating such parts tends to strip theory principles of much of their meaning. Moreover, authors of such syntheses seldom even try to demonstrate that the approaches they have synthesized are in fact compatible (Vuyk,

1981; Kendler, 1986). Difficulties such as these undermine most attempts to synthesize theories.

The Case for Theoretical Purity: Theory Incompatibility

Theories within the same paradigm tend to describe similar though not identical assumptions, problems of study, internal and bridge principles, and change mechanisms. Consequently, their structural components tend to reflect *intra*paradigm consistency.

A theoretical **purist** contends that because theories in different paradigms are inconsistent, only a *single theory* or a *single paradigm* should be used in one's professional practice. It is not necessary that one actually believe a preferred theory to be "true," but for matters of consistency, it is important to adopt one theory or one paradigm in order to interpret data, diagnose problems, and formulate educational plans or therapeutic strategies.

Underlying the purist's position is the belief that some theories rely on mutually exclusive assumptions, thus rendering the theories themselves logically incompatible. Logical incompatibility occurs when two theories assert claims about human nature that cannot both be true. Conversely, two theories are logically compatible if both can be right about a claim. Of course, it is possible for all theories to be wrong as a matter of empirical evidence in their claims about human nature. The issue here, however, is a logical one; if two or more theories make mutually exclusive claims, it is possible for only one at most to be right.

Consider, for example, the claims made by endogenous and exogenous theories. Endogenous theories claim that the primary forces that determine human nature are to be found inside the individual. In contrast, exogenous theories claim that primary forces external to the individual are responsible for shaping human development. These two positions (paradigms) pose logically contradictory positions about human development.

In this vein, theoretical purists believe that paradigms stake out mutually exclusive perspectives, and for this reason, theories in different paradigms pose mutually exclusive explanations of development. In his classical analysis of the history of science, Kuhn (1962, pp. 103–109) argues this point in the following manner. Paradigmatic differences are both necessary and irreconcilable. Paradigms determine the important problems to be solved, the methods of investigations to be employed, and the standards of solution accepted by a community of scientists. Problems in one paradigm may be thought to be irrelevant, trivial, or even nonproblems within a second paradigm. Competing paradigms disagree about what constitutes a problem, what is proper methodology, and what constitutes a solution. Moreover, because one paradigm will satisfy the criteria it sets for itself while failing criteria dictated by another paradigm, they are destined to debate endlessly about their respective merits and talk past each other without connecting.

Hultsch and Hickey (1978) have also attacked the eclectic's position in their analysis of psychological theories and paradigms. Specifically, they argue that different paradigms employ mutually exclusive definitions of external validity; theories in one paradigm actually define reality differently than theories in another paradigm. Paradigms see different psychological realities even when they appear to be looking at the same phenomena. For example, both Freud and Piaget emphasized the fact that infants tend to suck a variety of objects (apparently the same realities). However, recall that Freud viewed sucking as the channeling of psychic energy with the unconscious aim of reducing tension. For him, that was the psychological reality of sucking. Piaget, on the other hand, views sucking as a generalizable, organized action pattern—a schema—for relating to objects. In this view, sucking is seen as an intellectual event. The point here is much more important than simply claiming that different theorists collect only the data that interests them. Rather, competing paradigms may not only argue over interpretations of data, they may well view each other's data as invalid, irrelevant, or scientifically impermissible.

The importance of Hultsch and Hickey's point is that paradigms are paradigms precisely because they have different, mutually exclusive world views. Endogenous, exogenous, and constructivist paradigms (and their constituent theories) hold different assumptions about human nature, and they define it in terms of mutually exclusive qualities. To come full circle, the purist believes that the eclectic's puzzle analogy is a false analogy. Theories are not like pieces of a single puzzle; at best they are like pieces from *radically different* kinds of puzzles.

Following the puzzle analogy a bit further, what sometimes happens when one attempts to merge pieces from different puzzles is that the pieces get bent and no longer resemble their original shape. Something like this is what happened, according to Kendler (1986), with Lerner and Kauffman's (1985) attempt to synthesize two world views: the organismic and the contextualist. Despite their intended aim, Kendler shows that Lerner and Kauffman's revised concept of development distorted its original meanings in each paradigm. The consequence of this distortion is that Lerner and Kauffman end up with a concept of development that is not clearly related to or inclusive of either the organismic or the contextualist world view.

Unlike eclectics who stress complementarity, theoretical purists tend to concentrate on the logical inconsistencies that exist between families of theories. Table 13.2 shows an outline of some of the major paradigmatic claims whose logical inconsistencies underscore the purist's arguments. The most important of these claims are concerned with (1) assumptions made about the nature of the newborn human infant, (2) the contribution of the environment to the organism's development, (3) the relation between organism and environment, and (4) the location of the theory's change mechanism.

The table also shows that the three major paradigms begin with contradictory assumptions. For example, consider the infant's mind. Endogenous theories all assume that human infants have a mind in both form and content. Wilson assumes an evolved, species-specific mental capacity containing preprogrammed strategies for learning social rules. Freud and Erikson assume an unconscious mind, the id, which contains the psychic energy that motivates all goal-directed behavior. And

TABLE 13.2 Outline of Purist's Arguments

| Issue | Paradigm | | |
	Endogenous	Exogenous	Constructivist
Nature of organism	inborn mind irrational id	empty mind *tabula rasa*	no mind
Role of environment	minor	major	major
Organism–interaction environment	major emphasis on organism	major emphasis on environment	major emphasis on both
Change mechanism	maturation, genes, internal	consequences, external	equilibration interactional
Locus of change mechanism	inside	environment	interactional
Locus of significant problems	within organism	outside of organism	adaptive interaction
Type of change needed for development	organism	environment	interaction

Chomsky assumes an innate language faculty that directs linguistic acquisition and performance.

Exogenous theories presume a different type of mind, one with form but no content. This *tabula rasa* mind is logically incompatible with that proposed by endogenous theories. Constructivists propose no infantile mind at all, neither form nor content. Instead, these theorists show how it originates in actions on objects (Piaget) or in interpersonal commerce (Kohlberg). Constructivist proposals contradict both endogenous and exogenous theories' view of human nature at birth.

We see, then, that theories in different paradigms make logically contradictory assumptions about the neonate's mental capabilities. The most direct implication is that these theories view humans in *fundamentally different and irreconcilable ways*.

The three major paradigms also take contradictory positions with respect to the influence of the environment and the relationship between the organism and the environment. For example, the endogenous perspective holds that environment plays a *supportive but not causal* role in the scope and sequence of development. The environment is important, but only as a source of sustenance and variation for the maintenance of genetically programmed changes that unfold in a relatively fixed and rigid manner. Exogenous theories take the opposite position. The causes of human learning are believed to be environmental events that shape and mold innately flexible individuals. Finally, constructivist theories view the environment as important, but not in a deterministic sense. Without environment, a synthetic construction between sensations and organismic structures is not possible. Exogenous and endogenous theories take logically opposing positions with regard to the environment. The constructivist position is partially compatible with the exogenous position about the importance of the environment but not in viewing environmental events as determinants of developmental change. Rather, the environment is instrumental in development, not because it supplies reinforcement, but because its resistance to individual activity poses problems in need of adaptive solutions and because environmental objects can be organized and manipulated, thereby providing material for intellectual construction. At the same time, constructivist theories are logically incompatible with endogenous theories.

Endogenous and exogenous theories reflect contradictory positions with regard to the nature of organismic–environmental interaction and the nature and locus of change mechanisms that produce development. Moreover, endogenous theories locate developmental problems within the individual and specify developmental needs in terms of internal variables. In contrast, exogenous theories define problems in terms of environmental events that shape maladaptive behavior and specify developmental needs in terms of designing effective environments to control individual behavior. The constructivist position holds that both developmental problems and individual needs are functions of adaptive interactions between organism and environment.

In summary, the theoretical purists believe that while theories within a paradigm may be compatible with one another, theories from different paradigms hold logically contradictory positions about human nature. Endogenous and exogenous interpretations of human development cannot both be true. Constructivist theories cannot be true if either endogenous or exogenous interpretations are also true.

Resolving the Eclectic–Purist Debate

The debate between theoretical eclectics and theoretical purists is a controversy because good reasons exist for each position. The eclectic's strongest arguments derive from *pragmatic* considerations. Eclectics believe that different theories represent complementary visions and explanations of human nature that can be called upon to solve human problems in meaningful ways. This position has a common-sense appeal to it that cannot easily be ignored. After all, theories are necessarily limited in scope and explanatory power, and therein no theory by itself can provide a complete account of human development. By increasing the number of theories at one's disposal, the eclectic reasons, one can thereby vastly increase the range of problems one can deal with effectively.

The purist's arguments concentrate on *logical adequacy and consistency*. Purists, by definition, subscribe to a single theory or single paradigm. It is not important for our analysis which theory or paradigm a purist might adopt. What is important is that the purist maintains a theoretical alliance within rather than across paradigms. Nothing prevents the purist from changing alliances from time to time, so long as the change is treated as a stable, enduring commitment when it is made.

The preceding arguments reflect the respective strengths of each position: the logical superiority of the purist's position versus the pragmatic adequacy of the eclectic's. Each position has its weak points: the purist position is pragmatically inadequate, the eclectic logically inconsistent.

Certain fields such as physics, chemistry, and biology adhere to one predominant paradigm that unifies scientists in the questions they ask, the methods they use, and the interpretations they give to data. These fields do not exhibit the great controversies of developmental psychology: nature versus nurture, eclectic versus purist. Controversies occur in psychology largely due to the fact that members of the scientific community *dis*agree about the "rules of the game." The direct consequence is that there are multiple paradigms instead of a single, unifying paradigm.

Multiple paradigms, and multiple theories within each paradigm, give psychologists an amazing array of choices between interpretive devices. The issues raised by Kuhn (1962) earlier in this chapter indicate how difficult it is to get scientists to agree on the essential elements of human nature when they begin with different questions (problems of study), study different realities (phenomena and methods), maintain different rules of evidence for interpreting reality (internal and bridge principles), and speak different languages (theoretical jargon). In the absence of agreements about what should be studied, the range of permissible assumptions, the methodology for collecting data, and the rules for interpreting it, *psychology will remain unable to resolve the debate.* Consequently, no definitive resolution to the controversy is possible at this time. *If the controversy cannot be resolved, then how does one go about deciding whether to be an eclectic or a purist?*

Sandlot Seminar 13.1 provides you, the reader, with an opportunity to find your own way in the eclectic-versus-purist debate. Keeping in mind the arguments made here, complete the self-analysis posed in the exercise.

Sandlot Seminar 13.1

What Is Your Slant on the Eclectic-versus-Purist Debate?

Professionals, by their practice, invariably take a position on the debate. Even for those who attempt to bypass self-reflection and conscious choice, one position or the other is implied in their work. Working through the following steps may help the reader arrive at a personal decision about the eclectic–purist controversy. Keep a tally of your responses to each step, and when you have finished, weigh your evidence carefully. You should be able to arrive at a decision that is personally meaningful and professionally defensible.

Step 1. Identify and list the characteristics of human nature that you believe to be most important. A short list is better than a long one. Compare your list with the assumptions about human nature made by endogenous, exogenous, and constructivist theories. Do you find that your list matches closely the assumptions of only one paradigm or that they are scattered across the paradigms? A good match with one paradigm is one piece of evidence that you might be more closely aligned with theoretical purists than with eclectics. In contrast, finding your assumptions scattered among two or three paradigms is evidence that you might be more intellectually attuned to an eclectic position.

(continued)

Sandlot Seminar 13.1   Continued

Most Important Qualities of Human Development

_____

_____

_____

_____

_____

_____

Step 2. Carefully examine the kinds of problems addressed by theories in each paradigm and determine how relevant those problems are for your work. You might rank a theory's problems for study high, medium, or low for relevance. Next, examine your set of rankings. If you find that one paradigm tends to garner high rankings and the others low rankings, then you have a second piece of evidence that suggests a purist position. However, you may find that no single paradigm can be readily identified as high in relevance for its problems to your field of studies. In that case, you may have evidence suggesting an eclectic position.

Ranking of Problems	*Paradigm*
_____	_____
_____	_____
_____	_____
_____	_____

Step 3. Examine the methods used by theories in each paradigm to collect data. Do the methodologies used within a single paradigm seem to make better sense to you than methods used in the other paradigms? If so, does this match or mismatch earlier selections? If there is a consistent match with one paradigm throughout the first three steps, then you have consistent evidence supporting a purist's position. If, however, methods used by different paradigms seem to make equally good sense to you, or if you find yourself selecting different paradigms at different steps in this exercise, then this constitutes further evidence of an eclectic's stance.

Data Collection Methods	*Paradigm*
_____	_____
_____	_____
_____	_____
_____	_____

Step 4. Given the scope and limits of your profession, carefully review each theory's claims about the change mechanisms of human development. Rank the change mechanisms from highest to lowest. A high ranking means that it makes sense, and you have professional control over it. Do the change mechanisms in each paradigm seem to be equally relevant to your professional mission and make good sense as described and documented by the theorist? Affirmative answers indicate an eclectic orientation; negative answers are more closely associated with theoretical purity.

Ranking of Change Mechanism   *Paradigm*

_____   _____
_____   _____
_____   _____
_____   _____

Step 5. Finally, review the strongest arguments that support each side of the eclectic–purist controversy. Recall that the eclectic's position reflects a strong orientation toward pragmatic values, the purist's toward logical adequacy and consistency. Which set of arguments do you think makes the strongest case? Which set is the most personally compelling? Which position would you rather defend if challenged by someone who is informed? Your answers to these questions constitute the final piece of evidence needed to decide your own position on the debate.

Most Compelling Position

_____

Step 6. Tally the responses in your analysis. Your response to step 6 should probably be weighed more heavily than any other. If your responses tend to orient toward the purist's position, then there are probably personal assumptions, values, and beliefs that make that position more professionally meaningful for you. In contrast, if your responses tend to be aligned with the eclectic's position, it is likely that your intuitions and attitudes are more attuned to theoretical eclecticism.

Final Comment

From our point of view, the problems inherent in eclecticism, together with the logical inadequacy of that stance, persuade us that the purists occupy a more defensible position. Eclecticism is popular today, but many teacher education and counseling programs attempt to instill eclectic attitudes in their students without sufficient reflection or critical examination of the issues we've outlined in this chapter. The eclectic's belief that problems can be identified without making any prior assumptions is a hollow belief. Eclecticism leads to professional decisions marked by inconsistency and superficial common sense. For these reasons, we count ourselves as advocates for the logical consistency of the theoretical purists.

The ultimate goal of human service professionals is to be able to provide effective solutions to educational and clinical problems. Effectiveness is far more likely to follow understanding than precede it. In this vein, understanding the issues in the eclectic–purist controversy provides stepping-stones (rather than stumbling blocks) that lead to better understanding of the human condition. Learning about theories of development and the issues that accompany their study will, we believe, ultimately lead to better solutions to educational and clinical problems than are currently available.

Summary Points

1. Eclectics believe that their program is more pragmatic and applicable to a variety of problems than the purist program.
2. Purists believe that theories from different paradigms are mutually exclusive and logically contradictory.
3. Psychological paradigms claim mutually exclusive positions with regard to assumptions about the neonate, the role of the environment, the locus of the change mechanism, and the nature of human problems needing correction.
4. Given the multiplicity of theories and paradigms found in developmental psychology, there is no way to resolve the eclectic–purist controversy at this time. Such a resolution requires a unifying paradigm like those found in the natural sciences.

SUGGESTED READINGS

Hultsch, D. F., & Hickey, T. (1978). External validity in the study of human development: Theoretical and methodological issues. *Human Development, 21,* 76–91.

Kendler, T. S. (1986). World views and the concept of development: A reply to Lerner and Kauffman. *Developmental Review, 6,* 80–95.

Kuhn, T. S. (1970). *The structure of scientific revolutions,* 2nd ed. Chicago: University of Chicago Press.

Lerner, R. M., & Kauffman, M. B. (1985). The concept of development in contextualism. *Developmental Review, 5,* 309–333.

Sears, R. R., Whiting, J. W. M., Nowlis, V., & Sears, P. (1953). Some child-rearing antecedents of aggression and dependency in young children. *Genetic Psychology Monographs, 47,* 135–234.

CHAPTER
14

The Future of Developmental Psychology

Scenario

The year is 2035. At 3:10 A.M., Mrs. Cortez gives birth to her first child, Anna. The nurses clamp Anna's umbilical cord, suction mucus from her mouth and nose, and wrap her in a blanket before returning her to her mother's waiting arms. The birth has gone well.

Several hours later, a doctor enters the nursery carrying a small plastic case. He gently uncovers the sleeping Anna, opens her protruding umbilical cord, and carefully inserts a tiny plastic speck weighing less than a postage stamp. He carefully ties the umbilical cord, Anna's future belly button, covers the sleeping baby, and leaves the nursery. Anna will never feel and never be inconvenienced by the tiny chip, but she will grow up knowing it is there to help her if it is ever needed.

Like all newborns, Anna has just been fitted with her own personal identity chip containing her unique DNA. This information had first been extracted and then analyzed and electronically encoded on the tiny "genome" chip. An electronic copy of Anna's genetic information has already been transmitted to a secure government data bank in West Virginia.

Imagine the possibilities. Anna's chip, when activated, can be traced by global positioning satellites to find her if she is lost or kidnapped. Her physician can read the chip for allergies before prescribing drugs. In preparation for kindergarten, Anna's genome chip can be read at her neighborhood elementary school in order to set up her individualized learning program based on her personality, learning style, and aptitude tendencies. Later, when Anna is a young adult, her chip can also be read to determine bone marrow and organ compatibility without laborious clinical procedures. In preparation for raising a family, Anna and her spouse's chips can be read to determine the chances of passing on recessive genes and heritable birth defects. But the information the chip holds is double-edged. It can also be read by an insurance company before deciding whether to issue life or health insurance and at what rates.

While the moral and ethical issues raised by this scenario are certainly not trivial, we already possess elements of the technology to make it work. And as the following sections show, there are trends in developmental psychology that could help make something like this scenario become reality.

Throughout this text, we have kept to a consistent, detailed purpose: to explain in sufficient detail the most important concepts of developmental theories in order to draw well-informed comparisons both within and across paradigms. A subordinate aim has been both to provide living examples of each theory with sandlot seminars and to give a sense of a theory's value with ratings for scientific worthiness, developmental adequacy, and pedagogical usefulness. In spite of these efforts, we recognize that many readers will still wonder "So what?" That is, with so many theories *and* concepts *and* paradigms, where is it all leading? What is the future of developmental psychology?

In this chapter we attempt to provide some reasoned speculation about where developmental psychology is heading. While many factors will influence the future, we identify six specific themes that will likely change developmental psychology over the next several decades. As will be clear, we sometimes anticipate that scientific progress in other disciplines will have such a dramatic and sweeping impact that it spills over into developmental psychology. To show how such influences might play out, we occasionally drift into general descriptions of advances in other fields, but we always return to connecting them to potential changes in our primary discipline.

In our speculations here there is an essential missing element that no one can anticipate. That is the role of the individual, or as is more often the case today, teams of scientists who can generate new combinations of qualities. For example, Freud, Skinner, and Piaget all possessed (1) keen insights and (2) comprehensive visions of both details and the "big picture" of human nature. In addition, they had the (3) motivation and (4) personality to convey their images of human nature effectively and persistently. But they also had (5) sufficient data to support their theories. Historically, the combination of these traits was sufficient to shape and change developmental psychology. But as is clear from the historical sketches in each chapter, theories emerge and garner wider attention *only* if they address important issues and problems of the day. This interplay between the historical moment and an individual's characteristics is a delicate matter. Any strong move that fundamentally alters the future of developmental psychology will almost certainly be associated with individuals who exhibit these kinds of traits. There is simply no way to anticipate who will make such moves in the future.

Finally, we should be clear at this point that we do not envision a future for developmental psychology that is nothing more than a "roll of the dice." It is probably *not* the case that everything and anything is possible. But neither is it true that the future will become simply an extrapolation of the past. Somewhere between the two extremes lies a moderately predictable, somewhat knowable future for developmental psychology. We think the six themes that follow will become seminal problems for study and motivate significant changes in the landscape of development.

A Change in Paradigm Cases?

There is a reason that most readers have heard about Freud, Skinner, and Piaget even before reading this book. They are the theorists whose work provides the best examples, the prototypes, for the three paradigm cases in developmental psychology.

Skinner's operant conditioning does a good job of representing the exogenous paradigm. Reinforcers are delivered by environmental agents, and these external sources of development explain how individuals acquire new behaviors over time. There is no other theory on the horizon that competes with operant conditioning, so this theory will continue to be the paradigm case for the exogenous paradigm in developmental psychology.

Piaget's cognitive developmental theory is the paradigm case for the constructivist paradigm. Kohlberg offers a constructivist theory for moral development, but his theory is so limited in scope (to moral development) that it cannot replace Piaget's. Simply put, there is not another theorist in developmental psychology today who can match the scope or explanatory power of Piaget's theory. It will likely continue to be the paradigm case for the constructivist paradigm.

The endogenous paradigm is in flux. Freud's theory was the widely acknowledged paradigm case (which explains why it was so widely presented at university) in the twentieth century. But changes in this paradigm are already taking place. Psychology offers courses in the "biological basis of human behavior." Political science departments offer courses such as "the biological basis of human political behavior." Economic departments offer courses such as the "biological basis of human economic behavior." Finally, biology departments throughout the country are now teaching courses in sociobiology and human population genetics. The trend is clear.

Within the next two or three decades Freud will gradually disappear from the vocabulary of most undergraduates. Terms such as *ego* and *libido* will be replaced by other concepts such as *phylogenetic inertia* and *contest competition*. To put it boldly, we think Wilson's sociobiology will replace Freud's psychoanalysis as the paradigm case for the endogenous paradigm. One reason for this will be the success of the Human Genome Project (see Brain Research, this chapter). But another equally important reason is that sociobiology rests on the precision of scientific measurement, in contrast to the often immeasurable concepts encountered in psychoanalysis. Finally, we think how quickly this change occurs will be influenced in part by some of the other trends described in the following pages.

The Cognitive Revolution

Psychologists have long coveted the high esteem accorded natural scientists such as physicists, chemists, and biologists. After all, they have historically been the primary recipients of worldwide adulation and Nobel prizes. The idea that psychology could itself become a natural science originated in the early twentieth century in a Russian laboratory with a physiologist and his now-famous dog. Following Pavlov's conditioning experiments, American psychologists began to argue that by concentrating on observable and measurable behavior, and using mathematics to quantify their work, psychology could become a natural science. In single-minded pursuit of this goal, behaviorists dominated academic psychology in the United States for four decades, from the early 1920s to the late 1950s. During this time, questions about complex human planning, problem solving, and imagination were barely tolerated, unless approached stealthily (Gardner, 1985). After all, careful measurement, observable phenomena, and genuine experiments were the hallmarks of science, and behaviorists promised a genuinely "scientific" explanation of human nature. But two key events occurred in the 1950s and 1960s to change the direction of American psychology.

First, in 1957, B. F. Skinner published *Verbal Behavior*, an operant conditioning account of how children acquire and use language. Two years later, Noam Chomsky (1959) mounted a scathing critique of that work in which he showed how operant conditioning *could not possibly* account for language acquisition. While his critique of behaviorism was specific to language, Chomsky's point was not lost on other behaviorists who generalized its message to their own work. Without intending it, Chomsky had signaled the end of the behaviorists' grip on academic psychology, and he pointed ahead to what is now termed the *cognitive revolution* (Gardner, 1985).

The second key event occurred shortly after the invention of the computer; using this new machine, psychologists began to write computing programs that simulated various cognitive processes. While the early programs were creative inventions of machine logic and semilogic, they simply could not emulate decisions made by the human brain.

In 1955 a computer was first programmed to produce a mathematical proof from a theorem (Gardner, 1985). Several years later a new science called "information processing" had emerged. Its "problem of study" was to emulate human cognitive processes with computer programs that would (1) receive the same information, (2) process that information, and (3) make decisions based on that information that mimicked human decisions. Between 1960 and 1980 many psychologists used computer emulations to mimic or "test" human cognitive processes. It became clear, however, that such efforts were leading to better, more sophisticated computer programs, but aside from heuristic power, relatively modest progress was being made on understanding what actually goes on inside the human mind. No one can say exactly when, but some time in the 1990s the new field of "cognitive science" was born out of these early efforts.

Today, cognitive science is a very broad term that encompasses many different avenues for exploring human development. Looking over our historical shoulder, we see that psychologists have long wanted to become members of the natural science community, and cognitive science, by both name and method, has replaced behaviorism as psychology's best chance to become respectably scientific. The only real problem with cognitive science is that it just did not work.

We have not included cognitive science in this book because it is characterized more by methodological concerns than with theory. There never has been a single theory of cognitive science or information processing. What has happened is that information processing researchers and cognitive scientists have conducted experiments to test countless small, narrowly focused hypotheses. However, this approach replaced behaviorism as the dominant theme in American psychology because it made two implicit promises that behaviorism could not address (Erneling, 1997). First, cognitive science held out the promise of explaining the higher mental processes and states, such as those described by Vygotsky and Piaget. More specifically, the new field promised a scientific revival of mentalist concepts such as self-reflection and thinking about one's death, which had no voice in the behaviorist agenda.

In the second place, cognitive science sought to integrate disparate areas of psychology and different disciplines into a single paradigm. It was this more lofty promise to unite psychology within a single, new paradigm that led Baars (1986) to write, "It is only theory that gives a sense of unity to physics, chemistry, and other mature sciences. . . . [W]e may be moving toward the first major shared theory for psychological science" (p. 395).

By many accounts, the cognitive revolution has not fulfilled its promises. In the first place, cognitive science has delivered a fractured mosaic rather than a common understanding of "what constitutes the cognitive glue or shared conception of the mind" (Erneling, 1997, p. 379). Moreover, there has been no unifying paradigm of a common view of mind capable of holding all the disparate results together (Erneling, 1997). But the issue today is not merely that cognitive science failed to deliver on its promises. Rather, it cannot possibly succeed given its methodologies and competing views of how the mind works.

One problem is that cognitive science has concentrated on more and more trivialized aspects of cognition (Bruner, 1990). In this sense, the research agenda of cognitive science reflects a sustained agenda of solving trivial problems because they can be solved more readily than the big problems. The concern has been with getting the details right, almost as if once we get enough details, the big picture will begin to emerge. However, in at least one respect, the "failure" of the cognitive revolution is due precisely to the abandonment of pursuing the "big picture" of the mind's structure, organization, and processes for making meaning (Bruner, 1990).

Others believe the formal models employed by cognitive scientists fail to account for any important aspects of mental life, since they are mistaken about the very thing they try to model (Coulter, 1997; Harré, 1997; Shotter, 1997; Stenlund, 1997). And Bruner (1997) has begun to wonder if cognitive revolutions will ever stop.

Others view the current state of cognitive science with a less jaundiced eye. Bialystock (1997), for example, argues that the very fact that we can articulate the shortcomings, failed promises, and other concerns is actually evidence that the cognitive revolution has been a success. Here's why. Although the questions point to gaps in our current understanding of the mind, they arise from an "unquestioned assumption of the centrality, complexity, and diversity of the mind. These questions not only had no voice in the old behaviorist regime, they were inconceivable" (Bailystock, 1997, p. 112).

Our brief sketch of the cognitive revolution reveals an important lesson for the future of developmental psychology. It is this. No matter how good and timely the intent and no matter how bright the players, psychology will, by its very nature, continue to encounter tremendous conceptual and logical problems in the search for a unifying paradigm. Advances that provide clear answers to old questions will inevitably lead to new questions that either were not relevant or simply could not be asked. In this vein, Bruner's (1990) concern about whether cognitive revolutions will ever stop can be generalized. Will psychological revolutions ever stop? The answer is, probably not. While each revolution may lead to a better understanding of human nature, there will probably not be a genuinely unifying paradigm in developmental psychology.

The Age of Information

One of the most pervasive influences in the new millennium is the generation, storage, transmission, and analysis of information. We see this all around us. The vast data-storage and data-crunching capacity of modern computers, coupled with facile software programs for analyzing that information, have been the engine that is driving the information age. In addition, new technologies have given us the capacity to transmit data farther, faster, in greater quantities, and to more locations than could have been predicted a few decades ago. But the accumulation and handling of information is not simply growing, it is *accelerating*. Not only are we generating and using more information, we are discovering new *types* of and new *uses* for information in fields as diverse as business and economics, criminal science and forensics, and genetic biology and astrophysics. The growth of the Internet alone has made available vast quantities of information to more people in more places about more things than could ever have been imagined at the time most readers of this text were born. Will the *information age* have an impact on the future of developmental psychology? Absolutely.

Traditionally, theories of human development have attempted to explain changes over time in general patterns of behavior. In this vein the works described in this text reflect, to varying degrees, *macro*theories of development. There were good reasons for such an orientation. For example, because methods of collecting and analyzing data were so limited, theorists were naturally inclined to get the most "mileage" out of their work. That meant trying to maximize a theory's power to generalize, and generalization implied that they should concentrate on universal rather than individual qualities of human nature. Other considerations also influenced their work. For example, relatively fewer professional organizations and journals meant that they had to write for more general audiences in order to have their work disseminated. Today, the information age is exerting powerful influences on what developmental psychologists do and how they go about it.

The generation of increasing amounts of individual data taken from different sources and contexts will require new kinds of statistics and models. These, in turn, will provide better tools for analyzing not only behaviors in specific situations, but also long and complex *sequences* of behaviors in different contexts. In developmental psychology the immediate impact will be a diminished emphasis on macrotheories with general principles and an increased emphasis on *micro*theories that attempt to explain person-specific patterns of behavior, choice, and change over time. Of course, microtheories will lose explanatory power compared with macrotheories, but they will add a new dimension of precision in explaining and predicting individuals' behavior.

To some extent, what we are talking about here has already begun in the business world of *e-commerce*. Concerns about individual privacy and ownership of personal data have escalated in direct proportion to the type and amount of individualized data computers collect through Internet transactions. By sending a "cookie" to your home computer, an Internet site can track which sites you visit, when you visit them, and how long you remain at each site. That data can be easily stored and correlated with personal data derived from other sources. All this information can be used to build a personal *profile* of your interests, buying patterns, health, and insurance needs. The availability of millions of these personal profiles is a valuable business asset that can be used to selectively target mass mailings and other advertisements for business products and services. Imagine such possibilities if the information chip inserted into our newborn's navel actually becomes a reality.

It is certainly true that business motives to make a profit differ sharply from the psychologist's motive to explain phenomena. However, the capacity to build personal profiles from electronic data and the technology to analyze that data have important implications for the developmental psychologist.

We expect that, given the current growth of e-commerce, psychologists will become increasingly interested in and capable of building and analyzing personal profiles. The result will, we think, accelerate the shift from macrotheories of human development (like those of Freud, Skinner, and Piaget) to microtheories (like those found in the field of information processing and cognitive science). As the shift continues in the new millennium, developmental psychology will become even more fragmented and specialized than the current state of affairs in cognitive science.

The Human Genome Project

Several years ago, a visitor to Brookfield Zoo near Chicago captured an extraordinary event on video. A 3-year-old boy had fallen into a gorilla enclosure and was lying unconscious on the ground. Within moments, a female gorilla approached, sniffed, picked up the unconscious boy, and cradled him in her arms. Then she walked over and gently put him down in front of the caretaker's door. The event captivated the nation as the video played across millions of TV screens that evening. What had prompted the gorilla's behavior? Was it something she had learned, or had she, as some suggested, simply responded dispassionately to a deep-seated genetic urge?

We have long known that our genes can exert powerful, direct influences on physical traits (e.g., eye and hair color, prenatal growth of organs and structures, the timing and nature of growth spurts). Sometimes we take advantage of our limited knowledge, as when certain pet, livestock, or plant owners successfully manipulate gene-linked traits in breeding programs. Other times we are humbled by our powerless ignorance of the gene, as happens, for example, when reminded of profoundly disabling genetic diseases such as those shown in Table 14.1 on page 376.

TABLE 14.1   Well-Documented Genetic Diseases

Disease	Rate	Prognosis
Inheriting two abnormal recessive genes		
Sickle-cell anemia	1:65 African Americans	50 percent mortality before age 20
Cystic fibrosis	1:2,000 Caucasians 1:16,000 African Americans	Pancreatic enzymes are absent; many die in childhood, a few live to early adulthood
PKU (Phenlketonuria)	1:9,000 Caucasians	Nerve tissue destroyed; mental retardation
Tay-Sachs disease	1:3,600 Eastern European Jews	Nearly always death by age 3 or 4
Abnormal dominant gene		
Huntington disease	1:22,000 people	Central nervous system deterioration usually by age 35 to 40; death ten to twenty years after symptoms appear
Marfan syndrome	1:20,000 people	Heart and eye abnormalities; death from heart failure in young adulthood common
Genetic damage		
Down syndrome	1:600 infants	Mental retardation, abnormal appearance
Missing or extra chromosome		
Klinefelter's syndorme	1:1,000 males	Males receive extra X chromosome; mental retardation; may develop some female characteristics at puberty
Turner's syndrome	1:2,500 females	Girls have no or partial X chromosome; do not complete sexual development; low spatial IQ, average verbal intelligence

But genes are such tiny fragments of DNA themselves, they have remained elusively invisible. While we could examine their effects, we could not examine the very tiny specks exerting such power. All of our genetic information—the DNA—is packed onto twenty-three tiny pairs of chromosomes. For many decades, scientists have dreamed of unpacking this information so they could directly test and analyze the effects produced by specific genes and groups of genes.

But even as we write this, our ignorance is being overcome by the Human Genome Project, an ambitious undertaking to identify and map (1) the entire genetic composition of *Homo sapiens* and (2) the variations in genetic composition associated with different populations of humans. The first phase has been substantially completed, and the second is well underway.

At the time of this writing, researchers have already unpacked all the genetic details of one chromosome—number 22, the smallest of the twenty-three pairs. It turns out that chromosome number 22 contains 545 genes, 298 of them unknown to science until now. With such a script in hand, scientists can begin to examine the function of each gene.

Armed with the gene's script, we face the very real possibility within two decades of being able to perform genetic diagnoses and treatments of diseases such as those in Table 14.1. Gene-based designer drugs may become available for common conditions such as diabetes and high blood pressure. It is even plausible that scientists may develop successful genetic therapies for preventing mental illness and personality disorders altogether.

Back in the mid 1980s, when the first IBM PCs became available, no one predicted the development of portable laptops that could do ten thousand times more calculations per second and store ten thousand times more information. Similarly, scientists never expected the technology of DNA sequencing to advance so rapidly or its subsequent discoveries to explode at such a phenomenal rate.

As we look into the future of developmental psychology, we believe the Human Genome Project will magnify the effects of the information age in two specific ways. First, the idea of individualization and personal profile will take on new meanings. Rather than a personal identity or personality, individualization will come to reflect each person's specific genetic markers, the unique strands and sequences that comprise that person's DNA. In short, "genes" will no longer be a generalized collective noun; rather it will refer to the specific DNA sequences that identify and make each individual unique. The capability of mapping every individual's genetic markers will rapidly lead to identifying and quantifying the contributions of genetic markers to specific phenotypes (both in the Darwinian sense of physical traits and in Wilson's sense of social behaviors). Such work will lead naturally to a second important outcome.

The second outcome of the Human Genome Project will attempt to fashion a taxonomy of correlations between genetic markers and specific psychological states and phenomena. For example, given our knowledge of genetic diseases, it is only a short step to ponder the possibility of genetic links to more psychological phenomena such as aggressiveness, creativity, curiosity, intelligence, learning style, personality, shyness, and temperament. If anything like this comes out of the

Human Genome Project, then it is likely to have an immediate impact on how developmental psychologists are trained. We expect that graduate programs will be revised to include training in genetic analysis (a psychology graduate program in behavioral genetics already requires a course called "Analytical Methods for Quantitative Trait Loci"). And new generations will pursue a scientific agenda for developing clearly defined rules (microtheories) that explain psychological states and processes in terms of their underlying genetic sequences of DNA. But as we saw with the cognitive revolution, there are tremendous problems and difficulties still ahead in trying to map even simple relationships between DNA sequences and cognitive functioning (Heyes & Huber, 2000).

Brain Research

The mature human brain contains about one hundred billion (100,000,000,000) neurons or nerve cells, and the number of possible *interconnections* between them has been estimated by Churchland (1995) to be about 10 to the 100 trillionth power. This set of possible interconnections exceeds the number of atoms in the universe. But neurons decay, die, and atrophy through disuse at the rate of about 10,000 to 100,000 per day. A typical adult has about half the number of neurons as a 2-year-old (Jensen, 1998). With such an extensive array of possible interconnections, the adult brain exerts powerful learning, development, and understanding.

Current theories in developmental psychology represent a "domain" approach to explaining development. For example, Chomsky concentrates on language, Ainsworth on infant attachment, Skinner on behavior, and Piaget on cognitive development. In contrast, current research on the human brain, its structure and biochemistry, is attempting to explain psychological phenomena as manifestations of brain activities. It is possible that such efforts may succeed in integrating the domains of psychological development (e.g., language, cognition, emotions) at the level of biology and biochemistry. For example, we have long known that different areas of the brain display activity when we see, hear, talk, and taste. But in addition to our sensations, different parts of the brain are also involved in talking, solving complex problems, or rendering a drawing of a landscape. But beyond localizing the brain's various functions, researchers are delving into how specific kinds of brain activities render the brain's own developmental stages (Epstein, 1986), produce long-term memory of emotional events (Cahill, Prins, Weber, & McGaugh, 1994; Davidson & Sutton, 1995; LeDoux, 1993; Pert, 1997), activate speech centers for learning to talk (Tallal, Miller, & Fitch, 1993), and respond to environmental stimulation in promoting the brain's own development (Fuchs, Montemayor, & Greenough, 1990).

Searching for brain functions associated with psychological aspects of development is, of course, a reductionist enterprise. However, the new trend in brain research reflects a different type of reductionist orientation than that associated with the Human Genome Project. In fact, we expect that it will not take long for these two complementary fields of research to begin merging since they seem to have a natural affinity for biological and biochemical contributions to human nature. While much of the basic research will be undertaken by biologists and medical researchers, developmental psychologists will likely pursue their own interests in understanding how and in what capacity the brain controls various developmental domains and processes. The field of brain-based research is so full of potential that many educators have already begun outlining their own brain-based approaches to teaching and learning (Caine & Caine, 1994; Jensen, 1998; Sprenger, 1999; Sylwester, 1995).

We believe that the reductionist tendency of brain-based researchers will result in more microtheories about psychological functioning and development. Instead of relying on large, general theories of development which occupied twentieth-century psychology, increased precision will necessitate new techniques in collecting, storing, and analyzing vast amounts of information from very different domains of development. Here again, we believe such trends will require new kinds of statistical and other data-analytic models capable of finding patterns in large data sets with very different types of variables.

Ultimately these kinds of changes in research will lead to increasing fragmentation and specialization in psychology (Lewandowsky, 1998). However, as we discuss in the next section, science is a conservative process. So against the trend toward reductionism, fragmentation, and specialization will arise a small but vocal resistance against losing the explanatory power of macrotheories.

The Search for Unity in Developmental Psychology

For the past two hundred years philosophers have sought insight into the grand unifying themes that would explain human nature, the universe, and the relationship between them. They presumed that answers to their search would, even with some difficulties, eventually be forthcoming. A great deal of success has been achieved in the natural sciences (i.e., biology, chemistry, and physics) in large part because they tend to reduce physical phenomena to their constituent elements. Put differently, reducing phenomena to their essential components is one of two primary activities of science. The second activity is theory building. Once reduced, those essential components are then reconstituted from bottom to top in order to explain and predict the original phenomena. The Human Genome Project is a good example of this approach to the conduct of science.

The search for grand, unifying themes is called *consilience*. Wilson (1998b) argues that consilience is the world view that all phenomena, ranging from animal physiology and behavior at one extreme to the formation and structure of galaxies at the other, are based on underlying material processes. Moreover, these processes are "ultimately reducible, however long and tortuous the sequences, to the laws of physics" (Wilson, 1998, p. 266).

At the core of consilience is the inherent tendency of science to reduce phenomena at one level into well-understood phenomena at the next lower level. In this approach, the human mind might be understood as a network of causal links that begin with quantum physics and work upward through the levels of chemistry and neurology to arrive at an explanation of the human mind. Broadly speaking, physical atoms and forces would give rise to physiological structures and processes at the biological level, which in turn would give rise to psychological states and processes at the next. Here, for example, is Wilson's synopsis of the how this might happen.

> What is lacking is a sufficient grasp of the emergent, holistic properties of the neuron circuits, and of cognition, the way the circuits process information to create perception and knowledge . . . Mind is . . . at root the coded representation of sensory impressions and the memory and imagination of sensory impressions . . . Consciousness consists of the parallel processing of vast numbers of such coding networks. Many are linked by the synchronized firing of the nerve cells at forty cycles per second, allowing the simultaneous internal mapping of multiple sensory impressions. Some of the impressions are real, fed by ongoing stimulation from outside the nervous system, while others are recalled from the memory banks of the cortex. All together they create scenarios that flow realistically back and forth through time . . . The scenarios compose dense and finely differentiated patterns in the brain circuits. (Wilson, 1998b, p. 109)

But there is more. Wilson believes that consciousness is not like a remote "command center" that directs our thoughts, but rather is inherently part of the brain's own neural system, intimately wired to all the networks and circuits that regulate our physiology. Consistent with this view, he argues that the mind's capacity for *meaning* is created by spreading electrical excitations among the neural networks. In short, if scientific reductionism is ultimately successful, developmental psychology will evolve to the point where psychological development is analyzed in terms of neurological and biochemical processes and functions.

It is well understood that genes seldom act independently of one another. They almost always act in an orchestrated fashion, collectively exerting genetic influences over our lives. But understanding the ways in which DNA sequences produce subtle and sophisticated structures at both cellular and organismic levels is one thing. A much more ambitious enterprise, one that opposes the reductionism inherent in the natural sciences, seeks to understand how genes create structures and functions that *interact* with the environment to produce learning and development. While recent efforts in this regard can be found (see Griffiths & Gray, 2001; Wolf, Broie, & Wade, 2000), their ultimate success will depend in large part on how gene–environment interactions account for phenomena that are otherwise inexplicable by solely reductionist accounts.

Wertsch (1998) has argued, for example, that some kinds of phenomena simply cannot be understood or explained by their analytic decomposition into subordinate elements or units of analysis. Consider two examples, the first simple and the second more complex. For our purposes here, consider two interesting properties of unfrozen water: (1) it is a liquid and (2) it will extinguish a camp fire. But these properties disappear if we analyze a water molecule in terms of its constituent elements, hydrogen and oxygen. Hydrogen burns, and oxygen sustains combustion. In addition, both of these elements are gases in their natural state. The point here is that different characteristics and properties emerge at different levels of analysis, and higher levels cannot always be understood in terms of lower levels.

In our second example, we visit a young couple who have been dating each other for the better part of a year. Quite naturally, they have begun to discuss the possibility of getting married. Entering into this complex decision are all the historical, cultural, and personal experiences and memories of each. Simply examining the biochemical activities going on inside the young man and woman, we can learn little about each one's identity formation, personality, cognitive and moral development, or religious affiliation and convictions. Nor will any analysis of their biological systems and functions enable us to predict or explain the ebb and flow of their premarital conversations. In short, unless we analyze their interactions at either the social or psychological levels, we can never understand the forces and influences that contribute to their marriage decision.

Our examples, of course, are not themselves definitive. We concur with Wilson (1998) to the extent that we believe the first decades of the new millennium will be marked by further reductionism in developmental psychology and a corresponding emphasis on building microtheories of development. But we disagree on the ultimate outcome. There is a natural antagonism between microtheories and macrotheories, and Wilson's arguments notwithstanding, the latter cannot be easily reduced to the former.

A final example may be useful. In physics, gravity (a general principle) accounts for the behavior of bodies at intermediate and large distances, but it fails to account for the behavior of particles inside the atom. Within the atom, quantum physics takes over to explain how subatomic particles behave. The point is that physics needs both explanations. By way of analogy, developmental psychology probably needs both micro- and macrotheories of development because they explain different kinds of processes and states.

As the "natural" tendencies of science come to the forefront in developmental psychology, we think a small but respectable reaction against microtheories will emerge. We do not know what form it will take or how it will come about. But we are reminded of how Freud (Chapter 3) countered the neurological explanations of neuroses with his own theory of psychosexual origins and how Heinz Werner's *organicism* (see Chapter 11) offered a holistic orientation to human development to counter the reductionist attitude of American behaviorism. Given the geometric growth in data about human development, we think macrotheory-building will become increasingly more difficult than it was in the past. Nevertheless, macrotheories will continue to serve an important explanatory purpose in developmental psychology because they provide a "big picture" view of human nature.

Will the antagonism between micro- and macrotheories, between reductionism and holism, be eventually resolved in some type of friendly merger? Probably not. As we argued in Chapter 13, theories in different paradigms make incompatible assumptions, and these alone will prevent developmental psychology from achieving a unifying paradigm within the present landscape of developmental theory.

However, perhaps there are other new paradigms to be constructed. Perhaps some new paradigm might encompass the three world views described in this text. To be viable in the future, such a paradigm would have to reconcile two inherently antagonistic considerations. First, it would have to propose conceptual principles that somehow make compatible previously incompatible ideas (e.g., nature versus nurture). Second, it would have to contain sufficiently detailed and powerful explanatory concepts that could account for data at different levels of explanation (e.g., biochemical, biological, psychological, social). The future will tell us whether or not the same concepts can do all that, but we are skeptical. In closing, then, we believe developmental psychology will be stuck with its "multiple personalities." That means future generations will still have good reasons to study theories and paradigms of human development. Among the most important reasons are those we describe in the opening pages of Chapter 1.

REFERENCES

Abraham, K. (1927). The influence of oral eroticism on character formation. *Selected papers*. London: Hogarth.

Adams, A. K. (1987, January). "A penguin belongs to the bird family": Language games and the social transfer of categorical knowledge. Paper presented at the Third International Conference on Thinking, Honolulu.

Adams, G. R., & Fitch, S. A. (1982). Ego stage and identity status development: A cross-sequential analysis. *Journal of Personality and Social Psychology, 43*, 574–583.

Adams, G. R., & Montemayor, R. (1983). Identity formation during early adolescence. *Journal of Early Adolescence, 3*, 193–202.

Adams, G. R., Shea, J. A., & Fitch, S. A. (1979). The relationship between identity status, locus of control, and ego development. *Journal of Youth and Adolescence, 8*, 81–89.

Agassi, J. (1997). The novelty of Chomsky's theories. In D. M. Johnson & C. E. Erneling (Eds.), *The future of the cognitive revolution*, 136–148. New York: Oxford University Press.

Ainsworth, M. D. (1967). *Infancy in Uganda: Infant care and the growth of love*. Baltimore: Johns Hopkins Press.

———. (1973). The development of infant–mother attachment. In B. M. Caldwell & H. N. Riciuti (Eds.), *Review of Child Development Research*, Vol. 3, 1–94. Chicago: University of Chicago Press.

———. (1979). Infant–mother attachment. *American Psychologist, 34*, 932–937.

Ainsworth, M. D. S., Bell, S. M., & Stayton, D. J. (1972). Individual differences in the development of some attachment behaviors. *Merrill-Palmer Quarterly, 18*, 123–143.

Ainsworth, M. D. S., & Marvin, R. S. (1995). On the shaping of attachment theory and research: An interview with Mary D. S. Ainsworth (Fall 1994). In E. Waters, B. E. Vaughn, G. Posada, & K. Kondo-Ikemura (Eds.), *Caregiving, Cultural, and Cognitive Perspectives on Secure-Base Behavior and Working Models: New Growing Points of Attachment Theory and Research. Monographs of the Society for Research in Child Development, 60*, Serial No. 244, 3–21.

Ainsworth, M. D. S., & Wittig, B. A. (1969). Attachment and exploratory behavior of one-year-olds in a strange situation. In B. M. Foss (Ed.), *Determinants of infant behavior*, 111–136. London: Methuen.

Allen, E., Beckwith, B., Beckwith, J., Chorover, S., Culver, D., Duncan, M., Gould, S., Hubbard, R., Inouye, H., Leeds, A., Lewontin, R., Madansky, C., Miller, L., Pyeritz, R., Rosenthal, M., & Shreier, H. (1978). Against "sociobiology." In A. L. Caplan (Ed.), *The sociobiology debate: Readings on the ethical and scientific issues concerning sociobiology*, 259–264. New York: Harper and Row.

Allen, J. P., Leadbeater, B. J., & Aber, J. L. (1990). The relationship of adolescent's expectations and values to delinquency, hard drug use and unprotected sexual intercourse. *Development and Psychopathology, 2*, 85–98.

Alper, J., Beckwith, J., Chorover, S. L., Hunt, J., Inouye, H., Judd, T., Lange, R. V., & Sternberg, P. (1978). The implications of sociobiology. In A. L. Caplan (Ed.), *The sociobiology debate: Readings on the ethical and scientific issues concerning sociobiology*, 333–336. New York: Harper and Row.

Anderson, J. E. (1957). Dynamics of development: System in process. In D. B. Harris (Ed.), *The concept of development*, 25–46. Minneapolis: University of Minnesota Press.

Archer, S. L. (1982). The lower age boundaries of identity development. *Child Development, 53,* 1551–1556.

Armon, C. (1998). Adult moral development, experience and education. *Journal of Moral Education, 27,* 345–371.

Armon, C., & Dawson, T. L. (1997). Developmental trajectories in moral reasoning across the life span. *Journal of Moral Education, 26,* 433–455.

Azmitia, M. (1988). Peer interaction and problem solving: When are two heads better than one? *Child Development, 59,* 87–96.

Azrin, N., & Lindsley, O. (1956). The reinforcement of cooperation between children. *Journal of Abnormal and Social Psychology, 2,* 100–102.

Baars, B. J. (1986). *The cognitive revolution in psychology.* New York: Guilford Press.

Bailey, C. (1980). Morality, reason and feeling. *Journal of Moral Education, 9,* 114–121.

Bandura, A. (1986). *Social foundations of thought and action: A social cognitive theory.* Englewood Cliffs, NJ: Prentice-Hall.

———. (1992). Exercise of personal agency through the self-efficacy mechanism. In R. Schwarzer (Ed.), *Self-efficacy: Thought control of action,* 3–38. Washington, DC: Hemisphere.

———. (1993). Perceived self-efficacy in cognitive development and functioning. *Educational Psychologist, 28,* 117–148.

———. (1995). Exercise of personal and collective efficacy in changing societies. In A. Bandura (Ed.), *Self-efficacy in changing societies,* 1–45. New York: Cambridge University Press.

———. (1997). *Self-efficacy: The exercise of control.* New York: W. H. Freeman.

Bandura, A., & Walters, R. (1959). *Adolescent aggression.* New York: Ronald Press.

———. (1963). *Social learning and personality development.* New York: Holt, Rinehart and Winston.

Barash, D. P. (1977). *Sociobiology and behavior.* New York: Elsevier.

Barlow, G. W. (1980). The development of sociobiology: A biologist's perspective. In G. W. Barlow & J. Silverberg (Eds.), *Sociobiology: Beyond nature/nurture,* 3–24. Boulder, CO: Westview Press.

Barkow, J. H. (1982). Return to nepotism: The collapse of a Nigerian gerontocracy. *International Political Science Review, 3,* 33–49.

Barrouillet, P., & Poirier, L. (1997). Comparing and transforming: An application of Piaget's morphisms theory to the development of class inclusion and arithmetic problem-solving. *Human Development, 40,* 216–234.

Basen-Engquist, K., & Parcel, G. S. (1992). Attitudes, norms and self-efficacy: A model of adolescents' HIV-related sexual risk behavior. *Health Education Quarterly, 19,* 263–277.

Bates, J. E., Maslin, C. A., & Frankel, K. A. (1985). Attachment security, mother-child interaction, and temperament as predictors of behavior-problem ratings at age three years. In I. Bretherton & E. Waters (Eds.), Growing points of attachment theory and research. *Monographs of the Society for Research in Child Development, 50,* 167–193 (Whole No. 209).

Becker, W. C., Madsen, C. J., Jr., Arnold, R., & Thomas, D. R. (1967). The contingent use of teacher attention and praise in reducing classroom behavior problems. *Journal of Special Education, 1,* 287–307.

Behrend, D. A., Rosengren, K. S., & Perlmutter, M. (1992). The relation between private speech and parental interactive style. In R. M. Diaz & I. L. E. Berk (Eds.), *Private speech: From social interaction to self-regulation,* 85–100. Hillsdale, NJ: Erlbaum.

Beloff, H. (1957). The structure and origin of the anal character. *Genetic Psychology Monographs, 55,* 141–172.

Bereiter, C., & Englemann, S. (1966). *Teaching disadvantaged children in the preschool.* Englewood Cliffs, NJ: Prentice Hall.

Berk, L. E. (1992). Children's private speech: An overview of theory and the status of research. In R. M. Diaz & I. L. E. Berk (Eds.), *Private speech: From social interaction to self-regulation,* 17–53. Hillsdale, NJ: Erlbaum.

Berk, L. E., & Landau, S. (1993). Private speech of learning disabled and normally achieving children in classroom academic and laboratory contexts. *Child Development, 64,* 556–571.

Berk, L. E., & Spuhl, S. T. (1995). Maternal interaction, private speech, and task performance in preschool children. *Early Childhood Research Quarterly, 10,* 145–169.

Berkowitz, M. W., & Grych, J. H. (1998). Fostering goodness: Teaching parents to facilitate children's moral development. *Journal of Moral Education, 27,* 371–393.

Berlyne, D. E. (1960). *Conflict, arousal, and curiosity.* New York: McGraw-Hill.

———. (1965). Curiosity and education. In J. D. Krumboltz (Ed.), *Learning and the educational process,* 67–89. Chicago: Rand-McNally.

Bertrand, S., & Masling, J. (1969). Oral imagery and alcoholism. *Journal of Abnormal Psychology, 74,* 50–53.

Bettelheim, B. (1976). *The uses of enchantment: The meaning and importance of fairy tales.* New York: Knopf.

Bialystock, E. (1997). Anatomy of a revolution. In D. M. Johnson & C. E. Erneling (Eds.) *The future of the cognitive revolution,* 109–113. New York: Oxford University Press.

Bickard, M. H. (1978). The nature of developmental stages. *Human Development, 21,* 217–233.

Bijou, S. W. (1970). What psychology has to offer education—now. *Journal of Applied Behavior Analysis, 3,* 65–71.

Bivens, J. A., & Berk, L. E. (1990). A longitudinal study of the development of elementary children's private speech. *Merrill-Palmer Quarterly, 36,* 443–463.

Blake, J., & de Boysson-Bardies, B. (1992). Patterns of babbling: A cross-linguistic study. *Journal of Child Language, 19,* 51–74.

Blakemore, J. E., Larue, A. A., & Olejnik, A. B. (1979). Sex-appropriate toy preferences and the ability to conceptualize toys as sex-role related. *Developmental Psychology, 15,* 339–340.

Blatt, M., & Kohlberg, L. (1975). The effects of classroom moral discussion upon children's moral judgment. *Journal of Moral Education, 4,* 129–161.

Blum, G. S. (1949). A study of the psychoanalytic theory of psychosexual development. *Genetic Psychology Monographs, 39,* 3–99.

Boring, E. G. (1957). *A history of experimental psychology* (2nd ed.). New York: Appleton-Century-Crofts.

Bower, T. G. R. (1974). *Development in infancy.* San Francisco: W. H. Freeman.

———. (1977). *A primer of infant development.* San Francisco: W. H. Freeman.

Bower, T. G. R., & Wishart, J. G. (1972). The effects of motor skill on object permanence. *Cognition, 1,* 165–172.

Bowlby, J. (1951). *Maternal care and mental health.* WHO Monograph Series No. 2. Geneva: World Health Organization.

Bowlby, J. (1958). The nature of the child's tie to his mother. *International Journal of Psychoanalysis, 39,* 350–373.

Bowlby, J. (1969). *Attachment and Loss,* Vol. I, *Attachment.* New York: Basic Books.

Bowlby, J. (1973). *Attachment and Loss,* Vol. II, *Separation: Anxiety and anger.* New York: Basic Books.

Bowlby, J. (1980). *Attachment and Loss,* Vol. III, *Loss, sadness, and depression.* New York: Basic Books.

Brainerd, C. J. (1973). Neo-Piagetian training experiments revisited: Is there any support for the cognitive-development stage hypothesis? *Cognition, 2,* 349–370.

————. (1976). Does prior knowledge of the compensation rule increase susceptibility to conservation training? *Developmental Psychology, 12,* 1–5.

————. (1977). Cognitive development and concept learning: An interpretative review. *Psychological Bulletin, 84,* 919–939.

————. (1978a). Learning research and Piagetian theory. In L. S. Siegel & C. J. Brainerd (Eds.), *Alternatives to Piaget: Critical essays on the theory,* 69–109. New York: Academic Press.

————. (1978b). The stage question in cognitive-developmental theory. *The Behavioral and Brain Sciences, 1,* 173–213.

————. (1981). Working memory and the developmental analysis of probability judgments. *Psychological Review, 88,* 463–502.

Brainerd, C. J., & Brainerd, S. H. (1972). Order of acquisition of number and liquid quantity conservation. *Child Development, 43,* 1401–1405.

Brender, W.J., & Kramer, E. (1967). A comparative need analysis of immediately-recalled dreams and TAT responses. *Journal of projective techniques and personality assessment, 31,* 74–77.

Brenman-Gibson, M. (1984). Erik Erikson and the "ethics of survival." *Harvard Magazine, 87* (3), 58–64.

Bretherton, I. (1995). The origins of attachment theory: John Bowlby and Mary Ainsworth. In S. Goldberg, R. Muir, & J. Kerr (Eds.). *Attachment theory: Social, developmental and clinical perspectives,* 45–84. Hillsdale, NJ: The Analytic Press.

Broden, M., Bruce, C., Mitchell, M. A., Carter, V., & Hall, R. V. (1970). Effects of teacher attention on attending behavior of two boys at adjacent tables. *Journal of Applied Behavior Analysis, 3,* 199–203.

Brooks, J. (1969). The insecure personality: A factor analytic study. *British Journal of Medical Psychology, 42,* 395–403.

Brown, A. L., & Palincsar, A. S. (1989). Guided cooperative learning and individual knowledge acquisition. In L. B. Resnick (Ed.), *Knowing, learning, and instruction.* Hillsdale, NJ: Erlbaum.

Brown, R. (1973). *A first language: The early years.* Cambridge, MA: Harvard University Press.

Bruner, J. (1990). *Acts of meaning.* Cambridge, MA: Harvard University Press.

————. (1997). Will cognitive revolutions ever stop? In D. M. Johnson & C. E. Erneling (Eds.) *The future of the cognitive revolution,* 279–292. New York: Oxford University Press.

Bryan, J. H. (1975). Children's cooperation and helping behaviors. In E. M. Hetherington (Ed.), *Review of child development research,* Vol. 5, 127–181. Chicago: University of Chicago Press.

Butterworth, G., & Castillo, M. (1976). Coordination of auditory and visual space in newborn human infants. *Perception, 5,* 155–160.

Cahill, L., Prins, B., Weber, M., & McGaugh, J. (1994). Andrenergic activation and memory for emotional events. *Nature, 371,* 702–704.

Caine, R. N., & Caine, G. (1994). *Making connections: Teaching and the human brain.* Menlo Park, CA: Addison-Wesley.

Caplan, A. L. (1978). Introduction. In A. L. Caplan (Ed.), *The sociobiology debate: Readings on the ethical and scientific issues concerning sociobiology,* 1–13. New York: Harper and Row.

Carlson, V., Cicchetti, D., Barnett, D., & Braunwald, K. G. (1989). Finding order in disorganization: Lessons from research on maltreated infants' attachments to their caregivers. In D. Cicchetti & V. Carlson (Eds.), *Child maltreatment: Theory and research on the causes and consequences of maltreatment,* 494–528. New York: Cambridge University Press.

Chagnon, N. A. (1979). Mate competition, favoring close kin, and village fissioning among the Yanomamo Indians. In N. Chagnon & W. Irons (Eds.), *Evolutionary biology and human social behavior: An anthropological perspective,* 86–132. North Scituate, MA: Duxbury Press.

———. (1981). Terminological kinship, genealogical relatedness and village fissioning among the Yanomamo Indians. In R. Alexander & D. Tinkle (Eds.), *Natural selection and social behavior: Recent research and new theory,* 490–508. New York: Chiron Press.

———. (1982). Sociodemographic attributes of nepotism in tribal populations: Man the rule-breaker. In King's College Sociobiology Group (Ed.), *Current problems in sociobiology,* 291–318. Cambridge: Cambridge University Press.

Chomsky, N. (1957). *Syntactic structures.* The Hague: Mouton.

———. (1959). A review of *verbal behavior* by B. F. Skinner. *Language, 35,* 26–58.

———. (1965). *Aspects of a theory of syntax.* Cambridge, MA: MIT Press.

———. (1966). *Topics in the theory of generative grammar.* The Hague: Mouton.

———. (1972a). *Language and mind.* (2nd ed.). New York: Harcourt, Brace, Jovanovich.

———. (1972b). *Studies on semantics in generative grammar.* The Hague: Mouton.

———. (1975a). *The logical structure of linguistic theory.* London: Plenum.

———. (1975b). *Reflections on language.* New York: Pantheon Books.

———. (1982). *Lectures on government and binding.* Dordrecht, Holland: Foris.

———. (1983). Noam Chomsky's views on the psychology of language and thought. In R. W. Rieber (Ed.), *Dialogues on the psychology of language and thought,* 33–63. New York: Plenum.

———. (1986). *Knowledge of language: Its nature, origin, and use.* New York: Praeger.

———. (1988). *Language and problems of knowledge.* Cambridge, MA: MIT Press.

———. (1993). *Language and thought.* Wakefield, RI: Moyer Bell.

Churchland, P. (1995). *Engine of reason: Seat of the soul.* Cambridge, MA: MIT Press.

Clare, L., Gallimore, R., & Patthew-Chavez, G. G. (1996). Using moral dilemmas in children's literature as a vehicle for moral education and teaching reading comprehension. *Journal of Moral Education, 25,* 325–342.

Clifton, C., & Odum, P. (1966). Similarity relations among certain English sentence constructions. *Psychological Monographs, 80,* 1–35.

Clignet, R., & Sween, J. (1974). Urbanization, plural marriage, and family size in two African cities. *American Ethnologist, 1,* 221–242.

Cline, V. B., Croft, R. G., & Courrier, S. (1973). Desensitization of children to television violence. *Journal of Personality and Social Psychology, 27,* 360–365.

Colby, A., & Kohlberg, L. (1987). *The measurement of moral judgment.* (2 vols.). New York: Cambridge University Press.

Cole, M., & Scribner, S. (1978). Introduction. In M. Cole, V. John-Steiner, S. Scribner, & E. Souberman (Eds.), *Mind in Society: The development of higher psychological processes,* 1–14. Cambridge, MA: Harvard University Press.

Colin, V. L. (1996). *Human attachment.* New York: McGraw–Hill.

Commons, M. L., Richards, F. A., & Kuhn, D. (1982). Systematic and metasystematic reasoning: A case for levels of reasoning beyond Piaget's stage of formal operations. *Child Development, 53,* 1058–1069.

Comrey, A. L. (1965). Scales for measuring compulsion, hostility, neuroticism and shyness. *Psychological Reports, 16,* 697–700.

———. (1966). Comparison of personality and attitude variables. *Educational and Psychological Measurement, 26,* 853–860.

Connolly, J. (1989). Social self-efficacy in adolescence: Relations with self-concept, social adjustment, and mental health. *Canadian Journal of Behavioural Science, 21,* 258–269.

Cordua, G. D., McGraw, K. O., & Drabman, R. S. (1979). Doctor or nurse: Children's perception of sex typed occupations. *Child Development. 50,* 590–593.

Corey, J. R., & Shamow, J. (1972). The effects of fading on the acquisition and retention of oral reading. *Journal of Applied Behavior Analysis, 5,* 311–315.

Corman, H. H., & Escalona, S. K. (1969). Stages of sensorimotor development: A replication study. *Merrill-Palmer Quarterly, 15,* 351–361.

Cossairt, A., Hall, R. V., & Hopkins, B. L. (1973). The effects of experimenter's instructions, feedback, and praise on teacher praise and student attending behavior. *Journal of Applied Behavior Analysis, 6,* 89–100.

Coulter, J. (1997). Neural Cartesianism: Comments on the epistemology of the cognitive sciences. In D. M. Johnson & C. E. Erneling (Eds.) *The future of the cognitive revolution,* 293–301. New York: Oxford University Press.

Crain, S., & Thornton, R. (1998). *Investigations in universal grammar: A guide to experiments on the acquisition of syntax and semantics.* Cambridge, MA: MIT Press.

Crittenden, P. M. (1985). Maltreated infants: Vulnerability and resilience. *Journal of Child Psychology and Psychiatry, 26,* 85–96.

Crittenden, P. M. (1988). Relationships at risk. In J. Belsky & T. Nezworski (Eds.), *Clinical implications of attachment,* 136–174. Hillsdale, NJ: Lawrence Erlbaum.

Curcio, F., Kattef, E., Levine, D., & Robbins, O. (1977). Compensation and susceptibility to compensation training. *Developmental Psychology, 7,* 259–265.

Curtiss, S. (1977). *Genie.* New York: Academic Press.

———. (1981). Dissociations between language and cognition: Cases and implications. *Journal of Autism and Developmental Disorders, 11,* 15–30.

Czyzowska, D., & Niemczynski, A. (1996). Universality of socio-moral development: A cross-sectional study in Poland. *Journal of Moral Education, 25,* 441–455.

Daly, M., & Wilson, M. I. (1981). Abuse and neglect of children in evolutionary perspective. In R. Alexander & D. Tinkle (Eds.), *Natural selection and social behavior: Recent research and new theory,* 405–416. New York: Chiron Press.

———. (1985a). Competitiveness, risk taking, and violence: The young male syndrome. *Ethology and Sociobiology, 6,* 59–73.

———. (1985b). Child abuse and other risks of not living with both parents. *Ethology and Sociobiology, 6,* 197–210.

———. (1994). Some differential attributes of lethal assaults on small children by stepfathers versus genetic fathers. *Ethology and Sociobiology, 15,* 207–217.

Daniels, H. (1996). Introduction: Psychology in a social world. In H. Daniels (Ed.), *An introduction to Vygotsky,* 1–27. New York: Routledge.

Daniels, H., Lucas, N., Totterdell, M., & Fomina, O. (1995). Humanisation in Russian education: A transition between state determinism and individualism, *Educational Studies, 21,* 29–39.

Danto, E. A. (1998). The ambulatorium: Freud's free clinic in Vienna. *International Journal of Psycho-Analysis, 79,* 287–300.

Darley, J. M., Latane, B. (1968). Bystander intervention in emergencies: Diffusion of responsibility. *Journal of Personality and Social Psychology, 8,* 377–383.

Dasen, P. R. (1972). The development of conservation in aboriginal children: A replication study. *International Journal of Psychology, 7,* 75–85.

Davidson, R. J., & Sutton, S. K. (1995). Affective neuroscience: The emergence of a discipline. *Current Opinion in Neurobiology, 5,* 217–224.

Decarie, T. G. (1965). *Intelligence and affectivity in early childhood.* New York: International Universities Press.

Del Carmen, R., Pedersen, F., Huffman, L., & Bryan, Y. (1993). Dyadic distress management predicts security of attachment. *Infant Behavior and Development, 16,* 131–147.

Dement, W. C. (1960). The effect of dream deprivation. *Science, 131,* 1705–1707.

Dement, W. C., & Fisher, C. (1963). Experimental interference with the sleep cycle. *Canadian Psychiatric Association Journal, 8,* 400–405.

deVilliers, P., & deVilliers, J. (1972). Early judgments of semantic and syntactic acceptability by children. *Journal of Psycholinguistic Research, 1,* 299–310.

Diaz, R. M. (1987). The private speech of young children at risk: A test of three deficit hypotheses. *Early Childhood Research Quarterly, 2,* 181–197.

D'Odorico, L. (1984). Nonsegmental features in prelinguistic communications: An analysis of some types of infant cry and noncry vocalizations. *Journal of Child Language, 11,* 17–27.

Doland, D. J., & Adelberg, K. (1967). The learning of sharing behavior. *Child Development, 38,* 695–700.

Dorjahn, V. R. (1958). Fertility, polygyny and their interrelations in Temne society. *American Anthropologist, 60,* 838–860.

Drabman, R. S., & Thomas, M. H. (1974). Does media violence increase children's tolerance of real-life aggression? *Development Psychology, 10,* 418–421.

DuCharme, J., Koverola, C., & Battle, P. (1997). Intimacy development: The influence of abuse and gender. *Journal of Interpersonal Violence, 12,* 590–600.

Dukes, R. L., Martinez, R. O., & Stein, J. A. (1997). Precursors and consequences of membership in youth gangs. *Youth and Society, 29,* 139–165.

Egeland, B., & Farber, E. A. (1984). Infant–mother attachment: Factors related to its development and changes over time. *Child Development, 55,* 753–771.

Elkind, D. (1974). *Children and Adolescents.* New York: Oxford University Press.

Emerson, C. (1996). The outer word and inner speech: Bakhtin, Vygotsky, and the internalization of language. In H. Daniels (Ed.), *An introduction to Vygotsky,* 123–142. New York: Routledge.

Epstein, H. (1986). States in human brain development. *Developmental Brain Research, 30,* 114–119.

Erdley, C. A., & Asher, S. R. (1996). Children's social goals and self-efficacy perceptions as influences on their responses to ambiguous provocation. *Child Development, 67,* 1329–1344.

Erikson, E. (1958). *Young man Luther.* New York: Norton.

———. (1963). *Childhood and society* (2nd ed.). New York: Norton.

———. (1968). *Identity: Youth and crisis.* New York: Norton.

———. (1969). *Gandhi's truth: On the origins of militant nonviolence.* New York: Norton.

———. (1972). Autobiographical notes on the identity crisis. In G. Holton (Ed.), *The twentieth century sciences: Studies in the biography of ideas,* 3–32. New York: Norton.

———. (1980). *Identity and the life cycle.* New York: Norton.

———. (1983). Reflections. *Adolescent Psychiatry, 11,* 9–13.

———. (1984). Reflections on the last stage—and the first. *The Psychoanalytic Study of the Child, 39,* 155–165.

Erneling, C. (1997). Cognitive science and the future of psychology—Challenges and opportunities. In D. M. Johnson & C. E. Erneling (Eds.), *The future of the cognitive revolution,* 376–382. New York: Oxford University Press.

Eron, L. D., Lefkowitz, M. M., Huesmann, L. R., & Walder, L. O. (1972). Does television violence cause aggression? *American Psychologist, 27,* 253–263.

Essock-Vitale, S., & McGuire, M. T. (1980). Predictions derived from the theories of kin selection and reciprocation assessed by anthropological data. *Ethology and Sociobiology, 1,* 233–243.

Etaugh, C., Collins, G., & Gerson, A. (1975). Reinforcement of sex-typical behaviors of two-year-old children in a nursery school setting. *Developmental Psychology, 11,* 255.

Etzel, B. C., & Gewirtz, J. L. (1967). Experimental modification of caretaker-maintained high-rate operant crying in a 6- and 20-week old infant (Infans tyrannotearus): Extinction of crying with reinforcement of eye contact and smiling. *Journal of Experimental Child Psychology, 5,* 303–317.

Evans, R. I. (1968). *B. F. Skinner: The man and his ideas.* New York: E. P. Dutton.

Eyer, D. E. (1992). *Mother–infant bonding: A scientific fiction.* New Haven: Yale University Press.

Fancher, R. E. (1979). *Pioneers of psychology.* New York: Norton.

Feldman, C. F., Lee, B., McLean, J. D., Pillemer, D. B., & Murray, J. R. (1974). *The development of adaptive intelligence.* San Francisco: Jossey-Bass.

Ferster, C. B., & Skinner, B. F. (1957). *Schedules of reinforcement.* New York: Appleton.

Finney, J. C. (1961a). The MMPI as a measure of character structure as revealed by factor analysis. *Journal of Consulting Psychology, 25,* 327–336.

———. (1961b). Some maternal influences on children's personality and character. *Genetic Psychology Monographs, 63,* 199–278.

———. (1963). Maternal influences on anal or compulsive character in children. *Journal of Genetic Psychology, 103,* 351–367.

Fischer, W. F. (1963). Sharing in preschool children as a function of amount and type of reinforcement. *Psychology Monographs, 68,* 215–245.

Fisher, C. (1965a). Psychoanalytic implications of recent research on sleep and dreaming. Part I: Empirical findings. *Journal of American Psychoanalytic Association, 13,* 197–270.

———. (1965b). Psychoanalytic implications of recent research on sleep and dreaming. Part II: Implications for psychoanalytic theory. *Journal of American Psychoanalytic Association, 13,* 271–303.

Fisher, S. (1970). *Body experience in fantasy and behavior.* New York: Appleton-Century-Crofts.

———. (1973). *The female orgasm.* New York: Basic Books.

Fisher, S., & Greenberg, R. P. (1985). *The scientific credibility of Freud's theories and therapy.* New York: Columbia University Press.

Fiss, H., Klein, G. S., & Bokert, E. (1966). Waking fantasies following interruption of two types of sleep. *Archives of General Psychiatry, 14,* 543–551.

Flammer, A. (1995). Developmental analysis of control beliefs. In A. Bandura (Ed.), *Self-efficacy in changing societies,* 69–13. New York: Cambridge University Press.

Flavell, J. H. (1963). *The developmental theory of Jean Piaget.* New York: D. Van Nostrand.

———. (1993). Young children's understanding of thinking and consciousness. *Current Directions in Psychological Science, 2,* 40–43.

Flavell, J. H., Green, F. L., & Flavell, E. R. (1990). Developmental changes in children's knowledge about the mind. *Cognitive Development, 5,* 1–27.

———. (1993). Children's understanding of the stream of consciousness. *Child Development, 64,* 387–398.

———. (1995). Young children's knowledge about thinking. *Monographs of the Society for Research in Child Development, 60,* Serial No. 243.

Forrester, J. (1997). *Dispatches from the Freud wars: Psychoanalysis and its passions.* Cambridge, MA: Harvard University Press.

Foulkes, D. (1969). Drug research and the meaning of dreams. *Experimental Medicine and Surgery, 27,* 39–52.

Foulkes, D., & Rechtschaffen, A. (1964). Presleep determinants of dream content: Effects of two films. *Perceptual and Motor Skills, 19,* 983–1005.

Frauenglass, M. H., & Diaz, R. M. (1985). Self-regulatory functions of children's private speech: A critical analysis of recent challenges to Vygotsky's theory. *Developmental Psychology, 21,* 357–364.

Frawley, W. (1997). *Vygotsky and cognitive science: Language and the unification of the social and computational mind.* Cambridge, MA: Harvard University Press.

Freedman, D. G. (1979). *Human Sociobiology: A holistic approach.* New York: The Free Press.

Freud, A. (1946). *The ego and the mechanisms of defense.* New York: International Universities Press.

Freud, S.* (1900). *The interpretation of dreams.* Vols. 4 and 5.

———. (1908). *Character and anal eroticism.* Vol. 9.

———. (1909). *Analysis of a phobia in a five-year-old boy.* Vol. 10.

———. (1913). *Totem and taboo.* Vol. 13.

———. (1914). *The Moses of Michelangelo.* Vol. 13.

———. (1917). *On transformations of instinct as exemplified in anal eroticism.* Vol. 17.

———. (1920). *Beyond the pleasure principle.* Vol. 18.

———. (1923). *The ego and the id.* Vol. 19.

———. (1927). *The future of an illusion.* Vol. 21.

———. (1928). *Dostoevsky and parricide.* Vol. 21.

———. (1930). *Civilization and its discontents.* Vol. 21.

———. (1933a). *New introductory lectures on psychoanalysis.* Vol. 22.

———. (1933b). *Why war?* Vol. 22.

———. (1940). *An outline of psychoanalysis.* Vol. 23.

———. (1963). *A general introduction to psychoanalysis.* New York: Simon & Schuster.

Friedrich, L. K., & Stein, A. H. (1973). Aggressive and prosocial television programs and the natural behavior of preschool children. *Monographs of the Society for Research in Child Development, 39* (Whole No. 151).

Friedrich-Cofer, L. K., Huston-Stein, A., Kipnis, D. M., Susman, E. J., & Clewett, A. S. (1979). Environmental enhancement of prosocial television content: Effects on interpersonal behavior, imaginative play, and self-regulation in a natural setting. *Developmental Psychology, 15,* 637–646.

Frommer, E., & O'Shea, G. (1973). The importance of childhood experience in relation to problems of marriage and family building. *British Journal of Psychiatry, 123,* 161–167.

Fuchs, J. L., Montemayor, M., & Greenough, W. T. (1990). Effect of environmental complexity on the size of superior colliculus. *Behavioral and Neural Biology, 54,* 198–203.

Gallimore, R., & Tharp, R. (1990). Teaching mind in society: Teaching, schooling, and literate discourse. In L. C. Moll (Ed.), *Vygotsky and education: Instructional implications and applications of sociohistorical psychology,* 175–205. New York: Cambridge University Press.

Gardner, H. (1985). *The mind's new science: A history of the cognitive revolution.* New York: Basic Books.

Gardner, S. (1995). Psychoanalysis, science, and commonsense. *Philosophy, Psychiatry, and Psychology, 2,* 93–113.

Garret, M., Bever, T., & Fodor, J. (1966). The active use of grammar in speech perception. *Perception and Psychophysics, 1,* 30–32.

*Note: Unless otherwise noted, Sigmund Freud references are from: J. Strachey (Ed. and translator), *The standard edition of the complete psychological works of Sigmund Freud.* 24 vols. London: The Hogarth Press and the Institute of Psychoanalysis, 1953–1962.

Garrett, C. S., Ein, P. L., & Tremaine, L. (1977). The development of gender stereotyping of adult occupations in elementary school children. *Child Development, 48,* 507–512.

Gay, P. (1988). *Freud: A life for our time.* New York: Doubleday.

Gelfand, D. M., Hartmann, D. P., Cromer, C. C., Smith, C. L., & Page, B. C. (1975). The effects of instructional prompts and praise on children's donation rules. *Child Development, 46,* 980–983.

Gelfand, T., & Kerr, J. (Eds.). (1992). *Freud and the history of psychoanalysis.* Hillsdale, NJ: Analytic Press.

Gesell, A., & Ilg, F. L. (1949). *Child development.* New York: Harper & Row.

Gilligan, C. (1977). In a different voice: Women's conceptions of self and of morality. *Harvard Educational Review, 47,* 481–517.

Gilligan, C. (1982). *In a different voice: Psychological theory and women's development.* Cambridge, MA: Harvard University Press.

Ginsburg, H. J. (1992). Childhood injuries and Erikson's psychosocial stages. *Social Behavior and Personality, 20,* 95–100.

Givon, T. (1988). Toward a neurology of grammar. *Behavioral and Brain Sciences, 21,* 154–155.

Glick, J. (1975). Cognitive development in cross-cultural perspective. In F. D. Horowitz (Ed.), *Review of child development research,* Vol. 4, 595–654. Chicago: University of Chicago Press.

Goldberg, S. (1995). Introduction. In S. Goldberg, R. Muir, & J. Kerr (Eds.), *Attachment theory: Social, developmental, and clinical perspectives,* 1–15. Hillsdale, NJ: The Analytic Press.

Goldman, F. (1950–51). Breastfeeding and character formation. II. The etiology of the oral character in psychoanalytic theory. *Journal of Personality, 19,* 189–196.

Goldman-Eisler, F. (1951). The problem of "orality" and of its origin in early childhood. *Journal of Mental Science, 97,* 765–782.

Goodman, Y. M., & Goodman, K. S. (1990). Vygotsky in a whole-language perspective. In L. C. Moll (Ed.), *Vygotsky and education: Instructional implications and applications of sociohistorical psychology,* 223–250. New York: Cambridge University Press.

Gottheil, E., & Stone, G. C. (1968). Factor analytic study of orality and anality. *Journal of Nervous and Mental Disease, 146,* 1–17.

Gottlieb, R. M. (1989). Technique and countertransference in Freud's analysis of the Rat Man. *Psychoanalytic Quarterly, 58,* 29–62.

Gottschalk, L. A., Gleser, G. C., & Springer, K. J. (1963). Three hostility scales applicable to verbal samples. *Archives of General Psychiatry, 9,* 254–279.

Gould, S. J. (1977). *Ever since Darwin: Reflections in natural history.* New York: Norton.

———. (1980). Sociobiology and the theory of natural selection. In G. W. Barlow & J. Silverberg (Eds.), *Sociobiology: Beyond nature/nurture,* 257–269. Boulder, CO: Westview Press.

Gratch, G. A. (1972). A study of the relative dominance of vision and touch in six-month-old infants. *Child Development, 43,* 615–623.

Gratch, G., & Landers, W. F. (1971). Stage IV of Piaget's theory of infants' object concepts: A longitudinal study. *Child Development, 42,* 359–372.

Green, M. (1979). The developmental relation between cognitive stage and the comprehension of speaker uncertainty. *Child Development, 51,* 666–674.

———. (1984). Cognitive stage differences in types of speaker uncertainty markers. *Language and Speech, 27,* 323–331.

———. (1985). Talk and doubletalk: The development of metacommunication knowledge about oral language. *Research in the Teaching of English, 19,* 9–24.

———. (1990). Herbert Spencer's cognitive-developmental psychology: Historical connections with Piagetian theory. *Genetic Epistemologist, 18* (2), 41–45.

Greenberg, R., Pearlman, C., Fingar, R., Kantrowitz, J., & Kawliche, S. (1970). The effects of dream deprivation: Implications for a theory of the psychological function of dreaming. *British Journal of Medical Psychology, 43,* 1–11.

Griffiths, P. E., Gray, R. D. (Eds.) (2001). *Cycles of contingency: Developmental systems and evolution.* Cambridge, MA: MIT Press.

Grossmann, K. E. (1995). The evolution and history of attachment research and theory. In S. Goldberg, R. Muir, & J. Kerr (Eds.). *Attachment theory: Social, developmental, and clinical perspectives,* 85–121. Hillsdale, NJ: The Analytic Press.

Grossmann, K., Grossmann, K. E., Spangler, G., Suess, G., & Unzner, L. (1985). Maternal sensitivity and newborns' orientation responses as related to quality of attachment in Northern Germany. In I. Bretherton & E. Waters (Eds.), Growing points in attachment theory and research. *Monographs of the Society for Research in Child Development, 50,* 233–256 (Whole No. 209).

Grotevant, H. D. (1983). The contribution of the family to the facilitation of identity formation in early adolescence. *Journal of Early Adolescence, 3,* 225–237.

Grusec, J. E. (1972). Demand characteristics of the modeling experiment: Altruism as a function of age and aggression. *Journal of Personality and Social Psychology, 22,* 139–148.

Grusec, J. E., & Skubiski, S. L. (1970). Model nurturance, demand characteristics of the modeling experiment, and altruism. *Journal of Personality and Social Psychology, 14,* 352–359.

Haley, M. C., & Lunsford, R. F. (1994). *Noam Chomsky.* New York: Twayne.

Halford, G. S., & Fullerton, J. J. (1970). A discrimination task which induces conservation of number. *Child Development, 41,* 205–213.

Hall, C. S., & Van de Castle, R. L. (1965). An empirical investigation of the castration complex in dreams. *Journal of Personality, 33,* 20–29.

Hall, F., & Pawlby, S. (1981). Continuity and discontinuity in the behavior of British working-class mothers and their first born children. *International Journal of Behavioral Development, 4,* 13–36.

Hall, R. V., Lund, D., & Jackson, D. (1968). Effects of teacher attention on study behavior. *Journal of Applied Behavior Analysis, 1,* 1–12.

Hamburger, V. (1957). The concept of "development" in biology. In D. B. Harris (Ed.), *The concept of development,* 49–58. Minneapolis: University of Minnesota Press.

Hamel, B. R., & Riksen, B. O. M. (1973). Identity, reversibility, rule instruction, and conservation. *Developmental Psychology, 9,* 66–72.

Hames, R. B. (1979). Relatedness and interaction among the Ye'kwana: A preliminary analysis. In N. Chagnon & W. Irons (Eds.), *Evolutionary biology and human social behavior: An anthropological perspective,* 238–249. North Scituate, MA: Duxbury Press.

Hamilton, W. D. (1964). The genetical theory of social behavior, I, II. *Journal of Theoretical Biology, 7,* 1–52.

Hapkiewicz, W. G., & Roden, A. H. (1971). The effect of aggressive cartoons on children's interpersonal play. *Child Development, 42,* 1583–1585.

Hare, R. M. (1960). *The language of morals.* Oxford: Oxford University Press.

Harlow, H. (1958). The nature of love. *American Psychologist, 13,* 637–685.

———. (1971). *Learning to love.* New York: Ballantine Books.

Harlow, H., & Harlow, M. (1962). Social deprivation in monkeys. *Scientific American, 207,* 136–144.

Harlow, H., & Zimmerman, R. R. (1959). Affectual responses in the infant monkey. *Science, 130,* 421–432.

Harre', R. (1997). "Berkeleyan" arguments and the ontology of cognitive science. In D. M. Johnson & C. E. Erneling (Eds.), *The future of the cognitive revolution,* 335–352. New York: Oxford University Press.

Harris, D. B. (1957). Problems in formulating a scientific concept of development. In D. B. Harris (Ed.), *The concept of development*, 3–14. Minneapolis: University of Minnesota Press.

Harris, F. R., Johnston, M. K., Kelley, C. W., & Wolf, M. M. (1964). Effects of positive social reinforcement on regressed crawling of a nursery school child. *Journal of Educational Psychology, 55,* 35–41.

Harris, P. L. (1973). Perseverative errors in search by young children. *Child Development, 44,* 28–33.

———. (1974). Perseverative search at a visibly empty place by young children. *Journal of Experimental Child Psychology, 18,* 535–542.

Harris, T., & Bifulco, A. (1991). Loss of parent in childhood, attachment style, and depression in adulthood. In C. M. Parkes, J. Stevenson-Hinde, & P. Marris (Eds.), *Attachment across the life cycle,* 234–267. New York: Routledge.

Hart, B. M., Allen, K. E., Buell, J. S., Harris, F. R., & Wolf, M. M. (1964). Effects of social reinforcement on operant aging. *Journal of Experimental Child Psychology, 1,* 145–153.

Harwood, R. L., Miller, J. G., & Irizarry, N. L. (1995). *Culture and attachment.* New York: The Guilford Press.

Hayden, B., & Pickar, D. (1981). The impact of moral discussions on children's level of moral reasoning. *Journal of Moral Education, 10,* 131–134.

Hedegaard, M. (1996). The zone of proximal development as basis for instruction. In H. Daniels (Ed.), *An introduction to Vygotsky,* 171–195. New York: Routledge.

Heinrich, L. B. (1993). Contraceptive self-efficacy in college women. *Journal of Adolescent Health, 14,* 269–276.

Heinstein, M. I. (1963). Behavioral correlates of breast–bottle regimes under varying parent–infant relationships. *Monographs of the Society for Research in Child Development, 28,* Whole No. 88.

Hempel, C. G. (1966). *The philosophy of natural science.* Englewood Cliffs, NJ: Prentice-Hall.

Hetherington, E. M., & Brackbill, Y. (1963). Etiology and covariation of obstinacy, orderliness, and parsimony in young children. *Child Development, 34,* 919–943.

Heyes, C., & Huber, L. (Eds.). (2000). *The Evolution of Cognition.* Cambridge, MA: MIT Press.

Hill, J. P. (1980). The family. In M. Johnson (Ed.), *Toward adolescence: The middle school years. The seventy-ninth yearbook of the National Society for the Study of Education,* 32–55. Chicago: University of Chicago Press.

Hodgson, J. W., & Fischer, J. L. (1979). Sex differences in identity and intimacy development in college youth. *Journal of Youth and Adolescence, 8,* 37–50.

Hoffman, M. (1971). Identification and conscience development. *Child Development, 42,* 1071–1082.

———. (1975). Developmental synthesis of affect and cognition and its implications for altruistic motivation. *Developmental Psychology, 11,* 607–622.

———. (1983). Affective and cognitive processes in moral internalization. In E. T. Higgins, D. N. Ruble, & W. W. Hartup (Eds.), *Social cognition and social behavior: Developmental perspectives,* 236–274. New York: Cambridge University Press.

Hoffman, M. L., & Saltzstein, H. D. (1967). Parent discipline and the child's moral development. *Journal of Personality and Social Psychology, 5,* 45–47.

Hollos, M. (1975). Logical operations and role-taking abilities in two cultures: Hungary and Norway. *Child Development, 46,* 638–649.

Hollos, M., & Cowan, P. A. (1973). Social isolation and cognitive development: Logical operations and role-taking abilities in three Norwegian social settings. *Child Development, 44,* 630–641.

Holmes, J. (1995). "Something there is that doesn't love a wall": John Bowlby, attachment theory, and psychoanalysis. In S. Goldberg, R. Muir, & J. Kerr (Eds.). *Attachment theory: Social, developmental and clinical perspectives*, 19–43. Hillsdale, NJ: The Analytic Press.

Horney, K. (1967). *Feminine psychology*. New York: Norton.

Huffman, G., Edwards, B., & Green, M. (1982). Developmental stages of metalinguistic awareness related to reading. *Reading World, 21*, 193–200.

Hulit, L. M., & Howard, M. R. (1997). *Born to talk: An introduction to speech and language development*. Needham Heights, MA: Allyn & Bacon.

Hultsch, D. F., & Hickey, T. (1978). External validity in the study of human development. *Human Development, 21*, 76–91.

Hurley, P. J. (1982). *A concise introduction to logic*. Belmont, CA: Wadsworth.

Hyland, E. (1979). Towards a radical critique of morality and moral education. *Journal of Moral Education, 8*, 156–167.

Inhelder, B., Bovet, M., Sinclair, H., & Smock, C. D. (1966). On cognitive development. *American Psychologist, 21*, 160–164.

Inhelder, B., & Piaget, J. (1958). *The growth of logical thinking from childhood to adolescence*. New York: Basic Books.

Inhelder, B., & Sinclair, H. (1969). Learning cognitive structures. In P. H. Mussen, J. Langer, & M. Covington (Eds.), *Trends and issues in developmental psychology*, 1–21. New York: Holt, Rinehart & Winston.

Isaac, B. L., & Feinberg, W. E. (1982). Marital form and infant survival among the Mende of rural upper Bambara chiefdom, Sierra Leone. *Human Biology, 54*, 627–634.

Isabella, R. A. (1993). Origins of attachment: Maternal interactive behavior across the first year. *Child Development, 64*, 605–621.

Isen, A. M., Clark, M., & Schwartz, M. F. (1976). Duration of the effect of good mood on helping: "Foodprints in the sands of time." *Journal of Personality and Social Psychology, 34*, 385–393.

Ispa, J. M., Thornburg, K. R., & Gray, M. M. (1994). Relations between early childhood care arrangements and college students' psychosocial development and academic performance. *Adolescence, 25*, 529–542.

Jacob, T. (1974). Patterns of family conflict and dominance as a function of child age and social class. *Developmental Psychology, 10*, 1–12.

Jacobs, M. A., Knapp, P. H., Anderson, L. S., Karush, N., Meissner, R., & Richman, S. J. (1965). Relationship of oral frustration factors with heavy cigarette smoking in males. *Journal of Nervous and Mental Disease, 141*, 161–171.

Jacobs, M. A., & Spilken, A. Z. (1971). Personality patterns associated with heavy cigarette smoking in male college students. *Journal of Consulting and Clinical Psychology, 37*, 428–432.

Jeffrey, W. E. (1958). Variables in early discrimination learning. I: Motor responses in the training of a left–right discrimination. *Child Development, 29*, 269–275.

Jemmott, J. B., III, Jemmott, L. S., & Fong, G. T. (1992). Reductions in HIV risk-associated sexual behaviors among black male adolescents: Effects of an AIDS prevention intervention. *American Journal of Public Health, 82*, 372–277.

Jemmott, J. B., III, Jemmott, L. S., Spears, H., Hewitt, N., & Cruz-Collins, M. (1992). Self-efficacy, hedonistic expectancies, and condom-use intentions among inner-city black adolescent women: A social cognitive approach to AIDS risk behavior. *Journal of Adolescent Health, 13*, 512–519.

Jensen, E. (1998). *Teaching with the brain in mind*. Alexandria, VA: Association for Supervision and Curriculum Development.

Johnson, J., & Newport, E. (1989). Critical period effects in second language learning: The influence of maturational state on the acquisition of English as a second language. *Cognitive Psychology, 21*, 60–99.

Josselson, R. L. (1973). Psychodynamic aspects of identity formation in college women. *Journal of Youth and Adolescence, 2*, 3–52.

Josselson, R., Greenberger, E., & McConochie, D. (1977). Phenomenological aspects of psychosocial maturity in adolescence. Part II. Girls. *Journal of Youth and Adolescence, 6*, 145–167.

Jung, C. (1921). *The psychology of the unconscious.* London: Kegan Paul.

———. (1923) *Psychological types.* New York: Harcourt, Brace.

———. (1953). *Collected Works.* New York: Pantheon.

Kachigan, S. K. (1990). *The sexual matrix: Boy meets girl on the evolutionary scale.* New York: Radius Press.

Kagan, J., Kearsley, R., & Zelaso, P. (1978). *Infancy: Its place in human development.* Cambridge, MA: Harvard University Press.

Kasen, S., Vaughan, R. D., & Walter, H. J. (1992). Self-efficacy for AIDS preventive behaviors among tenth grade students. *Health Education Quarterly, 19*, 187–202.

Kempermann, G., Kuhn, H. G., & Gage, F. (1997). More hippocampal neurons in adult mice living in an enriched environment. *Nature, 38*, 493–495.

Kendler, T. S. (1986). World views and the concept of development: A reply to Lerner and Kauffman. *Developmental Review, 6*, 80–95.

Kennedy, H. (1986). Trauma in childhood: Signs and sequelae as seen in the analysis of an adolescent. *The Psychoanalytic Study of the Child, 41*, 209–219.

Kimeldorf, C., Geiwitz, P. J. (1966). Smoking and the Blacky orality factors. *Journal of Projective Techniques and Personality Assessment, 30*, 167–168.

Kline, P. (1969). The anal character: A cross-cultural study in Ghana. *British Journal of Social and Clinical Psychology, 8*, 201–210.

Kling, J. W. (1971). Learning: Introductory survey. In J. W. Kling & L. A. Riggs (Eds.), *Experimental psychology*, 3rd ed., 551–613. New York: Holt, Rinehart & Winston.

Kling, J. W., & Schrier, A. M. (1971). Positive reinforcement. In J. W. Kling & L. A. Riggs (Eds.), *Experimental psychology*, 3rd ed., 615–702. New York: Holt, Rinehart & Winston.

Knox, J. E., & Stevens, C. (1993). Vygotsky and Soviet Russian defectology: An introduction to Vygotsky, L. S. In R. W. Rieber & A. S. Carton (Eds.), *The collected works of L. S. Vygotsky. Vol. 2. Problems of abnormal psychology and learning disabilities*, 1–25. New York: Plenum.

Koblinsky, S. G., Cruse, D. F., & Sugowara, A. I. (1978). Sex role stereotypes and children's memory for story content. *Child Development, 49*, 452–458.

Kohlberg, L. (1966). Cognitive stages and preschool education. *Human Development, 9*, 5–17.

———. (1968a). The child as a moral philosopher. *Philosophy Today, 7*, 25–30.

———. (1968b). Early education: A cognitive-developmental view. *Child Development, 39*, 1013–1062.

———. (1969). Stage and sequence: The cognitive-developmental approach to socialization. In D. A. Goslin (Ed.), *Handbook of socialization theory and research*, 347–480. Chicago: Rand McNally.

———. (1971). From is to ought: How to commit the naturalistic fallacy and get away with it in the study of moral development. In T. Mischel (Ed.), *Cognitive development and epistemology*, 151–235. New York: Academic.

———. (1972). The cognitive-developmental approach to moral education. *Humanist, 32*, 13–16.

————. (1973). Contributions of developmental psychology to education: Examples from moral education. *Educational Psychologist, 10,* 2–14.

————. (1974). Education, moral development and faith. *Journal of Moral Education, 4,* 5–16.

————. (1975a). The cognitive-development approach to moral education. *Phi Delta Kappan, 61,* 670–677.

————. (1975b). Moral education for a society in moral transition. *Educational Leadership, 33,* 46–54.

————. (1977). The implications of moral stages for adult education. *Religious Education, 72,* 183–201.

————. (1984). *Essays on moral development* (Vol. II, The psychology of moral development). San Francisco: Harper & Row.

Kohlberg, L., & Gilligan, C. (1971). The adolescent as a philosopher: The discovery of self in a postconventional world. *Daedalus, 100,* 1051–1086.

Kohlberg, L., & Mayer, R. (1972). Development as the aim of education. *Harvard Educational Review, 42,* 449–496.

Kuhn, D. (1972). Role-taking abilities underlying the development of moral judgment. Unpublished manuscript, Columbia University.

Kuhn, D., Langer, J., Kohlberg, L., & Haan, N. S. (1977). The development of formal operations in logical and moral judgment. *Genetic Psychology Monographs, 95,* 97–188.

Kuhn, D., Nash, S. C., & Brucken, L. (1978). Sex role concepts of two- and three-year-olds. *Child Development, 49,* 445–451.

Kuhn, T. S. (1962). *The structure of scientific revolutions.* Chicago: University of Chicago Press.

Kurdek, L. A. (1978). Perspective taking as the cognitive basis of children's moral development: A review of the literature. *Merrill-Palmer Quarterly, 24,* 3–28.

Kurtines, W., & Grief, E. B. (1974). The development of moral thought: Review and evaluation of Kohlberg's approach. *Psychological Bulletin, 81,* 453–470.

Lana, R. E. (1976). *The foundations of psychological theory.* Hillsdale, NJ: Lawrence Erlbaum.

Lane, H. (1976). *The wild boy of Aveyron.* Cambridge, MA: Harvard University Press.

Langer, J. (1969). Disequilibrium as a source of development. In P. H. Mussen, J. Langer, & M. Covington (Eds.), *Trends and issues in developmental psychology,* 22–37. New York: Holt, Rinehart & Winston.

Langer, J. (1974). Interactional aspects of cognitive organization. *Cognition, 3,* 9–28.

Latane, B., & Rodin, J. (1969). A lady in distress: Inhibiting effects of friends and strangers on bystander intervention. *Journal of Experimental Social Psychology, 5,* 189–203.

La Voie, J. C. (1976). Ego identity formation in middle adolescence. *Journal of Youth and Adolescence, 5,* 371–385.

Lazare, A., Klerman, G. L., & Armor, D. J. (1966). Oral, obsessive, and hysterical personality patterns. *Archives of General Psychiatry, 14,* 624–630.

Leacock, E. (1980). Social behavior, biology, and the double standard. In G. W. Barlow & J. Silverberg (Eds.), *Sociobiology: Beyond nature/nurture,* 465–488. Boulder, CO: Westview Press.

LeDoux, J. (1993). Emotional memory systems in the brain. *Behavioral Brain Research, 58,* 69–79.

Lenington, S. (1981). Child abuse: The limits of sociobiology. *Ethology and sociobiology, 2,* 17–29.

Lenneberg, E. (1967). *Biological foundations of language.* New York: Wiley.

Lerner, R. M. (1998). Theories of human development: Contemporary perspectives. In W. Damon & R. M. Lerner (Eds.), *Handbook of child psychology,* Vol. 1, 1–24. New York: John Wiley & Sons.

Lerner, R. M., & Kauffman, M. B. (1985). The concept of development in contextualism. *Developmental Review, 5,* 309–333.

Levin, P. F., & Isen, A. M. (1975). Further studies on the effect of feeling good on helping. *Sociometry, 38,* 1141–1147.

Levine, C., Kohlberg, L., & Hewer, A. (1985). The current formulation of Kohlberg's theory and a response to critics. *Human Development, 28,* 94–100.

Levitt, A., & Uttman, J. (1992). From babbling towards the sound system of English and French: A longitudinal two-case study. *Journal of Child Language, 19,* 19–49.

Lewandowsky, S. (1998). Implicit learning and memory: Science, fiction, and a prospectus. In K. Kirsner, C. Spleelman, M. Maybery, A. O'Brien-Malone, M. Anderson, & C. MacLeod (Eds.), *Implicit and explicit mental processes,* 373–391. Mahwah, NJ: Erlbaum.

Liben, L. S., & Signorella, M. L. (1980). Gender-related schemata and constructive memory in children. *Child Development, 51,* 11–18.

Lightcap, J. L., Kurland, J. A., & Burgess, R. L. (1982). Child abuse: A test of some predictions from evolutionary theory. *Ethology and Sociobiology, 3,* 61–67.

Lightfoot, C. (1997). *The culture of adolescent risk-taking.* New York: Guilford.

Lincourt, J. L. (1986). Personal communication. Charlotte, NC.

Livingstone, F. B. (1980). Cultural causes of genetic change. In G. W. Barlow & J. Silverberg (Eds.), *Sociobiology: Beyond nature/nurture,* 307–329. Boulder, CO: Westview Press.

Lockard, J. S., & Adams, R. M. (1981). Human serial polygyny: Demographic, reproductive, marital, and divorce data. *Ethology and Sociobiology, 2,* 177–186.

Locke, D., (1979). Cognitive stages or developmental phases? A critique of Kohlberg's stage-structural theory of moral reasoning. *Journal of Moral Education, 8,* 168–181.

Locke, D. (1980). The illusion of stage six. *Journal of Moral Education, 9,* 103–109.

Lopez, B. G., & Lopez, R. G. (1998). The improvement of moral development through an increase in reflection: A training programme. *Journal of Moral Education, 27,* 225–243.

Lorenz, K. T. (1963). *On aggression.* New York: Harcourt, Brace, & World.

Low, B. S. (1979). Sexual selection and human ornamentation. In N. Chagnon & W. Irons (Eds.), *Evolutionary biology and human social behavior: An anthropological perspective,* 462–486. North Scituate, MA: Duxbury Press.

Macht, J. (1971). Operant measurement of subjective visual acuity in non-verbal children. *Journal of Applied Behavior Analysis, 4,* 23–36.

Macmillan, M. (1991). *Freud evaluated: The completed arc.* New York: Elsevier.

Madsen, C., Jr., Becker, W., & Thomas, D. (1968). Rules, praise, and ignoring: Elements of elementary classroom control. *Journal of Applied Behavior Analysis, 1,* 139–150.

Magid, B., et al. (Eds.). (1993). *Freud's case studies: Self-psychological perspectives.* Hillsdale, NJ: Analytic Press.

Maier, S. F. (1970). Failure to escape traumatic shock: Incompatible skeletal motor responses or learned helplessness? *Learning and Motivation, 1,* 157–170.

Maier, S. F., & Seligman, M. E. P. (1976). Learned helplessness: Theory and evidence. *Journal of Experimental Psychology, 105,* 3–46.

Main, M., & Solomon, J. (1986). Discovery of an insecure-disorganized/disoriented attachment pattern. In T. B. Brazelton & M. W. Yogman (Eds.), *Affective Development in Infancy,* 95–124. Norwood, NJ: Ablex.

Main, M., & Solomon, J. (1990). Procedures for identifying infants as disorganized/disoriented during the Ainsworth Strange Situation. In M. Greenberg, D. Cicchetti, & M. Cummings (Eds.), *Attachment in the preschool years: Theory, research, and intervention,* 121–160. Chicago: University of Chicago Press.

Maratsos, M. (1998). The acquisition of grammar. In D. Kuhn & S. R. Siegler (Eds.), *Handbook of child psychology: Vol. 2. Cognition, perception, and language* (5th ed., pp. 421–466). New York: Wiley.

Marcia, J. (1966). Development and validation of ego-identity status. *Journal of Personality and Social Psychology, 3*, 551–558.

Marr, M. J. (1979). Second-order schedules and the generational of unitary response sequences. In M. D. Zeiler & P. Harsem (Eds.), *Reinforcement and the organization of behavior*, 223–260. New York: Wiley.

Martin, C. L., & Halverson, C. F. (1981). A schematic processing model of sex typing and stereotyping in children. *Child Development, 52*, 1119–1134.

Masling, J., Rabie, L., & Blondheim, S. H. (1967). Obesity, level of aspiration, and Rorschach and TAT measures of oral dependence. *Journal of Consulting Psychology, 31*, 233–239.

Mattheson, D. R. (1974). Adolescent self-esteem, family communication, and marital satisfaction. *Journal of Psychology, 86*, 35–47.

Mazuka, R. (1996). Can a grammatical parameter be set before the first word? Prosodic contributions to early setting of a grammatical parameter. In J. L. Morgan & K. Demuth (Eds.), *Signal to syntax: Bootstrapping from speech to grammar in early acquisition* (pp. 313–330). Mahwah, NJ: Lawrence Erlbaum.

McAdams, D. P., de St. Aubin, E., & Logan, R. L. (1993). Generativity among young, midlife, and older adults. *Psychology and Aging, 8*, 221–230.

McAdams, D. P., Hart, H. M., & Maruna, S. (1998). The anatomy of generativity. In D. P. McAdams, E. de St. Aubin (Eds.). *Generativity and adult development: How and why we care for the next generation*, 7–43. Washington, DC: American Psychological Association.

McAdams, D. P., Ruetzel, K., & Foley, J. M. (1986). Complexity and generativity at mid-life: Relations among social motives, ego development, and adults' plans for the future. *Journal of Personality and Social Psychology, 50*, 800–807.

McCord, J. (1979). Some childrearing antecedents of criminal behavior in adult men. *Journal of Personality and Social Psychology, 37*, 1477–1486.

McCully, R. S., Glucksman, M. L., & Hirsch, J. (1968). Nutrition imagery in the Rorschach materials of food-deprived, obese patients. *Journal of Projective Techniques and Personality Assessment, 32*, 375–382.

McFarlane, A. H., Bellissimo, A., & Norman, G. R. (1995). The role of family and peers in social self-efficacy: Links to depression in adolescence. *American Journal of Orthopsychiatry, 65*, 402–410.

McGilly, K. (Ed.). (1996). *Classroom lessons: Integrating cognitive theory and classroom practice.* Cambridge, MA: MIT Press.

McNeill, D. (1970). *The acquisition of language.* New York: Wiley.

McReynolds, P., Landes, J., & Acker, M. (1966). Dream content as a function of personality incongruency and unsettledness. *Journal of General Psychology, 74*, 313–317.

Mehler, J., & Dupoux, E. (1994). *What infants know: The new cognitive science of early development.* Oxford, UK: Blackwell.

Meilman, P. W. (1979). Cross-sectional age changes in ego identity status during adolescence. *Child Development, 15*, 230–231.

Meredith, H. V. (1957). A descriptive concept of physical development. In D. B. Harris (Ed.), *The concept of development*, 109–122. Minneapolis: University of Minnesota Press.

Meyer, B. (1980). The development of girls' sex-role attitudes. *Child Development, 51*, 508–514.

Meyer, T. P. (1972). Effects of viewing justified and unjustified real film violence on aggressive behavior. *Journal of Personality and Social Psychology, 23*, 21–29.

Milgram, S. (1974). *Obedience to authority*. New York: Harper & Row.

Miller, D. R., & Swanson, G. E. (1966). *Inner conflict and defense*. New York: Schocken.

Minick, N. (1996). The development of Vygotsky's thought: An introduction to *Thinking and Speech*. In H. Daniels (Ed.), *An introduction to Vygotsky*, 28–52. New York: Routledge.

Mischel, T. (1976). Psychological explanations and their vicissitudes. In J. K. Cole (Ed.), *Nebraska Symposium on Motivation, 1975: Conceptual foundations of psychology*. Lincoln, NE: University of Nebraska Press.

Mithaug, E. D., & Burgess, R. L. (1968). The effects of different reinforcement contingencies in the development of social cooperation. *Journal of Experimental Child Psychology, 6*, 402–426.

Mittenburg, R., & Singer, E. (1999). Culturally mediated learning and the development of self-regulation by survivors of child abuse: A Vygotskian approach to the support of survivors of child abuse. *Developmental Review, 42*, 1–17.

Miyake, K., Chen, S., & Campos, J. J. (1985). Infant temperament, mother's mode of interaction, and attachment in Japan: An interim report. In I. Bretherton & E. Waters (Eds.), Growing points of attachment theory and research. *Monographs of the Society for Research in Child Development, 50*, 276–297 (Whole No. 209).

Molfese, V. J. (1989). *Perinatal risk and infant development*. New York: Guilford Press.

Moll, L. C. (Ed.). (1990). Vygotsky and education: Instructional implications and applications of sociohistorical psychology. New York: Cambridge University Press.

Moll, L. C., & Greenberg, J. B. (1990). Creating zones of possibilities: Combining social contexts for instruction. In L. C. Moll (Ed.), *Vygotsky and education: Instructional implications and applications of sociohistorical psychology* (pp. 319–348). New York: Cambridge University Press.

Moore, B. S., Underwood, B., & Rosenhan, D. L. (1973). Affect and altruism. *Developmental Psychology, 8*, 99–104.

Moore, S., & Boldero, J. (1991). Psychosocial development and friendship functions in adolescence. *Sex Roles, 25*, 521–536.

Morgan, J., Bonamo, K. M., & Travis, L. L. (1995). Negative evidence on negative evidence. *Developmental Psychology, 31*, 180–197.

Morgan, J. L., & Demuth, K. (1996). Signal to syntax: An overview. In J. L. Morgan & K. Demuth (Eds.), *Signal to syntax: Bootstrapping from speech to grammar in early acquisition* (1–22). Mahwah, NJ: Lawrence Erlbaum.

Morrison, J. W., Ispa, J. M., & Thornburg, K. R. (1994). African American college students' psychosocial development as related to care arrangements during infancy. *Journal of Black Psychology, 20*, 418–429.

Murray, F. B. (1972). The acquisition of conservation through social interaction. *Developmental Psychology, 6*, 1–6.

Murray, F. B., Ames, G. J., & Botvin, G. J. (1977). Acquisition of conservation through cognitive dissonance. *Journal of Educational Psychology, 69*, 519–527.

Musham, H. V. (1956). Fertility of polygynous marriages. *Population Studies, 10*, 3–16.

Nadel, C., & Schoeppe, A. (1973). Conservation of mass, weight and volume as evidenced by adolescent girls in eighth grade. *Journal of Genetic Psychology, 122*, 309–313.

Nagel, E. (1957). Determinism and development. In D. B. Harris (Ed.), *The concept of development*, 15–24. Minneapolis: University of Minnesota Press.

Nehrke, M. F., Bellucci, G., & Gabriel, S. J. (1977–78). Death anxiety, locus of control and life satisfaction in the elderly: Toward a definition of ego integrity. *Omega, 8*, 359–368.

Newman, F., & Holzman, L. (1993). *Lev Vygotsky: Revolutionary scientist*. New York: Routledge.

Nisan, J., & Kohlberg, L. (1982). Universality and variation in moral judgment: A longitudinal and cross-sectional study in Turkey. *Child Development, 53,* 865–876.

Nowlis, G. H., & Kessen, W. (1976). Human newborns differentiate differing concentrations of sucrose and glucose. *Science, 191,* 865–866.

O'Connor, M., Sigman, M., & Kasasi, C. (1992). Attachment behavior of infants exposed prenatally to alcohol. *Developmental Psychopathology, 4,* 243–356.

Onkjo, K. (1976). The dual-sex political system in operation: Igho women and community politics in midwestern Nigeria. In N. J. Hafkin & E. G. Bay (Eds.), *Women in Africa: Studies in social and economic change,* 45–58. Stanford, CA: Stanford University Press.

Oser, F. K. (1996). Kohlberg's dormant ghosts: The case of education. *Journal of Moral Education, 25,* 253–275.

Paranjpe, A. C. (1976). *In search of identity.* New York: Wiley.

Park, J. Y., & Johnson, R. C. (1984). Moral development in rural and urban Korea. *Journal of Cross-Cultural Psychology, 15,* 35–46.

Parke, R. D., Berkowitz., L., Leyens, J. P., West, S. G., & Sebastian, R. J. (1977). Some effects of violent and nonviolent movies on the behavior of juvenile delinquents. In L. Berkowitz (Ed.), *Advances in experimental social psychology,* Vol. 10, 135–172. New York: Academic Press.

Parkes, C. M. (1991). Attachment, bonding, and psychiatric problems after bereavement in adult life. In C. M. Parkes, J. Stevenson-Hinde, & P. Marris (Eds.), *Attachment across the life cycle,* 268–292. New York: Routledge.

Pastorelli, C., Barbaranelli, C., Bandura, A., & Caprara, G. V. (1996). Multi-faceted impact of self-efficacy beliefs on academic functioning. *Child Development, 67,* 1206–1222.

Paterson, C. E., & Pettijohn, T. F. (1982). Age and human mate selection. *Psychological Reports, 51,* 70.

Paterson, G. R., DeBaryshe, B. D., & Ramsey, E. (1989). A developmental perspective on antisocial behavior. *American Psychologist, 44,* 329–335.

Patterson, G. (1990). Freud's rhetoric: Persuasion and history in the 1909 Clark Lectures. *Metaphor and Symbolic Activities, 5,* 215–233.

Pert, C. (1997). *Molecules of emotion.* New York: Charles Scribner's Sons.

Piaget, J. (1952). Autobiography. In E. G. Boring et al. (Eds.), *History of psychology in autobiography,* Vol. 4, 237–256. Worcester, MA: Clark University Press.

——. (1962). *Play, dreams and imitation in childhood.* New York: Norton.

——. (1963). *The origins of intelligence in children* (2nd ed.). New York: Norton.

——. (1965a). *The child's conception of number.* New York: Norton.

——. (1965b). *The moral judgment of the child.* New York: The Free Press.

——. (1966). *Psychology of intelligence.* Totowa, NJ: Littlefield, Adams.

——. (1968). *On the development of memory and identity.* Barre, MA: Clark University Press.

——. (1969). *The mechanisms of perception.* London: Routledge & Kegan Paul.

——. (1971a). *Genetic epistemology.* New York: Norton.

——. (1971b). *Insights and illusions of philosophy.* New York: World Publishing Co.

——. (1972). Intellectual evolution from adolescence to adulthood. *Human Development., 15,* 1–12.

——. (1983). Piaget's theory. In P. H. Mussen (Ed.), *Handbook of child psychology,* Vol. 1 (4th ed., pp. 103–128). New York: Wiley.

Piaget, J., & Inhelder, B. (1969). Mental images. In P. Fraisse & J. Piaget (Eds.), *Experimental psychology: Its scope and method. Vol. VII: Intelligence,* 85–143. London: Routledge & Kegan Paul.

————. (1971). *Mental imagery in the child: A study of the development of imaginal representation.* New York: Basic.

————. (1973). *Memory and intelligence.* New York: Basic Books.

Piliavin, I. M., Rodin, J., & Piliavin, J. A. (1969). Good samaritanism: An underground phenomenon? *Journal of Personality and Social Psychology, 13,* 289–299.

Pinard, A., & Laurendau, M. (1969). "Stage" in Piaget's cognitive-developmental theory: Exegesis of a concept. In D. Elkind & J. H. Flavell (Eds.), *Studies in cognitive development: Essays in honor of Jean Piaget,* 121–170. New York: Oxford University Press.

Pinard, A., & Lavoie, G. (1974). Perception and conservation of length: Comparative study of Rwandese and French-Canadian children. *Perceptual and Motor Skills, 39,* 363–368.

Pines, M. (1989). On history and psychoanalysis. *Psychoanalytic Psychology, 6,* 121–135.

Pitcher, E. G., & Prelinger, E. (1963). *Children tell stories: An analysis of fantasy.* New York: International Universities Press.

Plumert, J. M., & Nichols-Whitehead, P. (1996). Parental scaffolding of young children's spatial communication. *Developmental Psychology, 32*(3), 523–532.

Pressley, M. (1995). More about the development of self-regulation: Complex, long-term, and thoroughly social. *Educational Psychologist, 30,* 207–212.

Price-Williams, D. A., Gordon, W., & Ramirez, M. (1969). Skill and conservation: A study of pottery-making children. *Developmental Psychology 1,* 769.

Quine, W. V., & Ullian, J. S. (1978). *The web of belief.* New York: Random House.

Radziszewska, B., & Rogoff, B. (1988). Influence of adult and peer collaboration on the development of children's planning skills. *Developmental Psychology, 24,* 840–848.

Rajecki, D., & Lamb, M. (1978). Toward a general theory of infantile attachment: A comparative review of aspects of the social bond. *Behavioral and Brain Sciences, 3,* 417–464.

Rao, P. S. S., & Inharaj, S. G. (1977). Inbreeding effects on human reproduction in Tamil Nadu of South India. *Annals of Human Genetics, 41,* 87–97.

Rawls, J. (1971). *A theory of justice.* Cambridge, MA: Harvard University Press.

Reed, G., & Liederman, P. (1983). Is imprinting an appropriate model for human infant attachment? *International Journal of Behavioral Development, 6*(1), 51–69.

Reese, E. P., Howard, J. S., & Rosenberger, P. B. (1977). Behavioral procedures for assessing visual capacities in nonverbal subjects. In B. C., Etzel, J. M. Leblanc, & D. M. Baer (Eds.), *New developments in behavioral research: Theory, method, and application,* 279–301. Hillsdale, NJ: Lawrence Erlbaum.

Rest, J. R. (1975). Longitudinal study of the Defining Issues Test: A strategy for analyzing developmental change. *Developmental Psychology, 11,* 738–748.

————. (1979). *Development in judging moral issues.* Minneapolis: University of Minnesota Press.

Rice, M. E., & Grusec, J. E. (1975). *Journal of Personality and Social Psychology, 32,* 584–593.

Rieser, J., Yonas, A., & Wikner, K. (1976). Rodent localization of odors by human newborns. *Child Development, 47,* 856–859.

Rogoff, B. (1990). *Apprenticeship in thinking: Cognitive development in social context.* New York: Oxford University Press.

————. (1998). Cognition as a collaborative process. In D. Kuhn & R. S. Siegler (Eds.), *Handbook of child psychology: Vol. 1. Theoretical models of human development* (5th ed., pp. 679–744). New York: Wiley.

Rogoff, B., & Gauvain, M. (1986). A method for the analysis of patterns illustrated with data on mother–child instructional interaction. In J. Valsiner (Ed.), *The role of the individual subject in scientific psychology,* 261–190. New York: Plenum Press.

Rosenhan, D. L., Underwood, B., & Moore, B. (1974). Affect mediates self-gratification and altruism. *Journal of Personality and Social Psychology, 30,* 546–552.

Royce, J. R. (1975). Psychology is multi-: methodological, variate, epistemic, world view, systematic, paradigmatic, theoretic, and disciplinary. In J. K. Cole (Ed.), *Nebraska Symposium on Motivation, 1975: Conceptual foundations of psychology,* 1–63. Lincoln: University of Nebraska Press.

Rushton, J. P. (1975). Generosity in children: Immediate and long-term effects of modeling, preaching, and moral judgment. *Journal of Personality and Social Psychology, 31,* 459–466.

Russell, E. S. (1945). *The directiveness of organic activities.* Cambridge, UK: Cambridge University Press.

Rychlak, J. F., & Brams, J. M. (1963). Personality dimensions in recalled dream content. *Journal of Projective Techniques, 27,* 226–234.

Ryff, C. D. (1982). Successful aging: A developmental approach. *The Gerontologist, 22,* 209–214.

Rymer, R. (1992). *Genie.* New York: Harper-Collins.

Sachs, J. (1967). Recognition memory for syntactic and semantic aspects of connected discourse. *Perception and Psychophysics, 2,* 437–442.

Sagi, A., Lamb, M. E., Lewkowicz, K. S., Shoham, R., Dvir., & Estes, D. (1985). Security of infant–mother, –father, and –metapelet attachments among kibbutz-reared Israeli children. In I. Bretherton & E. Waters (Eds.), Growing points of attachment theory and research. *Monographs of the Society for Research in Child Development, 50,* 257–275 (Whole No. 209).

Sagi, A., van Ijzendoorn, M. H., Aviezer, O., Donnell, F., & Mayseless, O. (1994). Sleeping out of home in a kibbutz communal arrangement: It makes a difference for infant–mother attachment. *Child Development, 65,* 992–1004.

Sanghvi, L. D. (1966). Inbreeding in India. *Eugenics Quarterly, 13,* 291–301.

Sarles, R. M. (1975). Incest. *Pediatrics Clinics of North America, 22,* 633–641.

Savage-Rumbaugh, E. S. (1990). Language acquisition in a nonhuman species: Implications for the innateness debate. *Developmental Psychobiology, 23,* 599–620.

Savin, H., & Perchonock, E. (1965). Grammatical structure and immediate recall of English sentences. *Journal of Verbal Learning and Verbal Behavior, 4,* 348–353.

Schaffer, H. R., & Emerson, P. R. (1964). The development of social attachments in infancy. *Child Development Monographs, 29* (No. 2).

Schultz, D. P. (1975). *A history of modern psychology,* 2nd ed. New York: Academic Press.

Schwanenflugel, P. J., Fabricius, W. V., & Noyes, C. R. (1996). Developing organization of mental verbs: Evidence for the development of a constructivist theory of mind in middle childhood. *Cognitive Development, 11,* 265–294.

Schwartz, B., & Lacey, H. (1982). *Behaviorism, science, and human nature.* New York: Norton.

Schwartz, B. J. (1956). An empirical test of two Freudian hypotheses concerning castration anxiety. *Journal of Personality, 24,* 318–327.

Schwebel, M. (1975). Formal operations in first year college students. *Journal of Psychology, 91,* 133–141.

Sears, R. R., Maccoby, E. E., & Levin, H. (1957). *Patterns of child rearing.* Evanston, IL: Row, Peterson.

Sears, R. R., Rau, L., & Alpert, R. (1965). *Identification and child rearing.* Stanford, CA: Stanford University Press.

Sears, R. R., Whiting, J. W. M., Nowlis, V., & Sears, P. S. (1953). Some child-rearing antecedents of aggression and dependency in young children. *Genetic Psychology Monographs, 47,* 135–234.

Seitz, J. A. (1997). Metaphor, symbolic play, and logical thought in early childhood. *Genetic, Social, and General Psychology Monographs, 123,* 373–391.

Seligman, M. E. P. (1975). *Helplessness.* San Francisco: W. H. Freeman.

Selman, R. L. (1971). The relation of role-taking to the development of moral judgment in children. *Child Development, 42,* 79–91.

Sheppard, E., & Karon, B. (1964). Systematic studies of dreams: Relationship between the manifest dream and associations to the dream elements. *Comprehensive Psychiatry, 5,* 335–344.

Shotter, J. (1997). Cognition as a social practice: From computer power to word power. In D. M. Johnson & C. E. Erneling (Eds.) *The future of the cognitive revolution,* 317–334. New York: Oxford University Press.

Sidman, M., & Stoddard, L. T. (1967). The effectiveness of fading in programming a simultaneous form discrimination for retarded children. *Journal of the Experimental Analysis of Behavior, 10,* 3–15.

Siegler, R. S., & Liebert, R. M. (1972). Effects of presenting relevant rules and complete feedback on the conservation of liquid quantity task. *Developmental Psychology, 7,* 133–138.

Silk, J. B. (1980). Adoption and kinship in Oceania. *American Anthropologist, 82,* 799–820.

Skinner, B. F. (1938). *The behavior of organisms.* Englewood Cliffs, NJ: Prentice-Hall.

———. (1950). Pigeons in a pelican. *American Psychologist, 15,* 28–37.

———. (1953). *Science and human behavior.* New York: Free Press.

———. (1967). B. F. Skinner . . . An autobiography. In E. G. Boring and G. Lindzey (Eds.), *A history of psychology in autobiography, Vol. 5,* 387–413. New York: Irvington Publishers.

———. (1971). *Beyond freedom and dignity.* New York: Bantam.

———. (1976). *Particulars of my life.* New York: Alfred A. Knopf.

Skinner, B. F., & Epstein, R. (1982). *Skinner for the classroom.* Champaign, IL: Research Press.

Skinner, B. F., & Krakower, S. A. (1968). *Handwriting with write and see.* Chicago: Lyons and Carnahan.

Slobin, D. (1966). The acquisition of Russian as a native language. In F. Smith & G. A. Miller (Eds.), *The genesis of language,* 129–148. Cambridge, MA: MIT Press.

———. (1982). Universal and particular in the acquisition of language. In E. Wanner & L. Gleitman (Eds.), *Language acquisition: The state of the art.* Cambridge, UK: Cambridge University Press.

Smith, M. E. (1979). Moral reasoning: Its relation to logical thinking and role-taking. *Journal of Moral Education, 8,* 41–49.

Smith, T. L. (1994). *Behavior and its causes: Philosophical foundations of operant psychology.* Dortrecht, Netherlands: Kluwer Academic Publishers.

Snarey, J. R. (1985). Cross-cultural universality of socio-moral development: A critical review of Kohlbergian research. *Psychological Bulletin, 97,* 202–232.

———. (1987). A question of morality. *Psychology Today, 21,* 6–8.

Snarey, J., & Clark, P. Y. (1998). A generative drama: Scenes from a father–son relationship. In D. P. McAdams, E. de St. Aubin (Eds.), *Generativity and adult development: How and why we care for the next generation,* 45–7. Washington, DC: American Psychological Association.

Snarey, J., Reimer, J., & Kohlberg, L. (1985). The kibbutz as a model for moral education: A longitudinal cross cultural study. *Journal of Applied Developmental Psychology, 6,* 161–172.

Spitz, R. (1965). *The first year of life.* New York: International Universities Press.

Sprenger, M. (1999). *Learning and memory: The brain in action.* Alexandria, VA: Association for Supervision and Curriculum Development.

Stafford-Clark, D. (1965). *What Freud really said.* New York: Schocken.

Stark, R., Bernstein, L., & Demorest, M. (1993). Vocal communication in the first 18 months of life. *Journal of Speech and Hearing Research, 36,* 548–558.

Staub, E. (1970). A child in distress: The influence of age and number of witnesses on children's attempts to help. *Journal of Personality and Social Psychology, 14,* 130–141.

Stein, A. H., & Friedrich, L. K. (1975). Impact of television on children and youth. In E. M. Hetherington (Ed.), *Review of child development research,* Vol. 5, 183–256. Chicago: University of Chicago Press.

Steinberg, L. D. (1981). Transformation in family relations at puberty. *Developmental Psychology, 17,* 833–840.

Stenlund, S. (1997). Language, action, and mind. In D. M. Johnson & C. E. Erneling (Eds.), *The future of the cognitive revolution,* 302–316. New York: Oxford University Press.

Steuer, F. B., Applefield, J. M., & Smith, R. (1971). Televised aggression and the interpersonal aggression of preschool children. *Journal of Experimental Child Psychology, 11,* 442–447.

Stone, A. A. (1997). Where will psychoanalysis survive? *Harvard Magazine, 99*(3), 35–39.

Story, R. I. (1968). Effects on thinking of relationships between conflict arousal and oral fixation. *Journal of Abnormal Psychology, 73,* 440–448.

Suppes, P., & Ginsberg, R. (1962). Experimental studies of mathematical concept formation in young children. *Science Education, 46,* 230–240.

Sylwester, R. (1995). *A celebration of neurons: An educator's guide to the human brain.* Alexandria, VA: Association for Supervision and Curriculum Development.

Tager-Flusberg, H. (1997). Putting words together: Morphology and syntax in the preschool years. In J. Berko Gleason (Ed.), *The development of language* (4th ed., pp. 159–209). Boston: Allyn and Bacon.

Tallal, P., Miller, S., & Fitch, R. H. (1993). Neurobiological basis for speech: A case for the preeminence of temporal processing. *Annals of the New York Academy of Sciences, 682,* 27–47.

Taylor, J. H., & Walker, L. J. (1997). Moral climate and the development of moral reasoning: The effects of dyadic discussions between young offenders. *Journal of Moral Education, 26,* 21–45.

Templeton, S., & Spivey, E. M. (1980). The concept of word in young children as a function of level of cognitive development. *Research in the Teaching of English, 14,* 265–278.

Tesch, S. A. (1985). Psychosocial development and subjective well-being in an age cross-section of adults. *The International Journal of Aging and Human Development, 21,* 109–120.

Teti, D. M., Nakagawa, M., Das, R., & Wirth, O. (1991). Security of attachment between preschoolers and their mothers: Relations among social interaction, parenting stress, and mothers' sorts of the Attachment Q-Set. *Developmental Psychology, 27,* 440–447.

Tharp, R. (1993). Institutional and social context of educational practice and reform. In E. A. Forman, N. Minick, & C. A. Stone (Eds.), *Contexts for learning: Sociocultural dynamics in children's development,* 269–282. Oxford, UK: Oxford University Press.

———. (1999). Therapist as teacher: A developmental model of psychotherapy. *Developmental Review, 42,* 18–25.

Thoma, S. J., & Rest, J. R. (1999). The relationship between moral decision making and patterns of consolidation and transition in moral judgment development. *Developmental Psychology, 35,* 323–334.

Thomas, K. R. (1992). The wolf–man case: Classical and self-psychological perspectives. *American Journal of Psychoanalysis, 52,* 213–225.

Thomas, M. H., Horton, R. W., Lippincott, E. L., & Drabman, R. S. (1977). Desensitization to portrayals of real-life aggression as a function of exposure to television violence. *Journal of Personality and Social Psychology, 35,* 430–458.

Thompson, C. (1957). Cultural pressures in the psychology of women. In P. Mullahy (Ed.), *A study of interpersonal relations,* 130–146. New York: Hermitage Press.

Thompson, P. R. (1980). "And who is my neighbor?" An answer from evolutionary genetics. *Social Science Information, 19,* 341–384.

Thorbecke, W., & Grotevant, H. D. (1982). Gender differences in adolescent interpersonal identity formation. *Journal of Youth and Adolescence, 11,* 479–492.

Thorndike, E. L. (1933). A proof of the law of effect. *Science, 77,* 173–175.

Toder, N. L., & Marcia, J. E. (1973). Ego identity status and response to conformity pressure in college women. *Journal of Personality and Social Psychology, 26,* 287–294.

Tomasello, M. (1995). Language is not an instinct. *Cognitive Development, 10,* 131–156.

Tomlinson-Keasey, C. (1972). Formal operations in females from eleven to fifty-four years of age. *Developmental Psychology, 6,* 364.

Touchette, P. E. (1968). The effects of graduated stimulus change on the acquisition of a simple discrimination in severely retarded boys. *Journal of the Experimental Analysis of Behavior, 11,* 39–48.

Triseliotis, J. P. (1973). *In search of origins.* London: Kegan Paul.

Trivers, R. L. (1971). The evolution of reciprocal altruism. *The Quarterly Review of Biology, 46,* 35–57.

Turiel, E. (1966). An experimental test of the sequentiality of developmental stages in the child's moral judgment. *Journal of Personality and Social Psychology, 3,* 611–618.

———. (1974). Conflict and transition in adolescent moral development. *Child Development, 45,* 14–29.

———. (1977). Conflict and transition in adolescent moral development. II. The resolution of disequilibrium through structural reorganization. *Child Development, 48,* 634–637.

Twardosz, S., & Sajwaj, T. E. (1972). Multiple effects of a procedure to increase sitting in a hyperactive, retarded boy. *Journal of Applied Behavior Analysis, 5,* 73–78.

Umiker-Sebeok, J., & Sebeok, T. (1980). Introduction. Questioning apes. In T. Sebeok & J. Umiker-Sebeok (Eds.), *Speaking of apes: A critical anthology of two-way communication with man* (pp. 1–59). New York: Plenum Press.

Urberg, K. A. (1979). Sex role conceptualizations in adolescents and adults. *Developmental Psychology, 15,* 90–92.

Uzgiris, I. C., & Hunt, J. McV. (1974). *Toward ordinal scales of psychological development in infancy.* Urbana, IL: University of Illinois Press.

Valsiner, J. (1984). Construction of the zone of proximal development in adult–child joint action: The socialization of meals. In B. Rogoff & J. V. Wertsch (Eds.), *Children's learning in the "zone of proximal development"* (pp. 65–76). San Francisco: Jossey-Bass.

van der Veer, R., & Valsiner, J. (1991). *Understanding Vygotsky: A quest for synthesis.* Cambridge, MA: Blackwell Publishers.

van Ijzendoorn, M., Goldberg, S., Kroonenberg, P., & Frenkel, O. (1992). The relative effects of maternal and child problems on the quality of attachment. *Child Development, 63,* 840–858.

Vasudev, J., & Hummel, R. C. (1987). Moral stage sequence and principled reasoning in an Indian sample. *Human Development, 30,* 105–118.

Veldman, D. J., Bown, O. H. (1969). Personality and performance characteristics associated with cigarette smoking among college freshmen. *Journal of Consulting and Clinical Psychology, 33,* 109–119.

Vogler, R. E., Masters, W. M., & Merrill, G. S. (1970). Shaping cooperative behavior in young children. *Journal of Psychology, 74,* 181–186.

———. (1971). Extinction of cooperative behavior as a function of acquisition by shaping or instruction. *Journal of Genetic Psychology, 119,* 233–240.

von Glasersfeld, E. (1979). Radical constructivism and Piaget's conception of knowledge. In F. B. Murray (Ed.), *The impact of Piagetian theory on education, philosophy, psychiatry, and psychology*, 109–122. Baltimore: University Park Press.

von Uexkull, J. (1957). A stroll through the worlds of animals and men. In C. H. Schiller (Ed.), *Instinctive Behavior* (pp. 5–80). New York: International Universities Press.

Voyat, G. (1977). In tribute to Piaget: A look at his scientific impact in the United States. In R. W. Rieber & K. Salzinger (Eds.), The roots of American psychology: Historical influences and implications for the future. *Annals of the New York Academy of Sciences, 291,* 342–349.

Vuyk, R. (1981). *Overview and critique of Piaget's genetic epistemology: 1965–1980.* London: Academic Press.

Vygotsky, L. S. (1962). *Thought and language.* E. Hanfmann & G. Vakar (Eds. & translators). Cambridge, MA.: MIT Press.

———. (1978). *Mind in society: The development of higher psychological processes.* Cambridge, MA: Harvard University Press.

———. (1981). The genesis of higher mental functions. In J. V. Wertsch (Ed.), *The concept of activity in soviet psychology,* 144–188. Armonk, NY: M. E. Sharpe.

———. (1997). (R. Silverman, translator) *Educational psychology.* Boca Raton, FL: St. Lucie Press.

Vygotsky, L. S., & Luria, A. (1993). Tool and symbol in child development. In R. Van der Veer & J. Valsiner, *The Vygotsky reader,* 99–174, translated by T. Prout & R. Van der Veer. Cambridge, MA: Blackwell.

———. (1994). Tool and symbol in child development. In R. Van der Veer & J. Valsiner, *The Vygotsky reader,* 99–174, translated by T. Prout & R. Van der Veer. Cambridge, MA: Blackwell.

Walaskay, M., Whitbourne, S. K., & Nehrke, M. F. (1983–84). Construction and validation of an ego integrity status interview. *International Journal of Aging and Human Development, 81,* 61–72.

Walker, L. J. (1982). The sequentiality of Kohlberg's stages of moral development. *Child Development, 53,* 1330–1336.

———. (1989). A longitudinal study of moral reasoning. *Child Development, 60,* 157–166.

Ward, M. H., & Baker, B. L. (1968). Reinforcement therapy in the classroom. *Journal of Applied Behavior Analysis, 1,* 323–328.

Waterman, A. S., & Goldman, J. A. (1976). A longitudinal study of ego development at a liberal arts college. *Journal of Youth and Adolescence, 5,* 361–375.

Waterman, A. S., & Waterman, C. K. (1971). A longitudinal study of changes in ego identity status during the freshman year of college. *Developmental Psychology, 5,* 167–173.

Watson, J. B. (1919). *Psychology from the standpoint of a behaviorist.* Philadelphia: Lippincott.

———. (1924). *Behaviorism.* New York: Norton.

———. (1928). *Psychological care of infant and child.* New York: Norton.

Watson, J. B., & Raynor, R. (1920). Conditioned emotional reactions. *Journal of Experimental Psychology, 3,* 1–14.

Wearden, J. H. (1988). Some neglected problems in the analysis of human operant behavior. In G. Davey & C. Cullen (Eds.), *Human operant conditioning and behavior modification,* 197–224. New York: John Wiley & Sons.

Webster, R. (1995). *Why Freud was wrong: Sin, science, and psychoanalysis.* New York: Basic Books.

Weiner, G. (1956). Neurotic depressives and alcoholics. Oral Rorschach percepts. *Journal of Projective Techniques, 20,* 435–455.

Weiss, L., & Masling, J. (1970). Further validation of a Rorschach measure of oral imagery: A study of six clinical groups. *Journal of Abnormal Psychology, 76,* 83–87.

Weissbrod, C. S. (1976). Noncontingent warmth induction, cognitive style, and children's imitative donation and rescue effort behaviors. *Journal of Personality and Social Psychology, 34,* 274–281.

Werner, E. E., & Smith, R. S. (1992). *Overcoming the odds: High risk children from birth to adulthood.* Ithica, NY: Cornell University Press.

Werner, H. (1948). *Comparative psychology of mental development.* New York: International Universities Press.

———. (1957). The concept of development from a comparative and organismic point of view. In D. B. Harris (Ed.), *The concept of development,* 125–148. Minneapolis: University of Minnesota Press.

Wertheimer, M. (1961). Psychomotor coordination of auditory and visual space at birth. *Science, 134,* 1692.

Wertsch, J. V. (1998). *Mind as action.* New York: Oxford University Press.

Wertsch, J. V., & Tulviste, P. (1996). L. S. Vygotsky and contemporary developmental psychology. In H. Daniels (Ed.), *An introduction to Vygotsky,* 53–74. New York: Routledge.

White, R. W. (1960). Competence and the psychosexual stages of development. In M. R. Jones (Ed.), *Nebraska Symposium on Motivation,* 97–141. Lincoln, NE: University of Nebraska Press.

White, S. H. (1976). The active organism in theoretical behaviorism. *Human Development, 19,* 99–107.

Whyte, M. K. (1978). Cross-cultural codes dealing with the relative status of women. *Ethnology, 17,* 211–237.

Wilson, E. O. (1975). *Sociobiology: The new synthesis.* Cambridge, MA: The Belknap Press of Harvard University Press.

———. (1978a). Academic vigilantism and the political significance of sociobiology. In A. L. Caplan (Ed.), *The sociobiology debate: Readings on the ethical and scientific issues concerning sociobiology,* 291–303. New York: Harper and Row.

———. (1978b). *On human nature.* Cambridge, MA: Harvard University Press.

———. (1998a). The biological basis of morality. *The Atlantic Monthly,* April, 53–70.

———. (1998b). *Consilience: The unity of knowledge.* New York: Alfred A. Knopf.

Wilson, G. D. (1997). Gender differences in sexual fantasy: An evolutionary analysis. *Personality and Individual Differences, 22,* 27–31.

Winestine, M. C. (1985). Weeping during the analysis of a latency-age girl. *The Psychoanalytic Study of the Child, 40,* 297–318.

Wohlwill, J. F. (1966). Comments in discussion on the developmental approach of Jean Piaget. *American Journal of Mental Deficiency, Monograph Supplements, 70,* 84–105.

Wolf, J. B., Broie, E. D., & Wade, M. J. (2000). *Epistasis and the evolutionary process.* New York: Oxford University Press.

Wolff, P. H. (1960). The developmental psychologies of Jean Piaget and psychoanalysis. *Psychological Issues, 2,* Monograph 5.

Wolman, B. (1981). *Contemporary theories and systems in psychology,* 2nd ed. New York: Plenum.

Youniss, J. (1980). *Parents and peers in social development: A Sullivan-Piaget perspective.* Chicago: University of Chicago Press.

Youniss, J., & Dean, A. (1974). Judgment and imagining aspects of operations: A Piagetian study with Korean and Costa Rican children. *Child Development, 45,* 1020–1031.

Zeiler, M. D. (1979). Output dynamics. In M. D. Zeiler & P. Harzem (Eds.), *Reinforcement and the organization of behavior,* 79–115. New York: Wiley.

Zimmerman, B. J., Bandura, A., & Martinez-Pons, M. (1992). Self-motivation for academic attainment: The role of self-efficacy beliefs and personal goal-setting. *American Educational Research Journal, 29,* 663–676.

Zuschlag, M. K., & Whitbourne, S. K. (1994). Psychosocial development in three generations of college students. *Journal of Youth and Adolescence, 23,* 567–577.

AUTHOR INDEX

SUBJECT INDEX